THE EVANGELICAL SUNDAY SCHOOL TEACHER'S GUIDE 1982–83

William Carey Moore

EDITOR

Fleming H. Revell Company
Old Tappan, New Jersey

Lessons and/or Readings are based on the International Sunday School Lessons. The International Bible Lessons for Christian Teaching, copyright © 1980 by the Committee on the Uniform Series.

Scripture quotations identified KJV are from the King James Version of the Bible.

Scripture quotations identified NIV are from HOLY BIBLE New International Version, copyright © New York International Bible Society, 1978. Used by permission.

Scripture quotations identified TLB are from The Living Bible, copyright © 1971 by Tyndale House Publishers, Wheaton, Illinois. Used by permission.

Scripture quotations identified NASB are from the New American Standard Bible, Copyright © The LOCKMAN FOUNDATION 1960, 1962, 1963, 1968, 1971, 1972, 1973, 1975 and are used by permission.

Scripture quotations identified TEV are from the *Good News Bible*—Old Testament: Copyright © American Bible Society 1976: New Testament: Copyright © American Bible Society 1966, 1971, 1976.

Scripture quotations identified PHILLIPS are from THE NEW TESTAMENT IN MODERN ENGLISH (Revised Edition), translated by J. B. Phillips. © J. B. Phillips 1958, 1960, 1972. Used by permission of Macmillan Publishing Co., Inc.

Scripture quotations identified RSV are from the Revised Standard Version of the Bible, copyrighted 1946, 1952, © 1971 and 1973.

Scripture quotations identified NEB are from *The New English Bible*. © The Delegates of the Oxford University Press and the Syndics of the Cambridge University Press 1961 and 1970. Reprinted by permission.

Scripture quotations identified MOFFATT are from THE BIBLE: A NEW TRANSLATION by James Moffatt. Copyright 1954 by James A. R. Moffatt. By permission of Harper & Row, Publishers, Inc.

Excerpt from "Ease on Down the Road" by Charlie Smalls. Copyright © 1974, 1975 by Fox Fan-Fare, Inc. All rights reserved. Used by permission.

ISBN: 0-8007-1310-9
ISSN: 0731-0463

Copyright © 1982 Fleming H. Revell Company
All rights reserved
Printed in the United States of America

Contents

International Sunday School Lesson Topics 5
Publisher's Foreword 6
How to Use This Book 7
A Few Basic Books for the Teacher 11
The Lessons for September 1982–August 1983 14

LIST OF LESSONS

FALL QUARTER   Origins of God's Chosen People

LESSON				Page
1.	Sept. 5.	**God Creates Persons**	Genesis 2:4-9,18-25	14
2.	Sept. 12.	**God Makes a Covenant**	Genesis 15:1-6,12-18	22
3.	Sept. 19.	**God Gives Jacob a New Name**	Genesis 32:9-12,22-30	31
4.	Sept. 26.	**God Preserves His People**	Genesis 50:15-26	39
5.	Oct. 3.	**God Reaffirms His Promise**	Exodus 5:22-6:9,13	48
6.	Oct. 10.	**God Establishes the Passover**	Exodus 12:11-17,24-27	56
7.	Oct. 17.	**God Forgives His People**	Exodus 32:9-14;34:5-9	65
8.	Oct. 24.	**God Proclaims the Year of Jubilee**	Leviticus 25:1,2,8-12,23,24, 39-43	72
9.	Oct. 31.	**God Speaks Through a Gentile**	Numbers 22:4-6;23:7-12; 24:17	80
10.	Nov. 7.	**God Leads His People into the Promised Land**	Joshua 3:14-4:7	89
11.	Nov. 14.	**God Provides Judges for His People**	Judges 2:6,7,11-19	97
12.	Nov. 21.	**God Empowers Gideon**	Judges 6:3-6,11-16;17:20,21	105
13.	Nov. 28.	**God Is Israel's True King**	Judges 8:22,23;9:6-15,55-57	114

WINTER QUARTER   The Gospel of Luke

#	Date	Title	Reference	Page
1.	Dec. 5.	*The Nature of Luke's Gospel*	Luke 1:1-4; 5:29-32;8:19-21; 9:18-22	124
2.	Dec. 12.	*Promise of Jesus' Birth*	Luke 1:39-56	133
3.	Dec. 19.	*Jesus' Early Life*	Luke 2:22-35,51,52	141
4.	Dec. 26.	*Jesus Begins His Ministry*	Luke 4:1-15	149
5.	Jan. 2.	*Teaching About Forgiveness*	Luke 7:36-50	158
6.	Jan. 9.	*Teaching About Compassion*	Luke 10:25-37	166
7.	Jan. 16.	*Teaching About Priorities*	Luke 12:13-21,35-40	174
8.	Jan. 23.	*Teaching About Lostness*	Luke 15:11-24	182
9.	Jan. 30.	*Teaching About Stewardship*	Luke 16:1-13	190
10.	Feb. 6.	*Going up to Jerusalem*	Luke 19:29-40,45-48	199
11.	Feb. 13.	*Observing the Last Supper*	Luke 22:1,2,7-20	207
12.	Feb. 20.	*Suffering Crucifixion*	Luke 23:32-46	215
13.	Feb. 27.	*Standing Among His Disciples*	Luke 24:36-53	223

SPRING QUARTER   The Book of Acts

#	Date	Title	Reference	Page
1.	Mar. 6.	*An Expectant Fellowship*	Acts 1:4-14	234
2.	Mar. 13.	*An Empowered Fellowship*	Acts 2:1-4,12-18,37,38	242
3.	Mar. 20.	*An Expanding Fellowship*	Acts 2:43-47;6:1-7	250
4.	Mar. 27.	*Good News for Outsiders*	Acts 8:25-38	259
5.	Apr. 3.	*Confronted by the Risen Lord*	Acts 9:1-16	268
6.	Apr. 10.	*Good News for Former Enemies*	Acts 11:2-18	276
7.	Apr. 17.	*Missionaries on the Move*	Acts 13:1-3;14:8-18	284
8.	Apr. 24.	*Good News for all People*	Acts 15:4-14,19-21	291
9.	May 1.	*Breakthrough in Macedonia*	Acts 16:9-18	300
10.	May 8.	*Conflict in Corinth*	Acts 18:1,4-17	308
11.	May 15.	*Riot in Ephesus*	Acts 19:23-29,35-40	317
12.	May 22.	*On Trial in Jerusalem*	Acts 22:30-23:11	325
13.	May 29.	*Paul in Rome*	Acts 28:11-23	333

SUMMER QUARTER   Old Testament Personalities

1.	June 5.	**Aaron: Spokesman and Priest**	Exodus 4:14-16,27-30;17:9-13;28:1-3	344
2.	June 12.	**Jethro: Wise Adviser**	Exodus 18:13-24	353
3.	June 19.	**Caleb: Loyal and Patient**	Numbers 13:30-33;14:24;32:10-12; Joshua 14:8,9	361
4.	June 26.	**Deborah: Supporter and Leader**	Judges 4:4-9,14-16;5:1-3	369
5.	July 3.	**Jephthah: Zeal Without Wisdom**	Judges 11:7-10,29-35	377
6.	July 10.	**Samson: Unfulfilled Destiny**	Judges 13:2-5,24,25;16:15-17,28-30	385
7.	July 17.	**Hannah: A Promise Kept**	1 Samuel 1:9-11,19,20,24-28; 2:1,2	393
8.	July 24.	**Naaman: Reluctant Follower**	2 Kings 5:1-5,9-14	401
9.	July 31.	**Joash: A King Led Astray**	2 Chronicles 24:1-7,17-20	408
10.	Aug. 7.	**Naomi and Ruth: Shared Loyalty**	Ruth 1:16-20;3:1-5;4:13-17	417
11.	Aug. 14.	**Hophni and Phineas: Corrupt Priests**	1 Samuel 1:3;2:12-17,22-25; 4:11	425
12.	Aug. 21.	**Jonathan and David: Loyal Friends**	1 Samuel 18:1-4;19:4-6; 23:15-18;2 Samuel 1:26	433
13.	Aug. 28.	**Mordecai and Esther: Challenge and Commitment**	Esther 2:7;4:13-16;8:3-8	441

International Sunday School Lesson Topics
September 1982–August 1986

	FALL QUARTER (Sept., Oct., Nov.)	WINTER QUARTER (Dec., Jan., Feb.)	SPRING QUARTER (Mar., Apr., May)	SUMMER QUARTER (June, July, Aug.)
1982–1983	Origins of God's Chosen People	The Gospel of Luke	The Book of Acts	Old Testament Personalities
1983–1984	Our Biblical Faith	Studies in Isaiah	The Gospel of Mark / The Letter of James	The Rise and Fall of a Nation
1984–1985	The Letters of Paul (Part 1)	What the Bible Is / The Gospel of John	The Gospel of John (cont'd) / Studies in Wisdom Literature	The Minor Prophets
1985–1986	The Letters of Paul (Part 2)	To You a Savior / Jesus Teaches About Living	The Christian Hope / The Holy Spirit and the Church	Jeremiah, Ezekiel, and Daniel

Foreword

For three years we have worked to produce *The Evangelical Sunday School Teacher's Guide*. Our research showed the need for a teacher's guide to the year's International Sunday School Lessons that combines thoroughly conservative commentary on the Scripture with strong emphasis on the practical application of God's Word. So, we commissioned William Carey Moore, an ordained evangelical minister (M. Div.) and writer of wide experience, to prepare such a guide.

This first volume has received enthusiastic comments from a variety of church leaders; for example: "One of the great strengths of *The Evangelical Sunday School Teacher's Guide* is its practical application of biblical truths to everyday life," says Dr. Carl H. Lundquist, president of Bethel College and Seminary, and formerly president of The National Association of Evangelicals.

"The Bible is meant not only to be read but to be obeyed," he adds. "Obedience to the Word of God is the ultimate proof of our orthodoxy. Hence Willam Carey Moore's stress on living the Bible makes this volume of unusual value to both Sunday School teachers and students. I commend it highly."

Dr. W. A. Criswell says of this volume "It is exactly what the title declares—a conservative, evangelical, and systematic approach to the study of God's Word." He praises its "abundant helps for the teacher that make application of Scripture to daily life much easier." As pastor of the First Baptist Church of Dallas, Texas, a church known for its large, vital Sunday School, Criswell points out two other significant features: "the old-fashioned practice of learning a memory verse each week," and the incorporation of "daily home Bible readings designed to prepare the pupil for the following Sunday's lesson."

C. Stephen Board, executive editor of *Eternity*, tells us, "This guide offers the teacher what is needed most—good illustrations, quotes, cross-references, and discussion questions. It wisely declines to be a 'script' for a class lecture, permitting instead the teacher's own personality to package the insights for each class."

We heartily and prayerfully commend this publication to you. It is written from a biblical, evangelical and conservative perspective with the aim that Christ's followers, everywhere, may "grow in the grace and knowledge of our Lord and Savior Jesus Christ."

The Publisher

How to Use This Book

We might think the Prophet Habakkuk lived in our own times for he wrote: "The Lord answered me, 'Write the vision; make it plain upon tablets so he may run who reads it.'"

This volume is written in that same spirit. A *Guide* to the universally popular International Sunday School Lessons, its objective is to make clear and plain the point of the passage so that he "who reads it" may run in obedience to the Word of God. It has been written for the teacher of the eighties, a person so often *on the run*, who is charged with the responsibility in a Sunday School class or weekly home Bible study to teach adult Christians—and young people—who themselves also are *on the run*.

The lessons in this Guide are laid out to give the teacher aid in two most important functions—*understanding* the revelation of God and *imparting* the central truths of a Bible Text for life-changing, character-building, Christ-glorifying results.

A Brief Look at the Lesson Format—Since many churches organize their church educational year according to the school calendar, the lessons in this book follow that same plan. The fifty-two Bible lessons in this Guide are scheduled for the year September 1982 through August 1983. By looking on page 5, the teacher will see at a glance that the lessons in this book are arranged in four quarters, each with thirteen Sundays, each quarter divided into three or four units.

The Lesson Text printed at the start of each lesson is the Scripture portion to be studied and discussed during class. This is usually a passage or group of verses from two or three chapters. Immediately under the Lesson Title, reference is made to *Background Scripture*. By reading these the teacher will better understand the setting of the Lesson Text.

A *Key Verse* is printed at the close of each lesson. Usually this is taken from the Text itself and in some way summarizes one major theme of the Text. The teacher is encouraged to use the *Key Verse* as a memory verse. Perhaps no other one thing the teacher and class do will contribute as much to their continued growth in Christ as memorizing these selected Scriptures.

Also printed with each lesson are the *Home Daily Bible Readings*. Most class members are not following a regular plan of Bible reading. By making frequent reference to what is contained in these readings, the teacher can encourage members to seek to form a habit of daily devotions. Often the *Home Daily Bible Readings* are from the passages included in your *Background Scripture*. The teacher who already uses another plan of daily Bible reading should not feel constrained to adopt these readings for daily use also. On the other hand, if the teacher has no regular plan, he or she will find that the daily reading of these texts will be a vital part of his or her preparation for teaching the lesson.

Next follows the *Lesson Aim*, the suggested object or goal the teacher will want to reach in teaching the lesson. The teacher should begin each class session with the *Lesson Aim* clearly in mind; however he or she may want to select a *Lesson Aim* that is different from the one suggested.

The *Lesson Outline* organizes the Text for the teacher. Often the Text lends itself to alliterative titles (each beginning with the same sound or letter), such have been used as an added teaching aid and in order to help the student recall the particular lesson. But when such a device was not obvious to the writer no attempt has been made to force it.

If the teacher were to imagine that the Scripture Text is the "house" for the class to live in, the *Background to the Scripture* would serve as the "front porch." The *Background* is often a bit of historical, geographical, or biographical information essential to the teacher in feeling "at home" in the Text.

Looking at the Scripture Text is a commentary on the verses to be studied, usually written in the form of a narrative. This commentary should supply what is needed for an understanding of and appreciation for the Text. Often, conservative Bible scholars are quoted as well as modern language versions. The teacher should seek to master this material and strive to reach his or her own conclusion where more than one interpretation is given in the commentary.

Of equal importance to the commentary is the section entitled *Applying the Scripture.* This points the way to one or more practical steps class members may take to be "doers of the word, and not hearers only."

The teacher will need to be careful to allow time for this vital step. Class members may unconsciously think that since they have listened to the Bible lesson they have learned all that the Lord expects of them. By regularly pointing to the practical application, the teacher will stimulate class members to continued growth.

During your study time you will want to prayerfully select the application you want the class members to make. You will see that many of the lessons suggest more than one application, but you may feel you can only adequately direct your class to a single application.

Each lesson contains *Questions for Discussion*. The answers to these questions are almost always found within the *Background* or *Looking at the Scripture Text,* though sometimes there are questions included that will draw on a person's general knowledge of the Bible. Think of these *Questions* as "spades" with which to dig beneath the surface of the Text, or "hooks" which can grab the attention of your class members and stimulate class participation and class learning.

While preparing the lesson the teacher will want to underline certain *Questions* for use in class.

To further assist the teacher, each lesson concludes with carefully chosen material under the headings: *Illustrating the Scripture* and *Topics for Youth*. Think on these as "windows," letting in light and fresh air to the discussion. By a judicious use of this material, the teacher can amplify a point of the lesson or bring a central truth into the "now" with a contemporary illustration.

Preparing To Teach. Because we all are on the run, the teacher will want to reserve time each week to adequately prepare the lesson. In order for the lesson to mature in the mind and heart of the teacher, time ought to be set aside for an initial reading of the lesson several days before the lesson is to be taught.

Some teachers, having taught Lesson 1 on Sunday morning, read through Lesson 2 in the *Guide* on Sunday afternoon or evening, a full week ahead of class time. This allows the teacher to meditate on the Text for six days, to think through any problem areas and to find original illustrative material he or she may wish to use.

Begin with prayer. Teaching the Bible is preeminently a spiritual task; it is not merely a matter of mentally mastering a unit of knowledge. Because it is a spiritual task, the teacher must prepare in prayer, seeking the Spirit's enlightening and guiding help as he or she "thinks God's thoughts after Him." The teacher ought to pray especially for the class members by name and seek to suit the Lesson Aim to their particular needs. Let Ezra be an example: "For Ezra had *prepared his heart* to seek the law of the Lord, and to do it, and to teach in Israel statutes and judgments" (7:10).

Time. During the week, the teacher should set aside two hours of uninterrupted time for study and classroom preparation. A time should be chosen that can be "reserved" for Sunday School study every week. Some will select a time in the early morning, before the work of the day; others will find a time during the day or evening.

A regular place is important for consistent study. At the desk or table where the teacher studies in this two-hour period, he should have close at hand the helps he will use frequently: a study Bible with maps; a concordance; other translations of the Bible or New Testament; a dictionary; a Bible dictionary or handbook, and a note pad.

Read. After prayer, read through the Text once more and then read the commentary carefully. Let a plan form in your mind for teaching this particular lesson—a plan that is right for you and for your class. The *Guide* is intended to assist you, but is not a textbook from which you read the lesson word for word in class. You will find your class members more attentive if you maintain eye contact with them.

You may want to write out an outline from the *Guide* on a sheet of notepaper, along with your own thoughts and material you find from your own study sources. Scan the *Questions* and mark on your paper which questions you plan to use, and when.

Many teachers prefer to teach from their open Bible and notes, referring to the *Guide* in class only to share an illustration or to read a quote in the commentary. Teaching from an open Bible encourages class members to bring their Bibles and to follow the Text with the teacher.

Visual Aids. Give thought to the visual aids that would enhance the lesson. Decide to make your teaching *interesting.* Often the lessons will suggest the use of a chalkboard, especially at the point of application. You may not have access to a chalkboard, so you may want to improvise with a large sheet of paper on which you can write so that class members can read it.

Sometimes you will want the class members to do some writing—some lessons call for this in the application. Be prepared for those times by having paper and pencils with you. But be aware of other imaginative visual aids—color slides of Bible scenes or Bible lands—filmstrips (your church library may have these, or a Christian bookstore or Sunday School publisher may supply what you need)—maps—charts—newspaper and magazine clippings, and so on.

Think ahead of ways to relate the lesson to the church. For example, in teaching the lessons on Paul's missionary journeys (Spring quarter), you may want to place a photo of one or more of the church's missionaries on the wall and trace their route of travel in carrying out their ministry in the city or country where they are.

Above all, aim for interest. Some texts in God's Word may be as familiar as the proverbial "old shoe," but they need never be boring.

Seek a specific application. Just as "everybody's responsibility" is "nobody's responsibility," a vague, general resolution to "be a better witness" will rarely do much good. During your study time, give prayerful thought to the needs of individual class members and be ready to suggest a practical step they can follow toward full obedience to Christ.

Finally, remember you are in the classroom on Christ's mission. He has said, "Go, then, to all peoples everywhere and make them my disciples ... and teach them to obey everything I have commanded you. And I will be with you always, to the end of the age" (Matthew 28:19, 20 TEV).

Abbreviations in this Guide. The Scripture Text printed at the beginning of each lesson is taken from the King James Version. Where other versions are quoted within the Lesson, the name of the version is abbreviated and follows the chapter and verse (for example, Matthew 6:33 NASB). The following are standard abbreviations for versions used in the *Guide:* New International Version (NIV); New American Standard Bible (NASB); Today's English Version or Good News Bible (TEV); The Living Bible (TLB); New English Bible (NEB).

WM. CAREY MOORE, EDITOR

A Few Basic Books for the Teacher

Every teacher needs a few basic reference books as he or she prepares to teach God's Word. A *concordance* aids the teacher in locating Bible verses on any subject. With the help of a *Bible dictionary* the teacher can find definitions of biblical terms and brief summary articles on nearly every subject in the Bible. A *biblical encyclopedia* offers much more detail, while a *Bible handbook* is usually more brief and often includes maps and excellent summary articles to assist the teacher year in and year out. The Loose-Leaf Bible allows the teacher to develop his or her study notes on blank sheets that can be placed alongside the Scripture section being studied. And a *commentary* makes available to the teacher the results of devout study by Bible scholars, often pointing the way to the meaning of difficult texts.

Cruden's Unabridged Concordance to the Old and New Testaments and the Apocrypha. Old Tappan: Fleming H. Revell Company.

Davis Dictionary of the Bible, Fifth Revised Edition. Old Tappan: Fleming H. Revell Company, 1972.

Eerdman's Handbook to the Bible, edited by David Alexander and Patricia Alexander. Grand Rapids: Wm. B. Eerdmans Publishing Company, 1973.

The Loose-Leaf Bible, King James Version. Old Tappan: Fleming H. Revell Company.

The New Bible Commentary Revised, edited by D. Guthrie and J. A. Motyer. Grand Rapids: Wm. B. Eerdmans Publishing Company, 1970.

Wycliffe Bible Encyclopedia, Vols. 1–2, edited by Charles R. Pfeiffer, Howard F. Vos, and John Rea. Chicago: Moody Press, 1975.

1982–1983 YEAR

FALL QUARTER: ORIGINS OF GOD'S CHOSEN PEOPLE

Morgan, G. Campbell, *Notes on the Pentateuch.* Old Tappan: Fleming H. Revell Company.

Young, Edward J., *Introduction to the Old Testament,* Revised Edition. Grand Rapids: Wm. B. Eerdmans Publishing Company, 1949.

WINTER QUARTER: THE GOSPEL OF LUKE

Marshall, I. Howard, *The Gospel of Luke. New International Greek Testament Commentary.* Grand Rapids: Wm. B. Eerdmans Publishing Company, 1978.

Morgan, G. Campbell, *The Gospel According to Luke.* Old Tappan: Fleming H. Revell Company.

SPRING QUARTER: THE BOOK OF ACTS
Blaiklock, E. M., *Acts: The Birth of the Church.* Old Tappan: Fleming H. Revell Company, 1980.
Morgan, G. Campbell, *The Acts of the Apostles.* Old Tappan: Fleming H. Revell Company.

SUMMER QUARTER: OLD TESTAMENT PERSONALITIES
Foster, David and Stern, Jossi, *People of the Book.* Elgin: David C. Cook Publishing Company, 1979.
Wright, J. Stafford, *Dictionary of Bible People.* Old Tappan: Fleming H. Revell Company, 1978.

FALL

September, October, November

Origins of God's Chosen People

UNIT I

God Creates and Calls His People

LESSON 1 SEPTEMBER 5

God Creates Persons

Background Scripture: Genesis 2:4b–25
Devotional Reading: Genesis 1:26–2:4a

Genesis 2:4b–9, 18–25

4 These are the generations of the heavens and of the earth when they were created, in the day that the Lord God made the earth and the heavens,

5 And every plant of the field before it was in the earth, and every herb of the field before it grew: for the Lord God had not caused it to rain upon the earth, and there was not a man to till the ground.

6 But there went up a mist from the earth, and watered the whole face of the ground.

7 And the Lord God formed man of the dust of the ground, and breathed into his nostrils the breath of life; and man became a living soul.

LESSON FOR SEPTEMBER 5

8 And the LORD God planted a garden eastward in Eden; and there he put the man whom he had formed.

9 And out of the ground made the LORD God to grow every tree that is pleasant to the sight, and good for food; the tree of life also in the midst of the garden, and the tree of knowledge of good and evil.

18 And the LORD God said, It is not good that the man should be alone; I will make him an help meet for him.

19 And out of the ground the LORD God formed every beast of the field, and every fowl of the air; and brought them unto Adam to see what he would call them: and whatsoever Adam called every living creature, that was the name thereof.

20 And Adam gave names to all cattle, and to the fowl of the air, and to every beast of the field; but for Adam there was not found an help meet for him.

21 And the LORD God caused a deep sleep to fall upon Adam, and he slept: and he took one of his ribs, and closed up the flesh instead thereof;

22 And the rib, which the LORD God had taken from man, made he a woman, and brought her unto the man.

23 And Adam said, This is now bone of my bones, and flesh of my flesh: she shall be called Woman, because she was taken out of Man.

24 Therefore shall a man leave his father and his mother, and shall cleave unto his wife: and they shall be one flesh.

25 And they were both naked, the man and his wife, and were not ashamed.

KEY VERSE: "And the LORD God formed man of the dust of the ground, and breathed into his nostrils the breath of life; and man became a living soul." Genesis 2:7.

Home Daily Bible Readings
Aug. 30   M.   In the Beginning God, Genesis 1:1–8.
Aug. 31   T.   God Created Natural Wonders, Genesis 1:9–19.
Sept. 1   W.   God Declared His Creation Good, Genesis 1:20–25.
Sept. 2   T.   God Created People, Genesis 1:26–2:4a.
Sept. 3   F.   God Provided for People's Needs, Genesis 2:4b–9.
Sept. 4   S.   God Set Standards, Genesis 2:10–17.
Sept. 5   S.   Man and Woman—Complementary, Genesis 2:18–25.

Lesson Aim: As a result of this study, adults should more highly esteem themselves and others as persons.

LESSON OUTLINE
Background to the Scripture
Looking at the Scripture Text

I. Man Is Created (Genesis 2:4b-9)
II. Finding a Companion for Man (Genesis 2:18-25)
Applying the Scripture

Background to the Scripture

Following the grand, sweeping account of the Creation of the world in Genesis 1, the writer proceeds to a more particular description of God's crowning creative work. Many Bible students are bothered by what appear to be two Creation stories in chapters 1 and 2.

James Orr in *The Problem of the Old Testament* agrees that "the narratives in Genesis 1-2:4 and chapter 2 are quite different in character and style, and view the work of creation from different standpoints. But they are not 'contradictory'; they are in fact, bound together in the closest manner as complementary."

The passage under discussion in today's lesson, he says, "taken by itself, begins abruptly, with manifest reference to the first: 'In the day that the Lord God made the earth and the heavens' (v. 4). It is, in truth, a misnomer to speak of chapter 2 as an account of the 'creation' at all, in the same sense as chapter 1. It contains no account of the creation of either earth or heaven, or of the general world of vegetation; its interest centers in the making of man and woman, and everything in the narrative is regarded from that point of view."

Looking at the Scripture Text

Man Is Created (vv. 4b-9) Later versions of the American Standard Bible acknowledge a pause or change of direction in the middle of Genesis 2:4. They begin this more particular, expanded creation narrative with "in the day that the Lord God made earth and heaven." Some versions include all of the words from verse 4b through verse 7 in one sentence. The effect is similar to that of a zoom lens, bringing us rapidly to the focus of the story—the creation of man and woman.

The stage was set for the creation of man when "there were no plants on the earth and no seeds had sprouted, because he (God) had not sent any rain . . ." (v. 5 TEV). As verse 6 states, the Lord took care of the plant life by natural means, causing a "mist" or subterranean waters to water the earth. Commenting on these verses, Basil F. C. Atkinson says, "when we come to the formation of man, nothing lies behind but the Creator Himself and the virgin earth of which He formed him. These facts prove . . . that the creation of man was the real purpose of God in making the earth" and that "man has no connection by descent or otherwise with the plant or animal life that preceded him. The implication is that they were all made for him, to supply his need, to afford him pleasure, or to teach moral lessons" (*Genesis*, Moody Press).

Perhaps nothing in all of English literature is so profound, so pregnant with significance as are the twenty-seven words of verse 7. In words mostly of single syllable, unencumbered by myth or magic, Moses describes the creation of the first man. The Hebrew word for man (*adam*) and the word for ground (*adamah*) are obviously linked linguistically, showing man's oneness with the created world. The KJV word *dust* is more accurately translated "clay" or "lumps of clay."

Instead of employing the word *create* as in chapter 1, here the writer says the Lord "formed" or "built" man. A modern Jewish scholar has pointed out that the word *formed* is "the same from which the Hebrew word for 'potter' is drawn," adding that "the terms for 'creator' and 'potter' may be expressed in Hebrew by one and the same word (*yoser*)" (Nahum Sarna, *Understanding Genesis*). The potter is a well known biblical image of God; it seems permissible to imagine Jehovah fashioning man as a potter does a vessel.

Genesis 1 simply states that Creation was by divine fiat. But in the creation of man we find the deliberate mention of the substance from which man was formed. Does this not imply the unique position for man among created things, and a special relationship to God?

The same can be said of the act of God's breathing into man's nostrils "the breath of life." It is used only in the case of man. Conservative Scripture scholars, including Atkinson and the late Addison Leitch, believed that this reference to God's inbreathing has only to do with physical life. One even points out that God breathed "into man's nostrils, not his heart." Yet the next statement, that the result was "a living soul," leads us to wonder if the resultant immortality is not directly to be associated with this inbreathing. The word *nephesh* is most often translated "soul" in the Old Testament, but can be translated "person" or "life." "The creature thus animated was not previously alive and it was nothing short of man, the image of God, that now by this immediate divine action first became a living being" (*New Bible Commentary, Revised*, Eerdmans).

Man, being specially prepared by his Creator out of clay and brought to life by the breath of the Almighty, was then led or transported to a garden specially prepared for him. Eden may be a loan-word from Sumero-Akkadian, meaning "steppe" or "plain," but more likely its meaning is "delight." The description that follows in verse 9 supports such an interpretation. Subsequent references to Eden call it the garden of God (Isaiah 5:3; Ezekiel 28:13, 31:9). It is impossible to imagine the beauty and luxurious foliage and fruit the Supreme Gardener bestowed upon Eden.

With the statement that the garden was planted in Eden "in the east," (NIV) comes the first biblical allusion to an actual geographical site. From the description that follows in verses 10–14, it is clear that Moses had no poetic myth in hand; he was telling real history and intended that his readers understand it as such. All that followed—the creation of woman, the temptation by Satan, man's fall and banishment from Eden—are to be interpreted as they would naturally be understood; they were real events that happened to real people in real time.

The Holy Spirit, who inspired this writing, seems only casually concerned with all of the trees in Eden—except for the tree of life and the tree of the knowledge of everything ("good and evil"). Space does not permit the various interpretations of these trees to be treated here. But we agree with the writer of the *Pulpit Commentary* when he argues that man was endowed from the beginning with immortality and that he was permitted to eat of the tree of life "as a symbol and guarantee of that immortality with which he had been endowed, and which would continue to be his so long as he maintained his personal integrity" (that is, abstain from eating of the second tree). He further states that the "incapacity to know good and evil . . . is not conceivable in the case of one who was created in God's image, invested with world-dominion and himself constituted the subject of moral government. Hence . . . the true character which belonged to these trees was symbolical or sacramental, suggestive of the conditions under which he was placed in Eden. The tree of knowledge was placed in the garden to give man the opportunity to exercise his freedom of choice."

Finding a Companion for Man (vv. 18–25) Following the statement of God's rules for man's conduct in the garden, the writer directs his attention to how God provides for man yet in his incomplete state. There is no hint here of God's proceeding to find a suitable partner for man in the same manner as a scientist goes about his or her research in a lab. The Lord knows what He will do, but only through experience will the man also keenly sense that his being alone is "not good."

The word *help meet* in the King James Version is variously translated, "a suitable companion to help him" (TEV), "a helper suitable for him" (NIV). The term literally means one "along side" and suggests correspondence, likeness, one "in every way adapted to be his co-partner and companion" (*Pulpit Commentary*).

After stating that the man was created, verse 19 says that the Lord *then* formed the beasts of the field and the birds. A contradiction of chapter one? No. The verb here translated "formed" can and should be read "had formed." The NIV has it: "Now the Lord God had formed out of the ground. . . ."

We are not told how the Lord caused the various land animals and birds which He had created to assemble before Adam. Very possibly, they gathered by instinct much as they did at the ark. As they came, the Lord is not to be pictured as coyly waiting "to see" what names Adam will give to each. The marvel is that the Lord should entrust such a task to man. From ancient cultures and the Old Testament Scriptures, we know that names of persons and places were not given willy nilly. The name given a person or thing denoted its character. One can scarcely imagine the most worldly-wise, the most brilliant intellectual on earth today being given such a task. Matthew Poole said of this that it demonstrates man's authority and "vast knowledge" to be able to name them according to their natures. No doubt this activity tells us something of man's perception and wisdom in his sinless state, a condition into which we can only occasionally glimpse; but a state which does not measure up fully to what we shall know when we are glorified.

Although the text does not say so, it is suggested by some Bible students that the creatures came to Adam two by two, male and female. If Adam's naming of the beasts and birds carried further to the naming of buck and doe, of ram and ewe, then of necessity he must have observed them in pairs. Would not this suggest to him that a partner similar to him would be the ideal companion? At this point, the Lord caused Adam to go to sleep, perhaps much the same way anesthesia acts upon a person undergoing surgery. Some suggest that while he slept Adam knew what the Lord was doing, "seeing" it all take place as in a dream.

From the man's "side" (more accurate than "rib"), the Lord took bone and flesh (v. 23) and from this He "built" woman. The King James translation fails to transmit the depth of emotion evidently expressed by Adam when he awakened to see Eve. It may not have been, "Whoopee!" as some paraphrases suggest, but it was more like the *Abingdon Bible Commentary* has it—"This is absolutely it!" John Calvin translated it, "At last one has come who is suitable to be my partner." The Lord knew and Adam knew that finally here was a companion and helper for the man. Having named each of the animals, Adam declares "she shall be called Woman (*ishshah* in Hebrew, meaning to be soft) because she was taken out of Man (*ish*, to exercise power)."

The words that follow in verse 24 seem more reflective and may not be intended as the words of Adam. We wonder how he would know at that time of the concept of "father and mother." But we can press this statement too far. Jesus quoted this text in defending the original divine purpose of marriage and attributed the words to Moses (Matthew 19:5). From their earliest usage, they were held to be a divine directive incumbent on all who marry. Man and woman are to part with their parents and "cleave" to one another. The "one flesh" state resulting "signifies unity of persons and not simply a conjunction of bodies" (*Pulpit Commentary*).

Our sinless parents were "naked . . . but . . . not embarrassed" (TEV). As one commentator says: "they were naked, but yet they were not so. Their bodies were the clothing of their internal glory; and their internal glory was the clothing of their nakedness" (Delitzsch).

Applying the Scripture
Two applications are suggested by this study—one concerning individual self-esteem and one concerning marriage.
1. A High but Humble Self-Esteem—To ponder the fact that we are the specially created handiwork of the Creator of the universe should bring us to our knees in humility while at the same time engendering in us a feeling of pride. We *are* special. With David we may declare:

> What is man, that you think of him;
> mere man, that you care for him? (Psalms 8:4 TEV).

So conscious are we of our sins and our failures, we forget our truly noble heritage. As Christians, we are the children of God and as Peter said, "a chosen generation, a royal priesthood, a holy nation." There is a sense in which we can believe in ourselves. God believed enough in man to allow him to name all of the animals.

Albert McClellan, a Southern Baptist, notes that "in the beginning God said to Adam, 'I will drive the animals by and you name them as you will.' Later He said to Adam and Eve to replenish the earth and to subdue it. It is a confidence that God has never forsaken. Not so man, for he has often lost it, both in God and in others. We see this most often in man's thoughtless cynicism, constant negativism, proud egotism, impetuous judgmentalism, and slick caustic analyses of other people and their motives. Man in judging other men still looks on the outward appearance, while God looks into the heart. God . . . believed in men more than men have believed in themselves, or in each other. He trusts them, so he made them free."

2. Man and Woman—Meant for Each Other—God intended, in making the woman from man's side that she should be near to the man's heart so that he would feel deeply for her, love her, and empathize with her. And He took her from man's rib so that she might stand beside him as an equal. Man is seen as her protector, not her lord. She is seen as his helper, not his slave. Wherever a man and a woman put forth the effort to live up to these ideals, the most beautiful of all creations is a possibility—a family where happiness and contentment and mutual love is experienced and where children are nurtured and given security.

Harold Francis Branch in his booklet on the happy home asks: "What is to be required of two people if marriage is to prove to them the blessing God intended it to be? They must have *patience . . . determination . . . politeness and courtesy . . . unity of interest . . . vision to avoid misunderstandings . . . and the abiding presence of Jesus Christ in the home.*" One cannot do it alone, but he or she should never give up following the example Jesus set. It is something *they* must both seek after with all of the strength they have and with all of the grace Christ gives. Ask your class to pick one quality (among the six listed above) and make an effort to develop it in a particular way this week.

Questions for Discussion
Make use of these questions to involve your students in learning and to test their understanding of the lesson.
1. What qualities mark this story as a real bit of human history? 2. What might the tree of life be? 3. The "tree of the knowledge of good and evil" is referred to only in the biblical account of Creation. Why do you think it is an important part of the Genesis story? 4. What are the implications of man being made first? (Consider what the New Testament says in 1 Corinthians 11:3, 7-12; 1 Corinthians 15:45, 47; and 1 Timothy 2:11-13.) Of woman being made of man? 5. Scientists today report that certain animals share a like genetic "code" with man. What might this mean in the light of the Genesis account of Creation? 6. What are the implications of man's being created before a garden was formed for him and the woman to live in? 7. What does this account of special creation do to the theory of evolution? Can we believe both or must we choose one and reject the other?

Illustrating the Scripture
Examples and quotations to help the teacher communicate the lesson.

AIN'T I A WONDER! A few years ago a popular self-help book came out under the name *Ain't I a Wonder!* with the added subtitle—"and Ain't You a Wonder Too!" The writer could have been speaking about the human body. This marvelous thing called life, science has learned, is built of very small minimicroscopic building blocks in humans. Nicknamed DNA, these building blocks are located along the chromosomes of the human cell in the shape of a twisting double helix. Some have called DNA a tiny computer. In our day, when everything from computers to sewing machines to radios are being miniaturized, we can appreciate this statement from Jeremy Rifkin and Ted Howard in their book, *Who Should Play God?* "A single thread of DNA located in just one human cell may house as much information as one thousand books, each 600 pages thick. . . . A teaspoon of DNA taken from simple bacteria has been equated to the storage capacity of a modern computer, 100 cubic miles in volume!" Yes, ain't *we* a wonder!

How great is our God!

THE CREATION OF MAN—GOD OR GORILLA "You have to make a choice. You cannot ride two horses in opposite directions. The Bible and the evolutionary hypothesis say two entirely different things.

"The Bible presents a world created in the hand of God. The Bible presents a personal Deity, through whose infinite power all of these things were made and devised and formed. The theory of evolution says that all of these things came through a materialistic, impersonal action process, for which process proponents of the theory can give no explanation. Impersonally, mechanically, these things just happened. They came to pass, and resulted in the marvelous phenomena you see today.

"We must believe one or the other. Even God Himself cannot deny Himself and God Himself cannot work on two opposite principles. The Bible says man was created perfect and walked in the Garden of Eden with all the faculties he possesses today, and he fell and went down. The theory of evolution says he started as a little primordial cell and has been coming up and up and up ever since. The ideas are diametrically opposite.

"What of this question of sin? According to the Bible, sin was a moral transgression of the law of God. What is sin in evolution? Sin is nothing but the drag of our ancestry, the stumbling upward. Evolution violates the whole Word of God, the atonement of Christ, the preaching of the gospel message of Jesus. It is nothing.

"I have never seen a theologian or a philosopher who could believe the Bible and at the same time believe the evolutionary hypothesis. The two are opposite. They are in one direction or the other, and we choose between.

"In the day it can be demonstrated that life came of spontaneous generation without God; in the day it can be demonstrated that there was no God in the creation of man, but he evolved upward by accident; in that day, my fellow religionists and I ought quietly to fold our tents and silently steal away.

"Well, preacher, are you expecting to resign your pulpit?

"Are you expecting to lay down your Bible?

"Are you expecting to quit preaching the Gospel?

"No, because I have already found to my heart's assurance that the hand that wrote the Book is the same hand that wrote His name across the sky and in the humblest little insect whose silver wings reflect a glory of the sun which shines upon him." W. A. Criswell, *Did Man Just Happen?* (Zondervan Publishing House, Grand Rapids, 1957).

Topics for Youth
EVOLUTION AND THE HIGH SCHOOL STUDENT—"What about theistic evolution: the belief that God used evolutionary processes such as natural selection to bring a man's body into being, and then at some point God placed a spirit into that man-like body, so that it became a true man, Adam?

"Well, if there is insufficient evidence for plain evolution, then there is also insufficient evidence for theistic evolution. But if you believe in evolution, can you still accept the Bible, or must you throw away your faith?

"No, don't throw away your faith! The Bible account can be read to harmonize with current science, if you insist! To me this seems unwise, unnecessary, and wrong, but here is the formula: Just assume that when I, as a creationist, read the first chapter of Genesis, I am reading into it something that isn't there. For I assume that it says that the creation of man was instantaneous. But when the Bible says, 'God created man in His own image,' perhaps this doesn't say or mean 'instantaneously,' but means instead that 'God created man (by a long process of evolution) in His own image.' You can argue that since the Bible is not quite clear on this point, it is not un-Biblical to believe either way you like. Among British evangelicals this view is fairly common—that God used evolution to form man. But it is not my own view at all. . . .

"Remember, too, that the Bible's principal purpose is to reveal to all mankind the kindness and power of God to forgive our sins under the conditions the Bible sets forth. There is no controversy about this. Whatever you decide about evolution has no relationship to this far-reaching, utterly basic fact of sin and salvation" (Kenneth N. Taylor).

LESSON 2 SEPTEMBER 12
God Makes a Covenant

Background Scripture: Genesis 15
Devotional Reading: Hebrews 6:13–20

Genesis 15:1–6, 12–18
1 After these things the word of the LORD came unto Abram in a vision, saying, Fear not, Abram: I am thy shield, and thy exceeding great reward.

2 And Abram said, Lord God, what wilt thou give me, seeing I go childless, and the steward of my house is this Eliezer of Damascus?

3 And Abram said, Behold, to me thou hast given no seed: and, lo, one born in my house is mine heir.

4 And, behold, the word of the Lord came unto him, saying, This shall not be thine heir; but he that shall come forth out of thine own bowels shall be thine heir.

5 And he brought him forth abroad, and said, Look now toward heaven, and tell the stars, if thou be able to number them: and he said unto him, So shall thy seed be.

6 And he believed in the Lord; and he counted it to him for righteousness.

12 And when the sun was going down, a deep sleep fell upon Abram; and, lo, an horror of great darkness fell upon him.

13 And he said unto Abram, Know of a surety that thy seed shall be a stranger in a land that is not theirs, and shall serve them; and they shall afflict them four hundred years;

14 And also that nation, whom they shall serve, will I judge: and afterward shall they come out with great substance.

15 And thou shalt go to thy fathers in peace; thou shalt be buried in a good old age.

16 But in the fourth generation they shall come hither again: for the iniquity of the Amorites is not yet full.

17 And it came to pass, that, when the sun went down, and it was dark, behold a smoking furnace, and a burning lamp that passed between those pieces.

18 In the same day the Lord made a covenant with Abram, saying, Unto thy seed have I given this land, from the river of Egypt unto the great river, the river Euphrates:

KEY VERSE: "In the same day the Lord made a covenant with Abram, saying, Unto thy seed have I given this land...." Genesis 15:18.

Home Daily Bible Readings
Sept. 6 M. God's Call to Abram, Genesis 12:1–5.
Sept. 7 T. God's Promise to Abram, Genesis 15:1–6.
Sept. 8 W. The Covenant Made, Genesis 15:7–21.
Sept. 9 T. The Covenant Restated, Genesis 17:1–8.
Sept. 10 F. The Birth of Isaac, Genesis 21:1–7.
Sept. 11 S. Abram Obeyed God, Genesis 22:15–19.
Sept. 12 S. God Kept His Promise, Hebrews 6:13–20.

Lesson Aim: That every student will understand what it means to be declared righteous and put their trust in God.

LESSON OUTLINE
Background to the Scripture
Looking at the Scripture Text
 I. Abram's Vision (Genesis 15:1)
 II. The Prayer of Abram (Genesis 15:2, 3)
 III. The Promise to Abram (Genesis 15:4-6)
 IV. The Covenant With Abram (Genesis 15:12-18)
Applying the Scripture

Background to the Scripture

Hebron, a town in modern Israel, is one of the oldest continually inhabited cities in the Bible lands. But it was not always known as Hebron. The Amorite people who inhabited that part of Canaan during Abram's lifetime called the place Mamre, after a prominent Amorite chieftain. In Mamre, Abram settled and there he received the vision which is the subject of today's lesson.

Abram (he did not receive the name Abraham until later) was about 80 years old at this point. He had passed his seventy-fifth birthday, we are certain, when he left Haran in the north. The next mention of his age is when Isaac is born; Abram was then 100.

Dating the lifetime of Abram is no easy matter. Many scholars place Abram in the twenty-first century, based on a fifteenth century date for the Exodus (approximately 1440 B.C.). William F. Albright preferred a twentieth-nineteenth century date for Abram, based on archaeological data. Dr. Edwin Yamauchi is one of a number of conservative evangelical scholars who believe a date of approximately 1970 B.C. "fits in well with the background of the patriarchal narratives." Perhaps archaeology will yet yield evidence that will enable us to be more certain of Abram's lifetime.

Looking at the Scripture Text

Abram's Vision (v. 1) Someone advises, "When you see a 'therefore' in the Bible, look to see what it is *there for*." The same could be said for the opening words of today's lesson, "After these things."

The previous chapter recounts Abram's swift counterattack upon the armies of five kings who had taken his nephew Lot and family captive when Sodom and Gomorrah were defeated. Returning to his home, Abram gave a tithe of the spoil to the priest Melchizedek, but refused to accept any reward from the now liberated king of Sodom for his rescue mission. In principle, he would not be enriched by the earthly possessions of this debauched people. But the Lord appeared to Abram and reassured him: "I am thy . . . exceeding great reward." Some Bible students suggest that the marauding enemy armies may have still been a threat, for the Lord also promises Abram to be his shield.

The reference in verse 1 to the "word of the Lord" is the first of the numerous appearances of this phrase in the Bible. How or in what manner the

Lord manifested Himself to Abram—whether in sleep or in human form or to his thoughts—we do not know. Some say that Abram first saw a vision of the Lord and heard the words recorded in verses 1-3 while asleep. Then, after he awoke, the Lord called him outside his tent to scan the star-filled skies and hear that grand promise: "So shall your offspring be."

The most acceptable interpretation may be that the vision occurred in the daytime and that it encompassed all that is described from verse 1 to verse 9. Then, after Abram had prepared the animals required for the covenant ritual and after fighting off vultures that sought to prey upon the carcasses, "as the sun was going down," he fell into a deep sleep during which further promises were made to him. Because of the concrete language contained in verse 17, we assume that Abram awakened in the dark, the promises of the Lord ringing in his mind. In a conscious state, he observed "a smoking fire pot with a blazing torch" (NIV) appearing and passing between the halves of the three slain animals.

The Prayer of Abram (vv. 2, 3) In response to the words of the Lord that were meant to encourage, we find the first recorded prayer of Abram. He could contain himself no longer. A man possessing great reverence for God, he had yet to give expression to his questioning fears. We do well to follow his example. The Lord never rebukes His children for asking Him what is going on. Indeed, we are invited to ask, seek, and knock.

With all of his attention on his "supreme personal problem," Abram confessed to the Lord that he did not understand how the promises God had made to him were going to be fulfilled since he had no son of his own. "The steward of my house . . . one born in my house is mine heir," he contended.

Evidently Eliezer was Abram's most trusted servant, one who was as close to Abram as a son, having grown up in Abram's household. Nowhere in Scripture is the man Eliezer named again. Following the Mesopotamian custom of which many examples can be found in the period 2000 to 1500 B.C., Abram and Sarai considered this adopted son to be the one who would carry on their name and establish the dynasty.

The Promise to Abram (vv. 4-6) But earnest prayer is not completed until the voice of God is heard. It was time for Abram to listen, and whether in an audible voice or in some other manner, the Lord spoke clearly to him. "A son coming from your own body will be your heir" (NIV) said Jehovah.

In recording the words of God, the writer of Genesis (whom we assume to be Moses) would have us believe that the Lord took pains to assure Abram that the heir to the promise would be his own flesh and blood. He said the heir would come "from your own body." This is all the more noteworthy when we consider that Abram was approximately eighty years old and Sarai only ten years younger. Twenty years later when the angel assured this aged couple that Isaac would be born the following year, they both laughed at the idea (17:17; 18:12). Evidently in ancient times, a woman could continue to bear children well beyond the age women usually experience menopause today; but at seventy or more, Sarai could hardly expect to give birth. Especially since she had always been barren (11:30). But they were to find out that nothing is too hard for the Lord (18:14). The miraculous nature of their son's birth prefigures the virgin birth of Jesus some eighteen centuries later in Bethlehem, a town not far from ancient Mamre.

In consideration of Eliezer, the question may arise, "If he was a legally adopted heir, how could his rights be set aside as long as he fulfilled his filial duties?" Unger in *Archeology and the Old Testament* explains that writings found at Nuzu, southeast of Nineveh, during explorations earlier in this century "give the answer. The Nuzu texts provide that if the adopter should afterward beget a son of his own, the adopted son must yield to him the place of the chief heir."

As if to answer questions of Abram's heart, the Lord made use of a quite remarkable visual aid—or shall we say millions of them!—to drive home the point of His promise. Taking Abram by the hand, He led him out of the tent and told him to look up into the heavens. "Count the stars—if indeed you can count them" (NIV) He said. "So shall your offspring be."

We should not think that the promise of numberless descendants speaks of the believing Jews only. Today more than twelve million Jews are alive on the earth. Proportionately few of them believe the Gospel and thus can be included in God's promise to Abram. But God's promise to Abram's "seed" clearly includes the whole of the Church throughout all ages.

The next fourteen words, in verse 6, speak volumes. In the immediate context, they assure us that the promise of God was met with belief, and that this trust was rewarded with the highest honor the Lord could bestow on Abram. He was, in effect, declared righteous. The key words are *believed*, *counted* and *righteousness*. Abram put his trust in the Word the Lord spoke and this act of faith was "counted" or reckoned ("imputed" in the New Testament) to his credit "for" righteousness or right standing with God.

This is the first statement in Scripture of the fundamental principle of justification by faith. Paul alluded to it in his letters to the Romans and the Galatians, showing that Abraham was not declared righteous by any works, but by his faith (*see* Romans 4:3-13, 22-24; Galatians 3:5, 6). Both Luther and Calvin agree that from this point God treated Abram as a righteous person, "now before God accepted and forgiven." Thus were believers in the Old Testament times saved, and thus are persons made right with God today.

The Covenant With Abram (vv. 12–18) To the promise of a son who would be the first of an innumerable crowd of descendants, God joined another promise—the land.

Not only would Abram's offspring be many, but they would inherit the land of Canaan where Abram was only a sojourner. Abram persisted in his prayer. He wanted to know how he could be sure that "the promised land" would be his one day. In answer to that prayer there follows a strange ritual. At the word of God, Abram killed a heifer, a goat, and a ram, cutting their bodies in halves. These were laid "opposite each other in two rows" says the TEV. Also he killed a dove and a pigeon and laid them with the other animal bodies.

Most translations bear out the sense of the King James Version when it speaks of a "horror of great darkness" falling upon Abram while asleep. The NIV says "dreadful darkness." Abram was gripped with terror and dread as though some evil was closing in upon him. Calvin thought this dread darkness was to symbolize the Egyptian bondage of which the Lord was to tell him momentarily. It may also have been an early foreboding signal of the sufferings of Christ since Abram's faith "embraced a larger sphere than Canaan (Hebrews 11:10, 14, 16) and a nobler seed than Sarah's son (John 8:56)" (*Pulpit Commentary*).

The words in verse 13, "Know of a surety" (literally, *knowing, know*) bring to mind the "verily, verily" of our Lord. Abram, already in a heightened sense of awareness from what has gone before, is now alerted to be absolutely sure of what he is to be told next. In rapid succession, he hears: (1) His descendants will be taken to a strange land. (2) They will be enslaved and mistreated 400 years. (3) God will punish the nation that is persecuting them. (4) Abram's descendants will come out of the country and bring great possessions with them. (5) Abram will die in a ripe old age and be buried. (6) His descendants will return to that very land to live, the sins of the Amorites then being too great for God to tolerate.

Every one of these promises made to the patriarch can be traced in Scripture. Egypt was the "strange country" where Israel would grow from seventy souls into a mighty nation during 400 years of enslavement. The 400 years (or four generations: "Caleb was the fourth from Judah, Moses the fourth from Levi") can be interpreted as a round number to represent 430 years as Moses (Exodus 12:40) and Stephen (Acts 7:6) say, and as does Paul (Galatians 3:17). The book of Exodus tells of the Hebrew enslavement under the pharaohs, documenting how the pressure grew to such an extent that the Lord brought terrible judgment on Egypt. A small detail that is not missed in the accounts of Israel's escape from Egypt is that the Israelites asked the Egyptians for jewelry and when they escaped they walked out of the land with abundant wealth, as the Lord here promises to Abram.

Clearly the supreme truth to be gained amid the flood of promises to Abram is the covenant which then was sealed. The sun having gone down and natural darkness fallen, Abram sees two objects. The one is an Oriental fire pot or furnace, probably cylindrical in shape, belching smoke; the other a flaming torch. Both of these well symbolize the presence of God who, Scripture says, is a "consuming fire." The fact that he saw these two objects "passing between those pieces" of the animal carcasses makes little sense to us, but it was customary in that time, when two parties made an important agreement with each other, for them to do as Abram did (*see* Jeremiah 34:18). God, being a spirit, passed between these animal bodies by means of these objects. In such an agreement between equals, both parties would walk between the carcasses. But this covenant was not between equals. It was a "settlement by a benefactor upon beneficiaries" and so Abram did not pass between the slain animals.

Having concluded the narrative, the writer declares that the Lord made a covenant (literally, cut a covenant) with Abram and solemnly promised the land of Canaan from "the river of Egypt" to the Euphrates to his descendants. A great promise indeed! In time, the nation Israel actually realized the potential for such expansion. David is said to have fought his enemies unto the border of the Euphrates (2 Samuel 8:3), and the boundaries in Solomon's reign actually reached from Egypt to the Euphrates (1 Kings 4:21; 2 Chronicles 9:26). Most scholars interpret the "river of Egypt" as the Wady el-Arish, not the Nile. The writer would not describe the Euphrates as "great" without using similar language if he intended the Nile.

Applying the Scripture

Two words sum up the action in this lesson. They are *believe* and *made*. "Abram believed God and it was counted unto him for righteousness." "The Lord made a covenant with Abram...." Direct your class's attention to these words.

1. Faith Reaches Out to God—The single most important response we can make to God's offer is to accept what He offers. Look at Abram's situation. He had heard a call from Jehovah and had followed His orders, even though it meant striking out for an unknown country and parting company with his family. More than once God told him that he would be the father of many nations, be greatly blessed, and have many children. Abram listened and worshiped God. But years went by and Sarai was unable to bear any children. The gap between the promised Word of God and the possibility of fulfillment seemed to grow greater and greater. Sooner or later Abram must either give up on any actual fulfillment of the promise the Lord had made, or he must accept the Word and await its fulfillment.

When the opportunity came for him to talk to God again about this, he raised the issue. "Where is my heir? I have no children. An adopted servant will inherit all my goods." But God simply stated even more clearly what He had been telling Abram all along. He *would* have a son of his own and of this son would come offspring as numerous as the stars. In effect, the Lord challenged Abram. Would he believe, or wouldn't he? He did. Abram reached out to God and believed. Forgetting all the reasons why it would not work, he accepted the Word of his Maker.

2. Faith Gained Acceptance With God—Because he trusted, Abram gained acceptance before God. We have various ways of saying what happened. He, a sinner, was declared righteous. He was acquitted of human sin, forgiven and placed in right standing with the holy God. His guilt was atoned for and he was deemed worthy of God's trust, for now God could make a covenant with him.

What about the members of your class? Do any of them still need to reach out to Him in faith? Use the opportunity of this lesson to invite any in your class who are not sure they are Christians to place their trust in God through Christ now. It may be helpful to show them the verses in Romans 4 that have to do with Genesis 15:6—"he believed in the Lord; and he counted it to him for righteousness."

3. "God's Work Done God's Way Will Not Lack His Supply"—Hudson Taylor, founder of the China Inland Mission (now known as the Overseas Missionary Society), told his fellow laborers this. It has a bearing on today's lesson. God had a purpose He would accomplish through Abram and He promised to carry out all of the terms of the covenant, even to the detail of supplying the people of Israel with the wealth of the Egyptians.

Invite your class members to examine what they know of God's covenant with them. Encourage them to talk to their Covenant-God about any complaint they have. Lead them to pray: "Teach Me Thy Way, O Lord, Teach Me Thy Way!"

Questions for Discussion
Make use of these questions to involve your students in learning and to test their understanding of the lesson.

1. How was Abram made right with God? Is there a different way to righteousness for people today?   2. Name two important aspects of Abram's prayer in this lesson.   3. What could be reasons for Abram being overcome with the great horror and darkness?   4. What is implied by the phrase that when Abram died he would "go to his fathers"?   5. What is the significance of the smoking furnace and the blazing fire in Abram's experience?   6. Who are the seed or descendants of Abram?

Illustrating the Scripture
Examples and quotations to help the teacher communicate the lesson.

"I AM THY SHIELD" (Genesis 15:1).   When was the last time you, as a child of God, were made aware of God's protection against danger?

In early 1981, a well-known newspaper carried a story of a World War II mortar shell exploding in the Alsatian village of Bremmelbach (France), killing five children and injuring three others.

Nearly every family in the small hamlet of 100 people near Strasbourg was affected by the accident, officials said.

The police said that the children, aged four to eleven, found the shell hidden under a wood pile in a courtyard and began playing with it after school. One of the children apparently threw the shell on its fuse, causing the explosion.

An immigrant from Germany, now an international banker in New York, tells a happier story. After the war he and a group of Friends (Quakers) erected a church building in Hanover for their use. Before putting a Quonset hut on the lot, they dug deep to lay the foundation. Also, they dug on the site for sand to use in making cement, and they drilled a well. Too, they dug holes for temporary outhouses. In 1950, they began using the building as a meeting place.

Ten years later, the banker learned that the city of Hanover had forced the

Friends to abandon their church. Reliable reports indicated that a 500-pound bomb lay buried on the grounds where the church had been built. After the church grounds were cleared of people, the bomb was found with the help of a Geiger counter, unearthed, and its arming mechanism disengaged without incident.

"COUNT THE STARS IF YOU CAN. SO MANY SHALL YOUR DESCENDANTS BE" (v. 5 NEB). When was the last time you were outside at night in the country or in the mountains or desert and were awestruck by the star-studded sky? I recall an incident from 1972; it always comes to mind when I read this verse. Our family was moving to California and we were camping along the way. As we entered Utah, we checked the map for our destination that night and immediately decided on the place with a name that was music to our ears—Dixie State Park, near St. George, Utah. Being Texans we warmed to the word *Dixie.*

That evening at dusk we arrived in the Dixie Canyon and decided because it looked like such natural terrain for rattlesnakes, scorpions, and such that we would bed down in the station wagon. Having a cot, I unrolled my sleeping bag upon it and slept under the open sky. I say "slept"—the Lord was putting on such a show in the heavens that night that I could scarcely close my eyes for fear I would miss something. The canyon was pitch black and the sky was cloudless. Never in my life have I seen so many stars. They filled the skies. And it was no doubt under such a sky that the Lord told Abram to "count the stars *if you can!*" What a promise!

Robert H. Baker in his book *Introducing the Constellations,* says there are only a "few thousand stars bright enough to be separately visible to the unaided eye." But "millions of fainter ones are revealed with a large telescope. As many as 100,000 million stars, suns if you please, are members of this galaxy to which the sun belongs."

Topics for Youth

PROMISES, PROMISES!—Count 'em! There are at least ten promises of God to Abram in the brief passage that makes up today's lesson. Can you find ten? Check the list below and see if they were all fulfilled.

1. A son of Abram's would be his heir.
2. He would have offspring as numerous as the stars.
3. His descendants would live a while in a foreign country.
4. In the foreign land, they would be slaves and suffer mistreatment.
5. Their exile would last 400 years.
6. At the end of that time, they will come out of the foreign country.
7. When they leave, they will bring with them "great possessions."
8. Abram will be buried after living to a ripe old age.
9. His descendants would live right there in Canaan.
10. The land, from Egypt to the Euphrates, is given to his descendants.

MORE PROMISES—Bishop J. Floyd Williams of the Pentecostal Holiness Church tells a story that illustrates what he means when he says, "A young person—or anyone—really isn't ready to pray until his heart is filled with the promises of God."

If ever any man lived to preach it is Bishop Williams. When he was still in elementary school, he used to gather the other children together on the steps of the schoolhouse and "preach" to them. For the past twenty-eight years, he has preached over 300 times a year. So it was acutely distressing to him one day in the late 1970s when a stroke left one side of his body lifeless.

"One eye wouldn't close," he said. "I couldn't talk without holding one side of my face and I couldn't eat without holding my mouth. I spent five sleepless nights and five terror-filled days like this. My wife could see that I was terribly depressed. I felt that if I couldn't preach I'd rather die."

The bishop was in this low state when the telephone rang. It was a fellow pastor calling. "Tell the bishop," the man said to Mrs. Williams, "we have prayed through. He's going to be all right."

"When I heard that, a promise from God came alive in my heart," the bishop says. "Why art thou cast down, O my soul? and why art thou disquieted within me? hope thou in God: for I shall yet praise him, who is the health of my countenance and my God" (Psalms 42:11).

The next Sunday the bishop preached. When he stumbled over a multisyllabic word, he said the devil whispered in his ear, "Your healing isn't complete." Stopping in his sermon, he said audibly, "Get behind me, Satan, I will run that one through again." And this time he enunciated the word perfectly. The bishop has been preaching ever since, his faith laying hold of great promises of God.

A young person can do no better thing to prepare for life ahead than fill his heart with the promises of God.

LESSON 3   SEPTEMBER 19
God Gives Jacob a New Name

Background Scripture: Genesis 27; 28; 31; 32
Devotional Reading: Genesis 35:1–15

Genesis 32:9–12, 22–30

9 And Jacob said, O God of my father Abraham, and God of my father Isaac, the LORD which saidst unto me, Return unto thy country, and to thy kindred, and I will deal well with thee:

10 I am not worthy of the least of all the mercies, and of all the truth, which thou hast shewed unto thy servant; for with my staff I passed over this Jordan; and now I am become two bands.

32 ORIGINS OF GOD'S CHOSEN PEOPLE

11 Deliver me, I pray thee, from the hand of my brother, from the hand of Esau; for I fear him, lest he will come and smite me, and the mother with the children.
12 And thou saidst, I will surely do thee good, and make thy seed as the sand of the sea, which cannot be numbered for multitude.
22 And he rose up that night, and took his two wives, and his two womenservants, and his eleven sons, and passed over the ford Jabbok.
23 And he took them, and sent them over the brook, and sent over that he had.
24 And Jacob was left alone; and there wrestled a man with him until the breaking of the day.
25 And when he saw that he prevailed not against him, he touched the hollow of his thigh; and the hollow of Jacob's thigh was out of joint, as he wrestled with him.
26 And he said, Let me go, for the day breaketh. And he said, I will not let thee go, except thou bless me.
27 And he said unto him, What is thy name? And he said, Jacob.
28 And he said, Thy name shall be called no more Jacob, but Israel: for as a prince hast thou power with God and with men, and hast prevailed.
29 And Jacob asked him, and said, Tell me, I pray thee, thy name. And he said, Wherefore is it that thou dost ask after my name? And he blessed him there.
30 And Jacob called the name of the place Peniel: for I have seen God face to face, and my life is preserved.

KEY VERSE: "And he said, Thy name shall be called no more Jacob, but Israel: for as a prince hast thou power with God and with men, and hast prevailed." Genesis 32:28.

Home Daily Bible Readings
Sept. 13   M.   Jacob Deceived Isaac, Genesis 27:19–29.
Sept. 14   T.   Esau Denied Birthright and Blessing, Genesis 27:30–36.
Sept. 15   W.   Jacob Sent to Laban, Genesis 28:1–5.
Sept. 16   T.   Jacob's Dream at Bethel, Genesis 28:10–22.
Sept. 17   F.   God Sent Jacob Home, Genesis 31:1–16.
Sept. 18   S.   Jacob Prepared to Meet Esau, Genesis 32:1–12.
Sept. 19   S.   Jacob Became Israel, Genesis 32:22–30.

Lesson Aim: That your students may yield themselves to God now and know the richest blessing of God.

LESSON OUTLINE
Background to the Scripture
Looking at the Scripture Text

I. Praying in a Panic (Genesis 32:9-12)
II. Striving in One's Strength Alone (Genesis 32:22-24)
III. Winning by Yielding (Genesis 32:25-30)
Applying the Scripture

Background to the Scripture
In our century, Israel the Land and Israel the people have again become one. As we watch to see what God will do with His ancient people in fulfillment of prophecy, it is helpful to remember the roots of that lovely name *Israel*.

Scholars place Jacob in the eighteenth century B.C. As today's lesson shows, Jacob, younger son of Isaac, first heard the name Israel breathed from the lips of a heavenly being at a critical juncture in his life. The Lord reaffirmed His intention that Jacob should henceforth be called Israel by appearing to him later at Bethel (Genesis 35:10). From that time, his offspring became known as "the children of Israel." The exodus from Egypt under Moses marked the birth of the nation Israel and subsequently the Promised Land, too, took on the name.

The sanctity of the Land Israel became established early in Jewish life. The Talmud, a collection of Jewish interpretations of the Law, stated, "The Land of Israel is holier than all other lands . . ." and declared that prophecy was possible only in the Land. Devout Jews were taught that only in the Land of Israel could they fulfill the Law.

Looking at the Scripture Text
Praying in a Panic (vv. 9-12) In one of his delightful stories, A. A. Milne has Winnie the Pooh invite himself into Rabbit's underground room for a midday feast of honey. As Pooh Bear was wont to do, he stuffed himself full—so full that, when he tried to wriggle out of Rabbit's doorway, he became stuck. A tear on his cheek, realizing he was going to have to remain there until he slimmed down a bit, he asked that a sustaining book be read to him, such a one that "would comfort a Wedged Bear in Great Tightness."

Our lesson for today finds Jacob in "great tightness." After living twenty years in Padan-aram in Mesopotamia, he has journeyed south on his way to Canaan at the command of God. But before he can take his large family and livestock across the Jordan into Canaan, he has one important matter to settle. Twenty years earlier, he had fled his home because he had cheated Esau out of the blessing that rightfully belonged to the firstborn, and Esau had sworn to kill Jacob in revenge. Jacob had now sent messengers ahead to find Esau, who had settled in the southern region called Seir (and Edom), and inform him of Jacob's arrival. The messengers did their duty and returned with ominous news: Esau was on his way to meet Jacob and with him were 400 men. As verse 7 says, "Jacob was greatly afraid and distressed."

But Jacob was never one to be without a plan. His wits were honed by twenty years of scheming to get rich while serving the crafty Laban, his father-in-law. And he had succeeded. It was natural that the resourceful Jacob thought of a plan. Fearing the worst, he split up his considerable caravan into two groups, thinking that if Esau meant to attack him, at least some of the women and children and cattle—and hopefully he—could escape. But having divided them, Jacob bursts into prayer in a most sincere petition for some form of divine deliverance.

Jacob knew to whom he was praying. In Mesopotamia, surrounded by idolaters, yet he had kept faith with the "God of Abraham and Isaac" and in his prayer he recalled the special personal Name, Jehovah (translated LORD), whereby God had revealed Himself. The pronunciation of this name is open to question, considering that the Hebrew script of that name deleted vowels (JHVH).

Jacob knew likewise that he was unworthy. Verse 10 reveals that a change has taken place in Jacob. He is more humble than before as can be seen by comparing his prayer with the self-centered vow he made at Bethel when the angels appeared to him on a ladder to heaven as he was fleeing from Esau (28:20-22). Jacob recalls how he had earlier crossed the Jordan "with nothing but a walking stick and now I have come back with these two groups" (TEV). He had two wives, Rachel and Leah, eleven sons and a daughter, numerous servants, and thousands of cattle. Shortly he would dispatch 220 goats, 220 sheep, 30 milk camels with their colts, 40 cows, 10 bulls and 30 asses with 10 foals as a gift to "appease" (v. 20) Esau. Yes, Jacob had been richly blessed!

Further, *Jacob knew for what to pray.* His request was specific: "Deliver me, I pray thee, from . . . Esau." The latter half of verse 11 suggests a most cruel fate. He feared that Esau's marauders would dash "the mother . . . in pieces upon her children" (Hosea 10:14) in the manner of raids in that day.

Lastly, Jacob's prayer shows that *he knew that the Lord could help him.* He may even have been quite confident, but his faith wavered. Pleading the promises made to him (31:3), he claimed the promise made earlier to his grandfather Abraham and confirmed with Isaac, that descendants "which cannot be numbered for multitude" were to be given him.

God, the spring of unfathomable goodness, would surely do him good (vv. 9, 12); this Jacob knew. Reminded of promises the Lord had made to him and his fathers, he took his stand on the promise and commanded God, so to speak, to fulfill His Word. This God takes great delight to do (Isaiah 43:26). Jacob's is a model prayer—first praise and worship, followed by thanksgiving, petition, and rest in the promise.

Striving in One's Strength Alone (vv. 22-24) Having obtained some peace through his communion with God, Jacob slept (v. 13) and then sent away, on the next day, the rich gifts by which he hoped to gain acceptance with Esau. The activities of the day kept Jacob occupied, but as darkness fell on the second day the tension mounted again—this time to a crisis. Verse 22 shows that they were at the brook Jabbok. This stream flows west into the Jordan about halfway between Lake Chinnereth (the Sea of Galilee) and the Salt (or Dead) Sea. Jacob took across its shallow waters Leah and Rachel and their servants,

Bilhah and Zilpah, and his eleven sons—Reuben, Simeon, Levi, Judah, Dan, Naphtali, Gad, Asher, Issachar, Zebulun, and Joseph. (Dinah, in typical custom of the day, was included but not named; Benjamin was yet to be born.)

Jacob sent all of these ahead of him and he remained all alone. We can almost see him, reviewing all of the plans he had carefully laid, pacing back and forth in the dark with nothing to do but wait. Esau was expected the following day. Then suddenly "a man" came and wrestled with Jacob all the night. We cannot be sure of the identity of this "man" though there is much to favor the view that this was the Son of God in one of His preincarnate appearances to man. Jacob had earlier seen a large body of angels (32:1, 2). Nowhere does the writer identify this "man" as an angel though years later the Prophet Hosea did (Hosea 12:4). But Scripture in numerous instances calls a heavenly visitor an angel or "the Angel of the Lord" when the context of the story leaves every impression that the visitor was the Lord Himself (Genesis 16:7; Exodus 3:2-6; Numbers 22:22-35; Judges 13:16, 17). As we shall see, Jacob came to sense that this "man" with whom he wrestled all night was God (v. 30).

But the fact of the struggle is probably more important for us than the identity of the stranger. This was a literal, physical wrestling match. If we had been there, we could have heard the grunts and groans of physical exertion. The Lord had intervened in Jacob's life, allowing a crushing crisis to face him, so as to bring the "supplanter"—scheming, conniving Jacob—to the end of himself. Spiritually, Jacob had already owned the Lord as his covenant God. We would say today that he had been born again at the time of his vision at Bethel in Genesis 28. But up to now he had continued to live by his wits. His struggle with the heavenly being symbolizes his striving in fleshly energies instead of relying on the Lord.

Winning by Yielding (vv. 25-30) Verse 25 in Today's English Version says that, "When the man saw that he was not winning the struggle, he hit Jacob on the hip, and it was thrown out of joint." Jacob showed great strength. The Other Man could not "prevail," so tenacious and determined was Jacob. The powerful "touch" of the heavenly visitor shows that He was not wrestling merely to win a contest; He could have done it easily much earlier.

Light was just beginning to appear on the eastern horizon signalling the coming day and the "man" begged Jacob to let him go; there was business ahead for Jacob. But Jacob, unable to wrestle any longer, had sensed something of God in this Wrestler and clung to the man all the more. He said "I will not let you go unless you bless me" (NIV).

The question, "What is your name?" was another way of asking, "Who are you? What are you really like?" The name was but an expression of one's personality. Jacob answered honestly, "Jacob," a name that means "supplanter" or "one that takes by the heel." At birth, he had reached out and taken his elder twin brother Esau by the heel, symbolic of what he would do later in life. Now he admitted what he was. He had nothing to hide. His primary concern was no longer about Esau, but that he should receive the blessing of God. This was the turning point in Jacob's life.

"Your name will no longer be Jacob, but Israel, because you have struggled with God and with men and have overcome" (NIV), said the heavenly Visitor. Greater than any blessing he could have possibly expected, Jacob received the name *Israel*—prince of El (Calvin), meaning wrestler with God or "God rules" (Oxford Annotated Bible). Having not been able to overcome God (in the form of this Heavenly Being), Jacob yielded to His power and thereby gained the blessing. Luther says of this verse: "we mustn't try to overcome God by our reason or natural powers. He is only overcome through faith in His promises."

Jacob knew now that this "man" was some heavenly Messenger and he pressed Him for His Name. In other words, he wanted the "Man" to identify himself. Instead of telling Jacob His Name, "he blessed him there." Evidently the Visitor invoked the old promise of blessing first given to Abraham and Isaac, telling Jacob that in his seed all the nations were to be blessed. Jacob had nothing to fear from Esau. Exclaiming that he had seen "God face to face" and his life had been preserved, he rose to meet the day. Verse 31 says that as he crossed at Penuel (the name given that hallowed spot), he limped on his lame hip, but that "the sun rose upon him," symbolic of the new man who bore the new name, Israel.

Applying the Scripture
Lead your students to be "doers of the Word" as they consider afresh this story from the life of the patriarch Jacob. Before class, assign the two wrong examples and the one positive example in this section to members of the class. Ask them to be ready to tell the class about one application their assignment suggests.

1. The Folly of Using Material Goods to Restore a Relationship—Jacob is a rather pitiful sight as he puts together a ransom from among his material possessions which he hopes will gain him favor with his offended brother. If he were sending all of these things out of the overflow of a heart of love—and not self-preservation—it would be different. Do we sometimes as parents attempt to make up to our children by inundating them with things? Or what about an employer who realizes that he has taken advantage of a subordinate and tries to make it right by showering the individual with flowery but empty praise? Or the husband or wife who tries to win back the affection of the other by lavish gifts and expensive clothing? There is a place for gifts and salary increases; yet these are empty without a face-to-face admission of wrongdoing and a sincere expression of apology.

2. Resorting to Prayer—Alexander Maclaren notes that in the story Jacob "schemes first, and prays second. The order might have been inverted with advantage, but is like the man—in the lowest phase of his character." Ouch! This does have a familiar ring to it! How often are we like Jacob, scheming and striving to come up with the answer, and only using prayer as a last re-

sort. God would have us trust Him fully first, last, and always. Give a modern example, perhaps something from your own life.

3. Standing on the Promises—If we can learn only one thing from Jacob's experience, and really learn it so that we begin to put it into practice in all circumstances, it should be this truth. In this prayer, he voiced his desperation, but he concluded by restating the promise he knew God had made to him. If we have a promise from God, our hearts can be kept through any storm, any disappointment, any loss. These trials are sure to come our way. Have we stored up God's promises in our hearts so we will be ready for the "rainy day"? Think of a modern-day example of this.

Questions for Discussion
Make use of these questions to involve your students in learning and to test their understanding of the lesson.
1. From Jacob's prayer, what evidence is there that he has begun to change (vv. 9-12)? 2. Why did Jacob have reason to fear Esau (vv. 6-8, 11)? 3. What gave Jacob ground on which to stand—and what can support us in our time of crisis (vv. 9, 12)? 4. What is the meaning to us of the wrestling match with the divine being (vv. 24-28)? 5. What is the significance of Jacob's new name (v. 28)?

Illustrating the Scripture
Examples and quotations to help the teacher communicate the lesson.
ISRAEL That masterful Bible expositor of an earlier day, Alexander Maclaren, sees in the bestowal of the name *Israel* upon Jacob a highly significant truth for us. After all, as Paul said, we are "the Israel of God" (Galatians 6:16).

"That name was transmitted to his (Jacob's) descendants, and has passed over to the company of believing men, who have been overcome by God, and have prevailed with God. It is a charter and a promise. It is a stringent reminder of duty and a lofty ideal. A true Christian is an 'Israel.' His office is to wrestle with God. Nor can we forget how this mysterious scene was repeated in yet more solemn fashion, beneath the gnarled olives of Gethsemane, glistening in the light of the paschal full moon, when the true Israel prayed with such sore crying and tears that His body partook of the struggle, and 'his sweat was as it were great drops of blood falling down to the ground.' The word which describes Christ's agony is that which is often rendered 'wrestling,' and perhaps is selected with intentional allusion to this incident. At all events, when we think of Jacob by the brook Jabbok, and of a 'greater than our father Jacob' by the brook Kedron, we may well learn what persistence, what earnestness and effort of the whole nature, go to make up the ideal of prayer, and may well blush for the miserable indifference and torpor of what we venture to call our prayers. These are our patterns, 'as many as walk according to this rule,' and are thereby shown to be 'the Israel of God'—upon them shall be peace."

IT'S ALL IN THE ATTITUDE   Our walk as Christians is warfare against the world, the flesh, and the devil. But if we are "doing our own thing," we shouldn't mistake the resistance we are meeting as coming from those sources. We are resisting God and He it is who is striving against us.

All of us have had the experience of putting our hand out the window of a speeding vehicle and feeling the wind resistance. If we tilt our flattened palm upward so that the wind strikes our hand on the under side, and if the car is going fast enough, the wind's force may drive our hand up. But if we exert ourselves to keep our palm at only a slightly positive angle of attack, the resistance of the wind will hardly be felt. It all depends on the angle of attack.

An Air Force pilot whose duty it was to orient new basic airmen to military life used to allude to this aeronautical law. "How you do in the Air Force all depends on your attitude," he used to tell them. "If you develop a positive angle of attack, nothing can stop you. Just think of how an airplane rolls out and assumes a positive angle of attack as it approaches the runway for a landing. The forces of gravity and drag would bring that multiton machine crashing into the runway but for one thing—the aircraft is moving at enough speed and with enough power and at *a positive angle of attack* so that the forces of gravity and drag are overcome."

For us, the positive angle of attack or positive attitude represents a life of trust in God, of relying on His power and grace. When we "go with the flow" of His Spirit then we, too, become overcomers for Christ (Galatians 5:16; Romans 8:37).

Topics for Youth

WHAT TO DO WHEN THE WRONG WE HAVE DONE CATCHES UP WITH US—Sooner or later the wrong we have done catches up with us. As a stepmother used to tell her teenaged stepson, "be sure your sin will find you out." Only later did the youth find out that that is a Bible verse (Numbers 32:23). But what do you do when your troubles "come home to roost"?

1. Know That You Are Not the Only Sinner in the World.
2. Go to Someone and Share Your Problem.
3. *Go to God!* Jacob, like so many of us, resorted to prayer after he took all the physical precautions he knew to take. But we should tell God our problems and earnestly wait for His answers. It may bring about the most important change in our life, as it did for Jacob!

CAN A PERSON REALLY CHANGE? REALLY?—One of the most difficult areas in which to expect change, society tells us, is in a person's sexual orientation. In its February 6, 1981 issue, *Christianity Today* carried an article by Tom Minnery entitled "Homosexuals Can Change." Several personal illustrations served to point out this truth: "Frank Worthen of Love in Action, the longest-running of the so-called ex-gay ministries, believes that overcoming homosexuality is extremely difficult. He believes most people who attempt it don't make it. Yet he's strongly convinced it can be done, and he offers himself as proof. He ended his homosexual lifestyle in 1973 by converting to Christ, yet his tortuous road out of it very nearly ended in suicide, so overwhelmingly severe were the emotional obstacles. He describes himself as happily celibate, although he does face the problem of keeping his psychic response to women under control, since he is not married.

"He said, 'I personally think (homosexuals) have an excellent chance of going on to marriage and a family. Not many of them do, however. They're usually held back by fear, inhibitions and the like. At Love in Action, we have seen a lot of marriages. I have seen all kinds of people come out of the gay lifestyle and develop a heterosexual response. This isn't to say it's easy. It's never easy. It requires a real heavy commitment to Christ. You actually have to lose your life to save it. A lot of people don't realize that.'"

LESSON 4 SEPTEMBER 26
God Preserves His People

Background Scripture: Genesis 37; 42–45; 50
Devotional Reading: Genesis 37:12–28

Genesis 50:15–26

15 And when Joseph's brethren saw that their father was dead, they said, Joseph will peradventure hate us, and will certainly requite us all the evil which we did unto him.

16 And they sent a messenger unto Joseph, saying, Thy father did command before he died, saying,

17 So shall ye say unto Joseph, Forgive, I pray thee now, the trespass of thy brethren, and their sin; for they did unto thee evil: and now, we pray thee, forgive the trespass of the servants of the God of thy father. And Joseph wept when they spake unto him.

18 And his brethren also went and fell down before his face; and they said, Behold, we be thy servants.

19 And Joseph said unto them, Fear not: for am I in the place of God?

20 But as for you, ye thought evil against me; but God meant it unto good, to bring to pass, as it is this day, to save much people alive.

21 Now therefore fear ye not: I will nourish you, and your little ones. And he comforted them, and spake kindly unto them.

22 And Joseph dwelt in Egypt, he, and his father's house: and Joseph lived a hundred and ten years.

23 And Joseph saw Ephraim's children of the third generation: the children also of Machir the son of Manasseh were brought up upon Joseph's knees.

24 And Joseph said unto his brethren, I die; and God will surely visit

you, and bring you out of this land unto the land which he sware to Abraham, to Isaac, and to Jacob.
25 And Joseph took an oath of the children of Israel, saying, God will surely visit you, and ye shall carry up my bones from hence.
26 So Joseph died, being an hundred and ten years old: and they embalmed him, and he was put in a coffin in Egypt.

KEY VERSE: "But as for you, ye thought evil against me; but God meant it unto good, to bring to pass, as it is this day, to save much people alive." Genesis 50:20.

Home Daily Bible Readings
Sept. 20 M. Joseph's Dreams About His Family, Genesis 37:1–11.
Sept. 21 T. Joseph Sold to Traders, Genesis 37:12–28.
Sept. 22 W. Joseph's Family Seeks Grain, Genesis 42:1–8.
Sept. 23 T. Back to Egypt for Grain Again, Genesis 43:1–15.
Sept. 24 F. Concern for a Father, Genesis 44:18–34.
Sept. 25 S. Joseph Reveals His Identity, Genesis 45:1–15.
Sept. 26 S. Joseph Reassured His Brothers, Genesis 50:15–26.

Lesson Aim: Because of the positive example of Joseph's life, adults should be able to face the future without fear.

LESSON OUTLINE
Background to the Scripture
Looking at the Scripture Text
 I. "Forgive, I Pray Thee" (Genesis 50:15–18)
 II. "God Meant It for Good" (Genesis 50:19–21)
 III. Joseph's Later Years (Genesis 50:22–26)
Applying the Scripture

Background to the Scripture

Wearing his "coat of many colors," seventeen-year-old Joseph had been sent on a mission by Jacob to see how his brothers were doing. He found them at Dothan tending their father's herds. Immediately, the brothers let go their jealous rage and stripped Joseph of his coat, throwing him like an animal into a deep pit. They would have killed him had not Reuben, the eldest, intervened. Instead, they sold him to merchants on their way to Egypt and sprinkled the blood of a young goat on Joseph's coat to cover their evil act. Then they lied to their father Jacob, telling him that they assumed a wild animal had mauled Joseph. Jacob, who bore the name Israel, grieved over his son Joseph for some dozen years until, forced by a harsh drought, he sent his sons to Egypt to buy grain. There they found not only grain, but their brother Joseph as governor of all Egypt.

Eventually they brought aged Israel down to Egypt to be joyfully reunited with Joseph and there Israel lived out his remaining seventeen years. But at his death, the ten older brothers and Benjamin feared for their lives. With Israel gone, would Joseph seek revenge "for all the harm (they) did to him" (Genesis 50:15 TEV)?

Looking at the Scripture Text
"Forgive, I Pray Thee" (vv. 15-18)   When Jacob's twelve sons returned to Egypt after the burial in Canaan, no doubt the eleven brothers of Joseph resumed their lives as the head of their clans in Goshen, in northeastern Egypt. Evidently Joseph went on to Pharaoh's court to carry on the affairs of state. But his brothers were worried. According to verse 16, they sent a messenger to Joseph stating that their father had commanded that he forgive the brothers their "trespass" and "their sin."

The patriarch could have so ordered his son Joseph, but it is doubtful that old Jacob actually ever issued such a command. What is more likely, the brothers chose to use their father's place of honor to secure forgiveness for their past deeds. "Their roundabout way of going to work by sending a messenger was an insult to their brother," says Maclaren. "The craft which was their father's by nature seems to have been amply transmitted . . . note, too, the ingenious way of slipping in motives for forgiving, first in putting the mention of their relationship into Jacob's mouth, and then claiming to be worshipers of 'thy (not our) father's God.'"

In the fourteen chapters of Genesis devoted to Joseph's life, there is little to suggest an unforgiving attitude on the part of Joseph. True, he was stern with his brothers when they first arrived in Egypt. He had been treated as a spy when he was sent to "see whether it be well" with his brothers (37:14) and, when they had arrived in Egypt to buy grain, Joseph accused them of spying. He even threw them in prison. At that time, the brothers confessed to each other that they were reaping trouble for their bad treatment of Joseph (42:21, 22; 44:16), but Joseph never showed any inclination toward revenge.

Later, when Joseph revealed his true identity to his brothers, he embraced them genuinely. He became the intermediary between them and the Egyptians, securing for them and their flocks the choice pasture land of Goshen. Nothing in his actions suggests that they had anything to fear. But their own guilty consciences would not allow them to trust Joseph. "Their fear that Jacob's death would be followed by an outbreak of long-smothered revenge betrayed too clearly their own base natures" (Maclaren).

Desperate in their attempt to stave off revenge, they also went to see Joseph in person and confessed their "trespass" and "their sin" (v. 17). Their words show "the depth of their humility, the sincerity of their repentance and the genuineness of their religion" says Thomas Whitelaw (*Pulpit Commentary*).

They even bowed down on the floor before Joseph. If their actions reminded Governor Joseph of the dream of his youth, now so literally fulfilled

(37:5-11), the text does not say so. Joseph did not revel in their servitude for a moment. Rather, he wept. On three previous occasions, Joseph was overcome with emotion and shed tears (42:24; 43:30; 45:2) when he met his brothers and was reunited with them. A sensitive man, Joseph was hurt deeply by their lack of trust in him.

"God Meant It for Good" (vv. 19-21) "Fear not, for am I in the place of God?" he asked. It may be true, as Lester Sumrall says, that there are 365 "fear nots" in the Bible—one for each day of the year. Joseph's "fear not," repeated in verse 21, was music to the ears of his brethren. His words carry the implied thought—"Am I in the place of God *to take revenge?*"

Verse 20 has been called *the grand golden key to the whole of Joseph's life history.* The past actions of Joseph's brothers were plain for all to see; they had "meant evil" against Joseph. But God, Joseph said, "meant it for good." The same Hebrew verb *to think, intend,* or *purpose* is used to express both ideas. Joseph, attributing to God the glory for working good out of the evil of man, takes no credit himself. His words here are consistent with what he said when first he and his brothers were reunited: "God sent me ahead of you to preserve for you a remnant on earth and to save your lives by a great deliverance. So then, it was not you who sent me here, but God. He made me father to Pharaoh, lord of his entire household and ruler of all Egypt" (Genesis 45:7, 8 NIV). These words tell more about Joseph's secret of survival during some thirteen years of isolation, imprisonment, and adversity than does anything else. He had developed the ability to look behind men and see God at work.

"*I will nourish you, and your little ones.*" The NIV and RSV say, "I will provide." The harsh famine had ended some years earlier, but Joseph evidently remained as the governor or prime minister over domestic affairs for all Egypt, including Goshen. He pledged to his blood kin his loyalty and devotion. As long as Joseph lived, the Israelite people enjoyed peace and plenty in a perfect setting for God to preserve for Himself a nation.

Joseph's Later Years (vv. 22-26) In the closing five verses of Genesis, the name Joseph appears seven times as if to emphasize the central place this man had in the plan of God at that time. We are told that he "dwelt in Egypt, he and his father's house," meaning that all of the children of Israel remained in Egypt even though the famine had ended and their patriarch Jacob had been buried in Canaan. It was now time for the sojourning sons of Abraham to put down roots and become a nation.

Next, we are told that Joseph lived "a hundred and ten years." Though he did not reach the advanced age of Abraham (175) or Isaac (180) or his father Jacob (147) Joseph's 110 years still outmeasured the seventy or eighty years which Scripture gives as an average life span (Psalms 90:10). God gave Joseph both a full and long life. In the words of Matthew Poole, Joseph's life is summed up—"for about thirteen years of affliction he enjoyed eighty years of honor and as much happiness as earth could afford him."

The next mention of Joseph's name is in connection with the primary source of that happiness—his family. It was his joy and that of his wife

Asenath to see three generations of his son Ephraim's children. These are named in the listing of the descendants of the twelve tribal elders in 1 Chronicles 7:20—Ephraim's son "Shuthelah, and Bered his son, and Tahath his son." Verse 23 further says that the grandchildren of Joseph's other son, Manasseh, were "born" or "brought up" on Joseph's knees. With what few words does the Bible show that to Joseph, his family came first! Though he was second in command in Egypt, he did not allow his position to keep him from his children and grandchildren. (Note in verse 23 that the firstborn, Manasseh, is listed after Ephraim in keeping with the surprising blessing the dying Jacob had pronounced upon the two boys [48:14–19].)

The next mention of Joseph is at his death. Though Scripture is silent on the point, it appears that when Joseph could carry the duties of his office no longer, he went to live with his family. As he saw death approaching, he reminded "his brothers" that "God will surely come to your aid and take you up out of this land to the land he promised on oath to Abraham, Isaac, and Jacob" (v. 24 NIV). Jacob had passed on to Joseph the hope of the Promised Land (48:21) and now Joseph "hands on the hope to his descendants."

The strength of Joseph's faith and conviction in this future deliverance is seen in the mention of Joseph's name in verse 25. Being confident that God would deliver the people Israel from Egypt, he made "the sons of Israel" swear solemnly to carry his bones out of Egypt when the people would leave that land. Neither Joseph nor the succeeding generation of Israel's leadership knew when God would "visit" the nation and take them out of Egypt. The "sons of Israel" who entered into the oath with Joseph were not the ones who later carried his bones out when Moses led the way (Exodus 13:19) or buried them in Shechem (Joshua 24:32). That was the duty of their sons or perhaps their grandsons.

The significant fact we should not overlook is Joseph's steadfast faith. He did not say, "if" God delivers you, but "when." Centuries later the writer to the Hebrews added Joseph's name to the honor roll of heroes of faith, remarking "by faith Joseph, when his end was near, spoke about the exodus of the Israelites from Egypt and gave instructions about his bones" (Hebrews 11:22 NIV).

With the final mention of Joseph's name, Moses reports Joseph's death in Egypt and draws the great book of Genesis to a close. Like his father Jacob, Joseph was embalmed after the traditions of the Egyptians.

Joseph might have been buried immediately in Canaan, as his father was, but the reasons for his wise choice are not hard to understand. In time, the people of Israel might forget that they were strangers in Egypt and that their true destiny lay in another land. The most natural thing for them would be to settle comfortably in Egypt. But Joseph's coffin remained as a profound witness to the promises of God. Also, the rulers of Egypt would not always look kindly on this growing nation of Hebrews. Indeed, this was the case in Moses' generation when a king came to the throne in Egypt, "who did not know Joseph" (Exodus 1:8). The coffin of the princely Joseph would be an eloquent, objective remembrance of the high respect paid to this son of Abraham and thus an Egyptian monarch might not hasten to crush the people of this former ruler.

With the words, "a coffin in Egypt," the scroll of Genesis ends. "This speaks to us vividly of the power of sin and death and the extent of man's fall," says Atkinson. "The book which begins 'In the beginning God created the heavens and the earth,' ends 'in a coffin in Egypt.' All seems lost, finished, reduced to dust and ashes, futility and vanity. This would be the story of man apart from Christ. We may thank God that it is not the end of the story."

Applying the Scripture

While we are coping with the present day's affairs, we are carrying "baggage" from our past and walking either confidently or without hope into the future. Challenge your class members to select the application that best fits their need and urge them to take action on it this week.

1. Unbelief Fears the Consequences of Past Sins—Joseph's brothers were afraid to see their aged father die for fear that at last Joseph would take revenge for their ill treatment of him. It did not matter that those events had taken place at least twenty years earlier.

One wonders if the seeds of this distrust were not planted in their hearts years earlier as they observed their father, Jacob. They saw how Jacob treated Joseph with favoritism. And was not Joseph's "spy mission" to check on his brothers, at his father's command, an evidence that Jacob did not trust his sons? The brothers of Joseph had developed a skeptical attitude and at Jacob's death it all came out.

A distrusting, disbelieving attitude provides fertile soil for the nourishment of fears. This story illustrates supremely that our trust in God should be such that we are free from fear. Ask: Are you building trusting relationships with the members of your families and others who are close to you? What can you do, if not, to avoid what happened to the brothers of Joseph?

2. Forgiveness Provides Peace Now—When we consider forgiveness we ought to think of it in two dimensions, from God and with our fellow man. Martin Luther knew what it was to be hounded by a guilty conscience. "Sin is so great an evil that it will never permit a sinner to rest until he has repented and has asked pardon of God and those whom he has wronged," he wrote in commenting on Genesis 50. "Only faith in Christ can calm our troubled conscience. I myself could not obtain an appeased conscience, despite all I did, until I learned to know Christ whose vicarious atonement now is so ever present to me as though He had redeemed me today. Sin will always torture our conscience until we have found pardon and peace through faith in our Redeemer."

There is another side to this truth. The brothers groveled in the dirt before Joseph and we, too, are inclined to "put on sackcloth and ashes" to show our deep repentance before God. He who looks on the heart knows if we have genuinely repented. As Maclaren says, "Our Brother (Christ), against whom we have sinned, wants love, not cowering; and if we believe in His forgiveness, we shall give Him the hearts which He desires. . . ." Ask: Have you accepted the forgiveness of God and of others?

3. Faith Plans Confidently for the Future—When it came time to die, Joseph reached back to the promises made to his forefathers and made his plans with confidence. So sure was he of the promises of God that he took an oath from his brethren requiring them to carry his remains out of Egypt when the day of deliverance finally came.

Ask: Are we that confident of the promises the Lord has given to us? Where do we need to apply this to our lives? Are we unsure that we are saved and that we have eternal life, even when God has promised? Are we unsure that He will provide for our family in these hard times? Are we nurturing our faith by spending time in God's Word so that the promises of God are planted deep within our hearts? This lesson should inspire us to trust God and look to Him for the future.

Questions for Discussion
Make use of these questions to involve your students in learning and to test their understanding of the lesson.
1. Was there anything in Joseph's life that led his brothers to think he would seek revenge?   2. When we see evil motives in others—even when they do not exist—what are we really seeing?   3. From the wording of the brothers' confession in verse 17, what leads us to believe they were sincere?   4. What was it in Joseph's idea of God that allowed him to forgive his brothers?   5. How is Joseph's forgiving attitude a reflection of God's forgiveness toward us?   6. How can we be sure that God forgives us our trespasses and our sins?   7. The sons of Israel were told that God would bring them out of Egypt. Why do you think Israel did not return to Canaan when Joseph died?   8. Why would Joseph care to have his bones buried in Canaan?

Illustrating the Scripture
Examples and quotations to help the teacher communicate the lesson.

"I AM SORRY"   The Reverend John R. W. Stott, in his little book *Confess Your Sins*, shows how forgiveness provides peace *now*. He says:

"D. L. Moody, the famous American evangelist of the last century, exhibited (the rare Christian grace of confession of sin) and I think I was more struck by this than by anything else about him when reading a recent biography. Let me give you two examples which impressed me.

"In the early days at their home in Northfield, Massachusetts, Moody was anxious to have a lawn like those he had greatly admired in England. But one day his two sons, Paul and Will, let the horses loose from the barn. They galloped over his precious lawn and ruined it. And Moody lost his temper with them. But the boys never forgot how, after they had gone to bed that night, they heard his heavy footsteps as he approached and entered their room, and, laying a heavy hand on their head, said to them: 'I want you to forgive me; that wasn't the way Christ taught.'

"On another occasion a theological student interrupted him during an address and Moody snapped an irritated retort. Let J. C. Pollock describe what happened at the end of the sermon: 'He reached his close. He paused. Then he said: "Friends, I want to confess before you all that I made a great mistake at the beginning of this meeting. I answered my young brother down there foolishly. I ask God to forgive me. I ask *him* to forgive me." And before anyone realized what was happening the world's most famous evangelist had stepped off the platform, dashed across to the insignificant anonymous youth and taken him by the hand. As another present said, "The man of iron will proved that he had mastered the hardest of all earth's languages, 'I am sorry.' " ' "

Topics for Youth

ON THE SOVEREIGNTY OF GOD—Dietrich Bonhoeffer, who spent the last two years of his life in prison, wrote to several of his friends of the lessons he had learned. "I believe that God both can and will bring good out of evil," he wrote. "For that purpose He needs men who make the best use of everything. I believe God will give us all the power we need to resist in all times of distress. But He never gives it in advance, lest we should rely upon ourselves and not on Him alone. A faith as strong as this should allay all our fears for the future. I believe that even our errors and mistakes are turned to good account. It is no harder for God to cope with them than with what we imagine to be our good deeds. I believe God is not just timeless fate, but that He waits upon and answers sincere prayer and responsible action." Pastor Bonhoeffer was hanged in April 1945 for his Christian testimony and resistance to the Nazi movement—*Letters and Papers from Prison.*

"ALL THAT BITTERNESS BEGAN TO MELT AWAY"—Not every crushing experience comes into our lives at the hands of people, as was Joseph's case. Sometimes an accident or illness intrudes into our lives. Joni Eareckson told free-lance writer Constance Radut the following in a recent interview:

Q. "Joni, what was your reaction as a seventeen-year-old girl when you found out that you would be paralyzed probably for the rest of your life?"

JONI: "It didn't register; it didn't compute. I was seventeen and very athletic at the time. To be told that I had to face the prospect of life without the use of my arms and legs just didn't make sense to me. It wasn't so much that I refused to accept it as much as it was that I listened to it and thought, yes, I'm hearing it, but it didn't click. It wasn't until two or three years later that finally the reality of the permanency of my paralysis began to sink in. Then came the depression, the bitterness and despair. Finally, however, I got back to the point where all that bitterness began to melt away under the crushing power of my friends' prayers and my family's love. That, I believe, is how God changed me."

Q. "How has your life changed through this experience?"

JONI: "It has forced a kind of maturity upon me that was a bit premature. It has also changed my whole value system. This paralysis has impressed upon me the virtue of empathy, the value of patience and perseverance and endurance and tolerance and self-control. These are the kinds of things that I really didn't care too much about when I was on my feet. In fact, I placed very little if any value at all on these kinds of attributes. The paralysis, however, has made it all too clear that this is the kind of value system that is paramount."

Q. "How do you see all of this in relation to God's plan?"

JONI: "I believe in a sovereign God who has control of all things, even of Satan's schemes. I don't believe that my paralysis was the result of some divine cruel joke. I don't believe that I was caught in some kind of cosmic game or war or battle between God and the devil. I believe that my paralysis was inspired by a plan of God that was initiated by His love. We are told in the Scriptures in Romans 8:28 that all things fit together in a pattern for good and this I stake my life on."

Q. "Your being a Christian through your handicap and being involved in a ministry to other handicapped persons must be very inspirational to a lot of people."

JONI: "I think a lot of these folks understand that I took many years to go through a great many questions and struggle, through a great deal of depression, and that I also took time to study and research the Word of God and see what the Bible really has to say to those who suffer.

"I believe that people can see that my struggle was honest and they identify with that. I do hope that it is that part of my life that is an encouragement to others and that is why I want to be so careful to give Him the glory and also to make plain to people who question me, the value of knowing God's Word. I don't want to simply share a testimony; I want to share a testimony that is illuminated by the Word of God so other people can hold on to it and gain the kind of comfort that God has comforted me with."

UNIT II

God Frees and Instructs His Chosen People

LESSON 5   OCTOBER 3

God Reaffirms His Promise

Background Scripture: Exodus 3:1–6:13
Devotional Reading: Exodus 1:1–14

Exodus 5:22–6:9, 13

22 And Moses returned unto the Lord, and said, Lord, wherefore hast thou so evil entreated this people? why is it that thou hast sent me?

23 For since I came to Pharaoh to speak in thy name, he hath done evil to this people; neither hast thou delivered thy people at all.

6:1 Then the Lord said unto Moses, Now shalt thou see what I will do to Pharaoh: for with a strong hand shall he let them go, and with a strong hand shall he drive them out of his land.

2 And God spake unto Moses, and said unto him, I am the Lord:

3 And I appeared unto Abraham, unto Isaac, and unto Jacob, by the

name of God Almighty, but by my name Jehovah was I not known to them.

4 And I have also established my covenant with them, to give them the land of Canaan, the land of their pilgrimage, wherein they were strangers.

5 And I have also heard the groaning of the children of Israel, whom the Egyptians keep in bondage; and I have remembered my covenant.

6 Wherefore say unto the children of Israel, I am the LORD, and I will bring you out from under the burdens of the Egyptians, and I will rid you out of their bondage, and I will redeem you with a stretched out arm, and with great judgments:

7 And I will take you to me for a people, and I will be to you a God: and ye shall know that I am the LORD your God, which bringeth you out from under the burdens of the Egyptians.

8 And I will bring you in unto the land, concerning the which I did swear to give it to Abraham, to Isaac, and to Jacob; and I will give it you for an heritage: I am the LORD.

9 And Moses spake so unto the children of Israel: but they hearkened not unto Moses for anguish of spirit, and for cruel bondage.

13 And the LORD spake unto Moses and unto Aaron, and gave them a charge unto the children of Israel, and unto Pharaoh king of Egypt, to bring the children of Israel out of the land of Egypt.

KEY VERSE: "I am the LORD, and I will bring you out from under the burdens of the Egyptians . . . and I will take you to me for a people, and I will be to you a God." Exodus 6:6, 7.

Home Daily Bible Readings
Sept. 27 M. Cruel Treatment, Exodus 1:1–14.
Sept. 28 T. God Intervenes, Exodus 3:1–10.
Sept. 29 W. The God of Abraham, Isaac, and Jacob, Exodus 3:11–17.
Sept. 30 T. Clear Evidence, Exodus 4:1–9.
Oct. 1 F. Needed Help, Exodus 4:14–16, 27–31.
Oct. 2 S. Confrontation, Exodus 5:1–5.
Oct. 3 S. Complaining, Exodus 5:15–23.

Lesson Aim: That your students will seek to know God in a personal way.

LESSON OUTLINE
Background to the Scripture
Looking at the Scripture Text

I. Moses' Complaint (Exodus 5:22, 23)
II. Jehovah's Self-Revelation (Exodus 6:1-5)
III. Jehovah, the God Who Acts (Exodus 6:6-8)
IV. Command to Leave Egypt Restated (Exodus 6:9, 13)
Applying the Scripture

Background to the Scripture

Today's lesson brings us swiftly to that hour in history when God said, "Enough!" to Egypt, for her sin and her cruelty, and "Enough!" to Israel, in her prolonged wait for deliverance promised 400 years earlier to Abraham.

According to Exodus 1, the people of Israel had become the slaves of Pharaoh and were hard at work constructing the cities of Rameses and Pithom. A hundred years ago, a French explorer excavated a mound of ancient ruins some sixty miles northeast of modern Cairo and found evidence of these two cities. Inscriptions indicated that the name of one was Pi-Tum, or House of Tum (a solar deity).

The view that Amenhotep was the pharaoh of the Exodus seems now to be giving way to an early thirteenth century date, approximately 1290 B.C. The archaeologists who explored Pi-Tum fixed an approximate date for the mound of 1300-1234, during the reign of Rameses II. This would fit approximately with the 1290 date for the Exodus; scholars suggest that Merenptah was the pharaoh with whom Moses had to deal.

Looking at the Scripture Text

Moses' Complaint (5:22, 23) Moses' first encounter with Pharaoh only accomplished one thing. He stirred up the monarch's anger against the Israelites. Pharaoh interpreted Moses' request for permission to go into the desert as an indication that the people were idle. So he decreed that the slaves must continue to make their daily quota of bricks plus gather their own stubble for their brick-making. To stress the determination of his will, he ordered the Israelite foremen to be soundly whipped.

In their angry and demeaned condition, these foremen turned on Moses and Aaron for making Israel "a stench" in the nostrils of Pharaoh. Moses had nowhere to turn but to God. "Why have you brought trouble upon this people?" (NIV) he cried. Or, as Today's English Version has it, "Why do you mistreat your people?" In words bordering on irreverence, he sounded off, seeming to accuse the Lord and not Pharaoh alone for the worsened lot of the covenant people.

The Moses we see here is not the seasoned, tempered veteran of the wilderness wanderings. There, on more than one occasion, his impassioned intercession for the nation Israel actually dissuaded the Lord from carrying out His threat to destroy the people. But in Egypt, having run into the meat grinder of Pharaoh's obstinence and Israel's despair, he complained, "and you have not rescued your people at all" (NIV). The impetuous Moses had expected a quick deliverance though the Lord had earlier told him to expect resistance from Pharaoh (3:19).

Jehovah's Self-Revelation (6:1-5) The Lord did not rebuke Moses for his complaint. He evidently delights to see His servant getting under the burden. Instead, He encouraged him by saying, "Now you are going to see what I will do . . ." (TEV). The assurance Moses received is reminiscent of the original terms of his call.

Modern translations help explain the sense of verse 1. "Because of my mighty hand he will let them go" says the NIV. The second clause of the sentence alludes to Pharaoh's might, which is considerable; the pharaoh "shall drive them out" (NIV, RSV, and NEB). God is the cause, Pharaoh the agent. As the Lord twists Pharaoh's arm behind his back, the stubborn monarch will finally be forced to send Israel away. Commenting on the verb *drive*, the *Pulpit Commentary* adds that the "phrase well expresses the final anxiety of Pharaoh to be rid of the Israelites."

"There appears to have been an interval of some months between the preceding events" and what follows in verses 2-8, says Canon F. C. Cook in *The Speakers Commentary*. "The oppression in the meantime was not merely driving the people to desperation but preparing them by severe labor, varied by hasty wanderings in search of stubble, for the exertions and privations of the wilderness."

In the furnace of Moses' great need, the Lord again came and said, I AM THE LORD. He was about to reveal Himself more fully to His servant. We learn from this passage that God can only be known as He chooses to reveal Himself to man. Abraham, Isaac, and Jacob *knew about* the Lord as Jehovah ("I am who I am" 3:14 NIV). The Name *Jehovah* appears in Genesis; but as God here tells Moses, He had revealed Himself to them largely as God Almighty (*El Shaddai*—"the One who provided for all their needs"). As the *New Bible Commentary* says, "the full significance of God's character thus designated (by Jehovah) was to be revealed to these afflicted and embittered slaves by a powerful, compassionate deliverance with positively enriching consequences." They would know Him as the "One who redeems her from sin and delivers her from Egypt" (Scofield) and thus call Him by this newly revealed Name.

Jehovah, or Yahweh, is a transliteration from the Hebrew of this new Name. It is formed from the same root as the verb to be, *hayah*, thus it means I AM WHO I AM. In many translations, where Yahweh appears in the Hebrew text (traditionally spelled Jehovah) it is usually printed in capital letters—LORD.

Some interpreters of Scripture point to this verse in defense of the theory that at least four editors compiled the Pentateuch. They say that the writer here obviously is ignorant of the fact that *Jehovah* appears in Genesis. But the writer here is saying that *Jehovah* is the medium whereby the Lord further reveals Himself in relation to the covenant of which now Moses was the mediator (*Speaker's Commentary*).

The words of verses 4 and 5 show further the faithfulness of God. He reminds Moses that He established the covenant with the patriarchs. He promised to give them Canaan, and now He assures Moses that He has heard the "groaning" of His people. Moses knew, of course, that this scheme to deliver Israel was the Lord's idea, not his own. He could not help but be encouraged to hear Jehovah reaffirm: "I have remembered my covenant." Twice it is here referred to as "my" covenant. The Lord had initiated this "bond" with Abraham and as we learned in studying Genesis 15:18, the covenant was not an agreement between two equals. It was the Lord's covenant, entirely dependent upon His ability and purpose. (For the dimensions of the Promised Land of the covenant, Canaan, *see* Genesis 15:18 and Deuteronomy 1:7, 8.)

Jehovah, the God Who Acts (vv. 6–8) The verbs in this section are worth noting. "I will bring" . . . "rid" . . . "redeem" . . . "take" . . . "bring" . . . "did swear" . . . "I will give." That generation of Israel was about to find out that Jehovah is a God who acts. The language in this discourse is energetic. What God has promised, He is about to perform.

"I will redeem you with a stretched out arm." The Hebrew word *redeem* here used, says Clements in the *Cambridge Bible Commentary*, "denotes the right of a member of a family to acquire persons or property belonging to that family which was in danger of falling to outside claimants." No longer are the people of Israel to be "under the burdens" of Egypt; the Lord is going to take them for His people.

Canon Cook makes an interesting observation about the phrase—"stretched out arm." In the hieroglyphic writing of that day, two outstretched arms signified might. From infancy, Moses would have been familiar with this symbol on the obelisk at Heliopolis where it bore witness to the strength of Ra, a sun god. In Jehovah, Moses would experience the true measure of that "outstretched arm."

The idea that "ye shall know that I am the Lord" is a strong biblical theme and especially so in the immediate context. God purposed that His people get to know Him; over and over it is stated that He did His mighty acts in the ten plagues so that Pharaoh would know "that I, the Lord, am at work in this land" (8:22 TEV).

The Lord promised to bring the people of Israel "in unto the land." Most later translations say "to the land." Actually, Moses did not enter the land, but the people (that is, the succeeding generation) did under Joshua's leadership.

Command to Leave Egypt Restated (vv. 9, 13) Israel was in no frame of mind to hear Moses. Conditioned by "the deafening power of sorrow," they did not, and probably could not, listen to Moses. Perhaps no other words in this section of Exodus portray so graphically the desperate and seemingly hopeless condition of the nation Israel. "For anguish of spirit" means literally shortness of spirit; their spirits were crushed. If their escape had been dependent on their own might, they would be no match for their oppressors. They were too far down in the slough of despond to even think about getting out.

At this point, Moses would have probably given anything to be released from his commission. But instead, God issued a firm command. The thirteenth verse reminds one of situations in life when the only thing that will get action is for the person in authority to assert himself, to "pull rank." The Lord specifically ordered Moses and Aaron to press the battle against Pharaoh. Obedience was the path to victory. Moses and Aaron would find that as they took the step of faith, the Lord would demonstrate His presence in remarkable ways. And when He began to act, then the spirit of the people would be revived and they would be able to follow Moses out of Egypt, through the Red Sea, and to the foot of the Mount of God to receive further revelation of Jehovah.

Applying the Scripture
The first application gets to the point of the lesson. Assign two class members to be prepared ahead of time.

1. Knowing About God or Knowing Him—To know about someone is one thing. To *know* that someone is something else. We can learn a lot about another person by reading about him or seeing him on television or occasionally in person. But we must live with that person to really get to know him. It is the same way with God. Many people use the name of God and know a lot about "the Man upstairs." But they really do not know Him well enough to understand Him. They are the ones who would rarely ever refer to Him as Lord or speak of His Son, the Lord Jesus Christ.

Moses and the children of Israel came to know the Lord through the experiences they had in Egypt and the wilderness. Take time in your class to stress the importance of knowing God personally. Invite two persons in class to tell of an experience that enabled them to become personally acquainted with the Lord at a deeper level than before.

2. Waiting for His Time—Moses complained because the Lord had not delivered his people. "For 80 years, God honed and polished Moses, first as a dignitary in Egypt, then as a desert shepherd in Midian, to prepare him for the task ahead. Finally, at the burning bush, God reminded Moses that his God was a consuming fire, majestic in His holiness, true to His word and sensitive to the cries of His children. Deliverance was at hand and Moses was the man!" (*The Daily Walk*). So, no wonder Moses was disappointed when after he had faced Pharaoh, nothing happened.

Are we like Moses? Many new Christians are thrilled by the sudden change in their lives at conversion. They walk around—or float on "cloud nine"—for several weeks after giving their lives to Christ, only to awaken one day and realize that they have not been completely delivered from the bondage of old habits. We need to realize that God's salvation, His deliverance, is a daily, ongoing thing. We *have been saved* from the penalty of sin, we *are being saved* from the power of sin, and we *will* (*one day*) *be saved* from the presence of sin.

3. Being His Covenant People—With each lesson in this unit, we are reminded that God made a covenant with His people. In Egypt after Moses had

become initially discouraged, God reaffirmed that He had "established" His covenant and that He now "remembered" this covenant. In a later text, God is spoken of as the One who "keepeth covenant and mercy with them that love Him and keep his commandments to a thousand generations" (Deuteronomy 7:9).

We, too, are covenant people. By grace through Christ, we are people of the "new covenant" and we gave witness to this covenant between us and the Lord at our baptism. When we receive the elements of bread and wine in communion, we renew our covenant vows. Think about what this means. To be His covenant people means that we are His possession and in everything we are to acknowledge Him first. We live not only because of Him; we live *for* Him.

Questions for Discussion
Make use of these questions to involve your students in learning and to test their understanding of the lesson.
1. Did Moses obtain an answer for his question of "why"? Should we expect to get answers when we ask God why?   2. What is the meaning of the word *Jehovah*?   3. What is meant by "appearing" or "being known" by a certain name?   4. What reason does Moses have to be comforted by the words of the Lord?   5. When the Lord told Moses that He would redeem him with "a stretched out arm," what did He mean by the expression?   6. If the Lord's purpose in delivering Israel is that "they might know" Him, what do you think is His purpose for us today?   7. Does this imply that not everyone knows God and that the Lord is not everyone's God?   8. Perhaps someone—or a group of someones—will not listen to the Gospel of redemption today because they are so broken in spirit. How can we go about bringing them to the spiritual freedom that is in Christ?

Illustrating the Scripture
Examples and quotations to help the teacher communicate the lesson.
ENCOURAGEMENT FOR MODERN-DAY HOSTAGES Moses responded positively to the assurances the Lord gave Him at this discouraging point in his life. A modern example of how words and actions bring encouragement to people in prison or enslaved to some cruel master was seen when the fifty-two American hostages returned home to America after 444 days as prisoners in Iran. One of them, Bruce Laingen, the chargée d'affaires of the American embassy in Teheran, said at a press conference upon returning home:

"I think never has so small a group owed so much to so many. The countless prayers from countless synagogues and churches all across this country, the expressions of love, many of them that have come through to us by mail from children all across this country.

"Things like a Valentine that reached some of us in August, but nonetheless, very welcome. From a schoolgirl in California, who told us: 'It's just not

America without you.' That was a beautiful expression in simple children's words that reached some of us and I think were felt by all of us.

"Countless messages from groups all over the country. The yellow ribbons. The church bells that we gather have rung in many places all across this country, church bells that in the future will add, I think, I hope, certainly for us, a new dimension, not only of the blessings of Almighty God but a reminder, refurbished by this experience, of the blessings of freedom that we enjoy in this country...." (*The New York Times*, January 28, 1981.)

LET'S NOT LIMIT GOD Moses was great because he knew how to let God be all that He could be. After all, in just a few words, the Lord told Moses that He had appeared to Abraham, Isaac, and Jacob. He had established His covenant, He had heard the groaning of Israel and remembered His promises. Then He told him what He intended to do—"I will bring them out . . . I will free . . . I will redeem . . . I will take you . . . I will bring you to Canaan . . . I will give it to you for a heritage."

D. L. Moody used to say, "Christ is all to us that we make Him to be." Then he would add—"I want to emphasize that word *all*. Some men make Him to be 'a root out of a dry ground,' 'without form or comeliness.' He is nothing to them; they do not want Him. Some Christians have a very small Savior for they are not willing to receive Him fully and let Him do great and mighty things for them. Others have a mighty Savior, because they make Him to be great and mighty."

NOR UNDERESTIMATE SATAN Moses was about to admit defeat because he failed to measure the real strength of his enemy, Pharaoh. "The reason why so many Christians fail all through life is just this—they underestimate the strength of the enemy. We have a terrible enemy to contend with. Don't let Satan deceive you. Unless we are spiritually dead, it means warfare. Nearly everything around tends to draw us away from God. *We do not step clear out of Egypt on to the throne of God.* There is the wilderness journey, and there are enemies in the land" (D. L. Moody).

Topics for Youth

THINGS OFTEN GET WORSE BEFORE THEY GET BETTER—Israel was having it hard enough. Perceived as a dangerous threat by their overlords, the Egyptians, they became a nation of slaves overnight. To keep the population from increasing and to prevent Israel from developing a fighting force, Pharaoh ordered all Hebrew baby boys to be thrown into the Nile. The people were forced to work all day long, constructing cities for the Pharaoh.

But when Moses began demanding, "Let my people go!" things grew worse. The taskmasters were even more cruel. Instead of gathering the straw for the Israelites' brick-making, the taskmasters made the Israelites do it themselves while demanding that they produce the same number of bricks as before. It was an impossible order. But in addition, the Israelite foremen were whipped badly.

Moses was discouraged and he had reason to be. He complained to God:

"You are treating your people so badly! Why did You send me here anyway. Pharaoh has done nothing but evil to the people since I came and You have not delivered them at all!" If only Moses could have seen what great things were just around the corner—a plague of locusts, widespread hail, water turning to blood, flies swarming, frogs leaping into bed and bread, darkness descending on the Egyptians. And then—death; every firstborn Egyptian would die and Israel would march out of Egypt a free people.

When we feel down, discouraged, and are tempted to quit, let's not! And, when we do pray to God and things get even worse, let's not be discouraged. This is often the way life is. Even as these words are being written, a plumber is working in my house. To fix a leaky pipe, he is making an awful mess—knocking out plaster, removing ceiling tiles, cutting old pipe. But soon he will replace the old pipe with new copper tubing and the walls and ceilings will all be repaired. Things do get worse before they get better in lots of situations—when we have to have an operation or if a person has to give up a drug habit. But in time, as we obey the Lord, things do get better. He has promised to bless everyone who trusts in Him.

TO WHOM ARE YOU LISTENING?—If God were trying to talk to you, do you think you would listen? Don't answer so quickly. The answer may not be all that obvious.

In the lesson today, the Lord spoke very clearly to Moses. What He said was positive. He was going to do some tremendous things for Israel, such as liberate them from the slave-driving Egyptians and give them a land of their own. But did Israel listen when Moses relayed these words to them?

We sometimes turn a deaf ear to the ones through whom God is speaking to us. For young people, this means we often will not listen to our parents; but if they are our parents, we owe it to them to hear them out. Give a listen. You may hear God talking!

LESSON 6　　　　　　　　　OCTOBER 10
God Establishes the Passover

Background Scripture: Exodus 11, 12
Devotional Reading: Exodus 12:37–42

Exodus 12:11–17, 24–27
11 And thus shall ye eat it; with your loins girded, your shoes on your feet, and your staff in your hand; and ye shall eat it in haste: it is the LORD's passover.
12 For I will pass through the land of Egypt this night, and will smite all

the firstborn in the land of Egypt, both man and beast; and against all the gods of Egypt I will execute judgment: I am the Lord.

13 And the blood shall be to you for a token upon the houses where ye are: and when I see the blood, I will pass over you, and the plague shall not be upon you to destroy you, when I smite the land of Egypt.

14 And this day shall be unto you for a memorial; and ye shall keep it a feast to the Lord throughout your generations; ye shall keep it a feast by an ordinance for ever.

15 Seven days shall ye eat unleavened bread; even the first day ye shall put away leaven out of your houses: for whosoever eateth leavened bread from the first day until the seventh day, that soul shall be cut off from Israel.

16 And in the first day there shall be an holy convocation; and in the seventh day there shall be an holy convocation to you; no manner of work shall be done in them, save that which every man must eat, that only may be done of you.

17 And ye shall observe the feast of unleavened bread; for in this self-same day have I brought your armies out of the land of Egypt: therefore shall ye observe this day in your generations by an ordinance for ever.

24 And ye shall observe this thing for an ordinance to thee and to thy sons for ever.

25 And it shall come to pass, when ye be come to the land which the Lord will give you, according as he hath promised, that ye shall keep this service.

26 And it shall come to pass, when your children shall say unto you, What mean ye by this service?

27 That ye shall say, It is the sacrifice of the Lord's passover, who passed over the houses of the children of Israel in Egypt, when he smote the Egyptians, and delivered our houses. And the people bowed the head and worshipped.

KEY VERSE: "And this day shall be unto you for a memorial; and ye shall keep it a feast to the Lord throughout your generations; ye shall keep it a feast by an ordinance for ever." Exodus 12:14.

Home Daily Bible Readings
Oct. 4 M. One More Punishment, Exodus 11:1–8.
Oct. 5 T. A Lasting Memorial, Exodus 12:1–14.
Oct. 6 W. Once Slaves, Deuteronomy 16:1–12.
Oct. 7 T. Seeing the Blood, Exodus 12:21–28.
Oct. 8 F. The Final Straw, Exodus 12:29–36.
Oct. 9 S. Setting Out, Exodus 12:37–42.
Oct. 10 S. Participation, Exodus 12:43–50.

Lesson Aim: As a result of this study, your class members should give serious consideration to keeping an annual spiritual retreat with God.

LESSON OUTLINE
Background to the Scripture
Looking at the Scripture Text
  I. How to Observe the Passover (Exodus 12:11)
  II. How to Avoid the Plague (Exodus 12:12, 13)
  III. How to Perpetuate the Feast (Exodus 12:14-17, 24-27)
Applying the Scripture

Background to the Scripture
In our studies of the Old Testament so far, we are able to trace clearly the steps the Lord God took toward the saving and redeeming of man. Following the fall of man, He appeared to Abraham, whose faith gained a righteous standing with God. With Abraham, the covenant was made which encompassed all of time and included Abraham's descendants who were to be as numerous as sands on the seashore. In Jacob, God gave the covenant people a name—Israel. In Joseph, He preserved the remnant of Jacob's offspring and brought them to Egypt where they might become a nation.

Last week's study is most important because at a critical point, when Israel was about to think her God had forgotten her, He revealed Himself as Jehovah, the great I AM, the self-existent, all-sufficient LORD.

The lesson today introduces us to two great truths in stereo—the great event of the Exodus and the high, holy convocation of the Passover. Whereas the Exodus was a great act never to be repeated, the memorial supper became the perpetual feast whereby God's merciful deliverance is celebrated even to this day. Let us observe carefully how God established the Passover.

Looking at the Scripture Text
How to Observe the Passover (v. 11)   The opening verse of today's text, which explains how the members of the Israelite family were to eat the Passover, will not seem unusual to the typical American. We are all so accustomed to eating our meals "in haste." But in the households of the East, then and now, the evening meal was taken leisurely and so this observance stands in stark contrast to their usual custom.

Men and women both dressed in long flowing robes. This outer garment was to be gathered and collected at the waist; the NIV says, "tucked into your belt." Sandals were usually not worn in the house or at mealtime, but for this meal they were to have their shoes on their feet. And they were even to have their walking stick in hand.

There would be no reason for this preparedness if the people did not believe that on that night they were to leave. By following these simple orders, each member of each household amply demonstrated his or her faith in the deliverance promised by Jehovah through Moses.

With the words, "It is the Lord's Passover," Jehovah gave a most significant name to the whole ordinance. "The word Passover renders as nearly as possible the true meaning of the original," says the *Speaker's Commentary*. "The primary sense is generally held to be 'pass rapidly,' like a bird with outstretched wings, but it undoubtedly includes the idea of sparing." Isaiah 31:5 sheds light on the meaning here intended: "As birds flying, so will the Lord of hosts defend Jerusalem; defending also he will deliver it; and passing over he will preserve it."

How to Avoid the Plague (vv. 12, 13) Exodus 12 opens with the declaration: "This month is to be for you the first month of your year" (NIV). Actually, as other Scriptures show, the Passover was installed in the seventh month of the civil year; what we see here is the origin of the ecclesiastical year in Israel. The Passover was to be observed between the fourteenth and twenty-first days (vv. 6, 15, 18) of the month Abib (later called Nisan). Since the observance began on the evening of the fourteenth day, it was actually the beginning of the fifteenth day, since Israel marked its days from sunset to sunset (v. 6).

At midnight (v. 29), the Lord would pass through Egypt. A deliberate play on words seems intended. In the *passover*, Jehovah would spare His chosen people; in *passing through*, He would judge Egypt.

The Lord is to strike Egypt with a terrible judgment. Every firstborn, "from the firstborn of Pharaoh that sat on his throne unto the firstborn of the captive that was in the dungeon" (v. 29), would be killed—and *of the animals*. We shall see that this was not to be taken lightly. The words, "I will bring judgment on all the gods" amply justify God's awesome destruction and slaughter. The biblical record does not reveal very much about Egypt's religious life, but sufficient artifacts are available to show that the whole country was filled with sacred idols. In its discussion of the religion of Egypt in ancient times, the *Encyclopaedia Britannica* names more than forty major and minor gods and goddesses. Each reigning pharaoh assumed the title of deity incarnate. No wonder the pharaoh of Moses' day scoffed and said, "Who is the Lord? . . . I know not the Lord" (5:2).

Every deity was represented by some creature—either a bull or a jackal or a cat or a goat or a lion or a crocodile or a hippopotamus or something else. Even the lowest forms of animal life, the frog and the beetle, were specially revered. "In smiting the firstborn of all living beings, man and beast, God smote the objects of Egyptian worship," notes the *Speaker's Commentary*. God had given sufficient warning to Pharaoh and the Egyptians in the plagues which preceded this night of death and in the specific words about the visit of the "death angel." In the consummating plague, He established His right to the absolute claim: "I am the Lord."

Earlier, Moses had received instructions that each Israelite household would follow in securing adequate protection for themselves against the plague of death. They were to kill a lamb and sprinkle its blood on either sides of the door frame and above the door of their homes. By obeying this order, they would show their faith in Jehovah who said that this blood would be a "sign" for that household.

***How to Perpetuate the Feast* (vv. 14–17, 24–27)** Having told Moses what He would do to Egypt as punishment for its sins and how to safeguard the people of Israel, Jehovah declared that the Passover was to be observed regularly in the years to come. It was to be "a lasting ordinance" expected of each and every generation of Israel's children. In later Scriptures, it would always be listed as the first of Israel's three annual festivals (Deuteronomy 16:16) because it came first on the calendar and, more importantly, it represented the Lord's redemption of the nation by the intervention of blood.

The seven-day extent of the feast is thought to take in the number of days required for Israel to travel from their homes to safety on the other side of the Red Sea. In future observances, the people would keep the first and last days of the festival as a sabbath, except that the work of food preparation was allowed. In time, this feast would be called the Feast of Unleavened Bread (v. 17).

A twofold symbolism is apparent in the rule regarding leaven (or yeast; in biblical times a bit of old dough in a high state of fermentation was used as leaven to make the new dough rise). The Israelites ate the Passover meal, consisting of roast lamb, bitter herbs, and unleavened bread and carried what remained of the uncooked dough with them when they left their homes (12:34). This was their chief food during the journey out of Egypt. From a practical standpoint, they did not have time to wait for the bread to rise and so the ordinance prohibiting the use of leaven.

But a spiritual and sacramental symbolism perhaps also was intended by the instructions. Leaven, being incipient corruption, was absolutely forbidden. Anyone violating this rule would be "cut off" or excommunicated from the community of faith. This was to teach the partaker that the meal was to be an occasion of separating from all sin.

"The requirement to 'put away leaven out of their houses' " says the *Pulpit Commentary*, was probably intended "to teach that for family worship to be acceptable, the entire household must be pure, and that to effect this result the head of the household must, so far as he can, eject the leaven of sin from his establishment."

Though the Passover was to be observed of necessity as a family feast in Egypt, in the future, it was forever to be an occasion of corporate celebration. The people were to be summoned, probably by the blast of trumpets, to a "sacred assembly" or "convocation." The Lord wanted the people to remember that "it was on this very day that I brought your divisions out of Egypt" (NIV). The past tense in verse 17 may indicate that this section does not represent the actual words of Jehovah given to Moses at this time, but rather a "recasting of the words after the event took place" (*Pulpit Commentary*).

Verses 24–27 form a part of the instructions Moses in turn gave to the "elders" or chiefs of the twelve tribes of Israel. Having explained to them the necessity of applying the blood of the lamb on the outside of the houses, he charged them: "Obey these instructions as a lasting ordinance for you and your descendants." His words, "when you enter the land" are evidence of his abiding faith that God would keep His promises and bring them to Canaan.

For centuries, Judaism has religiously observed the Passover and in the home of the devout today at Passover, the youngest person present asks the questions which the father or some older person answers, explaining, "It is the sacrifice of the Passover to Jehovah." The word *sacrifice* pointed to the lamb on the table. How beautifully does the Lamb of God, Jesus, "which taketh away the sin of the world" answer to the meaning of the Passover sacrifice.

One cannot but contrast the attitude of the elders after Moses gave them these instructions with the attitude of the people earlier when Moses and Aaron had only begun to plead with Pharaoh for Israel's deliverance. Then the people were so discouraged and crushed in spirit by their slavery that they did not listen to Moses (6:9). Now they humbly bow and worship God. Their attitude was transformed after witnessing the mighty acts of Jehovah in the punishing plagues. That night they were to witness one more ultimate act of deliverance and forever enshrine that deliverance in the Feast of the Passover.

Applying the Scripture
It is better to follow through in depth on one application than to try two or three. Devote time at the end of your class period for the first suggested item. Treat 2 and 3 only if time permits.
1. Why Did the Lord Establish the Passover?—We can see that the Passover prefigures the atoning sacrifice of Jesus Christ for our sins, and we are actually keeping the Passover when we partake of the Lord's Supper.

But why did Jehovah instill this festival as an annual thing? Look again of what it consisted. He wanted each of His covenant people to *remember* the great deliverance that He had wrought for them. He wanted each of them, at least once a year, to search their own lives as they would search the household for every trace of leaven, in order to *be purged* of sin and made more pure for His service. And, He wanted them to *impart* the rich core of their faith to the youth and children coming after them.

There is no reason why we as Christians today should not keep some kind of annual tryst with the Lord for these same reasons. Ask the members of the class if they have established a habit of annual spiritual inventory. Suggest that they may want to use the occasion of their birthday for such a thing. Or, they may want to do so on the anniversary of their spiritual "birthday." Urge your class members to make definite plans to keep the spirit of this teaching in their own personal lives.
2. He Is Either Lord of All, or He Is Not Lord at All!—When God told

Moses what He was going to do to the Egyptian firstborn and to all the hosts of Egypt's gods, He followed that up with the simple declaration: "I am the Lord." Jehovah certainly proved it by His mighty deeds which showed He was absolutely in control of things. Someone has said that if we call Jesus Christ Lord—and we do—then He ought to be in control of *what we are, what we do*, and *what we have*. He is either Lord of all or He is not Lord at all. Invite your class to think about the implications of this statement. Ask them what this means in regard to the plans we make for life (since it is His life), what we put into these bodies (since our body is His temple), what our hearts should be centered on (since "as a man thinketh in his heart so is he"), and what we should do with "our" possessions (since we are but stewards for a little while of what is truly His).

3. How Is Your W. Q.?—Yes, how is your Worship Quotient? Our text today closes with the quiet little sentence: "And the people bowed the head and worshipped." To close the discussion in your class, ask the members if they know why this sentence seems appropriate after Moses' words to the elders. What is the significance of their outward posture, such as bowing the head? And most important, what is the meaning of worship? How often should it happen to us? Will it happen automatically when we enter a service of worship? If your group meets just prior to a Sunday worship service, urge the members to carry a worshipful attitude into the service and be ready to share the following week what difference they noticed in their own experience of the presence of God.

Questions for Discussion
Make use of these questions to involve your students in learning and to test their understanding of the lesson.
1. Of what did the Passover meal consist?   2. Why were the people required to eat it "in haste"?   3. In verse 12, what might be an intended connection between the words *beasts* (or animals) and *gods*?   4. If the Passover is to be a continuing memorial (v. 14) and remembered "for ever," how is it observed today? Among Jews? Among Christians?   5. The Israelites were to eat unleavened bread because of the necessity of having to travel immediately; what other reason can be given for the regulation against leavened bread and even possessing leaven in the household during the festival?   6. What provision did the Lord make in the rules for the Passover to ensure that it would be observed by succeeding generations?

Illustrating the Scripture
Examples and quotations to help the teacher communicate the lesson.
CHRIST, THE PERFECT FULFILLMENT OF THE PASSOVER "The Passover was typical of the justice of God's passing over and sparing such who are sprinkled with the blood of Christ (1 Corinthians 5:7). As the destroying angel passed over the houses marked with the blood of the

paschal lamb, so the wrath of God passes over them whose souls are sprinkled with the blood of Christ.

"As the paschal lamb was killed before Israel was delivered; so it was necessary that Christ should suffer before we could be redeemed. It was killed before Moses' Law, or Aaron's sacrifices, were enjoined; to show that deliverance comes to mankind by none of them, but only by the true Passover, that Lamb of God slain from the foundation of the world (Romans 3:25; Hebrews 9:14).

"It was killed the first month of the year, which prefigured that Christ should suffer death in that month. It was killed in the evening, so Christ suffered in the last days, and at that time of the day (Matthew 27:46; Hebrews 1:2). At evening also the sun sets, which shows that it was the Sun of righteousness who was to suffer and die; and that at His passion universal darkness should be upon the whole earth.

"The passover was roast with fire, to note the sharp and dreadful pains which Christ should suffer, not only from men, but from God also. It was to be eaten with bitter herbs, not only to put them in remembrance of their bitter bondage in Egypt, but also to testify our mortification to sin, and readiness to undergo afflictions for Christ and likewise to teach us the absolute necessity of true repentance in all that would profitably feed on Christ" (Alexander Cruden).

HOW WE SHIELD AGAINST DEATH TODAY What if the Israelite households decided they would do as they pleased on the night the Lord passed through Egypt to kill the firstborn in every household? They would have surely met death, unless they had placed the blood as a token upon their doorposts. People in situations today have to apply a shield, much like the applying of blood, or else they would die.

A fire fighter would never think of trying to perform his task without preparing himself first. If he is on duty at one of the large airports served by jet aircraft, he must be ready to combat the superheated flame of jet fuel. Wearing an asbestos suit coated with aluminum, to reflect heat, he can expose himself to fire as hot as 2000° F, but inside the suit his body will be no warmer than on a hot summer day.

Workmen in nuclear reactor plants, or anyone handling radioactive material must take careful precautions. Allowing themselves to be exposed only once to several hundred roentgens of radiation will almost certainly mean death. How do they protect themselves against the plague of radioactive material? In many ways. They work behind thick concrete shields which absorb most of the damaging radiation and they handle such things as fission fragments by remote control. On their clothing, they carry a meter that tells them the amount of radiation to which they have been exposed. They cannot ignore the indications of that meter; to do so would endanger their health. They know the high-energy radiation that comes so near their bodies is a deadly plague, unless they are shielded.

Topics for Youth

CHRISTIAN FEASTS—By the memorial of the Passover, Jewish families have kept alive for centuries the miraculous deliverance of Israel by the Lord. Have you ever thought of the numerous memorials and symbols we enjoy in the Christian faith that serve to remind us of the meaning of our faith? Not all of our churches observe these, by any means; usually the more liturgical and formal the church, the more prone is it to keep many "holy days" and make use of visible symbols.

The Episcopal (or Anglican) and Lutheran churches will be marking All Saints Day soon, on November 1. That observance dates back to A.D. 615 when Pope Boniface IV introduced All Martyrs Day. For two hundred years, it was celebrated in May, but Pope Gregory IV moved it to November 1 in 844, not to "christianize" a pagan German celebration but for the practical reason that the many pilgrims who went to Rome for the Feast could be fed more easily after the harvest than in the spring. It is a day for remembering the great number of martyrs and "saints" as designated by the Catholic Church.

Among the celebrations that take place at the Advent season, one with a long history is the Christmas Pageant. Many churches again this year will produce a drama or play enacting the Christmas story or a portion of it—the visit of the Magi, the birth of Christ, the announcement to the shepherds. "In early centuries, the story of the Nativity was dramatized in churches within the framework of so-called 'miracle plays.' These semidramatic services consisted in pious representations of the 'mystery' of Christ's birth, accompanied by song, prayer, and other acts of devotion. (Mystery, in this connection, is the religious term for any episode of Christ's life related in the Gospels.) In those days, of course, books and pictures were not available to most of the common people, so these plays served not only as acts of worship, but also as a means of religious instruction" says Francis Weiser's *Handbook of Christian Feasts and Customs*.

EASTER LILY—Forming a part of nearly every church celebration of Easter is the Easter lily. One wonders if much use is made of the lily in teaching purity and the glory of the Lord. Weiser says: "In 1882, the florist W. K. Harris brought this lily to the United States (from Bermuda).... Since it flowers first around Easter time in this part of the world, it soon came to be called the "Easter lily." The American public immediately accepted the implied suggestion and made it a symbolic feature of the Easter celebration....

"Although the Easter lily did not directly originate from religious symbolism, it has acquired that symbolism, and quite appropriately so. Its radiant whiteness, the delicate beauty of shape and form, its joyful and solemn aspect, certainly make it an eloquent herald of the Easter celebration. Besides, lilies have always been symbols of beauty, perfection and goodness.... Since the Lord Himself stated that lilies are more glorious than the greatest earthly splendor, it certainly is fitting that we use these beautiful flowers to glorify Him on the day of His resurrection."

LESSON 7   OCTOBER 17

God Forgives His People

Background Scripture: Exodus 32:1–34:10
Devotional Reading: Exodus 20:1–17

Exodus 32:9–14; 34:5–9

9 And the LORD said unto Moses, I have seen this people, and, behold, it is a stiffnecked people:

10 Now therefore let me alone, that my wrath may wax hot against them, and that I may consume them: and I will make of thee a great nation.

11 And Moses besought the LORD his God, and said, LORD, why doth thy wrath wax hot against thy people, which thou hast brought forth out of the land of Egypt with great power, and with a mighty hand?

12 Wherefore should the Egyptians speak, and say, For mischief did he bring them out, to slay them in the mountains, and to consume them from the face of the earth? Turn from thy fierce wrath, and repent of this evil against thy people.

13 Remember Abraham, Isaac, and Israel, thy servants, to whom thou swarest by thine own self, and saidst unto them, I will multiply your seed as the stars of heaven, and all this land that I have spoken of will I give unto your seed, and they shall inherit it for ever.

14 And the LORD repented of the evil which he thought to do unto his people.

34:5 And the LORD descended in the cloud, and stood with him there, and proclaimed the name of the LORD.

6 And the LORD passed by before him, and proclaimed, The LORD, The LORD God, merciful and gracious, longsuffering, and abundant in goodness and truth,

7 Keeping mercy for thousands, forgiving iniquity and transgression and sin, and that will by no means clear the guilty; visiting the iniquity of the fathers upon the children, and upon the children's children, unto the third and to the fourth generation.

8 And Moses made haste, and bowed his head toward the earth, and worshipped.

9 And he said, If now I have found grace in thy sight, O Lord, let my Lord, I pray thee, go among us; for it is a stiffnecked people; and pardon our iniquity and our sin, and take us for thine inheritance.

KEY VERSE: "The LORD is merciful and gracious, slow to anger, and plenteous in mercy." Psalms 103:8.

Home Daily Bible Readings
Oct. 11 M. God's Commands, Exodus 20:1-17.
Oct. 12 T. Disobedience, Exodus 32:1-6.
Oct. 13 W. Justifiable Anger, Exodus 32:15-24.
Oct. 14 T. Punishment, Exodus 32:30-35.
Oct. 15 F. Not Angry Forever, Psalms 103:1-12.
Oct. 16 S. Father, Forgive Them, Luke 23:26-34.
Oct. 17 S. Forgiving Presence, Exodus 33:12-23.

Lesson Aim: That your class members may be assured of God's forgiveness.

LESSON OUTLINE
Background to the Scripture
Looking at the Scripture Text
  I. Wrath Intended (Exodus 32:9, 10)
  II. Man Interceded (Exodus 32:11-14)
  III. Mercy Intervened (Exodus 34:5-9)
Applying the Scripture

Background to the Scripture

The lesson today finds Moses alone with God on Mount Sinai. At the foot of the mountain, camped in their tents in that rugged desert, are the people of Israel. They have just passed through the most exhilarating days of their lives only to blow their truly golden opportunity—almost!

In rapid succession, they marched out of Egypt and through the Red Sea, looking back to see the waters of the sea sweep over Pharaoh's menacing hordes. On their march toward Sinai, they have experienced the manna supply and water from the rock, always with the pillar of cloud going before them by day and the pillar of fire at night. Their senses awakened, they arrived at Sinai only to be positively frightened by the awesome display of God's presence on the mount. The ground shook and the mount quaked as smoke billowed from its summit, accompanied by thunder and lightning. In dreadful fear, they pled with Moses to speak with God alone and to convey to them His messages.

For an extended time, Moses was "in the mount," receiving the Ten Commandments and the Law. Wearying of his absence, the people persuaded Aaron to make them a golden calf. Hailing it as their god, they let go their inhibitions in a wild party. It was this blasphemy and idolatry that almost cost the chosen people their place in God's plan and their very lives.

Looking at the Scripture Text

Teacher: Be sure you emphasize the result of not keeping one's word.

When will we ever learn that "talk is cheap"; that if we make a boast with our mouths, sooner or later we will have to face up to what we have said? At

Sinai's mountain, Moses elicited a ready commitment from the whole nation of Israel. "All that the Lord has spoken we will do," they said. At the moment, they meant every word. But shortly they would be tested and they would see how weak man is when his boasting is not in the power of God.

Wrath Intended (32:9, 10) Moses had been on the mount with God forty days. Jehovah gave His servant the two stone tablets on which the Ten Commandments were inscribed and was ready to send Moses down the mountain when the waiting Israelites decided they could wait no longer. Outraged by their idolatry, the Lord suddenly disowned them, calling them "your people, whom you brought up out of Egypt" (v. 7 NIV) in speaking to Moses. Seeing that they had rejected Him and replaced Him with a heathen idol, the Lord identified Israel as a "stiffnecked people," that is, a nation with a wilful, stubborn nature like the ox which will not bend its neck to receive the yoke.

"Don't try to stop me" (TEV) the Lord said to Moses, fully intent in His anger to "consume" the whole people. The verse raises interesting questions that cannot be fully answered. Scripture plainly shows that God reserves to Himself all power and that He is not limited by His Creation. "The Lord does whatever pleases him, in the heavens and on the earth, in the seas and all their depths" (Psalms 135:6 NIV). Yet on the mount, Moses found himself in a position of having an impact upon God, of being "in the way," having to be dealt with. Because he knew the Lord as no other man, he was in a position to stand his ground with the Almighty God and answer Him.

Man Interceded (vv. 11-14) It is a tribute to the character of Moses that he did not for a moment entertain the thought of the Lord's magnificent offer to make of him a great nation. His intercession shows his deep burden and care for the people of Israel. As a true "Israel," he now wrestles with God and prevails, standing his ground with three convincing arguments: (1) Israel was Jehovah's people, (2) the Egyptians would have no reason to believe in Jehovah if the people were annihilated, and (3) He had promised to Abraham, Isaac, and Israel that He would make a great nation out of their descendants.

Lord, they are your people. Moses' first argument was that the Lord could not vent the fury of His anger on Israel for they were His people. He reminded God that already He had a sizable investment in Israel; He had expended immense energies in delivering them from Egypt. True, Moses did not yet know the extent of the idolatry and debauchery of Israel, dancing as they were around the golden calf, and his anger would be hot enough (*see* vv. 19, 20; 26-28), but he argued that the Lord ought to turn from His fierce anger. In saying that Israel was His people, Moses was not denying that they were also his people.

Lord, what will the Egyptians say? Moses further argued that the Egyptians would be sure to misinterpret this entire experience if the Lord chose "to wipe them off the face of the earth" (NIV). Moses shows here an evangelical concern for the spiritual welfare of these enemies of Israel. He knew that the Lord had done all of those mighty miracles in Egypt so that the people, Egypt as well as Israel, might know that there is an Almighty God in heaven.

Lord, remember Abraham, Isaac, and Israel! With this, Moses was on the most solid ground of all—arguing on the basis of Jehovah's covenant with his forefathers. He even used Jacob's covenant name, Israel. When he was called at the burning bush on the back side of the desert, Moses was told that Jehovah was "the God of Abraham, the God of Isaac, and the God of Jacob" (3:15).

We must remember that Jehovah had not fully revealed His nature to Moses. On the mount, standing his ground in intercession, he could not be sure that the Lord would act in mercy. He knew that the Lord could indeed wipe out the whole nation and start all over with Moses to fulfill His sacred covenant.

The word *repent* in our text is translated "relent" in the New International Version; The Living Bible says "changed his mind." The word is best substituted today because of the contemporary understanding of *repent*—to feel sorry for sin and to change one's inner attitude. Human language cannot do justice to the divine character. "When He is said (by an anthropormorphic description) to repent, He changes not His purposes, but a course of events previously threatened, because the altered conduct of His people no longer calls forth what He had originally promised," says the *New Bible Commentary, Revised*. "It is a change in His dealings with people, not a change in His character or His purposes." Fourteen centuries later, Israel would reject their Messiah and be cut off, their place taken by the Church; God's judgments, though long in coming, are sure.

Mercy Intervened (34:5-9) Like Israel of old, Moses had prevailed with God. Having dealt with the sin in the Israelite camp, Moses returned to the tent of meeting outside of the encampment and pleaded for the abiding presence of Jehovah to be with them: "If thy presence go not with me, carry us not up hence" (33:15). And he prayed for the Lord to show him His glory. God granted these requests, promising to resume His presence among Israel's people and telling Moses that he would see the Lord's glory. In chapter 34 the second mountaintop experience of Moses is described.

On the mount, the Lord descended as was His usual custom in a cloud. By the plain expression, "the Lord passed by before him," Moses describes the height of his spiritual experience. Hiding in a cleft of a rock, he beheld the back side of Jehovah revealed in glory. It is from this time with the Lord that Moses' face radiantly reflected God's glory (34:29ff).

But Jehovah's self-revelation on the mount was not a silent thing. He "proclaimed His name." Or, He "announced the meaning of his name" (TLB). Until then Israel knew the Lord as the eternal, uncaused, unconditioned, self-sufficient, all powerful Lord; He was known by what He would *do*. Now He tells Moses who He *is*. Note the words used to fill in the gap in Israel's understanding of His nature: "merciful" or compassionate . . . "gracious" . . . "longsuffering" or slow to anger . . . "abounding in goodness" (He is generally better than His word, said Matthew Poole).

He is also abundant in truth or "faithfulness," that is, He is utterly trustworthy ... "maintaining love to thousands" ... and forgiving. The Lord declared that he forgives "wickedness, rebellion, and sin," using here the three most common words for sin in the Hebrew language. "No difference of any importance is discoverable in the Old Testament use of these three words," says Kenneth Grayston in *A Theological Word Book of the Bible*. "Behind the diversity of derivation there is a fundamental, unified conception of sin characterized in part as failure, in part as irregularity or crookedness, and in part as infringement of the psychic totality of the soul." God pledged Himself to forgive all, foreshadowing the great passages in the Old and New Testament on His forgiveness (Psalms 103:10–12; Isaiah 44:22; 1 John 1:9).

But that is not all; the Lord declared also that He will not "leave the guilty unpunished." Mercy is not mercy if there is no alternative of punishment. A righteous God can scarcely look the other way as man sins. He declared that He "punishes the children and their children for the sin of the fathers to the third and fourth generation" (NIV). He is not saying that the children bear the guilt of the sins of their parents, for we are each responsible before God. But sin is such that its consequences are felt by those closest to us.

At the revelation of God's glory and the proclamation of who He is, Moses bowed his head "at once." The only thing a man can do when coming to know God more perfectly is to worship. The mention of his bowed head suggests ample reason for us to pray in this manner, though it is not everywhere appropriate. Here Moses was overwhelmed as were the three disciples when the Lord Jesus was transfigured before their eyes on a mountain.

Having come more intimately into God's holy presence than any other human, Moses did not presume on the Lord's favor. "If now I have found grace (or favor) in thy sight...." He still interceded for his people, agreeing with God "it is a stiffnecked people." In the verse which follows, the Lord reaffirmed His covenant with Israel and promised to do wonders never before done in any nation and to enlarge their territory once they have possessed the Promised Land. Wrath had been intended against thousands, but one man interceded before God who intervened in mercy and blessing.

Applying the Scripture
Ask: What has ever happened or been accomplished for God in answer to your prayers?

That is a provoking question. But it is not an impertinent one. It does not apply only to pastors and missionaries and so-called saints. The New Testament teaches that God wants us to be like Christ in all respects. What does that mean when you consider that Christ's chief work in the heavens now is that of intercession?

To intercede is "to plead in behalf of another." Moses was a great intercessor. In this lesson, it can be seen that his "standing in the gap" made the difference at a critical point in the life of the young nation Israel. The members of your class will be challenged by his example and see their need to be greater intercessors. Here are some suggestions:

1. Get to know the mind of the God with whom you are dealing. Moses was an effective intercessor because he held God to His Word.

2. Interceding for others often frees God to bless us. Note the example of Job (Job 42:10). It certainly gets us out of our small, little selfish world.

3. Intercede for particular needs of your friends, your family, your pastor, your teacher(s), those whom you win to Christ. You may want to write missionaries you know to receive their prayer letters. Obtain an inexpensive world atlas and pray through it, perhaps a continent each day of the week. "Prayer is the slender nerve that moves the hand of God." (Appreciation is expressed to Robert D. Foster and his monthly "Challenge" letter for some of his ideas expressed here.)

Questions for Discussion
Make use of these questions to involve your students in learning and to test their understanding of the lesson.
1. Moses interceded for the children of Israel on the basis of three things. What were they? **2.** What does this passage show us about the influence a single individual may have with God when he or she intercedes on behalf of others? **3.** Does God really repent? Explain the meaning of the words, "the Lord repented of the evil which he thought to do." **4.** The phrase, "proclaimed the name of the Lord," sounds strange to us. What do you think is the meaning? **5.** What especially important attributes of God's moral nature were revealed to Moses on the mountain?

Illustrating the Scripture
Examples and quotations to help the teacher communicate the lesson.
GOD WILL FORGIVE ANY MAN   Billy Graham says, "If His conditions are met, God is bound by His Word to forgive any man or any woman of any sin because of Christ." And Oswald Chambers is quoted as writing: "Never build your preaching of forgiveness on the fact that God is our Father and He will forgive us because He loves us. . . . It is shallow nonsense to say that God forgives us because He is love. The only ground on which God can forgive me is through the cross of my Lord" (*Living Quotations for Christians*).

Last week's lesson taught us that God promised to pass over the sins of His people if they applied the blood to their houses. This symbolized the fact of God's forgiveness of all men today who will meet His conditions of genuine repentance and faith, whereby the blood of Christ washes us of all sin and we are accepted as righteous sons and daughters in His love.

MOVING BEYOND OUR FAILURES   Dr. George W. Truett was the pastor of the First Baptist Church in Dallas, Texas, for forty years. He was so greatly loved and respected that his radio sermons continued on the air in Dallas into the 1970s. He was a world figure in the Christian missionary cause, a leader in the Baptist World Alliance, and a dynamic evangelist throughout churches of the Southern Baptist Convention. He built the downtown Baptist church by his impassioned preaching and personal example. Few of the members of the church realized that in the early days of his pastorate in Dallas, Truett shot a man accidentally while they were on a hunting trip. The man, a great friend of the preacher, died. But Truett did not let the accident defeat him. If anything, the loss of his friend intensified Truett's motivation to do the work of two men. Assured of God's forgiveness, he was able to stand before people Sunday after Sunday and point them to God.

Topics for Youth
AN ARAB YOUTH WHO FOUND FORGIVENESS—"He had failed in what he had set out to do. His conscience and the fear of judgment and hell had defeated him. He had always hated admitting defeat on any score, but this was the ultimate failure. He couldn't even be successful at suicide.

"It was long past dark when he fell into his mother's arms. 'Anis, I'm so glad you're home,' she sobbed. 'I was so worried. Why did you go off without telling anyone where you were going? I died a thousand deaths not knowing.'

" 'Please give me food and water,' he croaked, collapsing onto a mat by the low kitchen table.

"Em Assad brought water and some cabbage rolls drenched in yogurt. Despite his hunger Anis ate little before dropping into an exhausted sleep on the cement floor of the kitchen.

"The next day was Easter Sunday. Anis refused to leave the house. He spent the entire day lying on his mat and reading his mother's Bible. For three days he read and read stories he had heard all his life. Somehow they seemed different now. For the first time he began to think that the Bible might be Supreme Truth, not just a collection of old traditions. He came to the Sermon on the Mount, which he had memorized years before, and stopped at: 'Seek ye first the kingdom of God, and his righteousness; and all these things shall be added unto you' (Matthew 6:33). He closed the Bible and lay staring at the ceiling for a long while.

"The battle flared again in his soul. Could this promise be believed? Could God 'add' to his miserable life all that he had been seeking—peace, purpose, hope, meaning? Could God lift the guilt that was knifing his heart?

"He would have to seek God *first*. That was what Jesus demanded—first place. His life would no longer be his own. He would not be free to lust, to scheme, to hate for any reason.

"He could fight no longer. In true contrition he knelt beside his mat and prayed, 'God, if You are real, You will keep Your word. I am holding You to this verse. From this day on I will seek Your kingdom, Your way, and I will depend on You to take care of me. I have made such a mess of my life, but I know You can forgive me and put me on the right road. Please begin by giving me a job. . . .'

"He rose from his knees and walked into the kitchen where Em Assad was at work. 'I'm hungry,' he said quietly.

"His mother smiled, 'Well, finally your appetite has returned.'

"Anis smiled at her.

" 'What has happened, Son? You seem different.'

" 'Oh, I'll tell you later,' he grinned and plunged into the food she had set before him.

"With his stomach content, he went outside for a walk. The world looked different that April 1951 day. The birds sang sweeter. 'A happy afternoon to you,' he called to an old man passing by.

"He walked boldly, confident in the future, though he was a youth of 18 without a job in a country (Jordan) where unemployment was pushing 40 percent.

"That evening he went gladly to prayer services and shared with the believers his new joy. His shining face convinced everyone that he had indeed experienced the new birth which Jesus said all must have to enter the kingdom of heaven.

"Afterward he floated home, ecstatic in his new faith, singing all the way. Too happy to go to bed, he dropped in next door and stayed up past midnight discussing the miracle of salvation with his brother-in-law Naji.

"At home again, he knelt beside his mat and thanked God once more for the new life. 'Let me be happy and rejoicing,' he asked." (From *The Liberated Palestinian: the Anis Shorrosh Story*, by James and Marti Hefley.)

LESSON 8   OCTOBER 24

God Proclaims the Year of Jubilee

Background Scripture: Leviticus 25
Devotional Reading: Leviticus 26:3–5, 40–46

Leviticus 25:1, 2, 8–12, 23, 24, 39–43
1. And the LORD spake unto Moses in mount Sinai, saying,
2. Speak unto the children of Israel, and say unto them, When ye come into the land which I give you, then shall the land keep a sabbath unto the LORD.
8. And thou shalt number seven sabbaths of years unto thee, seven times seven years; and the space of the seven sabbaths of years shall be unto thee forty and nine years.
9. Then shalt thou cause the trumpet of the jubile to sound on the tenth day of the seventh month, in the day of atonement shall ye make the trumpet sound throughout all your land.
10. And ye shall hallow the fiftieth year, and proclaim liberty throughout all the land unto all the inhabitants thereof: it shall be a jubile unto

you; and ye shall return every man unto his possession, and ye shall return every man unto his family.

11   A jubile shall that fiftieth year be unto you: ye shall not sow, neither reap that which groweth of itself in it, nor gather the grapes in it of thy vine undressed.
12   For it is the jubile; it shall be holy unto you: ye shall eat the increase thereof out of the field.
23   The land shall not be sold for ever: for the land is mine; for ye are strangers and sojourners with me.
24   And in all the land of your possession ye shall grant a redemption for the land.
39   And if thy brother that dwelleth by thee be waxen poor, and be sold unto thee; thou shalt not compel him to serve as a bondservant:
40   But as an hired servant, and as a sojourner, he shall be with thee, and shall serve thee unto the year of jubile:
41   And then shall he depart from thee, both he and his children with him, and shall return unto his own family, and unto the possession of his fathers shall he return.
42   For they are my servants, which I brought forth out of the land of Egypt: they shall not be sold as bondmen.
43   Thou shalt not rule over him with rigour; but shalt fear thy God.

KEY VERSE: "And ye shall hallow the fiftieth year, and proclaim liberty throughout all the land unto all the inhabitants thereof: it shall be a jubile unto you; and ye shall return every man unto his possession, and ye shall return every man unto his family." Leviticus 25:10.

Home Daily Bible Readings
Oct. 18   M.   The Year of Jubilee, Leviticus 25:1-6, 10, 18, 19.
Oct. 19   T.   The Blessings of Obedience, Leviticus 26:3-13.
Oct. 20   W.   The Consequences of Disobedience, Leviticus 26:14-20.
Oct. 21   T.   The Results of Repentance, Leviticus 26:40-46.
Oct. 22   F.   The Year of the Lord's Favor, Isaiah 61:1-7.
Oct. 23   S.   The Acceptable Year of the Lord, Luke 4:16-21.
Oct. 24   S.   God's Ultimate Plan for Liberty, John 8:31-36.

Lesson Aim: That adults, realizing that they are stewards of God's blessings, will lead their church to look out for the needy in their community.

LESSON OUTLINE
Background to the Scripture
Looking at the Scripture Text
  I. A Sabbatical Rest for the Land (Leviticus 25:1, 2)

II. The Jubilee Restoration of the Land (Leviticus 25:8-12)
III. The Land Is the Lord's (Leviticus 25:23, 24)
IV. The People Are the Lord's (Leviticus 25:39-43)
Applying the Scripture

Background to the Scripture
As its name implies, Leviticus was especially intended for the priestly tribe, the Levites. Within its pages are spelled out the careful instructions Israel was to observe in order to be an acceptable, separated people for Jehovah. The offerings and rituals would mark Israel as a uniquely chosen nation. Flowing out of that special relationship with the Lord is the Year of the Jubilee which reveals several significant truths regarding man's dependence upon God and his enjoyment of liberty in this life as well as in the hereafter.

The third of the five books that compose the Law of Moses, Leviticus bears the distinctive mark of Moses' pen. Some thirty times the phrase "and the Lord said to Moses" occurs. "These instructions, which so vitally concerned the welfare of God's people, and many of which are so precise and even minute in their requirements as clearly to require careful recording, were committed to writing either by Moses himself or at his command and under his supervision," says the *New Bible Commentary, Revised*.

Looking at the Scripture Text
A Sabbatical Rest for the Land (vv. 1, 2)   Children especially grow weary on long journeys—unless they have something wonderful to look forward to. The people of Israel were not children, but yet they often grew tired of the journey into Canaan and on several occasions wanted to turn back to Egypt. How quickly they had forgotten the cruel bondage of their taskmasters. In Egypt, liberty must have seemed an idle dream, an impossible dream. But God had in mind not only their freedom from cruel bondage, but their complete enjoyment of liberty in a land of their own. In giving Moses the instructions for the sabbatical year and the Year of the Jubilee, the Lord would show His people what wonderful liberty lay before them. It was to be His gift as a part of His covenant with Israel.

The guidelines Moses received at this point were for observance when the people had settled in Canaan. On the mountain of Sinai, Jehovah had already told Moses that they were to observe every seventh year as a sabbath rest (Exodus 23:10, 11). These more detailed instructions apparently were given while still in the region of Sinai. They follow on the heels of numerous rules and examples to follow affecting the whole of life. As they were already observing the sabbath day, the Lord said "the land itself must observe a sabbath to the Lord."

Three things may be noted about the Law concerning the sabbatical rest for the land. First, from the time they entered Canaan, Israel's people were to observe each seventh year by not sowing seed or pruning their vineyards or reaping a harvest. Second, the land itself was the Lord's and He was going to "lease" it to them. It was His right to tell them how to treat the land. Third, they were to observe the sabbath year "unto the Lord." While they would enjoy leisure during the year, they were to use that year in ways that would please Jehovah and they were to trust Him to take care of them while their fields lay fallow.

The Jubilee Restoration of the Land (vv. 8-12) When Israel settled Canaan after the conquest, Joshua supervised the orderly dispersal of all of the land among the eleven tribes (the tribe of Levi did not receive land as an inheritance since "the Lord was their inheritance"). Joshua indicated the boundaries for each tribe and then parceled out the land to families within that tribe (Joshua 13:15, 24, 29). Jehovah intended that the land remain the perpetual inheritance of each family within each tribe and so instituted a novel and truly wonderful thing—the Year of the Jubilee.

The nation would observe the sabbath year each seventh year, allowing the tilled earth to rest and refraining from harvesting what grew of itself. After seven cycles of seven years each, the trumpets were to sound all over the land to announce the fiftieth year, the Jubilee. The timing of Jubilee's beginning, coming on the Day of Atonement, would be rich with meaning and spiritual uplift. The text says the Jubilee would begin in the seventh month in the ecclesiastical year which began in March-April with the Passover. Thus with Yom Kippur, the Day of Atonement, coming in September-October, the Jubilee actually would be at the start of the Jewish civil year. The Jubilee, having to do with the social life rather than religious duties, would extend from the New Year just prior to autumn planting to the following autumn.

On the Day of Atonement, the holiest day of the Jewish year, the high priest offered sacrifices within the holy of holies for the entire nation. The people fasted and prayed and were in a restored relationship with Jehovah if they observed the Law. What a wonderful way to begin the year of liberty! Having been forgiven by God for their trespasses, they were, in the Jubilee, to cancel the debts of their brethren and allow any who had become servants to return to possess their family property. At the Jubilee, "there was a general restoration of heart and hope throughout the land ... *a bloodless revolution giving to the entire nation the opportunity of a new departure*" says the *Pulpit Commentary*.

The trumpet used for such occasions was a ram's horn, *yobel* in Hebrew; its name was adapted in the word *Jubilee* as the title of this year-long celebration.

The people were to "hallow" or "consecrate" the year with their families on the land originally given their tribal forefathers. Allowance was made here for the change in circumstances which would undoubtedly affect the people. If a man (or woman) could no longer keep his land in cultivation or his herds, he could sell himself to a neighbor. The price would be determined by the total net income from a year's crops multiplied by the number of years until the next Jubilee (*see* vv. 14-16). If his fortunes changed and he were able, he could redeem his home and property at any time, or a close kin could do so. But if he remained a servant until the Jubilee, then his debt was cancelled and he and the family would be liberated to return to their own land. A case in point, which almost necessitated the takeover of a widow's land, was alleviated by God's miraculous intervention in the person of Elisha (*see* 2 Kings 4:1ff).

In the Jubilee, the Lord would hope to show Israel that He is the Proprietor and Owner of the land. Since the Jubilee would come at least once in each person's lifetime, every generation would experience the direct relationship of serving Jehovah and looking to Him. The Jubilee was obviously meant to test the faith of God's people, as well, and to curb their natural tendency to "join house to house and field to field" (Isaiah 5:8) in greed and avaricious lust for material things. The Jubilee followed a sabbath year in which the people were not allowed to sow or reap. To embark on another year of the same would require careful planning and faith. Jehovah promised to bless the crop of the "sixth year" preceding the sabbath year (vv. 20-22). Some scholars, because of the difficulty of missing the harvest two years in a row, imagine that the Jubilee was actually the forty-ninth year, simultaneous with a sabbath. But the text explicitly says it was to be the fiftieth (vv. 10, 11).

Since the sabbath symbolizes God's rest, it would appear that the Jubilee was also intended to show a glimpse of heaven to the people of God. If the people observed the Law and entered into the Jubilee as they should, it would certainly be a little bit of heaven—joy, freedom, forgiveness, and unbroken fellowship with God. Sadly, no sure evidence exists that Israel ever observed the Jubilee in the land. It is spoken of in Numbers 36:4, but that is prior to their entrance into Canaan. Ezekiel mentions the "year of liberty," but again it is in reference to a future time and may have referred to the sabbath year.

The Land Is the Lord's (vv. 23, 24) Though it would be observed but every fifty years, the Jubilee made a difference in Israel's everyday life. For one thing, in the Jubilee, the Lord declared that the land belonged to Him. He absolutely forbade anyone to sell their land permanently. If by good fortune an Israelite acquired much land, he knew that it was "his" for only a few years. By this, the people would understand that they were but stewards of the Owner's property, "aliens and tenants" (NIV).

The People Are the Lord's (vv. 39-43) As much as the Owner was concerned for His land, He was equally and even more watchful for His people. It is impossible to miss the special attention and love He lavished on Israel. Here He places safeguards against any mistreatment of an Israelite by his fellow Israelite. "Do not make him work as a slave," the Lord commands. In the event a Hebrew became poor and had to sell himself to his neighbor, he was not to be treated as a slave; that was the position of an alien, for Israel was permitted to use them as slaves. Jehovah cautioned the people of Israel not to "take advantage of" their brothers (vv. 14, 17), but to guard their dignity and respect their pride. The *Westminster Dictionary of the Bible* says the Year of the Jubilee was instituted to teach "personal liberty, restitution of property and the simple life." It could add one other reason—respect for one's fellow man.

Note the explicit reason given for the prohibition of slavery among the Israelites: "For I brought you from the land of Egypt, and you are my servants; so you may not be sold as ordinary slaves" (v. 42 TLB). The following verse explains what the Lord intends. He does not want any "ruthlessly" (NIV) or "harshness" (RSV) treatment to be allowed. The rules of God among His people have never really changed. In the New Testament, the masters of slaves are enjoined, by reverence to God, to "treat your slaves in the same way. Do not threaten them, since you know that he who is both their Master and yours is in heaven, and there is no favoritism with him" (Ephesians 6:9 NIV).

Applying the Scripture
Teacher, two applications—one for the church body and one for the individual Christian—are suggested by today's lesson.

1. We Are Our Brother's Keeper—During the Year of the Jubilee each prosperous Israelite knew something of what it was to be poor. For two entire years, he did not have a crop to harvest. He was reduced to dependence upon God. In this way, he would not only be forced to look to the Lord for his provisions—he would be caused to look more compassionately on those within Israel who never had a crop to harvest.

Being laid off one's job, after consecutive years of earning good wages, has the same effect. We grow spiritually as we learn to look directly to God to meet our needs, and we gain sympathy for the less fortunate.

The Israelite community was encouraged to provide work for the less fortunate within their tribes. They were not to take advantage of them nor treat them harshly. Is this example being carried out by your church? What provision does the local assembly make for the unfortunate, the poor, the victims of job cutbacks and inflation in the community? As times grow increasingly worse, it will be all the more important for churches and volunteer agencies to show that *we are our brother's keeper*.

2. How Much Is Enough?—The Year of the Jubilee served to place a ceiling on the acquisitions of the Israelite householder. During the intervening years, a man was encouraged to prosper and increase his earnings. If he could help some poor Israelite by buying his land, well and good. He could expect God to bless him with abundance as the Lord did Abraham, surely one of the richest men of his day. But at the Jubilee, the servants who had been forced to sell out to him were set free and the lands he had acquired went back to their original owners. In such a way, avarice and greed were curbed.

No Jubilee observance will do that for us in present-day America. What can we do to control our natural tendency to acquire more things? We can examine our lives to see if we are giving the Lord His tithe of our income. If that still leaves us with plenty, we may want to adopt a plan of graduated giving and determine what portion of our budget we will live on. With the rest, we can seek to put it where it will enable God's Good News to be given to all men. This may involve assisting in the financial needs of a local Christian college, helping one of the Christian relief agencies, assisting in the work of Bible societies and Bible translation ministries for the poorest of all people—those who do not have the Scriptures in their own language.

We can allow the Scriptures to tell us how much is enough. Paul wrote to the Corinthians: "At the present time your plenty will supply what they need, so that in turn their plenty will supply what you need. Then there will be equality" (2 Corinthians 8:14 NIV).

Questions for Discussion
Make use of these questions to involve your students in learning and to test their understanding of the lesson.
1. What is the meaning of Jubilee? 2. How did the keeping of the Jubilee serve to test the faith of the Israelites? 3. If the Jubilee year began on the Day of Atonement, in what season was that and when did the year end? 4. Does the timing of Jubilee have a special spiritual significance, seeing that it was to commence on the Day of Atonement? What is the significance? 5. What values did the Jubilee teach besides showing that the Lord is the Proprietor of all and that men are directly His servants? 6. If the people could not plant crops or reap, how did they eat in the Year of Jubilee? 7. What are some of the economic implications of the Jubilee year for Christian stewards today? 8. From the record of Scripture, was the Jubilee observed very faithfully?

Illustrating the Scripture
Examples and quotations to help the teacher communicate the lesson.
PROCLAIM LIBERTY THRO' ALL THE LAND In 1976, Philadelphia played host to the entire nation as people from every state and every ethnic background within the United States went to pay homage to their country's birth 200 years earlier. In order to accommodate the throngs who would want to see the Liberty Bell, a glass-enclosed pavilion was erected near Independence Hall and there the historic bell was put on exhibit. Many of the sightseers did not realize that a verse of Scripture is emblazoned on the bell. That verse was there because of the request of a devout Quaker named Isaac Norris who may have drawn his inspiration from none other than Benjamin Franklin.

Norris, a member of the Society of Friends and a keen student of the Bible, ascended to the position of Speaker of the Assembly in Pennsylvania Colony in 1750 and was chosen to conduct the colony's correspondence with England. When the Assembly decided it wanted to hang a bell in the Statehouse then under construction, it looked to England to supply the bell; no American foundries at that time could produce a bell of the 2,000-pound size required. So Norris composed a letter on November 1, 1751, and requested from the colony's agent in London that he "get us a good Bell." The sum was to be "about one hundred pounds Sterling." Norris preserved a copy of his letter in a book of letters and in that letter he said, "Let the Bell be cast by the best Workmen and examined carefully before it is Shipped with the following words well shaped in large letters round it *viz:* 'By order of the Assembly of the Province of Pensylvania(sic) for the Statehouse in the City of Philadelphia, 1752.' and underneath, 'Proclaim Liberty thro' all the Land to all the Inhabitants Thereof—Levit. XXV 10.' " With those words in the inscription, the great Liberty Bell was hung in the Pennsylvania Statehouse where it tolled a nation's independence some twenty-four years later.

SURVIVALISTS   There could be no more stark contrast in attitude than to compare what we may call the "Jubilee" attitude with that of modern-day "survivalists." A special series on these people, reported by Peter Arnett of the Associated Press, revealed their repudiation of the idea that man is his brother's keeper. Excerpts follow:

"Apocalyptic writers such as the late survivalist Mel Tappan . . . have predicted potential disaster from nuclear war, a failed economy or natural disaster.

" 'The concept most fundamental to long-term disaster preparedness, in retreating, is having a safe place to go in order to avoid the concentrated violence destined to erupt in the cities,' Tappan wrote (in 1978) in his survival newsletter, Personal Survival Letter. . . .

"For his last place on Earth, Tappan chose the lush forests of southern Oregon. 'Mel thought it was the safest place in America,' said Mrs. Tappan. . . .

"Security dominates Richard Johnson's existence. He is a farmer and mechanic whose frame home is in O'Brien, a truckstop in the forests of southern Oregon.

"Johnson's mind is usually on 'Camp One,' a three-hour climb away from ridges topped with ice-fringed conifers, down steep slopes studded with pines, through rocky stream beds and up narrow, shaded valleys.

" 'Nobody could find this place, not tracking dogs, not the National Guard, not fighter bombers,' the rifle-carrying Johnson said, his baggy green fatigues slapping in the wind as he pointed to a large pile of branches that concealed his family's stored survival supplies.

"Johnson crawled into a bunker dug out of the rocky soil and revealed about 1,000 pounds of tinned food and army C-rations, freeze-dried meats, seeds, shovels, axes and saws, bedding and cookers.

" 'We have medical gear because most survivalists believe they will eventually take casualties,' Johnson said. 'We know how to remove bullets and stitch people up.' "

Topics for Youth

"THE TITHE IS THE LORD'S"—"Madam H. of Tokyo had no faith in Buddhism and was indeed an atheist, but a woman of high ideals and strong convictions. She became impressed with the reasonableness of setting aside a certain part of her income for philanthropy and after considerable deliberation decided on one-tenth as a just proportion. This she made her practice. When she was over sixty, she was brought into contact with Christianity and became a disciple of the Master. One day in reading the Bible, she came for the first time upon the command and promise in Malachi (3:10). She was startled.

" 'Why,' she said, 'I supposed that was my discovery that the tenth was a reasonable proportion, but I find that God had commanded it thousands of years ago!'

"If this principle had not been a good one for our development would God have so ordained it? It is not that He needs this tithe for Himself. All the cattle in the thousand hills are His. It is all His. He is the owner. It is the fact that we need this discipline. To become stewards means to accept responsibility, and responsibility strengthens character. Ruskin writes in *The Seven Lamps of Architecture:*

> Let us not now lose sight of this broad and unabrogated principle—I might say incapable of being abrogated so long as man shall receive earthly gifts from God: of all that they have His tithe must be rendered to Him, or in so far and insomuch He is forgotten; of the skill and of the treasure, of the strength and of the mind, of the time and of the toil offering must be made reverently; and if there be any difference between the Levitical and the Christian offering, it is that the later may be just so much the wider in its range as it is typical in its meaning, as it is thankful instead of sacrificial.

"The consciousness of being used, the sense of working in harmony with God's will, which is but another name for His good, wise and loving law, is one of the most heartening and satisfying experiences in the life of the normal Christian. Instead of saying, with downcast eyes and folded hands: 'Thy will be done,' to be able and willing, with squared shoulders, steady eye and firm lip to say courageously: 'Thy will be done and I am ready to help in having it done,' transforms duty into privilege." Clementina Butler, *Ownership: God Is the Owner, I Am His Steward* (Fleming H. Revell, Old Tappan, N.J., 1927).

LESSON 9   OCTOBER 31

God Speaks Through a Gentile

Background Scripture: Numbers 22–24
Devotional Reading: Proverbs 16:1–11

Numbers 22:4b–6; 23:7–12; 24:17b

22:4b   And Balak the son of Zippor was king of the Moabites at that time.

   5   He sent messengers therefore unto Balaam the son of Beor to Pethor, which is by the river of the land of the children of his people, to call him, saying, Behold, there is a people come out

from Egypt: behold, they cover the face of the earth, and they abide over against me.

6 Come now therefore, I pray thee, curse me this people; for they are too mighty for me: peradventure I shall prevail, that we may smite them, and that I may drive them out of the land: for I wot that he whom thou blessest is blessed, and he whom thou cursest is cursed.

23:7 And he took up his parable, and said, Balak the king of Moab hath brought me from Aram, out of the mountains of the east, saying, Come, curse me Jacob, and come, defy Israel.

8 How shall I curse, whom God hath not cursed? Or how shall I defy, whom the LORD hath not defied?

9 For from the top of the rocks I see him, and from the hills I behold him: lo, the people shall dwell alone, and shall not be reckoned among the nations.

10 Who can count the dust of Jacob, and the number of the fourth part of Israel? Let me die the death of the righteous, and let my last end be like his!

11 And Balak said unto Balaam, What hast thou done unto me? I took thee to curse mine enemies, and, behold, thou hast blessed them altogether.

12 And he answered and said, Must I not take heed to speak that which the LORD hath put in my mouth?

24:17b There shall come a Star out of Jacob, and a Scepter shall rise out of Israel, and shall smite the corners of Moab, and destroy all the children of Sheth.

KEY VERSE: "And he answered and said, Must I not take heed to speak that which the LORD hath put in my mouth?" Numbers 23:12.

Home Daily Bible Readings
Oct. 25 M. A Spokesman for God, Numbers 22:31-38.
Oct. 26 T. Careful to Obey, Numbers 23:4-12.
Oct. 27 W. The Power of God's Word, Numbers 23:16-23.
Oct. 28 T. Power Without Limit, Isaiah 45:1-7.
Oct. 29 F. God Enables Those He Calls, Jeremiah 1:4-10.
Oct. 30 S. The Source of Sound Speech, Proverbs 16:1-11.
Oct. 31 S. No Need to Worry, Matthew 10:7-20.

Lesson Aim: That students learn to discern the will of God whenever danger is near.

LESSON OUTLINE
Background to the Scripture
Looking at the Scripture Text

I. Fear Rises Out of Insecurity (Numbers 22:4b, 5)
II. Fear Resorts to Prophecy (Numbers 22:6)
III. The Essence of Prophecy (Numbers 23:7-12; 24:17b)
Applying the Scripture

Background to the Scripture

Look at a map of the Holy Land. If possible, get a map showing Canaan at the time of Israel's wilderness wanderings.

The Jordan River is Canaan's natural boundary on the east. Spreading east of the river, from a point halfway down the Dead Sea to the Jabbok River in the north, is the vast desert territory of the Amorites. Their king, Sihon, defied Moses when he sought passage through his land and in a series of military victories Israel crushed the king and his armies. Israel put to death all of the people and occupied their land and cities across from Jericho all along the Jordan, in preparation for entering the Promised Land.

Now imagine that you are King Balak, chief potentate of the Moabites, the Amorites' neighbors to the south. In recent years, your people lost a chunk of land to the Amorites and now this strange nation that has destroyed Sihon's forces is camped near your borders. It looks as if you are next on the list. Would you be a bit anxious?

Looking at the Scripture Text

Fear Rises Out of Insecurity (22:4b, 5) If Balak had only known, he actually had nothing to fear from Israel. The Lord had commanded Israel not to fight the people of Moab for they were Israel's distant cousins. The founder of their nation, Moab, was a son of Lot, Abraham's nephew and God was not going to give Israel any of the land that belonged to Moab; there was no reason to fight (Deuteronomy 2:8, 9; Judges 11:14, 18).

Besides, if Israel were to attack Moab, it would seem that now was not the time. To reach "the plains of Moab" where they camped, they would have had to travel north from the Wilderness and pass through Balak's territory. Evidently they had skirted Moab. Nevertheless the people of Moab were sick with fear as Moses had foretold in his prophetic song years earlier (Exodus 15:15).

Little is known about the size of the Moabite nation. They probably numbered a few thousand. They considered themselves no match for Israel, which is why the king summoned Balaam to come to his aid. This enigmatic figure lived a great distance away, "in the land of the Amavites" (NEB) or "the land of Amaw" (TEV) in the vicinity of the Euphrates River. Archaeologists believe his city, Pethor, is identical with Pitru which has been rediscovered in Mesopotamia. The messengers who were sent to fetch Balaam did not succeed on their first trip. The fact that Balak persisted in bringing Balaam demonstrates the intensity of his feelings of insecurity—"a whole nation has come from Egypt; its people are spreading out everywhere and threatening to take over our land" (TEV). The last words of verse 5 say it all. Israel was at Moab's door.

Fear Resorts to Prophecy (v. 6) Balak's message to Balaam, through the messengers he sent, was "come ... curse me this people." The New English Bible has it: "lay a curse on them." The steps Balak is taking reveal his steadfast belief that he needed supernatural help. He could not have failed to know something of the miraculous powers Israel had in her favor, so he sought a "holy man" to do for him what his armies could not do. Somehow the reputation of Balaam was known to him—"I know that when you pronounce a blessing, people are blessed, and when you pronounce a curse, they are placed under a curse" (TEV).

The man Balaam is a paradox. As we shall see, he did speak the Word of the Lord. The text indicates that God listened to his prayers and put the very words into his mouth. When Balak's messengers reached him, he made them wait until he had obtained guidance from God. And when the Lord said, "Don't go," he didn't. However, when more important leaders returned to plead with him, and offered to reward him richly, Balaam agreed to go (vv. 7-19), but only after again asking the Lord. To their offer of a reward, Balaam said, "If Balak would give me his house full of silver and gold, I cannot go beyond the word of the Lord my God, to do less or more" (v. 18). But evidently the offer of riches had turned his head.

On the journey to meet King Balak, the angel of the Lord withstood him. Not being able to gain Balaam's attention in any other way, he caused the ass on which Balaam rode to speak out. Balaam got the message, being fearfully humbled; he would go to Balak, but he would not say anything except what the Lord would tell him to say. In each of the four oracles which follow (23:7-12, 18-24; 24:3-9, 15-24), he pronounced nothing but blessings on God's people.

Was Balaam a man of God, since his mouth uttered God's words? The testimony of Scripture says *no*. Joshua described him as a soothsayer (Joshua 13:22). In the New Testament, Peter called him a prophet (2 Peter 2:16), but the description he gave of Balaam certainly is not complimentary. His name was used in the context as a symbol of avarice.

The letter of Jude speaks of people who "rushed for profit into Balaam's error" (v. 11 NIV) and his memory is blasted in Revelation as one "who taught Balak to entice the Israelites to sin by eating food sacrificed to idols and by committing sexual immorality" (Revelation 2:14 NIV). Nowhere is there a good word said about Balaam. We conclude that he was a false prophet and a soothsayer (in Numbers 24:1 we learn that he used enchantments and omens in his divination) who happened to come under God's sovereign power for a time. Just as Caiaphas the high priest, an enemy of the Gospel, uttered prophetic truth because his was the chief prophetic office in Israel (John 11:49-52), so Balaam in his oracles spoke God's truth. Is that too hard to accept, since Jehovah had to use a donkey to speak to Balaam?

The Essence of Prophecy (23:7-12; 24:17b) This, the first of Balaam's oracles, forms the heart of the lesson. In modern translations, this is treated as poetry and it is some of the oldest poetry in the Bible. William F. Albright concluded that the language of the story of Balaam and the grammatical and syntactical characteristics of the poetry bear the marks of twelfth or eleventh century B.C. times, the period to which Balaam belongs. The teacher will want to show this poetry to the class as it appears in modern versions which set it off in type as poetry; yet, the language of the King James can hardly be improved upon.

The word *parable* (v. 7) is sometimes translated "discourse," "prophecy," or "oracle"; the latter word appears most appropriate.

Some interpreters believe that Balaam had come from a city near Moab, especially since two trips were required to bring him there. But the oracle agrees with our introduction to Balaam; he came from the land of the Amavites—"Syria" or "Amaw" (NEB, TEV).

In the oracle, almost every statement is restated, a technique seen very much in the Psalms and in the Song of Solomon. "Curse me, Jacob, and *come defy Israel* . . . from the top of the rocks I see him, and *from the hills I behold him* . . . Let me die the death of the righteous, and *let my last end be like his!*" This literary form is known as "parallelism"; Hebrew poetry did not rhyme in sound, but in thought.

From Bamoth-baal, where pagan sacrifices were customarily offered, Balak caused Balaam to look down on "a part of the people of Israel" (TEV). After offering up seven bulls and seven rams, Balaam went aside to meet the Lord "and the Lord put a word" in his mouth. This message Balaam courageously proclaimed, to Balak's consternation.

By the words, "a people dwelling alone . . . not reckoning itself among the nations" he pointed out their uniqueness among all other peoples. It was like saying "these are separated from all other nations, as in religion and laws, so also in divine protection . . . my enchantments cannot have that power against them which they have against other persons and people" (Matthew Poole).

From where Balaam stood, Israel's companies were spread out below as far as the eye could see—"Who can count the dust . . . ?" he asked, an allusion to Israel's size that recalls God's firm promise to Abraham to make his descendants like the stars of heaven and the dust of the earth in number. The words "fourth part" (KJV) can also be translated "sands" or "dust clouds."

Balaam continued to bless Israel. They were a special people, a numerous people and were to be a happy people. Balaam wished aloud that he could die "the death of the righteous" as Israel would, that his "end" would be like theirs. But as Poole said, "as he would not live as God's people did, so he died by the sword." Balaam met a violent death at the hand of Joshua's conquerors (Numbers 31:8; Joshua 13:22). Though he was unwilling to yield to Satan in Moab and curse Israel, he ultimately contributed to Balak's goal by advising the bedouin Midianites to lure Israel into cultic worship and immorality (Numbers 31:16; Revelation 2:14).

Balak was outraged by Balaam's "curses." "I brought you here to curse my enemies," he said, "but all you have done is bless them" (v. 11 TEV). "I can say only what the Lord tells me to say," responded Balaam. His answer is classic. It is the essence of prophecy.

As Israel's Ahab of a later day, Balak would not listen to the Word of God. Twice more he took Balaam to a different place, but Balaam still had only blessings for Israel. Finally, Balaam clapped his hands in anger and sent this obstinate guest home. But not without Balaam's parting shot—"I am warning you what the people of Israel will do to your people in the future" (24:14 TEV).

"I shall see him, but not now" (v. 17). Not immediately, Balaam was saying, but "in the latter days" a Star would come out of the nation Israel—a prince of great eminence. He would come as One who treads down his enemies, as One who treads the winepress. "A Scepter" would be in his hand. Though some translations say "a comet," the Hebrew word here is *staff* or *rod* of a leader. This prince will "crush the forehead (or corners) of Moab" (RSV). This could refer to the borders of Moab or its leaders who were sometimes called the chief cornerstone. Did Balaam's prophecy find fulfillment in David, who did subdue Moab in his reign (2 Samuel 8:2; Psalms 60:8)?

Yes—and no. It seems entirely possible that the Word of God here looks beyond David to one greater—to David's Chief Son, the princely Messiah Jesus. One of the names of Jesus Christ is "morning star" (Revelation 22:16). As Moab stood here for the world's system opposed to God's Kingdom, it is no wonder that both Jews and Christians have seen a messianic connection in these words from Balaam.

Balak had been driven by his insecurities to fear, and his fears led him to resort to prophecy. But the prophecy he sought was not what he received. His was the curse, Israel's was the blessing.

Applying the Scripture
Two questions and a statement can help you suggest the proper application your students should make of their lesson. They are in italics below:

Since Scripture is silent about it, we are free to speculate how Balaam and his "prophecies" were regarded in Pethor, his hometown. Having the reputation that he did, he may have been well regarded by the folk who knew him best. But if he did have the respect of his own people, he does not fit the mold of a prophet. Didn't Jesus have something to say about a prophet being without honor in his own country?

This serves to point up our tendency to really listen to the outsider, someone who comes as an authority figure from either outside our native boundaries or from outside the Establishment. When Jimmy Carter ran for president in 1976, his being an "outsider" actually worked in his favor; people wanted to hear what he had to say and enough of them did listen so that he was able to win the election.

1. *How many of us are gullible enough to hearken to outsiders, especially in spiritual matters?* An outsider may have the Word of the Lord—Balaam certainly did—but then again, he may not. He may do like the false prophets have al-

ways done, tell us the things we want to hear. Could the success Sun Myung Moon has and the growth Islamic teaching has in America be partly attributed to people's gullibility to listen to the outsider?

2. *Do you only seek a favorable word from God?* Being a Christian means being a seeker, a learner, a disciple. And if we place ourselves in that category, then we are patently admitting that we don't have all the answers.

Yet many people in church are like Balak who only wanted the soothsayer Balaam to say what *he* wanted to hear. Many people, in seeking to make a decision about some matter, will listen only to the verses in God's Word that agree with what they want to do. Caution your class members to watch out for this deceitful delusion. Encourage them to seek the opinion of others, even those whom they think may be opposed to their own ideas. Then they can more objectively decide what is the best course to follow.

Dare to be a Balaam, dare to stand alone! That's not how the song goes; it is actually sung of Daniel who had the courage to stand against the king and princes of Persia. But Balaam offers a worthy example to us also, not in what he was but in how he withstood all the bribes and pressures and arm-twisting of King Balak. And remember, he was out of his element, too; he was a guest of the king and could have been harmed or even put to death for not doing as the king decreed.

Many of your class members may be in positions where they are tempted to compromise. Many of them may be working among those who are forever cursing the people of God. A Christian in that situation is constantly pressured to join them. Take time to allow class members to share how they have been able to take a stand for Christ and for good among others, either at work or in family relations or in other contexts. Encourage them to let others know they belong to Christ and let their true colors fly.

Questions for Discussion
Make use of these questions to involve your students in learning and to test their understanding of the lesson.
1. Whose son was Moab, the progenitor of the Moabite people? 2. Did Israel attack Moab on their way to the Promised Land, as Balak feared? 3. From what region of the Middle East did Balaam come? 4. Which term best describes Balaam—prophet, man of God, soothsayer? 5. How do we know that the Lord spoke through Balaam? 6. Why did the angel threaten Balaam as he rode on his ass to meet Balak? 7. Can a person be a foe of God and yet be a spokesman for Him, too? 8. Did Balaam's wish for a peaceful death like Israel's come true? How did Balaam die?

Illustrating the Scripture
Examples and quotations to help the teacher communicate the lesson.
RASPUTIN, A MODERN-DAY BALAAM? Grigori Efimovich Novykh —better known as Rasputin—bears certain similarities to Balaam. He, too, exerted immense power in an imperial court, the palace of Emperor

Nicholas II and his wife Alexandra in Russia. Born a peasant in Siberia, Rasputin arrived in St. Petersburg, the seat of power in Russia, in 1903. At the time, he was approximately thirty years old. Already he boasted of unusual powers. Claiming to be divinely inspired, this man with an extraordinary magnetic personality had a reputation as a miracle worker. In particular, he preached that physical contact with his own body had a healing and purifying effect, a "doctrine which served him as a convenient means of gratifying his phenomenal sexual appetite," says the *Encyclopaedia Britannica*.

Rasputin was accused of heresy by the Russian Orthodox Church, but the charges were dismissed.

Unlike Balaam, he was not summoned from a great distance to help at a time of an international crisis. Rasputin got himself known in the capital, befriended high-ranking Orthodox prelates, and attained admission into the aristocratic society, ultimately being introduced to the Tsar and the Tsarina in November 1905. Because his powers of suggestion had a soothing effect on Alexis, the *tsarevitch* who suffered from hemophilia, Rasputin became a court favorite, especially in the eyes of the Tsarina. She came to look on Rasputin as "a saint sent by God to save the dynasty."

After the outbreak of World War I and Nicholas's decision to assume command of the troops in the field in 1915, the empress and Rasputin were left in virtual control of domestic affairs in the capital. Historians attribute his dark presence as contributing to the downfall of the aristocracy. In 1916, Rasputin met a violent death as extreme conservatives in St. Petersburg tried first to poison him and then shot him to death.

CONFESS YOUR FREEDOM FROM FEAR   Balak and the people of Moab were sick with fear. We know what Balak did about it. Pastor Lester Sumrall has far better advice in overcoming fear:

"For most of my life, I have been gloriously free of fear. Once, while on my first preaching trip around the world, I was forced to walk a trail in China for three hours with a gun to my head. But I was not afraid; I did not collapse in fear, because the peace of God filled my heart. God told me that I would live, so I turned around and laughed in the faces of the soldiers.

"On that same trip, Howard Carter and I entered forbidden Tibet, traveling on muleback. For three months, we lived in that country, often sleeping in the dark pagan temples with their evil-looking idols. I do not remember being afraid. On another occasion, a small plane in which I was flying in Mexico went down and turned over. I was shaken up, but not hurt. Had I listened to some of the people who saw what had happened, I would never have flown again. But why should I limit myself? I took the next plane out and have flown hundreds of thousands of miles since then.

"If the devil tells me not to do something, that's the very thing I will do. If he tells me that a door is shut, I will kick the door down. We must not be afraid of the devil. The Bible tells us, 'Resist the devil, and he will flee from you' (James 4:7). Testify daily that you are free, saying, 'I am free from all my fears. I am not afraid.'" Lester Sumrall, *Living Free* (Thomas Nelson Publishers, Nashville. Copyright 1979 by Lester Sumrall Evangelistic Association).

Topics for Youth

DON'T FORGET TO BE A BLESSING!—Young people often cannot grasp the truth that they can be a means of blessing someone else. But why not? God has promised that He would bless all of the children of Abraham, and if a youth has put his or her trust in Christ, he or she can lay claim to that blessing. And the only requirement to meet in blessing others, is to be blessed ourselves!

Perhaps a song can help here. "Count your many blessings, name them one by one, and it will surprise you what the Lord hath done . . . count your blessings . . . see what God hath done!"

A missionary pilot flying out to remote mission villages was often the only English-speaking Christian the remote Bible translators saw in months while they lived in the village. As the pilot took off one day to take supplies to that translation team, over the radio came the voice of the dispatcher: "And don't forget to be a blessing at Pico Puerto!" The words struck him strangely. He had often asked God to bless him; but now he was ready to ask God to make *him* a blessing to others.

BREAKING THE POWER OF THE CURSE—A nationally known authority on youth and their development tells audiences of a young woman who attended one of his meetings and afterward asked to speak with him. When he counseled with her, he could see that she was in distress and seemed to be utterly lacking in self-confidence. He learned that when she was a small girl she had overheard her mother say that a fortune-teller had predicted she would never get married. That suggestion overheard by the girl became like a curse to her and she grew up believing that she would never marry.

The counselor showed her that what the fortune-teller told her was a lie and that such a prediction had really come from Satan who sought to bind her and control her life. It took time, as he opened the Bible and showed her promises having to do with the greater power of God, but the woman was able to reach out and claim the promises of God and begin to move out of her hang-up.

In such subtle ways, the devil seeks to bring a curse upon people today. One of the most "acceptable" ways of doing it is through the daily horoscopes people read in the newspapers. If he can get us to believe what these predictions say, then he has gained the initiative and effectively cursed our life. Make no doubt about it. Satan's power is real. He still seeks to "steal, and to kill, and to destroy" (John 10:10).

UNIT III

God Leads and Delivers His Chosen People

LESSON 10   NOVEMBER 7

God Leads His People into the Promised Land

Background Scripture: Joshua 3, 4
Devotional Reading: Joshua 4:19–24

Joshua 3:14–4:7

14 And it came to pass, when the people removed from their tents, to pass over Jordan, and the priests bearing the ark of the covenant before the people;

15 And as they that bare the ark were come unto Jordan, and the feet of the priests that bare the ark were dipped in the brim of the water, (for Jordan overfloweth all his banks all the time of harvest,)

16 That the waters which came down from above stood and rose up

upon an heap very far from the city Adam, that is beside Zaretan: and those that came down toward the sea of the plain, even the salt sea, failed, and were cut off: and the people passed over right against Jericho.

17 And the priests that bare the ark of the covenant of the LORD stood firm on dry ground in the midst of Jordan, and all the Israelites passed over on dry ground, until all the people were passed clean over Jordan.

4:1 And it came to pass, when all the people were clean passed over Jordan, that the LORD spake unto Joshua, saying,

2 Take you twelve men out of the people, out of every tribe a man,

3 And command ye them, saying, Take you hence out of the midst of Jordan, out of the place where the priests' feet stood firm, twelve stones, and ye shall carry them over with you, and leave them in the lodging place, where ye shall lodge this night.

4 Then Joshua called the twelve men, whom he had prepared of the children of Israel, out of every tribe a man:

5 And Joshua said unto them, Pass over before the ark of the LORD your God into the midst of Jordan, and take ye up every man of you a stone upon his shoulder, according unto the number of the tribes of the children of Israel:

6 That this may be a sign among you, that when your children ask their fathers in time to come, saying, What mean ye by these stones?

7 Then ye shall answer them, That the waters of Jordan were cut off before the ark of the covenant of the LORD; when it passed over Jordan, the waters of Jordan were cut off: and these stones shall be for a memorial unto the children of Israel for ever.

KEY VERSE: "Behold, the ark of the covenant of the LORD of all the earth passeth over before you into Jordan." Joshua 3:11.

Home Daily Bible Readings
Nov. 1   M.   God Promises His Presence, Joshua 1:1–9.
Nov. 2   T.   God Calls to Action, Joshua 3:5–13.
Nov. 3   W.   God Honors His Word, Joshua 4:11–18.
Nov. 4   T.   Remembering God's Faithfulness, Joshua 4:19–24.
Nov. 5   F.   Assurance of God's Direction, Psalms 23:1–6.
Nov. 6   S.   Assurance of God's Provision, Matthew 6:25–34.
Nov. 7   S.   God's Ultimate Presence and Provision, Ephesians 1:3–14.

Lesson Aim: That each student will establish a memorial of some kind to remember God's special blessing in his life.

LESSON OUTLINE
Background to the Scripture
Looking at the Scripture Text
  I. A Highly Religious Event (Joshua 3:14)
  II. A Most Propitious Time (Joshua 3:15)
  III. An Unforgettable Passage (Joshua 3:16, 17)
  IV. An Everlasting Memorial (Joshua 4:1–7)
Applying the Scripture

Background to the Scripture

At last! After wavering in their belief in Jehovah and wandering forty years in the wilderness, Israel miraculously stood ready to move into the land the Lord had promised her when she was still in Egypt. God had said He would give her the land and we have seen that she would have never made it this far, but for Him.

The Book of Joshua is important, not only because it records the culmination of the people's long journey, but for what it shows us of God. In Joshua, we see *God's faithfulness*—His plan ultimately won out over Israel's unbelief and her enemies' resistance; *God's holiness*—"the iniquity of the Amorites at last was full and Israel became the instrument of His punishment . . . Israel would succeed in the task committed to her only as every evil thing is put away from her" (*New Bible Commentary, Revised*); and *God's salvation*—the Exodus portrays the sinner's deliverance from sin's bondage while crossing Jordan pictures the abundant life God gives His people, a life of "victory and possession and rest."

Looking at the Scripture Text

A Highly Religious Event (3:14) Have you noticed how the Lord always gave very precise orders to His people? And it seems the more significant a thing was, the more carefully did He spell out what He expected. This is certainly true of today's lesson. And the writer, whom we presume to be Joshua, tells and retells each step in the dramatic crossing. One thing that becomes clear is that this is one event with tremendous religious associations.

On the morning of the tenth day of the month, which happened to be the first month in their calendar year (4:19), the people were told by their leaders to watch the priests who would soon carry the Ark of the Covenant in the direction of the Jordan River west of them. They were to follow.

The Ark of the Covenant (Today's English Version calls it the Covenant Box) was the centerpiece of Israel's religious life. Constructed of acacia wood and overlaid with gold, it rested inside the veil in the "holy of holies" when the tabernacle was set up in camp. In it were the two tablets on which were written the Ten Commandments, and Aaron's staff. On its covering of gold rested two large winged figures of solid gold. Upon the mercy seat, as this lid was called, the priest sprinkled sacrificial blood on the Day of Atonement and God said He met and communed with His people there. A holy God, He could only be in touch with His people by means of the sacrifice that atoned for their sins continually and appeased His wrath.

Only the Levites, the priestly tribe, were allowed to minister at the Ark. Throughout Israel's pilgrimage, the priests took turns transporting the Ark, carrying it on two long poles overlaid with gold. The usual place for the Ark was in the center of the camp and when traveling, six of the tribes went before it and six tribes followed in a train behind. But on this day, the Ark went ahead of all the people, symbolizing that the Lord was leading His people in a new way.

The people were to maintain a distance of one-half mile between the Ark and themselves (3:4) "Do not get near the Covenant Box" (TEV), they were warned. God's holiness demanded this separation. At Sinai, the people were taught to keep their distance from Jehovah and their doing so at the Jordan demonstrated reverence and godly fear. The distance also served a practical purpose, however. By waiting to see where the priests went, the people would see where to go. An estimated two million people were to move across into Canaan that day so it was absolutely essential they follow an orderly, direct course.

A Most Propitious Time **(v. 15)** The Lord's timing in an event so spectacular is worth noting. The first hint of the season is found in the words—"the Jordan is in full flood in all its reaches throughout the time of harvest" (NEB). We might at first be puzzled, accustomed as we are to think of "harvest" as the autumn season, wondering how the river could be at flood stage after the long dry summer. But the season is actually springtime. We are sure of that because only four days later the people observed the Passover (5:10).

But what is being harvested? Commentators suggest the barley crop, and the evidence does seem satisfactory. From Exodus 9:31, we see that barley and flax were harvested at the same time. And Joshua's spies who had returned from Jericho only days before the crossing reported that they were forced to hide on Rahab's roof under "sheaves of flax"! Jehovah had promised His people "a land flowing with milk and honey." In His gracious plan, the timing of their entry was that season when all of the countryside was coming alive. The flowers were abloom, the barley swayed in the wind, the bird was on the wing, the streams were brim full—a most propitious time.

But the waters of the Jordan posed a problem to Israel. Not being a large river, it could be forded at certain points in the dry season, but usually not in the springtime. Its reputation to swell during the spring run-off of snow from mountains in the north is well established. A superheroic feat would be required to bring the nation Israel with all her flocks and herds across the Jordan at flood stage.

Yet another factor also comes into play as we consider the timing of this event. Moses, who led the people all of the way, had only recently died. Into that great vacuum stepped God's man, Joshua. Born in Egypt, he had served at Moses' side evidently all the years in the wilderness. Moses chose Joshua among the twelve men to spy on Canaan (Numbers 13:8) and on that occasion gave him the name *Joshua* which means "Jehovah is salvation." This son of Nun, of Ephraim's tribe, distinguished himself on that spy operation and for his faith and courage was selected by the Lord as one of only two adult Hebrews to enter the Promised Land (two out of 603,550 men; *see* Numbers 2:32). Despite all of this, Joshua was not Moses. The people might not be confident in him. The Lord would, by means of the crossing of the Jordan, honor Joshua in the sight of Israel. "They will realize that I am with you as I was with Moses" (v. 8 TEV), He told Joshua.

An Unforgettable Passage (vv. 16, 17) The priests, far out in front of the people, did as Joshua commanded and walked into the waters of the Jordan, carrying the Ark with them. As they did, the river ceased to flow. Upstream, as if held by an invisible hand, they stood up and backed up at an obscure place called Adam "beside Zaretan" (or Zarethan, possibly Zarthan). Meanwhile the waters downstream, toward the Dead Sea, "failed . . . were cut off." From the manner in which this supernatural parting is described, it seems that the waters must have disappeared immediately. As the priests proceeded to a point in the middle of the riverbed, they walked on dry ground. Twice the text states that the bed was dry. The priests stood "firm" in the river and the people, "all Israel," passed over near Jericho.

There is no attempt in the text to account for the miracle by any natural means as Moses did when saying that the Lord used a "strong east wind" to part the Red Sea. Of course, many have volunteered explanations, chiefly suggesting that an earthquake or landslide might have checked the waters upstream. An Arabic historian is reported to have described "how in A.D. 1266 near Tell ed-Damiyeh, which many experts have identified with Adam, the bed of the river was left dry for ten hours in consequence of a landslide," says the *New Bible Commentary, Revised*. "In 1927, an earthquake caused the west bank to collapse near the location of Adam, and the Jordan was dammed up for more than twenty-one hours. These events may indicate a 'natural explanation' of what happened centuries earlier, but to accept that explanation does not detract in any way from the supernatural intervention which opened the way to Israel just at the moment when they needed to cross."

An Everlasting Memorial (4:1-7) Joshua had already ordered each tribe to select one man for a special duty (3:12) and when the crossing was accomplished the Lord told Joshua what that duty was. "Command them to take twelve stones out of the middle of the Jordan . . . carry these stones with them and to put them down where you camp tonight" (TEV).

The stones were to be taken from "the very place" of the riverbed where the priests stood and they were evidently of great size for each man was to hoist one upon his shoulder. These were carried that same day to Gilgal, very near Jericho, and there Joshua himself arranged them in a heap as a memorial (vv. 7, 19, 20). As the Lord had done several times before—administering the nation through the twelve tribal chiefs, selecting a spy from each of the twelve tribes, designating that the names of the twelve tribes be inscribed on the high priest's holy garments—so at the Jordan He ordered the entire nation to be represented in the acts of the twelve men.

Some commentators say that two different accounts of the crossing are woven together in chapters 3 and 4. They point to 4:5 as evidence that the men who were sent to carry the stones out of the Jordan had not yet crossed over the river. But that explanation does not seem necessary at all. Verse 5 can as well be translated: "pass over to where the Ark of the Lord your God is in the midst" (*New Bible Commentary, Revised*). Others point to the confusion about the twelve stones, implying that Joshua's subsequent act of heaping up a dozen stones in the Jordan (4:9) contradicts the earlier account. Why not accept them both? One memorial was made in Gilgal and another in the midst of the Jordan which might be seen when the waters were running low.

Jehovah wanted Israel to long remember the day they entered the Promised Land and the supernatural means of that entrance. As the Passover would serve as an object lesson to teach the future generations of Israel's deliverance from Egyptian bondage, so the stone memorial was to be used. It was hoped that children would ask, "What mean ye by these stones?" (It is worth noting that the Lord did not intend that they merely ask, "What do these stones mean?" but "what do they mean *to you*?")

Applying the Scripture
Teacher: Two directions for application are suggested by this lesson. One concerns remembering God's goodness; the other emphasizes the deeper Christian life. You may want to use both.
1. Where Is Your "Conversation Piece"?—By setting up the memorial of twelve stones, Joshua created a "conversation piece." True, he could not very easily take this one around with him and he didn't have a coffee table for it to rest upon, but we can be sure that it served its purpose.

Actually, Israel had acquired several symbols or "conversation pieces" since leaving Egypt. The Ark of the Covenant was one. The entire tabernacle in its several parts and in its entirety was meant to stir deep devotional desires in Israel, and to portray redemptive truth. Certainly the Passover was another. The embalmed body of Joseph which they carried up from Egypt must have afforded many an occasion to recount God's goodness to the nation and recite His providential acts in the hearing of a younger generation.

Urge your class members to share their thoughts on this matter. Do any of them have a personal or family spiritual memorial that helps them remember a gracious blessing from God in the past? If you or your family has such a "conversation piece" share it with your class members.

2. Crossing Over the Jordan in *This* Life—Christian songs such as "I Won't Have to Cross Jordan Alone" and "On Jordan's Stormy Banks"—as well as much sermonizing on the subject—take the symbolism of Israel's crossing the Jordan River to mean the believer's passing into Heaven, the Promised Land. But that's not it at all. The entrance into Canaan was in order to con-

quer the land and gain full victory as well as rest. It typifies powerfully what God wills for the life of every one of His children—the abundant life. Jesus said, "I have come that they may have life, and have it to the full" (John 10:10 NIV).

The shame was that Israel, having been given the land by so wonderful an act of the Lord, faltered and failed to rout all her enemies and live in glorious prosperity as the Lord said she could. But what about us? Have we an answer to those who ask—"Is there life after (the second) birth? Is there an abundant, blessedly happy, increasingly more victorious life?" Challenge your class to think upon those three key words from the "Background to the Scripture"—God's faithfulness, holiness, and salvation—and invite them to expect more of the fulness of Christ in their life this week.

Your church may have a special view of this topic. Some refer to it as the second blessing. Others think of it as sanctification. Beware of the tendency your class members will have to rely upon the motivation of the moment or to try to experience a fuller life in their own self-effort. Remind them that God brought Israel out of Egypt and God brought them into the Promised Land and that by His Spirit He will bring the believer into the abundant life. But it will be a life marked by our trust in God's faithfulness and our willingness to stop the trends of sin as God shows them to us.

Questions for Discussion
Make use of these questions to involve your students in learning and to test their understanding of the lesson.
1. Why do you think the Lord commanded Joshua to have the Ark of the Covenant brought into the Jordan ahead of the people? **2.** For what reason(s) were the people to keep their distance from the Ark? **3.** The waters did not part until the priests had placed their feet in the water at the bank. What does this suggest for us today in regard to things God may be asking of us? **4.** How can we explain the damming of the waters? **5.** Why was it necessary for all of the tribes to be represented by the men who took up stones from the riverbed? **6.** What provision was being made to keep this event alive for future Jewish generations? **7.** What other symbols did the Israelite community now have for their religious and national life, that they did not possess when they left Egypt? What symbols does the Church have to perpetuate the meaning of its faith?

Illustrating the Scripture
Examples and quotations to help the teacher communicate the lesson.
GOD IN MY OWN ROOM " 'Then Samuel took a stone, and set it between Mizpeh and Shen, and called the name of it Ebenezer, saying, Hitherto hath the Lord helped us' (1 Samuel 7:12).

"In many Eastern lands, you will find numerous stone pillars set up, or heaps of stones, which mark the spot where some traveler or worshiper has on some particular occasion received some help from his God. Each time he passes that spot, he stops to throw another stone on the pile, to remind himself and others that God had been good to him. These are called stones of remembrance, reminder stones. . . .

"Samuel called the stone which he set up, 'Ebenezer,' that is, 'the witnessing stone of God's help.' Always when he looked upon this stone, he remembered God and said, 'By this, shall we be reminded of God's good help.' . . . You may . . . have a *remembrance spot* in your own room. Every time God is good to you or gives you some gift, you could, if you planned, have some spot in your room where you might go and stand and look up and thank God for His goodness and His gifts." Guy L. Morrill, *More Stewardship Stories* (Harper and Brothers, New York, 1941).

A CREED FOR A CRISIS   From today's key verse, we get the creed: we believe in "the Lord of all the earth."

"No local deity, like those heathen deities whose sovereignty was often as limited as a German duchy; no limited being; but master of all powers of nature, master of all tribes of men, with the government upon His shoulder of all things; able to open a path where all passage seemed denied; so that his and Israel's future would not depend on their own wisdom, strength, or fortunes, but would depend supremely on the favor of God. Aye, and that is the sort of creed which we all need for the crises we have to face. God living and reigning; earth alive with His presence and His work; all events dependent on His will.

"Oh, let us catch from heroic souls at least their creed. Their faith, which works such wonders, must be the true faith. *God is living*, His heart is alive with tenderness. He is not the great grave into which all things fall, but the great fount of life from which all things live. So alive that He could become incarnate and take infinite trouble to redeem us. So alive He is here today, ready to help us . . . if you are in any crisis of your life, do not assume that so far as you are concerned God is dead or unable to control the elements of nature. The fair results of your opportunity will be lost because it passes unused. If you have come to Jordan, cross over it; and if you want strength to do it, find it in this creed: God is the living God, and the Lord of all the earth" (*The Pulpit Commentary*).

Topics for Youth

SHE WAS SUSTAINED BY A PROMISE IN THE BIBLE—" 'I felt from the very beginning that I would go free. I didn't know whether it was going to be five days, five months, or fifteen years, but I was pretty sure I was going to walk away from that place.'

"That place—the U.S. Embassy in Tehran—separated hostage Kathryn Koob from freedom for 444 days, but it never separated her from the love of Christ. Her testimony to faith in God as a primary source of strength and comfort during captivity affirms a devotion that has been an integral part of her life.

"Confirmation of her optimism about eventual release came from the Bible. 'I received a promise verse,' she said, 'when my Bible fell open to

Psalms 118, verses 17 and 18: "I shall not die, but live, and declare the works of the Lord. The Lord hath chastened me sore: but he hath not given me over unto death." ' The passage sustained Koob throughout the monotonous days of confinement.

"While she was confined, Koob said she perceived God as a 'golden column, a pillar of support and strength. My day revolved around that golden column, and I looked to God as the source of everything.'

". . . The impact of the experience on her spiritual life crystallized for her the importance of Christian education at an early age. 'Young people should have the opportunity and be required to do memory work,' she said. Lay leaders and pastors would do well to make sure that 'very basic, simple concepts of Christian faith are understood.' As she wrote to a nephew in Florida, 'Be sure and study your catechism, because you never know when it's going to come in handy.' " (Excerpted from a news story in *Christianity Today*, March 13, 1981, by Beth Spring. Used with permission.)

Note to the teacher: This modern example of God's faithfulness to keep His promises can be used to underscore the truth in today's lesson; God brought Israel into the Promised Land according to His promise.

LESSON 11   NOVEMBER 14
God Provides Judges for His People

Background Scripture: Judges 1, 2
Devotional Reading: Joshua 24:19–29

Judges 2:6, 7, 11–19
6 And when Joshua had let the people go, the children of Israel went every man unto his inheritance to possess the land.
7 And the people served the LORD all the days of Joshua, and all the days of the elders that outlived Joshua, who had seen all the great works of the LORD, that he did for Israel.
11 And the children of Israel did evil in the sight of the LORD, and served Baalim:
12 And they forsook the LORD God of their fathers, which brought them out of the land of Egypt, and followed other gods, of the gods of the people that were round about them, and bowed themselves unto them, and provoked the LORD to anger.
13 And they forsook the LORD, and served Baal and Ashtaroth.
14 And the anger of the LORD was hot against Israel, and he delivered them into the hands of spoilers that spoiled them, and he sold them into the hands of their enemies round about, so that they could not any longer stand before their enemies.

15 Whithersoever they went out, the hand of the LORD was against them for evil, as the LORD had said, and as the LORD had sworn unto them: and they were greatly distressed.
16 Nevertheless the LORD raised up judges, which delivered them out of the hand of those that spoiled them.
17 And yet they would not hearken unto their judges, but they went a whoring after other gods, and bowed themselves unto them: they turned quickly out of the way which their fathers walked in, obeying the commandments of the LORD; but they did not so.
18 And when the LORD raised them up judges, then the LORD was with the judges, and delivered them out of the hand of their enemies all the days of the judge: for it repented the LORD because of their groanings by reason of them that oppressed them and vexed them.
19 And it came to pass, when the judge was dead, that they returned, and corrupted themselves more than their fathers, in following other gods to serve them, and to bow down unto them; they ceased not from their own doings, nor from their stubborn way.

KEY VERSE: "And when the LORD raised them up judges, then the LORD was with the judges." Judges 2:18.

Home Daily Bible Readings
Nov. 8 M. Remember Your Past, Joshua 24:1-13.
Nov. 9 T. Serve the Lord, Joshua 24:14-25.
Nov. 10 W. New Direction, Judges 1:1-8.
Nov. 11 T. United to Fight, Judges 1:9-17.
Nov. 12 F. Failure to Obey, Judges 1:27-36.
Nov. 13 S. A Time for Weeping, Judges 2:1-6.
Nov. 14 S. The Lord Raised Up Judges, Judges 2:16-19.

Lesson Aim: As a result of this lesson the church should take first steps to evaluate its teaching and training of the next generation.

LESSON OUTLINE
Background to the Scripture
Looking at the Scripture Text
 I. Jehovah Served by His People (Judges 2:6, 7)
 II. Jehovah Forsaken by His People (Judges 2:11-15)
 III. Jehovah Sends Judges for His People (Judges 2:16-19)
Applying the Scripture

Background to the Scripture
Israel's united campaign under the leadership of Joshua broke the back of Canaanite resistance. The individual tribes were now charged with the re-

sponsibility of possessing the land allotted to each of them. So began that crucial period of Israel's history—following Moses and the Conquest of Canaan and preceding the monarchy—known as the Period of the Judges. If we choose the later date for the Exodus, this period may be dated from approximately 1250 B.C. to 1020 B.C. when Saul became Israel's first king.

Joshua had died and so had that generation of leaders who had entered Canaan with him. But Israel would "follow on to know the Lord"—wouldn't they? A warning of what was to come lies hidden as a land mine in the midst of our text: "and there arose another generation after them, which knew not the Lord, nor yet the works which he had done for Israel" (2:10). The writers of Scripture are always careful to plot the course of God's people—whether Israel in the Old Testament or the Church—and show where they are in relation to their Lord. Having been alerted to the spiritual condition of the new generation, does anyone need to guess what lay ahead?

Looking at the Scripture Text

Jehovah Served by His People **(vv. 6, 7)** The writer or final editor of the Book of Judges tied the period of the judges to that of the latest great leader of Israel—Joshua. After the introduction to his book (1:1-2:5), he resumed the record of Israel's history where the Book of Joshua ended. In fact, he incorporated some of the last chapter of Joshua (24:28-31) into his own record.

Before his death, Joshua assembled Israel's top leadership ("elders," "heads," "judges," "officers") and probably a large representation of the people at Shechem for the purpose of reviewing the conditions Jehovah had laid down in His covenant. There the people pledged, "The Lord our God will we serve, and his voice will we obey" (Joshua 24:24). And, as he did when Israel crossed the Jordan, Joshua set up a memorial rock on that occasion. Then he dismissed the people, each to his own inheritance.

Those of the tribes of Simeon and Judah headed south to their lands. Benjamin and Dan also walked south, though not so far. Reuben and Gad's clans and half of Manasseh went east to their possessions across the Jordan River. The other half of Manasseh's tribe spread out in the land immediately north and west of Shechem while those of Asher, Naphtali, Zebulun, and Issachar traveled further north. The Ephraimites spread out to their homes immediately south of Shechem and the Levites, who had no lands for their inheritance, went to the several cities in each tribe which the Lord had given them.

"The tribes had a considerable amount of hard fighting to do before the land could properly be said to be conquered," says Arthur E. Cundall in his commentary on Judges. As Judges 1 shows, the Canaanites put up a stiff fight and Israel seemed all too quickly to forget that the Lord had promised them victory. By appearing to Israel in the form of an angel (2:1-5), Jehovah rebuked the people, but the effect was not lasting.

Israel's slide into apostasy did not happen overnight. The period in which "the people served the Lord" (v. 7) must have lasted forty to fifty years. Inspired by the elders who had seen the great works of Jehovah, the people continued to observe the Passover and the Sabbath and offered the sacrifices according to the Law of Moses. They sought to walk obediently to the Word which was proclaimed to them on special occasions.

But with each passing year, the great works of the Lord faded further into history. Fewer warriors who had walked in amazement over Jordan's dry bed remained to tell about it. Few priests and soldiers who had encircled Jericho and had seen its walls collapse were still alive to recount this miracle. In time, the great victory God gave Joshua over the five Amorite kings in the day the sun stood still (Joshua 10:1–14) was forgotten as each family adapted to life in Canaan.

The inconspicuous words, "every man" (v. 6), provide an important key for our understanding of what was transpiring. Until Israel crossed into Canaan and actually during the early, united conquest of the land, there was little opportunity for one's individual expression. Everything was done en masse. Camped together with his or her tribe, near the entire assembly of the nation, the Israelite took instructions from the elders and watched for the cloud of Jehovah's presence.

But once they were sent away from Shechem to possess their inheritance, they began to taste the heady wine of liberty. It was a tall order for them to luxuriate in their newfound freedom and keep the faith while living miles away from the sacred tabernacle in Shiloh. And their carefree, sensual, cultured Canaanite neighbors had their own life-style on full display before them day and night.

Jehovah Forsaken by His People (vv. 11–15) Chapter 2 serves to introduce in broad strokes what is to follow in the next nineteen chapters. Israel begins to move into "a recurring cycle of four phases . . . apostasy, servitude, supplication, and deliverance," says Cundall.

"Did evil in the sight of the Lord" (v. 11). In a sense that was not true of any other people, the Lord watched everything Israel did; His people were in His view constantly as the children in any household are in the view of their watching mother. Other people served false gods, but for Israel to do so was tragic. The Baals she learned to serve in Canaan were many—Baal-berith (Judges 9:4), Baal-peor (Numbers 25:3); Baal-gad (Joshua 11:17) and Baal-zebub (2 Kings 1:2) were the most prominent. They seemed to have been local variations of the chief Canaanite fertility god, Baal, son of El. The Canaanites invested in Baal powers to control storms and rains and thus, the harvests.

"Baal worship . . . was conducted by priests in temples and outdoors in fields and on hilltops called 'high places,'" says the Criswell Study Bible. Accustomed as the Israelites were to sacrificing animals, they probably reasoned that the sacrifices of their Canaanite neighbors were equally as acceptable. There had evidently been a breakdown of the vital instructions about how to worship and serve Jehovah and this new generation became vulnerable to pagan religion. The ritual meals and risque dances that were a part of the service of Baal proved to be irresistible. Once the people of Israel began to join in, they were inevitably drawn to the chambers on the hillsides where temple prostitutes and sodomites initiated them into sensuous forms of "worship" of which they had never dreamed.

The worship of Ashtaroth, a female deity, the chief "consort" of Baal, was especially strong in Canaan also. Called Ishtar in Babylonia and Anath in northern Syria, Ashtaroth held such power over the people that they offered their children on her altars. Her name often appears as Ashtoreth in Hebrew; the vowels of the word *boseth* ("shame") replaced the usual vowels to indicate "the worship of this goddess was a shameful thing" (*Abingdon Bible Commentary*).

The verbs in this section describe how Israel went down to the depths of immorality. She "did evil" and "forsook the Lord." She "followed other gods" and "bowed themselves unto them." Conversely, Jehovah acted and His response can be traced in the verbs in verses 14-16. Provoked to anger, the Lord "delivered them to raiders who plundered" them. "He sold them into the hands of their enemies (*see* Isaiah 50:1). His hand "was against them to defeat them" (NIV). But in grace, *He raised up judges.*"

Jehovah Sends Judges for His People (vv. 16-19) Her soul panting, not after God, but after the hot sex sold in Baal's chambers, Israel had little claim on the Lord. She had broken the covenant in the most wanton manner. But God did a merciful thing. God is like that—a God of surprises and grace. "The Lord raised up judges to save them from their enemies" (TLB). The verse alludes to the difficult conditions to which Israel's apostasy had brought her. Because she did not rid the country of the heathen nations and because she forsook the true God to worship at the pagan altars, the Lord used these Canaanite nations to raid and plunder and enslave His people.

Over the period of more than 200 years, Jehovah sent one woman and a dozen men (not counting Abimelech) to lead rescue operations, regain lost liberties and to punish God's foes. These judges were "raised up" from first one tribe and then another. Some are well known—Gideon, Deborah, Barak, Samson, Jephthah—all of whom are named in the "Hall of Fame" of Faith (Hebrews 11:32). Most are altogether unknown—Othniel, Ehud, Elon, and others.

The judges were not so much rulers as they were "religious reformers and patriots," says C. I. Scofield, "because national security and prosperity were inseparably connected with loyalty and obedience to Jehovah . . . they were the spiritual ancestors of the prophets." Their title, *judges*, literally meant "saviors, deliverers," says Edward J. Young.

While they lived, "God was with them" (v. 18); the Scripture does not say His presence was with the people as a whole. During this period, "every man did what was right in his own eyes" (17:6; 21:25). "They ceased not from their own doings, nor from their stubborn way" (v. 19) until they were in major trouble. But then their prayers were more like the cries of men in foxholes and trenches during the world wars; once the crisis passed, the people "turned back and behaved worse."

Because the Lord's relationship with His people is described in the terms of a marriage, to abandon Him was to commit adultery spiritually. God had made covenant vows with His people and from time to time He caused them to repeat these vows. This Joshua had done at Shechem before his death. When the people turned their back on the Lord and ran after the gods of Canaan, the writer described it as "a whoring" after other gods. The New International Version has it: "prostituted themselves." This idea is further supported by the meaning of Baalim—"husbands" or "owners." The Lord, jealous for His own people, could not watch impassively as His bride went after others. He was driven to anger, "hot anger" that moved Him to resist Israel and to vow that He would not drive out the enemy nations any more but leave them "to test my people, to see whether or not they will obey the Lord as their ancestors did" (v. 22 TLB). The testing would be severe, but the Lord only intended to compel His people to return to Him. He even does this today when we who claim to be His Church do not obey Him.

Applying the Scripture
Begin class discussion with: "How much time did you give each of your children during the past week?"
1. The Power of an Example—When a vacuum occurred in the leadership of Israel, when Joshua and his contemporaries died off, Israel's masses were left without the dynamic influence of an example to follow. Their heroes were no more. They were in a transitional time, having just routed the main body of Canaanites and begun to settle for the first time in their own lands. They needed an example, a person who could exert so strong an influence upon their lives that they would not yield to the temptations around them.

Who needs a dynamic example today? Who needs the influence of a godly Christian? What about your children? The children and young people in your church? The young marrieds who are facing a host of adjustments and are hit from all sides with the world's alternative arrangements for their lifestyle? The middle-aged men and women who began well in their Christian life but who now are apparently ready to "chuck it all"? The divorcée or widow who does not think anyone understands or cares? The older person who is isolated from genuinely fulfilling work and activity?

To bring this lesson to a practical application, discuss with your adults what they can do to set a better example before the young people. Or, confine your discussion to the children and youth in the homes of your class members. If it really is true that we are always just one generation away from paganism—and today's lesson seems to bear this out—then parents have an essential responsibility to rightly influence the coming generation.
Ask: Is our church following a comprehensive Christian educational plan to make sure that God's revelation is imparted to persons in our church?
2. Influence Is Not Enough—Moses did not stop with just setting an example. He imparted the Law. Jesus did not only inspire with His influence. He taught. He constantly taught truth. So, the Church must today impart knowledge; influence and examples are not enough. It is easy for us to see how Is-

rael failed in her second generation in Canaan because she was unschooled in the things of God. Take time in your class to enumerate the actual ways you as adults are carrying out the part of the Great Commission that says "teach all nations . . . teaching them to observe all things whatsoever I have commanded you" (Matthew 28:19, 20).

Let this lesson stimulate your church to improve and upgrade the teaching program for the adults who come to your church without adequate Christian training as well as for the children growing up in the church.

Questions for Discussion
Make use of these questions to involve your students in learning and to test their understanding of the lesson.
1. Where were the people of Israel when Joshua "let them go"? What had they been doing there? 2. How did "every man" know what "his inheritance" was? 3. What "great works" might the elders have seen? 4. How would you describe the worship practices of those who served Baal? 5. Who was Ashtaroth and how was she served? 6. What verbs in the lesson identify what the people did in relation to the Lord and to the gods of Canaan? Similarly, what verbs identify Jehovah's actions in relation to Israel? 7. What was the purpose of the judges and who sent them?

Illustrating the Scripture
Examples and quotations to help the teacher communicate the lesson.

MODELING " 'What you do speaks so loudly that I cannot hear what you say,' is a truism with which we are all familiar. But applied positively, it is a basic lesson in education. Most of what we learn happens at an informal, unconscious level. It follows that the way we 'teach' people is by letting them observe what needs to be done and how to do it as we go about the everyday business of doing our job. A basic requirement of leadership is to train (educate), and a basic method of training is modeling.

"By modeling we mean a conscious effort on the part of the leader to speak and act in such a way that when he or she is emulated by followers that their actions will be recognized by the leader as being appropriate and honoring to Christ.

"In what follows we will try to draw attention to the many ways and situations in which we can model.

"Probably nothing impresses our followers as much as the way we respond to situations, particularly emergencies. If they see a Spirit-filled calmness in the way we meet unforeseen and difficult crises, they will be inclined to follow our example. If our regular response to others' mistakes is, 'How stupid can you be!' we should not be surprised if they respond the same way in front of their subordinates.

" 'Remaining calm' usually means not responding too quickly. If you are one of those people who tend to overrespond to situations maybe the old adage about counting to ten will help you have enough time to really understand what the situation is.

"Leaders talk too much. If we dominate conversations or find it necessary to take the lead in solving every problem that a group has, if we are quick to define solutions for other people rather than let them find their own, others will follow our lead.

"We are all impressed by the leader who seems to have the time and ability to hear others out. It takes practice. . . .

"In your modeling give careful attention to how you give directions, how you deal with subordinates, the memos you write, your integrity (does your staff believe it will really happen just because you said so?), openness, keeping confidences, attitudes, concern for others and prayer. . . .

"One way that we have found effective is to ask each member of the staff to give us an anonymous piece of paper that has a sentence on it which begins with, 'I wish Ed would. . . .' We then gather the staff together and read out loud the things that they 'wished' and attempt to answer the questions as best we can. Questions can at times be startling and very threatening, but in giving our staff an opportunity to comment on our performance we are already beginning to model a willingness to listen, to change and to become the kind of leader that God wants us to become." (Excerpted from "Modeling," *Christian Leadership Letter*, Ted W. Engstrom and Edward R. Dayton, editors, July 1978, Monrovia, California. Used with permission.)

Topics for Youth

ARE YOU A THERMOSTAT OR A THERMOMETER?—Once the children of Israel reached Canaan, they gave in to the pressures of the people around them. They became like thermometers, registering the spiritual temperatures of their environment, rather than thermostats, changing and controlling how they lived. The following true story from pilot Bernie May helps illustrate this:

"Recently Dave Wike, Eastern Airlines pilot, and I were flying a Helio Courier down V-93 en route from Hampton, New Hampshire to Philadelphia. The weather was marginal. Freezing level was 8,000 feet, right where we had been cleared to fly.

"As Dave flew I kept my eye on the outside air temperature gauge (OAT)—which is nothing more than an old-fashioned thermometer. A change of one or two degrees could mean the difference between wings and prop covered with ice or smooth sailing.

"As the ice began to build up, I reached for the mike and requested a change of altitude from New York Center. Another five minutes at 8,000 feet would have been disastrous.

"'What we need,' I shouted to Dave as we dropped down to warmer air at 6,000 feet, 'is a thermostat out there, not just a thermometer.'

"Thermometers measure the environment. Thermostats change it. Our house has a thermostat. It measures, reacts, and brings change. It makes our house comfortable.

"There seem to be a lot of thermometers in the Kingdom these days. It's easy to get a reading on everything from the charismatics to the Catholics. Everyone seems to have an opinion. Sometimes I think the church is in danger of paralysis by analysis.

"Rare are the thermostat people. Those who are not content with simply measuring, but are in the business of bringing change. Those who can cool down an explosive situation or build a fire under a cold church.

"Recently a nearby church renovated its building. When they put up the new steeple, they left off the cross and installed a weathervane. Weathervanes, like thermometers, only measure the environment. Crosses change things.

"There is nothing wrong with measuring and evaluating. Every thermostat has a built-in thermometer. But the need in the Kingdom today is for men and women who will do more than analyze. The cry is for men and women who will take an uncomfortable situation and change it to meet needs and glorify God. Otherwise, we have no choice but to request a change of flight plan to a lower altitude." Bernie May, *Climbing on Course* (Multnomah Press, Portland, Oregon, 1979. Used with permission).

LESSON 12   NOVEMBER 21

God Empowers Gideon

Background Scripture: Judges 6:1–8:21
Devotional Reading: Psalms 105:7–15

Judges 6:3–6, 11–16; 7:20, 21

3 And so it was, when Israel had sown, that the Midianites came up, and the Amalekites, and the children of the east, even they came up against them;

4 And they encamped against them, and destroyed the increase of the earth, till thou come unto Gaza, and left no sustenance for Israel, neither sheep, nor ox, nor ass.

5 For they came up with their cattle and their tents, and they came as grasshoppers for multitude; for both they and their camels were without number: and they entered into the land to destroy it.

6 And Israel was greatly impoverished because of the Midianites; and the children of Israel cried unto the LORD.

11 And there came an angel of the LORD, and sat under an oak which was in Ophrah, that pertained unto Joash the Abiezrite: and his son Gideon threshed wheat by the winepress, to hide it from the Midianites.

12 And the angel of the LORD appeared unto him, and said unto him, The LORD is with thee, thou mighty man of valour.

13 And Gideon said unto him, Oh my Lord, if the LORD be with us, why then is all this befallen us? and where be all his miracles which our fathers told us of, saying, Did not the LORD bring us up from Egypt? but now the LORD hath forsaken us, and delivered us into the hands of the Midianites.

14 And the LORD looked upon him, and said, Go in this thy might, and thou shalt save Israel from the hand of the Midianites: have not I sent thee?

15 And he said unto him, Oh my LORD, wherewith shall I save Israel? behold, my family is poor in Manasseh, and I am the least in my father's house.

16 And the LORD said unto him, Surely I will be with thee, and thou shalt smite the Midianites as one man.

7:20 And the three companies blew the trumpets, and brake the pitchers, and held lamps in their left hands, and the trumpets in their right hands to blow withal: and they cried, The sword of the LORD, and of Gideon.

21 And they stood every man in his place round about the camp: and all the host ran, and cried, and fled.

KEY VERSE: "And the angel of the LORD appeared unto him, and said unto him, The LORD is with thee, thou mighty man of valour." Judges 6:12.

Home Daily Bible Readings		
Nov. 15	M.	One Among Many, Judges 3:1–6.
Nov. 16	T.	Othniel the Judge, Judges 3:7–11.
Nov. 17	W.	Ehud Delivers, Judges 3:12–30.
Nov. 18	T.	Deborah and Barak Prepare, Judges 4:1–9.
Nov. 19	F.	A Victory Song, Judges 5:1–5, 31.
Nov. 20	S.	Away With False Gods, Judges 6:25–32.
Nov. 21	S.	The Victory Gained, Judges 7:9–22.

Lesson Aim: As a result of your lesson, your class members should memorize the key verse so they will remember the Mighty One who has sent them.

LESSON OUTLINE
Background to the Scripture
Looking at the Scripture Text
  I. The Cry of a Humiliated People (Judges 6:3–6)
 II. The Call of a Humbled Man (Judges 6:11–16)
III. The Conquest of a Heathen Foe (Judges 7:20, 21)
Applying the Scripture

Background to the Scripture

Gideon is the best known of all the judges who served Israel. More space (100 verses) is devoted to him in the Book of Judges than to any of the others. This is due as much to the character of the man Gideon as it is to the marked degree of Israel's suffering at that particular time.

The historical record of the judges is a selective one. Some judges are passed over with a few words. Others, like Deborah and Samson and Jephthah, receive more detailed treatment. What we find in Judges meets exactly with the overriding purpose of the Spirit of God who inspired these writings: "These things happened to them as examples and were written down as warnings for us, on whom the fulfillment of the ages has come" (1 Corinthians 10:11 NIV).

The student of Judges must find a way of reconciling the approximate span of years assigned to this period with the actual contents of the book. Conservative scholars who hold to the later date of the Exodus (1290 B.C.) allot approximately 210 years to the period of the judges. But the sum of all the years of the various judges as given throughout the book approximates 350 years. On looking closer, we find that a number of the judges held sway over only a few of the tribes and it seems that the time of one judge often overlapped with that of another elsewhere in Canaan.

Looking at the Scripture Text

The Cry of a Humiliated People (6:3-6) The previous lesson concluded with Jehovah's words to Israel—"Because you have forsaken Me, I will leave your enemies to test you, to see whether you will return to Me."

For seven years, no people "tested" Israel so severely as did the combined marauding forces of Midian and Amalek. These seminomadic people swept into the central hill country of Canaan—Amalek coming from the south and Midian from east of the Jordan in the vast Arabian desert region. Although they were distinctly different tribes, during this period they evidently traveled together and had found in Israel a common enemy. Since the Midianites are usually mentioned alone in the story of Gideon, though both Midian and Amalek are intended, it is safe to assume that the Midianites were the stronger, more numerous, and more aggressive of the two.

The desert-dwelling Midianites who made such trouble for Israel had apparently been neutral toward Israel until she settled in Canaan. Having descended from Abraham by his second wife, Keturah, their ancestors had been sent away from Isaac into the "east country" (Arabia) while Abraham yet lived (Genesis 25:1, 2, 6). It was to their tribal camps that Moses fled when he had killed the Egyptian (Exodus 2:15). For a wife, he chose Zipporah, daughter of Jethro, a Midianite priest. The Midianites caused no direct harm to Israel as she traveled through the desert although they were drawn into Balak's counsel when he sought to curse Israel (Numbers 22:4). Evidently they camped adjacent to Israel in the plains of Moab and Israel imbibed their idol worship and immoral ways.

The Amalekites, on the other hand, were a cursed people of the Lord when they showed their faces at this time. These descendants of Esau were the first nation to make war with Israel after she left Egypt. Because they fought against Israel, the Lord vowed to "utterly put out the remembrance of Amalek from under heaven." Balaam in his final oracle described Amalek as "the first of the nations" at that time, but he also foresaw their doom (Numbers 24:20). Israel would not actually be rid of this implacable foe until King Saul and his army wiped them out.

United with these two peoples against Israel were an unnamed bedouin people, the "children of the east (desert)." The Midianites and Amalekites were not farmers. In the springtime when Israel's crops were maturing, they would roll across Canaan like a sandstorm. What was growing they took for themselves. Their cattle filled their bellies on the rich grasses of the Jezreel valley. The fact that they brought their cattle indicates that when they came they evidently remained for months at a time. The names of two of their princes, Oreb (raven) and Zeeb (wolf) are clues to the predatory ways of these people. They totally deprived the Israelites even of grazing land so that their herds of sheep, oxen, and donkeys were depleted. They were a vast horde, as "grasshoppers for multitude."

"The simile of *locusts* (RSV) is an appropriate one," says Cundall in his commentary, "indicating the absolute devastation of these rapacious hordes as they moved from one area to another. The cumulative effect of these raids would be considerable: all agriculture would be affected and the plundering of Israel's herds, crops and fruits would make for long, lean winters."

The focus of their occupation seems to have been the upper hill country west of the Sea of Chinnereth (Galilee) for Gideon recruited his original 32,000 warriors from the tribes of Asher, Zebulun, and Naphtali as well as Manasseh. They ranged through the central region and extended their dominion southwest "till thou come to Gaza" along the Mediterranean.

What their livestock did not consume, their camels did. These angular beasts have been called Midian's "secret weapon," affording Midian unusual mobility and speed for that day. Cundall remarks that this is the first documentation of the large-scale use of camels in a military campaign.

In her "greatly impoverished" condition, Israel "cried unto Jehovah" (v. 6). Though in a hopeless state, the people did remember the Lord and wailed to Him for relief. The cycle of apostasy, servitude, and supplication was about to give way to the fourth phase—deliverance!

The Call of a Humble Man (vv. 11-16)   The more perceptive people in Israel must have recognized the beginnings of a reply from Jehovah in the message a prophet gave (vv. 7-10). But, hoping in His mercy, they continued to cry. One of those undoubtedly was Gideon whose angry, frustrated state of mind is revealed in the conversation he had with "an angel of the Lord" who paid him a visit.

Gideon was of the tribe of Manasseh, of the clan of Abiezer; his father, Joash, must have been a man of some means and certainly was respected in the little town of Ophrah where they lived. As the story shows, Joash also had compromised the covenant with the Lord; in his courtyard stood an idol to Baal and an image of worship devoted to Ashtaroth. The people had evidently embraced these Canaanite gods while thinking they were still honoring Jehovah as one among the many.

Gideon's soul was in anguish over the extremity to which the Midianite invasion had driven them, but nevertheless he went on with his daily chores, beating the wheat grains from the stalks. Normally he would have been threshing wheat in a clearing, with the aid of oxen, but the fact that he was doing this at the winepress reveals both the smallness of the harvest and the risks involved ("so that the Midianites would not see him" TEV). A hollowed-out rock served normally as a winepress and there Gideon worked near a huge oak tree which for some reason must have been revered as a sacred tree (see 9:6, 37 RSV). The writer refers to it as "the oak tree," evidently one well known in that day. To this spot already hallowed by previous experience, "the angel of the Lord" came and sat.

What follows is a "theophany," God revealing Himself to man in human form. Gideon did not at first recognize anything extra-human about his guest. His initial reply, "my Lord," is probably accurately translated "sir." His answer, which pours out as well-aged wine from a tight wineskin, is remarkable for its bitter honesty; it is telling in its despair.

But "the Lord" (the writer dropping the word *angel*) then "looked on him." Other translations say "turned to him" (v. 14). For the first time, Gideon met the "settled and pleasant" gaze of his guest, seeing in his "countenance ... a readiness to help him" (Poole). And on speaking a second time, the Lord commanded him: "go in this thy might," possibly an allusion to Gideon's physical powers that were to be enveloped in the Spirit's might (6:34). "Do not I send you?" The emphasis is on the sender: "*I myself* am sending you" (TEV).

Gideon's reply, so similar to that of other men at the point of their call—Moses, Saul, Jeremiah, Amos, Peter—contrasts extremely with what the Lord saw in him. Gideon was aware of his inadequacy; his family was poor and he was "the least" in the household. But the Lord had seen vast potential, calling him "a mighty man of valour."

"*I will be with you*" promised the Lord. With certainty, He promised that Gideon would "crush the Midianites as easily as if they were only one man" (TEV).

The Conquest of a Heathen Foe (7:20, 21) Our text captures but the climax of what followed Gideon's call. At the Lord's command, he tore down the heathen altars at home. Still unsure of himself, he put out the original "fleece" before the Lord (6:36–40). Gideon's activities caught the attention of the Midianites at this time for they assembled in the valley of Jezreel (6:33) for battle. Gideon issued a call to arms, possibly after the Midianites had murdered his brothers (8:18, 19). Thirty-two thousand Israelites volunteered—the pruning down of that number until Gideon's 300 emerged is a story in itself.

From a vantage point, Gideon and his men spied "the host of Midian"

(7:8) in the valley as the sun went down. Moving under cover of darkness, Gideon's army carried strange battle gear—"a trumpet in every man's hand, with empty pitchers, and lamps (or torches) within the pitchers" (v. 16). Though it is not stated, they evidently also carried a sword. The trumpet or ram's horn hung by a leather cord from their shoulder or belt and if they did bear a sword, this would have been in a scabbard at their waist.

The strategy was for three groups of 100 men each to completely encircle Midian's camp, each man holding the pitcher over his torch. At Gideon's signal, the soldiers were to break the clay pot, hoist the flaming torch, and give a loud blast on the trumpet. They would also shout, "A sword for the Lord and for Gideon" (v. 20 RSV). The surprise attack would so startle the slumbering Midianites that they would panic. Seeing a line of fire on the perimeter all around them, they would assume that a host of innumerable size awaited them, and they would flee.

The timing of the attack was no accident. It was "in the beginning of the middle watch" (v. 19), about ten o'clock. "Those not involved in the first or second watches would be in the deep sleep of the earlier part of the night, whilst those who had just been relieved would still be moving about the camp, thus increasing the fear of those awakened by the din, that the enemy had already penetrated the camp. The clamor would also cause unrest among the large numbers of camels, possibly leading to a stampede. It is not surprising that in the resultant confusion soldiers lashed out at everyone who loomed up in the darkness, not knowing who was friend or foe; 'all the host ran, and cried, and fled' " (Cundall).

The ensuing words of chapters seven and eight document the thorough victory God gave His people that night and the following day. "As one man" the ferocious Midianites turned tail and ran. Gideon caught the two princes Oreb and Zeeb and beheaded them (7:25) and tracked down the kings Zebah and Zalmunna and killed them. When the fighting was over, "Midian (was) subdued before the children of Israel, so that they lifted up their heads no more. And the country was in quietness forty years in the days of Gideon" (8:28).

Applying the Scripture
Two "remembers" open the way for our lesson application. Use both as you complete this lesson.
1. Remember Who Sent You—Look back over the call of Gideon for a moment. What made the difference? What transformed him from a solitary, self-conscious weakling into a bold and daring leader? Where did he gain the confidence to meet a fierce foe, to break with the religious loyalties of his own father, and to head up an army? It was the assurance that the Lord was the One who had sent him.

How about us today? We are sent into the world. The words of Jesus remind us: "As Thou didst send Me into the world, I also have sent them into the world" (John 17:18 NASB). Jesus' last words were, "Go into all the world and preach the gospel to all creation" (Mark 16:15 NASB).

He sends us into the world of missions, but also into the world of education. He sends us as pastors, but also as scientists, as politicians, as business and professional people, as artists and musicians and engineers, as men and women of law, as athletes. To do what? To deliver people held captive by one who is the epitome of Midianite evil, Satan. Sure, the odds are tough and the world system seems completely closed to the Gospel.

But—who has sent us? If He has sent us, what does it matter if the world is against us? "If God be for us, who can be against us?"

Seek to bring this truth down to practical application for your class. Some in your group may be struggling with a "call" to go into some "world" where God wants to use them. Encourage them not to fear, but to say *yes*, remembering who sent them.

2. Remember Who Promised to Be With You—"There is might in the consciousness of the Lord's commission; there is greater might in the consciousness of divine companionship."

A song writer has penned the words: "If Jesus goes with me, I'll go, anywhere." Is the Lord's promise to Gideon any more special than His assurance to us of "Lo, I am with you alway"?

Ask the class to discuss how Gideon became conscious of Jehovah's presence. Does the Lord work that way today? Allow time for one or two present to tell of an experience when the assurance of God's presence with them made the difference.

You may also want to ask for discussion on the subject of how to "practice the presence of God," how to live day by day knowing that God is with you. One friend tells how he allowed the hands of his watch, by their various positions, to remind him to pray, to praise, to think of others. (That's a little difficult with a digital watch.)

Another man carries several verses of Scripture with him which he "affirms" each day, especially when facing a spiritual challenge, when seeking to lead a person to Christ, or when exposed to certain temptations.

God is Spirit. We should not trust in material objects as good-luck pieces, such as crosses or images. But what about "Christian" bumper stickers, crosses, and lapel pins that remind us of His presence? If our motive is to keep ourselves close to God, these things can be useful.

Questions for Discussion
Make use of these questions to involve your students in learning and to test their understanding of the lesson.
1. Who were the Midianites and the Amalekites? And where was their homeland? 2. In what region of Palestine did the Midianite raids occur? 3. Explain how the text leads us to believe that the angel who spoke to Gideon was "more than an angel." 4. What is the significance of Gideon's beating out the wheat in the wine press? 5. Do we also take bad times

to mean that the Lord has abandoned us? Why is this response usually not accurate?   6. What essentially was the one promise the Lord made to Gideon?   7. Some scholars contend that Gideon's men could not have handled their torch and a clay pot and a trumpet—plus a sword—all at one time, and that such "confusion" indicates that two accounts are woven together in chapter seven. How could these difficulties be explained?

Illustrating the Scripture
Examples and quotations to help the teacher communicate the lesson.

Bill Terrill* couldn't see it coming, but a week in August 1979 was to be the beginning of the end for him, or the beginning of The Beginning.

A Christian living in a big city back East, Bill thought nothing of it when the bathroom shower began to leak on Monday and the goldfish died on Tuesday. But on Wednesday evening when the family car caught fire and almost exploded fifteen feet away from a gas pump, the Lord had his attention. But not nearly so thoroughly as on Friday when his boss laid him off. Immediately, Bill began the humbling, toilsome task of seeking a job. For the first time, he had to go on unemployment. In a few weeks, the car was restored (thanks to the insurance) so that was not a matter for worry. But eating away at Bill was an ache not many people knew about.

He and his wife had grown further and further apart and when he lost his job, she began pressing him to leave her. He received no support emotionally from her and to make matters worse he realized for the first time how he had ignored her and taken her for granted for fifteen years while he had devoted all of his energies to his work. He felt terribly guilty.

Bill had known that things were not well, but the job loss exposed the problem to him as he had never seen it before. It was like ripping the bandages off an open wound. Besides that, the opportunities he had had for Christian service suddenly dried up. Everywhere the job market was tight as the proverbial drum. The emotional distance between him and his eldest son seemed impossible to bridge. He was like Israel in our text today—"greatly impoverished."

What did he do? He had made a few close friends, and with them he shared his domestic agony. They prayed for him. A friend gave him a copy of Andrew Murray's little book, *Waiting on God*, and he began reading it daily. He filled the pages of his journal with his thoughts, promises he felt God was giving him, events good and bad—mostly bad. But he felt God telling him not to leave his family and not to take a job out of town if it meant having to live elsewhere. God honored that.

He took part-time work. Finally, in mid-winter a job came his way and he saw some stability return to his finances. Then through a circumstance completely beyond his control, his wife agreed to join him for professional Christian counseling, and they began talking once again. He still has a long

(*A fictitious name is substituted to protect the persons involved.)

way to go, but he is still with his family, working happily, and cherishing the hope of a restored marriage and complete wholeness. He would say God is rescuing him from the plague of the Midianites.

Topics for Youth
ANOTHER GENERAL WHO ROSE FROM POVERTY TO POWER—Gideon was given a humanly impossible job, it would seem. But actually his heroics were just the kind of stuff of which man is made. An American president's life bears some striking similarities to that of Gideon.

Andrew Jackson, the "baby" of his family, was born in 1767, a few days after his father Andrew passed away. Only two years earlier had his mother, Elizabeth Hutchinson Jackson, immigrated from Ireland with their two sons, Hugh and Robert. His mother, now a widow, was forced to earn the family's keep by helping care for the eight children of her sister.

Andrew had little opportunity for an education, but he learned to read early. In fact, when the Declaration of Independence was published, nine-year-old Andrew had the honor of reading it to the town meeting of their small settlement in South Carolina. At thirteen, he and his brother Robert joined the militia under the command of their uncle, Major Robert Crawford. Andrew's older brother Hugh had already died fighting in the Revolution and in a year both Andrew and Robert were captured by the British. Always a fiercely independent battler, he refused to polish a British soldier's shoes, contending that was a task unsuited for a prisoner to perform. After he and his brother contracted smallpox, they were both sent home to what should have been a happier day. Instead, both his mother and Robert died, leaving Andrew the sole survivor in his family; he was only sixteen.

Undaunted, Andrew found his purpose for living irrevocably bound up in the destiny of the young country he loved. True, he did squander an inheritance from Ireland while a young man, but soon he settled into the study of law. He was ready, when frontier territories opened in what is now Tennessee, and he became an aggressive attorney in Nashville. His leadership capabilities were noticed and he served capably in military uniform. When his country needed deliverance from a menacing British attack force at New Orleans in 1815, General Jackson was there, leading his fighting men to the greatest military victory his country's soldiers had achieved to that time. His country never forgot this patriot. Thirteen years later, a majority of its citizens offered Andrew Jackson the nation's highest office. As the seventh president, from 1829–1836, he led his country with courage and dedication. "The common people," it was said, "loved him as their fathers and grandfathers had loved George Washington." Though many doubted that President Jackson would live long enough to fill his term of office, the old scarred battler reached the age of seventy-five, with his country's blessing, before he died at The Hermitage.

LESSON 13   NOVEMBER 28

God Is Israel's True King

Background Scripture: Judges 8:22–9:57
Devotional Reading: Isaiah 12:1–6

Judges 8:22, 23; 9:6–15, 55–57

22 Then the men of Israel said unto Gideon, Rule thou over us, both thou, and thy son, and thy son's son also: for thou hast delivered us from the hand of Midian.

23 And Gideon said unto them, I will not rule over you, neither shall my son rule over you: the LORD shall rule over you.

9:6 And all the men of Shechem gathered together, and all the house of Millo, and went, and made Abimelech king, by the plain of the pillar that was in Shechem.

7 And when they told it to Jotham, he went and stood in the top of mount Gerizim, and lifted up his voice, and cried, and said unto them, Hearken unto me, ye men of Shechem, that God may hearken unto you.

8 The trees went forth on a time to anoint a king over them; and they said unto the olive tree, Reign thou over us.

9 But the olive tree said unto them, Should I leave my fatness, wherewith by me they honour God and man, and go to be promoted over the trees?

10 And the trees said to the fig tree, Come thou, and reign over us.

11 But the fig tree said unto them, Should I forsake my sweetness, and my good fruit, and go to be promoted over the trees?

12 Then said the trees unto the vine, Come thou, and reign over us.

13 And the vine said unto them, Should I leave my wine, which cheereth God and man, and go to be promoted over the trees?

14 Then said all the trees unto the bramble, Come thou, and reign over us.

15 And the bramble said unto the trees, If in truth ye anoint me king over you, then come and put your trust in my shadow: and if not, let fire come out of the bramble, and devour the cedars of Lebanon.

55 And when the men of Israel saw that Abimelech was dead, they departed every man unto his place.

56 Thus God rendered the wickedness of Abimelech, which he did unto his father, in slaying his seventy brethren:

57 And all the evil of the men of Shechem did God render upon their heads: and upon them came the curse of Jotham the son of Jerubbaal.

LESSON FOR NOVEMBER 28   **115**

KEY VERSE: "And Gideon said unto them, I will not rule over you, neither shall my son rule over you: the LORD shall rule over you." Judges 8:23.

Home Daily Bible Readings
Nov. 22   M.   King Over All, Psalm 47.
Nov. 23   T.   A Song to the King, Psalms 74:1–12.
Nov. 24   W.   The Lord Is Our King, Psalms 89:8–18.
Nov. 25   T.   King of Glory, Psalm 24.
Nov. 26   F.   The King Remembers, Isaiah 43:14–21.
Nov. 27   S.   Treachery by the King's Son, Judges 9:1–15.
Nov. 28   S.   The Meaning of Jotham's Fable, Judges 9:16–21.

Lesson Aim: Because of this study your class members should seek ways to warn this present generation of the perilous course of wrong choices.

LESSON OUTLINE
Background to the Scripture
Looking at the Scripture Text
  I. The Kingdom Offered to a Worthy Man (Judges 8:22, 23)
  II. The Kingship Entrusted to an Ignoble Man (Judges 9:6–15)
  III. The Lord Shows He Is King (Judges 9:55–57)
Applying the Scripture

Background to the Scripture

We do not often think of Moses as a prophet, but he did fulfill that office as well as being the lawgiver. Toward the end of his life, he took a long look forward and foretold that Israel would one day say, "I will set a king over me, like as all the nations that are about me" (Deuteronomy 17:14). In making such a pronouncement, he was not declaring that it was God's will; rather, he was prophesying the hard cold facts: Israel would be intent on having a king.

The ill-fated first attempt to install a king is the subject of today's lesson. Abimelech, a son of Gideon, achieved his ambition to become king though his "reign" lasted but three years and probably did not extend much beyond the valley of Shechem in the tribal boundaries of Ephraim's territory. The greater part of Israel was not even involved in the story. The actual establishment of a monarchy in Israel would come in time, as the period of the judges reached its climax in Samuel and a greater emergency, involving a majority of the tribes, would precipitate the selection of a single ruler to coordinate the forces of all of Israel's tribes.

Looking at the Scripture Text

The Kingdom Offered to a Worthy Man (8:22, 23) In 1952, America sought for a man to lead her out of the entanglements of a costly police action in Korea and to restore a postwar normalcy. She turned to her most popular general, Dwight D. Eisenhower. A similar thing happened in Israel after General Gideon and his army vanquished the hated Midianites. The nation, represented by her elders, offered to Gideon the supreme place of leadership. So strong was the mood running, at least in the northern and central tribes where the Midianites had done the most harm, that the people asked Gideon to be the first of a dynasty: "thou, and thy son, and thy son's son" shall be our king.

Such a turn of events prove of what a man is made. Gideon was worthy of their trust. He had defeated the enemy with a singleness of purpose that belied no selfish ambitions. A humble man who was raised out of mediocrity by the sovereign Lord Himself, he staunchly turned down the offer and returned to his village of Ophrah to live out his days. In recognition of his influence, the Scripture says "the country was in quietness forty years in the days of Gideon" (8:28).

Unfortunately, that is only the good part. As so many men of faith, Gideon had some critical weaknesses and it seems that in the quiet, prosperous years that followed, he gave in to those weaknesses. In doing so, he sowed the seeds destined to bring on the horrible and bloody events that followed his death.

After his victory over Midian, Gideon could have had anything he desired from his grateful fellow Israelites, and so he asked them to give him the golden earrings they had taken from the Midianites. In an inexplicable act that reminds us of Aaron's golden calf, he fashioned a golden idol out of the jewelry and set it up in his village. The writer says this idol "became a snare to Gideon and his family." How quickly did Gideon forget the lessons the Lord had sought to teach him when he destroyed the heathen idols of his father's household (6:27).

Evidently revelling in the good times, Gideon began taking many wives. The text attributes to him "seventy sons," and then adds that he also had a son by a mistress who lived in Shechem some thirty miles away. This unnamed "concubine" was probably not an Israelite at all, but a pagan Canaanite, which might explain why he never married her. To their son, Gideon gave the name Abimelech, meaning "my father a king." Though Gideon had declined the offer of the kingdom, he lived like a king; as he grew near death, there were still those in Israel who were hankering after a king and Abimelech was all too ready to oblige them.

The Kingship Entrusted to an Ignoble Man (9:6–15) The words "all the men of Shechem gathered . . . and made Abimelech king" take on special meaning as we realize that Shechem was Abimelech's hometown. He had evidently never gone to live with his father and his seventy half-brothers; they probably despised him.

After Gideon died Abimelech took advantage of the prestige of his father's name and made an offer to the citizens of Shechem. Assuming that the people of central Israel wanted someone to lead them, and assuming that one or more of Gideon's sons would declare himself king, Abimelech asked his mother's clan to spread the word throughout Shechem that he would be glad to be their king. "Wouldn't you rather have one of your own people rule over you?" he suggested. They would.

But what about those "seventy sons"? Abimelech had a plan for them. With money the people of Shechem gave him from the city's Baal shrine, he hired a bunch of "worthless scoundrels" (v. 4 TEV) and they went to Ophrah and killed all but one of the seventy sons of Gideon. This act of Abimelech's bears the stamp of heathen practice. Peculiarly, Shechem was not designated as a town already possessed by either Ephraim or Manasseh when the land was divided by Joshua's orders. Levites were assigned to live there, but the context in this passage shows that the townspeople traced their ancestry to one Hamor (9:28; *see* also Joshua 24:32). It was an Amorite city-state that had not yielded to Israel's rule or to Israel's God.

Modern Nablus is near the site of ancient Shechem. It has been called "the natural capital of Canaan," the "uncrowned queen of Palestine." It was situated on the trade routes and took its name from its being a "shoulder" between the mountains Gerizim and Ebal. Hallowed as the place where Abram built his first altar in Canaan and where Jacob seized land for his settlement, Shechem was the site of Israel's final assembly before dispersing to possess the land. There Joshua led the nation in reaffirming the covenant with Jehovah, and as a memorial, he set up a stone near a specially revered oak tree.

To this "oak of the pillar" (v. 6 RSV), Shechem's men gathered to anoint Abimelech king. A modern version calls this tree "the Diviners' Oak."

The "house of Millo"—meaning "house of the fortress"—evidently was that portion of the citizenry that lived in and around the Tower of Shechem. The entire township made Abimelech king, but, while they celebrated, a loud voice broke in upon them from mount Gerizim. The sole survivor of the slaughter at Ophrah, Gideon's youngest son, Jotham, stood on a ledge on the 1,000 foot mount and addressed Shechem. Taking advantage of the unusual acoustical qualities of this natural amphitheater, he spoke the Word of God in a fable. "Listen to me, you men of Shechem," he said, "and may God listen to you!" (TEV).

If Jotham's voice from the safe distance on the mount startled the people, his use of a fable as the vehicle of his message must have captured their attention. They were anointing a king, a familiar allusion to the pouring of oil on the head of the one named king—he would tell them what happened "once upon a time" when the trees once tried to do the same. The olive and fig and grapevine were all worthy of the promotion; their fruit was vital to man's very life. Two of them—the olive for its oil and the vine for its wine—were also of service to "the gods." But if they were promoted (literally, "sway" or "move hither and thither") over the trees, they would sacrifice the essence of their existence. No, they could not do it.

The trees, Jotham went on, did not know any better than to offer the honor to the bramble. So flattered by this was the lowly thornbush that it immediately laid out its conditions for agreeing. "If in truth ye anoint me king over you," it said, "then come and put your trust in my shadow: and if not, let fire come out of the bramble, and devour the cedars of Lebanon" (v. 15). Its response was laughable. How could the trees gain any shelter from the thorny bush? And how could Shechem's people gain any protection from Abimelech? In the bramble's response, there was also a two-edged warning. Notorious for its vulnerability to the intense Mideastern heat, the bramble was a real menace to the other trees. A grass fire would soon become a forest fire, fed along by these low shrubs. Even the kingly "cedars of Lebanon" would fall prey to their mischief. So would the noblemen of Shechem fall prey to Abimelech if they turned against him. But did Abimelech catch the warning of Jotham's fable intended for him? Had he considered that these people would not actually "put their trust" in him?

The Lord Shows He Is King (vv. 55-57) Not only was Jotham looking down on Shechem to see what her citizens would do, Jehovah was also watching. The writer explains what took place in terms expressing his conviction that the Lord is sovereign. "God sent an evil spirit between Abimelech and the men of Shechem" (v. 23), turning them against him. But the governor of the city, Zebul, was Abimelech's ally and he kept Abimelech informed of events. With his help, Abimelech's bloodthirsty warriors rushed upon Shechem and in two days took the city and burned it to the ground, sowing salt over its ruins, symbolic of its destruction. It would be rebuilt by Jeroboam (1 Kings 12:25). Almost a thousand of Shechem's men and women, surely a major portion of the population, took refuge in the Tower of Shechem. To Abimelech, they were easy prey as he and his men torched the Tower and killed everyone that survived the blaze. In this act, he effectively stopped the rebellion, but he also had eradicated his own constituency.

The nearby village of Thebez had been in league against Abimelech and its residents fled to a tower evidently on the wall of the town. Abimelech thought to do to them what he had done to Shechem, but a woman "happened" to carry with her to the top of the tower a millstone (approximately 18 inches in diameter, 2-3 inches thick) and it "happened" to find its mark when she dropped it over the edge. It crushed Abimelech's skull. "The justice of God is remarkable in suiting the punishment to his sin," remarks Poole. "He slew his brethren upon a stone (v. 5) and he loseth his own life by a stone."

"And so it was that God paid Abimelech back for the crime that he committed against his father in killing his seventy brothers," says the writer (v. 56 TEV). As Cundall comments, "The Hebrews overlooked what might be called secondary causes and saw in these events the direct action of *God*...."

Applying the Scripture
Three statements as "food for thought"—and action.

Gideon's words were so true. "The Lord shall rule over you." This story points out in a powerful way that God is in control of human events. "Alleluia: for the Lord God omnipotent reigneth!" declare the heavenly hosts (Revelation 19:6). The Psalmist said the same thing: "For promotion and power come from nowhere on earth, but only from God. He promotes one and deposes another" (Psalms 75:6, 7 TLB).

All of the lessons in this autumn quarter have illustrated the fact of God's sovereignty. He created and called His people. He freed and instructed them. And He led and delivered them. This particular lesson emphasizes the justice He renders. We see at least three significant meanings in it:

1. God is the ruler yet. God places over a people the leader that he chooses. A nation tends to get the kind of leadership it deserves. Shechem's selection of a "bramble" for a king showed their "poor opinion of the value of kingship" says the *New Bible Commentary, Revised.* They chose freely in setting up Abimelech, hardly recognizing that the Lord was giving them one suited to them. He gives us justice tempered with mercy. A century or so later when they chose a son of Jesse as king, His full blessing would be upon the whole nation, not just upon a small portion of one tribe.

2. We must be careful whom we elect to office. The fact of Abimelech's blood kinship blinded the minds of the people of Shechem to what kind of person he was. It is easy to be swayed by prejudices and favoritism, against our better judgment. Christians are not to vote a party line or go with the status quo. We are to make a difference, just as salt and light make a difference.

3. We must warn this generation of wrong decisions. If we were to try to find a person in this story who represented the Lord, we would undoubtedly choose Jotham. He was spared by the providence of God, but he did not evade the responsibility God gave him. Sure, he did run for his life. But first he risked his life to deliver a message of warning. He didn't know how things would work out, although he had good reason to believe that in choosing Abimelech they were choosing a "bramble." But he said that if they were happy with him, let them "rejoice in him." He also warned them and his half-brother of the treachery and death that were to come.

Call attention in class to what risks he took and to the creative, bold way he confronted the men of Shechem. His example is worth emulating. Allow your class to discuss how Jotham's use of a fable might lead modern-day followers of Christ to employ the arts in addressing the moral evils in American society. Are there plays or songs or books that are now speaking to America's conscience in a way Jotham's fable sought to touch the conscience of his contemporaries?

Or, think of the meaning of his example for all of us today. Are we speaking out—in whatever means are at our disposal—against the moral and spiritual evils of our local area? Our city? Our state? Our nation? What bold, creative actions would the Lord have you and your class take to warn others of God's righteous judgment and loving forgiveness?

Questions for Discussion
Make use of these questions to involve your students in learning and to test their understanding of the lesson.
1. Name at least three actions which Gideon took in later life that led to the tragic and disgraceful episode of Abimelech's rise to power. 2. Who were

the father and mother of Abimelech? What was the meaning of his name?
3. Who was Jotham? 4. How could the populace of Shechem hear Jotham speak from Mount Gerizim? 5. Was Jotham realistic about the preoccupations and demands of governing a people? 6. In his fable, who is intended as the bramble? 7. How did the curse in Jotham's fable actually find fulfillment? 8. How does this episode illustrate the fact that the Lord is really the King? 9. What is the warning to us today concerning the people we elect to office?

Illustrating the Scripture
Examples and quotations to help the teacher communicate the lesson.

A nineteenth century book recently republished under the title *540 Little Known Facts About the Bible* contains a careful description of the topographical features of the vicinity of Shechem as well as ample evidence that Jotham's voice could have carried from Mount Gerizim to the valley below. The following excerpt is from a report by a Colonel Wilson.

"On the 6th of March (1866), Lieut. Anderson and I arrived at Nablous (the ancient Shechem), with the view of carrying out some excavations on Mount Gerizim. Before, however, attempting to describe the results of our labours, it will be as well to give a general sketch of the locality.

"At Nablous, the range of hills which traverses Palestine from north to south is pierced by a remarkable pass, running nearly east and west; on the north, the pass is flanked by the range of Mount Ebal, rising at its highest point to 3,029 feet above the sea, or 1,200 feet above the level of the valley; on the south by the range of Mount Gerizim, rising to 2,898 feet. Between these two mountains, the valley rises gently towards the east, to the water-parting between the Mediterranean and the Jordan, at which point there is a remarkable topographical feature which is not often met with—a recess on either side of the valley, forming a grand natural amphitheatre, probably the scene of the events described in Joshua 8:30–35.... It is hardly too much to say of this natural amphitheatre that there is no place in Palestine so suitable for the assembly of an immense body of men within the limits to which a human voice could reach, where at the same time each individual would be able to see what was being done....

"The valley has no peculiar acoustic properties, but the air in Palestine is so clear (homogeneous is a better word, for *clearness* of air does not assist the passage of sound), that the voice can be easily heard at a distance which would seem impossible in England; and as a case in point it may be mentioned that during the excavations on Mount Gerizim the Arab workmen were on more than one occasion heard conversing with men passing along the valley below."

SOVEREIGNTY = LORDSHIP What are we saying when we declare, "Jesus Christ is Lord!"? We are saying He is sovereign. If one dictionary's definition is any indication, modern man does not care very much for the idea that God is sovereign. Note the definition of the word: "*Sovereign:* 1. Exercising or possessing supreme jurisdiction or power. 2. Free; independent, autonomous. . . . 3. Supremely excellent, great or exalted . . . of chief importance . . . one who possesses sovereign authority; a monarch. . . ." Of course, all of these describe our Lord, but the dictionary does not allude once to the Lord being sovereign.

Someone asked the Bible teacher, Arthur W. Pink, what sovereignty meant, and he replied: ". . . the supremacy of God, the kingship of God, the godhood of God. To say that God is sovereign is to declare that God is God. He is the Most High, doing according to his will, so that none can stay his hand, defeat his counsels, or thwart his purpose" (*Living Quotations for Christians*).

Topics for Youth

WHY NOT WRITE A FABLE!—The great majority of Aesop's fables have to do with conversations between animals. But a few are like Jotham's—they give voice to the trees. Like the one called, "The Trees and the Axe."

"A man came into a forest and asked the Trees to provide him a handle for his axe. The Trees consented to his request and gave him a young ash-tree. No sooner had the man fitted a new handle to his axe from it, than he began to use it and quickly felled with his strokes the noblest giants of the forest. An old oak, lamenting when too late the destruction of his companions, said to a neighboring cedar, 'The first step has lost all. If we had not given up the rights of the ash, we might yet have retained our own privileges and have stood for ages.' "

Another even includes a bramble and, interestingly, takes for granted that it is the most worthless of all "trees." That fable is called "The Fir-Tree and the Bramble."

"A Fir-Tree said boastingly to the Bramble, 'You are useful for nothing at all; while I am everywhere used for roofs and houses.' The Bramble answered: 'You poor creature, if you would only call to mind the axes and saws which are about to hew you down, you would have reason to wish that you had grown up a Bramble, not a Fir-Tree.'

"Better poverty without care, than riches with."

Introducing Doubleday's new version of the ancient Aesop's Fables, Isaac Bashevis Singer forecasts that "there is no reason why some modern fabulist should not deal with jet planes, rockets, and in the not too distant future, even with animals that may exist on one of the planets." Or maybe with endangered species, or unborn babies threatened by the abortionist's knife, or prayer, or nuclear wastes lying on the ocean floor, or child pornography, or child abuse, or . . . ? The fable is a powerful method of ridiculing immoral or unwise actions. A generation of young people, with their consciences sensitive to what is wrong with our world, could help make it a better place perhaps—by writing a Christian fable.

WINTER

December, January, February

The Gospel of Luke

UNIT I

The Nature of Luke's Gospel

LESSON 1 — DECEMBER 5

The Nature of Luke's Gospel

Background Scripture: Luke 1:1–4; 5:29–32; 8:19–21; 9:18–22
Devotional Reading: 2 Timothy 4:1–8

Luke 1:1–4; 5:29–32; 8:19–21; 9:18–22
1 Forasmuch as many have taken in hand to set forth in order a declaration of those things which are most surely believed among us,
2 Even as they delivered them unto us, which from the beginning were eyewitnesses, and ministers of the word;
3 It seemed good to me also, having had perfect understanding of all things from the very first, to write unto thee in order, most excellent Theophilus,
4 That thou mightest know the certainty of those things, wherein thou hast been instructed.
5:29 And Levi made him a great feast in his own house: and there was a great company of publicans and of others that sat down with them.
30 But their scribes and Pharisees murmured against his disciples, saying, Why do ye eat and drink with publicans and sinners?

31 And Jesus answering said unto them, They that are whole need not a physician; but they that are sick.
32 I came not to call the righteous, but sinners to repentance.
8:19 Then came to him his mother and his brethren, and could not come at him for the press.
20 And it was told him by certain which said, Thy mother and thy brethren stand without, desiring to see thee.
21 And he answered and said unto them, My mother and my brethren are these which hear the word of God, and do it.
9:18 And it came to pass, as he was alone praying, his disciples were with him: and he asked them, saying, Whom say the people that I am?
19 They answering said, John the Baptist; but some say, Elias; and others say, that one of the old prophets is risen again.
20 He said unto them, But whom say ye that I am? Peter answering said, The Christ of God.
21 And he straitly charged them, and commanded them to tell no man that thing;
22 Saying, The Son of man must suffer many things, and be rejected of the elders and chief priests and scribes, and be slain, and be raised the third day.

KEY VERSE: "I came not to call the righteous, but sinners to repentance." Luke 5:32.

Home Daily Bible Readings			
Nov. 29	M.	A Writer Led by God, Luke 1:1–4; Acts 1:1–3.
Nov. 30	T.	Luke, Faithful Friend, 2 Timothy 4:6–11.
Dec. 1	W.	The Guide for Believers' Growth, 2 Timothy 3:12–17.
Dec. 2	T.	A Doctor for the Sick, Luke 5:27–32.
Dec. 3	F.	A Family of Believers, Matthew 12:46–50.
Dec. 4	S.	A Leader Who Must Die, Luke 9:18–22.
Dec. 5	S.	The Lord Is Merciful, Psalms 103:1–12.

Lesson Aim: That your class members develop an attitude of hearty obedience to Scripture, saying to Christ: "What will You have me to do?"

LESSON OUTLINE
Background to the Scripture
Looking at the Scripture Text
  I. A Most Reliable Record (Luke 1:1–4)
 II. A Most Universal Appeal (Luke 5:29–32)
III. A Most Demanding Discipleship (Luke 8:19–21)

IV. A Most Radical Belief (Luke 9:18-22)
Applying the Scripture

Background to the Scripture

There has never been any real quarrel over the authorship of the Gospel of Luke. As the writer in the *Pulpit Commentary* says, "The earliest traditions of the church and the writings which we possess of her teachers, of men who lived in the century following the death of St. John—the 'remains,' too, of the great heretical teachers who taught for the most part in the first half of the second century—all bear witness that the author of the third Gospel was identical with the writer of the Acts, and that this person was Luke."

The Canon of Muratori, found in a library in Milan and dated approximately A.D. 170, shows what books were generally accepted as Scripture by the early Church. Luke was among them. That portion of the Canon referring to Luke reads: "The Gospel of St. Luke stands third in order having been written by St. Luke the physician, the companion of St. Paul, who, not being himself an eye-witness, based his narrative on such information as he could obtain...."

Though Luke's name nowhere appears in his Gospel, he is named in three of Paul's letters written from Rome. In Colossians, he is called "Luke, the beloved physician" (4:14). Paul closed the brief letter to Philemon by naming Luke and other "fellow workers" (v. 24) and in 2 Timothy he says, "only Luke is with me" (4:11). Since Acts is universally attributed to Luke, one can learn more about this "kindly, evangelistic literary genius and first-century physician" by tracing the passages in Acts that are cast in first person, beginning with "Therefore putting out to sea from Troas, *we* ran a straight course from Samothrace" (16:11 NASB).

Looking at the Scripture Text

Anyone who raises the question, why are there four Gospels? amply shows that he hasn't taken the time yet to examine Matthew, Mark, Luke, and John closely. They have striking similarities, especially the first three "synoptic" Gospels, but each is unique. During the next three months we will have opportunity to study one of these books carefully. The experience promises to be rewarding.

A Most Reliable Record (1:1-4) Luke opened his account of the life, ministry, death, and resurrection of Jesus with a formal introduction, much like the classical Greek writers. Since his introduction is all in one sentence in Greek—and is an example of the common Greek tongue at its best—we might gain a more accurate sense of what he is saying by reading this in one of the modern English translations which reproduces it all in one sentence. We have chosen J. B. Phillips:

> Dear Theophilus,
> Many people have already written an account of the events which have happened among us, basing their work on the evidence of those who, we know, were eye-witnesses as well as teachers of the Message. I

have decided, since I have traced the course of these happenings carefully from the beginning, to set them down for you myself in their proper order, so that you may have reliable information about the matters in which you have already had instruction.

Luke's Gospel is most often dated at A.D. 80 though it may have been written at least a decade earlier. As Luke indicates, "many people" had already written their accounts of the life of Jesus and various of these were circulating around the Mediterranean region, from Jerusalem to Asia Minor and to Rome. The Gospel of Mark and possibly the Gospel of Matthew were among these. As he indicates, these works were based on the word of "eyewitnesses." Luke classified himself among those who were not eyewitnesses; he was a second generation Christian dependent on those closer to the Lord Jesus for his sources.

Scholars translate the words *most surely believed* in two ways; the traditional expression ends up as a marginal reference in the NIV which chooses instead to express the meaning, "the things . . . fulfilled among us." There is no real problem with either of these translations. Luke stresses at the outset that the things "believed" by the churches were actual historic "events." Yet he could see that none of the narratives (literal meaning of *declaration* in v. 1) in circulation were thorough in their treatment or sufficiently broad in their perspective to serve the larger non-Jewish public. Without boasting, he recognized himself as one who had "perfect understanding of all things from the very first." Phillips translates this, "I have *traced* the course of these happenings," expressing the literal meaning of the Greek—"to follow along beside."

How was Luke able to trace the story of Jesus to its beginnings? In Acts, he included himself in the party which accompanied Paul to Jerusalem. Then we lose track of him, it being his purpose to tell of Paul's arrest and subsequent two-year imprisonment in Caesarea. But Luke is again in the party with Paul when they board ship to sail to Rome (Acts 27:1). It is believed that Luke spent the greater part of that two years gathering firsthand story material from eyewitnesses in Palestine. That, together with his travels with Paul in Asia Minor, afforded him the opportunity to read virtually all of the fragmentary accounts that were reliable, while giving him a "world view" which colors his Gospel in its appeal to all men everywhere.

"A comparison with Mark and Matthew shows Luke's dependence on Mark and many agreements with Matthew," says the *Harper's Bible Dictionary*. "A third of Luke's Gospel" seems to be drawn from Mark, but "nearly half of Luke's material is peculiar to his Gospel."

Luke has been called "the most carefully composed of the Gospels," and the author "much more of a self-conscious historian than the other Evangelists." *The New Bible Commentary, Revised* says Luke "believed that Christian faith was based on historical events which could be regarded as the acts of God, and he was trying to establish a firm historical foundation for the faith of his readers."

His purpose in writing was to enable his friend Theophilus "to know the full truth about everything which you have been taught" (v. 4 TEV). False gospels had already begun to float around, purporting to be genuine; Luke would provide an accurate, reliable document.

We cannot be certain of the identity of Theophilus, to whom the Gospel and Acts are addressed. Since the name means "lover of God" any of us who fit that description may take the letter as being personally addressed to us! But since Luke salutes him as "most excellent" and indicates that he had already been instructed in the faith, we are correct to believe Luke had a specific person in mind. One commentator says "he was most likely, from Luke's connection with Antioch, a noble of that great and wealthy city, and may fairly be taken as a representative of that cultured, thoughtful class for whom in a measure St. Luke especially wrote."

A Most Universal Appeal (5:29-32) In this lesson's "sampling" of the Book of Luke, three encounters have been selected from the ministry of our Lord in Galilee to give us a taste of what we find in Luke. This story shows what kind of people Jesus called to salvation, and justified His doing so.

Not long before Levi's "great feast," Jesus had walked by his money table and called this tax collector to be His disciple. Levi, whose name was also Matthew (Matthew 9:9) and who is generally regarded as the author of the first Gospel, was probably a typical tax collector.

Considered religiously unclean because he worked for the pagan Romans, he had few social contacts among the Jewish upper class. The common people hated him because tax collecters had the reputation of fleecing their own people and lining their pockets with the takings (*see* Zaccheus's confession, chapter 19:8). With their fat income, they could afford a house large enough to entertain grand parties, as we see here; yet it could be that his alienation had kept this house empty and unhappy. No wonder he hosted a banquet and seemed not at all concerned that the "riff-raff" of society were climbing over one another to take part.

At the center of the festivities, Jesus and His disciples reclined at the table with Levi and his family and close associates. In the East, a large meal was no private occasion. Others who were not invited would look in, and did. Among them were the persnickety Pharisees and "the teachers of the law who belonged to their sect" (NIV). These whose sect name meant "separated" could not believe that a good "rabbi" like Jesus would associate with "publicans and . . . others" (Luke does not call them sinners; the terms would include prostitutes and any person of the common folk).

Though they complained to the disciples, Jesus saw that they were really questioning Him, so He came to their defense in a few words. "It is not the healthy who need a doctor, but the sick" (v. 31 NIV). Matthew (9:12) and Mark (2:17) give Jesus' answer word for word as Luke has it. The next thing Jesus says reveals how He conceived His mission—He had come to call sinners, not the righteous. Did the Pharisees grasp the irony in His statement?

A Most Demanding Discipleship (8:19-21) As did Matthew (12:46-50) and Mark (3:31-35), Luke included in his Gospel this brief encounter between Jesus' mother and brethren and Himself. Luke's account is brief, suggesting that he had no original material to add to what he may have borrowed from Mark. Yet this incident shows what Jesus expected and expects of any who would respond to His call stated so broadly at Levi's feast.

Luke places this event after the parables, showing how a man is to respond to His teaching. This may have happened in Capernaum; the story shows that Jesus was deluged by the throng. Mark in his account recorded that at about this time Jesus' family had sought to restrain Jesus, fearing that He was "beside himself," since He was not even taking time to eat. From Matthew and Mark, we learn the names of Jesus' half-brothers—James, Joseph, Simon, and Judas (Mark 6:3). They were evidently born to Mary after Jesus; by the time of our story, Joseph had died.

The reply of Jesus would have hurt Mary, no doubt reminding her of the prophetic words of Simeon (Luke 2:35); but Jesus intended no slight. Rather, He took the occasion to emphasize obedience and declare that everyone who obeys Him enjoys the closest relationship to Him.

A Most Radical Belief (*9:18-22*)   Whereas the first two scriptural selections dealt with *whom* Jesus was calling and *how* to respond, this third vignette focuses on *who Jesus is*. It also is fully stated in Matthew (16:13-16) and Mark (8:27-29).

Luke alone mentions that this discourse took place after a time of prayer. Alone in the company of the twelve, He asked them what the people were saying about Him. Of course, He didn't need information; He was preparing to draw them out on life's most important question. (Luke already had told his readers that Herod was asking the same things because of the widespread and enthusiastic following of Jesus, vv. 7-9.)

To His question, "Who do you say I am?" Peter replied, "You are God's Messiah" (TEV). That Jesus accepted Peter's estimate of Himself is evidence that He approved of this singular confession. He would not have hesitated to set Peter straight if He had not agreed with his words. Indeed, when Peter vigorously disputed with the Messiah's statements that He "must suffer . . . and be rejected . . . and be slain," Jesus immediately condemned Peter's point of view (Matthew 16:23). Jesus' strict warning for them to tell no man may have been in order to prevent their misunderstanding the Messianic claim in a political sense.

Applying the Scripture

Teacher: Ask each class member to choose one application *action* to begin putting into effect this week.

Jesus' words, as quoted in Luke 8:21, capture the essence of what we should be striving for in applying the Scripture to our lives. This is why it is so vital to follow instruction with practical ideas of how to put His teaching into practice. Have your class consider two questions from today's lesson.
1.   Do you, or does your church, practice Jesus' example of reaching out to the "sick" and the "sinners" of the world?

A Sunday School class in New Jersey pondered a hypothetical situation.

"What if," a member asked, "a house of prostitution were near our church and down the street in the other direction, a bunch of drug pushers hung out. And what if some of these people came to our church. How would we treat them?" An uneasy silence followed. No one was sure that these "sinners" would receive a friendly and warm welcome, even if they came in repentance and sought salvation.

When was the last time you or your church had a "Levi's feast" and invited people who were truly in need, economically and morally and spiritually, and who had no way of returning the favor?

Or, how many of the class members put forth effort to befriend and remain in contact with other adults who are not Christians, in order to influence them for Christ. All too many church members have little direct and daily contact with the "outcasts" of society. Would this please Jesus?

2. What are people saying today about Jesus? Who is He? And, who do *you* say Jesus is? If you know your class members well, you may still be surprised to learn that not all of them have believed in Jesus Christ as the Son of God and have followed Him in Christian baptism. Find opportunity in class to confront the persons in attendance with life's all-important question. Invite them to be "doers of the Word" by believing in Jesus Christ as the "Christ, the Son of the living God."

Questions for Discussion
Make use of these questions to involve your students in learning and to test their understanding of the lesson.
1. Although Luke's name nowhere appears in this Gospel, it is universally accepted as his work. Why?   2. What is the advantage of an eyewitness?   3. Who was Theophilus?   4. What are some of the distinguishing characteristics of Luke's Gospel?   5. What is Luke's purpose in writing this Gospel?   6. What was it about the Pharisees and scribes that made their question significant? Why would they be concerned about who was eating with Jesus and the disciples?   7. In the three passages from Jesus' ministry, what does Luke suggest about the mission and the person of Jesus?   8. From the context in chapter 8, and the parallel accounts in Matthew and Mark, what do we learn that shows that Jesus' treatment of His mother was not improper?

Illustrating the Scripture
Examples and quotations to help the teacher communicate the lesson.
We can be thankful that Luke obeyed the impulse of the Holy Spirit and recorded his thoroughly documented Gospel narrative. Not only were many erroneous stories circulating in his lifetime—a great many letters and tracts were produced in the next 100 years that wandered far from the truth.

Many were named after a prominent Christian, like the *Apocryphon of John* and the *Gospel of Mary*. The latter of these pretended to record visions that Mary, the mother of Jesus, had which differed from and challenged what the early Church had accepted. *The Letter of Peter to Philip* and the authoritatively titled *Wisdom of Jesus Christ* said that Jesus appeared after His Resurrection as "a great angel of light" offering to teach His disciples "the secret of the holy plan" of the universe. The *Acts of John* claimed that Jesus was not human at all, but "a spiritual being who appeared to each believer in a different form appropriate to his or her own understanding," says Elaine Pagels in *The Gnostic Gospels.*

Another of these gnostic (from *gnosis* or "knowledge") texts was the *Apocalypse of Peter.* Note how this excerpt differs from the New Testament. " 'Is it really you (Jesus) whom they take? And are you holding on to me? And are they hammering the feet and hands of another? Who is this one above the cross, who is glad and laughing?' The Savior said to me, 'He whom you saw being glad and laughing above the cross is the Living Jesus. But he into whose hands and feet they are driving the nails is his fleshly part, which is the substitute. They put to shame that which remained in his likeness. And look at him, and (look at) me'!"

Early, the false teachers tried to deny that the Son of God actually was put to death. While these false gospels faded out, the heresies they taught remain alive in cults today.

A FAVORITE THEME   *"They that are whole need not a physician; but they that are sick."*

"This was one of those sayings of the Lord which sank very deep into the hearts of the hearers. All three—Matthew, Mark, and Luke—repeat it with very slight variations; it was evidently a favorite theme with the great first teachers who followed Christ. It has borne rich fruit in the Master's church; for this vindication of Jesus of his conduct in going so often into the society of the moral waifs and strays of the population has been the real 'foundation of all those philanthropic movements which enlist the upper classes of society in the blessed work of bending down to meet in love the lower classes, so that the snapped circle of humanity may be restored; it is the philosophy in a nutshell of all home and missionary operations' " (*Pulpit Commentary*).

Topics for Youth

"I WANT TO MAKE ONE THING PERFECTLY CLEAR"—One of the most significant battles Christian youth will be involved in this decade, and perhaps in their lifetime, has to do with the authority of the Bible. Youth are susceptible to Satan's tactics to undermine the Bible's credibility. Let's face it—the Bible is a miracle book, and it requires faith to, well—*believe it!* But not unenlightened faith, not blind faith, not foolish faith. Take Luke, for example; he introduces his letter, stating his intention to make all things perfectly clear. That pledge of honest reporting ought to be honored as highly as any claim of a modern-day skeptic. Let the youth be encouraged to read Luke for themselves, noting his careful use of historical personages, his essential agreement with the other Gospel writers, though his was an original work. And let them ponder how long his narrative has survived the attacks of man.

Dare them to read a chapter in Luke every day of this month and see for themselves if God does indeed speak to them from these pages!

RAVE REVIEWS FOR LUKE'S GOSPEL—Have you noticed the advertising copy that appears in announcements of new books? Often, some personality is quoted, a critic also describes the book in glowing terms, an "authority" hypes it also. What might the reviewers have said about Luke if they were asked to write it up for the Jerusalem Tribune? "The most carefully composed history of the life of Jesus." "The fullest account of the life of Jesus of Galilee, the only Gospel to report the miraculous appearance of the angel and the actual birth of Jesus. Traces His family all the way back to Adam!" "CAREFULLY DOCUMENTED. Agrees with what is known of historical events and names. Outstanding!" Invite your young people to write their own "rave reviews."

UNIT II

Jesus' Preparation for Ministry

LESSON 2 **DECEMBER 12**

Promise of Jesus' Birth

Background Scripture: Luke 1:26–56
Devotional Reading: Hebrews 3:1–6

Luke 1:39–56
39 And Mary arose in those days, and went into the hill country with haste, into a city of Judah;
40 And entered into the house of Zechariah, and saluted Elisabeth.
41 And it came to pass, that, when Elisabeth heard the salutation of Mary, the babe leaped in her womb; and Elisabeth was filled with the Holy Ghost:
42 And she spake out with a loud voice, and said, Blessed art thou among women, and blessed is the fruit of thy womb.
43 And whence is this to me, that the mother of my Lord should come to me?

133

44 For, lo, as soon as the voice of thy salutation sounded in mine ears, the babe leaped in my womb for joy.
45 And blessed is she that believed: for there shall be a performance of those things which were told her from the Lord.
46 And Mary said, My soul doth magnify the Lord,
47 And my spirit hath rejoiced in God my Saviour.
48 For he hath regarded the low estate of his handmaiden: for behold, from henceforth all generations shall call me blessed.
49 For he that is mighty hath done to me great things; and holy is his name.
50 And his mercy is on them that fear him from generation to generation.
51 He hath showed strength with his arm; he hath scattered the proud in the imagination of their hearts.
52 He hath put down the mighty from their seats, and exalted them of low degree.
53 He hath filled the hungry with good things; and the rich he hath sent empty away.
54 He hath holpen his servant Israel, in remembrance of his mercy;
55 As he spake to our fathers, to Abraham, and to his seed for ever.
56 And Mary abode with her about three months, and returned to her own house.

KEY VERSE: "And she spake out with a loud voice, and said, Blessed art thou among women, and blessed is the fruit of thy womb." Luke 1:42.

Home Daily Bible Readings:
Dec. 6   M.   Preparing the Lord's Way, Isaiah 40:3–5, 10, 11.
Dec. 7   T.   New Growth From David's Line, Isaiah 11:1–5, 10.
Dec. 8   W.   A Child Will Be Born, Isaiah 9:2–4, 6, 7.
Dec. 9   T.   Gabriel's Startling Word to Mary, Luke 1:26–33.
Dec. 10 F.   Mary's Song of Wonder, Luke 1:46–55.
Dec. 11 S.   The Angel's Message to Joseph, Matthew 1:18–25.
Dec. 12 S.   Christ and God's House, Hebrews 3:1–6.

Lesson Aim: That your class members will seek a way to magnify Christ through their lives this week.

LESSON OUTLINE
Background to the Scripture
Looking at the Scripture Text
   I. Mary Goes to Elisabeth (Luke 1:39, 40)
  II. Elisabeth's Prophetic Outburst (Luke 1:41–45)

III. Mary's Praise Song (Luke 1:46-56)
Applying the Scripture

Background to the Scripture
After the silent centuries, the Spirit of God began to move once again among His covenant people. To an unpretentious dwelling in Nazareth of Galilee, the angel Gabriel was dispatched on a mission from heaven. Mary, a young woman engaged to a Joseph "of the house of David," received Gabriel's startling news in solitude. Nothing is said concerning her family. Luke only records that she was a virgin promised to be wed to a man of the tribe of Judah.

To David the king, the Lord had promised . . . I will make for "thee a great name, like unto the name of the great men that are in the earth . . . and thine house and thy kingdom shall be established for ever before thee; thy throne shall be established for ever" (2 Samuel 7:9, 16). In bringing Mary and Joseph together, He was about to fulfill the next step in that glorious prophecy. But that step did not involve any human parent. Understanding that she was to become pregnant and give birth to One who is to be called "Jesus," Mary only questioned how this could be. "I have no husband," she responded.

To that Gabriel answered, "The Holy Spirit will come upon you, and the power of the Most High will overshadow you. . . ." In hearing news too wonderful for human ears, she bowed and said, "Let it be." With that the angel departed.

Looking at the Scripture Text
Mary Goes to Elisabeth (*vv. 39, 40*)   Mary's unbelievably good news had to be shared. And Mary knew the one person with whom she could share her secret—Elisabeth. Luke says she hurried to a town in the "hill country of Judah" and entered the house of Zechariah.

Zechariah and Elisabeth may have lived in Hebron, but we cannot be certain. Joshua did describe Hebron in a similar way (Joshua 21:11). It was a city of refuge belonging to the Levites. Zechariah the priest and his wife, who was "of the daughters of Aaron," could well have lived there. But the location of their home is secondary in importance to what took place in the first minutes the two women faced one another.

Elisabeth was older than Mary. From the angel's pronouncement to Mary, we learn that they were "kinswomen." One translation says they were cousins. Mary, rushing to Elisabeth's door, her heart in her throat, knew already that her relative was six months along in her first pregnancy. After many years, she was to bear a child! That of itself was reason enough for Mary to go to her, but Mary must have felt acutely the need not only to share her good news, but also to think aloud with this dear older woman about all that lay ahead for her, for her espoused husband—indeed, for Israel.

Elisabeth's Prophetic Outburst (*vv. 41-45*)   Some imagine that, because Elisabeth's first words reveal a knowledge of Mary's great good news, Mary must have told her this much in her greeting. But that is placing too much of a burden on Luke's simple statement, she "saluted Elisabeth."

The first response to Mary's greeting at the door was the swift movement of Elisabeth's unborn child John within her womb. Simultaneously Luke says Elisabeth was "filled with the Holy Ghost," the only explanation he offers for the prophetic revelation which follows. It is one of the distinguishing characteristics of Luke's Gospel that he gives emphasis to the work of the Holy Spirit. Note the several instances of this in his opening chapters.

- "he (John) shall be filled with the Holy Ghost" (1:15)
- "The Holy Ghost shall come upon thee" (1:35)
- "Elisabeth was filled with the Holy Ghost" (1:41)
- "Zechariah was filled with the Holy Ghost" (1:67)
- "the Holy Ghost was upon him" (2:25)
- "came by the Spirit" (2:27)
- "the Holy Ghost descended . . . upon him" (3:22)
- "Jesus being full of the Holy Ghost" (4:1)
- "Jesus . . . in the power of the Spirit" (4:14)
- "The Spirit of the Lord is upon me" (4:18)

A new age, a new way of God's working among men, is about to dawn, and Luke freely attributes to the Spirit the wonderful stirrings taking place.

Elisabeth's behavior under the power of the Holy Spirit is very forceful. Her words and her "loud voice," point to "an unrestrained utterance under the influence of irrepressible feelings" says the *Expositor's Greek Testament*. Essentially she declared three truths.

1. *Mary's unparalleled happiness.* "Blessed art thou among women. . . ." No woman on earth in any age would be so favored as Mary. She had every reason to be very happy. Poole comments, "Elisabeth's words are certainly a great confirmation of what the angel had before told her." If Mary had been anxious, afraid to trust her own confidence in what the angel had said, now she would undoubtedly be encouraged.

2. *Mary's son is "my" Lord.* We might miss the implication of Elisabeth's words. It seems evident that already Mary is with child. The NIV translates "blessed is the fruit of thy womb" this way: "blessed is the child you will bear!" As the Spirit gave utterance, Elisabeth announced a like blessedness upon Mary's child and asks, "Why am I so favored" (NIV) "that the mother of my Lord should come to me?" The word *lord* was a title of respect for one's father or husband or ruler. It was the most common form of address the disciples used when speaking to Jesus. In the Greek translation of the Old Testament, the Septuagint, Jehovah is translated Lord. So, to see in Elisabeth's words a reference to God is not to put in meaning that is not there.

3. *Mary's blessedness for believing.* When we recall that for six months Zechariah had been "stealing about the house dumb," these words carry an even greater feeling. Zechariah had been startled by an angel appearing to him in his regular rounds of ministry at the Temple in Jerusalem. The angel told Zechariah that his wife would bear him a son, but Zechariah could

not take the word of the angel. He asked for a sign. "Now you will be silent and not able to speak until the day this happens," the angel answered, "because you did not believe my words, which will come true at their proper time" (v. 20 NIV). He could have had the full use of all his faculties if only he had believed. He is a warning to any who are afraid to take God at His Word, while Mary is our example. On hearing even more impossible news, that she a virgin was to have a child, the "Son of God," she said: "Behold the handmaid of the Lord; be it unto me according to thy word."

Interpreters differ in their translation of verse 45. Some follow the KJV which states that Mary's blessedness is because now the promises will be fulfilled. Others state that she is blessed because she believed; for example, the NASB: "blessed is she who believed that there would be a fulfillment of what had been spoken to her by the Lord."

Mary's Praise Song (vv. 46-56) This song of Mary's is well known, especially among the liturgical churches where it is called *Magnificat* from the Latin word which in our English versions reads *magnify*. It is an apt title. Mary's response to Elisabeth's prophetic outburst was to give expression to the greatness of the Lord. In contrast to Elisabeth, Mary's hymn is quiet in tone; its primary note is joy and the chief cause of that joy is God.

Mary's praise song has been compared with Hannah's hymn at the time she offered her child Samuel to Jehovah's service (1 Samuel 2:1-10). Many think that it takes its inspiration from that hymn. Following as it does the announcement by the angel, it also reminds us of the triumph songs of Moses (Exodus 15) and Deborah (Judges 5). It is a regular part of the ritual of the Catholic Church, and certainly its chief benefit, as with any Scripture, comes to the one who meditates upon it. Nevertheless, being literature, it has not escaped analysis.

Two views are generally held regarding its origin. The most popular view is that this was a spontaneous Spirit-inspired song that Luke recorded as it was passed on to him, possibly from the lips of Mary herself. Yet, because its scope breaks far out of the bounds of Mary's circumstances, this song is thought to be a familiar Jewish psalm. Contained in the song are two identifiable portions from the Psalms (103:17; 107:9).

Four verses can be seen in the song.

First, Mary declared her chief reason for joy to be God Himself. "My spirit hath rejoiced in God my Saviour." Her choice of the word *Saviour* suggests the rich idea of Jehovah as Redeemer of Israel. She declares Him to be *her* Saviour; *her* Deliverer. That she felt unworthy of the honor bestowed on her is expressed next: "for he hath regarded (looked upon) the low state of his handmaiden." She used the common word for a bond slave.

How literally true are her next words: "all generations shall call me blessed." That many have venerated Mary far beyond what was intended does not take away from the fact that Mary is universally believed to be blessed of God.

Next, Mary stated the cause of her gladness (vv. 49, 50). She glorified God for His power, His holiness, and His mercy. "Surely in all the records of the

Lord's works since the world's creation, his might had never been shown as it was now about to be manifest in her," says the *Pulpit Commentary.*

Then Mary gloried in God as the mighty Sovereign over all the world (vv. 51-53). In words similar to what can be found in the Sermon on the Mount, the Lord is revealed as He who had "performed mighty deeds" and "brought down rulers" and "lifted up the humble." Her words remind us that "all is *not* right with this world" as the poet declared. Most everywhere truth and righteousness and justice have been turned upside down. Mary prophesied as if all of this had already been made right (note the past tenses of the verbs).

Finally, Mary praised God for His eternal faithfulness to His chosen people. "He has helped his servant Israel, remembering to be merciful to Abraham and his descendants forever, even as he said to our fathers" (vv. 54, 55 NIV). Two millennia had passed since Jehovah had made a covenant with Abraham. When the angel appeared to Zechariah and to Mary to announce the coming of the Messiah, it had been 400 years since a prophet had spoken out in Israel. But the Lord had not forgotten His covenant people. As Poole points out, "He remembered them not for their merits, but in His mercy."

Mary's faith had not wavered. It is one thing to be told something "in the dark." It is quite another to keep on believing it in the light of other circumstances. In mercy, God gave Mary a believing companion in Elisabeth. As they shared the next three months together, we can imagine the joy and mutual encouragement each received from the other as they believed in their God.

Applying the Scripture
Teacher: In this lesson you want to encourage true friendships and help your class magnify Christ.
1. A Friend Indeed—When we think of what application the Lord would have us make in response to the truth of His Word, we can use no surer guide than the action verbs within that particular passage of Scripture. In today's lesson, we can draw an application from the opening verses—Mary "arose . . . and went . . . with haste . . . and entered into the house . . . and saluted Elisabeth."

It has been often said that with a friend we can lighten the load of our problems and double the joy of our blessings. Both Mary and Elisabeth experienced this. Clearly the emphasis in this passage is on the blessings, but Mary must have gained a needed encouragement and strength through long conversations with Elisabeth.

Friendship is one of those things the Church needs to encourage today. Take time in class to emphasize the importance of cultivating a friendship. Some people are without close friends, and thus they have no one to whom they can turn in time of need as well as in times of gladness. Maybe someone in the class needs to "rise up and go" as Mary did to Elisabeth's.

2. "O Magnify the Lord"—Ask your class, "Have you ever magnified

the Lord?" They may come back with a question of their own: "How?" Give it some thought.

A piece of glass passed over a page of fine print has the effect of making that print appear larger than it is. So, our lives can be magnifying glasses through which others can see the Lord in His glory and greatness. If the world around us could only see how great the Lord is to us, then they might believe Him, too. But how?

Perhaps no greater example can be found of a person who magnified the Lord than Mary. She believed His word and acted accordingly. What she did is summed up in the familiar words of the hymn, "Trust and Obey." It follows, that the more we trust Him and obey everything He tells us, the more we are able to show forth His glory.

A teenaged girl, taking part in a Sunday youth service in her church, read Romans 8:28 and said that the Lord had given her that promise. Only a week earlier, her father had experienced a massive heart attack and was still in the hospital. All of the people in the audience who knew about her father were able to "magnify" the Lord as they heard this youth testify.

If one of us can magnify God by obeying Him, think what effect a whole church could have upon its surrounding community if all its members sought to walk in faith and obedience. It is futile to pray for a mighty moving of God in our midst unless each of us individually is seeking to walk in the light. His light, passing through the body of His Church, will cause sinners to turn their gaze toward the Savior and be saved.

Challenge your class members to memorize the following verse as a reminder to "magnify" Him: "O magnify the Lord with me, and let us exalt his name together" (Psalms 34:3).

Questions for Discussion
Make use of these questions to involve your students in learning and to test their understanding of the lesson.
1. What was Mary's family relation to Elisabeth? 2. Since Elisabeth greeted Mary with a prophecy declaring "blessed be the fruit of thy womb" she already knew that Mary was to bear the Messiah. How did she know this? 3. What reason would Luke have to bring the Holy Spirit into this narrative? 4. What effect would Elisabeth's words have on Mary? 5. Who is the central figure in Mary's song? 6. How does Mary's song reveal that she was believing what was promised to her? 7. What qualities of character can be seen in Mary from her "Magnificat"? 8. What other outbursts of spiritual song can this song be compared to in the Bible?

Illustrating the Scripture
Examples and quotations to help the teacher communicate the lesson.
HOLY IS HIS NAME   "We often say, 'God hates the sin but loves the sinner.' This is blessedly true, but too often we quickly rush over the first half of this statement to get to the second. We cannot escape the fact that

God hates our sins. We may trifle with our sins or excuse them, but God hates them.

"Therefore every time we sin, we are doing something God hates. He hates our lustful thoughts, our pride and jealousy, our outbursts of temper, and our rationalization that the end justifies the means. We need to be gripped by the fact that God hates all these things. We become so accustomed to our sins we sometimes lapse into a state of peaceful coexistence with them, but God never ceases to hate them.

"We need to cultivate in our own hearts the same hatred of sin God has. Hatred of sin as sin, not just as something disquieting or defeating to ourselves, but as displeasing to God, lies at the root of all true holiness. We must cultivate the attitude of Joseph, who said when he was tempted, 'How then could I do this great evil, and sin against God?' (Genesis 39:9).

"God hates sin wherever He finds it, in saint and sinner alike. He does not hate sin in one person and overlook it in another. He judges each man's works impartially (1 Peter 1:17). In fact, biblical evidence indicates that God may judge the sins of His saints more severely than those of the world....

"Frequent contemplation on the holiness of God and His consequent hatred of sin is a strong deterrent against trifling with sin. We are told to live our lives on earth as strangers in reverence and fear (1 Peter 1:17). Granted, the love of God to us through Jesus Christ should be our primary motivation to holiness. But a motivation prompted by God's hatred of sin and His consequent judgment on it is no less biblical." (From *The Pursuit of Holiness* by Jerry Bridges, Colorado Springs, Colorado: Navpress, 1978, pp. 32, 33. Used by permission.)

THE VIRGIN BIRTH—IMPOSSIBLE? "A shovel of dirt analyzed in a chemical laboratory, we are told, contains thirteen chemicals identical with those found in the human body. So we see, that without the instrumentality of man or woman, God created man. In Genesis 2:22, we read, 'And the rib, which the Lord God had taken from the man, made he a woman.' God, having only the instrumentality of a man, made a woman.

"Surely you must believe that each of us was not born merely by the reproductive process. It is God that gives us life. Having man and woman, He creates each one of us. Nobody will argue that Abraham was not the progenitor of the people of Israel. He is called, 'Abraham, our father,' but how did he become their forefather?

"'And God said unto Abraham, As for Sarai thy wife, thou shalt not call her name Sarai, but Sarah shall her name be. And I will bless her, and give thee a son also of her: yea, I will bless her, and she shall be a mother of nations; kings of peoples shall be of her. Then Abraham fell upon his face, and laughed...' (Genesis 17:15–17).

"Abraham and Sarah laughed. Unthinkable! Impossible! But God did it by a miracle.... Could it be possible for her to bear a child? Why, such a thing was absurd—was laughable! That is exactly why God told them that they should call their son 'Isaac,' because Sarah laughed, and the Hebrew word for *laugh* is to be found in the name *Isaac*....

"To summarize, God made Adam out of the dust of the earth without the instrumentality of man or woman. He made Eve when He had only man. He made each one of us when He had both man and woman. He made the first Jew when He had a barren old woman and an old man. Is it so difficult for God who did all this to make man through a young virgin? The prophet Isaiah said, 'Behold, a virgin shall conceive, and bear a son, and shall call his name Immanuel' (7:14)" —Sanford C. Mills.

Topics for Youth

WHY NOT WRITE YOUR OWN "MAGNIFICAT"?—Young people may put up resistance at first, but most of them—if not every one—will like writing their own praise song. If they need a pattern to follow, suggest that they use Mary's hymn and write in their own words what they would like to say.

They don't need to worry about verses or rhyming, but these ideas may help them:

1. Begin by praising God for loving you. Bless God for the special, personal way He has of noticing you.

2. Then, bless Him for His attributes. Mary named His mighty power and His holiness and His mercy. You may want to praise Him for His faithfulness or for His love or other qualities in Himself.

3. The next part of your praise song can praise the Lord for His workings in the world, in nature, in history, in the nations of the world.

4. Then, conclude your song with praise to Him for His covenant people Israel and for His Church which now carries His truth to man everywhere.

Let this be your very own praise song!

LESSON 3   DECEMBER 19

Jesus' Early Life

Background Scripture: Luke 2
Devotional Reading: Proverbs 23:15–25

Luke 2:22–35, 51, 52

22 And when the days of her purification according to the law of Moses were accomplished, they brought him to Jerusalem, to present him to the Lord;

23 (As it is written in the law of the Lord, Every male that openeth the womb shall be called holy to the Lord;)

24 And to offer a sacrifice according to that which is said in the law of the Lord, A pair of turtledoves, or two young pigeons.

25 And, behold, there was a man in Jerusalem, whose name was Simeon; and the same man was just and devout, waiting for the consolation of Israel: and the Holy Ghost was upon him.

26 And it was revealed unto him by the Holy Ghost, that he should not see death, before he had seen the Lord's Christ.
27 And he came by the Spirit into the temple: and when the parents brought in the child Jesus, to do for him after the custom of the law,
28 Then took he him up in his arms, and blessed God, and said,
29 Lord, now lettest thou thy servant depart in peace, according to thy word:
30 For mine eyes have seen thy salvation,
31 Which thou hast prepared before the face of all people;
32 A light to lighten the Gentiles, and the glory of thy people Israel.
33 And Joseph and his mother marvelled at those things which were spoken of him.
34 And Simeon blessed them, and said unto Mary his mother, Behold, this child is set for the fall and rising again of many in Israel; and for a sign which shall be spoken against;
35 (Yea, a sword shall pierce through thy own soul also,) that the thoughts of many hearts may be revealed.
51 And he went down with them, and came to Nazareth, and was subject unto them: but his mother kept all these sayings in her heart.
52 And Jesus increased in wisdom and stature, and in favour with God and man.

KEY VERSE: "And Jesus increased in wisdom and stature, and in favour with God and man." Luke 2:52.

Home Daily Bible Readings
Dec. 13 M. Born in a Stable, Luke 2:1–7.
Dec. 14 T. Glory to God in the Highest, Luke 2:8–14.
Dec. 15 W. Let Us Go Over to Bethlehem, Luke 2:15–20.
Dec. 16 T. Dedication, Luke 2:22–28.
Dec. 17 F. A Song of Praise, Luke 2:29–35.
Dec. 18 S. A Widow's Testimony, Luke 2:36–40.
Dec. 19 S. Jesus in the Temple, Luke 2:41–52.

Lesson Aim: That your class members will see that God meets them in surprising ways when they attend services faithfully.

LESSON OUTLINE
Background to the Scripture
Looking at the Scripture Text
  I. In Jerusalem for Ceremonial Offerings (Luke 2:22–24)
 II. In Simeon's Arms for Revealing Prophecies (Luke 2:25–35)
III. In Nazareth, Subject to His Parents (Luke 2:51, 52)
Applying the Scripture

Background to the Scripture

About the only time we give much thought to the birth of the Lord Jesus Christ is during the Advent season. During the rest of the year, we do not hear sermons about the Incarnation and the Virgin Birth. And when Christmastime arrives, very little attention is given to the events before us in this lesson. We are more familiar with the nativity story, the visit of the wise men, the announcement to the shepherds than we are with the prophetic words uttered over the baby Jesus when His parents took Him to the Temple in Jerusalem.

The devout Joseph and Mary were traveling to Jerusalem to offer the sacrifices for Mary's "purification" and to pay the required redemption price for their firstborn male son. Little did they realize how God would meet them in the performance of their religious duties and show them some things highly significant that lay immediately before them and the baby Jesus.

Looking at the Scripture Text

In Jerusalem for Ceremonial Offerings (vv. 22–24)   Mary and Joseph made the journey from Bethlehem to Jerusalem forty days after Jesus' birth. Luke's mention of "her purification" assures us of this. When a Hebrew woman gave birth to a male child, she was denied access to Temple worship for a total of forty days (Leviticus 12:2–4) after which time she was to present a sin offering and a burnt offering at the Temple.

To us, this aspect of the Law will seem strange until we understand its purpose. The word *purification* points to defilement, not that childbirth was in any way sinful, but because the sufferings a woman endures in labor are a part of the curse God declared in the Fall (Genesis 3:16). Travail at birth was intended to remind man and woman of their sinful condition before God. They are helpless in preventing their newborn child from inheriting their fallen nature, or in preventing the further spread of the plague of sin. "Although the birth of a child is a joyous event, it is also a solemn one. For the birth of the child will inevitably be followed ultimately by its death, and by eternal death unless the child is made an heir of life through the redemption which is in Christ.... According to the law, everything connected with parenthood is treated as unclean, and especially as rendering the person unfit for the performance of religious duties" (*New Bible Commentary, Revised*).

Because of this, the Law commanded that every new mother was to remain in isolation until forty days passed (a different length of time in the case of female child). Then she was to bring a lamb and either a pigeon or a turtledove to the priest for offerings. The lamb would be sacrificed as a sin offering to purify her; the bird would be consumed as a burnt offering, symbolizing her renewing of vows to Jehovah.

That Mary and Joseph brought two fowl as their offerings is an indication that they were too poor to afford a lamb. The Law made exception in such cases (Leviticus 12:8).

Two ceremonies brought Joseph and Mary to Jerusalem, and a third purpose should be listed, too, if we allow a special significance to the words "to present him to the Lord." Some suggest that Mary was bringing Jesus to the Temple to dedicate Him to the Lord as Hannah did with Samuel. The word *present* is the same term used by Paul in calling believers to "present your bodies a living sacrifice" (Romans 12:1).

The second ceremonial duty which they would fulfill at the Temple was the payment of the redemption price. Mindful of his non-Jewish readers, Luke quoted from the Mosaic Law—"As it is written in the law of the Lord, Every male that openeth the womb shall be called holy to the Lord" (v. 23)—which said the firstborn of every Israelite family and of the cattle belonged to the Lord. The first of the herds was offered on the altar; the firstborn son was "redeemed" by a payment of five shekels to the priest. In this way, each set of parents was reminded that they were the people of God, were bought with a price, and that their children were given them as a trust from the Lord.

In Simeon's Arms for Revealing Prophecies (vv. 25-35) In fulfilling the Law's decree, Mary and Joseph had a surprising encounter. Simeon, an aged man, came where they were as surely as if he had a guide. And the text indicates he did! Some have speculated that Simeon was a priest, but as one commentator says, he had his worthy title: "a just and devout man." His spirituality is well attested to: "the Holy Spirit was upon him . . . revealed to him by the Holy Spirit . . . moved by the Spirit, he went into the temple" (NIV).

Simeon was of that faithful remnant who waited for ("looked for" NASB) the Messiah. The rabbis called Messiah "the Comforter" and a common Jewish prayer of the day was, "May I see the consolation of Israel." Isaiah had prophesied, "Comfort, comfort my people, says your God. Speak tenderly to Jerusalem, and cry to her that her warfare is ended . . ." (40:1, 2 RSV). To this hope Simeon and other Jews clung (Anna, v. 38; also Joseph, Mark 15:43). Simeon's special distinction was that the Spirit had revealed to him that he would live to see the Messiah (or the Christ, the anointed one; the words "the Lord's Christ" point unmistakably to the Messiah).

The Spirit who had assured Simeon that he would live to see the Messiah now came upon him to utter a prophecy much as the Spirit came on Mary, Elisabeth, and Zechariah in the previous chapter.

"My eyes have seen your salvation" (NIV)—he was confident that he held in his arms the Savior of his people.

"In the sight of all people"—he saw that this Savior was not sent alone to Israel, but to Jews and Gentiles alike.

"A light for revelation to the Gentiles"—the nations of the world were always portrayed as walking in darkness (Isaiah 60:1-3; 62:6). Christ "the light of the world" (John 8:12) would enlighten all the world as the Gospel penetrated that darkness.

"Glory to your people Israel"—though He would be a light for all people, the Messiah had been promised to Israel, was born of Israel, would live among and do mighty works and teach His marvelous words—to Israel. Christ is forever the noblest son to come of Abraham's seed.

The mother and her husband (older manuscripts do not name Joseph) "marveled" at the extraordinary words of Simeon. This appears as a natural explanation of their reaction to hearing this stranger speak such a prophecy. But Simeon was not through. To Mary personally he delivered the darker message:

"This child is destined to cause the falling and rising of many in Israel"—this difficult statement must be taken in the context of the balance of verses 34 and 35. It surely could apply to the way in which Christ brought Israel to decision and there is no reason to limit the meaning to Jesus' lifetime. Jesus' own statement that He had "come to bring . . . a sword" (Matthew 10:34) would agree with the intent of this prophecy. Wherever He would go, men and women would be forced to decide for Jesus or against Him. It is the same today. Finally, in Jesus' lifetime every man's hidden thoughts were exposed. Those who loved Him became His followers even though it meant martyrdom. Those who hated Him helped put Him to death. The Gospel of Jesus Christ when it is declared in the power of the Spirit cuts to the heart of its hearers, exposing to the sinner his or her own sins. But this awareness that one stands naked in the presence of God, who knows all, is the first step toward salvation, possibly alluded to in the words *rising again* or *resurrection.*

"And a sword will pierce your own soul too"—these words Simeon spoke to Mary. She would have cause to remember them, even as the very next incident shows (2:41–50). The anecdote from our first lesson in Luke fits this description, showing Mary's mother heart reaching out to a son whom she did not fully understand. But no greater anguish could come than what she endured on Calvary's hill during the hours of His passion. The substance of Simeon's brief, but powerful, prophecy was remarkable, coming as it did as he held what looked like but a fragile baby in his trembling arms.

In Nazareth, Subject to His Parents (vv. 51, 52)   There is nothing remarkable about these words—until we remember who Jesus was. The key for our study is "these things" (*sayings,* literally *words*). What things? Obviously Luke is referring to the events just described. In Jerusalem, standing among the teachers in the Temple, Jesus said to His mother, "Why were you searching for me? Didn't you know I had to be in my Father's house?" This is the only statement from Jesus' boyhood that is preserved for us. Perhaps Mary told this to Luke.

From the anecdote, isn't it reasonable to conclude that Jesus' behavior as a boy had been much like that of any other child? If He had been a one-dimensional religious fanatic, a boy obsessed only with mastering the Law and the religious traditions, would not Mary and Joseph sought for Him first at the Temple?

Or was Jesus' question more nearly "Why were you searching for me *at all?*" We cannot understand, even as Mary and Joseph did not, how the divine and human natures blended in Jesus and it is beyond us to trace the arousal of the God-consciousness in Him. In awe and wonder, we watch Him "go down" to Nazareth (the traveler always went *down* from Jerusalem to anywhere, literally and figuratively) and honor His parents with obedience. These were the silent years. Nothing more is known of Him until He is thirty years of age.

Luke sums up the growth and development of Jesus into manhood in the oft-quoted fifty-second verse. He kept advancing intellectually, physically, spiritually, and socially. He was the only Perfect Man, the only Whole Person, an example as well as a Savior for us all.

Applying the Scripture
Two applications to ponder—emphasize these in this lesson.
1. The encounter with Simeon ought to encourage us to continue faithfully practicing our Christian faith by attending the services and taking part in ministries as provided in our local church. A seminarian and his wife were tempted not to go to church on Sunday evenings. But invariably they found that once they had made the effort, God had blessed them in a remarkable way.

It is often easy to withdraw from services of the church. We may think we have "our reasons." But this narrative of Mary and Joseph's visit to the Temple for a regularly prescribed service shows us that we can never tell when God may have something "special" for us there. Ask your class: "Wouldn't it be a great loss for us if God had something special for our lives, and we were not there to even hear about it?" True, God does meet us in many places, and we don't have to go to church to be in His presence, but if we call ourselves a part of the Church we need to remember by definition it is a "called out" body and we should make effort to be there when the body is called to assemble.

2. A second application is suggested from the words: "the thoughts of many hearts may be revealed." If we are watching for our Lord's return we cannot be harboring sinful thoughts.

Ask your class: "Does God really care as much what we think about as He does what we say or do?" Try to press your members for answers that show support in the Scriptures.

A powerful example can be taken from Jesus' words in the Sermon on the Mount. He showed that God does not condone lustful thoughts (that is the same as committing adultery); He does not accept hatred in our hearts (that is the same as murder).

Lead your class members to begin consciously committing their thought life to God. Discuss ways they can replace evil and negative thoughts with good and positive ideas. One way many have found to overcome evil thoughts is to memorize Scripture verses or whole chapters so that they can be available for meditation, for witnessing, for feeding our prayer life, and fostering our spiritual growth. Suggest that the simplest way to begin is for each person to try to form the habit of confessing to God immediately when he becomes aware of harboring evil thoughts. "As a man thinketh in his heart, so is he."

Questions for Discussion
Make use of these questions to involve your students in learning and to test their understanding of the lesson.
1. What two purposes brought Mary and Joseph to the Temple with the Baby Jesus? 2. What was the rite of purification of the mother? How would you explain its meaning? 3. What can we assume about Joseph and Mary from the fact that they offered two birds rather than a lamb? 4. What is meant by "the consolation of Israel"? 5. Define the term *Christ*. 6. Why did the statement of Simeon seem to surprise Joseph and Mary? 7. How does the closing verse of the chapter describe the way the youthful Jesus grew to maturity?

Illustrating the Scripture
Examples and quotations to help the teacher communicate the lesson.

"THE CHILD'S FATHER AND MOTHER *MARVELED* AT WHAT WAS SAID ABOUT HIM" (Luke 2:33 NIV). "To marvel is one of the first experiences of the true disciple," says Dr. Eugene A. Nida in *God's Word in Man's Languages*. "But to express this emotional attitude is not always easy, for languages employ so many different ways of describing what seems to us such a self-evident kind of emotion. The Kekchis say that 'to marvel' is literally 'to lose one's heart.' In one's amazement the heart seems to disappear completely. The Tzeltals describe this experience even more vividly by the words 'he felt like dying.' We might speak of 'dying' from fright, or wishing we could die in cases of great embarrassment, but we would not think of dying from amazement.

"The Tarascans in central Mexico describe astonishment as 'to shut one's mouth, thinking.' One is so overwhelmed with thoughts that there is nothing to say. The Mixtecos, farther to the south, talk about 'marveling' in quite a different way. They say 'to forget, listening.' That is, the report is so marvelous that it makes one completely forget everything else.

"In the Loma language the report of Jesus' astonishment at the belief of the people (Mark 6:6—the same word used in our text in Luke) is expressed as 'their unbelief was so great that his mind walked away.' His thoughts simply could not endure the willful unbelief of the multitude."

"HE IS *THE LIGHT* THAT WILL SHINE UPON THE NATIONS, AND HE WILL BE THE GLORY OF YOUR PEOPLE ISRAEL!" (v. 32 TLB). Samuel Shoemaker said in *How to Become a Christian* that "a good historic case could be made for stating that the impulse back of practically every move for the betterment of man in the past twenty centuries has been a Christian motive, directly or indirectly." While He was in the world, Christ was the Light of the world (John 8:12). He said that every one who follows Him is a light in the world (Matthew 5:14–16). His Word is "a lamp unto (our) feet ... a light unto (our) path" (Psalms 119:105). His words are now translated into more tongues than any other book—over 1,700 languages have at least one book of the Bible in their native tongue. Today, though the world is a dark place, Christ the Light is shining upon the nations through His people, His Church, and His Word!

Topics for Youth

MAKE YOUR LIFE REFLECT THAT OF JESUS—"Take out that small computer which is your brain and put it in a little box and shoot it to the moon. Then let God use your heart." That is how one evangelist instructed Christians a few years ago. If we would *really* be used of God, he said, we should disregard the rational process and go straight for feeling.

It's easy to see the danger in such an extreme action. A young person, though, in the zeal of newfound faith especially, can unconsciously adopt such an unbalanced attitude toward life. And adults are not immune to it either.

The example Jesus set in His life ought to be our own goal—to advance in wisdom and in bodily development and in favor with God and our fellow man. That is the well-balanced, *whole* life.

Enthusiasm is a great thing and should never be dampened. But to be just a "Jesus freak" or a "Jesus jock" is not His purpose for the young person following Christ. *Time* magazine said a few years ago, "There is little evangelical leverage in the great universities or communications outlets in America." To enter those positions of reponsibility takes discipline, hard work, study, and determination. But the goal is worth it.

Today the Lord is calling young people to be the best they can be in all phases of their lives. The closer we get to Jesus, the more His balanced life should be reflected in ours. Some young people get tagged with the label "egghead" or "bookworm." They probably need to develop their social life. Others are the "party" type—they always like to have a good time, but seldom buckle down to the work at hand. While they should not quit partying altogether, they need to commit themselves to some solid study goals and intellectual or vocational aims. All of us have our strengths and weaknesses—that is why we need Jesus—but wouldn't He be glorified by our development in all four basic areas?

A word of caution: if we took a survey we would probably discover that of the four areas, the spiritual side of man is the one most likely to be neglected. Society has a way of pushing us to grow socially and physically. And there are certain incentives the family and society stress to encourage intellectual development. But the spirit can be neglected. Young people will respond to encouragement to read spiritual books and develop habits of daily devotions.

"He (Jesus) went down with them, and came to Nazareth, and was *subject* unto them" (Luke 2:51).

Wow! Think what that means. Jesus, the Son of God, was submissive to His parents. Knowing more than they did, He did not *teach* them. Seeing things they could not see, yet He *respected* them. Evidently, He worked in the household carpentry shop. And more than that—He waited. He waited for the right time to leave home and begin His ministry, and that was not until

He was thirty. It is thought that Jesus' father Joseph died leaving Jesus as the eldest son with responsibilities to provide for the home. Being like Jesus today is following His example—honoring our parents in submission and obedience.

LESSON 4 DECEMBER 26

Jesus Begins His Ministry

Background Scripture: Luke 3:21–4:15
Devotional Reading: Luke 3:15–20

Luke 4:1–15

1 And Jesus being full of the Holy Ghost returned from Jordan, and was led by the Spirit into the wilderness,
2 Being forty days tempted of the devil. And in those days he did eat nothing: and when they were ended, he afterward hungered.
3 And the devil said unto him, If thou be the Son of God, command this stone that it be made bread.
4 And Jesus answered him, saying, It is written, That man shall not live by bread alone, but by every word of God.
5 And the devil, taking him up into an high mountain, shewed unto him all the kingdoms of the world in a moment of time.
6 And the devil said unto him, All this power will I give thee, and the glory of them: for that is delivered unto me; and to whomsoever I will I give it.
7 If thou therefore wilt worship me, all shall be thine.
8 And Jesus answered and said unto him, Get thee behind me, Satan: for it is written, Thou shalt worship the Lord thy God, and him only shalt thou serve.
9 And he brought him to Jerusalem, and set him on a pinnacle of the temple, and said unto him, If thou be the Son of God, cast thyself down from hence:
10 For it is written, He shall give his angels charge over thee, to keep thee:
11 And in their hands they shall bear thee up, lest at any time thou dash thy foot against a stone.
12 And Jesus answering said unto him, It is said, Thou shalt not tempt the Lord thy God.
13 And when the devil had ended all the temptation, he departed from him for a season.

14 And Jesus returned in the power of the Spirit into Galilee: and there went out a fame of him through all the region round about.
15 And he taught in their synagogues, being glorified of all.

KEY VERSE: "And Jesus returned in the power of the Spirit into Galilee: and there went out a fame of him through all the region round about." Luke 4:14.

Home Daily Bible Readings		
Dec. 20	M.	A Call to Repentance, Luke 3:1–6.
Dec. 21	T.	Proof of Repentance, Luke 3:7–14.
Dec. 22	W.	My Beloved Son, Luke 3:15–22.
Dec. 23	T.	Victory in Temptation, Luke 4:1–15.
Dec. 24	F.	Behold the Lamb of God, John 1:29–36.
Dec. 25	S.	Two Interested Men, John 1:37–42.
Dec. 26	S.	Follow Me, John 1:43–51.

Lesson Aim: Challenge your class members to learn one thing from the temptations of Jesus that they can put in practice as a safeguard against temptation.

LESSON OUTLINE
Background to the Scripture
Looking at the Scripture Text
 I. Tested in the Desert (Luke 4:1, 2)
 II. Temptation to Use Power to Selfish Advantage (Luke 4:3, 4)
 III. Temptation to Expediency to Obtain Power (Luke 4:5–8)
 IV. Temptation to Assert His Powers as Messiah (Luke 4:9–12)
 V. Teaching in the Spirit's Power (Luke 4:13–15)
Applying the Scripture

Background to the Scripture

Planet Earth is a battlefield. Unseen and unrecognized by human senses, the forces of evil are engaged in deadly combat with the forces of righteousness. A few selections in Scripture draw back the veil and show the "conflict of the ages" that is raging around us. The fourth chapter of Luke, and the fourth chapter of Matthew are such passages (Job 1 and 2, Daniel 10, and Revelation are others).

Satan had not ignored the Messiah at His birth. Stirring King Herod, he sought to put the young Babe to death. But we know of no other attempt on Jesus' life until He stood fullgrown in Jordan's waters and the voice of God said, "Thou art my beloved Son." That was like declaring war. Christ had invaded enemy territory and succeeded in bringing the devil out of hiding.

The temptation of Jesus which ensued is rich in the insights it provides us into the cosmic battle. It is equally rich in the practical instruction it offers us, for we, too, are caught up in the spiritual warfare.

Looking at the Scripture Text

Tested in the Desert (vv. 1, 2) From the obscurity of Nazareth, the Lord Jesus had emerged to be baptized by John, only to withdraw once again, this time to the desert. We must remember that before Him lay His entire ministry, and beyond that, the Cross. To prepare for that brief three-year period that would change the course of history, He sought solitude. For forty days, He separated Himself from all social contact and even went without food. His body was under the control of His spirit. Without distraction, He devoted Himself to prayer and contemplation of His work.

According to Luke's account, the devil tempted Jesus throughout the entire forty days. Perhaps he assumed that by catching Jesus alone and weakened without sustenance he would more easily trap the Lord.

We have already noted the importance placed on the Holy Spirit's presence in the events surrounding Jesus' advent. With marked emphasis on the Spirit, Luke introduces the temptation experience—"Jesus, full of the Holy Spirit . . . was led by the Spirit" (NIV). Whereas Matthew (4:1-11) and Mark (1:12, 13) indicate a certain compulsion of the Spirit, driving Jesus into the desert, Luke describes the act as one of voluntary movement. He was "led by" (literally "in") the Spirit.

Normally we would interpret "being filled" and "in the Spirit" as indicating a state of being fully controlled by the Spirit, as those expressions are used in the Epistles and Acts. But Scripture testifies that God's Spirit was never limited in any way in our Lord's life (John 3:34). Luke may have intended a special meaning in these words, similar to John's description of his vision (Revelation 1:10). This would help us understand how the devil presented the three temptations to the Lord. Nowhere does the Bible say that Satan appears to man. The accounts of Matthew and Luke do not describe an appearance of Satan. Further, the second temptation clearly fits an "out-of-the-body" experience. It is impossible of physical fulfillment. The *Pulpit Commentary* says that these temptations must have come to Jesus in a higher realm than to the physical senses; Jesus was "especially under the influence of the Spirit so that His eyes were open to see visions and sights not usually visible to mortal eyes and His ears were unlocked to hear voices not audible to ordinary mortal ears." This does not make the temptation any less real. In fact, this seems to be the way the devil tempts every man, remaining out of sight, whispering his deceits to our inner man.

Temptation to Use Power to Selfish Advantage (vv. 3, 4) As we have seen, Luke described the devil as constantly tempting Jesus during the forty days. The three singular bouts may have taken place at the end of the period (Matthew 4:2) and as a climax to this duel. Jesus related His experience to the twelve and chose these three temptations for their broad application to our condition. He "has been tempted in every way, just as we are—yet was without sin" (Hebrews 4:15 NIV). But His temptations—and ours—might be classified in three types.

The first temptation is strictly a slur against the Messiah. No other person would be tempted to change a stone into a loaf of bread. But in kind, it is like what every man faces: the enticement to use what privilege he has to serve himself. This is the siren song of *self-preservation*.

In so far as we know, Jesus had not exercised His supernatural powers yet. What Satan urged Him to do was within His power, and it could have been justified as meeting a legitimate need. But Jesus answered the devil by paying honor to a higher need. He would please His Father. "Man shall not live by bread alone," He answered. The best manuscripts do not show the remainder of the verse.

Although many have done it before, it is worth pointing out that Jesus answered the devil on all three occasions by repeating Scripture. This is good advice for every follower of His. In the temptations, He drew from the Book of Deuteronomy a scroll familiar to every Israelite because it was used in religious instruction. One commentator says, "The Lord simply chose to frame His answers from . . . the maxims and precepts of Deuteronomy (which) . . . were written on the phylacteries or frontlets which so many pious Jews were in the habit of wearing."

Temptation to Expediency to Obtain Power (vv. 5–8) For some reason, Matthew placed this as the last of the three temptations. It is essentially the same in both Gospels although Luke added more to the boasting of Satan. This is the temptation of the shortcut; to do the expedient thing, not the right thing. It is the temptation to power, the siren song of *self-achievement*.

Showing Him in some manner "all the kingdoms of the world," the devil tells Jesus, "I will give you all their authority (power) and splendor . . . if you will worship me" (NIV). What did our Lord see? The inhabited places of the first-century earth? Or did His vision catch sight of all empires of all times, including the empires of the East and of the Aztecs, the British and the Spanish, the Islamic world and the Soviet Union and its satellites? The devil was playing for high stakes and it seems reasonable to believe that he tempted Jesus with *all* of the earth's kingdoms and dominions. It was a genuine temptation, for He had come to claim the uttermost parts of the earth as the King of kings.

But was it Satan's to give? It could not have been a real temptation otherwise. Jesus later recognized publicly that the world was under a satanic ruler (John 12:31). The theme is consistently borne out in the Epistles and the reversal of Satan's authority is the theme of the Revelation. Yes, it was his to give, in a sense, though the devil's own words show that his authority was limited. "It has been delivered to me" he said, conveniently neglecting to say who had given him this authority.

In resisting Satan, the Lord showed that the end cannot justify the means. No price was so rich as to make Him bow to Satan. Again, from Deuteronomy, He quoted: "Thou shalt fear the Lord thy God, and serve him, and shalt swear by his name" (6:13).

Temptation to Assert His Powers as Messiah (vv. 9–12) Again, this temptation loses nothing of its reality if we consider that it took place, not on the highest pinnacle of Jerusalem's Temple, but in the realm of the spirit. Satan again insinuated, "If thou be the Son of God," trying to find some small chink in His armor. Until now Jesus had lived in relative obscurity in Nazareth. Satan hoped to cast doubt in Jesus' mind, to make Him not believe He was really on earth, God in the flesh, as he tempted Eve with the insinuation in the Garden, "Yea, hath God said . . . ?" His final tactic was to lure Jesus to employ His alleged powers to demonstrate that He really was Who He claimed to be. There is no mention of any crowd at the Temple so this could not have been a temptation to make a splashy showing and thus launch His mission with immediate popular support. Instead, this is the temptation to presume upon the Father's promised protection. It was a temptation to pride, the siren song of *self-adulation*.

The subtle deceiver resorted to Scripture in presenting this final temptation to the Lord, quoting from Psalms 91:11, 12. Mark's brief reference to the temptation says that angels were ministering to Jesus while He was being tempted. Possibly this prompted Satan's selection of the passage from the Psalms. Yet he handily omitted seven words that lay in the midst of the verses quoted—*"to keep thee in all thy ways."* Our Lord had to determine whether the voice He heard was from above or from the devil. In His ministry, He would do rather spectacular things, such as multiply the loaves, raise the dead, and walk on the water. But a motive of service that would glorify God lay behind each miracle; He could see no such motive in the suggestion Satan offered and so rebuked him: "Ye shall not tempt the Lord your God" (Deuteronomy 6:16).

Teaching in the Spirit's Power (vv. 13–15) Moffatt's version captures the sense of Luke's meaning well—"after exhausting every kind of temptation, the devil left him till a fit opportunity arrived." We cannot doubt that the testing was severe, just as is ours, but the Lord won the victory, as we are promised in 1 Corinthians 10:13.

In summary, it can be seen that the temptations came to Jesus from outside His person. He met them each with the revealed Word of God and Satan could not defeat that kind of authority. The temptations show these truths about the devil. He is the ruler over the kingdoms of this world and is by nature one who tempts man to evil. He has his power by grant from a higher authority and he desires worship, jealously craves it. He has access to religious halls of worship (the Temple) and knows at least some Scripture. He knows man's weaknesses and works on those vulnerable points. He speaks to the inner thoughts and the spirit of man. But, comforting thought, he does not hang on forever; his visitations are seasonal. In overcoming him, it should be noted that the power of the Spirit is absolutely essential.

Having concluded the temptation account, Luke hurries to introduce the auspicious event in Nazareth. In doing so, He seems to be saying that Jesus returned directly from the wilderness to His hometown and the Sabbath day encounter. But in comparing the remaining three Gospels, it is plain that Luke has chosen to skip over the earliest ministry of Jesus in Galilee. Only John records this. During this time, which may have been a six-month period, Jesus called Andrew, Peter, Philip, and Nathanael as disciples, visited Cana and Capernaum, went to Jerusalem for the Passover and cleansed the Temple for the first time (meeting with Nicodemus while there) and then ministered in Samaria on the way to Galilee. "Rapidly the report of what He had done at Cana, the fame of His marvelous words at Jerusalem, Samaria, and other places spread through all the central districts of the Holy Land," notes one commentator. This helps explain Luke's words in verse 15: "And he taught in their synagogues, being glorified of all." Returning from the testing experience in the desert, He launched His ministry in a whirlwind, gladly acclaimed by the people.

Applying the Scripture
Ask your class why the temptations of Jesus were included in the Scriptures. You will probably receive several answers:

"To show us how to meet temptation."

"To teach us how the devil operates."

"To show us that the Lord was tempted as we are."

All of these replies are true. Perhaps they can be summed up in one sentence. They were written so that we would know to expect temptation and know how to overcome the tempter.

Some of your class members may not be convinced that a being known as the devil actually exists. In their case, the devil's strategy is working perfectly. If they do not think he exists, they will surely be confused in trying to overcome temptation.

Several approaches might be appropriate in applying this lesson. Some may need to do a topical study in their Bible on the subject of the devil. Suggest that, with the aid of a good concordance, they look up a large selection of verses where the devil (or Satan, or the prince of the power of the air, or Lucifer) is named. Have them write out a part of the verse with the reference and then a brief statement about it. For example:

1 Peter 5:8, 9   "be vigilant; because your adversary the devil, as a roaring lion, walketh about, seeking whom he may devour: Whom resist stedfast in the faith...."   *Satan is out to attack believers. Be alert and resist him.*

Invite one or two in the class to talk about a temptation that they have faced, even if they did not win a victory at the time. Share openly how your class can resist temptations to cheat, to lie, to gossip, to yield to physical pleasures that are forbidden. Some suggestions offered may be:

Make up your mind beforehand; resolutely commit yourself to obey the Lord.

Stay away from people and places of temptation to you.

Realize that you cannot withstand Satan by yourself.

Encourage all class members to study the Scriptures and to memorize portions of the Word—promises especially. "To be forearmed is better than being forewarned!"

Questions for Discussion
Make use of these questions to involve your students in learning and to test their understanding of the lesson.

1. What momentous event in the life of Jesus had taken place just prior to the temptation experience? 2. Why is it important that Luke described Jesus as "being full of the Holy Spirit"? 3. What were the three temptations? How are they typical of the sort of temptations every person experiences? 4. Is it a sin to be tempted? 5. Can you name at least five characteristics of the devil that are revealed in this passage of Scripture? 6. How can Jesus' temptations, and the victory He won over Satan, enable us to withstand the temptations in our lives?

Illustrating the Scripture
Examples and quotations to help the teacher communicate the lesson.

WHO IS THE DEVIL? "The devil's best defense has been his successful delusion of mankind into thinking he does not really exist. If we swallow that lie, we are simply proving how clever he is and how unbelievably naive we humans can be.

"In the Bible, Satan is directly mentioned more than two hundred times. Satan enters the realm of human activity in Genesis 3. In Job 1, he is an oppressor of good people. In Matthew 4, Satan audaciously tempts Jesus. His final incarceration and eternal confinement are described in Revelation 20.

"We have the full story of the fall, the words and the destiny of the devil in Ezekiel 28:12–19. Satan was created an archangel, one of the highest order of God's creation. This description in Ezekiel can only be applied to a superbeing, not a man who ruled Tyre.

"The prophet Isaiah describes the devil's actual fall from his place of honor and glory as one of the archangels. The apostle John supplies more description of Satan's fall in Revelation 12:7–10, 12.

"Not content to be the beautiful, intelligent creature of God's creation and the highest order of angels, Satan aspired to a position of equality with God. His contest seems to have been most specifically with Jesus Christ, although the entire Godhead was challenged. This conflict has endured through the ages and will not be entirely consummated until Satan is cast into the lake of fire for ever and ever. . . .

"The devil is not an influence or an idea or some abstract design. He is a person. Personal names and titles are given to him (Revelation 20:2). Personal acts and attributes are ascribed to him (Isaiah 14:12-15). Jesus dealt with the devil as a person (Matthew 4:1-11) and waged war against him as against a person (Luke 13:16). Paul, in his Epistles, described the believer's battle with Satan as with a real person (Ephesians 6:10-18). The devil is spoken of as possessing personal characteristics—heart, pride, speech, knowledge, power, desire and lusts." (Reprinted by permission of Thomas Nelson Publishers from *Demons: The Answer Book* by Lester Sumrall, Copyright 1979 by the Lester Sumrall Evangelistic Association.)

KNOW YOUR ENEMY! "Enticement to sin attacks you with an open Bible in the solitude of your church as well as upon the streets of Paris or before your TV set. Meet your attacker with the proper and the God-given approach.... Know your enemy!

"If it is the flesh ... flee! If in doubt, read Galatians 5:19-21 and then run for your life. Get out of the place. If the building is on fire, look for the EXIT sign. When trouble is brewing, head for the nearest escape door! God makes the way to escape; we have to run through to the place of safety.

"If your temptation is the world ... fellowship! You are being molded to whomever you yield. The world squeezes! Allow God to remold. Fellowship with Christ and hence ... occupied with Him is your solid defense against the world system of greed, ambition, selfishness and pleasure.

"If tempted by Satan ... fight! Stand in God's strength and let him have both barrels. Resist. This is no time to run. Hold all ground gained. But I warn you, don't go into the ring with this enemy barehanded. Grab the Sword of the Spirit. As soon as Satanic temptation hits you, start swinging the Word. It has never lost a man yet. 'More than conquerors through him....' " (Foster, Robert D., *The Challenge*, Colorado Springs, Colorado.)

Topics for Youth

"THE DEVIL MADE ME DO IT"?—The flip phrase doesn't seem very funny when people realize that an evil spiritual being is behind the violence in modern society. In early 1981, three years after David Berkowitz had pleaded guilty to a series of "Son of Sam" murders, reporter Maury Terry of Gannett News Service made the following disclosure:

" 'David Berkowitz says he did not kill alone.

" 'In a series of signed statements and letters he said the Son of Sam murders that terrorized New York in 1976-77, to which he pleaded guilty in 1978, were committed by members of a satanic cult he belonged to, the Westchester Rockland Newspapers reported....'

"In the letters, sent to this reporter, he also described details of the cult's operation, plans and activities....

"According to Berkowitz, the Yonkers (N.Y.) cult included both male and female members. The group practiced a variety of rituals and followed the teaching of 'occultists Eliphas Levi and Aleister Crowley, as well as certain concepts as Black Magic, ancient Druidism, the Order of the Golden Dawn and the Basque witches of Spain'."

IS IT REALLY HARMLESS?—"Much of Satan's activity dazzles the senses. It seems so harmless. But is it?

"When one of our three sons was thirteen, he and his friends became enamored with the Beatles's music for a time. Word got around high school that there was a secret message on one of their records if it were played backwards, so the boys tried it. All Sunday afternoon they tried to decipher a message.

"My wife and I were sitting downstairs that evening as my son rushed into the room, frightened, and cried, 'Dad, the devil's in my room!'

"I didn't know what to make of it. 'Well, if he's there, then you're going to have to tell me how he got there,' I said.

"He told me what he and his friends had been doing. I could see that he was in no shape to return to the room, so I prayed with him and told him he would sleep with his mother and I would go upstairs to his room.

"When I reached the room I knew a devil was there. The feeling was strange. It made my flesh seem to crawl. But I had dealt with the devil before and so I wasted no time in taking charge. Slamming the door, I said, 'You wicked devil, what right do you have coming into my house! This house is cleansed by the blood of Jesus Christ. I want you to know I've already claimed the covering of Jesus' blood for my son, and now I'm ordering you to get out of this house and never return. Furthermore, I'm sleeping in this room and I will not be bothered by you. I'm not afraid of you; now get out, in the name of Jesus.'

"I slept in my son's room that night, and the devil never bothered us again." (Reprinted by permission of Thomas Nelson Publishers from *Demons: The Answer Book* by Lester Sumrall, Copyright 1979 by the Lester Sumrall Evangelistic Association.)

UNIT III

Jesus' Ministry Through Teaching

LESSON 5   **JANUARY 2**

Teaching About Forgiveness

Background Scripture: Luke 7:36–50
Devotional Reading: Luke 5:17–26

Luke 7:36–50
36 And one of the Pharisees desired him that he would eat with him. And he went into the Pharisee's house, and sat down to meat.
37 And, behold, a woman in the city, which was a sinner, when she knew that Jesus sat at meat in the Pharisee's house, brought an alabaster box of ointment,
38 And stood at his feet behind him weeping, and began to wash his feet with tears, and did wipe them with the hairs of her head, and kissed his feet, and anointed them with the ointment.
39 Now when the Pharisee which had bidden him saw it, he spake within

himself, saying, This man, if he were a prophet, would have known who and what manner of woman this is that toucheth him: for she is a sinner.

40 And Jesus answering said unto him, Simon, I have somewhat to say unto thee. And he saith, Master, say on.

41 There was a certain creditor which had two debtors: the one owed five hundred pence, and the other fifty.

42 And when they had nothing to pay, he frankly forgave them both. Tell me therefore, which of them will love him most?

43 Simon answered and said, I suppose that he, to whom he forgave most. And he said unto him, Thou hast rightly judged.

44 And he turned to the woman, and said unto Simon, Seest thou this woman? I entered into thine house, thou gavest me no water for my feet: but she hath washed my feet with tears, and wiped them with the hairs of her head.

45 Thou gavest me no kiss: but this woman since the time I came in hath not ceased to kiss my feet.

46 My head with oil thou didst not anoint: but this woman hath anointed my feet with ointment.

47 Wherefore I say unto thee, Her sins, which are many, are forgiven; for she loved much: but to whom little is forgiven, the same loveth little.

48 And he said unto her, Thy sins are forgiven.

49 And they that sat at meat with him began to say within themselves, Who is this that forgiveth sins also?

50 And he said to the woman, Thy faith hath saved thee; go in peace.

KEY VERSE: "Wherefore I say unto thee, Her sins, which are many, are forgiven; for she loved much: but to whom little is forgiven, the same loveth little." Luke 7:47.

Home Daily Bible Readings
Dec. 27   M.   The Authority of Jesus, Luke 4:16–30.
Dec. 28   T.   His Authority Demonstrated, Luke 4:31–37.
Dec. 29   W.   Jesus' Love for All People, Luke 4:38–44.
Dec. 30   T.   Leaving Everything to Follow Jesus, Luke 5:1–11.
Dec. 31   F.   Which Is Easier, Luke 5:17–26.
Jan. 1   S.   They Found the Slave Well, Luke 7:1–10.
Jan. 2   S.   Teaching About Forgiveness, Luke 7:36–50.

Lesson Aim: As a result of this lesson the members of your class should be more confident that God has freely forgiven them and they should take time this week to consider how much God has forgiven them.

LESSON OUTLINE
Background to the Scripture
Looking at the Scripture Text
  I. Two People in Need of Forgiveness (Luke 7:36-39)
  II. The Fact of Forgiveness (Luke 7:40-43)
  III. The Effect of Forgiveness (Luke 7:44-47)
  IV. The Forgiver (Luke 7:48-50)
Applying the Scripture

Background to the Scripture

From the previous lesson's close look at the temptation experience, we move now to five lessons on the teaching ministry of Jesus—teaching about forgiveness, compassion, priorities, lostness, and stewardship.

The discussion of forgiveness could grow out of many of the experiences and teachings of our Lord. As we shall see, this particular one is inspired by an early reputation he received as a "friend of publicans and sinners." The *Expositor's Greek Testament* says of today's Scripture:

"This section, peculiar to Luke, one of the golden evangelic incidents we owe to him, is introduced here with much tact, as it serves to illustrate how Jesus came to be called the friend of publicans and sinners, and to be calumniated as such, and at the same time to show the true nature of the relations He sustained to these classes. It serves further to exhibit Jesus as One whose genial, gracious spirit could bridge gulfs of social cleavage, and make Him the friend, not of one class only, but of all classes, the friend of *man*, not merely of the degraded."

Looking at the Scripture Text

Two People in Need of Forgiveness (vv. 36-39)   This is one of three occasions described by Luke telling of the Lord going to dine as a guest in the home of a Pharisee. The others, treated in the eleventh and fourteenth chapters, took place in an atmosphere much more caustic than this event; the legalistic sect had not quite taken its measure of Jesus when Simon (v. 30) invited Him home for a meal. As the preceding verses show, the Pharisees had made up their minds that John the Baptist had nothing to offer them. They were well on their way to closing their minds toward Jesus. Possibly Simon had asked Jesus to go to his home so that he and his fellow Pharisees could reach a persuasion about the identity of the young rabbi from Nazareth.

This dinner probably took place in Capernaum. We should not confuse it with the story of Mary of Bethany which, though similar in some respects, is agreed upon by scholars as a different event altogether (*see* Matthew 26, Mark 14, John 12).

Jesus, having acquired the reputation of being a friend of sinners and publicans, a class of people from whom the Pharisees always maintained a respectable distance, accepted Simon's invitation. He never turned down an opportunity to do some good.

Understanding the prevailing customs in Palestine is important for us if we would know what went on in Simon's house. A dinner guest, on arriving, would leave his sandals at the door and proceed to the room set aside for dining. If several guests were invited, there might be three tables laden with food joined in the form of a U. On one side of each table, toward the walls, couches were arranged capable of "seating" three or four guests each. On these, the guests and their host reclined with their feet turned outward. The Jews had learned this posture "from their various masters, the Persians, the Greeks, and the Romans," says the *Expositor's New Testament.* The opposite "open" side of the tables allowed servants to come and go as they served the food.

Such a feast was usually not a private affair. As the various mealtime experiences narrated in the Gospels show, people from the town were free to look in or enter. On occasion, benches were provided along the walls for their use. A popular teacher such as Jesus would draw a number of onlookers desiring to hear what He had to say.

On this occasion, a woman of the city who had an immoral reputation entered Simon's house, probably with the group of guests so as not to be singled out and expelled before she had accomplished her purpose. She had come to pour perfume on Jesus, perhaps intending to anoint His head, and she evidently went directly to Jesus soon after He had reclined at the table. But there she lost her composure completely. Tears flooded down her cheeks and fell on Jesus' feet. It wasn't going at all as she had planned. Instinctively, she bent over and taking her long, flowing hair began wiping the tear-stained feet. Intense devotion to Jesus, being this close to Him, caused her to bend further and kiss His feet again and again. Only then did she regain her composure enough to pour out the perfume. She spoke not a word as the pungent fragrance wafted over the room.

All of this caught the steely gaze of Simon, the other key figure in the story. Two more opposite characters could not be imagined—a shameless, disheveled prostitute and a peacock-proud religionist.

Luke's use of the word *behold* connotes something of the shock Simon felt. The woman's appearance broadcast the fact of her loose ways. Luke records that Simon wondered to himself that this "prophet" would not know what kind of woman was "touching" him, the implication being that *if* He knew He would tell her to keep her distance.

The Fact of Forgiveness (vv. 40–43) While Simon wondered that Jesus could not read character, Jesus read Simon's thoughts. Interestingly, Luke says He "answered" Simon. The expression of self-righteous disapproval was written all over his face.

Clearly Jesus had to do something. The weeping, affectionate woman at His feet had probably gotten the attention of all in the room. There was an uneasy quiet as guests muffled their comments to one another. Jesus skillfully opened the conversation in a way to respect the dignity of both the woman and Simon while at the same time driving home His point to both.

The parable He told requires no explanation. Most versions tell us the sums forgiven were 500 and 50 denarii and that a single denarius was equivalent then to one day's wages. Neither party could pay their debt. Both were "forgiven" (debt cancelled) all. But Jesus' question was surprising: "Which of them will love him most?" using the word *agape* for the highest form of love.

The Effect of Forgiveness (vv. 44-47) Only at this point, did the Lord turn and look upon the woman. Gesturing toward her He drew a stinging comparison between the Pharisee's "cold courtesy" and her voluntary and abundant display of hospitality.

"Thou gavest me no water for my feet." Simon had evidently omitted the customary basin of water and towel for the guests. He himself may have been under scrutiny by other Pharisees, possibly from Jerusalem, to spy on Jesus. A fearing man, Simon dared not show too much approval of Jesus. But the woman washed Jesus' feet with her tears and wiped them with her hair.

"Thou gavest me no kiss." The kiss on the cheek when greeting a guest on his or her arrival was as commonplace as a handshake in our day—or as a kiss still is in many cultures. The host had withheld this obvious token of hospitality. But the woman more than made up for it. The expression Jesus used of her repeated kisses is found in the New Testament only when speaking of Judas (Matthew 26:49), of the prodigal's father (Luke 15:20) and of the Ephesian elders (Acts 20:37) when they knew they were saying goodby to Paul for the last time.

"My head with oil thou didst not anoint." After being exposed to the hot Palestinian sun, to have one's head anointed with oil was indeed a welcome part of the usual greeting. Wealthy Simon had not bothered to pour the inexpensive olive oil on Jesus' head. But the woman anointed His feet with a perfume. Some have concluded that she had paid for it with her earnings as a prostitute. It was a treasured possession to her, but she lavished it on Jesus.

So that Simon would not miss His point, Jesus said, "Her sins, which are many, are forgiven." Identifying her with the debtor who owed the 500 denarii, He said, "for she loved much." The NIV translation of His next words is helpful—"he who has been forgiven little loves little." The fact, He said, was that whatever she had done before, she was now forgiven. And the effect of that forgiveness was love. All the dammed-up emotions of a sinful life gushed out in love to the One who had forgiven her.

The Forgiver (vv. 48-50) The unnamed woman had perhaps only recently been changed, probably as a result of hearing Jesus teach. The important message of her actions, and the parable, was the keen sense of needing forgiveness. Great sinners are always that way. She had already been forgiven when her heart was changed. The profusive show of love for the Teacher proved her forgiveness. But she needed to hear His words, "Thy sins are forgiven." Simon had little or no sense of even needing to be forgiven.

As in other contexts, when Jesus uttered the fateful words, "Your sins have been forgiven" (note the past tense), the dinner guests were even more alarmed. This was an exercise of Jesus' unique personhood. He was assuming a position in their thinking dangerously close to Deity. Whenever He did this, His audience would be divided as they were at Simon's house.

But Jesus ignored their dis-ease and finished with the woman who stood, quiet and listening, at His feet. "Thy faith hath saved thee; go in peace." That is, "depart in a lasting condition of peace." To others, her love so demonstrably shown was the proof of her forgiveness. To the woman, as she disappeared into the night, the peace "that passeth understanding" was forgiveness' abiding effect.

To be forgiven is to be saved. The *Pulpit Commentary* comments: "We can conceive the joy of Paul when this 'memory of the Master' came across him. It so admirably illustrates what this great teacher felt was his Master's mind on the all-important subject—the freeness and universality of salvation." This universal and free salvation, as we have seen, is a distinguishing characteristic of Luke's Gospel.

Applying the Scripture
At the close of your class period suggest several relevant applications your students may draw from this text. Recommend they choose one that speaks to their own personal needs.
1. Sensing Our Sinfulness—Jesus was as concerned for Simon as He was for the woman. He held her up as an example because she knew she was a great sinner. Simon's sins, though not at all like the woman's, were just as great, were they not? Only, he did not know that. He seems largely self-satisfied. A lot of church members are that way. We are not aware of how sinful we are because we have "respectable" sins. Therefore we miss out on knowing how much we have been forgiven. And as a result, we don't love our Lord as we should.

Discuss in class what can be done about this.
2. Knowing That We Are Forgiven—One of the most common needs people have in any age is an assurance that they are forgiven. It seems that people need for God to write in the heavens the words—*You Are Forgiven!* But He does not have to. Point out to your class the words of Jesus to the woman—"Thy sins are forgiven" and then have them read aloud His closing message to her in verse 50. Ask the class if they do not see that the point of the parable was that God's forgiveness is entirely free. If it is free then all we have to do is believe Him, and keep on believing Him every day. Encourage any students who have a problem with this to study 1 John 1:9 and memorize it along with verse 50.
3. Being a Friend of Sinners—Would you go to a "block party" to be a friend to your neighbors, even if everyone were drinking beer and they were playing rock music on their radios? Would you accept an invitation to lunch with someone whom you know would order cocktails—just so you could show them love? Would you have gone to the house of one who seemed to be your enemy, as Jesus did?

Open this subject for discussion. Perhaps someone has a real-life illustration to share. Ask someone to point out the significant steps Jesus took to communciate His meaning while at the same time showing love and respect.
4. Practicing Hospitality—Perhaps someone has an experience to share similar to the dinner at Simon's, where they received the cold shoulder instead of warm hospitality for some reason. Or, someone may be willing to share a time when they were less than hospitable with guests. This could be for religious or racial or other reasons. Invite those who are interested in this subject to examine the words of Jesus closely in Matthew 25:34-46, and to consider what Paul wrote in Romans 12:13, 1 Timothy 3:2 and Titus 1:8. Peter may have had this incident in Simon's house in mind when he said "Use hospitality one to another without grudging" (1 Peter 4:9).

Questions for Discussion
Make use of these questions to involve your students in learning and to test their understanding of the lesson.
1. Why do you think Jesus' going to eat with a Pharisee was worthy of mention?   2. In the parable, who is the money lender? Who might the two debtors in the story be?   3. Why would Simon be expected to give Jesus water for His feet, or greet Him with a kiss or anoint His head with oil?   4. As Jesus compared the one forgiven much with the one forgiven little, what do you think was the point He was making?   5. How did Jesus communicate His gentle rebuke to Simon without rudeness?   6. By her actions, what did the woman prove?   7. Why did the guests react negatively when Jesus told the woman she had been forgiven?

Illustrating the Scripture
Examples and quotations to help the teacher communicate the lesson.
PERFUMES "Perfumes were associated with almost every action and event in the life of the ancients," says the Rev. Hugh Macmillan. "The free use of them was peculiarly delightful and refreshing to the Orientals. A bouquet of fragrant flowers was carried in the hand; or rooms were fumigated with the odorous vapors of burning resins; or the body was anointed with oil mixed with the aromatic qualities of some plant extracted by boiling; or scents were worn about the person in gold or silver boxes, or in alabaster vials in which the delicious aroma was best preserved. Beds, garments, hair, and articles of furniture were perfumed with myrrh, aloes, and cinnamon; and so indispensable were perfumes considered to the feminine toilet, that the Talmud directs the apportioning of one-tenth of a bride's dowry for their purchase. When entertainments were given, the rooms were fumigated; and it was customary for a servant to attend every guest as he seated himself, and anoint his head, sprinkle his person with rose-water or apply incense to his face and beard; and so entirely was the use of perfumes on such occasions in accordance with the customs of the people, that the Savior reproached Simon for the omissions of this mark of attention, leaving it to be performed by a

woman." (From *Biblical Things Not Generally Known*, published in 1879 in London.)

HE UNDERSTOOD THE MEANING OF THE VERSE: "Her many sins were forgiven—for she loved much."—An engineering student on the campus of Texas University was one of the most active members of the Inter-Varsity chapter. He also was a part of the core group of Navigators seeking to disciple other students and he regularly attended the meetings of the Baptist Student Union on campus. When the Campus Crusade for Christ representative asked him to give his testimony at a dormitory, Jim was always willing.

One day Jim expressed aloud a thought he was having. He had realized that his religious involvement was a bit much. Without assuming an attitude of pride at all, he admitted that he just couldn't do enough to show his love for his Lord. When he looked around and compared his life with that of the other Christian students, he couldn't help wonder if he were a fanatic. But then he discovered the verse quoted above, and he knew he had his answer. Jim looked at the lack of enthusiasm in the lives of "good Christian kids" on campus and realized that many of them were the products of Christian homes and they had never known the sinful life he had experienced. Older than most of them, he had joined the navy after finishing high school and had lived purely for personal pleasure. He had married a young girl after a tempestuous love affair and then had left her. Only after a number of years of this kind of life did he find Christ and the love for which he was longing. "I guess I just realize what a sinner I was and that Christ has now forgiven all my sin," he said. "I've never been so happy as I am now that Christ is in my heart."

Topics for Youth
WHAT OTHERS HAVE SAID ABOUT FORGIVENESS—

"To err is human, to forgive divine"—Alexander Pope.

"Nothing in this lost world bears the impress of the Son of God so surely as forgiveness"—Alice Cary.

"Dynamic psychology (teaches) that we can achieve inner health only through forgiveness—the forgiveness not only of others but also of ourselves"—Joshua Loth Liebman.

"If his conditions are met, God is bound by his Word to forgive any man or any woman of any sin because of Christ"—Billy Graham.

"The noblest vengeance is to forgive"—an English Proverb.

"Humanity is never so beautiful as when praying for forgiveness or else forgiving another"—Jean Paul Richter.

"THE ONLY SOLUTION TO THE PROBLEM OF TRANSGRESSION IS FORGIVENESS—With God, forgiveness is complete; we need never be troubled by guilt again. 'As far as the east is from the west, so far hath he removed our transgressions from us' (Psalms 103:12).

"We must beware of continual fretting and brooding over past sins. If we have confessed and have asked forgiveness, let us not continue to condemn ourselves. To do so indicates a lack of faith. Be as gracious with yourself as God is with you. Paul said, 'Therefore being justified by faith, we have peace with God through our Lord Jesus Christ.... There is therefore now no condemnation to them which are in Christ Jesus, who walk not after the flesh, but after the Spirit" (Romans 5:1; 8:1).

"The third source of guilt is closely related to the second—regret and sorrow. Many people browbeat themselves. They are broken and unable to function properly, sad of countenance and heart because of their past. It is true that we have all made mistakes in the past, but when we have found forgiveness, we need also to forget. The Apostle Paul is our example. Admitting that he had made mistakes, he said, 'One thing I do, forgetting the things which are behind, and stretching forward to the things which are before, I press on toward the goal unto the prize of the high calling of God in Christ Jesus' (Philippians 3:13, 14).... Forgiveness of sin involves more than God's willingness to forgive us. It also involves our willingness to accept God's forgiveness and to forget the past." (Used with permission of Zondervan Publishing House from *The Silent Thousands Suddenly Speak* by Charles E. Blair, Copyright 1968.)

LESSON 6   JANUARY 9

Teaching About Compassion

Background Scripture: Luke 7:11–23; 10:25–37
Devotional Reading: Luke 6:6–11

Luke 10:25–37

25 And, behold, a certain lawyer stood up, and tempted him, saying, Master, what shall I do to inherit eternal life?
26 He said unto him, What is written in the law? how readest thou?
27 And he answering said, Thou shalt love the Lord thy God with all thy heart, and with all thy soul, and with all thy strength, and with all thy mind; and thy neighbour as thyself.
28 And he said unto him, Thou hast answered right: this do, and thou shalt live.
29 But he, willing to justify himself, said unto Jesus, And who is my neighbour?
30 And Jesus answering said, A certain man went down from Jerusalem to Jericho, and fell among thieves, which stripped him of his raiment, and wounded him, and departed, leaving him half dead.
31 And by chance there came down a certain priest that way: and when he saw him, he passed by on the other side.

32 And likewise a Levite, when he was at the place, came and looked on him, and passed by on the other side.
33 But a certain Samaritan, as he journeyed, came where he was: and when he saw him, he had compassion on him.
34 And went to him, and bound up his wounds, pouring in oil and wine, and set him on his own beast, and brought him to an inn, and took care of him.
35 And on the morrow when he departed, he took out two pence, and gave them to the host, and said unto him, Take care of him; and whatsoever thou spendest more, when I come again, I will repay thee.
36 Which now of these three, thinkest thou, was neighbour unto him that fell among the thieves?
37 And he said, He that shewed mercy on him. Then said Jesus unto him, Go, and do thou likewise.

KEY VERSE: "Thou shalt love the Lord thy God with all thy heart, and with all thy soul, and with all thy strength, and with all thy mind; and thy neighbour as thyself." Luke 10:27.

Home Daily Bible Readings		
Jan. 3	M.	A Demonstration of Compassion, Luke 7:11–17.
Jan. 4	T.	From Bondage to Freedom, Luke 8:26–39.
Jan. 5	W.	A Plea for Help, Luke 8:40–42a; 49–56.
Jan. 6	T.	Jesus' Response to Faith, Luke 8:42b–48.
Jan. 7	F.	Because He Cared, Luke 9:1–6.
Jan. 8	S.	Feeding the Hungry, Luke 9:10–17.
Jan. 9	S.	Who Is My Neighbour? Luke 10:25–37.

Lesson Aim: That students will commit themselves to becoming neighbors who are more merciful, compassionate persons.

LESSON OUTLINE
Background to the Scripture
Looking at the Scripture Text
  I. The Question of Eternal Life (Luke 10:25–28)
 II. The Question of Loving a Neighbor (Luke 10:29–35)
III. The Question of Being a Neighbor (Luke 10:36, 37)
Applying the Scripture

Background to the Scripture

Jesus "rejoiced greatly." Just prior to recording the enduring story of the Good Samaritan, Luke reports a high moment of joy in the life of our Lord. If we doubt that, all we have to do is note the times the Evangelist mentions joy in verses 17–22 of chapter 10.

And what was it that gave Jesus such joy? The joy of His disciples! The seventy had returned from their first ministry trip to say that they had experienced the power of God firsthand. The air was electric with excitement as the new followers testified of the victory they had tasted. Encouraging them to reserve their highest joy for the sheer knowledge that their names were "written in heaven" (v. 20), Jesus burst out in an unusual expression of praise, thanking His Father for revealing Himself to these "babes" while hiding the things of the Spirit from the "wise and learned."

Almost as if to illustrate the spiritual blindness of the intelligentsia, Luke introduces the questioning lawyer. This event, though similar to that recorded in Matthew 22:35ff and Mark 12:28ff is of a separate and earlier happening in Jesus' teaching ministry.

Looking at the Scripture Text

The Question of Eternal Life (vv. 25-28) The story of the Good Samaritan, preserved for us only by Luke, came to be told as the indirect result of a question put to Jesus by a lawyer. Some have suggested that the question arose in one of the synagogues of Judea, because the lawyer "stood up." Other commentators think the lawyer may have been among those gathered in a home and a few even speculate that it may have happened in the home of Mary and Martha of Bethany since the next incident in Luke's narrative takes place there and since Bethany was on the road leading from Jericho to Jerusalem.

The lawyer asked Life's Greatest Question. But it appears that he did so insincerely to "test" Jesus' ability as a teacher as well as His orthodoxy. Moses' Law was the authority in the land, in so far as every Jew was concerned. This expert in the Law wanted to see if the Galileean Rabbi would uphold the Law. He may have been doing what many of the religious leadership later did—laying a trap so as to accuse Jesus.

As so often happened when Jesus was questioned, He replied with a question. "What is written in the Law? . . . How do you read it?" (NIV). The lawyer did not fumble for an answer. He answered directly from the Book of Deuteronomy, from the *Shema* used daily in a devout Hebrew's worship—"And thou shalt love the Lord thy God with all thine heart, and with all thy soul, and with all thy might" (Deuteronomy 6:5), adding with it the words of Leviticus 19:18—"and thou shalt love thy neighbour as thyself." By the first century, the two concepts of religious and ethical duties had become wedded. The highest duty of man was to love God with heart and soul and might (the New Testament added "mind") and his highest ethical duty was summed up in the seven words: "Love your neighbour as you love yourself." The man had reasoned that if these were the requirements God made of man, then to live up to them would surely be the way to gain eternal life.

Before rushing on to what follows, it would be good to stop and consider the two great commandments. What other "god" asks its worshipers to love?

To be devoted to a god, yes; to revere it, yes; even to sacrifice, yes. But only the Lord God asks love. This must be because He is love.

Note that He demands full rendering of all the powers He has given man—the affections, the will, all of his physical energy, and even his intellect. He asks that we utilize all our powers all of the time as expressions of love to Him. Jesus' answer in the present tense shows this—"continually do this" (v. 28). And this isn't all. He demands that we love our fellow man with the same depth of feeling and concern we give ourselves.

If Jesus seems here to approve a salvation by good works it is because of what is left unsaid. (Note Paul's answer to almost the same question in Acts 16:30, 31.) If anyone could love God in this way all of the time and love his or her neighbor as himself, then he would surely please God. But no one has ever done this or ever will—except Jesus. The man must have seen this, for his next question indicates that while he may have assumed he met all of the Law's requirements for the love of God, he was not sure he was doing right by his neighbor.

The Question of Loving a Neighbor (vv. 29-35) This man does not have a monopoly on asking the wrong questions; we do our share of it also. But he batted zero on the questions he asked here. His first one should have been: "In whom must I trust to inherit eternal life?" and his second question ought to have been, "How can I prove myself a neighbor?"

If the man was honest, he knew he gave favored treatment to some people while holding himself aloof from others. Perhaps his conscience was awakening to a responsibility toward the common folk or even the despised Roman occupational forces. It is likely that he had not even considered any responsibility he ought to feel toward such persons as the Samaritans.

The story of the Good Samaritan must have imprinted itself indelibly on the man's conscience. If it has all of the moral force it contains today after 2,000 years, we can imagine the force with which this story arrested its hearers, uttered as it was from the pure lips of Jesus, His clear eyes giving expression to the sorrowful treatment of man to his fellow man. The story is not so much a parable as it is an example. It may well have been a real event.

The certain man in Jesus' words was surely a Jew though Luke's omission of that fact allows for the story's universal application; it could have been a German or an Hispanic-American, a Mongolian or a Quechua. This "Jew" was traveling, probably from Jerusalem to Jericho on the winding road that took all its travelers to the Jordan Valley, some 3,300 feet below Jerusalem's lofty heights. This road had earned the name "The Way of Blood" because of the frequency with which robbers victimized those who traveled this way. Falling among thieves (that is, they were all around him), the man was robbed, stripped, and beaten. Half-dead he lay beside the path. One commentator says, "He will soon be *whole dead* unless someone comes to his help—he cannot help himself or move."

A priest was the first traveler to happen upon this wounded, bleeding man. Jericho was a residence of many priests and it is safe to assume that this priest was returning to his home after officiating at services in the Temple (*see* Luke 1:23). Seeing the man, he may have presumed him dead and not willing to defile himself by touching a dead body, he passed on.

The next traveler, a Levite, proved even more heartless. This priest of a "second rank" evidently came right to the man, looked him over, and then stepped aside. That Jesus cast these two priests in a bad light seems evidence that it was a factual story. He usually refrained from criticizing the Jewish religious leaders, except when confronting them to their faces.

Like racial hatred wherever it is found, the animosity between Jew and Samaritan had a long history. Samaritans were a racially mixed people. When Assyria defeated Samaria in approximately 700 B.C., its king took the leading families of Israel out of the country and brought in foreigners, from Babylon and Syria and elsewhere. These people intermarried with the peasant remnant of Israel. Though remaining monotheistic, they did not join in the worship of Jehovah in Jerusalem. They feuded with the Jews who returned with Nehemiah to rebuild Jerusalem and later erected a temple of their own at Mt. Gerizim to prevent a reunification with the Jews in Judea. John's Gospel tells us that in Jesus' days the Jews "have no dealings with the Samaritans" (John 4:9).

One of this hated "half-breed" happened along the road and showed compassion for the beaten man. Luke says he bound up his wounds, pouring in a mixture of oil and wine—oil to soothe the wounds, the wine to serve as an antiseptic. He cared for the stranger, placing him on his beast, taking him to an inn where he remained with him and leaving money with the innkeeper the next day so that the man could have whatever was needed.

The Question of Being a Neighbor (vv. 36, 37) Jesus' story shattered the lawyer's attempt to discriminate between "neighbors." Jesus turned the lawyer's question around and tossed it back in his lap: "Which of these three do you think proved to be a neighbor . . . ?" (NASB.)

The answer to Jesus' question was obvious. What is not obvious is that the kind of love the Samaritan showed was the counterpart of his love to God. A nineteenth century commentator has expressed it well: "Love requires the perception of what is lovable. It requires, too, that there shall be some link connecting one personality with another. But to summon us to love the neighbor, in Christ's sense of the phrase, is to insist on love before the discovery of any such link. . . . We cannot love by commandment; we cannot go beyond the prompting of our own natures. Some we can embrace with affection, but from others we turn away. . . .

"Christ, in commanding, has indicated the way of assistance. In the sentence reported by St. Matthew, 'The second commandment is *like to* the first.' To the first, 'Thou shalt love the Lord thy God . . .' we must look for the significance of the measure which the second proposes, 'Thou shalt love thy neighbour as thyself.'

"What do we mean when we speak of loving God? Surely we mean a delight in God for what he is; for his righteousness, his goodness, his holy and loving will.... Such a longing necessarily takes beyond self. It embraces the desire that the Eternal Name be hallowed, the eternal will be done in earth as it is in heaven, and the eternal kingdom of the Father come.

"In the love of God, our love for our friend has been quickened and intensified.... Observe, when we have gained the second commandment through the first; when the love of the neighbor proceeds out of the love whose first and greatest is God, such links are always at hand. There are interests and sympathies which serve as points of approach to all, to any one."

The lawyer could not bring himself to utter the word *Samaritan* in reply. "He that showed mercy" was his answer. The compassionate Master commanded—"Go and do the same," as a lifelong commitment. He says the same to us.

Applying the Scripture
Help your class members hear the Savior, as if speaking to them alone. "Go and do thou likewise."

Ask your class to imagine that they are the lawyer who asked the questions. Have them see themselves as the one to whom he addressed the story of the Good Samaritan.

Ask: Where do you fit in the story? Do you see yourself as the priest, or as the Levite, or as the Samaritan?

Perhaps two or three in the class will be willing to share in their own words how someone in real life has been like the priests or like the Samaritan. It may be an incident from their own experience. To prompt them to remember, suggest they think of a time when they had car trouble and were in need of aid. Or ask them to think of a time when they were too busy to stop and help someone. It may have been someone in their own family—a child needing help with his homework or a husband or wife in need of some individual attention.

Invite a brief discussion of the reasons we give today for not getting involved with a stranger. Some are afraid to serve as a witness to an accident because they know that many people are sued or personally injured in such ways. If some of your class members contend that Christians have to play it safe and protect themselves, ask them if they think the Samaritan took undue risks in stopping to help the stranger on the Jericho road. Ask if Jesus would commend our rationalizations for not taking risks or if He would point us to His own example.

You may want to conclude the discussion with a prayer, confessing the failure of Christians today to show pity on others and asking God to sensitize us for being more compassionate neighbors.

How Do You Develop Compassion?—As a further part of the application, lead the class in a discussion of this question. Some in your class may feel genuinely the need for becoming more compassionate, merciful persons, but they have grown to accept the notion that they are "just not very demonstrative people."

Suggest two approaches (you may want to add more):

1. Pray—If we recognize that we are not very expressive people and that we tend to withhold feelings from others, this is a need for which we can pray. It is not the only thing such a person can do, but it will be a start for him to pray, "Lord, give me Your compassion, let me feel pity and love for others." One man prayed, "Lord, break my heart with the things that break the heart of God."

2. Exercise compassion—Muscles of the body are developed through use. When a person is laid up in bed for a long while, the best therapy for him is to make use of his disabled limbs. Little by little, a weak arm or leg becomes strong through daily exercise. In the same way, if we would develop a merciful life-style, we should begin to do something to help someone in need. If a member of our family needs a good massage, to rub them voluntarily will be to exercise compassion. If we learn of a church member or acquaintance who has entered the hospital, to go visit them is to exercise compassion. By doing the small daily things and praying for a sensitivity to other people, we will find ourselves developing the quality of compassion which so characterizes the Lord Jesus Christ.

Questions for Discussion
Make use of these questions to involve your students in learning and to test their understanding of the lesson.
1. What was the lawyer's original question? How does the wording of his question reveal a wrong understanding? 2. How can you reconcile Jesus' answer with the scriptural teaching that faith alone is the way to eternal life? 3. Where are the two great commandments found in the Old Testament? 4. How do you love God with your mind? 5. What may have been Jesus' reason for including a Samaritan in His story? Why not a Roman or a Greek? 6. How did Jesus turn around the man's second question? 7. Why would Jesus command doing and not emphasize believing? 8. How is Christ like the Good Samaritan?

Illustrating the Scripture
Examples and quotations to help the teacher communicate the lesson.
THE GOOD SAMARITAN Many have expressed the point Jesus made in the story of the Good Samaritan. Wordsworth said, "It is not place, but love, which makes neighborhood." Teresa of Avila said, "Though we do not have our Lord with us in bodily presence, we have our neighbor, who, for the ends of love and loving service, is as good as our Lord Himself."

Another has said, "Neighborhood is coextensive with humanity." Still another said, "Neighbor is as neighbor does." Finally one commentator said: "Failure to keep the commandment doesn't spring from lack of information (who is my neighbor?), but from lack of love."

A man who works in New York City tells the true story of encountering a "Good Samaritan" once, when he became ill in the city. He was walking toward his office in midtown Manhattan when he realized that he was too dizzy to go to work. Ahead of him was Grand Central Station and, knowing that he could gain access to a rest room there, he made for the station. By the time he reached the rest room, his dizziness had brought on nausea. For some time he became immobilized, unable to move for fear of aggravating the nauseous feelings.

Finally, in a weakened condition, he slowly began the ascent from the rest room to the waiting room on the ground level. Two or three men stopped to ask if he was all right, but one young salesman named Nathan took his briefcase and helped him walk to the waiting room. Nathan then went to a refreshment stand and brought back a Coke which the man sipped to help settle his stomach. Making conversation and showing friendship, Nathan asked the man where he wanted to go. "To Penn Station, to return home," was the answer.

After still more waiting, Nathan accompanied the man to the outside door, summoned a taxi, and rode with him to Penn Station. By this time, they had become acquainted with each other. The man, a Christian, learned that Nathan was a Jew. He was working as a salesman, but was in "no rush." Paying the cab fare, he further helped the man find the train for his return trip to New Jersey and didn't leave until the man had safely boarded the train. That Christian will probably never forget "Good Samaritan" Nathan!

LOVE THY NEIGHBOR   "It is a serious thing to live in a society of possible gods and goddesses, to remember that the dullest and most uninteresting person you talk to may one day be a creature which, if you saw it now, you would be strongly tempted to worship, or else a horror and a corruption such as you now meet, if at all, only in a nightmare.

"All day long we are, in some degree, helping each other to one or other of these destinations. It is in the light of these overwhelming possibilities, it is with the awe and the circumspection proper to them, that we should conduct all our dealings with one another, all friendships, all loves, all play, all politics.

"There are no ordinary people. You have never talked to a mere mortal. Nations, cultures, arts, civilization—these are mortal, and their life is to ours as the life of a gnat. But it is immortals whom we joke with, work with, marry, snub, and exploit—immortal horrors or everlasting splendors. This does not mean that we are to be perpetually solemn. We must play. But our merriment must be of that kind (and it is, in fact, the merriest kind) which exists between people who have, from the outset, taken each other seriously—no flippancy, no superiority, no presumption. And our charity must be a real and costly love, with deep feeling for the sins in spite of which we love the sinner—no mere tolerance or indulgence which parodies love as flippancy parodies merriment. Next to the Blessed Sacrament itself, your neighbor is the holiest object presented to your senses." (Reprinted by permission of Macmillan Publishing Company from *The Joyful Christian* by C. S. Lewis, copyright 1977, Macmillan Publishing Co.)

Topics for Youth
GO AHEAD—LOVE YOURSELF!—As a natural instinct, God built into us the quality of self-preservation. A facet of that instinct is self-acceptance. Might we even say: self-love? This truth is implied in today's passage. How can we love our neighbors as we love ourselves, if we don't love ourselves?

This is no proof text either. The Scriptures take for granted that we will love ourselves. Paul wrote to the Ephesians: "Men ought to love their wives just as they love their own bodies . . . (no one ever hates his own body. Instead, he feeds it and takes care of it . . .)" (5:28, 29 TEV).

The teen years are often characterized by a great deal of self-hate. Partly due to peer pressures, partly due to unwise parental nagging, and partly because of an intense idealism, youths today are often down on themselves. It would be good if young people could look through this depressive cloud that hangs over them and see behind it their archenemy—Satan. He is the one who seeks to discourage and destroy them. For fear that self-love and self-esteem will get out of hand and grow into conceited, arrogant attitudes, youths are constantly being told to lower themselves in their own eyes.

Let the truth be shouted: GOD LOVES YOU. HE ACCEPTS YOU. A CERTAIN MEASURE OF SELF-LOVE IS GREAT! A HEALTHY SELF-ESTEEM IS A MARK OF A HEALTHY CHRISTIAN LIFE!"

Loving and accepting yourself just may be the key that will unlock the door and free you to love others with a good Samaritan kind of love.

LESSON 7   JANUARY 16
Teaching About Priorities

Background Scripture: Luke 12:13–40
Devotional Reading: Luke 6:46–49

Luke 12:13–21, 35–40
13 And one of the company said unto him, Master, speak to my brother, that he divide the inheritance with me.
14 And he said unto him, Man, who made me a judge or a divider over you?
15 And he said unto them, Take heed, and beware of covetousness: for a man's life consisteth not in the abundance of the things which he possesseth.

16 And he spake a parable unto them, saying, The ground of a certain rich man brought forth plentifully:
17 And he thought within himself, saying, What shall I do, because I have no room where to bestow my fruits?
18 And he said, This will I do: I will pull down my barns, and build greater; and there will I bestow all my fruits and my goods.
19 And I will say to my soul, Soul, thou hast much goods laid up for many years; take thine ease, eat, drink, and be merry.
20 But God said unto him, Thou fool, this night thy soul shall be required of thee: then whose shall those things be, which thou hast provided?
21 So is he that layeth up treasure for himself, and is not rich toward God.
35 Let your loins be girded about, and your lights burning;
36 And ye yourselves like unto men that wait for their lord, when he will return from the wedding; that when he cometh and knocketh, they may open unto him immediately.
37 Blessed are those servants, whom the lord when he cometh shall find watching: verily I say unto you, that he shall gird himself, and make them to sit down to meat, and will come forth and serve them.
38 And if he shall come in the second watch, or come in the third watch, and find them so, blessed are those servants.
39 And this know, that if the goodman of the house had known what hour the thief would come, he would have watched, and not have suffered his house to be broken through.
40 Be ye therefore ready also: for the Son of man cometh at an hour when ye think not.

KEY VERSE: "Be ye therefore ready also: for the Son of man cometh at an hour when ye think not." Luke 12:40.

Home Daily Bible Readings
Jan. 10   M.   Concerned About Things, Luke 10:38–42.
Jan. 11   T.   God's Supply, Luke 11:1–13.
Jan. 12   W.   A Test of Genuineness, Luke 11:37–44.
Jan. 13   T.   Determining Priorities, Luke 12:1–12.
Jan. 14   F.   Full Barn and Empty Life, Luke 12:13–21.
Jan. 15   S.   Seek God's Kingdom First, Luke 12:22–31.
Jan. 16   S.   Expecting His Return, Luke 12:32–40.

Lesson Aim: That each adult will examine his life and establish priorities to assure readiness for death or the Coming of Christ.

LESSON OUTLINE
Background to the Scripture
Looking at the Scripture Text
  I. The Obsession With Possessions (Luke 12:13-15)
  II. Fools With Wrong Priorities (Luke 12:16-21)
  III. Readiness the Top Priority (Luke 12:35-40)
Applying the Scripture

Background to the Scripture
When we speak of priorities, we are talking about putting things in their proper order. We have in mind a ranking according to importance. "First things first," we say.

In the attempted assassination of President Reagan on March 30, 1981, three other men were wounded besides Mr. Reagan. Jim Brady, the press secretary, was the most critically wounded of all. But Mr. Reagan was rushed to the hospital and was in the emergency room six minutes after the shooting while the other men still lay on the pavement outside the Washington Hilton. Why? It was a simple matter of priorities. In such events, the President takes precedence over all others because of the high office he holds. The unspoken assumption would be that others can do the job of the policemen and the press secretary, but only very few can fulfill the office of the president.

Priorities have to do with choices. Every one of us lives by a set of priorities—some more consciously chosen than others. Today we observe the Lord Jesus as He seeks to give the people of His day priorities to live by. These words spoken over 1,900 years ago are alarmingly relevant today. We should make it our first priority to listen for what He would say to us.

Looking at the Scripture Text
The Obsession With Possessions (vv. 13-15) The individual in the crowd had a way of getting Jesus' attention. Blind Bartimaeus, sitting beside the road as Jesus left Jericho, cried incessantly to the "Son of David" and received his sight. Feisty Zaccheus, perched on the limb of a sycamore tree because he was too short to see Jesus among the throng, was singled out by Jesus and received salvation. A woman plagued by a hemorrhage twelve years touched the hem of Jesus' garment and received healing. All of these, and more, reached out to Jesus as He was passing by and in that one opportunity had their deepest need satisfied.

But the man in our story took advantage of his one chance to address Jesus and what did he ask? "Master, tell my brother he'd better give me my share of the inheritance." Jesus had been teaching a very large crowd and evidently, in the lull between His discourses, the question arose. The unnamed questioner probably had an older brother who (according to the Law; Deuteronomy 21:17) received a double share of the estate and had not given this man his due.

Jesus' reply was sharp. "Man," he said, "who appointed me a judge or an arbiter between you?" (NIV.) The people habitually took these kinds of concerns to their rabbis—and Jesus was considered a rabbi—but there were judges who were to resolve such disputes. Jesus was not going to involve Himself in a petty squabble. That the man asked Him to do it reveals his lack of perception of who the Teacher was.

While Jesus did not pursue the surface problem of the man's inheritance, He did use the occasion to get to the bottom of the issue of worldly possessions. Notice that He turned from addressing "him" to address "them," the people.

Covetousness was and is such an evil that it was singled out for warning in the Ten Commandments: "You shall not covet your neighbour's house; you shall not covet your neighbour's wife, his slave, his slave-girl, his ox, his ass, or anything that belongs to him" (Exodus 20:17 NEB). In the modern translations of verse 15 of our text, we see that Jesus warned against "all kinds" or "every form" of covetousness. The large letters spelling BEWARE OF DOG warn a person of real danger. Jesus placed a BEWARE sign at the front door of covetousness.

Scripture is replete with examples of the Balaams and Achans and Gehazis who ruined their lives because of their obsession with possessions. To His hearers and to us, He declared: "accumulation of material good doesn't equal LIFE." A person's life, He said, is made up of much more than things.

Fools With Wrong Priorities (vv. 16-21) Luke is the only Evangelist to record the Parable of the Rich Fool. There is no condemnation of wealth per se here. Folk often misquote Paul and say, "Money is the root of all evil," but of course Paul said what Scripture consistently teaches: *"the love of money* is the root of all evil" (1 Timothy 6:10, italics added).

The picture Jesus painted of the stupid wealthy man was of one completely wrapped up in himself. Note the "I" and "my" in the story—"what shall I do? . . . I have no room . . . my fruits . . . my barns . . . my fruits . . . my goods." Most of us are concerned with getting more money. Then once we have it, we, like this rich man, worry what to do with it. This man reasoned or debated with himself, "What shall I do?" This portrait is of a man whose "body and soul have become the slaves of his wealth." Blind to the desperate needs of others, he was consumed with the desire for more. He is a man without the compassion Jesus commanded in the lesson on the Good Samaritan.

Such a fool, Jesus said, eventually thinks he has enough. "Lucky man!" he will say to himself. "You have all the good things you need for many years. Take life easy" (v. 19 TEV). But Jesus pointed out two fatal flaws in the materialist's philosophy, flaws that earn him the name *Fool,* a term Jesus did not use lightly (Matthew 5:22).

First, he thought that things would satisfy. To his soul, he says, "you have all the good things," but a man's soulish needs are not satisfied by palatial mansions or silver and gold. A man's soul cries out for relational, emotional, personal satisfaction. Ultimately it cries out for the Person of Christ as Pascal said: "Inside every human heart is a God-shaped vacuum that cannot be filled by any created thing, but only God made known through Jesus Christ."

Second, he forgot that he is not in charge. God says to him, "this night thy soul shall be required of thee." This is a solemn interruption. Literally it reads: "they require" your soul. Perhaps Jesus was alluding to the angels who come for a person at death. The meaning is that, just when he has outfitted his ship for a long cruise, he has to cash in, boat and all. "This man hoped to give death the lie: 'Eat, drink, and be merry, for the future is yours,' " says Frederick Danker in his commentary on Luke. "Before the day was out in which he planned his bigger barns, they changed the wording back—'Eat, drink and be merry, for tomorrow you will be dead.' "

The shame of such a life is that it is not necessary. C. S. Lewis said, "Aim at heaven, and you get earth thrown in; aim at earth and you get neither." The fool could have provided amply for himself while trusting God. Jesus was not denying the rightful place of providing for oneself and one's loved ones; He was warning against piling up riches while not being "rich toward God." On these words, the Pulpit Commentary says such richness includes *"a wealth of right feeling toward God*—reverence, trust and gratitude—*a wealth in qualities which are divine*—righteousness, truth, faithfulness, goodness—and *a wealth in God Himself*—His presence and the transforming power of His Holy Spirit."

Readiness the Top Priority (vv. 35-40)   Jesus' words recorded here, continuing the theme of priorities for living, were spoken primarily to His disciples. The theme of worldly possessions gives way to preparedness. To those early disciples standing in Jesus' presence, this teaching had an immediate meaning with a special future significance. They were to adopt an attitude of living for God in the present, an attitude that would prepare them for the day when Jesus would be taken from them. It would be the attitude that would please God in every generation as the Church waits for His coming again. Jesus symbolized this by two figures of speech: "let your loins be girded about, and your lights burning." They can be summarized as "being engaged in service" and "expecting the Savior."

Engaged in service—Having their "loins girt" refers again to the dress of that day. When doing physical work or running, a man would gather his garments and tuck them into the belt. Jesus, addressing His disciples as "bond slaves" (vv. 37, 38), told them that they were to be as servants awaiting their master's return from a round of wedding feasts (not His own). They were to be busily engaged in their household duties in His absence.

Expecting the Savior—The wedding feast would be at night. The servants, their lamps alight for the services they rendered and immediately accessible for welcoming their master at the first sound of his arrival, were to be ready to usher him in from the dark to his well-lighted house. Though these hearers would not be familiar with the symbolism, such a reference to a wedding became in later Scripture synonymous with Christ's building His Church (Ephesians 5:26, 27; Revelation 19:7-9; 22:17). The "lord" would be so happy, Jesus said, to be greeted by serving, watchful slaves, that he would do something unheard of. Reversing the role of master and servant (seen in its usual customs in Luke 17:7-10) he will "gird himself" with the garments of a servant and wait on his slaves as he would his friends. By using the Beatitude word *blessed*, Jesus placed a premium on the industry and attitude of His servants.

The night customarily was divided into four watches by the Romans. Jesus selected the second and third watches, approximately the hours from 9:00 P.M.—midnight and midnight—3:00 A.M., because those are the most difficult. Servants in the "still and weary hours" were most likely to be overtaken by sleep. He commended those who would remain watchful and active even into the third watch.

In verse 39, the metaphor changes to that of a thief in the night. Climaxing His lesson, He challenged His close followers to be just like the master of the house who, because he did not know when a thief might "dig through" the mud walls of his house, remained alert. This statement is contained in Matthew 24:43, 44. Jesus' talk of a thief in the night must have made quite an impression on the disciples. Peter and John, who would have been in the crowd that day, later wrote similar words (2 Peter 3:10; Revelation 3:3; 16:15) and Paul, possibly hearing this narrative from Luke, warned the Thessalonian church (1 Thessalonians 5:1, 2).

Both "exits" from this life—death and the Coming of Christ—are treated in these words of Jesus, given to stir all men to think about their priorities. We may not live to see Christ come, but we are to be watching for Him and engaged in His work even in this "third watch." Since death could cut us off from our possessions at any time, we can see the urgency of ordering our priorities now to please God.

Applying the Scripture
Before the close of class, give priority to these two priorities! Putting God first and putting things in their order.

The "carry-over" from this lesson into our lives is so obvious that it requires effort to miss it. Each section of the text concludes with a moral.

1. Put God first. Jesus said, "So is he that layeth up treasure for himself, and is not rich toward God." Positively stated, this is, "Put God first." From the negative side, it is, "Don't set your heart on things."

Putting God first, above all, means a right relationship with Him. Perhaps you will want to speak privately with that person in your class who has never identified himself or herself as a believer in Christ. He or she may need someone to ask them about their relationship to Christ. Be ready to point that one to Christ. Explain that the point of Jesus' parable was that we forget God at our peril. If we have not let Christ become our Savior, we are fools who will lose everything at death.

2. Put things in their proper order. Jesus said, "Be ye therefore ready also: for the Son of man cometh at an hour when ye think not." Knowing that Christ's return is imminent, and being freshly reminded that He expects us to be ready, we should not wait to put our house in order. Ask your class to do the following exercise on a separate piece of paper.

List your six personal goals for your life for the next three to five years.
1.
2.
3.
4.
5.
6.

Now, beside each goal write the word that best describes the category: *family, work* (vocation or profession), *spiritual* (Christian growth, service), *personal enrichment,* and *money* (possessions, finances).

Ask each class member to review what they have written. Ask them what their list reveals about their preparedness and their priorities for living. Suggest they make changes after careful review, and then carefully lay plans for carrying out the priorities.

Questions for Discussion
Make use of these questions to involve your students in learning and to test their understanding of the lesson.
1. Why would Jesus not arbitrate the dispute over an inheritance? **2.** What did Jesus' warning about covetousness imply about the man in verse 13? What is covetousness? **3.** What could the man have done with the surplus of his crops? **4.** What does the parable have to teach us regarding the provision of future security via insurance, trusts, and other means? **5.** What is the meaning of the phrase "thy soul shall be required of thee"? **6.** What is it to be "rich toward God"? **7.** What "coming" is Jesus speaking of in verse 40? **8.** What is the significance of His words about a "second watch" and a "third watch"?

Illustrating the Scripture
Examples and quotations to help the teacher communicate the lesson.
"COOL THESE FIRES OF WANTING" Marjorie Holmes says: "Help me not to put too much stock in possessions, Lord. Mere possessions.

"I want things, sure I want things. Life seems to be a continual round of wanting things, from the first toys we fight over as children, on through our thrilled counting of the wedding presents.... Not primarily love and friends and pride in what we can do, but *things.*

"Sometimes I'm ashamed of how much I want things. For my husband and the house and the children. Yes, and for myself. And this hunger is enhanced every time I turn on the TV or walk through a shopping mall. My senses are tormented by the dazzling world of *things.*

"Lord, cool these fires of wanting. Help me to realize how futile is this passion for possession. Because—and this is what strips my values to the bone—one of my best friends died today in the very midst of her possessions.

"The beautiful home she and her husband worked so hard to achieve, finally finished; furnished the way she wanted it, with the best of everything.... The oriental rugs she was so proud of. The formal French sofas. The paintings. The china and glass and handsome silver service.... She has been snatched away, while silently, almost cruelly, they remain.

"Lord, I grieve for my friend. My heart hurts that she had so little time to enjoy her things. Things she had earned and that meant so much to her. But let me learn something from this loss:

"That possessions are meant to enhance life, not to become the main focus of living. That we come into the world with nothing, we leave with nothing.

"Help me not to put too much stock in mere possessions." (Possessions from HOLD ME UP A LITTLE LONGER, LORD, by Marjorie Holmes. Copyright © 1974 by Marjorie Holmes Mighell. Reprinted by permission of Doubleday & Company, Inc.)

BEING READY David Copperfield said, "You'll find us rough, Sir, but you'll find us ready." Can we say that to our Lord and Master?

Missionaries to Ethiopia (and to the Seychelles, and Rwanda and Kenya) told on a recent furlough of the "blessing" of being in a country they knew they might have to exit any day. The reason these Southern Baptist missionaries had served parts of a term in three other places was that the door closed to them in Ethiopia as it did to most foreign missionaries in the mid-70s. Overnight their household furnishings were confiscated and they had to leave Addis Ababa with few of their belongings. In America, they purchased things they would need and found an open door for service in the Seychelles Islands of the Indian Ocean. But as soon as the government there found that they intended to preach the Gospel, they were forbidden to do that, so they returned to the continent of Africa, for a while filling a need in Rwanda. But their hearts longed to return to their people in Ethiopia. In 1980, the chance came and they remain there at this writing.

"It's sort of good in a way," said the wife, "not knowing how long we are going to get work in that country. It keeps us from getting involved in a lot of unimportant things. We major on teaching the people the Bible and training their leaders to guide the Church. We do a lot of one-to-one counseling and recently we were reunited for a weekend retreat with the church leaders out in the country where we lived earlier—but where we can no longer go."

Lord, help us to know we do not have a guarantee of many days to do what You want us to do. Show us what to do today!

Topics for Youth

WHAT CAN MONEY DO FOR YOU?—" 'Millionaires who heartily laugh are rare! What then are they doing if they are not laughing? They are carrying burdens which crush all laughter out of them. They are carrying the thing which promised to carry them,' says Dr. J. H. Jowett.

" 'In 1923, a very important meeting was held at the Edgewater Beach Hotel in Chicago. Attending this meeting were nine of the world's most successful financiers. Those present were: the president of the largest independent steel company, the president of the largest utility company, the president of the largest gas company, the great wheat speculator, the president of the New York Stock Exchange, a member of the President's cabinet, the greatest "bear" in Wall Street, the head of the world's greatest monopoly and the president of the bank of international settlements.

" 'Men who had found *the secret of making money*. Twenty-five years later let's see where these same men are:

" '*Charles Schwab*, died a bankrupt and had lived on borrowed money. *Samuel Insull*, died a fugitive from justice and penniless. *Howard Hopson*, now insane. *Arthur Cutten*, died abroad, insolvent. *Richard Whitney*, recently released from prison. *Albert Fall*, pardoned from prison so he could die at home. *Jesse Livermore*, died a suicide. *Ivar Krueger*, died a suicide. *Leon Fraser*, died a suicide! All these men learned well the art of making money, but *not one of them learned how to live.*' " (From *The Challenge*, by Robert D. Foster, Colorado Springs, Colorado, April 27, 1963.)

SOME THOUGHTS ON MONEY—"Benjamin Franklin said, 'Money never made a man happy yet, nor will it. There is nothing in its nature to produce happiness. The more a man has, the more he wants. That was a true proverb of the wise man, rely upon it: "Better is little with the fear of the Lord, than great treasure, and trouble therewith." '

" 'The man who loves money is the man who has never grown up,' said Robert Lynd.

" 'No man is really consecrated until his money is dedicated,' said Roy L. Smith.

" 'The real measure of our wealth is how much we'd be worth if we lost all our money,' said John Henry Jowett.

"Samuel Johnson advised: 'Resolve not to be poor; whatever you have, spend less.'

"Money buys everything except love, personality, freedom and immortality." (Quotes are taken from *Living Quotations for Christians*, ed. by Sherwood Eliot Wirt and Kersten Beckstrom, Harper & Row, New York, 1974.)

LESSON 8   JANUARY 23
Teaching About Lostness

Background Scripture: Luke 15
Devotional Reading: Luke 15:4–7

Luke 15:11–24
11 And he said, A certain man had two sons:
12 And the younger of them said to his father, Father, give me the portion of goods that falleth to me. And he divided unto them his living.

LESSON FOR JANUARY 23   183

13 And not many days after the younger son gathered all together, and took his journey into a far country, and there wasted his substance with riotous living.
14 And when he had spent all, there arose a mighty famine in that land; and he began to be in want.
15 And he went and joined himself to a citizen of that country; and he sent him into his fields to feed swine.
16 And he would fain have filled his belly with the husks that the swine did eat: and no man gave unto him.
17 And when he came to himself, he said, How many hired servants of my father's have bread enough and to spare, and I perish with hunger!
18 I will arise and go to my father, and will say unto him, Father, I have sinned against heaven, and before thee,
19 And am no more worthy to be called thy son: make me as one of thy hired servants.
20 And he arose, and came to his father. But when he was yet a great way off, his father saw him, and had compassion, and ran, and fell on his neck, and kissed him.
21 And the son said unto him, Father, I have sinned against heaven, and in thy sight, and am no more worthy to be called thy son.
22 But the father said to his servants, Bring forth the best robe, and put it on him; and put a ring on his hand, and shoes on his feet:
23 And bring hither the fatted calf, and kill it; and let us eat, and be merry:
24 For this my son was dead, and is alive again: he was lost, and is found. And they began to be merry.

KEY VERSE: "For this my son was dead, and is alive again: he was lost, and is found." Luke 15:24.

Home Daily Bible Readings
Jan. 17 M. The Lost Sheep, Luke 15:1–7.
Jan. 18 T. The Lost Coin, Luke 15:8–10.
Jan. 19 W. The Lost Son, Luke 15:11–17.
Jan. 20 T. The Father's Compassion, Luke 15:18–24.
Jan. 21 F. The Unforgiving Son, Luke 15:25–32.
Jan. 22 S. "To Seek and to Save," Luke 19:1–10.
Jan. 23 S. God Seeks His Sheep, Ezekiel 34:11–16.

Lesson Aim: That adults may comprehend the awful condition of being lost so that they may rejoice more heartily when anyone is found.

LESSON OUTLINE
Background to the Scripture
Looking at the Scripture Text

I. The Impatient Son (Luke 15:11, 12)
II. What It's Like to Be Lost (Luke 15:13-16)
III. The Inner Change (Luke 15:17-19, 21)
IV. The Loving Father (Luke 15:20)
V. The Joy of Being Found (Luke 15:22-24)
Applying the Scripture

Background to the Scripture

If you are using the Good News Bible in your study of Luke the first words of today's text—"Jesus went on to say"—sent you scurrying to examine the context. Virtually every version starts out either with "And" or "Jesus continued," pointing back to earlier verses which tell us the purpose of this story. It is actually a piece of a triad, three parables to illustrate lostness. Their reason for being is the fact that Jesus was under heavy criticism for habitually associating with sinners and outcasts. Seeming to participate in their careless ways, He even ate with them.

Poole explains that the scribes and Pharisees assumed that there was no mercy for "bold and presumptuous sinners" because the Law appointed no sacrifice for such. Thus, to them, these outcasts were excommunicated; "therefore Christ sinned in eating or drinking with them, or in any degree receiving them." They concluded Christ was not a prophet. But to show why it was necessary for the Savior to be accessible to sinners, Jesus told the parable of the lost sheep, the lost coin, and the lost son. Through them all He was saying, "The welcome I give to outcasts and sinners is justified."

Looking at the Scripture Text

The Impatient Son (vv. 11, 12)   In the story of the Prodigal Son, the father might be considered more the main figure than the son. But at least in the first part, the Savior focuses on the son. It is a classic treatment of the sort of real-life drama being played out in all its various stages at any time. The younger son, eager for his independence, asks his father to divide up the inheritance he and his brother are to share. He does not consider that, with time, his share might be worth a great deal more. Whatever allowance he is receiving is not nearly enough to finance what he wants to do. The only way he can get that kind of money is to demand a premature payment of his inheritance—which he does.

The father divides up his wealth (some versions say "property") between the two sons, evidently keeping control of the older son's assets while giving the younger what he requested. Along with some treasured items which would represent dollars to the eager young man, and cash from the estate, there was probably a share of the land and even a building or two. These the son liquidated for easy mobility "in not many days," leaving nothing of material value that would cause him to want to return. Self-confident and immature, he left home. His modern day counterpart rolls through the front gate in a purring Corvette; this one struck out on foot, a far-away look in his eye. In his heart, he had already left home long before. A sad father must have watched him as he disappeared down the road.

What It's Like to Be Lost (vv. 13-16) Like young adults of every generation, this one thought virtue lay in his being as far from home as he could get. Jesus' listeners might have pictured the man heading for Alexandria or Antioch or Rome. Whatever his destination, the unfolding of the story shows that he was going to a foreign land.

The restraints of his home and homeland removed, he immediately gave in to whatever pleasures appealed to him. The duration of the "good life" for him was not long as he "squandered" all he had in "wild living" (NIV)—"reckless living" (TEV), "on parties and prostitutes" says The Living Bible. He proved the Scriptural point that there is pleasure in sin *for a season* (Hebrews 11:25).

Living for the moment, he did not take note of how quickly he was running out of capital and his host country was running out of food. One commentator notes: "The working of Providence is manifested in coincidences. Just when he had spent everything, a famine, a severe one, arose in precisely that land to which he had gone to enjoy himself" (*International Critical Commentary*). But the young man would have to go much lower before he would be willing to recognize any Providence.

Hunger forced him, at last, to work. But he had few marketable skills. With no degree or experience, he had to take a job paying the minimum wage. From the words, "joined himself to a citizen," we conclude that he took room and board in exchange for feeding the man's pigs. His father, a good Jew, would not have kept swine, they being considered an abomination for their filthy ways and forbidden by the Law as food. In caring for them, the cocky young man had to deal with pangs of conscience as well as hunger pangs. Before long he even craved the carob pods which were the pigs' staple diet—his employer being either unable or unwilling to give him enough to eat. "Neither food nor love abounded in that country."

His condition is a graphic picture of what it means to be lost in spirit. He was underfed, unclean, unwanted, unknown, and undone. As the father would say later, he was "dead" (v. 24), for that is the ultimate description of lostness. And the worst part for the sinner was that in his lucid moments he knew that he had brought it upon himself.

The Inner Change (vv. 17-19, 21) A person who is lost would laugh at any suggestion that he is not in his right mind. He thinks of religious people as "nuts" and "crazies." But the words of our Lord give grounds for the opposite view. The prodigal "came to himself" or "came to his senses." That is, he began to get a glimpse of reality in his destitute state. He was now at the point of conversion, of turning, of the inner change. His awakening is not unrelated to his physical existence. Hunger drove him to think of making a change, but everything about this turn-around marks it as sincere.

In the stories of the sheep and the coin, the lost item needed merely to be brought back to its owner, but with the son "there has to be a self-recovery—a sinning man may not be brought back to God like a straying sheep to the fold," notes the *Expositor's Greek Testament*. The sinner had to take an active part.

Note the indications of inner change. First, *repentance*. In his mind, he began to formulate the words he would tell his father. "I have sinned against heaven and against you." Rarely does sin work its evil against God alone. It almost always hurts others. In rehearsing his confession, he may have been drawing from the teaching he had received as a child from the Psalms: "I acknowledged my sin unto thee, and mine iniquity have I not hid. I said, I will confess my transgressions unto the Lord; and thou forgavest the iniquity of my sin" (32:5).

Second, *contrition*. He considered himself so great a sinner that he said, "I am no more worthy to be called thy son." Realizing that in taking all of his inheritance he had no claim on his father, he went a third step—*humility*. Far from demanding his share as he did when he left home, he was now willing to accept any conditions his father would permit—and he was so low in his own estimation that he imagined that condition to be that of a household slave.

All of this circulated through his mind as he resolved to return home. Repentance began its work in the inner heart and was actually achieved long before he fell into his father's arms and blurted out his confession. As long as he sat with the pigs and held out any hope of finding himself there, he would have remained lost. But the moment he arose and set his face toward home, the inner change took place.

His resolve appears to be his own doing in this story but elsewhere in the Bible we learn that faith is a gift from God and "no man can come to (Christ) except the Father . . . draw him" (John 6:44).

The Loving Father (v. 20) The father-figure in this story is not just any father. He represents God the Father. Jesus spoke frequently and affectionately of His Father. In Jerusalem when He was twelve, He asked His parents, "Didn't you know I had to be in my Father's house?" He taught His disciples to pray, "Our Father, which art in heaven. . . ." This story agrees with the words Luke earlier recorded: "Be merciful, just as your Father is merciful" (6:36 NIV).

The prodigal was not a runaway, but his position was not a great deal different from that of a runaway. Just as those young people may fear what their parents will do should they return, this son must have feared the worst. He had no assurance of mercy. But as Jesus described what took place, the man had no grounds for fear. Every day, the father had looked down that road for his son. When he saw the figure "a great way off" (indicating how far the young man had gone in his lostness), he recognized him immediately. He "saw" and in seeing he "was filled with compassion." Though he may have been aged, he "ran to his son, threw his arms around him and kissed him" (fervently and frequently). The description of the father says Poole "magnifies the grace of God" showing the "exceeding readiness of our heavenly Father to receive penitent sinners."

The Joy of Being Found (vv. 22-24) Overcome with emotion, the son did manage to voice his confession. But in the warm embrace of his father, he could not go further. His father was issuing commands: "Quick! Bring the best robe . . . a ring . . . sandals." Each was a distinguishing mark of authority. Sandals were the prerogative of free men; slaves went without shoes.

A feast was in order and the fattened calf reserved for special occasions was killed. Joy engulfed the whole occasion. The father wanted no remembrance made of his son's terrible waste. "Let us eat and be merry" (NASB) he said. Music and dancing filled the air. In the father's words, "For this son of mine was dead, and has come to life again; he was lost, and has been found." Each of the stories climaxes with the joy of heaven. Perhaps this rejoicing in the highest realms is the highest reason of all for Jesus' association with sinners.

Not included in our text is the tale of the elder brother who, jealous of his ne'er-do-well brother, sulked outside the house. "Did the elder brother eventually join in the celebration and accept his brother back as a member of the family?" asks the *New Bible Commentary*. "The omission is deliberate. For the elder brother represents the Pharisees and their spiritual kin, and the parable is an appeal to them to receive the outcasts. Jesus was waiting for their verdict."

Applying the Scripture

Two applications are suggested for today's lesson. One has to do with your classroom time, the other is for consideration by a church committee or should perhaps be brought to the pastor's attention.

1. For a particularly enriching class period, plan ahead of time for a member of the class to relate his or her own "prodigal" story at the close of your teaching period.

Scripture admonishes us to remember our salvation, "Consider the quarry from which you were mined, the rock from which you were cut!" (Isaiah 51:1 TLB). Israel told and retold the story of their Lord's deliverance. So, while we should not dwell on the past or sensationalize our "old life"—it is right for us to remember "all the way the Lord thy God led . . ." (Deuteronomy 8:2).

Consider this an opportunity to help a class member grow as a disciple. You will not want to ask the person who is your most frequent talker or the one who has often told his or her conversion experience. Choose a person whose story is perhaps not known by the class members. Suggest that he or she be ready to share a testimony of being lost and found. You may ask them to write out what they will say, at least in outline form, but stress that you only want them to speak a couple of minutes—a lot can be said in that amount of time.

It will help them if you suggest a plan, such as:

1. Tell what my life was like before I met Christ.

2. Tell how I came to know Christ (encourage them to use a Scripture that will contain the Gospel, for this is to benefit others who will hear).

3. Tell what my life is like now that I know Christ.

Following this time of sharing, why not suggest to all your class members that they write out their testimony and be looking for an opportunity to share it with someone this week!

2. Ask: How do we as a Church celebrate the salvation of a lost soul? If there is rejoicing in heaven when one soul repents, ought there not to be much joy here on earth?

One church in New Jersey marked the baptism of a young couple in a special way. First the man had publicly confessed his faith in Christ, and three weeks later his wife went forward and did the same. Tears were shed by many in the congregation—tears of joy, for many had prayed. A large number of people went up to the couple and expressed their joy. Then a baptismal service was scheduled for a few weeks later. Following the baptism and the evening preaching service, the couple was again called to the front of the auditorium. With prayer, the minister dismissed the service and everyone went to the reception hall for an informal time of rejoicing with one another and this new pair of Christians. This is not always done in this church; but they are thinking of making it a regular practice.

Have your class consider how the Church can make such times a genuine time of rejoicing and celebration. The new Christian needs the encouragement, and the Church needs to remember what a great salvation we have from such an awful lostness.

Questions for Discussion
Make use of these questions to involve your students in learning and to test their understanding of the lesson.
1. What prompted Jesus to tell the story of the prodigal? 2. How would you characterize the younger son at the start of the story? 3. Why would feeding the pigs be especially loathsome to this Jewish young man? 4. What was the primary motivating force leading to the man's decision to return home? 5. How had the son changed as he began the journey home? What qualities were uppermost in him? 6. Describe the waiting father. What characteristics are dominant in him? 7. What does the parable teach us about lostness? About the grace of God?

Illustrating the Scripture
Examples and quotations to help the teacher communicate the lesson.
ARE YOU STILL ALIVE? LET SOMEBODY KNOW! These words grab attention on a poster. They appear above a teenage girl who is thumbing a ride to "Anywhere." For every prodigal who has a settlement with his parents in today's society and then leaves home, there are thousands of runaways who don't. Considering the very young who run away but many of whom return, there are either 1 million of them a year or almost 2 million, depending on which authority is being quoted.

Newsweek in its January 29, 1979, issue told of a nationwide telephone hotline for runaways. Located in Houston, Texas, it is called Operation Peace of Mind and is directed by Marilyn Davidson. At that time, this center received 5,000 calls a month on toll-free numbers. Ms. Davidson said there are an " 'estimated two million kids who run away each year from their families in the U.S.

" 'The typical runaway who phones in is a fifteen-year-old girl who left home less than a week before. Some runaway callers want the volunteers (phone answerers) to break the ice with their parents, passing on a message without disclosing the youngster's location.

" 'We can be a buffer,' says Ms. Davidson. 'It allows the kid to save face. Others aren't ready to make contact with their families, but need medical advice or a place to stay. Approximately ten percent of the runaways turn out to be "throwaways" whose parents don't want them back. When hotline staffers learn that,' says Ms. Davidson, 'they inform the child. There is no point saying everything's rosy and have them go back home and be beaten again. But we don't just leave them hanging. We urge them to call a child-welfare worker.'

"The hotline has no figures on its success rate but does try to make a spot check and occasionally gets a call from a former runaway or a contribution from grateful parents."

CONVERSION   "It is well to remember that the Bible's word for "conversion" is *repentance*. Any real turning to the Lord is a turning away from sin. For converts, this repentance is often wrought with tears. When converts come at last to the Lord, they bring to Him the sorrows not of a week or a year but of a lifetime. At times the sins they confess are so dark and hateful to themselves that they have never looked honestly at them, but have repressed even the memory of their own wrongdoing. And it seems they have repressed it—tried to pretend that evil was good—because of a kind of hopelessness and despair. Until now, they had not dared to hope that they could do or be other than what they have done or been.

"Before I became a Christian this notion of confessing my sins was hateful to me. It was not a question of unwillingness to confess my sins before another human being; it was in fact an unwillingness to confess my sins at all. I could not admit myself to be a sinner. . . .

"The confession which Christians make—have made since the earliest times—was for me (when I discovered it) a refreshing piece of honesty. It was a kind of release. And in doing so, I also found I had a great deal of company, which oddly enough gave me enormous hope." (From *Turning* by Emilie Griffin, Doubleday & Co.: New York, 1980.)

Topics for Youth

"JOY IN HEAVEN OVER ONE SINNER WHO REPENTS"—A Christian sometimes needs to repent and "head for home," too. Youth Sunday in a church in the Northeast gave occasion for a sixteen-year-old girl to do just that, and it was one of the happiest days in the life of that church.

Elaine was the worship leader in a Baptist church for the service in which all of the duties were given for that day to the church's young people. The youth group sang a special call to worship and a young man prayed. Another young man led in the congregational singing and Elaine gave the announcements. Youths served as ushers and again offered more music. Then it came time for the sermon.

First Vic spoke a few minutes, telling what the Lord meant to him. When Elaine got up to speak, laying her notes on the pulpit before her, nothing unusual had transpired and the service was running far ahead of schedule. She jokingly said that no one had to worry about their roast burning today!

No one knew how her heart must have been pounding. Halfway into her talk, she said that she had caused her parents a lot of grief in recent months. "I've been running around with some kids my parents had forbidden me to be with," she said. Then she told of being with these young people on the highway when an accident occurred. Luckily, or providentially, no one was injured.

"I said at the time, 'Why me, Lord! Why did this have to happen when I was in the car?' I had to tell my mom and dad and for that I was grounded."

Elaine had been a believer for a few years and she struggled with the Lord during the next few weeks.

"I just want to say today," she went on, pausing to gain her composure, "that I'm coming home. I'm giving my heart and life to the Lord today in a way I never have before." It was all she could say. When the invitation was given by the minister, Elaine went to the altar, responding to her own message. A girl friend joined her there as almost everyone in the church wiped tears from their eyes. One visitor, the mother of one of the youths, said: "I thought I was coming today just to witness my son's participation. But this is why the Lord had me here."

It was a homecoming for a girl on the verge of being a prodigal.

LESSON 9   JANUARY 30
Teaching About Stewardship

Background Scripture: Luke 16:1–13, 19–31
Devotional Reading: Amos 5:6–15

Luke 16:1-13

1 And he said also unto his disciples, There was a certain rich man, which had a steward; and the same was accused unto him that he had wasted his goods.

2 And he called him, and said unto him, How is it that I hear this of thee? give an account of thy stewardship; for thou mayest be no longer steward.
3 Then the steward said within himself, What shall I do? for my lord taketh away from me the stewardship: I cannot dig; to beg I am ashamed.
4 I am resolved what to do, that, when I am put out of the stewardship, they may receive me into their houses.
5 So he called every one of his lord's debtors unto him, and said unto the first, How much owest thou unto my lord?
6 And he said, A hundred measures of oil. And he said unto him, Take thy bill, and sit down quickly, and write fifty.
7 Then said he to another, And how much owest thou? And he said, A hundred measures of wheat. And he said unto him, Take thy bill, and write fourscore.
8 And the lord commended the unjust steward, because he had done wisely: for the children of this world are in their generation wiser than the children of light.
9 And I say unto you, Make to yourselves friends of the mammon of unrighteousness; that, when ye fail, they may receive you into everlasting habitations.
10 He that is faithful in that which is least is faithful also in much: and he that is unjust in the least is unjust also in much.
11 If therefore ye have not been faithful in the unrighteous mammon, who will commit to your trust the true riches?
12 And if ye have not been faithful in that which is another man's, who shall give you that which is your own?
13 No servant can serve two masters: for either he will hate the one, and love the other; or else he will hold to the one, and despise the other. Ye cannot serve God and mammon.

KEY VERSE: "No servant can serve two masters: for either he will hate the one, and love the other; or else he will hold to the one, and despise the other. Ye cannot serve God and mammon." Luke 16:13.

Home Daily Bible Readings		
Jan. 24	M.	The Shrewd Steward, Luke 16:1–9.
Jan. 25	T.	The Faithful Steward, Luke 16:10–17.
Jan. 26	W.	Unconditional Service, Luke 17:5–10.
Jan. 27	T.	The Rich and the Kingdom, Luke 18:18–25.
Jan. 28	F.	Not to Use Is to Lose, Luke 19:12–26.
Jan. 29	S.	Stewardship Determines Destiny, Luke 16:19–31.
Jan. 30	S.	A Plea for Justice, Amos 5:6–15.

Lesson Aim: That adults will decide to use all material things of value to God's advantage as trustworthy managers.

LESSON OUTLINE
Background to the Scripture
Looking at the Scripture Text
 I. The Dishonest Manager (Luke 16:1–8)
 II. The Lord's Management Lesson (Luke 16:9–13)
Applying the Scripture

Background to the Scripture

This is the fifth and final lesson under the general theme of Jesus' teaching ministry—and again we confront a parable. Some of your students may not have been familiar with the parables of the Lord before now and these lessons are serving to show them something of the way which a parable frequently suited His purposes. We have looked at but a few of them.

Yet by this time some of your class members may be puzzled by the parables. And this particular one, admittedly more difficult than any of those we considered in Luke 15 or the one which follows in verses 19–31, could dampen their interests. It may help them to rethink what a parable is. We ought not to demand too much of this literary form. Matthew Poole said it well—"a parable is not designed to inform us in a matter of fact, but to describe to us our duty, under a fictitious representation." Someone has said a parable is "an earthly story with a heavenly meaning."

We get into trouble when we try to nail down every detail with some specific person or corresponding fact in human history. This is apparent from the treatment this Parable of the Unjust Steward has received. Men have labored to find out who the steward in the story is and, believe it or not, they have variously concluded that he is the Jewish hierarchy or tax-collectors or Pilate or Judas or Satan or penitents or Paul, or even Christ! In our study, we will not try to determine such ultimately unrewarding details—but we will attempt to see through the apparent difficulties to the Savior's meaning and thus, "our duty."

Looking at the Scripture Text

The Dishonest Manager (vv. 1–8) A first reading of this parable leaves us with mixed emotions. We are happy for the encouragement to wise stewardship, but we have a queasy feeling that praise is being doled out for rather shady dealings. And that Jesus is the one doing the praising. Let us be quick to say that the conduct of the steward in the story is more than shady. It is fraudulent. And Jesus characterized him as such, calling him an "unjust steward." What the Lord praised in the man was not his conduct but his shrewd foresight in looking out for himself.

We encounter the role of the steward commonly throughout the Bible.

Abraham had a steward and it was he who was sent on the very important mission to acquire a bride for Isaac. Abraham's great grandson Joseph, when taken into Egypt, served for a time as steward to Potiphar. So great was his master's trust in him that he could say: "My master does not have to concern himself with anything in the house, because I am here. He has put me in charge of everything he has" (Genesis 39:8 TEV).

The New Testament words for *house* and *steward* have identical roots. A steward was the manager of a large household. Probably in the story Jesus told, the wealthy landowner did not live on his estate. Leaving that in the hands of his trusted steward, he may have resided in the city.

But a day came when he could no longer trust this steward. When that happens, drastic action is necessary for as Paul says, "it is required in stewards, that a man be found faithful" (1 Corinthians 4:2). The text suggests that the owner called his steward in after hearing complaints about his waste and dismissed him on the spot. That could be. Or, the complaints may have been coming for some time and the lord could no longer ignore them. The words "give an account of thy stewardship" indicate that the owner may have listened to the steward's side of the story. But evidence against him must have been convincing so the relationship of trust was ended abruptly.

Trying to determine why the steward could think of only two alternatives—either digging or begging—is a vain exercise. On many details of the parables, we cannot be certain of possessing the one accurate interpretation. One commentator has said of such attempts to explain all of the points in this one parable that "the literature on the subject is voluminous and unrepaying." Suffice it to say that Jesus portrayed the steward as thinking of two alternatives only, neither of them satisfactory.

Then the proverbial light went on in the steward's mind. "I know what I'll do" he told himself smugly. Most Bible students agree that his ingenious idea was an immediate measure only. He would do something for his master's debtors that would ingratiate them to himself so that when he was turned out, he would have a temporary place to stay—"people will welcome me into their houses" (v. 4 NIV).

One by one, the debtors came to see him. The scene is one of urgency. He would know these debtors well, probably being the one who collected from them all along. To each he asked, "How much do you owe my master?" though he himself had the books. By such little ways, he made known his crookedness. Whatever their answer was, the steward, no doubt glancing at the books, discounted the total owed in an arbitrary manner. To the first he said, "Cut the total by 50 percent" and had him "quickly" sit down and write out a new bill. The second bill he reduced 20 percent. These two examples were given to suggest how he handled all the debtors.

"Was there not a risk of offence when the debtors began to compare notes?" asks the *Expositor's Greek Testament*. "Not much; they would not look on it as mere arbitrariness or partiality, but as policy: variety would look more like a true account than uniformity. He had not merely to benefit them, but to put himself in as good a light as possible before his master."

The "100 measures" of olive oil would be approximately 800 gallons, say modern versions. The hundred "cors" of wheat would be about 1,000 bushels, worth possibly ten times the value of the oil.

The steward may have charged these debtors an unfair rate of interest in his earlier dealings, skimming the extra cash for himself. In reducing their debts, he may have simply been charging them what they really owed. This dishonest twist was the latest in a habit of crookedness that had earned him the epithet "unjust." Some of the debtors may well have been the ones who accused him to his master, but now they were not about to tell on the steward.

Some scholars believe that with verse 7 the parable ended and that "the lord" spoken of in verse 8 is Jesus. This would have Jesus commending the unjust steward and allow us to believe that the landowner may not have known that his steward discounted all his debtors' accounts. But the usual interpretation is that the landowner is the one who praised the steward. The significant point is that he praised the steward because he had acted wisely or prudently.

Jesus' commentary on the parable begins with the words: "for the children of this world are in their generation wiser than the children of light." Identifying these groups should be easy to determine. The former are all men in their natural state—worldly men, particularly the "shakers" and "movers" of any period in history. The latter are the believers, those made righteous through faith, who "walk in the light" (1 John 1:7).

The difficulty in understanding this verse stems from the words "in their generation." Here, the NIV translation helps: "the people of this world are more shrewd in dealing *with their own kind* than are the people of light." W. E. Vine in his dictionary of New Testament words says the words mean any "race of people, possessed of similar characteristics, pursuits." The translation "with their own kind" or "to men of their own kind" seems to answer the difficulty. The truth of Jesus' assessment is everywhere apparent. Men of this world, who claim no inheritances in the hereafter, outdo the godly in their investing and improving upon wealth so their future is provided for. Man will work and dream with gargantuan effort to be wealthy and exercise power in this world.

The Lord's Management Lesson (vv. 9–13) If verse 8 has caused difficulties, verse 9 has led to even more. Jesus' words, "I tell you," point up the importance of what He has to say. "Use worldly wealth to gain friends for yourselves, so that when it is gone, you will be welcomed into eternal dwellings" (NIV). Moffatt's translation of the same verse—"use mammon, dishonest as it is, to make friends for yourselves, so that when you die they may welcome you...." Mammon is universally understood to be riches or money. It is characterized as unrighteous because of the great many temptations to evil that usually come to the person who has wealth. Scripture warns of the "deceitfulness of riches."

Our Lord's meaning is that the children of light should use all the worldly wealth to which they can rightfully gain access and distribute it to the poor ("the friends") who, when the believer dies (and the money fails, as it must at death), these poor will welcome them into heaven. The "eternal tents" of heaven are so much more to be valued and desired than any transitory dwellings that our debtors on earth may have to offer. Our word *distribute* should not be thought of literally, but in the sense of making available to the poor through diligent investment and industrious management.

In verses 10-12, an admonition to faithfulness follows. "Earthly wealth is not only trivial and unreal," says one commentator. "It does not belong to us." With this in mind, we can see why Jesus underscores faithfulness. Being trustworthy in the menial, small things, Jesus said, would lead to faithfulness in larger things. Verse 11 emphasizes faithfulness with money, the next verse stresses faithfulness with other people's goods as preparation for having our own, to do with as we please.

In verses 10-12, Jesus puts the mammon of unrighteousness over against the "true riches." The contrast is a stark one. Mammon is likened to "little," is called unjust and the implication is that it is fleeting for it belongs to another (v. 12). But the Gospel or Christ is likened to "much," is called true riches and is "our own," therefore it cannot be taken away.

Our Lord's management lesson concludes with the statement of objective fact—no one can serve two masters at the same time. The steward indulged his own greedy interests while employed by his master. His service turned out to be mere lip service. We are in danger of treating our Lord and Master in the same way. Christ ever calls us to serve Him as Lord alone.

Applying the Scripture
Two applications suggest themselves from today's lesson—the primary one could be termed wise stewardship; the secondary one, faithfulness.
1. "Money talks—it says good-bye." How true is that statement! But it could be put another way. "Money talks—it says *use me!*" In one of the Bible readings for the week, Luke 19:12-26, Jesus tells the parable of the three men who received talents from their lord who then went on a far journey. Two of them invested their talents and made more while one hid his in a handkerchief, afraid of losing it. He should have used it. One day the master returned and asked for an accounting. The two who had invested their talents were given more responsibility and received the praise of their master. But the third one was scolded and had to give up the one talent entrusted to him. Verse 9 commands us to use money and riches.

Ask your class what their attitude is toward money. You may want to write their answers on the chalkboard. Probably their answers will fall in one of four areas: a. a trust from God; b. a dangerous evil; c. a substance with great potential for good; d. life's most important object. After some discussion, see if everyone agrees that money is chiefly "a trust from God" and "a substance with great potential for good."

Now, ask your class if they agree with John Wesley who said of money—"make all you can, save all you can, give all you can."

Discuss ways they as children of light can be wise in making all the money they can. Here, reliability on the job would be suggested, as well as further study or courses to advance. Or some may suggest "moonlighting" or profitable hobbies.

Discuss also ways of "saving"—including specific things an adult should do to accrue basic savings and then, as further funds become available, what additional methods may be employed. Here, savings accounts, bonds, stocks, real estate, and other things may be mentioned. Seek to make the session generally stimulating and helpful while keeping control of the course of conversation. As a result, the church may want to schedule a brief seminar on stewardship for its members. Perhaps it can be taught by men and women of the church. Its aim should be to help all believers be shrewd stewards.

If this sounds "dangerous," it is well to remember Jesus' words about covetousness, studied two lessons earlier. The motivation for your study and application on stewardship should be "for the glory of God." Conclude this session with the key verse: Luke 16:13.

2. Suggest a word study on the theme of faithfulness. Some in your class will want to look further at what the Bible has to say about this subject. Recommend that they use a good concordance, preferably *Strong's* or *Cruden's*, and look up the words *faithful, steward, service, trust,* and *unfaithfulness.* Invite them to share the findings of their study with the class next week.

Questions for Discussion
Make use of these questions to involve your students in learning and to test their understanding of the lesson.
1. Jesus called the man "the unjust steward." Why? 2. Who are the "people of this world" and the "people of light"? 3. Explain how the sons of this world are wiser toward their own kind than the people of the light? 4. The term *mammon of unrighteousness* is important in this story. What is its meaning? 5. How do the "everlasting habitations" find their fulfillment? With what do they contrast in the parable? 6. Can you name three ways the unrighteous mammon contrasts with true riches? 7. If we are not to serve money, what are we to do with it?

Illustrating the Scripture
Examples and quotations to help the teacher communicate the lesson.

A STRATEGY FOR THE FUTURE These words from Drs. Ted Engstrom and Edward Dayton were intended originally for Christian leaders, but they have application to all Christians in the matter of good management.

"The most effective preparation for the future is done by clearly stating the vision, putting a time frame around it and then planning *backwards* from that desirable future to the present....

"It seems to us that fear always relates to the future. (We never fear the past.) When asked about preparing about tomorrow, Sir William Oster, the great Canadian physicist, answered, *'If we throw all of our energy, intelligence and enthusiasm into doing superb work today, there will be nothing to fear tomorrow. In other words, present action generates future security.'*

"We recognize as Christians that God is very much in control of both the present and the future. Our confidence is not in man or his ability, but rather in God's sovereign rule and overrule. We must, as Christian servants, continually exercise faith to believe that He is mightily at work in all of history and all of our future....

"In the eighties let us be bold to suggest some possible hard choices most of us need to face.

"First, we need to recognize the importance of *qualitative* growth which must continue alongside of any quantitative growth.... Christians are in the people business.... It is not poor stewardship to spend God's resources on building the individual strengths of that portion of the Body of Christ which we are called to lead.

"Second, in these 'turbulent times,' we must be able to be flexible without in any way losing integrity. We must be responsive to the needs of those to whom we minister and with whom we work.

"This calls for a constant rethinking of what we are called to do, a continuous updating of the initial vision. Such rethinking cannot be done on a casual basis. We have to *plan* to think. We have to *plan* times of reflection and discussion....

"Third, we must effectively use all of the available resources given to us, with wisdom and creativity, in order to insure the blessing of success, under God, of the ministry which is ours." (From *Christian Leadership Letter*, October 1980, published by World Vision International, 919 West Huntington Drive, Monrovia, California.)

YOU CARRY IT ROUND IN YOUR POCKET! "Many years ago an old United States Senator was talking to me. He had had a lot of money, and lost it, but his wife went on spending it. What to do? I said, 'Senator, you have lived a lot longer than I. But I believe if you could really bring God in on the situation, it would clear up. So many human relations are like dots at the end of a line, and they ought to be like base-angles at the bottom of a triangle, with God at the top. If, instead of trying to work out your problems in the horizontal, you would go up to God, and she would go up to God....' He finished the sentence himself, 'Then she wouldn't put anything over on me, and I wouldn't put anything over on her!' This happened just after the present form of dollar bill was issued. He drew a dollar from his pocket and said, 'The Founding Fathers knew about the triangle. Look at the pyramid of the Great Seal, with the Eye of God at the top!' And there it was, and there it is. You carry it round in your pocket. Let's begin carrying it round in our minds and hearts and relationships!" (From *How to Become a Christian* by Samuel M. Shoemaker, Harper and Brothers, New York, 1953.)

Topics for Youth

"YE CANNOT SERVE GOD AND MAMMON"—So—*serve God!* "Dr. William Stidger has given us the beautiful story of Saint Anthony. He was a good man. He prayed and read his Bible for hours every day, but one day the Lord told Anthony that he was not as good as he might be. There was one other man in the world better than he. Anthony very anxiously asked the Lord to tell him who this man was. If he could only know the secret of this man's life, he would apply it to his own. The Lord told him the man was Conrad, the cobbler, who lived in Jerusalem.

"Bright and early one morning Saint Anthony entered Conrad's shop in Jerusalem and was cordially welcomed. Conrad inquired if he could be of service. Anthony told Conrad that he understood that he was the best man in the world and would like to know what he did to be so good. Conrad remonstrated concerning his goodness, but said, 'If you wish to know what I do, I don't mind telling you. I mend shoes for a living, and I mend every pair as if I were mending them for Jesus.'

"Jesus says very clearly, 'Whosoever will be chief among you, let him be your servant" (Matthew 20:27). The greatest in the kingdom, according to Jesus, are those who serve the most. Service is the rent we owe for the space we occupy in God's world. It is the most eloquent thing on earth.

"Every person should earnestly desire to make this a better world in which to live. This is our debt to oncoming generations. What a pity to live for self when one can live for Jesus!

"But no person can live for and serve Jesus who does not live for and serve others. They who live for Jesus would rather live a life than make a living, rather serve than be served. They prefer giving to receiving and losing their lives to saving them. Their prayer is:

> Help me in all the work I do
> To ever be sincere and true,
> And know that all I'd do for You
> Must needs be done for Others.

(James P. Wesberry, *Meditations for Happy Christians* [Nashville: Broadman Press, 1973] pp. 50, 51. All rights reserved. Used by permission.)

UNIT IV

Jesus' Earthly Ministry Completed

LESSON 10 — FEBRUARY 6

Going Up to Jerusalem

Background Scripture: Luke 19:28–48
Devotional Reading: Lamentations 3:21–33

Luke 19:29–40, 45–48

29 And it came to pass, when he was come nigh to Bethphage and Bethany, at the mount called the mount of Olives, he sent two of his disciples,
30 Saying, Go ye into the village over against you; in the which at your entering ye shall find a colt tied, whereon yet never man sat: loose him, and bring him hither.
31 And if any man ask you, Why do ye loose him? thus shall ye say unto him, Because the Lord hath need of him.
32 And they that were sent went their way, and found even as he had said unto them.

33 And as they were loosing the colt, the owners thereof said unto them, Why loose ye the colt?
34 And they said, The Lord hath need of him.
35 And they brought him to Jesus: and they cast their garments upon the colt, and they set Jesus thereon.
36 And as he went, they spread their clothes in the way.
37 And when he was come nigh, even now at the descent of the mount of Olives, the whole multitude of the disciples began to rejoice and praise God with a loud voice for all the mighty works that they had seen;
38 Saying, Blessed be the King that cometh in the name of the Lord: peace in heaven, and glory in the highest.
39 And some of the Pharisees from among the multitude said unto him, Master, rebuke thy disciples.
40 And he answered and said unto them, I tell you that, if these should hold their peace, the stones would immediately cry out.
45 And he went into the temple, and began to cast out them that sold therein, and them that bought;
46 Saying unto them, It is written, My house is the house of prayer: but ye have made it a den of thieves.
47 And he taught daily in the temple. But the chief priests and the scribes and the chief of the people sought to destroy him,
48 And could not find what they might do: for all the people were very attentive to hear him.

KEY VERSE: "And it came to pass, when the time was come that he should be received up, he stedfastly set his face to go to Jerusalem." Luke 9:51.

Home Daily Bible Readings
Jan. 31 M. "The Lord Has Need," Luke 19:28–40.
Feb. 1 T. A Place to Pray and Teach, Luke 19:41–48.
Feb. 2 W. The Question of Authority, Luke 20:1–8.
Feb. 3 T. A Parable of Judgment, Luke 20:9–18.
Feb. 4 F. Give God His Own, Luke 20:19–26.
Feb. 5 S. God of the Living, Luke 20:27–40.
Feb. 6 S. The Lord Is Good, Lamentations 3:22–33.

Lesson Aim: That your students will praise the Lord Jesus Christ in public ways as well as in private.

LESSON OUTLINE
Background to the Scripture
Looking at the Scripture Text
 I. A Colt for the King (Luke 19:29-36)

II. A Song for the King (Luke 19:37-40)
III. A House for the King (Luke 19:45-48)
Applying the Scripture

Background to the Scripture

Luke does not inform his readers what day the events now described took place. For a time reference, we must look at John's Gospel. There, in the opening verse of chapter 12, he indicates that Jesus arrived at Bethany "six days before the Passover." After telling of the feast in Jesus' honor at the home of Mary, Martha, and Lazarus, John says that on the following day—five days before the Passover—Jesus made his triumphal entry (12:12).

If we can determine on what day the Passover was observed that year, we can know whether Jesus entered Jerusalem on the first day of the week (and we would know whether the Church's tradition of celebrating Palm Sunday has support in Scripture). Since the Law declared that the seven-day Feast of the Passover was to begin on the fourteenth day of the month, the Passover might occur on any day of the week.

In the year of our Lord's Crucifixion, the Passover began at the close of the fifth day of the week because Jesus' body was on the cross the following day and was taken down before sundown because the next day was a Sabbath (*see* John 19:31). Considering the fifth day of the week (our Thursday) as the fifth day before Passover—since the Passover would commence at sundown—we count back and find that the day of Jesus' entry apparently was the first day of the week. It was one of the most joyful days in the life of Jesus' followers.

Looking at the Scripture Text

A Colt for the King (vv. 29-36) With his account of Jesus' entry into Jerusalem, Luke rejoins the other Gospel writers in a careful description of the final week in the life of the Lord.

From the opening verse of this section, we would assume that Jesus proceeded into Jerusalem without interruption upon arriving in the vicinity of Bethany. Luke does not recount the feast in Mary and Martha's house, wanting now to describe how Jesus made preparations for a distinctive entry. Bethany lay just east of the Mount of Olives, on Jerusalem's eastern side. To an unknown village in that region, Jesus dispatched two of the twelve to bring Him a young donkey. He had a particular "colt" in mind—an unbroken colt which would be tied to a post near the entrance of the village.

Nothing in Luke's account rules out a natural explanation of Jesus' prescience in this. He might have arranged with the owner for the use of the colt or it may have been offered Him by one of the devoted followers of the Lord. However, in the absence of any such explanation in Luke or in Matthew and Mark, this seems rather a case of the Lord's prophetic knowlege. Jesus exercised His gift of knowledge on many occasions and we can see instances of its use in the life of God's servants as well (*see* 1 Corinthians 12:8; Acts 21:10, 11; 2 Kings 6:12).

Jesus did not send His disciples on a dishonorable errand. They were to explain their purpose to anyone who asked what they were doing. The Lord would have them "be careful to do what is right in the sight of everybody" (Romans 12:17 NIV). After being with Jesus all this time, the disciples would not have thought inadequate His answer: "the Lord needs it." We wonder if "the owners" (v. 33) recognized the disciples and knew for Whom the donkey was intended. Mark says that the disciples told the owners that they would return the animal when the Master needed it no longer.

Why did Jesus *need* a donkey? In all of His journeyings through Galilee and Judea, He went by foot. The answer lies in the purpose of Jesus. He intended to assume a regal bearing as He entered Jerusalem. The time was right and the place was right for Him to receive the adulation of His followers. All who would see in Him the Person of the Messiah would recognize His actions as perfectly fitting. Too, He *needed* the colt because Scripture had to be fulfilled. Long before, the Prophet Zechariah had foretold: "Shout for joy, you people of Jerusalem! Look, your king is coming to you! He comes triumphant and victorious, but humble and riding on a donkey—on a colt, the foal of a donkey" (Zechariah 9:9 TEV).

To Luke's account that the people spread their clothes in the way, the other Gospels add that the people waved palm branches. This "practice of carrying palm leaves was an act of honor to a victorious person" says the *New Bible Commentary, Revised*. The people were hailing Him as if He were a king. But, by choosing a lowly beast of burden instead of a stallion, Jesus was saying, "My Kingdom is not of this world."

A Song for the King (vv. 37-40) The story of the "triumphal entry" should not be read in Luke alone. That would be like playing a stereo record on a mono player. John's account particularly adds color to Luke's description, communicating the rising degree of opposition against Jesus as He neared Jerusalem. To John alone, we owe the debt of the details of Lazarus's miraculous resurrection. This sensational miracle, which happened not long before, stirred enormous interest among the followers of Jesus and at the same time it drove the chief priests and scribes into a firm determination to seize the "Teacher." The word went out—if anyone knew of Jesus' whereabouts they were to report it to the authorities so they could arrest Jesus (John 11:57). Note the "audacity of the whole transaction . . . here are His disciples bringing Him in triumph into Jerusalem, and the populace enthusiastically joining with them. Moreover, all this had been arranged by Jesus Himself, when He sent for the colt. What He had hitherto concealed, or obscurely indicated, or revealed only to a chosen few, He now, seeing that the fulness of time is come, makes known to the whole world. He publicly claims to be the Messiah. This triumphal procession is the Holy One of God making solemn entry into the Holy City" (*International Critical Commentary*).

Pilgrims coming near Jerusalem for one of the three high feasts in the year customarily broke out in song. It would not be unusual on this occasion, nor were those followers immediately surrounding Jesus the only ones singing.

As they brought Jesus to the summit of the Mount of Olives and began the descent toward the Kidron Valley and to the East Gate, the people began to shout and sing loudly. John's account says that as soon as people within Jerusalem learned that Jesus was coming many of them went out to meet Him, waving palm branches. The cause of their rejoicing was, according to Luke, "for all the mighty works that they had seen," not just Lazarus's recovery from death but the healing of the blind in Jericho only days before and the many individual "mighty works" that each remembered in his own way. Their songs of joyful praise drifted across the whole valley:

"Blessed is the king who comes in the name of the Lord; Peace in heaven and glory in the highest!" (NIV).

The words, called the "earliest hymn of Christian devotion," are those of Psalms 118:25, 26. Each Gospel writer records the words differently, perhaps to meet the needs of his intended audience. The distinctive Hebrew word *Hosanna* (meaning Save! Now!) that Matthew uses for his Jewish readers is absent from Luke's narrative. All include the phrase "who comes in the name of the Lord." One commentator explains, "the blessing of the psalm was on all pilgrims coming up to the feast, but it was especially appropriate for the Son of David who came as the supreme Pilgrim to enter His kingdom."

All of this praise was quite spontaneous. In a sense it was Jesus' finest hour, a time when men rendered to Him the praise and glory due His Name. John later wrote that he and his fellow disciples did not realize till "after Jesus was glorified (His Resurrection) . . . that these things had been written about him . . ." (John 12:16 NIV), meaning the prophecy concerning the colt and the prophetic words of the pilgrims' song.

With few words, Luke gave his readers a measure of the tension that was mounting. Pharisees among the throng shouted over the singing, demanding that He rebuke His disciples. But it was impossible. Jesus answered them effectively: "If they keep quiet the stones will cry out." The next passage, not in our lesson, reveals the mood of Jesus during the procession. In this His finest hour, He was overcome with compassion and wept. He could see in the not too distant future the brutal atrocities and the massacre of the Jewish people in this city because "they did not recognize the time of God's coming."

A House for the King (vv. 45-48) Jesus "went into the temple"—more accurately, the Temple area. This large pavilion immediately inside the East Gate was called the Court of the Gentiles. It was on a level lower than the Temple proper. Along the walls were dozens of shops where pilgrims could purchase a lamb or goat or dove for the required sacrifices. In prominent places were the moneychangers, eager to give Temple coinage in exchange for the money the pilgrims brought. It was a lucrative commercial enterprise and, because the shopkeepers charged exorbitant fees and the changers exceeded the fair rate of exchange, it was indeed a "den of robbers."

The King, for that is what He was, did not assert His own authority in clearing out this motley crew. Instead He appealed to Scripture, an authority all of the people would honor. Quoting a part of Isaiah 56:7 (NIV), He spoke of the exalted purpose for the Temple. It was to be a "house of prayer for all nations." Obviously the hubbub would have made prayer impossible. Quoting from Jeremiah 7:11 (NIV), He said "You have made (my house) a den of robbers." He would have been just as angry at the chief priests and scribes and leaders of the people (a third group not before mentioned, in v. 47), for they did nothing to stop the commercialization of the Temple. They were probably receiving some of the shopkeepers' income.

Luke's account of the Temple cleansing is brief. Convinced that both Matthew and Mark had covered this event fully, he was anxious rather to present the bulk of Jesus' teaching which followed during the final four days of Jesus' life. Before he moves on to the subjects of our Lord's instruction, he takes note of the darkening clouds of opposition gathering against Jesus. In verse 47, he says the scribes and chief priests and leading laypeople were trying to kill Jesus, the first time he has been this explicit. Yet they could not succeed. Even though they knew the King would come to His house and teach daily—staying at night in Bethany (or possibly on the Mount of Olives, *see* Luke 21:37; Matthew 21:7)—they could not figure out a way to catch Jesus "for he was a hero to the people—they hung on every word he said" (v. 48 TLB).

Applying the Scripture
Two applications are suggested for this lesson. Both are personal in nature. You may want to add a third that would be a group application, for instance, from the example of the disciples joining together in song and praise.

1. Ask your class the question:

"If Jesus were to come to your town today, which crowd do you think you would be a part of?"

The crowd of disciples shouting, "Hosanna"?

Or, the Pharisees shouting, "Rebuke your followers"?

The throng of followers praising Him and proclaiming Him King?

Or, the scribes and leaders plotting to kill Him?

A preacher pointed out that for a long while he was bewildered by the fickle behavior of the people in Jerusalem during Holy Week. He wondered how the crowd could be shouting praises to Jesus one day and "Crucify Him!" a few days later. Then he realized that these were not the same people.

Challenge the persons in your class to ask themselves now and during the coming week, "Am I a follower or am I a part of the opposition?" To help them carry this question with them through the week, why not prepare beforehand a red ribbon for each class member. Letter on it with a marking pen the letters: *F or O?* This signifies "followers" or "opposition." Then give each class member a ribbon at the end of the class and ask them to place it in a prominent spot during the coming days so they will see it and be reminded of the application to today's lesson.

2. Ask your class:

Are you Available Jones? Are you ready to do something or give something, go somewhere when a neighbor calls on you for help? Do you recognize sometimes the call of God in the call of your neighbor, or a family member?

The disciples had but one answer to the owner of the colt—"the Lord needs it." And evidently that was all the owner needed to hear. He must have been pleased to learn that Jesus needed his little animal.

How about us? Are we so intent on keeping "our" car and "our" house and "our" things that they are not available to the Lord? If He never asks us, maybe it is because He knows from previous experience that we are not available.

The Lord does not so much need our ability as He does our *availability*. Encourage your class members to watch the church bulletin and bulletin board for announcements of needs the Lord may be asking them to fill. Invite discussion of the subject. Perhaps someone in class won't be too modest to share a recent experience when they, like the owners of the colt, were asked to give something of theirs for the Lord's service.

Questions for Discussion
Make use of these questions to involve your students in learning and to test their understanding of the lesson.
1. How did Jesus know that a colt fitting His description would be where He said it would be?   **2.** In what ways was the triumphal entry similar to that of a king? How did it differ from what would be expected of a king?   **3.** What two features of Luke's account link the triumphal entry to Old Testament prophecies concerning the Messiah?   **4.** What particular miracles would be fresh in their minds for which they glorified God?   **5.** Why would they be singing the words of Psalms 118?   **6.** Why did Jesus throw people out of the Temple?   **7.** What three Old Testament books are quoted in these verses of study?

Illustrating the Scripture
Examples and quotations to help the teacher communicate the lesson.
ON BEING AVAILABLE!   " 'We felt we should share what we have. Everything we have is the Lord's anyway.'

"Those words express the particular sentiments of Winston and Chris Creel of Anaheim, California—and the general feelings of a lot of other people all over the United States who have been and are involved in the Hospitality Roster. That is a roster of homes in which missionaries of an evangelical Bible translation society may find hospitality when home on furlough or when traveling across America.

"The Creel family wanted to introduce their preschool triplets to missionaries. One year their girls sent valentines to two missionary families they had hosted in their home. 'The children really enjoy missionaries,' says their mother. 'They want them to speak the foreign language and they keep talking about their slides.'

"The Hospitality Roster was set up to offer mutual blessing for hosts and guests. Many of God's people wanted to help and this was something they could do right in their own homes. The hosts could gain firsthand knowledge of Bible translation while having a share in the ministry by taking care of a vital need. The missionaries could share the excitement of Bible translation with new friends and save high motel/restaurant costs. The program was so popular that in 1975 more than 3,000 homes were on the Hospitality Roster.

"A number of roster friends use the opportunity to set up meetings for their missionary guests, helping them to obtain needed financial and prayer support. This has been a tremendous encouragement and in some cases has made it possible for them to get to their fields sooner." (From *The Wycliffe Associates Newsletter*, May 1975, Orange, California.)

MY HOUSE SHALL BE CALLED THE HOUSE OF PRAYER   "One of the preparations for prayer is *stillness* of the soul. 'Be still, and know that I am God,' is an admonition too few of us heed. If we were in the presence of an earthly king, we would keep silent until spoken to. How much more should we give the King of kings the opportunity to speak to us!

". . . Prayer not only means stillness in God's presence, it also means waiting, a difficult thing for those of us who are caught up in the whirl of earthly affairs.

"But the reward of waiting in God's presence is rich: 'they that wait for Jehovah shall renew their strength; they shall mount up with wings as eagles; they shall run and not be weary; they shall walk and not faint.' In prayer, we renew our strength, we are enabled to rise above the trials and contingencies of life. . . .

"Prayer also includes confession. 'If I regard iniquity in my heart the Lord will not hear me' carries with it a warning. Unconfessed sin is a deadly deterrent to prayer, whether viewed from the standpoint of our petition or God's response.

"Another aspect of prayer is restitution. How often we have offended others, even defrauded them. 'Therefore if thou bring thy gift to the altar, and there rememberest that thy brother hath ought against thee: leave therefore thy gift before the altar, and go thy way: first be reconciled to thy brother and then come offer thy gift.' Some revivals have started in local churches when Christians prayed and were reconciled to fellow Christians through confession and apology.

"Prayer also involves surrender . . . faith . . . importunity . . . thanksgiving. And finally . . . prayer is an attitude. The Apostle Paul meant a spiritual reality when he said we should pray without ceasing for it is the privilege of a Christian to live in such close contact with God that at all times the way is open into His presence." (From "A Layman and His Faith," L. Nelson Bell, *Christianity Today*, April 24, 1961, used with permission.)

Topics for Youth

YOU CAN WRITE A SONG!—Yes, you can. And this week, after studying the lesson in which a song played so vital a part in a day's events, it is just the time to sit down and put pen to paper.

But you don't write a song about the first thing that comes to your mind. That probably would not be the sort of idea that would express your deeper feelings—or minister to others for that matter.

First, look at the song in today's lesson: "Blessed be the King that cometh in the name of the Lord: peace in heaven, and glory in the highest."

You may want to look at this same song in the other Gospels and write out the words, noting how they are similar and how they are different.

This song we have learned is inspired from Scripture. Bits of verses from the Psalms can be found in the lyrics. That is a good tip. Many songs have been written today that incorporate a song or verse from the Bible, especially the Psalms. But there remain many, many biblical ideas and Scripture truths to be expressed in song.

Why don't you decide on writing a praise song? Don't worry about the music first. Just begin to put expressions on paper with a pencil. Draw from an experience that recently gave you encouragement from God. Or draw from a verse you read in the Bible which spoke heavily to your heart. This will get you past "writer's block"!

Don't make it too complex or all-inclusive. Some of the best loved are such praise songs as "Bless the Lord, O My Soul!" But let the words express *you*. Don't just copy words out of the Bible. Put them in the way you talk and then begin to read them aloud for rhyming and rhythm. Soon you'll be ready to "sing to the Lord a new song."

LESSON 11 FEBRUARY 13

Observing the Last Supper

Background Scripture: Luke 22:1–23
Devotional Reading: 1 Corinthians 11:23–26

Luke 22:1, 2, 7–20
1 Now the feast of unleavened bread drew nigh, which is called the Passover.
2 And the chief priests and scribes sought how they might kill him; for they feared the people.
7 Then came the day of unleavened bread, when the passover must be killed.

8 And he sent Peter and John, saying, Go and prepare us the passover, that we may eat.
9 And they said unto him, Where wilt thou that we prepare?
10 And he said unto them, Behold, when ye are entered into the city, there shall a man meet you, bearing a pitcher of water; follow him into the house where he entereth in.
11 And ye shall say unto the goodman of the house, The Master saith unto thee, Where is the guestchamber, where I shall eat the passover with my disciples?
12 And he shall shew you a large upper room furnished: there make ready.
13 And they went, and found as he had said unto them: and they made ready the passover.
14 And when the hour was come, he sat down, and the twelve apostles with him.
15 And he said unto them, With desire I have desired to eat this passover with you before I suffer:
16 For I say unto you, I will not any more eat thereof, until it be fulfilled in the kingdom of God.
17 And he took the cup, and gave thanks, and said, Take this, and divide it among yourselves:
18 For I say unto you, I will not drink of the fruit of the vine, until the kingdom of God shall come.
19 And he took bread, and gave thanks, and brake it, and gave unto them, saying, This is my body which is given for you: this do in remembrance of me.
20 Likewise also the cup after supper, saying, This cup is the new testament in my blood, which is shed for you.

KEY VERSE: "And he took bread, and gave thanks, and brake it, and gave unto them, saying, This is my body which is given for you: this do in remembrance of me." Luke 22:19.

Home Daily Bible Readings
Feb. 7	M.	Institution of the Passover, Exodus 12:1–13.
Feb. 8	T.	Plotting Against Jesus, John 11:45–53.
Feb. 9	W.	Judas Agrees to Help Jesus' Enemies, Luke 22:1–6.
Feb. 10	T.	Jesus Prepares for the Passover, Luke 22:7–13.
Feb. 11	F.	The Lord's Supper, Luke 22:14–23.
Feb. 12	S.	The Meal Anticipates God's Kingdom, Luke 13:28, 29; 14:15; 22:28–30.
Feb. 13	S.	Memorializing the Supper, 1 Corinthians 11:23–32.

Lesson Aim: As a result of this study your class members should appreciate more keenly the significance of the Lord's Supper and resolve faithfully to observe it in remembrance of Christ.

LESSON OUTLINE
Background to the Scripture
Looking at the Scripture Text
   I. As Passover Approaches, a Plot Continues (Luke 22:1, 2)
  II. As Passover Day Arrives, a Plan Unfolds (Luke 22:7-13)
 III. At Passover Hour, a New Testament (Luke 22:14-20)
Applying the Scripture

Background to the Scripture
Do you remember our lesson last quarter on the institution of the Passover? You may want to refer to that lesson to refresh your memory about how the Passover was established. You will recall that on the fourteenth day of the first month of the ecclesiastical year, Passover would be observed in each home. Since the Jews reckoned their days from sunset to sunset, the Passover meal would actually be eaten at the beginning of the fifteenth day. That first day of the Passover, or the Feast of Unleavened Bread as it was called, and the twenty-first day of the month which ended the feast, were "holy days"— no work was done on those days.

As we discovered in our preceding lesson, Jesus arrived in Jerusalem on the first day of the week (the tenth day of the month Nisan) and was received by a jubilant crowd with an outpouring of love and adoration. Knowing well the great climactic Act which awaited Him five days later, He established a pattern for the days that were left to Him on earth.

Lodging outside the city, He went to the Temple early each day and taught the people. Evidently He did not devote as much attention to the disciples during this time, with one exception. One day, possibly as they left the city in the afternoon, He took the twelve to the Mount of Olives and spoke to them of what was to come—the destruction of the city and the end of the world and His return. Luke records those words in chapter 21.

Looking at the Scripture Text
As Passover Approaches, a Plot Continues (vv. 1, 2)   In chapter 22, Luke uses three time references. The first of these is in verse 1, "the Passover was approaching." Matthew and Mark fix this time more exactly, reporting that two days before the Passover the Jewish leaders gathered in the court of Caiaphas, the high priest, to work out a strategy for seizing Jesus. "But they were saying, 'Not during the festival, lest a riot occur among the people'" (Matthew 26:1-5 NASB; Mark 14:1, 2).

Luke notes that the chief priests and scribes were continuing to seek (literal meaning of *sought*) to "remove" or "get rid of" Jesus. But it was no easy matter. The population of Jerusalem had swelled by the time of the festival to perhaps 100,000 people. Jesus was highly popular among them. From reports of riots in our cities in recent times, we can well understand the fear of the hierarchy. If they were to arrest Jesus openly, they would face explosive and immense resistance from His followers. The results would be hard to predict. No, the scribes and elders needed to take Him by stealth and they were frustrated until Judas Iscariot surprisingly supplied the necessary element to allow their plot to succeed (vv. 3–6).

As Passover Day Arrives, a Plan Unfolds (vv. 7–13) With verse 7 comes Luke's second reference to time—"then came the day of unleavened bread." Sometime on the fourteenth day, in the early afternoon perhaps, Jesus began to reveal to the twelve something of the careful plans He had in mind for their observance of the Passover meal. For Him, it would be the Last Supper.

That day, according to the Law, the paschal lamb was to be slaughtered for the supper meal. Edersheim says that lambs were killed at the Temple between 2:00 and 5:30 P.M. on this day by the head of the family or company that would later share the meal. No fewer than ten were to share in the meal. The blood of the lamb was to be caught and poured out at the foot of the altar of burnt offering. Then each family head would be responsible for the roasting of the lamb.

Jesus perhaps was unofficially recognizing Peter and John as the heads of the disciples by sending them to prepare the Passover meal. His order for them to go is characteristic of Jesus, reminding us of another mealtime when 5,000 men and women and children stood hungry on a hillside and Jesus said, "You feed them." He had a plan then and He had a plan now. It will encourage us as His followers to know that He always has a plan for our good.

Again at this instance, He exhibited the prophetic knowledge we have remarked on in previous lessons. He told Peter and John exactly how they were to know where to find the guest chamber. They were to proceed to the city and upon entering they would see a man carrying water. "Follow him," Jesus said. If He had said for them to follow a woman carrying water, He would have needed to be more specific. Hauling water was customarily the chore of women, or of slaves. But when they cast their gaze upon the crowded city street, there would be but one man carrying a jug of water. He would lead them to the house where they would find a large upper room furnished and available for the Lord. One wonders if the water the man carried was to be used in washing the paschal lamb after its slaughter. Or was it the water Jesus would use in washing the disciples' feet? (*see* John 13).

How did the owner of the house know to whom he was giving his guest chamber? Did he recognize Peter and John as disciples of Jesus? Was he himself a follower of the Lord? Was his "upper room" the same one to which the disciples retreated behind closed doors after the Resurrection and Ascension (Acts 1:13)? Luke gives us no answers to these questions. He merely pursues his story, stating that the disciples found the room "as he had said unto them."

The word used to designate *guest chamber* appears here and only in Mark 14:14 (the same story) with the exception of the Nativity account. There the word for *inn* is the same word. It literally means a lodging place for "loosening down"—used of a "place where travelers and their beasts untied their packages, girdles, and sandals" says W. E. Vine. It could be that Jesus was only asking for a guest chamber on the lower floor and the generous master of the house gave Him rather the best room, the "upper room." The rabbis boasted, says Hastings in his Bible Dictionary, that notwithstanding the enormous crowds in Jerusalem for the feast, no man could say to his fellow, "I have not found a fire where to roast my paschal lamb in Jerusalem." Peter and John must have recognized at once, on seeing the room, how wise was the Lord's plan.

At the Passover Hour, a New Testament (vv. 14-20) The "hour" of which Luke writes would be approximately six o'clock. The Master arrived with the remaining ten disciples and proceeded to the room where they reclined around tables in the upper room.

"The normal course of the Passover meal," notes the *New Bible Commentary*, called for an inaugural blessing and prayer "followed by the first of four cups of wine and a dish of herbs and sauce." Then one in the room would recite the story of the institution of the Passover and all would sing the 113th Psalm. After a second cup of wine was consumed and grace said for "the main meal of roast lamb with unleavened bread and bitter herbs," another prayer was offered. Then "the third cup of wine was drunk" followed by the singing of the 114th-118th Psalms. A fourth cup of wine was often drunk to conclude the meal.

As the meal proceeded, Jesus revealed the intensity of His desire to share this Supper with the disciples. "I have looked forward to this hour with deep longing, anxious to eat this Passover meal with you before my suffering begins" (TLB), He said. The agony of the cross was only hours away, but Jesus devoted His attention to the men in the room with Him. They could not have realized the importance of this occasion and none of them would have known it was His last supper even though He had warned them. We wonder what meaning they put on the words of Jesus when He said He would not eat of the Passover any more until "it be fulfilled in the kingdom of God."

The phrases "fulfilled in the kingdom of God" and "until the kingdom of God shall come" are identical in meaning. In the upper room, Jesus was signaling the end of the observance of the Passover. It would be fulfilled on the following day when Jesus offered His sinless body and His life blood as the sacrifice for man's sin ("For Christ, our Passover lamb, has been sacrificed" 1 Corinthians 5:7 NIV), inaugurating a new covenant. This new covenant would be perpetually reaffirmed as the disciples of each generation obey His command to do this "in remembrance of me."

Looking ever to the glory of the new day, He said the Passover's ultimate fulfillment would be found in the great Messianic banquet, the "marriage supper of the lamb." This meal John describes in Revelation 19:6-9, but it is alluded to in the Gospels also. In verses 29, 30, Jesus promised "a kingdom . . . that ye may eat and drink at my table in my kingdom, and sit on thrones judging the twelve tribes of Israel."

Some conclude that because Luke refers to a cup in verse 17 and another in verse 20 that Luke must not have written verse 20; that it was included at a later date. One ancient Greek manuscript does omit the verse, but almost 3,000 Greek manuscripts as well as Latin and Syriac manuscripts include it. To omit the verse would be to reverse the order in which the bread and wine are received as the other Gospels state, and as Paul later wrote (1 Corinthians 11:23-26). Criswell offers as a solution that the first cup was the "cup of blessing" (1 Corinthians 10:16).

The Last Supper superseded the Passover in that upper room. Jesus Himself inaugurated this ordinance or sacrament with such few words and only the two elements—the bread and wine. The bread, as He said, stood for His body to be broken on the tree. The cup, or wine, symbolized His blood. By commanding them to eat the bread and drink the wine, He was assuring His disciples of His perpetual presence with them. We do the same and Paul charges the Church to so remember the Lord in this manner "until he comes."

Applying the Scripture
Close your class period by allowing time for personal reflection on the words, THIS DO IN REMEMBRANCE OF ME.
1. "This Do"—The child of God can do many things as an individual that are pleasing to God—but the Lord's Supper is not one of them.

Ask your class how recently they heard someone contend that he or she does not need to attend church, that being a Christian is a private matter, and that God can be worshiped alone out in the grandeur of nature (even a golf course!), away from all those "hypocrites" in church?

We ought to grant that a good deal of Christian discipleship is within the reach of the individual. We are to witness as individuals. We ought to pray and read our Bibles and do loving service. But the child of God cannot keep this command of His Savior and Lord unless he makes the effort to be in the presence of other believers when the Lord's Supper is observed.

Recently an evangelical church announced a Maundy Thursday communion service. Families gathered for the evening's solemn observance. A class meeting and studying the subject of worship had planned the evening program which began with a song and commenced with Scripture readings and personal messages from three laymen who had not spoken at a service of the church. At either side of the altar stood a low table on which were placed a loaf of bread and communion cups filled with grape juice. After the presentation of the messages and singing of two hymns, the people were invited to come forward, to pray at the altar and to receive the elements.

One mother and her teenage daughter were seen kneeling at the altar for long minutes and while no one knew what might have been their cause of prayer, it occurred to one observer that the missing father was the object of their prayers. For months, he had absented himself from the services. Even on this holy occasion, this man who professes to be a Christian had not been there. How lightly we take Jesus' command to "do this."

2. "In Remembrance of Me"—Ask your class to think on the words Jesus spoke in the upper room. The whole event of a communion service or Lord's Supper should be to focus upon Jesus, to remember Him. The observance is in vain and will yield no blessing to us if we leave Him out of our ritual.

Some suggestions for remembering Him are:

Bring your Bible to communion service. Turn to the Scriptures that are read during the service and meditate upon the words, especially as they relate to who Jesus is and what He has done.

Let the music minister to you. Often the musical instruments play hymns that speak of Jesus' sacrifice. Let the words of these hymns go over and over in your mind as the hymn is played. If this is not a practice in your church, you may want to suggest it.

Examine yourselves. The Scripture says, "let every one examine himself and not partake of the bread and the cup in an unworthy manner." By reflecting upon Jesus and His perfect sacrifice, and His promise of total forgiveness, we can invite the Lord to search our hearts and minds, confident that for what we confess to Him we receive forgiveness.

Questions for Discussion

Make use of these questions to involve your students in learning and to test their understanding of the lesson.
1. How does the phrase, "sought how they might kill him" link up in meaning with the statement that the Jewish hierarchy "feared the people"? 2. How do you explain Jesus' knowledge that Peter and John would meet a man carrying a jug of water? 3. What would be extraordinary about finding a man carrying water? 4. What would be involved in making "ready the passover"? 5. Approximately what hour would the meal commence? 6. How will the Passover be fulfilled in the Kingdom of God? 7. According to Jesus, what is the meaning of the bread? What is the meaning of the cup, or wine?

Illustrating the Scripture

Examples and quotations to help the teacher communicate the lesson.

IN JEWISH HOMES TODAY "During the eight days of Passover, Jewish people refrain from eating bread or any dishes prepared with leaven, symbolizing their haste and sacrifice when they marched out of Egypt. Instead, matzoh is substituted for bread, and matzoh meal for leaven.

"Beginning at sundown, Jewish families will gather in their homes to participate in the traditional Passover meal, called a seder, during which the story of the deliverance from Egyptian bondage is retold in the form of a dialogue between the head of the household and the youngest child present capable of asking questions.

"After the opening blessing, the child begins the seder by reciting the traditional 'four questions,' the first of which is, 'Why is this night different from all other nights?'

"The seder, which means 'order,' is conducted in accordance with the traditional format and sequence in a booklet called the Haggadah.

"The seder table holds a sumptuous meal with many courses, including sweet wine for everyone. Symbolic foods are eaten as well, such as a mixture of apples, nuts, and wine, resembling the mortar used in the buildings of Egypt, and bitter herbs, a reminder of the bitterness of life in slavery.

"Not only is the pace of the seder leisurely, but the festive mood of the holiday is underscored with resounding choruses of traditional Passover songs, which all seder participants sing together.

"The seder service is repeated on the second night of Passover. The holiday continues for eight days." (From *The Somerset Messenger-Gazette*, Somerville, New Jersey, April 16, 1981.)

HOW FREQUENTLY SHOULD THE LORD'S SUPPER BE OBSERVED? Dr. Andrew W. Blackwood, professor of preaching and Bible at Temple University, said, "Ideally, many think with Calvin we should follow the apostolic church in observing Communion every Lord's day. Many, like him, have compromised on once a month, not always at the same hour of the day. Special services of the sort on Christmas, Maundy Thursday and other high days are increasingly common. Almost every pastor stands ready to administer this sacrament (a term not acceptable to many churches) to sick or shut-in friends. Communion on the evening before a marriage has become fairly common. All sorts of churches are becoming like liturgical bodies that believe in frequent Communion. This involves the possibility of its becoming only a form. The facts call for special training in communicants' classes, pastoral work, personal counseling, and sermons about the meaning of the Supper."

Topics for Youth

WHAT DO YOU DO AT THE LORD'S TABLE?—Blessed are the pastors who take pains to teach their young people how to prepare themselves for the Lord's Supper, for they shall point them to Christ!

Youth are not unable to take seriously the Communion table, but they often act bored or play silly games—or fail to be present—when Communion is served. Let them know that:

THE LORD'S TABLE IS DESIGNED FOR A SPECIAL PURPOSE—Jesus chose "what his enemies thought was the one thing in his career he would have his disciples forget—his death—and bade his followers keep that event in mind and commemorate it often," says W. W. Hamilton. Communion is not a "magical mystery by which in some supernatural way the elements are linked to and filled with Christ, the bread and wine producing some magical effect of cleansing or of life-giving power."

THE LORD'S TABLE IS AN OCCASION FOR REMEMBRANCE—He said, "this do in remembrance of me," not "each other." He did not invite His mother or sisters and brothers or Mary and Martha or Nicodemus or others of His friends. No, only the disciples. "Love for all Christians is beautiful and good, but he who at the Lord's Table eats and drinks to show this is eating and drinking unworthily 'not discerning the Lord's body.' We are not assembling to remember each other, but . . . Christ."

THE LORD'S TABLE IS A PICTURE OF LOVING SACRIFICE—"The woman's portrait on the wall, with its kind and constant gaze upon a man of business as he goes out to his daily toil, is a tender reminder to him of a mother's love and of the life which was sacrificed one night in rescuing her boy from a horrible death in a burning building. He looks now and then upon the portrait, recalls her love, her life, her death, and each time he is more determined to be a stronger and braver and better man. So at the Lord's Table we remember Him who loved us and gave Himself for us. We do this in remembrance of the Lord Jesus Christ."

The act of Communion, receiving the bread and the cup, draws us near the Savior. It is the time for us to confess our shortcomings and cling closer to Him.

LESSON 12   FEBRUARY 20

Suffering Crucifixion

Background Scripture: Luke 23
Devotional Reading: Luke 23:18–25

Luke 23:32–46

32 And there were also two others, malefactors, led with him to be put to death.

33 And when they were come to the place, which is called Calvary, there they crucified him, and the malefactors, one on the right hand, and the other on the left.

34 Then said Jesus, Father, forgive them; for they know not what they do. And they parted his raiment, and cast lots.

35 And the people stood beholding. And the rulers also with them derided him, saying, He saved others; let him save himself, if he be Christ, the chosen of God.

36 And the soldiers also mocked him, coming to him, and offering him vinegar,
37 And saying, If thou be the king of the Jews, save thyself.
38 And a superscription also was written over him in letters of Greek, and Latin, and Hebrew, THIS IS THE KING OF THE JEWS.
39 And one of the malefactors which were hanged railed on him, saying, If thou be Christ, save thyself and us.
40 But the other answering rebuked him, saying, Dost not thou fear God, seeing thou art in the same condemnation?
41 And we indeed justly; for we receive the due reward of our deeds: but this man hath done nothing amiss.
42 And he said unto Jesus, Lord, remember me when thou comest into thy kingdom.
43 And Jesus said unto him, Verily I say unto thee, To day shalt thou be with me in paradise.
44 And it was about the sixth hour, and there was a darkness over all the earth until the ninth hour.
45 And the sun was darkened, and the veil of the temple was rent in the midst.
46 And when Jesus had cried with a loud voice, he said, Father, into thy hands I commend my spirit: and having said thus, he gave up the ghost.

KEY VERSE: "And when Jesus had cried with a loud voice, he said, Father, into thy hands I commend my spirit: and having said thus, he gave up the ghost." Luke 23:46.

Home Daily Bible Readings
Feb. 14 M. Jesus Before the Council, Luke 22:66–71.
Feb. 15 T. Jesus Before Pilate, Luke 23:1–5.
Feb. 16 W. Jesus Before Herod, Luke 23:6–12.
Feb. 17 T. Jesus Is Sentenced to Death, Luke 23:13–25.
Feb. 18 F. Jesus Is Crucified, Luke 23:26–43.
Feb. 19 S. The Death of Jesus, Luke 23:44–49.
Feb. 20 S. The Burial of Jesus, Luke 23:50–56.

Lesson Aim: As a result of this lesson, the students in your class who have Christ in their hearts should treasure Him even more, and those who are unconverted should face the fact of their need of Him.

LESSON OUTLINE
Background to the Scripture
Looking at the Scripture Text
  I. Crucified With Two Criminals (Luke 23:32, 33)
  II. Father, Forgive Them (Luke 23:34–39)

III. Today, With Me (Luke 23:40-43)
IV. Father, Into Thy Hands (Luke 23:44-46)
Applying the Scripture

Background to the Scripture
So much happened after the Lord shared His Last Supper with the disciples that it is easy to confuse the events that led to His death. At night, following the supper, Jesus led the eleven disciples out of Jerusalem and into the Garden of Gethsemane. There He prayed, well knowing what lay before Him. We believe He won the victory over the forces of evil there in the garden on His knees.

Into the garden next came Judas leading a band of the Jewish rulers and Roman soldiers and Jesus was taken by force to Annas the high priest. After false witnesses leveled charges and the Sanhedrin condemned Him to death (Peter denying Him meanwhile), it was necessary to persuade the Roman authorities to exact the death penalty. It must have been very early in the morning when Jesus was brought before Pilate. After a brief examination, Pilate sent Him to Herod, but soon received Him back and faced the awful decision of what to do with a man against whom he could find no charge. He sentenced Jesus to die and had Him whipped. After mocking Him, the soldiers laid on Jesus the heavy cross and the procession headed for Golgotha where they would execute Him. But He fell beneath the load and another man was forced to carry the cross for Him. All of this happened in less than twelve hours. It was approximately nine o'clock in the morning when Jesus was brought to the hill of Calvary.

Looking at the Scripture Text
Crucified With Two Criminals (vv. 32, 33)   Each year at Easter, Christians in Jerusalem retrace the steps of Jesus from Pilate's court to the site of the Crucifixion. In Aramaic, this hill was named Golgotha (Matthew 27:33). Luke avoided that word in his account, knowing that it would be meaningless to his Gentile readers, choosing rather to call it "the place of the skull" which it was called by the distinctive skull-like appearance of the hill. From Latin versions, the word *Calvary* slipped into English texts.

We do not know the exact location of this hill. For many years one site, called "Gordon's Calvary," was thought to be it but that theory is generally rejected today.

From Luke's simple statement, "they crucified him," offered with no descriptive detail, we must conclude that crucifixion was such a common occurrence throughout the Empire that the writer saw no necessity of explaining how it was performed. However, we feel the need today for more background. A brief description ought to help us picture what happened so that we can comprehend what Jesus suffered in dying for us.

The Romans adopted this form of execution from the Persians and Phoenicians. They used it rarely on a Roman citizen, reserving it primarily for slaves and foreigners. In Palestine, this cruel means of death was employed to punish robbers and those found guilty of sedition. Two such criminals stood condemned on the day Jesus was crucified.

A prisoner so condemned carried the transverse beam of the cross to the site of execution. This may have weighed as much as 100 pounds. This heavy coarse beam the soldiers placed on Jesus' shoulders, but He needed help in carrying it. Matthew and Mark with Luke record that Simon of Cyrene carried the cross of Jesus. The Lord, weary from lack of sleep and having had nothing to eat since the Last Supper, had been further deprived of strength by the whipping at the hands of Roman soldiers.

At the site of the execution, the victim would be forced to lie down, his shoulders against the cross piece and either arm stretched out. The executioners drove a nail through the hand (or the wrist, some say) into the wood. Raising the victim by the cross beam, the soldiers affixed this beam either by rope or nails to the stationary stake in the ground. Whether the victims always had their feet nailed to the cross seems open to question. Perhaps Luke 24:39 can best be interpreted in the light of the piercing of Jesus' feet. An American Lutheran anatomist, Dr. Howard A. Matzke, who made a thorough study of the Crucifixion, said that if Jesus' feet were nailed, it would have been done in this way: "With the knees slightly flexed, one foot was placed over the other, and a single spike driven through both. Riveted to the rough timbers, the holy Victim was left to die."

With Jesus on that stark Judean hill were two criminals who also met death by crucifixion, fulfilling the prophecy Isaiah had uttered centuries earlier, "he was numbered with the transgressors."

Father, Forgive Them (vv. 34–39) The sayings of Jesus on the cross are themselves rich sources for meditation. Luke alone gives us the first and the last utterance as well as the reply of Jesus to the thief beside Him.

For whom did Jesus pray: "Father, forgive them; for they know not what they do"? The answer seems obvious at first. The soldiers, who were perhaps even then driving the nails into His gentle hands, surely must be intended. They were only carrying out their duty, horrible as it was. They were calloused by their task; they would not "know what they do."

But Jesus' prayer could just as well have been intended for those, His enemies, among the Jewish rulers, too. They *thought* they knew what they were doing, disposing of a fanatical Nazarene, a self-styled prophet, a blasphemer who pretended to be the Son of God. But the later testimony of Peter agrees with Jesus' prayer; the Jewish hierarchy opposed Him and crucified Him "in ignorance" (Acts 3:17).

Yet the prayer cannot even be limited to these active participants. His prayer was for us all. Inasmuch as the rulers and the soldiers and the crowd represent mankind, He was praying for fallen man. And His prayer again was a fulfillment of Isaiah's words: He "made intercession for the transgressors" (53:12). He lived out what He had taught His disciples—"pray for them which despitefully use you, and persecute you" (Matthew 5:44).

Death by crucifixion was a shameful thing (note Hebrews 12:2; 13:13). Added to the humiliation of having to carry one's own cross to the site of execution was the fact that the victim's clothing would be removed. John in his Gospel says that four soldiers each took one of Jesus' garments, but that they were loathe to tear apart the seamless robe. For this they gambled, as all the Gospels indicate, once more fulfilling a prophecy spoken in Psalms 22:18. "This dividing of clothes is one more detail in the treatment of Christ as a criminal," says the *International Critical Commentary*.

In portraying the death of Jesus, Luke identified four groups of people on Golgotha's hill—the crowd, the rulers, the soldiers, and the criminals. Each formed a part of the tragic mosaic of his depiction of Jesus' death. Omitted are Mary and John and other disciples who stood by and extended loving sympathy.

The *crowd* stared in stark unbelief and vulgar curiosity. The *rulers* of the Jews, their purpose accomplished, would not shut their hateful mouths but chided Jesus to prove He was the Messiah by coming down from the cross. Luke's account suggests that the religionists' taunts egged on the *soldiers*. Prompted by the inscription which declared His crime—THE KING OF THE JEWS—they mocked Him. "If you are the king of the Jews, save yourself" (NIV). The offer of sour wine, probably a compassionate gesture earlier in the crucifixion, was part of their cruel mockery.

Closer at hand, one of the *criminals* mouthed off at Jesus. "Aren't you the Christ?" he griped. "Save yourself and us" (*see* v. 39). From all sides, man was pleading with Jesus to save himself. It is not a very pretty picture of human nature, cruel and selfish and blind.

Today, With Me (vv. 40-43) The two thieves were but hours away from death. Being evidently Jews, they knew that God's judgment awaited them. This may explain the second thief's rebuke: "Don't you even *fear* God?" not to speak of any higher feelings toward the Creator. The second thief confessed his guilt (vv. 40, 41) and Jesus' innocence. Poole remarks that "Christ had that honor from a thief which was denied Him by the chief priests and elders."

"Lord, remember me when thou comest into thy kingdom" was the desperate cry of a dying man. But it was accepted because of his faith. That prayer could be taken to mean, "when You return as king" or "when You come in the glory and power of Your kingdom," probably the latter. Both the man's question and Jesus' reply confirm belief in life after death. "Jesus' use of the word (*paradise*) neither confirms nor corrects Jewish beliefs on the subject," remarks one commentator. "He assures the penitent that He will do far more than remember him at some unknown time . . . this very day He will have him in His company in a place of security and bliss." Paradise was thought variously to be a park or pleasure ground, the garden of Eden, the resting place of the souls of the just until the Resurrection ("Abraham's bosom") or a region in heaven (*see* 2 Corinthians 12:4).

Father, Into Thy Hands (vv. 44-46) Our text says that at "about the sixth hour" (noon) . . . a darkness" covered the land (the land of Palestine is the best interpretation). The word Luke used for the sun's failure is *eclipse*, though, with a full moon in the sky at Passover, a normal eclipse would not have been possible. Some have suggested that a desert sandstorm might have caused the strange darkness and the rending of the veil as well. We do not know. The best explanation may be that God intervened in a supernatural way to cause such a darkness to shield the indignities done to His Son and to show the sympathetic grief of the universe over His death.

Matthew reports that an earthquake shook the city. This also could account for the splitting of the veil. This thick curtain hung between the Holy Place and the Holy of Holies. It stood as a barrier, not allowing man into the central place where God's presence was made manifest. Matthew's words that the veil was torn from top to bottom suggests a heavenly Hand removing this barrier once for all. It marked the end of an era. Man no longer had to go to another as mediator between himself and God. Christ at His death fulfilled the type of the priest and made access to the Father possible through His shed blood (*see* Hebrews 10:19, 10).

All of the Evangelists agree that Jesus' last words were a shout or loud cry, indicating that He died of His free will as He said He would (John 10:18). He faced death courageously, holding off the enemy until all around Him were cared for. He faced death sweetly, harboring no enmity toward His executioners. He faced death confidently, knowing that He would awaken in paradise. He faced death triumphantly, with a shout.

Applying the Scripture

Ask the members of your class: With which of the thieves do you identify? The first one, who said, "Aren't you the Christ? Save yourself and us!" Or the second one, who said, "We are getting what our deeds deserve. But this man has done nothing wrong . . . Jesus, remember me when you come into your kingdom."

Preachers have made the comparison. All of mankind can be seen represented by these two men. Both are alike—sinners, guilty and condemned, their deeds having brought them to the moment of truth. There the similarities end.

One is impenitent, the other is sorry for his sins.

One does not see anything in Christ for him. The other sees in Him his one hope.

One is bitter. The other is bitterly remorseful.

One shows no stirrings of faith. The other acts in faith.

Elsewhere in the Bible this division of all mankind is made. Some walk in darkness, others in light. Some are goats, others are the redeemed sheep. Many are on the broad road that leads to destruction. Few are on the narrow road that leads to life.

Tell your class: While God does not encourage "deathbed repentance," this passage clearly shows that a sinner who truly reaches out in faith to Christ—even at death, when there is no opportunity to do good or be baptized—is assured of eternal life in heaven with God. Encourage everyone to decide today to call upon the name of the Lord and be saved.

Ask your class: Do you want a worship experience that will transform your life? Set aside a block of time and go to a place where you will not be disturbed. Take your Bible and a hymn book.

Read the accounts of the Crucifixion in each of the Gospels. In Matthew, read chapters 26, 27; in Mark, chapters 14, 15; in Luke, chapters 22, 23; and in John, chapters 18, 19.

Worship the Savior by quietly meditating on the words you have read. Close your eyes and allow the scenes of which you have read to take place before your eyes. Let your emotions freely express how you feel. "Worship the Lord in the beauty of holiness." Read then a hymn or two that speak of His Passion. You will find rich thought for your worship and praise in, "When I Survey the Wondrous Cross" or perhaps in, "There Is a Fountain Filled With Blood."

Remain in the quiet place for a while. Commune with your Savior, knowing now that He is alive. Thank Him afresh for all His suffering and His dying love.

Questions for Discussion
Make use of these questions to involve your students in learning and to test their understanding of the lesson.

1. Can you name at least three things the Lord did or that were done to Him in this passage that fulfilled specific prophesies? **2.** Since Jesus did not save Himself from this cruel death, it was either because He could not or chose not to. Which do you think is the best answer? State your reasons. **3.** What quality is shown in the penitent thief's question to Jesus? **4.** What is revealed about life beyond death by Jesus' answer to the man? **5.** What is the meaning of "paradise"? **6.** How would you explain the meaning of the darkness and other cataclysmic conditions in nature that took place at the time Jesus was on the cross? **7.** Do you think an important significance should be given to the statement, "the veil of the temple was rent in the midst"? If so, what is the significance? **8.** How would you describe the way Jesus met death?

Illustrating the Scripture
Examples and quotations to help the teacher communicate the lesson.

A MEDICAL EXPLANATION FOR HIS DEATH   "Crucifixion resulted in severe pain because the body was hanging on the nails through the hands. It also placed considerable stretch on the muscles extending from the chest to the arms, muscles which are very important in breathing. Crucifixion thus prevented normal expiration, for it held the chest expanded. Impaired breathing results in a decreased oxygen supply to the muscles. These in turn accumulate an excess amount of lactic acid. Severe tetany follows. These are muscle spasms comparable to muscle cramps.

"To alleviate the pain of severed nerves and the muscle spasms, the victim would try to push himself up by using the nails through his feet as a brace. Within a few minutes, the pain in the feet would become unbearable, and the body would sag again. For Christ this went on for six hours—until He sank in death.

"The most plausible medical explanation for the immediate, natural cause of His death would be asphyxia. His body no longer received enough oxygen to sustain life. At death the muscle spasms would convulse the body, and the head would slump forward because of the pull of the muscles extending from the arms and chest to the neck.

"John, who watched Jesus die, records that Jesus willingly yielded Himself to death because His mission was accomplished: 'When Jesus therefore had received the vinegar, he said, It is finished; and he bowed his head and gave up the ghost' (John 19:30)." (From "An Anatomist Looks at the Physical Sufferings of Our Lord" by Howard A. Matzke, *The Lutheran Witness*, February 21, 1961.)

LOVE IS NOT ABLE TO SAVE ITSELF   "The mystery of love is that it cannot save itself. The taunts of the priests were correct: love is not able to save itself. Christ can't come down and save himself. He is not concerned to save himself. Love is never concerned with itself, to save itself.

"Christ on the Cross was there because he was obedient to love. If you are obedient to love you do not save yourself. To obey love means to renounce all power to save yourself. Christ saves you. It means to renounce all rights to protect yourself. Christ protects you. That is part of the mystery of the Cross and Christ—that he revealed the mystery of love by giving up his authority as King. And so he finally came to reign as King.

"His power and his worth are seen in this: his refusal to exercise his power or to show forth his worth in any way except by love. He gave up himself.

"Ever since then, whenever we have given up ourselves in love because of love, we have revealed that truth. 'Vicarious suffering,' it is sometimes called, on behalf of others with no return expected. That is the mystery of God and of us." (From *Christ's Life: Our Life* by John B. Coburn, The Seabury Press, New York, 1978.)

Topics for Youth

FIRST EASTER—"The crowd hurled His own words back at Him, but they were barbs, dipped in venom and shot from snarling lips, like poisoned arrows.

'He saved others, himself he cannot save.

Yes, he healed the cripples.

Yes, he gave sight to the blind.

He even brought back the dead, but he cannot save himself.'

"They were willing now to grant the truth of His miracles.

Out of the mouths of His enemies comes this testimony to His power—'He saved others'. . . .

"Yes, they were saved—those others . . .
  saved from the land of shadows
    saved from the caves of derangement
      from the couches of pain
      from the leprous touch of sickness
    saved from the enslaving grip of vice
  saved even from the jaws of death.
Yes, He had saved others—His enemies admitted it. . . .
"But now their taunt rose to its crescendo—
  'Perform a miracle now, Miracle Man! Come down from the cross, and we will believe thee.
  Aha, thou who wouldst build the temple in three days,
  Thou hast nails in thy hands now . . .
  Thou hast wood . . . go on and build thy temple.'
  'If thou be the Christ . . . prove it to us. . . . Come on down from the cross!'
"They shouted until they were hoarse.
The noise was so great that only a few of them standing near the Cross heard what He said when His lips moved in prayer:
  'Father, forgive them, for they know not what they do.' "
(From *The First Easter* by Peter Marshall, McGraw-Hill Book Company, Inc., New York, 1959.)

LESSON 13   FEBRUARY 27

Standing Among His Disciples

Background Scripture: Luke 24:1–11, 36–53
Devotional Reading: 1 Corinthians 15:1–11

Luke 24:36–53

36 And as they thus spake, Jesus himself stood in the midst of them, and saith unto them, Peace be unto you.
37 But they were terrified and affrighted, and supposed that they had seen a spirit.
38 And he said unto them, Why are ye troubled? and why do thoughts arise in your hearts?
39 Behold my hands and my feet, that it is I myself: handle me, and see; for a spirit hath not flesh and bones, as ye see me have.
40 And when he had thus spoken, he shewed them his hands and his feet.
41 And while they yet believed not for joy, and wondered, he said unto them, Have ye here any meat?
42 And they gave him a piece of a broiled fish, and of an honeycomb.

43 And he took it, and did eat before them.
44 And he said unto them, These are the words which I spake unto you, while I was yet with you, that all things must be fulfilled, which were written in the law of Moses, and in the prophets, and in the psalms, concerning me.
45 Then opened he their understanding, that they might understand the scriptures,
46 And said unto them, Thus it is written, and thus it behooved Christ to suffer, and to rise from the dead the third day:
47 And that repentance and remission of sins should be preached in his name among all nations, beginning at Jerusalem.
48 And ye are witnesses of these things.
49 And, behold, I send the promise of my Father upon you: but tarry ye in the city of Jerusalem, until ye be endued with power from on high.
50 And he led them out as far as to Bethany, and he lifted up his hands, and blessed them.
51 And it came to pass, while he blessed them, he was parted from them, and carried up into heaven.
52 And they worshipped him, and returned to Jerusalem with great joy:
53 And were continually in the temple, praising and blessing God. Amen.

KEY VERSE: "Behold my hands and my feet, that it is I myself: handle me, and see; for a spirit hath not flesh and bones, as ye see me have." Luke 24:39.

Home Daily Bible Readings		
Feb. 21	M.	The Resurrection, Luke 24:1–12.
Feb. 22	T.	The Walk to Emmaus, Luke 24:13–24.
Feb. 23	W.	Explanation, Luke 24:25–35.
Feb. 24	T.	Appearance to His Disciples, Luke 24:36–43.
Feb. 25	F.	Commissioning His Disciples, Luke 24:44–49.
Feb. 26	S.	The Ascension, Luke 24:50–53; Acts 1:9–11.
Feb. 27	S.	Paul's Testimony, 1 Corinthians 15:1–11.

Lesson Aim: As a result of this study each individual in the class should commit himself or herself to telling one individual in their "Jerusalem" of the repentance and pardon in Christ's Name.

LESSON OUTLINE
Background to the Scripture
Looking at the Scripture Text
  I. Persuades Them He Is Alive (Luke 24:36–43)
  II. Imparts to Them the Gospel (Luke 24:44–48)

III. Empowers Them With the Spirit (Luke 24:49)
IV. Ascends From Them to Heaven (Luke 24:50-53)
Applying the Scripture

Background to the Scripture

With today's lesson, we conclude Luke's account of the life of Jesus, a remarkable and careful biography—perhaps the best "life of our Lord" ever written. With the characteristic precision of a physician, Luke relates the final appearances and words of the Lord. He ends his account on a high note of joy. Jesus, ever the focus of his pen, is now the one subject demanding all of his attention. No words of the disciples are recorded after verse 34. Only Jesus' words and Luke's narrative remain to complete the book.

Luke introduces Jesus in the passage by His earthly name, but that name does not appear again. The one time Jesus refers to Himself He does so not as the Son of Man, but as Christ. Having conquered death and the tomb, fulfilling all the prophecies concerning His life, He took His rightful name as the Anointed One of God. But He did not go immediately to heaven. Important business awaited the risen Christ during the forty days after His Resurrection in which He met with His disciples on numerous occasions (*see* Luke's introductory words to the Book of Acts).

Looking at the Scripture Text

Persuades Them He Is Alive (*vv. 36-43*)   A man once said to his friend that he was not content with any of the religions of the world and that he was going to found a new religion. To that the friend replied, "All you have to do is die and come back to life!"

That proposition has a way of thinning out the competition. But as difficult as it is to come back from the grave, there remains the almost impossible task of convincing people that you are alive. Jesus, in the story of the rich man and Lazarus, said, "If they do not listen to Moses and the Prophets, they will not be convinced even if someone rises from the dead" (Luke 16:31 NIV).

His experience demonstrated the truth of the statement. Only with evidence heaped upon evidence did the disciples come to believe that Jesus had risen. None of them were expecting the Resurrection and they had to be persuaded against a prejudice all of us have: dead people don't live again. Their attitude as portrayed by all four Evangelists is a feature that makes the account of the Resurrection credible.

When Jesus suddenly "stood in the midst" of the disciples, they were in Jerusalem, perhaps in the upper room where the Last Supper had been observed. The time was about 8:00 P.M. or later, on the day the Lord had risen—Easter Sunday. While Cleopas (v. 18) and his friend, all out of breath from their hurried return to the city, listened to the startling news that Peter had seen the risen Lord, the same Person all of a sudden was there in the room with them.

Jesus presented Himself to their senses. They *heard* Him say, "Peace be with you." Noting the frightened and bewildered expression on their faces, He said "Behold me." To their *sight*, He "showed them his hands and feet." "Handle me," He added, encouraging them to *touch* Him. They spoke not a word—not even Peter.

We do not know how long this group of stunned men and women stood and looked at Jesus. As He said, "Behold my hands and feet," He must have stretched out His hands toward them. His feet also. This action certainly implies that His feet had suffered the nail wounds as well as His hands, and by seeing those marks the disciples would make positive identification of the Lord. (John says He showed His hands and side, he being the only Evangelist to record how Jesus received that wound from the Roman soldier.)

Reading their questioning minds, Jesus said, "Handle me, and see . . . a spirit hath not flesh and bones as ye see me have." Touching Him, as they must have, they would discover that He had a body though they could not comprehend how He suddenly materialized in the room without using the door (John 20:19). Nor can we comprehend it.

The King James expression of Luke's next words have not been improved upon by modern translators: "they yet believed not for joy, and wondered." A huge bubble of joy—like a lump in their throats—awaited to burst within them, but their minds were telling them this could not be true. As they gaped, Jesus said, "Do you have anything eatable?" Still silent, one reached for a piece of broiled fish and gave it to Him. (The words "and of an honeycomb" are not in the most reliable manuscripts.) He ate the fish, not to sustain His life, but to persuade them He was alive and not a mere spirit.

Eating, of course, is inconsistent with the existence of spirit forms as we know them. And His instantaneous appearances rule out any explanation that He had a normal physical body. But what is not ruled out is a third possibility—a glorified body. In this resurrected body, He stood before them, not dazzling them, appearing ever so much like Himself and yet we wonder if He did not have a glorious appearance to some degree. (Note Paul's words about the body of the Resurrection in 1 Corinthians 15:35–49: "the body that is sown is perishable, it is raised imperishable; it is sown in dishonor, it is raised in glory; it is sown in weakness, it is raised in power; it is sown a natural body, it is raised a spiritual body. If there is a natural body, there is also a spiritual body" NIV.)

Imparts to Them the Gospel (vv. 44–48)   If we read Luke's account to the end of the book, we might conclude that all of this took place on the same day. But from his statement about "forty days" at the beginning of Acts we know that Jesus made several appearances to the disciples. Luke has here telescoped some of Jesus' parting instruction and the final event of His Ascension into a strong, powerful ending.

The verses that follow in this section are appropriate in subject matter to what has gone before and may well be the continuation of the activities of that evening. As they began to allow themselves to believe it was really Jesus, their minds needed to be opened; that is, their understanding needed enlightening about all the events that had taken place.

Jesus began by reminding them of the earlier occasions when He foretold His suffering and His Resurrection (9:22; 18:31–33). Note that He said, "while I was yet with you," using the past tense. He was no longer with them as before. That was in the past—a new relationship awaited.

Having appealed to their senses to prove He was alive, He then appealed to the Word of God. Scholars believe that He took them on an extended "tour" through the Old Testament Scriptures, pointing out what they said about Him. It would have been a teaching lesson all of us could wish for. He pointed out the threefold makeup of the Old Testament—the Law of Moses and the Prophets and the Psalms (usually referred to as the Writings, including all of the books of poetry) and no doubt cited verses from all three.

The expression "opened he their understanding" is used earlier, of His dealing with Cleopus (vv. 27, 31, 32) and is quite similar to that which Luke uses in Acts to refer to Lydia's conversion (16:14). This illumination is undoubtedly the work of the Spirit, leading some to see in this a parallel to Jesus' words ("Receive ye the Holy Ghost") in John 20:22.

From the summary of this teaching, Luke returns in verses 46–49 to quote the Lord. He spoke of the Gospel, His death and Resurrection, already accomplished. And He spoke of the unfinished work—that the necessity of changing one's whole attitude toward God and being pardoned for one's sins must be proclaimed to all nations (literally, to all ethnic peoples). This Good News must be declared in Christ's Name, that is, preaching Him as the Way to the Father. And they were to begin at home, in Jerusalem. While the message was for all men, it is clear that the Lord intended His own people, the Jews, to hear it first. This commission is repeated more familiarly in Acts ("and you will be my witnesses in Jerusalem, and in all Judea and Samaria, and to the ends of the earth" 1:8 NIV).

Empowers Them With the Spirit (v. 49) Jesus had taught His disciples about the Holy Spirit though John, not Luke, records this instruction (*see* John 14:16, 26; 15:26; 16:7–13). His words about the Holy Spirit were among His last and deserved their closest attention. "I will send down on you what my Father has promised; wait in the city till you are endued with power from on high" (v. 49 MOFFATT). The Spirit, He said, was "the promise of the Father." Jesus Himself promised to send the Spirit of truth "down" from heaven. He would come upon the disciples who were to remain in one place, in Jerusalem, until this happened. The command to "tarry in Jerusalem" was specifically for the first disciples. At Pentecost, the "promise" of the Father was gloriously poured out on them and He has been in the world ever since, coming upon each and every person who believes in Christ as Savior.

Ascends From Them to Heaven (vv. 50–53) Some time elapsed certainly between what is recorded in verse 50 and the preceding verses. On the day of His Ascension, Jesus led the disciples "out as far as Bethany," the words implying that they went from Jerusalem to Bethany, which was at the foot of the

Mount of Olives, on the eastern slope. But since Jesus did not appear after His Resurrection to any but believers, it is difficult to be specific about Luke's words here.

Luke says in Acts that they returned after His Ascension "from the mount called Olivet" (1:12). This favorite place was evidently the scene of His Ascension. To this mountain, He is to return when He comes again (Zechariah 14:4). Lifting up His hands in blessing the disciples, He left them and was taken up into heaven. His last act before leaving them was blessing them.

The disciples worshiped Him as they watched Him ascend, being taken in a cloud out of their sight (Acts 1:9). Evidently they gazed heavenward for some time because according to Luke's account in Acts, two angels spoke to them and promised, "This same Jesus, which is taken up from you into heaven, shall so come in like manner as ye have seen him go into heaven" (1:11).

Jesus had instructed them to wait in Jerusalem and, to the city, they then returned "with great joy." As much as they were able, they remained in the Temple, continually praising God. It was not yet time for them to share their splendid secret with others—but that day was very close.

Applying the Scripture
In closing the lesson today, ask your class: Maybe you cannot witness to the peoples of Asia or Europe or some other place overseas, but where can you witness? Ask them: Where is it often the hardest to witness? And finally, ask: Where did Jesus tell His disciples to begin their witnessing?

If they are listening closely, your class members should all come up with one answer—"my Jerusalem." We are to witness of Christ where we are, not where we would one day hope to be. And that surely means beginning with those closest to us—our family, our friends, and associates. Jesus said that everyone (almost) will listen to a prophet except his hometown crowd and his own people. We will find it the same way. But that does not mean that we are to avoid them and try to reach complete strangers first.

He knew that the majority of His own people would reject the message, but He charged the disciples with the task of telling them first. There is a principle here: if we have a true message and have experienced a true conversion then we need not be afraid of sharing it with those who know us better than anyone else. Their immediate reaction may be negative, but because we are witnesses to them day by day, and are praying for them, they have the best opportunity to know that our rebirth is genuine.

Expect everyone in your class to be willing to sharpen his witness in his Jerusalem, which certainly includes the town or city in which he lives as well as his family and associates. Two tips may be helpful.
1. Talk about what it is to "witness." Some Christians have an erroneous conception of this responsibility. They conjure up visions of preaching or going door-to-door or learning some formula and using it from rote memory.

Encourage your class to explore the meaning of the Word and to think of new ways to tell the Good News. Stress that our responsibility is not to convert the world, but to tell the Good News.

2. Second, emphasize what it is we are witnesses of. Jesus said, "you are witnesses of *these things.*" What things? That Christ suffered and died and rose again on the third day and that repentance and forgiveness of sins is declared in His Name. We are not primarily witnesses of a church or a denomination. We have the happy privilege of announcing to "our Jerusalem" that we have awakened to the fact that we were hopeless sinners, that we found forgiveness from God and that all of this was made possible through Jesus Christ—His death and His Resurrection. Knowing that this is what it means to witness should free up your class members to look for opportunities to share the News with someone often—maybe every day!

Questions for Discussion
Make use of these questions to involve your students in learning and to test their understanding of the lesson.
1. Do you think the disciples' reaction upon seeing Jesus is what you would expect? Does it help you believe Luke is giving an accurate account of a supernatural event? 2. How did Christ seek to overcome the obstacles of their unbelief? 3. Why did Jesus invite them to look at His hands and feet to prove His identity? 4. What did He do to open their minds to understand the Scripture? 5. In summing up God's plan of redemption (vv. 46, 47), what did Christ say had been accomplished already? What even yet remains to be done so that the Scriptures will be fulfilled? 6. In what way are we also witnesses? 7. What is the "promise" of the Father?

Illustrating the Scripture
Examples and quotations to help the teacher communicate the lesson.
THE OLD TESTAMENT'S WITNESS TO THE MESSIAH For one of the most comprehensive and easily readable studies on this vital subject, the teacher is referred to *Evidence That Demands a Verdict* by Josh McDowell (Campus Crusade for Christ, 1972). McDowell lists sixty-one prophecies and cites the New Testament reference showing how each was fulfilled, often quoting Jewish sources that interpreted the Old Testament prophecy as pointing to the Messiah.

The first reference, out of the Law of Moses, on virtually every such list is Genesis 3:15—"And I will put enmity between you and the woman, And between your seed and her seed; He shall bruise you on the head, and you shall bruise him on the heel" (NASB). Did Jesus cite this verse to the disciples? We do not know; but the Spirit did inspire Paul later to write: "But when the fulness of time came, God sent forth His Son, born of a woman, born under the Law" (Galatians 4:4 NASB).

Another verse from the Law, which Jesus almost certainly quoted was Deuteronomy 18:18—"I will send them a prophet like you from among their own people; I will tell him what to say, and he will tell the people everything I command" (TEV). Jesus was often called a prophet. Commenting on the statement in John 4:19—"Sir, I perceive that thou (Jesus) art a prophet"— Aaron Judah Kligerman says, "The use of the term *prophet* by the Jews of Jesus' day shows not only that they expected the Messiah to be a prophet in accordance with the promise in Deuteronomy 18, but also that He who performed these miracles was indeed the Promised Prophet."

To the surprise of many Bible students, the Psalms have much to say concerning the Messiah. Did Jesus cite the passages from Psalm 22 and Psalm 69, relating to His suffering on the cross? Did He quote from Psalm 2: " 'I will announce,' says the king, 'what the Lord has declared. He said to me: "You are my son; today I have become your father" ' " (verse 7 TEV)? Or did He again cite the first verse of Psalm 110 which He had used in His teaching in the Temple during the last week of His ministry (Luke 20:41–44)?

Since the disciples and all the first followers were totally unprepared for the concept of the suffering Servant, we can be sure that Jesus "opened their understanding" concerning the prophets' messages dealing with that aspect. The prophets foretold that Jesus would be sold for thirty pieces of silver (Zechariah 11:12), forsaken by His disciples (Zechariah 13:7), wounded and bruised (Isaiah 53:5), His side would be pierced (Zechariah 12:10), He would be buried in a rich man's tomb (Isaiah 53:9), a worker of miracles (Isaiah 35:5, 6), anointed by the Spirit (Isaiah 11:2), a light to the Gentiles (Isaiah 60:3) and much more.

Topics for Youth

HOW CAN YOU BE SURE JESUS AROSE?—Young people may be confused and puzzled from time to time by the reports of "new" evidence in the assassination deaths of President John F. Kennedy and the Reverend Martin Luther King. After all of the investigations, it would seem that everyone would believe the preponderance of testimony favoring the accepted view. But not so.

In 1981, the wire services issued a report that "some speculation can never be resolved to the satisfaction of all" regarding "one of the most exhaustively documented cases" in the twentieth century. That report was concerned with the 1932 kidnapping of the twenty-month-old son of Charles and Anne Morrow Lindbergh. "After reviewing the 90,000 documents and evidence in the case, state police (in New Jersey) concluded that 'the Lindbergh kidnapping must rank as one of the most exhaustively documented cases of the era' " the wire services said.

But what of the most exhaustively documented case in the history of mankind—the death and Resurrection of Jesus? Is the jury still out? Do we await new evidence? Or is the evidence there and faith is required? In writing on this subject in *Christianity Today* in the late 1960s J.N.D. Anderson observed:

"Not so very long ago there was in England a young man barrister, or what you would call a trial lawyer, by the name of Frank Morison. He was an unbeliever. For years he promised himself that one day he would write a book to disprove the Resurrection finally and forever. At last he got the leisure. He was an honest man and he did the necessary study. Eventually (after accepting Christ) he wrote a book that you can buy as a paperback, *Who Moved the Stone?* Starting from the most critical possible approach to the New Testament documents, he concludes *inter alia* that you can explain the trial and the conviction of Jesus only on the basis that he himself had foretold his death and resurrection."

We believe that a person can know whether Jesus truly lives. The way to that assurance is to reach out to Him in faith as He is revealed in Scripture. Everyone who has reached for Him has found Him alive and able to save.

SPRING
March, April, May

The Book of Acts

UNIT I

Beginning at Jerusalem

LESSON 1   MARCH 6

An Expectant Fellowship

*Background Scripture: Exodus 33:15, 16; Luke 1:1–4;
24:36–53; Acts 1
Devotional Reading: Exodus 17:1–7*

Acts 1:4–14

4 And, being assembled together with them, commanded them that they should not depart from Jerusalem, but wait for the promise of the Father, which, saith he, ye have heard of me.

5 For John truly baptized with water; but ye shall be baptized with the Holy Ghost not many days hence.

6 When they therefore were come together, they asked of him, saying, Lord, wilt thou at this time restore again the kingdom to Israel?

7 And he said unto them, It is not for you to know the times or the seasons, which the Father hath put in his own power.

8 But ye shall receive power, after that the Holy Ghost is come upon you: and ye shall be witnesses unto me both in Jerusalem, and in all

Judea, and in Samaria, and unto the uttermost part of the earth.
9 And when he had spoken these things, while they beheld, he was taken up; and a cloud received him out of their sight.
10 And while they looked stedfastly toward heaven as he went up, behold, two men stood by them in white apparel;
11 Which also said, Ye men of Galilee, why stand ye gazing up into heaven? this same Jesus, which is taken up from you into heaven, shall so come in like manner as ye have seen him go into heaven.
12 Then returned they unto Jerusalem from the mount called Olivet, which is from Jerusalem a sabbath day's journey.
13 And when they were come in, they went up into an upper room, where abode both Peter, and James, and John, and Andrew, Philip, and Thomas, Bartholomew, and Matthew, James the son of Alpheus, and Simon Zelotes, and Judas the brother of James.
14 These all continued with one accord in prayer and supplication, with the women, and Mary the mother of Jesus, and with his brethren.

KEY VERSE: "But ye shall receive power, after that the Holy Ghost is come upon you: and ye shall be witnesses unto me both in Jerusalem, and in all Judea, and in Samaria, and unto the uttermost part of the earth." Acts 1:8.

Home Daily Bible Readings
Feb. 28 M. The Presence of the Lord, Exodus 33:12–16.
Mar. 1 T. Proof of the Resurrection, Luke 1:1–3.
Mar. 2 W. The Fellowship of Witness, 1 Thessalonians 1:2–9.
Mar. 3 T. All People Are Welcome, Romans 15:7–13.
Mar. 4 F. The Living Hope, 1 Peter 1:3–9.
Mar. 5 S. Living in Readiness, 2 Peter 3:9–14.
Mar. 6 S. Sharing Our Hope, Titus 2:11–15.

Lesson Aim: That your class members face the question personally of their own responsibility in response to Christ's commission.

LESSON OUTLINE
Background to the Scripture
Looking at the Scripture Text
  I. Wait (Acts 1:4, 5)
  II. Power (Acts 1:6–8)
  III. Promise (Acts 1:9–11)
  IV. Prayer (Acts 1:12–14)
Applying the Scripture

Background to the Scripture

The fifth book of the New Testament is appropriately named. Action characterizes its contents. Though its formal title is The Acts of the Apostles, a more literal translation would be "Acts of Apostles" for the Greek title has no definite articles. Many recent translations simply call this book *Acts*.

Today's lesson is a prelude to the action, taking as its subject the quiet before the storm of explosive Church growth into the first-century world. But we will find many currents flowing in the eleven verses of this lesson. We will hear Jesus utter His last words, endearing words of His Father and deliberate words about the promised Holy Spirit. We will see, if we watch closely, the interplay of the Trinity—Father, Son, and Holy Spirit—in this transitional time. Our gaze fixed on Jesus, we will not take for granted the appearance of two angels, nor their message about our Lord's Second Coming. We will scan the number of the Eleven as they regroup in Jerusalem and we will take note of the last mention of Mary, Jesus' mother.

A. T. Pierson is credited with having first called this book The Acts of the Holy Spirit! In the Gospel, Luke wrote "about all that Jesus began to do and teach" (v. 1). In Acts, Luke writes about all that Jesus continued to do, exalted in glory, through the ministry of the Holy Spirit.

Looking at the Scripture Text

Wait (vv. 4, 5) In reading the first few verses of Acts 1, we need to remind ourselves that Luke is writing of the supernatural, postresurrection appearances of our Lord. His testimony that Jesus "shewed himself alive after his passion by many infallible proofs, being seen of them (the apostles) forty days" is rejected outright by skeptics. Humanly speaking, the things he describes—Christ arising from a grave, ascending in clouds to heaven, angels appearing and speaking—are incredible. But we cannot pick and choose what we want to believe in the Gospels or in Acts. Luke wrote sincerely and seriously, accepting the testimony of his sources because, no doubt, he believed the Resurrection had to be true because it was the only adequate explanation of what had happened to the little band of apostles.

After Jesus' death, the natural inclination of the apostles would have been to return to Galilee and there try to pick up the shattered remains of their lives. But once they had seen the risen Christ, they could not leave one another; they never knew when He might appear again.

The events of verses 4 and 5 seem to fit best into the first Easter day, a day already described in the last lesson. Except for the time when they traveled to Galilee to meet Jesus (Matthew 28:10), the apostles and the women who were with them remained in Jerusalem. In his Gospel, Luke says they "were continually in the temple, praising and blessing God" (24:53).

Micah had foretold that "the law will go out from Zion, the word of the Lord from Jerusalem" (4:2 NIV) and so they were to remain there, waiting for the promise of the Father.

Before His Crucifixion, in the final hours He had with the apostles, Jesus told them that though He was going away, He would send the Holy Spirit to them. John records the substance of those parting words in John 14:16, 17, 26; 15:26 and 16:7-13. To that instruction He alluded after His Resurrection, picking up a familiar expression which seems only to have been used in the beginning of Jesus' ministry: "John baptized with water, but in a few days you will be baptized with the Holy Spirit" (Acts 1:5 NIV).

John the Baptist had been dead, perhaps two years, and the Gospels are silent concerning any continuation of His practice of baptism (except in John 4:1, 2). Nevertheless, "John's baptism" remained as a picture in the apostles' memories—if indeed they did not continue to baptize. Jesus jogged that mental picture with a new fact—the baptism in the Spirit was just days away. If these words were spoken at the close of the "forty days," they had but ten more days to wait for Pentecost.

Power (vv. 6-8) Luke makes a transition at verse 6, beginning with "When they therefore were come together." This section definitely belongs to the events of Jesus' last day on earth, His last appearance, perhaps the last minutes of that appearance. The apostles asked Him if He were at last going to restore the kingdom to Israel. "In view of the recent resurrection and other demonstrations of supernaturalism, it is not surprising that the disciples expected one further victory," says the Criswell Study Bible—"the deliverance from Rome and possibly the setting up of the messianic kingdom." This belief was a persistent one. The Pharisees had asked about it, near the end of Jesus' life there was a general expectation of it (Luke 19:11) and the disciples had set their hopes on it (24:21).

Jesus could have corrected them—and no doubt would have—if their messianic expectations were totally unfounded. But He did not. He had fed those expectations Himself, telling them that they would sit on twelve thrones ruling the twelve tribes. His answer fits consistently with a literal interpretation of other prophecies pointing to a yet future blessing on Israel under her Messiah Jesus.

While He did not correct their belief in the ultimate establishment of a kingdom, Jesus did correct their focus. As one commentator says, "they speculated *when* but Jesus gave them *work*." His answer in verse 7 reminds us of the words He spoke earlier, that the only one who knows the hour of Jesus' return is the Father. Part of the disciples' duty of "letting God be God" was to rest the "when" in His hands. The Lord has never rescinded that prohibition; it is still good today as is the command of verse 8.

This truly marvelous statement is viewed by virtually every student of the New Testament as the key to Acts. Indeed, it expresses the organizing principle of Luke's history: "in *Jerusalem*, and in all *Judea and in Samaria* and unto *the uttermost part* of the earth." "Acts may be divided into three principal parts, reflecting the ever widening area in which the Good News about Jesus was proclaimed and the church established" says the Today's English Version: "(1) the beginning of the Christian movement in Jerusalem following the ascension ..." (chap. 2–8:3); "(2) expansion into other parts of Palestine" (chap. 8:4–12:25); "(3) and further expansion, into the Mediterranean world as far as Rome" (chap. 13–28).

In words at once a command and a prediction, Jesus told the apostles what they should be able to do. He was commissioning them to be witnesses—that is, they were to tell all they knew about Jesus Christ. They were to start in Jerusalem and spread out from there into the whole region of Judea, its neighboring province of Samaria and keep going until the whole world knew. The *Expositor's Greek Testament* notes that they were to begin in Jerusalem; "their testimony should be delivered not to men unacquainted with the facts, but to inhabitants of the city where Jesus had been crucified and buried."

Their superhuman task called for suprahuman powers and those powers He promised when "the Holy Ghost is come upon you." No man had been indwelt by the Spirit except Jesus until this time. In Old Testament times, He had come temporarily upon certain individuals for a particular task. Jesus had said earlier he "shall be in you" (John 14:17). In a matter of days, these few apostles and the band of disciples with them would know what Jesus meant and set out to carry His Name around the world.

Promise (vv. 9–11) By the time Luke wrote Acts, he seems to be better informed about the Ascension of our Lord than when he wrote his Gospel. His account is the most complete record we have. We can appreciate the importance of Jesus' ascending in full view of the disciples. Since His Resurrection He had made at least ten appearances to them (see a list of these in "Illustrating the Scripture") so they needed to know not to expect this to continue. Artists of the Renaissance era have captured the Ascension event gloriously—it was a golden moment and made an indelible impression upon the apostles. Peter wrote of it (1 Peter 3:22) as did Paul (Ephesians 4:8, 9; Philippians 2:9; 1 Timothy 3:16).

Lange speaks of the "rapture" of the disciples as they beheld Him taken up into the cloud (using the word in its most common meaning, of a feeling of ecstasy). Anyone who has had to say farewell to one whom they loved can understand the "painful longing" and homesickness the disciples felt at that time. Compassionately the Father attended to their needs. Jesus could not come back nor could they go to Him yet. But God assured them through two angels that the same Jesus would come again. The promise is yet to be fulfilled that Jesus will return visibly, in a cloud, by His own power, in majesty and with the same body and soul. This is the Church's blessed hope.

Prayer (vv. 12–14) Angels having diverted the gaze of the disciples from the sky back to earth, they did the only thing they knew to do—returned to Jerusalem. As we would say, "The ball was now in God's court"; they were to wait.

Luke's list of the apostles agrees with his earlier one in his Gospel (Luke 6:14–16) except the order is different and, of course, Judas is omitted. John, according to recent versions, is listed second after Peter, reflecting perhaps the leadership these two assumed (*see* Acts 3:1; 8:14). All of these and the women "joined together constantly in prayer" (NIV), probably in the upper room where they had met Jesus behind locked doors after His Resurrection. They were growing in expectancy of the coming of the Holy Spirit with the passing of each hour, but their communion with the risen Christ gave them strength to wait.

Luke's account is valuable for its mention of the women who were a part of the company of disciples, and especially for his report that Jesus' brethren were now believers. They had not believed in Him at first (*see* John 7:5), but by the time the Church began growing, one of them, James, became a leader in the Jerusalem assembly (Acts 15:13; 1 Corinthians 15:7; Galatians 1:19).

Mary, the mother of Jesus, is the only woman named in the group which numbered approximately 120 disciples (v. 15). But several women were named in the Gospel accounts of the Crucifixion and Resurrection—Mary Magdalene, Mary the mother of James and Joses (Zebedee's wife), Salome, Joanna, and at least one other Mary. Others were included in the phrase "women from Galilee."

Applying the Scripture
Ask the class: Has the great commission been fulfilled? The Gospel has surely been carried to the "uttermost part of the earth," hasn't it?

You should get a variety of answers, but be prepared for the shock when you tell them that current missionary research continues to say—*2 billion people have little or no opportunity to hear about Jesus today*. Thus, they are unevangelized and to that degree the great commission has not been carried out in our generation.

These unreached peoples exist everywhere, but especially in the world's metropolitan centers, Asia, and the islands. We think because radio is broadcasting the Gospel into most of the habitable earth and because satellites are carrying television signals into remote parts of the globe that everybody who wants to know Christ has the opportunity to do so. But how can people who are so different linguistically, socially, economically, or culturally make a commitment to Christ when they could not realistically become members of an existing church?

Wycliffe Bible Translators estimates that more than 2,000 minority language groups in the world are without a *single verse of God's Word* in their language. They comprise only 3–5 percent of the world's population, but that's almost *200 million* men, women, boys, and girls—just like you and me!

Dr. Ralph Winter, director of the U.S. Center for World Mission in Pasadena, says 16,750 subnations of people—groups identifiable either by language or culture or social level—exist as "hidden people," without access to Christ. They add up to 2.4 billion people, more than half of the world's population.

"Three thousand of these nations are in India," says Dr. Winter. "The Gospel has really substantially penetrated only 21 of these 3,000 human societies. There are some Christians in about 50 others, but there are 2,900 social traditions in India within which there is not a church. . . .

"People have just sort of lost interest in mission," he says. "Mission work seems to be no longer all that interesting to local Christians. But I believe that once the Hidden Peoples become visible, become known to local churches, the Church is going to be electrified."

What would it take to electrify your church? Lead the class in the closing moments in a serious confrontation with the question: Have you personally faced the issue squarely—what am I doing in the light of Jesus' command to be His witness to the "uttermost part of the earth"? Call on your class members to search their hearts this week as they meditate on Acts 1:8. For future follow-up, ask your pastor or denomination or mission societies to supply you with current reading matter to distribute. Or, write the U.S. Center for World Mission for their current mailings (1605 E. Elizabeth St., Pasadena, CA 91104).

Questions for Discussion
Make use of these questions to involve your students in learning and to test their understanding of the lesson.
1. In what passages in the Gospels can we find what Jesus said to the disciples about the "promise of the Father"?   2. What was to happen "not many days hence" as Jesus said? About how many days were they to wait?   3. What may have prompted the disciples to ask about the restoration of the kingdom to Israel? What does Jesus' reply indicate?   4. In the "great commission" what is the order in which the disciples were to carry out the Lord's command? Why did He give such an order?   5. What do we learn of the manner of the Second Coming from the angels' words?   6. What purpose is served by the list of the eleven disciples in verse 13?   7. Why is the mention of "his brethren" significant here?

Illustrating the Scripture
Examples and quotations to help the teacher communicate the lesson.
JESUS CHRIST? I MAY HAVE HEARD OF HIM   "Hearing a Chinese woman say she 'might have heard the name of Christ' helped Barton Starr decide to become a missionary" reported the Baptist Press.

"Starr, a Florida native, was one of 24 persons commissioned as missionaries by the Southern Baptist Foreign Mission Board at the Lakeland (Florida) Civic Center in April 1981.

"While on a trip into China during the year he and his wife spent as Mission Service Corps volunteers in Hong Kong, Starr made friends with his guide, a young woman who wanted to learn English.

"Asking her if she had ever known any Christians, he learned that she didn't know what they were. Not finding the word *Christian* in his Chinese-

English dictionary, he showed her the word *Christ* and learned that she had only heard the name.

"A college history teacher, Starr said her reply brought to mind a song which says that Christ is only history for some people. Realizing this was true for 85 percent of the students at Hong Kong Baptist College, where he was teaching, was one of the things that made him consider mission service after returning to the United States."

RESURRECTION APPEARANCES OF JESUS CHRIST "Ten distinct resurrection appearances of Christ prior to His ascension can be documented in Scripture. The order of those appearances follows:

1. To Mary Magdalene near the tomb (John 20:11-18).
2. To the women returning from the tomb (Matthew 28:9, 10).
3. To Peter (Luke 24:34).
4. To the disciples approaching Emmaus in the evening (Luke 24:13-22).
5. To all the disciples except Thomas, who was absent (Luke 24:36-43).
6. To the disciples, including Thomas, on Sunday night one week later (John 20:26-31).
7. To seven disciples beside the Sea of Galilee (John 21:1-25).
8. To more than 500 people on an appointed mountain in Galilee (Matthew 28:16-20; 1 Corinthians 15:6).
9. To James the half brother of Jesus (1 Corinthians 15:7).
10. To the apostles at the ascension (Acts 1:3-11)."

(From the Criswell Study Bible.)

The Great Commission in the Other Gospels: for comparison with Acts 1:8, have each of these verses printed on 3x5 cards and pass them around to your class while teaching the lesson. Matthew 28:18-20; Mark 16:15; Luke 24:46-48; John 20:21.

Topics for Youth

YOUNG PEOPLE AND MISSIONS—"Eager bright young people—the most potent force on this planet"—that is what Ralph Winter says when he thinks of the unfinished task of the Church today. In an interview in 1980 in London, with *Buzz* magazine, Dr. Winter spoke of the current surge of interest in world missions among the young people of America. He pointed to the Inter-Varsity Student Missions Convention held at Urbana, Illinois, noting that at each convention the young people attending were asked to sign a card saying they were available for overseas missionary work.

In 1970, only 8 percent of the 12,000 people in attendance said they would work overseas. In 1973, a noticeable difference was apparent. Attendance had grown to 14,000. With no alteration in the theme of the convention and no special appeal for missionary work, the percentage of those interested in going overseas jumped from 8 percent to 28 percent. Then in 1976, when the next convention was held, it jumped again to 51 percent!

"There is a new openness and availability to mission," said Winter. "If these young people ever get their teeth into the problem, the American church would never know what had happened to it. It would just be shaken to the core by the number of young people who are open to go to the very ends of the earth. They are fearless, they are not afraid. It's a very exciting era....

"If any generation in history has ever been so clearly capable of doing its job, it is ours. We have a much stronger base to work from than ever before. The number of Christians around the world is truly astronomical.

"There are more Christians today than there were people in the world a few centuries ago. All these vital, earnest, eager, bright young people are the salt of the earth. They are the most potent force on this planet. Just get them headed in the right direction and every people—every nation—will have a church by the year 2000."

LESSON 2   MARCH 13

An Empowered Fellowship

Background Scripture: Numbers 11:24–29; Joel 2:28–32; Acts 2:1–42
Devotional Reading: Ephesians 1:3–10

Acts 2:1–4, 12–18, 37, 38

1 And when the day of Pentecost was fully come, they were all with one accord in one place.
2 And suddenly there came a sound from heaven as of a rushing mighty wind, and it filled all the house where they were sitting.
3 And there appeared unto them cloven tongues like as of fire, and it sat upon each of them.
4 And they were all filled with the Holy Ghost, and began to speak with other tongues, as the Spirit gave them utterance.
12 And they were all amazed, and were in doubt, saying one to another, What meaneth this?
13 Others mocking said, These men are full of new wine.
14 But Peter, standing up with the eleven, lifted up his voice, and said unto them, Ye men of Judea, and all ye that dwell at Jerusalem, be this known unto you, and hearken to my words:
15 For these are not drunken, as ye suppose, seeing it is but the third hour of the day.
16 But this is that which was spoken by the prophet Joel;
17 And it shall come to pass in the last days, saith God, I will pour out of my Spirit upon all flesh: and your sons and your daughters shall

prophesy, and your young men shall see visions, and your old men shall dream dreams:

18 And on my servants and on my handmaidens I will pour out in those days of my Spirit; and they shall prophesy:

37 Now when they heard this, they were pricked in their heart, and said unto Peter and to the rest of the apostles, Men and brethren, what shall we do?

38 Then Peter said unto them, Repent, and be baptized every one of you in the name of Jesus Christ for the remission of sins, and ye shall receive the gift of the Holy Ghost.

KEY VERSE: "Not by might, nor by power, but by my spirit, saith the Lord of hosts." Zechariah 4:6.

Home Daily Bible Readings
Mar. 7 M. The Promise of the Holy Spirit, John 14:15–24.
Mar. 8 T. The Promise of Peace, John 14:25–31.
Mar. 9 W. When the Spirit of Truth Comes, John 16: 4–11.
Mar. 10 T. The Illuminating Power of the Holy Spirit, John 16:12–15.
Mar. 11 F. Filled With the Holy Spirit, Acts 4:23–31.
Mar. 12 S. The Source and Varieties of Spiritual Gifts, Romans 12:1–11.
Mar. 13 S. The Promised Outpouring of the Spirit, Joel 2:28–32.

Lesson Aim: As a result of this study the members of your class should pray with strong desire for spiritual awakening in the Church.

LESSON OUTLINE
Background to the Scripture
Looking at the Scripture Text
 I. The Spirit Comes With Power (Acts 2:1–4)
 II. The Spirit's Coming Explained (Acts 2:12–18)
 III. Requisites for the Spirit's Coming to Man (Acts 2:37, 38)
Applying the Scripture

Background to the Scripture

After the tumultuous week of the Passover feast, life in Jerusalem returned to its normal pace. Buying and selling resumed in the markets, school continued in the Temple, and in the halls of the high priest's house Jewish dignitaries spoke with relief that the Galilean had been disposed of. Jews of the dispersion who had made their pilgrimage to their most favorite city for the Passover were enjoying an extended holiday with yet another festival to look forward to—the Feast of Weeks. After that they would return to Rome or Alexandria or Asia Minor or Mesopotamia—or wherever they called home.

Many of these sojourning Jews would have wished for a more satisfactory explanation of the events surrounding the Crucifixion. They had barely gotten acquainted with the facts about the remarkable Teacher when to their amazement He had been condemned. Now, whenever they visited the Temple, they saw a band of men and women whom they recognized as followers of the Teacher—and they wondered about them.

As for the disciples, they stayed in Jerusalem. At first they barred the door where they met, but soon they learned that the Jewish rulers were not interested in them and felt no threat from their numbers or their belief that Jesus was alive. These were waiting days for the disciples.

Looking at the Scripture Text

The Spirit Comes With Power (vv. 1-4) Whether the day of Pentecost found the disciples in any unusual sense of expectation, we do not know. As the word itself indicates, *Pentecost* marked the fiftieth day following the Passover observance, counting from the second day of the Passover feast. After His Resurrection Jesus had appeared to the disciples numerous times over a period of forty days and now almost ten days had elapsed since His Ascension.

From Leviticus 23:15, 16, it is clear that this day fell on the first day of the week. It commenced the annual Feast of Weeks in Jerusalem, marking the harvest of the "firstfruits" of Israel's wheat crop. On this auspicious day, God chose to pour out His Spirit on the waiting believers and harvest the firstfruits of His Church.

The 120 believers (1:15) were all together in a house in Jerusalem when suddenly, from the direction of the sky, a great noise enveloped the whole room. Luke describes it "like the roaring of a mighty windstorm" (TLB), a "sound from heaven like the rushing of a violent wind" (PHILLIPS). The closest association we might make to describe this sound that "filled all the house where they were sitting" may be the noise of a tornado in full force or the all-encompassing sound of huge rocket engines at lift-off.

Accompanied with the deafening sound was the appearance of a flame which seemed to divide into tongues of fire that rested upon each one in the room, probably upon their heads. The result of this powerful Presence was: "they were all filled with the Holy Ghost, and began to speak with other tongues, as the Spirit gave them utterance." Thus Luke describes the coming of the Holy Spirit.

Several important conclusions may be drawn from Luke's description. One, the symbol of wind is frequently used in God's Word when speaking of God (*see* John 3:7, 8; 1 Kings 19:11; Psalms 104:3). Two, the symbol of fire likewise represents God's presence (the "burning bush," the "pillar of fire"; the writer to the Hebrews says "our God is a consuming fire" 12:29). Three, Luke notes that all of the people in the room were filled with the Spirit. Four, the Spirit enabled them to tell "the wonderful works of God (v. 11) in languages other than their native Aramaic. In verses 9-11, Luke names seventeen regions and countries, telling us that Jews from those places were in Jerusalem and came to see what was happening, and that each understood these Spirit-filled believers "in his own native language" (v. 8 NIV).

The descent of the Spirit, here called His *filling*, corresponds to the *baptism* of which Jesus spoke earlier (1:5). The term *baptism of the Spirit* is no longer used in the New Testament, except once in Paul's letter to the Corinthians (1 Corinthians 12:13). The usual descriptive word now is *filling*. Kenneth S. Wuest, longtime teacher of Greek at Moody Bible Institute, said that to be filled with the Spirit is to be controlled by the Spirit. "The Holy Spirit is not a substance to fill an empty receptacle. He is a Person to control another person, the believer," he said. "He does not fill a person's life with Himself. He controls that person."

The Spirit's Coming Explained (vv. 12-18) Someone has said that in any human event three kinds of people are always involved. There are those who make things happen, others who watch things happen, and still others who don't know what is happening. In the case of Pentecost, God made it happen and all in the house watched it happen, knowing that this was what Jesus had told them to wait for.

Either the sound and the fire, or the subsequent speaking of the disciples (possibly both) attracted a large gathering of people immediately. No matter who they were, whether a Jew from Egypt or Babylon or Rome, each heard the disciples proclaiming God's praises in his own tongue. Clearly they did not know what was happening and so they asked, "What does this mean?" A few concluded that the disciples had had too much to drink, a dismally inadequate explanation. Someone needed to stand and explain what was going on.

In that moment, the Spirit granted boldness to Peter. Perhaps the apostles were seated together in the middle of the room (the text does not say whether they remained in the house or were now in an open area or a court of the Temple). When Peter stood, they all stood with him. His first words indicate a solemn mood: "let me explain this to you; listen carefully to what I say" (NIV).

Peter cast aside the opinion that they were drunk, noting that it was but nine o'clock. On a feast day, the custom was for the people to abstain from food and drink until noon at least. The association of being Spirit filled with being drunk is interesting, however. Paul would later write: "be not drunk with wine . . . but be filled with the Spirit" (Ephesians 5:18). Being filled with the Spirit is another way of saying, "be controlled by the Spirit." Did the disciples evidence by their uninhibited speech and behavior the sort of reckless liberty of an intoxicant?

Peter's certainty is a thing to behold. "Where so recently he had shown such cowardice he is now indeed a rock, as Jesus had said he would be," notes A. T. Robertson. Without hesitating he told the throng of people that

Joel, the Old Testament prophet, had foretold this. His ability to interpret the events in light of Scripture is a result of the Spirit's control in his life. The words he quotes are from Joel 2.

"I will pour out my spirit upon all flesh ... your sons and your daughters ... your old men ... your young men ... servants and ... handmaids." What Peter said was plainly demonstrated—without discrimination as to age or sex or station in life, the Spirit of God had been "poured out" on all.

In the Hebrew and Greek texts of the Joel passage, the term *afterwards* is found in place of Peter's words—"in the last days." By the Spirit, Peter saw in this outpouring the fulfillment of Joel's prophecy "and the dawn of the period preceding the return of Christ in glory," says the *Expositor's Greek Testament*. He declared that the Spirit's coming signified the beginning of the end-time.

Jesus had said, "ye shall receive power." That power was everywhere apparent now. (1) The sound of the wind and the tongues of fire showed God's power. (2) The witness in unknown tongues required power far beyond what the disciples had ever experienced. (3) Peter's message, delivered no doubt in the presence of Jewish rulers who had hated his Lord, would have been impossible without the Spirit's power. (4) And the effect of the message upon the people showed convincingly the power of the Spirit.

Requisites for the Spirit's Coming to Man (vv. 37, 38)   Peter's message on that day is probably condensed by Luke. Though it is not included in the lesson text, it would be well to read it in class, perhaps at this point in the lesson.

Luke marked the point where Peter's words had their greatest impact on the gathered assembly. After proving that David's words concerning life after death could only find their fulfillment in Christ, Peter declared (1) that Jesus was alive, (2) that the disciples had seen Him (v. 32) and (3) that this Jesus had been declared by God as the Lord and the Messiah. When he said this, Luke writes that his hearers "were pricked in their heart." They spontaneously asked of the disciples, "What shall we do?" The *Pulpit Commentary* notes that "it is a sign of the working of God's Spirit in the heart, renewing it to repentance, when men feel the need of changing their old course of thought and action, and inquire anxiously what they must do to inherit eternal life." The Spirit was in control as Peter told them what to do.

As John the Baptist and the Lord Jesus had charged in beginning their ministries, the first requisite for right standing with God was repentance, a change of heart and life. Coupled with it was Christian baptism. John's baptism had looked forward to the atoning sacrifice whereby man's forgiveness would be declared. Baptism in the name of Christ was an outward sign that the penitent sinner had been forgiven; it was a turning from the old life and the sign of a new birth. Faith was implied in the act of repentance. To all who would meet these two conditions, Peter declared "ye shall receive the gift of the Holy Ghost."

Three thousand souls responded to Peter's invitation that day. The Church was born! Looking over what took place on that historic day, we are impressed by the power of the Spirit and what may be accomplished when all of God's people are united and filled. Pentecost can never be repeated; it was the point in time when, as Peter preached, the ascended Christ received the promise from the Father and poured out the Spirit. But we cannot help believe that like results would happen if the Church in its local expression were to meet the conditions that this group of believers met.

Applying the Scripture
Ask your class: Does the title of today's lesson aptly describe our church? Is ours An Empowered Fellowship? If you can answer yes, your church is the exception.

Probably you would have to agree that you have seldom experienced anything even close to what those early Christians experienced, as our lesson explains. The inevitable question is why. Surely, the Lord is willing and His power is just as great as it has ever been. Probably all of your class would agree that the problem is *us*.

If you, the teacher, have been in a church that experienced the sort of power for witnessing and the kind of conviction of sin that fell upon Peter's listeners, now would be a good time to briefly relate what you recall. Or, if you have not had that sort of experience, ask members of the class if they would share a firsthand experience they had. Allow time for some discussion of this, but keep the sharing time on target. If in either case there was genuine revival and a sense of the Spirit filling the members of that body, ask if the class can trace the cause(s). What led to the spiritual outpouring and awakening?

The aim of your discussion should be to force the class to see that there is a blessed level on which the Church should exist in the Spirit's power. The way to that level of the Spirit's filling is the same way that Peter declared to his listeners.

Nothing short-circuits the power of the Spirit in a fellowship as effectively as sin. Repentance, the door to the new birth, is to be a constant way of life for the Church. The revivals that shook churches in Canada and in the Upper Midwest in the early '70s began with confession of sin and heartfelt repentance.

On the positive side, a church that really wants the presence and power of God in their midst will follow the example of the Jerusalem believers and pray for that. They were in prayer daily for some seven weeks—quite a length of time for a body of people to maintain unity and purpose. This is a point where your class can start something in the church. As many as want God's best—His presence and power in the fellowship—can begin to meet together for times of prayer.

If there is a weekly prayer meeting, that could be a regular meeting for members in which to take part. Possibly that meeting is attended by faithful workers and members who have long ago accepted the status quo in the church. But an injection of earnest *prayers* in that regular meeting can only bring positive results. However, it is wise to suggest that every member of the class seek out one individual with whom he or she can pray at another time, hopefully each week, and for them to devote a protracted time to pray together. Challenge them to look upon their prayer unit as a brush fire—many brush fires can set the whole church aflame in a conflagration of spiritual fervor. But it is so important, this matter of revival, that your class should accept a challenge to be the driving force behind this effort. Perhaps the class can set a weekly time, at the convenience of most members, for earnest prayer. An early morning hour, before work, is suggested, or a daybreak meeting on Sunday.

Revival can come, not through our half-heartedly singing "Revive us again" on Sunday mornings, but through earnest, united prayer over protracted times, and through repentance and confession of sin.

Questions for Discussion
Make use of these questions to involve your students in learning and to test their understanding of the lesson.
1. What feast did the Day of Pentecost inaugurate? How many days was Pentecost after the Passover? 2. For whom was the sign of speaking in tongues given? 3. What manifestations or proofs of the Spirit's power can you find in the text? 4. How did Peter explain the miraculous phenomena—the rushing, mighty wind and the flame and speaking in tongues? 5. Why was it significant that even sons and daughters, slaves and handmaidens would prophesy? 6. How does Christian baptism differ from John's baptism? 7. According to Peter, what must one do to receive the Holy Spirit?

Illustrating the Scripture
Examples and quotations to help the teacher communicate the lesson.
THE CENTRAL TRUTH OF PENTECOST "The question is: Are we to expect another Pentecost baptism—another outpouring, another shedding forth of the Spirit? Or what is the essential truth of Pentecost which we are to seize upon?

"The central fact of Pentecost was that they were FILLED with the Spirit and 'endued with power from on high' (Luke 24:49) enabling them to go everywhere *witnessing* with divine unction (Acts 1:8). We do not have to *tarry for the coming* of the Spirit, but it has certainly been the experience of the vast majority of Christians that this 'unction' (1 John 2:20) or 'anointing' (2 John 2:27) or 'fulness' (Ephesians 5:18) of the Spirit has come at some time *subsequent to conversion*, and it has usually been connected with special times of prayer and heart searching (Acts 4:31).

"Dr. R. A. Torrey taught that power of the Spirit for service was to be earnestly sought in prayer (Luke 11:13) and we believe this to be sound advice. Many are living without power because they have not earnestly sought it. There are doubtless some who, at the time of conversion, make such a complete surrender to God that they experience *fulness* of life simultaneously with the gift of life through the Spirit, but the majority are not brought to surrender until some special experience brings them to face their need of power for service" (Keith L. Brooks).

WHO OUGHT TO READ THE BOOK OF ACTS? "There are two types of people especially who should read and study this book (Acts). First, those intellectuals who assume that Christianity was founded on a myth and is in any case a spent force today. For this book of Luke's, whose authenticity no reputable scholar disputes, takes more than a little explaining away. This is the beginning of the Christian era. . . .

"The second group of people who should certainly study this book with the closest attention are what we might call the churchy-minded. They will find in this honest account of the early Church a corroboration of what Jesus meant when He said, 'The wind bloweth where it listeth, and thou hearest the sound thereof, but canst not tell whence it cometh, and whither it goeth: so is every one that is born of the Spirit.' For this is the story of Spirit-directed activities and there is what appears to be from the human point of view an arbitrariness, even a capriciousness, in the operation of the Holy Spirit. Of course from the real point of view, God's work is neither arbitrary nor capricious—and this will be plain to us one day. Yet it will often appear to be so in the present human set-up, for God's wisdom is working at a different level from our own. When we compare the strength and vigor of the Spirit-filled early Church with the confused and sometimes feeble performance of the Church today, we might perhaps conclude that when man's rigidity attempts to canalize the free and flexible flow of the Spirit he is left to his own devices." (From the Translator's Preface to *The Young Church in Action*, by J. B. Phillips.)

Topics for Youth

DAVID WILKERSON TALKS WITH HIS GRANDAD—"'Davie, you've got to keep your eye focused on the central heart of the Gospel. What would you say that is?'

"I looked him in the eye, 'I've heard my own grandfather often enough on this subject,' I said, 'to give him an answer from his own sermons. The heart of the Gospel is change. It is transformation. It is being born again to a new life.'

"'You rattle that off pretty smooth, David. Wait until you watch the Lord do it. Then you'll get even more excitement in your voice. But that's the theory. The heart of Christ's message is extremely simple: an encounter with God—a real one—means change.'

"'Davie,' said Grandpap with his hand on the farmhouse door, 'I'm still worried about you when you meet the raw life of the city. You've been sheltered. When you meet wickedness in the flesh it could petrify you.

"'You know . . .' and then Grandpap started off on a story that didn't seem to me to have any relation to his point. 'Some time ago I was taking a walk through the hills when I came across an enormous snake. He was a big one, David, three inches thick and four feet long, and he just lay there in the sun looking scary. I was afraid of this thing and I didn't move for a long time, and lo and behold, while I was watching, I saw a miracle. I saw a new birth. I saw that old snake shed its skin and leave it lying there in the sun and go off a new and really beautiful creature.

" 'When you start your work in the city, boy, don't you be like I was petrified by the outward appearance of your boys. God isn't. He's just waiting for each one of them to crawl right out of that old sin-shell and leave it behind. He's waiting and yearning for the new man to come out.' " (From *The Cross and the Switchblade* by David Wilkerson, with John and Elizabeth Sherrill; Copyright © 1963 by David Wilkerson. Published by Chosen Books, Lincoln, Va. Used by permission.)

LESSON 3　　　　　　　　　　　　MARCH 20

An Expanding Fellowship

Background Scripture: Acts 2:43–6:7
Devotional Reading: Isaiah 44:6–8

Acts 2:43–47; 6:1–7

43　And fear came upon every soul: and many wonders and signs were done by the apostles.

44　And all that believed were together, and had all things common;

45　And sold their possessions and goods, and parted them to all men, as every man had need.

46　And they, continuing daily with one accord in the temple, and breaking bread from house to house, did eat their meat with gladness and singleness of heart,

47　Praising God, and having favour with all the people. And the Lord added to the church daily such as should be saved.

6:1　And in those days, when the number of the disciples was multiplied, there arose a murmuring of the Grecians against the Hebrews, because their widows were neglected in the daily ministration.

2　Then the twelve called the multitude of the disciples unto them, and said, It is not reason that we should leave the word of God, and serve tables.

3　Wherefore, brethren, look ye out among you seven men of honest report, full of the Holy Ghost and wisdom, whom we may appoint over this business.

4　But we will give ourselves continually to prayer, and to the ministry of the word.

5　And the saying pleased the whole multitude: and they chose Stephen, a man full of faith and of the Holy Ghost, and Philip, and Prochorus,

and Nicanor, and Timon, and Parmenas, and Nicolas a proselyte of Antioch:
6 Whom they set before the apostles: and when they had prayed, they laid their hands on them.
7 And the word of God increased; and the number of the disciples multiplied in Jerusalem greatly; and a great company of the priests were obedient to the faith.

KEY VERSE: "And all that believed were together, and had all things common." Acts. 2:44.

> **Home Daily Bible Readings**
> Mar. 14 M. The First Ingathering of Souls, Acts 2:37–42.
> Mar. 15 T. The Faith Through Jesus Christ, Acts 3:11–16.
> Mar. 16 W. A Call to Repentance, Acts 3:17–26.
> Mar. 17 T. Preaching the Resurrection of Jesus, Acts 4:1–8.
> Mar. 18 F. Peter's Defense Before the Sanhedrin, Acts 4:5–12.
> Mar. 19 S. The Fearlessness of the Apostles, Acts 4:13–22.
> Mar. 20 S. Stephen Before the Sanhedrin, Acts 6:8–15.

Lesson Aim: That adults will name several qualities that make for healthy church growth and pray for these qualities in their church.

LESSON OUTLINE
Background to the Scripture
Looking at the Scripture Text
 I. Happily Growing (Acts 2:43–47)
 II. Peacefully Serving (Acts 6:1–7)
Applying the Scripture

Background to the Scripture

To adults who have lost their way in their careers, Barbara Sher advises tracing their life back to childhood to discover their *original self*. "The design of your life path is right there in miniature," she says, "like the genes in a seed. . . ." As an illustration, she notes that Linda Ronstadt's earliest memory is asking her parents to play her some music. In her years of career counseling, Ms. Sher says she has led people to discover inborn talents and drives and to realize "their own special kind of genius" as adults.

Does someone need to lead the Church of the late twentieth century back to find its original self? All about us are signs that it has lost its way. If we were to describe the Church today—how effective it is in reaching out to its community, how joyful is its fellowship, how liberal its generosity, how vibrant its worship—would we conclude that it is *An Expanding Fellowship?* The text for today allows us to peel back the historical, traditional, and cultural accretions which hide the Church's true nature. The early Church that appears here may well serve as a model of what Christ wants in our day.

Looking at the Scripture Text

Happily Growing (2:43-47) In these final verses of Acts 2, Luke gives "a wonderfully vivid description of the first days of activity after the enduement of the Holy Spirit," said the New Testament scholar A. T. Robertson. "The notes of a happy church were here (unity, instruction, fellowship or partnership, liberality, praise, prayer, gladness, singleness of heart). Small wonder that there was power in that church and the fear of God. It was a perpetual revival."

All of these "notes" or qualities of the growing Church can be found in our text except "instruction." That is found in verse 42 where it is named first. This summary of the life of the Church is one of nine such summaries Luke gives in his account of the early Church's history.

The NIV translation of verse 43a—"Every one was filled with awe"—is to be preferred to "fear came upon every soul." And it fits well with the fact that the apostles did "wonders and signs." For a period of time—perhaps several months, perhaps only a few weeks—the people of Jerusalem were in reverential awe of this growing group of disciples. The same sort of thing happened when Israel began to possess the Promised Land. As the nations melted for fear of Jehovah because of the miraculous works He demonstrated, so the enemies of the Gospel let the Church alone in its infancy, providentially allowing the Church to gain strength.

Fellowship—This mark of the Church, meaning to share in common, speaks of the total way the early disciples partook of the abundant life of Christ. They were filled with love for one another and so they congregated frequently, in the Temple and in the homes of those who resided in Jerusalem. The phrase "breaking bread from house to house" (translated "they broke bread in their homes"—NIV) suggests that many guests would be in the house for meals and that they probably kept the Lord's Supper rather frequently.

Joy—The mention of meals together and frequent gatherings—daily in many persons' lives—brings to mind a joyful quality in the early Church. Luke's word is *gladness*—exulting, boundless joy. And why should not they be glad? They knew Christ was alive, they had peace with God and a noble mission to fulfill. Their material needs being taken care of only added to their joy. "There is plentiful redemption in the blood that has been shed; there is joy for all the members in the sorrows of the Head."

Worship—The disciples (that word is for the first time applied to the group in Acts 6:1; they would not be called Christians until later, 11:26) continued to go to the Temple at the scheduled hour of prayer (3:1). Luke specifically notes that they were "praising God" which may primarily refer to the individual devotion and group worship experience in homes, but would no doubt include their Temple worship also. As proclamation is a part of worship today, so it was then; the apostles were evidently proclaiming the death and Resurrection of Christ in the Temple every day (5:20, 42). By this means the Lord added to the Church "those finding salvation."

Love—At this time the Church's fellowship found a deep expression that may not be meant for every church or at all times, but was nevertheless integral to their healthy life in Christ. "All the believers joined together and shared everything in common" (v. 44 PHILLIPS). This may have originated as a few sold their properties to aid new believers who had come to Jerusalem from distant countries and remained there for instruction. In whatever manner it began, everyone seems to have shared his possessions. F. F. Bruce says it was "in part a continuation of the practice of the twelve in the days when they had gone about with Jesus. They shared a common purse . . . (it) was also the spontaneous response of many of the new converts to the forgiving grace which they had experienced." The practice was voluntary and not permanent.

Favor—Luke's description of the young Church almost parallels the way he described the growth of Jesus—"Jesus kept increasing in wisdom and stature, and in favor with God and men" (Luke 2:52 NASB). God gave the young Church favor also. Their love, joy, charity, and sincerity, coupled with "the pure and simple life" they led "commended them to the people and made it easier for them to gain confidence . . . and converts" says one commentator.

Peacefully Serving (6:1-7) Our text is peppered with references to the Church's rapid growth—"the Lord added daily . . . number of the disciples was multiplied . . . word of God increased . . . disciples multiplied in Jerusalem greatly . . . great number of the priests were obedient to the faith." Some 3,000 converts entered the ranks of the Church on the day of Pentecost. A while later Luke says the men numbered 5,000 (4:4).

The mushrooming growth of the number of disciples strained the simple plans that had been made for the care of the people. As the believers "handed over their property" to the apostles, suggests Bruce, the proceeds were put into a common pool "from which a daily dole was distributed to the poorer members of the community." Among these poor were the widows. Very possibly, when they confessed their faith in the risen Christ and were baptized, they were cut off from the widows' fund administered by the Jewish priests. Among them were Grecian Jews, women who had come to Jerusalem from Greek-speaking countries.

A prejudice may well have existed among Palestinian Jews toward the Grecians. The latter spoke Greek and read a Greek translation of the Old Testament; they may have appeared to compromise the Jewish religion by their life-style and mode of worship since they were not near Jerusalem. The Gospel does eradicate prejudice, but not always overnight. As more and more Jews turned to Christ, the Hellenic or Grecian Jews realized that their widows were being neglected in the daily distribution of food (TEV says "funds"). So arose the first sign of conflict in the Church.

On learning of the problem, the apostles evidently responded immediately. Upon them lay the singular charge to bear witness by preaching the death and Resurrection of Christ. They could not "neglect" this ministry, just as the widows could not be neglected. Someone was needed to supervise the daily distribution.

Their solution is well-known. Men would be chosen *by the Church* and the *apostles* would commission them. They were to (1) be men from within the fellowship of believers, (2) have a good reputation, (3) be full of the Holy Spirit, and (4) be full of wisdom. Seven men were to meet these stringent spiritual and moral requirements.

Why seven were to be named is not clear. One attractive explanation is that there may have been seven "house churches" in Jerusalem and so one could oversee these matters at each. Equally compelling is the suggestion that the number seven was chosen because of its sacredness in Jewish thinking.

The Church cheered the decision of the apostles and proceeded to name the seven men. No mention is made of how this was done. Selected were Stephen, Philip, Prochorus, Nicanor, Timon, Parmenas, and Nicolas. All bear Greek names which, many say, shows that the Church took pains to appoint persons sympathetic to the plight of the Grecian widows. But we are not sure of such an interpretation; Greek names were common among Jews, even in Palestine, and these "deacons" would perform many tasks not related to the ethnic problem.

Of the seven, Stephen and Philip are the only ones of whom more is known. Stephen, who may have been one of the Seventy sent out by the Lord, became the Church's first martyr (chapter 7), and Philip is most noted for his evangelistic ministry (8:4–12; 26–40; 21:8).

Were the apostles intending to establish a permanent office of deacon in the Church? Probably not. But the Church looks primarily to this event as the historical roots of the deaconship. Paul's instructions regarding deacons (1 Timothy 3:12, 13) and his use of the word (Philippians 1:1; Romans 16:1) presupposes an ongoing office.

Blessed was that Church, whose spiritual leaders shared the ministry with other spiritual men and women. By doing so they could devote themselves to prayer and the ministry of the Word.

The laying on of hands is the common visible sign of the "bestowal of spiritual gifts in the apostolic church." We will observe it again and again in the early Church, most always in the context of prayer. (For references on this practice the teacher may want to examine Numbers 27:18; Exodus 29:15; 1 Timothy 5:22; 2 Timothy 1:6.)

Under such godly and wise leadership, no wonder the "word of God increased." By this rather strange wording, Luke indicates the steady growth of the Church, the expanding influence of the Gospel. This expansion so far is limited to Jerusalem and among the Jews—but that is good. Jesus commanded them to go about their outreach in this manner. The Church would need a strong base from which to launch its mission into the world.

Luke concludes our lesson text with another of his summaries, this one containing the highly significant fact that "very many of the priests adhered to the Faith" (NEB). That these men who were schooled in the Scriptures embraced the Gospel confirms the idea that they had found in Jesus their long-awaited Messiah. Luke does not even hint that they believed they were repudiating their Jewish faith in turning to Christ. Rather, they were finding fulfillment. The large movement of priests into the Church would, however, hasten the coming conflict between the Church and Judaism.

Applying the Scripture

In thinking of today's lesson you will want to guide each class member to consider first your own church's spiritual condition and second, how he or she can figure in making the church "An Expanding Fellowship."

Give each class member a sheet of paper and ask them to write out every quality of the first-century Church found in the text that contributed to the Church's being an expanding fellowship. As the teacher, you may want to write your list before class time. *Don't peek at the writer's list below* until you have drawn up your own list.

Qualities of An Expanding Fellowship:
1. Godly fear, reverence
2. Miracles
3. Faith ("believers")
4. Togetherness
5. Sharing of possessions
6. Unselfishness
7. Frequent attendance in God's house
8. A glad mood
9. Eating in homes
10. Simplicity
11. Praise of God
12. Good name in community
13. God's Spirit at work
14. Frequent conversions
15. Sensitive leaders
16. Sense of priorities (not neglect the Word)
17. Shared responsibilities
18. Wise leaders
19. Prayerful leaders
20. Unity
21. Obedient body

Ask one member of the class to read his or her list while you write the words on the chalkboard or on a large flipchart where everyone can see the entire list. When that person has completed, have others add qualities to this list, keeping in mind that they must all be qualities contributing to an expanding fellowship.

Now, see if you as a class can indicate the qualities on that list that would also describe your own church. Be honest here. Underline the ones that would apply to your church, emphasizing to the class that all of you want to see how the church measures up, should such a measurement be valid.

Finally, ask each member to examine the qualities that are underlined and circle the traits for which he or she has some responsibility. This will include most qualities, but will not include those having to do with leaders, unless you have church leaders in your class. The quality of a "good name in community" may be thought of as a collective testimony, but each member should include himself in that because each person contributes to the church's "reputation" in some way. Urge the class to note the qualities that could not be underlined and ask them to pray and act to bring those into reality in your church. Close in prayer, asking God to cause your church to be An Expanding Fellowship!

Questions for Discussion
Make use of these questions to involve your students in learning and to test their understanding of the lesson.
1. What is meant by the words, "fear came upon every soul"? 2. Did the disciples break away from Judaism and Jewish practices of worship immediately? Explain your answer. 3. Who were the "Grecians" and what was the cause of their complaint? 4. What office in the Church might be said to trace its origin to this passage? 5. Who selected the Seven? Who appointed them? 6. What four qualifications were established for the Seven? 7. From this passage (6:1–7) what do we learn about the extent of the growth of the young Church?

Illustrating the Scripture
Examples and quotations to help the teacher communicate the lesson.
DEACONS "Every clergyman begins as a deacon. This is right. But he never ceases to be a deacon. The priest is a deacon still. The bishop is a deacon still. Christ came as a deacon, lived as a deacon, died as a deacon" (Bishop Lightfoot).

"*Diakonos* and its derivatives are in use in the New Testament for any kind of 'ministry' or service. But in Philippians 1:1 the noun has become the title of particular officials, 'deacons.' In this passage and in 1 Timothy 3, the deacons are associated with the bishops (or overseers) and clearly exercise a subordinate ministry. This corresponds with the subsequent history of the office in the early centuries; deacons were the personal assistants of the bishop both in the conduct of public worship . . . and in the administration of church affairs.

"The two New Testament passages do not by themselves give a clear idea of the functions of deacons, but the list of qualifications for the office in 1 Timothy 3:8–13, as well as the general meaning of the word *diakonos*, suggests that among their duties, as in later times, was the administration of the charitable funds of the church. Perhaps the 'attendant' in the Jewish synagogue (Luke 4:20) supplied the model of the Christian deacon. More probably we should assume that the church, under the guidance of the apostles, created the subdivisions of its ministry in forms adapted for its mission to the world. . . ." (H. J. Carpenter, in *A Theological Word Book of the Bible*, edited by Alan Richardson.)

"HE GAVE HIMSELF WHOLLY TO PRAYER" (v. 4) "The year was A.D. 30. The city: Jerusalem. The evangelist: an untutored fisherman named Simon Peter. The occasion: the first great mass evangelistic meeting of the Christian era. The audience: a mixture of Jews and God-fearing Gentiles from all over the known world. The sermon: a forthright declaration of Jesus Christ, plus an urgent exhortation to repent. The result: 3,000 conversions that very day! The secret? The power of the Holy Spirit at work in answer to the prayers of the tiny band of disciples.

"Pentecost was no accident. It was the consequence of a ten-day-long prayer meeting. The pattern of evangelistic power set then has not varied down through the centuries. Whenever men and women have been converted by the power of the Holy Spirit through the preaching of the Gospel, the secret has been this: somebody has been fervently praying.

"Move on to the year 1830. The city: Rochester, New York. The evangelist: a young lawyer named Charles G. Finney. The results of this remarkable campaign: in one year, some thirty thousand people were converted. The secret? Somebody was praying. Finney himself attributed the blessing to the prayers of a minister named Abel Clary who did not attend a single meeting. He commented: 'This Mr. Clary continued in Rochester as long as I did, and did not leave until after I had left. He never, that I could learn, appeared in public, but gave himself wholly to prayer' " (Evangelist Leighton Ford).

Topics for Youth
"HEY, GANG! WE CAN DO IT—TOGETHER!"—The Living Bible says, "And all the believers met together constantly and shared everything with each other" (Acts 2:44). From an unknown source comes an illustration from nature of the power of teamwork.

"One of the intriguing mysteries of nature is a flock of wild geese flying in a V-shaped formation. When a group of aerodynamic engineers studied this phenomenon, they made an interesting discovery.

"As the geese fly in the V-formation, the flapping of the wings of each bird gives an uplift to the one before and behind him, and he in turn receives an uplift from them. This lift creates approximately 70 percent more forward thrust, so that as a group the geese can fly further than they can individually. If one goose slips out of formation and tries to fly on his own, he misses that uplift and falls behind. When he moves out on his own, he gives and receives nothing. . . .

"In these troubled days God is trying to pull us together and show us that as we move with one another, we can go further and accomplish more than we can by traveling alone. He is telling us that if we will walk side by side, love each other and feel for one another, we will be stronger and have a much more powerful thrust in our lives, both as a group and as individuals."

WHAT MAKES A LEADER?—Someone said, a good leader must first of all be a good follower. Today's lesson talks about leadership. At a critical time in the life of the young Church, they had to pick some leaders. Did you note carefully what the four qualifications were?

1. First, he or she must *be a member of the group;* "select seven . . . among yourselves." Companies have a habit of promoting within the ranks, rather than going outside the organization to pick leaders. Whether you aspire to

lead in the church or elsewhere, first, commit yourself to the group. Join!

2. Second, they must *have a good reputation;* "well thought of by everyone" (Acts 6:3 TLB). We can't all be perfect, but that is not what is implied by this quality. If we are to lead, we must take care to keep our name as clear of evil as we can.

3. Third, *be full of the Holy Spirit.* In other words, controlled by the Holy Spirit. This means that a person must yield control of her or his life to God, moment by moment, day by day, and live close to Him in prayer, the Scriptures, obedience, and fellowship with others.

4. Fourth, *be wise.* This can come as an answer to prayer. It can come also by associating with others who are truly wise. Wisdom is the right application of knowledge and the Bible says "the fear of God is the beginning of wisdom."

UNIT II

Beyond Old Barriers

LESSON 4   **MARCH 27**

Good News for Outsiders

Background Scripture: Isaiah 56:3–8; Acts 6:8–8:40
Devotional Reading: Isaiah 56:3–8

Acts 8:25–38

25 And they, when they had testified and preached the word of the Lord, returned to Jerusalem, and preached the gospel in many villages of the Samaritans.
26 And the angel of the Lord spake unto Philip, saying, Arise, and go toward the south unto the way that goeth down from Jerusalem unto Gaza, which is desert.
27 And he arose and went: and, behold, a man of Ethiopia, a eunuch of great authority under Candace queen of the Ethiopians, who had the charge of all her treasure, and had come to Jerusalem for to worship,
28 Was returning, and sitting in his chariot read Esaias the prophet.
29 Then the Spirit said unto Philip, Go near, and join thyself to this chariot.

260 THE BOOK OF ACTS

30 And Philip ran thither to him, and heard him read the prophet Esaias, and said, Understandest thou what thou readest?
31 And he said, How can I, except some man should guide me? And he desired Philip that he would come up and sit with him.
32 The place of the scripture which he read was this, He was led as a sheep to the slaughter; and like a lamb dumb before his shearer, so opened he not his mouth:
33 In his humiliation his judgment was taken away: and who shall declare his generation? for his life is taken from the earth.
34 And the eunuch answered Philip, and said, I pray thee, of whom speaketh the prophet this? of himself, or of some other man?
35 Then Philip opened his mouth, and began at the same scripture, and preached unto him Jesus.
36 And as they went on their way, they came unto a certain water: and the eunuch said, See, here is water; what doth hinder me to be baptized?
37 And Philip said, If thou believest with all thine heart, thou mayest. And he answered and said, I believe that Jesus Christ is the Son of God.
38 And he commanded the chariot to stand still: and they went down both into the water, both Philip and the eunuch; and he baptized him.

KEY VERSE: "Then Philip opened his mouth, and began at the same scripture, and preached unto him Jesus." Acts 8:35.

Home Daily Bible Readings
Mar. 21 M. The Promised Blessings to Outsiders, Isaiah 56:3-8.
Mar. 22 T. The Gospel Proclaimed in Samaria, Acts 8:4-8.
Mar. 23 W. The Gift of the Holy Spirit to Gentiles, Acts 8:14-17.
Mar. 24 T. The Good Tidings of Salvation, Isaiah 61:1-3.
Mar. 25 F. The Kingdom of God on Earth, Isaiah 2:1-4.
Mar. 26 S. An Apostle to the Gentiles, Romans 11:13-16.
Mar. 27 S. Standing Fast Through Faith, Romans 11:17-24.

Lesson Aim: That adults will be motivated to look for "outsiders" with whom they can share the Good News of salvation in Christ this week.

LESSON OUTLINE
Background to the Scripture
Looking at the Scripture Text
  I. To Many Samaritans (Acts 8:25)
 II. To One Ethiopian (Acts 8:26-30)
III. Using the Scriptures (Acts 8:31-35)

IV. Baptizing the New Convert (Acts 8:36-38)
Applying the Scripture

Background to the Scripture
It is almost impossible for us to imagine that the Good News of salvation in Jesus Christ was for so long the precious possession of only a few thousand people of one nation. In our century, Christianity has become the world's only universally accepted religion, with adherents in virtually every country on earth.

Do you recall the early lessons in this book which we studied a few months ago? They concentrated on God's covenant with Abraham. The Lord first "cut" His covenant with His chosen people 2,000 years before Christ. While Jesus walked this earth, ministered, and trained the Twelve, He devoted His ministry entirely to the house of Israel. And even when He was ready to ascend to heaven after His Resurrection, He still forbade the Twelve to leave Jerusalem. For the time being, they were not to share the Gospel with others than the Jews.

That "time being" is ended as we open our Bible to the eighth chapter of Acts. Here we see the young Church, empowered by the Holy Spirit, bursting out of Jerusalem into the neighboring district of Samaria. Beginning with this lesson and continuing for the next four sessions we move into that second section of Luke's broad framework—"ye shall be my witnesses . . . in all Judea and in Samaria" (1:8).

Looking at the Scripture Text
What caused the breakthrough? What motivated the Church, almost 100 percent Jewish in makeup, to go with the Gospel into the regions beyond? And what happened when they tried to confront "outsiders" with their message of salvation?

To Many Samaritans (v. 25) Stephen, one of the Seven, boldly testified before a called meeting of the Jewish hierarchy and was barely finished with his preaching when they seized him and stoned him to death. A young Pharisee named Saul witnessed the bloody stoning (7:57-8:1) and in his zeal for what he thought was the truth led a furious campaign throughout the city against the believers. The apostles went underground for a time, but many of the disciples scattered to escape being thrown in jail.

Luke records in chapter 8 the remarkable reception given the Gospel by the Samaritans when another one of the Seven, Philip, fled there and preached the Gospel. The people turned to Christ in such numbers that Peter and John were sent from Jerusalem to Samaria. Their chief mission there, while adding their testimony of the risen Lord, was to bring to the believers the empowering of the Holy Spirit. Laying their hands on the Samaritan believers, Peter and John prayed and the Spirit was given, thus linking this group with their brethren in Jerusalem into the one growing church body. Peter and John then returned to Jerusalem, preaching the Gospel in "many villages of the Samaritans" on their way, some versions say, although the text does not make clear whether they did so before or after returning to Jerusalem.

To One Ethiopian (vv. 26–30) It could be assumed that Philip is intended in the *they* of verse 25; the Greek text does not name him or Peter or John. But whether he was in Jerusalem or still in Samaria when the angel sent him on a special mission, makes little difference. By some means, perhaps a vision, "the angel of the Lord" said, "Get ready and go south to the road that goes from Jerusalem to Gaza" (v. 26 TEV). Philip did not stop to ask what reason lay behind the angel's command to him, or to doubt. The early Church, not yet in possession of the complete written revelation of God's will as we have it in the Bible, frequently received guidance by the intervention of angels. We may also expect angelic visits, but the normal course God follows in speaking to us is through the Scriptures.

Gaza does not sound all that unfamiliar to us today. Rather frequently we read of or hear of goings-on in the Gaza Strip which Israel occupied in the Six Day War. The ancient Philistine city of Gaza lay about fifty miles (eighty km) southwest of Jerusalem and was inland. Scholars think it was to this Gaza the desert road would lead; the Romans built a new Gaza, but it was on the seacoast. Luke points out that the road was "desert." On that road, perhaps not far from Jerusalem, Philip came upon a chariot whose occupant was the Ethiopian eunuch. The Gospel was about to bridge another gulf to the outside world.

What follows is one of the most moving, graphic accounts in all of Luke's writing. No doubt Luke had heard this story from Philip himself (Acts 21:8–10).

Some Bible students think that an official of such high rank as this Ethiopian would be accompanied by a retinue of attendants. That idea is appealing. But Luke does not concern himself with such matters. He focuses on the one man who for all we know was alone in his covered carriage. Luke describes him carefully. *An Ethiopian eunuch*—he was of the Nubian people of northeast Africa, a nation that inhabited the land along the Nile between modern Aswan and Khartoum in what is now Sudan. As was frequently the custom in the courts of kings in the East, this trusted steward was a eunuch. Another Ethiopian eunuch, Ebedmelech, is named in Scripture and like this man, he is well spoken of. That man had mercy on Jeremiah and helped free him from the awful dungeon (Jeremiah 38:7ff).

Candace—he served in the court of the queen or Candace (Kandake), as the queens of the Nubians were titled.

Great authority—he was a potentate, over the queen's entire treasury, "an important official" says the NIV.

He had traveled to Jerusalem on a pilgrimage and having worshiped there was returning on his long journey home. In the stillness of the desert, he read from a scroll of Isaiah which possibly he purchased in Jerusalem. His desire to worship in Jerusalem marks him as a proselyte. How his spirit was awakened to seek Jehovah is not told; his story is similar to those which foreign missionaries encounter upon entering unevangelized territory, finding there sincere men and women who are prepared to hear the Good News they bring.

From the verses of Isaiah quoted in our text it is fair to assume that this man read from the Greek Septuagint version. Those verses agree verbatim with the Greek translation which was made in Alexandria in the third century before Christ.

On seeing the Ethiopian, Philip sensed an immediate leading of the Spirit to approach the chariot "and stay near it" (NIV). This he did, running near enough so that he could hear the man read aloud. We cannot help but comment on Philip's eager obedience and ask if we respond as readily to what God asks of us. Consider the Spirit's timing in taking Philip to this chariot—here was a man, all alone in his quest for the true God, with the true Book on his lap and a servant of the Truth running beside him asking if he understood what he read! If ever a person was prepared to receive the Good News of salvation, the Ethiopian eunuch was the man.

Using the Scriptures (vv. 31–35)   Sometimes we are guilty of thinking, *"they have the Bible. They are without excuse."* It is astounding for some of us who have access to such fine teaching to judge others in this way. Would we be willing to forego the Christian teaching afforded us?

It is a mark of the Ethiopian's humility that he urged Philip to join him for the purpose of explaining the Scriptures to him. The word *guide* or *explain* (v. 31) is the same word used of the Holy Spirit whom Jesus promised would *"guide* you into all truth" (John 16:13). The eunuch, not knowing the Spirit, desired a man to be his guide.

The words he did not understand were these: "He was led like a sheep to the slaughter, and as a lamb before the shearer is silent, so he did not open his mouth. In his humiliation he was deprived of justice. Who can speak of his descendants? For his life was taken from the earth" (NIV).

The passage before his questioning traveling companion was a difficult one, but "as a text, Philip needed no better opening than this Messianic passage in Isaiah," notes A. T. Robertson. "Philip had no doubt about the Messianic meaning and he knew that Jesus was the Messiah. There are scholars who do not find Jesus in the Old Testament at all, but Jesus himself did (Luke 24:27) as Philip does here."

Philip must have pointed out that Jesus was the "Lamb of God" who silently endured the cross for mankind. He was the One "who in his humiliation . . . was deprived of justice" (NIV). He was the One who was prematurely cut off so that the world might well wonder, "who will be able to speak of his posterity?" (NEB). Philip, no doubt, would have testified of the life Jesus lived, but chiefly he would tell the eunuch of Jesus' sacrificial death accomplished only months earlier, the Resurrection, the Ascension and the Pentecostal outpouring. And he would have declared the Gospel imperative—repent and be baptized in the Name of Jesus Christ the Lord!

Baptizing the New Convert (vv. 36–38) From the eunuch's last question, it is plain that he knows that Jesus commanded all His followers to be baptized. We wonder if in Jerusalem this man had not heard apostolic preaching and witnessed baptism. Coming upon a spring or pool of water in the desert he asked, "Is there any reason why I should not be baptized?" (PHILLIPS). John Chrysostom comments on this verse—"mark the eager desire, mark the exact knowledge . . . see again his modesty; he does not say 'Baptize me,' neither does he hold his peace, but he utters somewhat between strong desire and reverent fear."

According to verse 37, Philip answered him with a plain question. This verse, though entirely biblical and acceptable, is unfortunately without sound basis in the best manuscripts. Irenaeus, in the later second century, and Cyprian in the third century, both quoted parts of the verse and Augustine held it to be genuine. But it may have been a part of a creed used in baptismal services. Many scholars believe a scribe inserted it into the text.

The chariot halted, both Philip and the Ethiopian disembarked and waded into the cool water. There Philip immersed the penitent eunuch. Those who believe that a corps of attendants traveled with the eunuch say that they, witnessing the baptism, were later converted themselves. One tradition says that the Ethiopian returned to his country and baptized the Candace into the faith.

It is quite characteristic of Luke's emphasis on the universal appeal of the Gospel that he should include this choice story in his account. In the old dispensation, a eunuch could not participate fully in worship; the Law forbade it (Deuteronomy 23:1). But now this man stood in the inner circle of those who worship God in Christ. God had promised such in a prophecy concerning the coming Kingdom: "A man who has been castrated should never think that because he cannot have children, he can never be part of God's people. The Lord says to such a man . . . your name will be remembered in my Temple and among my people longer than if you had sons and daughters. You will never be forgotten" (Isaiah 56:3–5 TEV).

Applying the Scripture
Do you remember this Bible School song?

> Jesus loves the little children,
> All the children of the world.
> Red and yellow, black and white,
> They are precious in His sight.
> Jesus loves the little children of the world.

You might recite the words of this simple, but profound chorus to your class as you think together of the meaning of today's lesson.

Now, ask your class to focus their attention on "outsiders" for the next few minutes. It is easy to see that the Ethiopian eunuch was an outsider. Ask your class to name some groups of people who may be considered such.

The list may include: refugees from Asia—people whose ethnic background differs from the more predominant group in a community—the handicapped—the poor—newcomers to a community—the aged—prisoners. . . .

It is surprising, isn't it, to think that so many people in our world might consider themselves or be considered *outsiders.*

An outsider to us is one who does not know our Lord and Savior and with whom we cannot have fellowship in Him. Can anyone in your class identify with the "outsider" in their own experience of coming to Christ? Perhaps that someone would talk briefly about what made them feel like an outsider and how they came to know God's love and Christian fellowship. *Note:* If you can find out what needs in their life Christ met, you may know better how to reach out to others.

Now ask the class to narrow their thinking down—to focus on individuals who are in their community who would be considered outsiders. You may want to list them on the chalkboard:

—the refugee family from North Vietnam who have just settled in town.
—the man from India who is cashier at the local news stand.
—the family from out of state who moved into your block.
—the young person who was recently placed in prison in your county.
—the servicemen and women who are stationed at a nearby military installation.

Encourage your class to know that God wants us to reach out to these and all outsiders who are within our sphere of influence. As you close the class period, ask one member to pray for the individuals listed on the board. Urge each member to take the name of one person to pray for daily and to look for opportunities to include the person in some ministry of the church so that they may come to know Christ.

Questions for Discussion
Make use of these questions to involve your students in learning and to test their understanding of the lesson.
1. What caused the disciples to spread out from Jerusalem, leading Philip to begin evangelizing Samaria?   2. By what means did God guide Philip to the eunuch? How does He lead us today to those who are seeking Christ?   3. How might the eunuch have obtained a scroll of Isaiah? From what passage was he reading?   4. What are the indications that he was prepared to receive Philip's witness?   5. In Philip's witness to the Ethiopian, what truths would he have been most certain to emphasize?   6. If verse 37 was not a part of Luke's account, what explanation might be offered for its existence?   7. Why would an Ethiopian eunuch's conversion particularly merit inclusion in the sacred Scripture?

Illustrating the Scripture
Examples and quotations to help the teacher communicate the lesson.
"Why was it needful that two apostles should come down to Samaria and pray, with laying on of hands, for the newly baptized that they might receive

the Holy Spirit? There is no mention of such prayer or such imposition of hands in the case of the first three thousand who were baptized. They were told by Peter, 'Be baptized every one of you . . . and ye shall receive the gift of the Holy Ghost" (2:38) and they were baptized, and doubtless did receive the Holy Spirit. Neither is there any mention of such things in the case of the subsequent thousands who were baptized at Jerusalem after the apostles' preaching. Why, then, was it so in Samaria?

"To answer this question, we must observe the difference in the circumstances. The baptisms at Jerusalem were performed by the apostles themselves. The Holy Spirit was given upon their promise and assurance. But in Samaria, the preaching and the baptizing were done by the scattered disciples. There was a danger of many independent bodies springing up, owing no allegiance to the apostles, and cemented by no bonds to the mother church. But Christ's church was to be one—many members, but one body. The apostolate was to be the governing power of the whole church, by the will and ordinance of Christ. Hence, there was a manifest reason why, when the Gospel spread beyond Judea, these visible spiritual gifts should be given only through the laying on of the apostles' hands, and by the intervention of their prayers. This had a manifest and striking influence in marking and preserving the unity of the church, and in marking and maintaining the sovereignty of the apostolic rule. . . . Observe, too, how prayer and the laying on of hands are tied together. Neither is valid without the other. In this case, as at Pentecost, the extraordinary gift of the Holy Spirit was conferred" (*Pulpit Commentary*).

THE INFLUENCE OF THE BIBLE   As our lesson points out, the eunuch found his way to God by finding his way in the Word. Equally important, Philip was able to help the eunuch because he knew the Bible. Here is what some men have said:

"The Christian feels that the tooth of time gnaws all books but the Bible. It has a pertinent relevance to every age. It has worked miracles by itself alone. It has made its way where no missionary had gone and has done the missionary's work. . . . Nineteen centuries of experience have tested the Book. It has passed through critical fires no other volume has suffered, and its spiritual truth has endured the flames and come out without so much as the *smell* of burning" (W. E. Sangster).

"Jesus Christ absolutely trusted the Bible, and though there are in it things inexplicable and intricate that have puzzled me much, I am going to trust the Book, not in a blind sense, but reverently, because of him" (H.C.G. Moule).

"If a man is not familiar with the Bible, he has suffered a loss which he had better make all possible haste to correct" (Theodore Roosevelt).

Topics for Youth

AN OUTSIDER COMES TO CHRIST—A COMMUNIST! AND THE BIBLE PLAYED A LARGE PART—"Roger Arienda was a nationally known communist agitator when sentenced to prison in 1972 in Manila, Philippines, for possession of illegal weapons. While in prison he became a Christian in 1975 and then a vibrant witness who has led more than 2,000 people to Christ. He was paroled from prison on Christmas Day, 1980. . . .

"Arienda's fiery speeches calling for an overthrow of the government and adoption of communism prompted several attempts on his life in the early 1970s. The weapons he carried led to a twelve-year prison sentence in 1972 after Philippine President Ferdinand Marcos declared martial law.

"Arienda had been in prison three years, fighting boredom and loneliness, when one day in the library he picked up a book to read. It had a red cover and he thought it was a communist book. Instead, it was a Bible. Out of sheer desperation he read it.

"He read about a new sort of revolution called for by Christ which included forgiving enemies instead of killing them as communism had taught. Peace and tranquility began replacing the hate, anger and loneliness in his heart. When he finally accepted Christ through his Bible reading, he actually visited the prison doctor because he thought something was wrong with his heart. It felt different, he said. Howard and Marjorie Olive, Southern Baptist missionaries, enrolled Arienda in Bible correspondence courses offered through the 'Baptist Hour' television program they direct and he completed every course in record time.

"He soon began witnessing and preaching in the national prison with dramatic results: over the five-year period more than 2,000 inmates, prison officials and their families were baptized in fish ponds or pools used to hold drinking water. Eventually Simbahan Kristiyano Southern Baptist Church was formed within the prison and Arienda became pastor. His cellmate, Cesar Guy, became a deacon and began leading Bible studies in the maximum security area.

"As knowledge of Arienda's dramatic conversion spread, lawyers, doctors, movie stars and writers began visiting him in prison and he led many of these outsiders to Christ. . . .

"Arienda no longer holds to his old political ideas for changing society. 'A utopian society is only possible when Christ is made the total leader,' he says." (Mike Creswell, Baptist Press, February 21, 1981, News Service of the Southern Baptist Convention. Used by permission.)

LESSON 5   APRIL 3

Confronted by the Risen Lord

Background Scripture: Acts 9:1–31; 22:1–21; 26:1–23
1 Corinthians 15:3–11
Devotional Reading: 1 Corinthians 15:1–11

Acts 9:1-16

1 And Saul, yet breathing out threatenings and slaughter against the disciples of the Lord, went unto the high priest,

2 And desired of him letters to Damascus to the synagogues, that if he found any of this way, whether they were men or women, he might bring them bound unto Jerusalem.

3 And as he journeyed, he came near Damascus: and suddenly there shined round about him a light from heaven:

4 And he fell to the earth, and heard a voice saying unto him, Saul, Saul, why persecutest thou me?

5 And he said, Who art thou, Lord? And the Lord said, I am Jesus whom thou persecutest: it is hard for thee to kick against the pricks.

6 And he trembling and astonished said, Lord, what wilt thou have me to do? And the Lord said unto him, Arise, and go into the city, and it shall be told thee what thou must do.

7 And the men which journeyed with him stood speechless, hearing a voice, but seeing no man.

8 And Saul arose from the earth; and when his eyes were opened, he saw no man: but they led him by the hand, and brought him into Damascus.

9 And he was three days without sight, and neither did eat nor drink.

10 And there was a certain disciple at Damascus, named Ananias; and to him said the Lord in a vision, Ananias. And he said, Behold, I am here, Lord.

11 And the Lord said unto him, Arise, and go into the street which is called Straight, and enquire in the house of Judas for one called Saul, of Tarsus: for, behold, he prayeth,

12 And hath seen in a vision a man named Ananias coming in, and putting his hand on him, that he might receive his sight.

13 Then Ananias answered, Lord, I have heard by many of this man, how much evil he hath done to thy saints at Jerusalem:

14 And here he hath authority from the chief priests to bind all that call on thy name.

15 But the Lord said unto him, Go thy way: for he is a chosen vessel

unto me, to bear my name before the Gentiles, and kings, and the children of Israel:
16 For I will shew him how great things he must suffer for my name's sake.

KEY VERSE: "And I said, Who art thou, Lord? And he said, I am Jesus whom thou persecutest." Acts 26:15.

Home Daily Bible Readings
Mar. 28 M. The Conversion of Saul, Acts 9:1-9.
Mar. 29 T. The Authority of Paul's Apostleship, Galatians 1:11-17.
Mar. 30 W. The Damascus Road—Revisited, Acts 22:1-10.
Mar. 31 T. The Divine Command, Acts 22:17-22.
Apr. 1 F. Paul's Defense Before Agrippa, Acts 26:1-8.
Apr. 2 S. By the Grace of God, 1 Corinthians 15:3-11.
Apr. 3 S. From Persecutor to Preacher, Galatians 1:18-24.

Lesson Aim: As a result your class members should be more able to recognize God's sovereign hand in carrying out His purpose.

LESSON OUTLINE
Background to the Scripture
Looking at the Scripture Text
  I. A Hateful Schemer (Acts 9:1, 2)
  II. A Heavenly Speaker (Acts 9:3-9)
  III. A Helping Servant (Acts 9:10-14)
  IV. A Heavy Sufferer (Acts 9:15, 16)
Applying the Scripture

Background to the Scripture

The opening word in Luke's account of Saul's conversion, *meanwhile* (NIV), reminds us that despite the joy on the Jerusalem-Gaza road and the spontaneous revival in Samaria, a frightening persecution of Christians continued in Jerusalem.

Our text picks up where 8:3 leaves off. Saul, a Pharisee present at the stoning of Stephen, became convinced that the new teaching of the apostles could never be reconciled with the ancestral traditions of his people. Believing that by locking up the Christians he was "doing God a service" (John 16:2), he proceeded to map an even more evil strategy. Doubtless knowing that many believers had fled Jerusalem, he decided to track them down. For some reason, he chose to chase them in Damascus where many of them might be mingling in the thirty to forty synagogues history tells us were there.

The prospect looked dim for the young Church. *But God!* In a matter of a few days, God was going to give one of His most prized gifts to the Church. Saul would return to Jerusalem a believer; in time he would become the Apostle Paul.

Looking at the Scripture Text

A Hateful Schemer (vv. 1, 2)   In his commentary on Acts, J. W. Packer calls attention to "the importance attached by Luke to the conversion of Saul . . . it is recounted in detail three times in Acts—here, in Paul's speech from the steps leading to the barracks (22:1-21); and in his defense before King Agrippa (26:1-23). If we bear in mind the restrictions imposed upon an early writer by the possible length of a scroll and the cost of writing material, this repetition is of great significance."

The three accounts of Saul's conversion differ in some details but agree in substance; combined, they give us a striking record of the original "Damascus Road experience." Saul in later years would write to the church at Philippi of his "zeal" in persecuting the Church. Luke describes him as "breathing out murderous threats against the Lord's disciples" (NIV).

In Judaism, the high priest was the supreme spiritual authority. His authority in religious matters was "upheld by the Roman powers," says the *New Bible Commentary (Revised)*. All of the synagogues everywhere respected the authority of this office. Knowing this, Saul had only to gain authorization from the high priest to search among the worshipers in Damascus and arrest any of "the Way" he found there. Before they were given the name *Christians*, the disciples were frequently called by this term, "the Way," to differentiate them from their fellow Jews whom they still joined in certain of the synagogue worship services but who did not accept Jesus as the Messiah. (See Acts 18:25, 26; 19:9, 23; 22:4; 24:14.) Its use in Luke is one mark of an early date for the writing of Acts.

A Heavenly Speaker (vv. 3-9)   Damascus, a very old city even in the first century, is situated approximately 140 miles north and east of Jerusalem. Celebrated for its gardens and orchards and fountains, at the crossroads of trade routes to Baghdad, Arabia, and Egypt, it hosted a considerable colony of Jews. The historian Josephus estimated that Nero had put 10,000 Jews to death (some thirty years after the events of today's lesson); it is possible that 40,000 Jews inhabited the city. When Saul chose Damascus as the next place for squelching the rising voice of Christian witness, little did he know that he was walking into a heavenly ambush. His party would have required seven or eight days to journey from Jerusalem. According to his own testimony later, it was noon (22:6) as they approached Damascus and Saul was struck down.

Luke describes the cause as an overpowering "light from heaven." Simultaneous with the light, a voice sounded: "Saul, Saul, why persecutest thou me?"

Hearing his name called out distinctly "in the Hebrew tongue" (26:14) stunned the determined Pharisee. He may have recognized that the source of the light and the voice was God, but his reply, "Who art thou, Lord?" tells us that he was not sure who was speaking to him. Robertson and others say "it is open to question whether the word should be translated 'sir' or 'Lord'." But in a moment Saul did know that it was the risen Christ who spoke with him: "I am Jesus whom thou persecutest."

The truth that in persecuting the Church he was in reality persecuting Jesus must have pained Saul acutely. Of course he had not accepted the teaching that Jesus was alive from the dead. To be confronted by Jesus, in glorified form, calling out to him like this must have devastated the Jewish zealot. The words Jesus said point to the mystic union between the Lord Jesus and His people ("He that receiveth you receiveth me, and he that receiveth me receiveth him that sent me," Matthew 10:40; *see* also Matthew 25:40, 45).

Luke does not say that Saul saw Jesus, but later, in one of his letters, the apostle affirms it: "Have I not seen Jesus Christ our Lord?" (1 Corinthians 9:1). This was "a vision so real that later he classed it as a resurrection appearance," says Packer, referring to Paul's words in 1 Corinthians 15:8—"I saw him too, long after the others, as though I had been born almost too late for this" (TLB). The vision reduced Saul instantly to submission. With his words, "What wilt thou have me to do?" Saul evidences a change of heart and his conversion could well be marked from that instant.

Modern versions omit the last sentence of verse 5 and the opening question of verse 6. They are genuine, scholars believe, but belong in Acts 26:14.

The Lord does not give us a blueprint for our lives, someone has said. He tells us what to do next, and this He did with Saul. "Get up and go into the city, and you will be told what you must do" (v. 6 NIV). Luke says that the men who accompanied him had seen the light, but though they heard the voice they did not comprehend what was said (*see* 22:9 NIV, NASB). They led blinded Saul by the hand into Damascus. Some suggest that this means the party had traveled on foot to Damascus, since no mention is made of animals. But what is more likely, they rode asses or mules—strict Jews rarely mounted horses—but at this point they were near the city and in such a subdued frame of mind by what had happened, that they traveled into the city on foot.

A *Helping Servant* (vv. 10–14) For three days, Saul was sequestered in the house of Judas on Straight Street in Damascus. He abstained from food and drink willfully in order to pray and understand what the vision meant. Sometime, perhaps on the third day, he saw "in his mind's eye," PHILLIPS says, a man come to him and lay his hands on him so that he can see again. Somewhere in the city, that man—a disciple named Ananias—received a vision. The Lord who had intersected Saul's life directly now chose a human instrument to bring Saul into the fulness of his Christian experience.

Ananias is remembered by this lone deed. The record does not spell out what other things he did in faithfulness to merit this responsible mission. He is typical of the thousands of unsung servants and handmaidens of the Lord whom the Lord counts as indispensable to His work. What God asked of him required strong faith. It would be like going across town to lay hands on Joseph Stalin or Idi Amin. The evil reputation Saul had gained for atrocities in Jerusalem had preceded him to Damascus and Ananias understandably questioned the Lord about that. He wanted to be sure he was hearing the right thing from God.

Commenting on verse 13 the *Pulpit Commentary* says, "Ananias's answer shows his profound astonishment, mixed with doubt and misgiving. . . . Little did Ananias suspect that this dreaded enemy would be the channel of God's richest blessings to his Church throughout all ages until the coming of Christ. How empty our fears often are!"

How did Ananias know what Saul's mission was in Damascus? An angel could have revealed it, or it may have been a gift of knowledge from the Holy Spirit. But the likely answer seems the "disciples' grapevine"; probably some of the believing priests had learned of the plot and had sent messengers ahead to Damascus to warn their brothers and sisters.

Ananias calls the believers *saints* in our text, the earliest appearance of that title in the New Testament. It literally means "holy ones" or "pure ones" and can be applied since the Cross to every believer. In the brief span of our text, believers are called "disciples" (v. 1), "the Way" (v. 2), "saints" and those "who call upon Thy name" (v. 14 NASB).

A Heavy Sufferer (vv. 15, 16) What Luke wrote in our text concerning God's answer to Ananias differs somewhat from how Paul described the same event when he addressed the throng at Jerusalem (22:12-16). What is of interest to us is the way the Lord described Saul to Ananias when He sent him to lay hands on him. The words "he is a chosen vessel" mean literally "he is my vessel of election." Modern versions translate this: he is "my chosen instrument." Here lies the secret to the unsurpassed achievement of Saul, later called Paul. The Lord had set him apart, elected him to be the apostle to the Gentiles (Romans 11:13); for this reason the Gentiles are named before "the children of Israel" (v. 15).

Paul was conscious, in defending his apostleship before the Galatian church, that he had been set apart from birth. Paul labored with all his might, but his unique office and powers lay in the fact of his election, and in Christ.

For some reason the Lord revealed to Ananias, too, that Saul would suffer greatly "for my name's sake." Perhaps He told Ananias this so that Ananias, instead of fearing Saul, would begin to love him. The manner in which he subsequently served Saul, addressing him as a brother, baptizing him and feeding him, speaks eloquently of that love. Saul would live to suffer as few believers have, but not as retribution for the suffering he brought on the Church. He became the chief exponent of a salvation of grace. In 2 Corinthians 11 and 12, after cataloging his sufferings, he glorified Christ in saying—"for Christ's sake, I delight in weaknesses, in insults, in hardships, in persecutions, in difficulties. For when I am weak, then I am strong" (12:10 NIV).

Applying the Scripture
Two applications may follow this lesson, but you will need determination to reserve time for them. This lesson is so rich and there is so much in Paul's letters you will be tempted to add, that you will easily run out of time before covering it all. Believing that no lesson is complete without application, plan to leave the last five to ten minutes to this.

1. Ask your class to think of others in the Bible to whom the Lord appeared and with whom He spoke. You may want to list them on the chalkboard. A list might include:

        a. Abraham   e. Isaiah   i. Joseph
        b. Moses   f. Jeremiah j. Zechariah
        c. Gideon   g. John
        d. Jacob   h. Mary

Now see if you can name some characteristics of the visions these received that are similar to Saul's vision.

    a. Light—a number of them include the figure of fire or a bright figure or bright light.

    b. Voice or speech—most represent God speaking aloud.

    c. Awe-inspiring effect—Moses removed his shoes and Isaiah cried out, "Woe is me!"

    d. Can you name others?

Finally, in what peculiar way did Paul's vision differ from the others? Someone may suggest that Saul's blindness is almost unique (Zechariah did lose his speech because he would not believe the angel Gabriel). Discuss this and seek to determine why Saul lost his vision. It may have had something to do with his spiritual state before God appeared to him and it no doubt served a purpose after Saul's conversion.

2. Two sentences in our text can provide your class members with easy-to-remember tools for Bible study. They are:

Who art thou, Lord?
What wilt thou have me to do?

Virtually every passage of Scripture can be approached with these tools, like a spade in each hand. By putting these questions to the text the Bible student will discover new truth and receive direction for the daily walk.

You may want to make up a simple book mark with one of these questions on each side, to give to your class as a reminder of this lesson. They can use these tools in their daily devotional time with the Lord, while listening to sermons or to help them prepare devotional talks or teach Bible study. It goes like this. Suggest they try this in their morning Bible reading. Read the passage. Then review the verses with the first question in mind, seeking to see what the passage has to say about the person of Christ, the Holy Spirit, God the Father.

Then review the verses again and ask, "What wilt thou have me to do?" Here the aim is to discover a command to obey, an example to follow, a deed to be done. By combining these two simple tools, the believer can be sure to grow in grace and become a "doer of the Word" and not a hearer only.

Questions for Discussion
Make use of these questions to involve your students in learning and to test their understanding of the lesson.
1. Who was Saul? Can you name several identifying marks of the man? 2. Who was intended in the group of people known as "of this way"? 3. Explain how Saul, in persecuting the Church, could be accused of persecuting Christ as is charged. 4. By what three names or designations, all used in our text, were the early Christians known? 5. How did Ananias know that Saul had authority from the high priest to arrest the believers? 6. In the Lord's instructions to Ananias, what is prophesied concerning Saul. Explain briefly if you think these prophecies came true. 7. What do we learn from this passage about the *election* of God?

Illustrating the Scripture
Examples and quotations to help the teacher communicate the lesson.
THE WAY   This was an early name given to the Christians. "In Acts 18:25, 26, the Christian faith is spoken of as 'the way of the Lord' and 'the way of God.' In other references (Acts 19:9, 23; 22:4; 24:14, 22) it is called simply 'the Way.' Evidently, therefore, for a time, 'the Way' was the term by which the faith of Christ was spoken of chiefly perhaps among the Jews. The term means a peculiar doctrine or sect. Its application to Christians apparently lasted only so long as Christianity was considered to be a modification or peculiar form of Judaism, and its frequent use in the Acts is therefore an evidence of the early composition of the book" (*Pulpit Commentary*).

SAUL OF TARSUS—*NO ORDINARY CITY!*   Saul is introduced in our text to Ananias as "Saul of Tarsus." In Acts 21:39, Paul is quoted as saying he was "a citizen of no mean city." Quite true. Tarsus, the capital of the province of Cilicia in Asia Minor, was "renowned as a commercial and educational center on the Cydnus River," says John Stirling, the distinguished British cartographer and Bible scholar. "Its wharves (in Saul's day) were crowded with the produce and people of every nation; educationally it was held in the highest repute and sent out from its university distinguished teachers of Stoic philosophy and Roman law."

Alexander the Great visited there in A.D. 334, fostering the Greek elements in its civilization which had long been there. Marc Antony bestowed full Roman citizenship on all its inhabitants and Caesar Augustus confirmed the privilege during his rule. Although Saul's strict upbringing as a Jew destined to become a Pharisee prevented him from taking part in the university life, he was no doubt affected deeply by this center of learning. Living in a city which was visited by maritime vessels from many nations helped create within him a vision for the whole world, a vision which God would amply use in later years.

ANANIAS'S UNLIKELY MISSION "Nothing which Christ could have given Ananias to do would have surprised him more than the duty with which he was entrusted. It filled him with astonishment and perplexity. Instead of immediately acquiescing, he raised a strong objection. It seemed impossible to him that this should be his mission; nevertheless it was so, and the obedient disciple of Damascus never did a better morning's work than when he conveyed sight to the eyes and gladness to the heart of the last and greatest of the apostles.

"We may be summoned by our Lord, either through the promptings of his own Spirit or through the instrumentality of his Church, to do work which at first seems surprising, undesirable, useless. We may be invited to appeal to those we deem unlikely to welcome us, to address ourselves to apparently unremunerative toil, to cultivate ground which looks sterile to our eye; but it may be that we are really called of Christ to do a most needed and useful work" (*Pulpit Commentary*).

Topics for Youth

"IF STEPHEN HADN'T PRAYED, PAUL HADN'T PREACHED"—So says one thoughtful observer of the events which led to the conversion of Saul. It ought to encourage us to keep praying and keep believing God for the salvation of that special someone whom we want to see saved more than anyone else.

Remember what Saul was doing when the first Christian was martyred? As the enraged Jews were stoning Stephen, the young Pharisee, Saul, was holding the men's coats and consenting to Stephen's death. He was saying in his heart, "He's getting what he deserves." If Saul were standing near enough to have heard Stephen's dying prayer, "Lord, do not hold this sin against them," it must have made a profound impression on him.

Not many days later Saul met Jesus on the Damascus Road and was gloriously saved. He had to be the least likely candidate for salvation, if the early Christians were to estimate such things in human terms. But did you ever stop to think that the tremendous energy he was exerting *against* the Gospel may have been caused by a mighty unrest and sense of conviction that was growing inside of him? This is very often the case and modern-day Christians have testified that when they really knew they were lost and felt the convicting power of God, that's when they began to put up a fight.

Be encouraged to keep loving, to keep praying for and to keep communicating with that person—maybe it's a friend, or a member of your family—for whom you are burdened. If they are fighting you and doing all kinds of things against the Church and the Gospel, that may be a good sign. May God grant you your heart's desire to see their salvation.

"It has been said that the true account of what happened to Saul of Tarsus was that he had an epileptic seizure in a thunderstorm. Then men ought always to pray for a multiplication of thunderstorms and an epidemic of epilepsy!" (G. Campbell Morgan.)

LESSON 6 APRIL 10

Good News for Former Enemies

Background Scripture: Acts 9:32–12:24
Devotional Reading: 1 John 5:1–12

Acts 11:2–18

2 And when Peter was come up to Jerusalem, they that were of the circumcision contended with him,
3 Saying, Thou wentest in to men uncircumcised, and didst eat with them.
4 But Peter rehearsed the matter from the beginning, and expounded it by order unto them, saying,
5 I was in the city of Joppa praying: and in a trance I saw a vision, A certain vessel descend, as it had been a great sheet, let down from heaven by four corners; and it came even to me:
6 Upon the which when I had fastened mine eyes, I considered, and saw fourfooted beasts of the earth, and wild beasts, and creeping things, and fowls of the air.
7 And I heard a voice saying unto me, Arise, Peter; slay and eat.
8 But I said, Not so, Lord: for nothing common or unclean hath at any time entered into my mouth.
9 But the voice answered me again from heaven, What God hath cleansed, that call not thou common.
10 And this was done three times: and all were drawn up again into heaven.
11 And, behold, immediately there were three men already come unto the house where I was, sent from Caesarea unto me.
12 And the spirit bade me go with them, nothing doubting. Moreover these six brethren accompanied me, and we entered into the man's house:
13 And he shewed us how he had seen an angel in his house, which stood and said unto him, Send men to Joppa, and call for Simon, whose surname is Peter;
14 Who shall tell thee words, whereby thou and all thy house shall be saved.
15 And as I began to speak, the Holy Ghost fell on them, as on us at the beginning.
16 Then remembered I the word of the Lord, how that he said, John indeed baptized with water; but ye shall be baptized with the Holy Ghost.

17 Forasmuch then as God gave them the like gift as he did unto us, who believed on the Lord Jesus Christ; what was I, that I could withstand God?
18 When they heard these things, they held their peace, and glorified God, saying, Then hath God also to the Gentiles granted repentance unto life.

KEY VERSE: "Then hath God also to the Gentiles granted repentance unto life." Acts 11:18.

Home Daily Bible Readings		
Apr. 4	M.	The Universality of Guilt, Romans 3:1–11.
Apr. 5	T.	Righteousness by Faith, Romans 3:21–26.
Apr. 6	W.	The Reign of Grace, Romans 5:17–21.
Apr. 7	T.	Saved by Grace, Ephesians 2:1–10.
Apr. 8	F.	Through Jesus Christ, Ephesians 2:11–18.
Apr. 9	S.	An Habitation of God, Ephesians 2:19–22.
Apr. 10	S.	A Light to the Gentiles, Acts 13:44–49.

Lesson Aim: That adults will be willing to open their lives to the control of God's Spirit.

LESSON OUTLINE
Background to the Scripture
Looking at the Scripture Text
  I. Peter Criticized in Jerusalem (Acts 11:2, 3)
 II. Peter Describes the Joppa Vision (Acts 11:4–10)
III. Peter Relates the Caesarean Breakthrough (Acts 11:11–15)
IV. Peter Interprets the Caesarean Event (Acts 11:16–18)
Applying the Scripture

Background to the Scripture

If the early Christians in Jerusalem had been "blessed" with television, one can imagine a newscaster breaking the day's top story: "Simon Peter, the respected leader of the Christian movement, today baptized a family of one of the Roman captains in Caesarea after eating in the home of that Gentile."

Watching in shocked amazement across town, an older believer may well have turned to his wife and said: "Sarah, if it ain't one thing, it's another."

Since Pentecost, nothing had remained the same—or so it seemed. First, the coming of God's Spirit had turned the city into an uproar and the Church grew large overnight. Next, because of the bigness, some Greek-speaking widows were neglected and the apostles had to step in and set apart seven deacons. Then one of those deacons, Stephen, caused such a turmoil when he disputed with the Jewish leaders that he was murdered and a wholesale assault started on the Church, led by a fiery young man, Saul. The Christians in Jerusalem thought they would not live to see another sabbath, but then Saul got converted and things returned to normal. But now, Peter, of all people, had "defiled" himself in the home of some Roman Gentile.

The viewer in his home might well say: "What on earth can happen next?" Then, turning back to his television set, he hears the announcer say, "Word is that Peter is on his way now to Jerusalem. When he arrives, we will keep you posted on this story that has all the Jewish Christians here upset."

Looking at the Scripture Text
Peter Criticized in Jerusalem (vv. 2, 3) The fresh winds of the Spirit were bringing rapid changes to the young Church. Some time after Saul's conversion, his subsequent arrival in Jerusalem (after three years in Arabia) and his departure to Tarsus (9:30), Peter visited some of the groups of believers in outlying areas. Luke records that he spent time in Lydda, northwest of Jerusalem, and then responded to an urgent call from believers in Joppa, on the shores of the Mediterranean. The Holy Spirit singularly blessed his ministry in both cities and Peter remained in Joppa for a while in the home of a leather craftsman, Simon. There he received the call to go up the coast to Caesarea, the seat of the provincial government of Judea, to the house of a Gentile. And not just *any* Gentile either—to Cornelius, "a captain of an Italian regiment. He was a godly man, deeply reverent, as was his entire household. He gave generously to charity and was a man of prayer" (10:1, 2 TLB).

Our text begins with Peter's return to Jerusalem. News of what had happened in Caesarea had traveled to the "apostles and brethren" in Christ (11:1) and as Luke points out, "they . . . of the circumcision" criticized Peter. Their bone of contention was that he had entered the house of uncircumcised men (Gentiles) and had eaten with them, in violation of ceremonial law.

But he had not disobeyed Scripture. God had demanded that His covenant people keep themselves separate from the nations of the world, and specifically forbade intermarriage. But the scribes had embellished Scripture and added all manner of rules prohibiting their socializing with "Gentile dogs." These rules got in the way of our Lord and nothing so angered the scribes and Pharisees as the way He seemed to trample over the Law. He was, instead, trampling over men's traditions. Indeed, one of the frequent accusations leveled against Him was "This man welcomes sinners and eats with them" (Luke 15:2 NIV). Peter was in good company. He was being accused of the same things his Lord was.

Jesus had set aside the ceremonial law and Peter's accusers should have known better. But habits die hard. This issue of the Gentiles' acceptance into the Church would spark controversy for a long time to come because well-meaning Jewish Christians were fearful of breaking with their ancient traditions.

Who were these of the "circumcision party"? It seems strange that Luke refers to them in this way, because they were Jewish believers and they comprised the entire Church so far as we know. These were evidently the most conservative or orthodox of the Jewish converts; we will encounter them again in our study of chapter 15.

Peter Describes the Joppa Vision (vv. 4–10) Peter, far from being a lord or bishop over the Church, proved that he was accountable to the Church for his actions. He had acted first, but he knew that he must answer to the Church for his acts. At some appropriate place, the apostles and evidently a large representation of the Church listened as he "explained everything to them precisely as it had happened."

Luke evidently placed much importance on this event since he chose to repeat, through the mouth of Peter, much of what is told in 10:9–24. Peter was in prayer on the flat housetop of Simon's home and fell into a trance. The word translated *trance* is very similar to our word *ecstasy* and means to stand outside oneself. Today we might say he had an out-of-the-body experience.

Entranced, he saw a great sheet lower from heaven and he "looked intently" to see what was on it. There he saw four-footed animals (literally, quadrapeds), beasts of prey, reptiles (or crawling creatures) and birds. And a voice commanded him by name to "kill and eat."

But Peter in his vision remonstrated: "Surely not, Lord! I have never eaten anything impure or unclean" (NIV). His reply reminds us that Jehovah had told His people what they could eat and what they could not. Certainly beasts of prey and reptiles and many kinds of birds were considered "unclean" and thus unapproved for the Jewish diet.

But, as Peter explained, the voice in the vision said clearly, "Do not call anything impure that God has made clean." This exchange was then repeated twice before the sheet was raised up out of sight. With that the trance ended and Peter was left to meditate upon its significance (10:17–19).

Peter Relates the Caesarean Breakthrough (vv. 11–15) Peter's listeners no doubt were giving him their undivided attention. They knew of Peter's going into Cornelius's house, but this was the first they had heard of the vision. Not stopping to interpret it, Peter went on to say that at that very instant three men arrived downstairs at Simon's house. They were asking for Peter and were hoping that he would accompany them from Joppa to Caesarea, to Cornelius's house.

Throughout his report, Peter leans on the authority of heaven for what actions he took. Here he said the Spirit told him to have no hesitation about going with them. If this had been the sole occasion for pointing to God's leading, Peter may have been guilty of mistaking his subjective feelings for God's leading. But besides the vision, there would be two more unmistakable marks of God's leading.

Peter wisely took six of the believers in Joppa with him. Verse 12 makes clear that he had brought these six with him to Jerusalem. Perhaps he was anticipating some opposition. The apostles and Jerusalem Christians could ask these "brethren" if what Peter said was so.

Summarizing what Luke tells in greater detail and omitting the worshipful welcome he received in this great house, Peter defers once again to heavenly authority. "He shewed us how he (Cornelius) had seen an angel in his house," Peter said. The angel had promised Cornelius further light (10:22, 33). Luke here states, after the fact, "He (Peter) will bring you a message through which you and all your household will be saved" (11:14 NIV). The text reminds us of Paul's words in the prison in Philippi (Acts 16:31).

Peter hurried to his climactic news: "As I began to speak, the Holy Ghost fell on them, as on us at the beginning." This was his ultimate call to authority. Luke describes how this astonished Peter and his six fellow believers. Before their eyes Cornelius and "all who heard the message ... (were) speaking in tongues and praising God" (10:44, 46 NIV).

From Peter's summary we miss completely the exposition he gave in Cornelius's home. This sermon is an excellent example of the primitive Christian message, declaring—(1) Peace had been preached throughout Judea; (2) Jesus was anointed with the Holy Spirit and did good deeds; (3) Jesus' Crucifixion; (4) the Resurrection; (5) His postresurrection appearances; (6) the command to proclaim Jesus as God's appointed Judge; (7) forgiveness of sins. In Luke's account, Peter prefaced his sermon with the statement that he now knew the meaning of the vision; God was no respecter of persons and welcomed people from every nation who worship Him (v. 34).

Peter Interprets the Caesarean Event (vv. 16-18) The words "at the beginning" no doubt look back to the Day of Pentecost. This "occasion has been well described as 'the Pentecost of the Gentile world.' No routine procedure would have availed for so unprecedented a situation as the acceptance of the Gospel by Gentiles; an unmediated act of God was required" (F. F. Bruce).

In interpreting the pouring out of the Spirit in Caesarea, Peter resorted once more to God's authority, citing the words of Jesus: "John baptized with water, but ye shall be baptized with the Holy Ghost." (See Acts 1:5.) It was obvious that God had given the gift of the Spirit to these Gentiles "as he did unto us who believed," he said, so "what was I, that I could withstand God!"

One further important truth stands out in our text. Peter's interpretation quieted the jealous prejudices of the Jewish believers and Luke says they "glorified God" after hearing his account. One of them, perhaps an apostle, voiced the response of the Church: "So then, God has even granted the Gentiles repentance unto life" (NIV). Packer notes that they may not have realized the full impact of what they said. "This approval given to Peter here was not meant to imply wholesale admission of Gentiles into the church." But the Church had taken a giant step in that direction. Note the wording of this final statement. Repentance is a *gift* of God, and it is a repentance that leads to and results in *life*, eternal life and abundant life.

Applying the Scripture
Ask your class: Is our church a "New Testament church"?

The Church of New Testament times was probably never intended to be a model or pattern of the perfect church. It was, after all, an infant organism and organization. The Epistles show clearly enough the problems that beset the churches. More pronounced, perhaps, in Corinth, nevertheless the weaknesses were there in Jerusalem, too. One of that church's continued stumbling blocks was its prejudice against non-Jewish believers.

But for all its flaws, most of us would opt for the Jerusalem church rather than the one where we presently fellowship. Why is that? We would probably state our reasons differently, but we might all agree on the one quality which makes that early Church so attractive. *It was alive.*

Our text is eloquent witness to that. Scan the Scripture and note how many times an element of the spiritual, the supernatural, the charismatic blends into the narrative.

"In a trance I saw a vision."

"The voice spoke from heaven."

"The Spirit told me."

"He told us how he had seen an angel."

"The Holy Spirit came on them."

Of course, there were reasons for the tremendous surgings of the Spirit just after Christ's death and Resurrection, and the Pentecostal outpouring. But are we to conclude that *all* of that was for the apostolic era?

It's been said that if God were to remove His Spirit from a lot of churches today they would go right on functioning, never knowing that God no longer is in their midst. To what degree do you think this is true of your local church?

Ask your class to identify the elements in our text that might prove to be keys to unlock spiritual power in your church. A list might include the following:

1. *Prayer.* Peter received a vision while in prayer. Cornelius, before he was saved, was "a man of prayer." Some things just are not brought down from heaven in any other way but prayer—consistent, believing, prevailing prayer.

2. *Obedience to the Spirit.* Peter heard the Spirit tell him to go to Caesarea and into the home of a Gentile. To obey meant to go against all his natural instincts and a lifetime of teaching. But he obeyed, risking criticism from others, in order to do the Spirit's bidding.

3. *Open-mindedness.* The church at Jerusalem questioned, even criticized, Peter's actions. But they listened to his whole explanation and then with an open mind agreed that God was doing a new thing. They were flexible to go in the new direction in which they sensed the Lord leading them.

See if your class can name still other qualities from today's lesson. Then conclude your class, asking in prayer that all of you may "go with God!"

Questions for Discussion

Make use of these questions to involve your students in learning and to test their understanding of the lesson.

1. Why were the people "of the circumcision" upset with Peter? Who were these people? 2. What did Peter mean by "common" or "unclean"?

3. What did Peter take to be the meaning of the vision he had, as he explained in 10:34, 35?   4. How did he and his fellow Christians know that the Holy Spirit had been given to Cornelius and his household?   5. To what day or event did Peter refer when he spoke of "at the beginning" (v. 15)?   6. Peter repeatedly resorted to an authority for his actions in baptizing the Gentiles in Caesarea. What was his source of authority?   7. In one sentence, can you sum up the meaning, for all time, of the giving of the Spirit to the household of Cornelius?

Illustrating the Scripture
Examples and quotations to help the teacher communicate the lesson.
"WHEN THEY HEARD THESE THINGS, THEY HELD THEIR PEACE, AND GLORIFIED GOD, SAYING, THEN HATH GOD ALSO TO THE GENTILES GRANTED REPENTANCE UNTO LIFE" (v. 18). "After Peter's explanation and impassioned plea these men had nothing else to say. They glorified God and made this admission. Peter gave to the Jerusalem church the most encouraging message any church will ever receive. He told them that souls were being saved at the other end of the line. There is rejoicing in heaven over one sinner that repenteth, and there should be the same rejoicing in our hearts, also.

"A telegraph operator in Cincinnati attended a revival service. In his sermon the preacher told how a telegraph operator in Zanesville had been converted. The Cincinnati operator was interested and when he returned to work that night, he decided to call the Zanesville operator and ask him if the story was true. When he did this the man replied, 'Yes, it is true. I am the man. Christ has saved me.' They talked over the wires for some time and the Cincinnati man asked the Zanesville man to pray for him.

"Before midnight he called him again and said, 'Everything is all right now. Your Savior is my Savior, too.' This was the message that Peter gave the Jerusalem church. This is the reason that they rejoiced and glorified God after the other matter had been straightened out." (From *Simple Sermons from the Book of Acts*, by W. Herschel Ford, published by Zondervan Publishing House, copyright 1950.)

REMOVING PREJUDICE   Peter's actions led the way for the early Church to deal with a deep prejudice against Gentiles. Many Christian blacks are still waiting for the courageous acts of their Christian white brothers, to take away the discrimination that persists. William Pannell, wrote in *My Friend, the Enemy*, "At the level where Christians like to live, namely, the 'spiritual,' there is an even better leverage for respectful relationships. Since the question ('Don't you have to earn their respect?'), seems to assume the colored man's second-class status, or at best to recognize it as a fact of contemporary life, it forces the believer to examine his concepts of creation and redemption. The Scriptures inform us that God created man. Not necessarily a white man either, assuming of course that Adam wasn't. If this is true and all men proceed from this beginning, then an essential brotherhood is established, and it must be recognized as valid even apart from redemption. Must I then earn respect from my *brother?*

"To my Christian brother this is unrealistic. 'It fails to take sin into account. You can't expect unsaved people to treat you like a brother. They don't possess the love of God.' Granted. But how then explain my need to earn the respect of my *Christian* brother? Why the wheelin' and dealin' before I can get help? Why the question in the first place? My suspicions lead me to deduce that the question is asked by those who do not intend to help anyhow....

"Le Rone T. Bennett, Jr., puts it straight when he declares that 'friendship in such a situation (of oppression) is not a pledge, it is an act. It is an address of one's total being to the destruction of the situation of oppression. One can say that one is a friend of the oppressed, but one can only mean it by doing something about it, by tearing down and building up. In the end friendship for the oppressed can only be proven in an extreme situation where one is forced to choose—once, finally, and for all—for either the oppressor or the oppressed.' " (From *My Friend, the Enemy* by William E. Pannell, copyright © 1968 by Word Books, Publishers, Waco, Texas; used with permission.)

Topics for Youth

"A PICTURE IS WORTH MORE THAN A THOUSAND WORDS"—We have all heard this until it is trite, trite, trite. But it still is true. Think of Peter's situation. When God chose to lead him—and through him the New Testament Church—to go to the Gentiles, He did not resort to words. He dramatized His intentions. He put on quite an audio-visual demonstration. He showed Peter "pictures." And Peter got the picture.

As young people grow up and see changes that need to be made, they should know that the head-on approach of talking and writing about change may not be the way to go about it. But drama, an acting out of the idea, can be effective. Think of the drama of the Southern Black's marches and bus boycotts that led the way to a lifting of discriminatory laws in the United States and awakened people to the power of their prejudices? A play, a mime, a demonstration may go a lot further than talk!

PREJUDICE—SOME QUOTES—"Passion and prejudice govern the world, only under the name of reason," said John Wesley.

"No person is strong enough to carry a cross and a prejudice at the same time"—William A. Ward.

"Prejudices are often carefully taught, and once established they are strengthened by superstitions, old wives' tales and downright lies"—Source unknown.

"Very few people take the trouble to use their brains as long as their prejudices are in working condition"—Roy L. Smith.

"A great many people think they are thinking when they are merely rearranging their prejudices"—William James.

"Beware lest we mistake our prejudices for our convictions"—H. A. Ironside.

"Prejudice is the child of ignorance"—William Hazlitt.

"Prejudice—a vagrant opinion without visible means of support"—Ambrose Bierce.

"The catastrophe of the atomic bombs which shook men out of cities and businesses and economic relations, shook them also out of their old-established habits of thought, and out of the lightly held beliefs and prejudices that came down to them from the past"—H. G. Wells.

LESSON 7   APRIL 17

Missionaries on the Move

Background Scripture: Acts 12:25–14:28
Devotional Reading: 1 Peter 1:19–25

Acts 13:1–3; 14:8–18

1 Now there were in the church that was at Antioch certain prophets and teachers; as Barnabas, and Simeon that was called Niger, and Lucius of Cyrene, and Manaen, which had been brought up with Herod the tetrarch, and Saul.

2 As they ministered to the Lord, and fasted, the Holy Ghost said, Separate me Barnabas and Saul for the work whereunto I have called them.

3 And when they had fasted and prayed, and laid their hands on them, they sent them away.

14:8 And there sat a certain man at Lystra, impotent in his feet, being a cripple from his mother's womb, who never had walked:

9 The same heard Paul speak: who stedfastly beholding him, and perceiving that he had faith to be healed,

10 Said with a loud voice, Stand upright on thy feet. And he leaped and walked.

11 And when the people saw what Paul had done, they lifted up their voices, saying in the speech of Lycaonia, The gods are come down to us in the likeness of men.

12 And they called Barnabas, Jupiter; and Paul, Mercurius, because he was the chief speaker.

13 Then the priest of Jupiter, which was before their city, brought oxen and garlands unto the gates, and would have done sacrifice with the people.

14 Which when the apostles, Barnabas and Paul, heard of, they rent their clothes, and ran in among the people, crying out,

15 And saying, Sirs, why do ye these things? We also are men of like passions with you, and preach unto you that ye should turn from these vanities unto the living God, which made heaven, and earth, and the sea, and all things that are therein:
16 Who in times past suffered all nations to walk in their own ways.
17 Nevertheless he left not himself without witness, in that he did good, and gave us rain from heaven, and fruitful seasons, filling our hearts with food and gladness.
18 And with these sayings scarce restrained they the people, that they had not done sacrifice unto them.

KEY VERSE: "I have set thee to be a light of the Gentiles, that thou shouldest be for salvation unto the ends of the earth." Acts 13:47.

Home Daily Bible Readings		
Apr. 11	M.	The Conversion of Simon the Sorcerer, Acts 8:9-13.
Apr. 12	T.	The Conversion of the Eunuch, Acts 8:26-40.
Apr. 13	W.	The Ministry of Peter at Lydda, Acts 9:32-35.
Apr. 14	T.	Barnabas at Antioch, Acts 11:19-26.
Apr. 15	F.	The Missionaries Driven Out of Town, Acts 14:1-7.
Apr. 16	S.	Through Much Tribulation, Acts 14:19-22.
Apr. 17	S.	The Missionary Report to the Church, Acts 14:23-28.

Lesson Aim: That adults will choose not to limit God, but believe Him to empower the workers whom He guides into His work.

LESSON OUTLINE
Background to the Scripture
Looking at the Scripture Text
  I. The Missionary Call (Acts 13:1-3)
  II. The Cripple Healed (Acts 14:8-10)
  III. A Tumultuous Heathen Response (Acts 14:11-13)
  IV. Worship Directed to the Living God (Acts 14:14-18)
Applying the Scripture

Background to the Scripture

Have you ever been on a job or in school where your boss or teacher assumed too much? He was discussing steps K through P, not realizing you didn't know steps A-J? No wonder you felt something was missing.

Well, today's lesson on the church at Antioch begins about with Step *D*—for Departure. Since we have not studied steps *A*, *B* and *C*, we do well to look at them now to understand how the church at Antioch became "the true center of direct mission to the heathen world."

Luke tells how the Gospel came to Antioch in Acts 11:20-26. Evidently driven out of Jerusalem by the persecution, believers traveled as far north as

Antioch with the Gospel, but they only witnessed to the Jews there. Some of them, however, from Cyprus and the north African city of Cyrene, found a responsive audience as soon as they began preaching the Gospel among Gentiles in Antioch. So great was the turning to Christ there that the Church in Jerusalem heard of it and sent Barnabas there. Seeing immediately that God was at work and knowing that the new believers needed sound doctrine, he went to Tarsus, which was near, found Saul and brought him back with him to Antioch. The two of them stayed for a year and taught the "great numbers" who were coming to know the Lord. Luke says the epithet *Christians* was first applied to the believers there in Antioch of Syria.

Looking at the Scripture Text

The Missionary Call (13:1-3) The names of the prophets and teachers in the Antiochan church immediately reveal that church's cosmopolitan composition. *Barnabas,* perhaps the leader of the leaders, was a Jew of the tribe of Levi, a native of the island of Cyprus (4:36). He must have committed his life to Christ at Pentecost or shortly afterward, for his name appears early in the life of the Jerusalem church. Though named Joses, he is always called Barnabas, "son of encouragement." He was the one who first had confidence in Saul and welcomed him into the church at Jerusalem; when that church sent him to Antioch, Luke described him as "a good man, full of the Holy Ghost and of faith" (11:24).

Simeon, also called Niger, is thought to be a Christian from Antioch. *Lucius* hailed from Cyrene, on Africa's northern coast, and some think he is one of those with Paul in Rome many years later (Romans 16:21). *Manaen* (or Menahem) is distinguished by the singular fact that he grew up with or was foster brother to Herod Antipas, tetrarch of Galilee (Luke 3:1; Matthew 14:1). If Herod's childhood was spent in Jerusalem when his father, Herod the Great, was king, then we may conclude that Manaen was a Jew, also from Jerusalem.

Last named is *Saul,* whom we shall call Paul from now on (13:9). Five spiritual leaders: one native of Antioch, one from neighboring Tarsus in Cilicia, one from Cyprus, one from Africa, and one from Jerusalem. These were "prophets and teachers," gifted men in the Church who were held in high esteem next to the apostles (Ephesians 4:11; 1 Corinthians 12:28). Prophets exercised the gift of prophecy, uttering truths not disclosed to everyone (such as Agabus's prophecy of the coming famine, 11:28) as well as preaching the Word of God. Teachers expounded Christian truth by the Spirit's enabling.

The term *ministered* (v. 2) seems best translated worshiped, though it is used in the New Testament of various kinds of service, including giving (Romans 15:27). The five might well have been in prayer together over some particular matter when the Holy Spirit made His will known. We cannot be sure how the Spirit "said, 'Separate me Barnabas and Saul for the work whereunto I have called them' " but it seems likely that the word came through a prophetic utterance from one of the men and was confirmed by all. The entire church would have taken part in the service commissioning Barnabas and Paul to their new role, but only the three other prophets and teachers would lay on hands.

J. W. Packer comments on this passage: "The Holy Spirit is the source of all direction in the church and to the waiting committee he speaks (through one of them). The setting, as usual in a great moment in the church's development, is one of prayer. This time a *fast* is added to it, as if waiting for the absent Lord to make his will known." The *Lord*, through the Spirit, called two men to the work. The *church* set them apart "and let them go."

The Cripple Healed (14:8-10) The events here described are a part of what is generally termed Paul's First Missionary Journey. Though Barnabas was the more experienced of the two and is listed first in the account, Paul's unusual gifts as a leader and speaker brought him to the forefront by the time this mission is complete. The two of them, accompanied for a time by John Mark, went through Cyprus and then sailed to Perga, entering the provinces of Pamphylia and Galatia in what is today southern Turkey.

Their efforts met with both a marked spiritual hunger among Gentiles and angry opposition from Jews in the two cities where they preached prior to Lystra, an obscure town of Galatia. In Lystra and its neighboring city, Derbe, "they preached the gospel" (v. 7). This is significant because it gives us necessary background for understanding the healing of a cripple. And it sets the record straight against any who contend that Paul did not preach the Gospel in Lystra.

If ever there seemed to be a hopeless human, the cripple would be one. The scene seems to take place at the city gate, suggested by what follows. Paul perhaps spoke in public nearby—there is no mention of a synagogue—and the man was listening as Paul was speaking (the verbs imply that Paul may have spoken two or more times). Sensing that the man was being drawn by the Holy Spirit and "had faith to be healed," Paul shouted to him, "Stand upright on thy feet!" In that instant, weak legs and feet that had never held him up received strength. He "leaped and walked." The effect was explosive.

If this story sounds familiar, it may be because of striking similarities between it and the healing of a man at the Beautiful Gate when Peter was the instrument God used (3:2-8). Both were crippled from birth, both had faith, on both the apostle looked intently, and both leaped and walked.

A Tumultuous Heathen Response (vv. 11-13) The miracles were given to the apostles to confirm the message they preached. As well, they opened doors for new growth by the Church. The citizens of Lystra were correct in attributing the healing of the cripple to a superhuman cause, but being superstitious and polytheistic, they saw this within the framework of their pantheon of gods. Scholars suggest that the action they took in naming Barnabas, Zeus, and Paul, Hermes (Jupiter and Mercury were the Latin names) stemmed from an old legend.

Ovid had written that two Phrygians, Philemon and Baucis, entertained Zeus and Hermes in the neighboring district of Phrygia. For their hospitality the two received the blessing of the gods. The moral of the legend—"them that honor me, I will honor"—seems to be what influenced the citizens of Lystra to honor Barnabas and Paul.

Modern translations indicate that the temple of Zeus was outside the city gates, as a protecting deity. From there the priest of Zeus, who would be a very powerful personage, came bringing oxen to sacrifice to these "gods" who had come in human form. The garlands or wreaths would be placed, during the sacrificial ritual, around the necks of the oxen.

Worship Directed to the Living God (vv. 14–18) There could be no greater contrast than the reaction of Herod when the crowd hailed him as a god (12:21–23) and the response of Paul and Barnabas. The apostles may not have understood the native speech of the people (v. 11) but they knew the meaning of the oxen. They "tore their clothes" to show their distress and "rushed into the crowd," shouting in horrified indignation.

The sermon that follows in verses 15–17 is more than likely a summary and Paul in all probability was the speaker. In the heat of excitement with the people evidently thronging around him loudly, what he said is in stark contrast to his addresses to mainly Jewish audiences. There he quotes the Old Testament and shows how Christ fulfills the prophecies. Now, he pleads with them to realize that he and Barnabas were "only human beings" of like nature with them, "equally prone to human weakness" as one commentator says. He called their idol worship and whole religious system "vanities"—meaningless, worthless things—and again reiterated the burden of what he had been preaching, that they should turn to "the living God."

Basic to the Judeo-Christian belief system is that there is one God and that He is the Creator. Paul declared that to this one, true, living God they owed every thing. He summoned the Creator's unfailing goodness as witness of His love, saying "He has shown kindness by giving you rain from heaven and crops in their seasons; he provides you with plenty of food and fills your hearts with joy" (v. 17 NIV).

Paul satisfied two "main objections these heathen idolaters might make against the Gospel," Poole notes regarding verse 16. They might argue that their worship is *universal*, everywhere observed, and *ancient*, that from antiquity man has so worshiped. The reason "why so many, and for so long a time had followed idols, was from the just judgment of God." He "let all nations go their own way."

"With these words," Luke concludes, Paul and Barnabas barely succeeded in stopping them from offering sacrifices. Whether on the same day or after a few days, Jews who had heard Paul and Barnabas in Pisidian Antioch and in Iconium arrived in Lystra. They so turned the majority of the people against the apostles that Paul was stoned and left for dead (v. 19). In truth stranger than fiction, a crowd in one moment was ready to worship Paul; the next moment they almost stoned him to death. The words of Jesus were coming true in Paul's experience. He was learning "how much he must suffer for (Jesus') name."

With this first journey of Paul and Barnabas from the missionary church in Antioch begins that large section of Luke's account fitting under the third division so broadly sketched in Acts 1:8—"ye shall be witnesses unto me both in Jerusalem, and in all Judea, and in Samaria, and *unto the uttermost part of the earth.*" In other places it would seem the success of the apostles was more apparent, but the verses following our text show that a group of disciples had been formed in Lystra and that before they left the region, Paul and Barnabas strengthened the disciples and encouraged them and ordained them elders in every church." On his next missionary journey to Lystra, young Timothy joins Paul. Apparently a growing church had taken root in Galatian soil to the glory of God.

Applying the Scripture
Ask: Do you know anybody who needs encouragement? (Don't everyone raise his hand at once!) Now ask your class to think about this:

Mary McLeod Bethune said, "Neither God nor man can use a discouraged person."

In the light of that, our brother Barnabas takes on a rather important position. Remember, his name was given to him because he was a "son of consolation" or "encouragement."

Someone has said, "It would have been easy for Barnabas to view Paul as a threat . . . to respond to him with envy rather than encouragement. After all, the Holy Ghost had said, 'Separate me *Barnabas and Saul* for the work' (13:2). Wasn't that a clear indication who was to be the leader? But as the gifted Paul's ministry blossomed on that first missionary journey, Barnabas rejoiced . . . encouraged . . . took a 'back seat.' Result: 'the word of the Lord was published throughout all the region' (13:49)."

It might be fearful to think what would have become of Paul, if he had not had an encourager with him on that critical first journey. Christ by His Spirit would have been with him and yet—God chooses to help us *through others.*

Allow your class to talk about persons who have encouraged them. Ask them particularly to name the quality or action which proved to be a source of encouragement. Was it a friendly call to ask, "How are you?" Was it a commendation? Was it a note in the mail, a gift, a gentle hug?

Close the class period with prayer that we might become encouragers of our brother or sister in Christ, but first suggest that as a tie-in to this lesson and missionary service that each class member choose one person in full-time Christian service whom they can encourage in the next few days. Perhaps they will want to write or telephone one of the church's home or foreign missionaries. Don't forget the pastor's family or other members of your church staff, such as the church secretary, custodian, or youth minister. "Be strong, and of a good courage!"

Questions for Discussion
Make use of these questions to involve your students in learning and to test their understanding of the lesson.

1. How did the church at Antioch come into existence?   2. What were the ministries and special functions of prophets? Of teachers?   3. From the five names of the leaders in the church, what can we learn about the kind of people who comprised its membership?   4. With the commissioning of Saul and Barnabas, what great step was the early Church taking?   5. How was Paul's preaching at Lystra so different? Why?   6. From Paul's message to the

people of Lystra, we are reminded of what God has done so that everyone knows that there is a God. What is it that provides such a witness to every person? 7. Did the Gospel message take root in Lystra, producing a church?

Illustrating the Scripture
Examples and quotations to help the teacher communicate the lesson.
"HE LEFT NOT HIMSELF WITHOUT WITNESS, IN THAT HE DID GOOD...." J. I. Packer has written, "Within the cluster of God's moral perfections there is one in particular to which the term 'goodness' points—the quality which God specially singled out from the whole when, proclaiming 'all his goodness' to Moses, He spoke of Himself as 'abundant in *goodness* and truth' (Exodus 34:6). This is the quality of *generosity*....

"God's generosity in bestowing natural blessings is acclaimed in Psalms 145. 'The Lord is good to all: and his tender mercies are over all his works.... The eyes of all wait upon thee; and thou givest them their meat in due season. Thou openest thine hand, and satisfiest the desire of every living thing' (vv. 9, 15, 16).

"The psalmist's point is that, since God controls all that happens in His world, every meal, every pleasure, every possession, every bit of sun, every night's sleep, every moment of health and safety, everything else that sustains and enriches life, is a divine gift. And how abundant these gifts are!

" 'Count your blessings, name them one by one,' urges the children's chorus, and anyone who seriously begins to list his natural blessings alone will soon feel the force of the next line—'and it will surprise you what the Lord has done.' But the mercies of God on the natural level, however abundant, are overshadowed by the greater mercies of spiritual redemption." (From *Knowing God* by J. I. Packer, InterVarsity Press, copyright 1973; used with permission.)

THE WITNESS OF "NATURE" IS NOT ENOUGH A missionary pilot was speaking to a church meeting in California. His Bible was open at Psalms 19, which he read in its entirety. But he drew contrasts between the witness of nature in verse 1 and the witness of Scripture in verse 7. "The heavens declare the glory of God.... The law of the Lord is perfect, converting the soul...."

"The witness of nature is universal," he said. In words similar to what Paul used in Lystra, he told how God has made Himself known partially through Creation. But it is *insufficient*.

"But the witness of the Word is sufficient. In the Bible there is everything a person needs to know about how to be saved and how to live a life of faith." But the witness of Scripture is *not universal*. The Bible has to be translated and the Word has to be preached and taught and explained. Both are needed—the witness of nature and the witness of words.

Topics for Youth
AMERICANS AND THE WORLD MISSION TASK—Dr. Henry Leiper has described our world this way—by reducing the total population proportion-

ately into a theoretical town of 1,000 people, it might look something like this:

"In this town, there would be 60 Americans; the remainder of the world would be represented by 940 persons. This is the proportion of the United States to the population of the world . . . 60 to 940. The 60 Americans would have half the income of the entire town, with the other 940 dividing the other half.

"About 330 people in the town would be classified as Christians; 670 would not. Fewer than 100 would be Protestant Christians, and some 230 would be Roman Catholics. At least 80 townspeople would be practicing Communists, and 370 others would be under Communist domination. White people would total 303, with 697 non-white.

"Half of the 1,000 people would never have heard of Jesus Christ or what He taught. On the other hand, more than half would be hearing about Karl Marx, Lenin, Stalin. . . .

"The 60 Americans would have an average life expectancy of 70 years; the other 940 less than 40 years on the average. The 60 Americans would have an average of 15 times as many possessions per person as all the rest of the people. The Americans would produce 16 percent of the town's total food supply. Although they eat 72 percent above the maximum food requirements, they would either eat most of what they grew, or store it for their own future use at enormous cost.

"Since most of the 940 non-Americans in the town would be hungry most of the time, it could lead to some ill feeling toward the 60 Americans, who would appear to be enormously rich and fed to the point of sheer disbelief by the great majority of the townspeople.

"The American families would be spending at least $850 a year for military defense, but less than $4 a year to share their religious faiths with the other people in the community." (Taken from *The Challenge*, a monthly letter by Robert D. Foster, Colorado Springs, Colorado. Used with permission.)

LESSON 8   APRIL 24

Good News for all People

Background Scripture: Genesis 17:9-14; Acts 15:1-35; Galatians 2:1-10
Devotional Reading: John 10:7-18

Acts 15:4-14; 19-21

4 And when they were come to Jerusalem, they were received of the church, and of the apostles and elders, and they declared all things that God had done with them.

5 But there rose up certain of the sect of the Pharisees which believed,

saying, That it was needful to circumcise them, and to command them to keep the law of Moses.

6 And the apostles and elders came together for to consider of this matter.

7 And when there had been much disputing, Peter rose up, and said unto them, Men and brethren, ye know how that a good while ago God made choice among us, that the Gentiles by my mouth should hear the word of the gospel, and believe.

8 And God, which knoweth the hearts, bare them witness, giving them the Holy Ghost, even as he did unto us;

9 And put no difference between us and them, purifying their hearts by faith.

10 Now therefore why tempt ye God, to put a yoke upon the neck of the disciples, which neither our fathers nor we were able to bear?

11 But we believe that through the grace of the Lord Jesus Christ we shall be saved, even as they.

12 Then all the multitude kept silence, and gave audience to Barnabas and Paul, declaring what miracles and wonders God had wrought among the Gentiles by them.

13 And after they had held their peace, James answered, saying, Men and brethren, hearken unto me:

14 Simeon hath declared how God at the first did visit the Gentiles, to take out of them a people for his name.

19 Wherefore my sentence is, that we trouble not them, which from among the Gentiles are turned to God:

20 But that we write unto them, that they abstain from pollutions of idols, and from fornications, and from things strangled, and from blood.

21 For Moses of old time hath in every city them that preach him, being read in the synagogues every sabbath day.

KEY VERSE: "For in Jesus Christ neither circumcision availeth any thing, nor uncircumcision; but faith which worketh by love." Galatians 5:6.

Home Daily Bible Readings		
Apr. 18	M.	God's Promise to Abraham, Genesis 17:1–8.
Apr. 19	T.	The Blessings of Obedience, Genesis 28:1–14.
Apr. 20	W.	A Great Light in Darkness, Matthew 4:12–17.
Apr. 21	T.	A Light to the Nations, Isaiah 42:5–9.
Apr. 22	F.	The Truth of the Gospel, Galatians 2:1–5.
Apr. 23	S.	The Apostleship to the Gentiles, Galatians 2:6–10.
Apr. 24	S.	One Fold and One Shepherd, John 10:14–16.

Lesson Aim: That adult Christians will examine their Christianity and free themselves of unnecessary legalistic baggage.

LESSON OUTLINE
Background to the Scripture
Looking at the Scripture Text
   I. A Crisis in the Early Church (Acts 15:4-6)
   II. Peter's Testimony (Acts 15:7-11)
   III. Barnabas and Paul's Experience (Acts 15:12)
   IV. James's Summary (Acts 15:13, 14, 19-21)
Applying the Scripture

Background to the Scripture
The yard next door is filled with dandelions. Only you would never know it today. Yesterday the lawn was mowed and all those wild flowering weeds were cut down to size. From a distance, you would never suspect that dandelions pose a problem in our neighbor's yard. But we know that their reappearance is guaranteed. For the mower did not get to the root of the problem.

Any difficulty or disagreement is just like that neighbor's yard. Dealt with in a superficial manner, it may not bother anyone for a while. But the problem often becomes more stubbornly entrenched if let go. It is best to take time to get to the root issue.

In today's lesson, the early Church deals with the problem that would not go away—whether to require non-Jewish Christians to adopt the customs of Jewish believers when becoming the people of God. The mission of Paul and Barnabas to Cyprus and Asia Minor had succeeded in bringing large numbers of Gentiles into the Church. They had been baptized and received the Spirit when they had repented and believed in Jesus Christ. But should the men be circumcised? Should they all have to "become Jews"? The Church had to decide.

Looking at the Scripture Text
A Crisis in the Early Church (vv. 4-6) This is now Paul's third visit to Jerusalem. He and Barnabas "caused great joy unto all the brethren" (v. 3) in the places they visited as they journeyed south from Antioch to Jerusalem, but inwardly the two apostles must have been preparing for a showdown. Previously in Antioch, where they had returned from their first missionary journey, a heated controversy broke out. On one side of the argument were men of Judea insisting that circumcision was essential to salvation. On the other side were Paul and Barnabas and others who were alarmed by such an idea and who taught rather that salvation was a free gift of grace. Wisely the church at Antioch decided to send a delegation to Jerusalem and call a meeting of the apostles to decide the issue.

On their arrival in the Holy City, Paul and Barnabas gave the church a report of their missionary work. One can almost picture the Jerusalem church assembled around the two men, listening with wonder and joy at the report of the conversion of Sergius Paulus, the proconsul on the isle of Cyprus, and of the great hunger for truth among the Gentiles of Galatia. Barnabas would no doubt have described the stoning of Paul in Lystra and his miraculous recovery. We sense in verse 4 that the church as a whole, and especially the apostles who were there and the elders gave them a warm welcome.

But the jubilant mood did not last. "Certain of the sect of the Pharisees which believed" could remain silent no longer. These men, who had so long upheld the Torah and all of the traditions before the Jewish people, were having difficulty living in the liberty of the Gospel. It did not fit the tight wineskins of their legalism. They were totally sincere in believing that something essential to the faith was being lost in the Church's rapid growth.

These Pharisees-turned-Christians may not have been the same ones who stirred up the sharp debate in Antioch (v. 1). We cannot be sure. But it is interesting to compare the dogmatic statement made in Antioch with the milder one before the church in Jerusalem. Did these "Judaizers," who went to Antioch, speak in such absolute terms because they were on their own, away from the authority of the apostles, and because they did not respect the Antiochan believers as equals?

One commentator describes the Pharisees' belief this way: they believed "that Jesus was the Messiah, and the fulfiller of the law—but still only as the Head of a glorified Judaism, from which Gentiles were to be rigidly excluded unless they conformed to the enactments relating to circumcision."

It was an explosive issue, threatening to split the young Church. Therefore a time was set for the apostles and elders to look into the matter.

Peter's Testimony (vv. 7-11) The context shows that not just the apostles and elders, but the Church also assembled for this Jerusalem Church Council (vv. 12, 22). It was fitting that Peter should introduce the subject since it was by his preaching that the first Gentiles embraced Christ. His opening words remind us of the conversion of Cornelius and his household (Acts 10) to which Peter is obviously referring. His use of "a good while ago" suggests that many years have passed since he preached the Good News in Caesarea to those gathered in the home of the Roman centurion. Perhaps it is ten to twelve years later now.

His testimony is first concerned with the action of God. "You know," he said, "that God *chose* me, Peter, to go to the Gentiles." God also *had given* them the Holy Spirit as He had done the Jewish believers. He *had "put no difference"* (v. 9) between the Jewish and Gentile believers, *"purifying* their hearts by faith." Peter's reasoning was similar here to that which he used when called upon to explain why he had gone into Cornelius's house. God was so obviously at work that he, Peter, could not be blamed for taking the initiative.

We might ask, "How did Peter or anyone know that the Gentiles had believed, and that they were made pure from all defilement of sin?" He would no doubt have several answers—the way these people had changed, their own spoken testimony and particularly, their being given the Holy Spirit. In Cornelius's house, which may be the only incident to which Peter is referring, this coming of the Spirit was accompanied by tongues-speaking as on the day of Pentecost. No one there questioned Peter's claim that God "showed that he accepted them by giving the Holy Spirit to them" (NIV).

Peter's confession before the Jerusalem church is truly remarkable. To hear him say that even though he was an apostle, he could not bear the yoke of the Law of Moses—and neither could the previous generations of Jews—would have a tremendously liberating effect upon his hearers. Some of the Pharisees might breathe a sigh of relief for such honesty. It is a good thing for any church in any age to hear such a confession from its leaders.

The words Luke quotes in verse 11 are the last from Peter in the book of Acts. They reveal a humility that is itself a mark of the transformation that has taken place in Peter's life. Note that he does not say cockily, "We believe that the Gentiles will be saved even as we are." No, he chooses instead to state the certainty of their salvation and base his own hope for salvation on the grace or "free gift" of the Lord Jesus. When we claim, as Peter does, to be saved by grace through faith, we are telling the world that nothing we have done deserves such kindness. Peter's testimony would seem to knock the Judaizers' demands into a cocked hat.

Barnabas and Paul's Experience (v. 12) Two things are noteworthy about how Luke describes what takes place next. Peter's address had strongly affected his hearers. They "kept silence." No more were they disputing and debating. Second, Barnabas and Paul report not of what *they* had done, but what the active Lord had done through them. This, built upon Peter's emphasis on God at work, would be impossible to refute. Luke gives no details of what Barnabas and Paul said. If we wanted to recreate their report of "miracles and wonders" we have only to turn back and read the two preceding chapters.

James's Summary (vv. 13, 14, 19-21) Luke evidently felt that James was so well known among his readers that he need not identify him. But we need help, for there were three Jameses in the New Testament. This is the brother of the Lord Jesus (Galatians 1:19), one to whom the Lord appeared after His Resurrection (1 Corinthians 15:7). He seems to be the acknowledged leader of the Jerusalem church, whether holding the post of apostle or elder, we cannot tell. As the president of the assembly it was his to conclude the debate.

Simon Peter (Simeon is the Hebrew form), Luke said, has described "how in the first place God chose a people from among the nations who should bear his name" (PHILLIPS). Since the statement is not in Peter's address recorded in verses 7-11, we assume that Luke only wrote down a part of what Peter said or that he did not have access to more. The difficulty with the verse lies in the time reference. Is Peter talking about how God "at the first" (KJV) called Abraham out from among the Gentiles and made a people for Himself? Or is he speaking of the "new thing," God's calling out of the Gentiles a people to form the church? We take him to mean the latter.

James cited Amos 9:11, 12 in the following verses evidently to show that by calling the Gentiles into the family of God the Lord is fulfilling His promise to "build again the tabernacle of David . . . that the residue of men might seek after the Lord." James's statement in verse 14 is a unique description of the missionary activity of the Spirit in the Church age. By the preaching of the Gospel, God takes the initiative in calling men and women to make up His own people. Those who answer His call "bear his name"—they are a people for Himself.

The summary which James makes of the action the Church will take is not his opinion alone. As the letter which they draft shows, it is the mind of the Church and of the Spirit (v. 28). Instead of laying heavy burdens on the Gentile Christians, the Church decides to lay on them only a few rules:

- keep away from things polluted by idols.
- be pure from all sexual immorality.
- eat no meat from which the blood has not been properly drained.
- abstain from blood.

Verse 21 is offered as an explanation of these stipulations. The Gentiles knew these basically Jewish rules as a result of the dispersion; synagogues were in virtually every city of the Empire. The customs of the Jews were widely known. If the Church were to keep its doors open for Jews to find their Messiah, they would do well at least to abide by these few rules. The first, third and fourth were relaxed in time. Paul in 1 Corinthians 8 no longer strictly forbade the eating of meat that had been offered to idols. The prohibitions against eating anything strangled, or eating blood, stem from the Old Testament (Genesis 9:4; Leviticus 17:13; Deuteronomy 12:16). Blood represented life and man was forbidden to partake of it out of respect for life. The extremely lax moral atmosphere of the empire made it necessary to stress sexual purity.

Applying the Scripture
Ask the class: Have we added anything to the Gospel that either distorts its true message or turns people off?

Of course, we are not talking about the "offense of the Gospel." God did not offer salvation and then allow man to write his own contract. He does require repentance and faith as necessary for salvation. And a life of selfless love and obedience is expected of His disciples. But we need to consider whether we, like the Judaizers, are adding any "baggage" to the Gospel that keeps people from receiving Christ.

The problem: The Church was preparing in the first century to go into the world with a message for all mankind. It needed to make the message clear, free of confusion. For instance, it would have been disastrous for the Church to appear to be for Jews only. Why limit itself in such a way? It might reach some Jews and some Gentiles, but think of the many who would never be touched because it was essentially too Jewish, or at least it appeared that way.

That brings up another side of this issue. A product or a thing may appear to be something it is not. A lot of people who may buy it for what it is won't touch it for what it appears to be. The advertisers of deodorants know that if their product appears to be for men and women, both will probably buy it and their sales will be larger. This goes for the Church. As we present Christ to the world, we want the Gospel of grace to appear to the world for what it is, without excess baggage of ritual, culture, or anything else.

The history of the church is largely the story of the Church's endeavor to keep on track, to be faithful to its holy mission of knowing Christ and making Him known. Which brings us to the application. Probably we do not need in our day to stop insisting that our converts be circumcised. That is not our problem. But can we think of anything which is a part of the message we preach and the ministry we carry out in the community that distorts the Gospel or turns people off?

Discuss this as a group. It was a problem that concerned the first group of believers, and so this is a problem which the Church as a body needs to discuss. Ask the class to ponder the question above. You may spark discussion by saying that in some places, the practice of living in community is a requirement of Christians. Anyone professing faith in Christ has to sell his material goods and put everything in the community pot. In other places, they teach that a person must be baptized in order to be saved. Both of these are additions to the Gospel.

Ask the question another way: what about appearances? In so far as your church is concerned, would the world perceive it as for the successful only, and not for the weak, the losers, the strugglers? Is your church seen as "for whites only" rather than a haven for people regardless of race? Is your church apparently for the middle class and not the poor, for women and old people rather than men and young people? Discuss how these also can be unnecessary baggage.

Questions for Discussion
Make use of these questions to involve your students in learning and to test their understanding of the lesson.
1. What events in Antioch prompted the so-called "Council at Jerusalem"? 2. What are the people of the "sect of the Pharisees" commonly called? What was their hang-up? 3. Check your students' comprehension: to what particular incident would Peter be referring when he says that God had chosen to give the Gospel to Gentiles through him? 4. According to Peter, would the Gentiles be saved by keeping the Law, or by some other means? How did he express this? 5. Who was James? 6. What is the meaning of James's statement in verse 14? How does this uniquely describe what God is doing today? 7. Why are they required to abstain from blood? What is the significance?

Illustrating the Scripture
Examples and quotations to help the teacher communicate the lesson.

"EASE ON DOWN THE ROAD"   The popular song from the Broadway musical has a message that fits our lesson today. The words say: "Ease on down, ease on down the road / Don't you carry nothin' that might be a load / Ease on down, ease on down the road."

Christ has not exactly called us to "ease on down the road"; He has rather commissioned us to march and to endure hardness. But He does not want us to carry "nothin' that might be a load." He does not want us making people obey laws that Christ has fulfilled in His bodily sacrifice. He does not want us to carry excess baggage of any kind—cultural, social, traditional—that will hinder the people around us from seeing Christ in us.

WHY BLOOD AS FOOD IS FORBIDDEN 1. "The prohibition is among the precepts given to Noah. God who reserved the tree of knowledge of good and evil in his grant of vegetables to man for food, reserved blood in his grant of animals (Genesis 9:4—'The one thing you must not eat is meat with blood still in it; I forbid this because the life is in the blood' TEV). Being a rule given to Noah, this law is obligatory upon the human family at large.

2. "The prohibition of blood was formally incorporated into the Levitical code (*see* Leviticus 17:10–13). The abrogation of the Levitical Law, however, does not repeal this rule. Unless it can be shown that the command God gave Noah is no longer in effect, it is still unlawful for Jew or Gentile to eat blood.

3. "So far from being repealed, this precept is reenforced under the Gospel. This *burden* our Lord still lays upon the churches...

"Two reasons for the prohibition are assigned: (1) That 'the life of the flesh is in the blood.' This is philosophically true. Cut a nerve, you paralyze a member, but it lives; cut off the blood, the member mortifies. Blood flows to a wound, becomes vascular there, knits the living parts, and it heals. The vitality of the blood is seen in its power of maintaining its temperature against the extremes of heat and cold. The lesson of this reason is to teach us the value of life.... (2) That 'it is the blood that maketh an atonement for the soul'—Leviticus 17:11. That should not be treated as a common thing which is the principle of atonement, and the type of the precious blood of Christ" (*Pulpit Commentary*, Leviticus).

Topics for Youth

SAVED BY GRACE—Peter said, "We believe and are saved by the grace of the Lord Jesus, just as they are" (Acts 15:11 TEV). We hear a lot about grace in church. We sing "Amazing Grace." What does it mean to be saved by grace?

Fritz Ridenour who has authored books that communicate with youth, once said: "Grace is getting another chance even though you haven't earned it or deserved it. (You may not even want it!)"

Martin Luther said: "Christ is no Moses, no exactor, no giver of laws, but a giver of grace, a Savior; he is infinite mercy and goodness, freely and bountifully giving to us."

Ready for a "heavy" definition? Well, this is not really all that deep, but *A Theological Word Book of the Bible* says—"Its main characteristic is of God's redemptive love which is always active to save sinners and maintain them in proper relationship with Him."

C. L. Mitton said: "Grace is God's unmerited, free, spontaneous love for sinful man, revealed and made effective in Jesus Christ."

IT'S A DIVINE MYSTERY!—Have you ever wondered why God chose you for salvation out of all of the people in your class, in your town, in the world? No one can really understand the favor God has shown us in putting us where we might learn of Christ and then graciously and kindly opening our hearts to believe and be saved—for all eternity!

James said that for a long time God has been "taking out a people for His name" from among the world's people. If we are one of the "chosen," it is not because we are special. It is all of His grace. And it does not mean that He has chosen others to damnation and hell. The invitation is to all—anyone who will trust Christ will be saved by His grace. But mysteriously the election and calling of God is at work. To be among the chosen ought to make us grateful every day. And it ought to spur us on to tell everybody about Christ so those whom God has called—those who will believe and receive the message—can say with Peter, "We believe that through the grace of the Lord Jesus Christ we shall be saved!"

UNIT III

Breaking Into the Rest of the World

LESSON 9 — MAY 1

Breakthrough in Macedonia

Background Scripture: Acts 15:36–17:34
Devotional Reading: John 15:1–8

Acts 16:9–18

9 And a vision appeared to Paul in the night; There stood a man of Macedonia, and prayed him, saying, Come over into Macedonia, and help us.

10 And after he had seen the vision, immediately we endeavoured to go into Macedonia, assuredly gathering that the Lord had called us for to preach the gospel unto them.

11 Therefore loosing from Troas, we came with a straight course to Samothracia, and the next day to Neapolis;

12 And from thence to Philippi, which is the chief city of that part of

Macedonia, and a colony: and we were in that city abiding certain days.
13 And on the sabbath we went out of the city by a river side, where prayer was wont to be made; and we sat down, and spake unto the women which resorted thither.
14 And a certain woman named Lydia, a seller of purple, of the city of Thyatira, which worshipped God, heard us: whose heart the Lord opened, that she attended unto the things which were spoken of Paul.
15 And when she was baptized, and her household, she besought us, saying, If ye have judged me to be faithful to the Lord, come into my house, and abide there. And she constrained us.
16 And it came to pass, as we went to prayer, a certain damsel possessed with a spirit of divination met us, which brought her masters much gain by soothsaying:
17 The same followed Paul and us, and cried, saying, These men are the servants of the most high God, which shew unto us the way of salvation.
18 And this did she many days. But Paul, being grieved, turned and said to the spirit, I command thee in the name of Jesus Christ to come out of her. And he came out the same hour.

KEY VERSE: "There is neither Jew nor Greek, there is neither bond nor free, there is neither male or female: for ye are all one in Christ Jesus." Galatians 3:28.

Home Daily Bible Readings
Apr. 25 M. The Compassionate Christ, Luke 13:10–13.
Apr. 26 T. Paul Chose Silas, Acts 15:36–41.
Apr. 27 W. A Disobedient Prophet, Jonah 1:1–6.
Apr. 28 T. The Prophet Had a Second Chance, Jonah 3:1–5.
Apr. 29 F. The Unlimited Mercy of God, Jonah 4:1–11.
Apr. 30 S. Go Preach the Gospel, Mark 16:9–16.
May 1 S. The Great Commission, Matthew 28:16–20.

Lesson Aim: As a result of this lesson your class members should be encouraged to seek the Holy Spirit's guidance in all that they do.

LESSON OUTLINE
Background to the Scripture
Looking at the Scripture Text
  I. "Come Over Into Macedonia" (Acts 16:9–12)
  II. "Come Into My House" (Acts 16:13–15)
  III. "Come Out of Her" (Acts 16:16–18)
Applying the Scripture

Background to the Scripture

Encouraged by the decision of the council in Jerusalem, Paul set out on what was to become known as his "Second Missionary Journey." His primary purpose was to visit the brothers and sisters in the cities of Asia Minor where he and Barnabas had planted churches.

Traveling with Paul was Silas, a prophet in the church at Jerusalem who had returned to Antioch with the apostle and confirmed Paul's report of the council. On their way, as they reached Lystra, Paul recruited a third member for his traveling evangelistic team, Timothy—a young man who would come to mean very much to Paul. As these three left the region where churches had been formed, traveling in a generally westerly direction, Paul met closed doors. On trying to preach in Asia, the large province that took in the southwest quarter of Asia Minor (modern Turkey), the Spirit prevented their entering. Next they tried to go into Bithynia, in the north, but again the Spirit did not allow them. Probably some circumstance prevented it, in addition to an inner conviction that God was not leading.

Paul and his two partners may have felt frustrated as they reached Troas, on the far western end of Asia Minor. But having found closed doors, they were about to discover a wide open window—to Europe!

Looking at the Scripture Text

"Come Over Into Macedonia" (vv. 9-12) Paul may well have wondered what purposes had brought him to Troas, and where he was to go from there. It was the end of the line—or a jumping-off place. Yet he must have encouraged himself in the knowledge that he was following the leading of the Spirit as he understood that leading. He must have sensed keenly the responsibility of leading young Timothy and Silas, who had not traveled with him before, on what looked like a wild goose chase.

Yet a third man joined them in Troas. From Luke's use of the first person in this section, it is apparent that this "beloved physician" is also a member of the team. When and under what circumstances he joined Paul, Silas, and Timothy, we are not told. "Luke's Christian modesty forbade his speaking of himself," notes the *Pulpit Commentary*.

The "we sections" of Acts show that Luke was a companion of Paul on this journey, on the return trip from Achaia to Jerusalem (20:5-15; 21:1-18), while Paul was prisoner in Caesarea, and on the voyage to Rome (27:1-28:16).

Perhaps with a prayer for guidance, the four of them bedded down for the night. Suddenly Paul saw a man in a vision, more real than a dream, standing at some distance from him. "Come over into Macedonia, and help us," the man said, a pleading, begging quality in his appeal. Paul had his answer. Luke records that the four got ready at once, unanimously convinced that God had called them to go to Macedonia and preach the Gospel. Only when they reached Troas were they ready to know what their next major move would be.

God had led them by the "closed doors" to the one open door He intended for them to enter. In the situations where they felt no peace to proceed, they acted on the principle, "If in doubt, don't!" Circumstances and timing, which always play an important part in God's guidance, were right at Troas. The "clincher" was the vision. Oftentimes today God will "clinch" His guidance for His child through the Scriptures; rarely does He seem to use a vision, but He does implore us through other people.

From Troas, the party sailed to the island of Samothrace and then on to Neapolis which served as the port for the important city of Philippi. Entering Philippi was like coming to a whole new world. As R. A. Redford said, "To touch Greece was to open a thousand doors to the world at large."

Rebuilt in 350 B.C. and named for Philip of Macedon, father of the illustrious Alexander, Philippi was decreed a Roman colony in the reign of Caesar Augustus (31 B.C.–A.D. 14). In his translation, J. B. Phillips takes note of the "colony status" of Philippi, calling it rather "a Roman garrison-town" from the presence of soldiers there. This city was "the leading city of that district of Macedonia" (NIV), a phrase which can also be translated, "a city of the first division of Macedonia" (*New Bible Commentary, Revised*); Rome had divided Macedonia into four administrative areas.

"Come Into My House" (vv. 13-15) Travelers could reach this bustling commercial center not only by sailing into Neapolis (modern Kavalla), but by way of the Roman highway, the Egnation Way, which crossed Macedonia from the Adriatic Sea on the west. In this city was a woman named Lydia. She was a devout woman, waiting in anticipation for spiritual light much as old Simeon used to go to the Temple in Jerusalem in hope of seeing the Messiah.

Lydia is called a worshiper of God. It could well be that she had learned of the true God in Thyatira, her hometown on the Asia Minor peninsula, for a number of Jews had settled there and history records that a synagogue was there. In Thyatira, she learned the art of dying cloth, for which the city was famous. Perhaps through marriage or by her own industry she now plied that trade in Philippi. "Women occupied positions of considerable freedom and social influence" in the Greek world, notes one commentator.

There being no synagogue in Philippi, Lydia and some women habitually went outside the city on the sabbath day to worship. Evidently her family went with her. A place beside the river served well because ritual washings, for purification, were a part of their worship. The historian, Josephus, pointed out that when a city had no synagogue, a place where there was water was usually preferred by Jews for their "ablutions." At this place, Paul and his company found Lydia and the others and joined them.

How did he know they were worshiping? Perhaps they were singing one of the Psalms, or reading from the Law, or praying. Hearts that seek to worship the Lord have a way of uniting with others of like mind.

The text says that Paul did not so much enter into conversation as he did preach. And when he spoke, God did a work in Lydia, opening her heart to respond—to attend unto, give heed to, pay attention to Paul's Good News. In other words, she believed. "The opening of the heart was God's work," said Chrysostom, "the attending was hers: so that it was both God's doing and man's."

Since Lydia's baptism is told next, we understand that Paul or one of the missionaries with him baptized her in the river that day. Luke employs the words "and her household," suggesting perhaps that a husband and children, and possibly servants also believed with her. Since we do not know if there were children present, it is impossible to build a case for infant baptism on this text. In making baptism the first duty of a believer, Paul was following the example of others before him—Peter (Acts 2:38, 41; 10:47), Philip (8:38), and Ananias, who had immersed Paul (22:16).

Peter exhorted the early Christians to "use hospitality to one another without grudging" (1 Peter 4:9). Before this Scripture was ever written, Lydia gave proof of the Law written in her heart by inviting Paul and the others to make her house their abiding place. She "prevailed upon us" (NASB), Luke says. To the traveling evangelists, this was but another confirmation of God's leading, a fulfillment of Jesus' words to all that leave everything for the sake of the Gospel that they will not fail "to receive . . . (homes, brothers, sisters, mothers, children and fields—and with them, persecutions) and in the age to come, eternal life" (Mark 10:30 NIV).

"Come Out of Her" (vv. 16–18) With the salvation of Lydia and her household, a church was planted in Philippi. This body of believers would always mean very much to Paul and to them he would pen his epistle of joy, Philippians. But Lydia's turning seems to have made little impact on Philippi. That impact would come about indirectly through another woman.

On their way to prayer, possibly on a sabbath, Paul and his companions encountered a young girl who was demon-possessed. The spirit gave her power to tell fortunes and in this way she earned a lot of money for her masters. For some time, she had been the slave of more than one man and a tool of Satan. Commentators believe that she had the powers of a ventriloquist. The Greek word for *divination* is *Python,* referring to the serpent or dragon in Greek mythology which dwelt in Pytho, at the foot of mount Parnassus, guarding the oracle of Delphi. This serpent Apollo killed and its name was thereafter used interchangeably with his name for this mythical god of prophecy. The word came to be applied to "diviners or soothsayers, regarded as inspired by Apollo," says W. E. Vine.

"It is a characteristic of the Gospel and Acts to note that beings of the demonic world were sensitive to the presence of an inspired person," notes the *Abingdon Bible Commentary.* This was true in the ministry of Jesus and it is what we encounter in our text. This girl's tongue became the instrument for the evil spirit within her as it cried out, "These men are servants of the Most High God, who are telling you the way to be saved" (NIV).

It should not surprise us to see the truth being spoken by a Satan-inspired person. The evil one even uses truth when it will serve his purposes. Perhaps he hoped, through telling the truth, she would attract more people to her and cause them to have confidence in her soothsaying. Or, he may have sought to flatter Paul and lead him into sin. Whatever the reason, Paul was not deceived. But he soon became annoyed by her persistence; evidently she kept this up several days. Turning to her, he spoke to the spirit and commanded it on the authority of Jesus Christ to come out of her.

The outcome of this encounter is well known. This "damsel" ceased being a slave to Satan and became a bond slave of Christ, joining Lydia and others in the young Philippian church. But because her masters saw their hope of gain was lost, they brought charges against Paul and Silas and had them beaten and put in jail. A defeat for the Gospel? A setback for the Philippian church? By no means. That night, when an earthquake shook the prison, the jailor fell in fright to the feet of Paul and Silas and asked the Question of all Questions: "Sirs, what must I do to be saved?" He, too, found Christ, and all his household, and on the next day the authorities granted a reprieve to Paul and apologized for whipping a Roman citizen. The Gospel had broken through all barriers in Macedonia.

Applying the Scripture

Ask: Do you have difficulty discerning God's will? If your class members answered in the affirmative, tell them they should not feel alone.

Most of us would agree with Lorne C. Sanny, president of The Navigators, when he said, "The older I get the more difficult it becomes for me to know God's will."

We may wish for the days when God showed the way by visions and voices, but the Lord does not operate that way today. "Nevertheless He does direct our steps," says one nineteenth-century commentator.

"He either calls us or 'suffers us not' to go where we had designed to work, by some method, of His divine procedure.

"1. He may enlighten our minds by enlarging our faculties; so that, though we are not conscious of any special influence, we see clearly what is the right and wise course to pursue.

"2. He may inspire us with such promptings that we feel assured that we are being moved by His own hand.

"3. He may, by His providential ordering, shut us out from, or shut us up to, the path in which He would not, or would, have us walk. It is for us to inquire reverently what is His will, which way He does not desire us to take, when He calls us to preach the Gospel, and then promptly and cheerfully to obey."

Suggest to your class the following three essentials in determining God's will—*the Word of God, circumstances,* and *the peace of God.*

The story is told of a seaman who never ran aground when piloting his ship into a harbor at night. It was all the more remarkable because the channel was narrow and treacherous coral rose to shallow levels on either side. When asked, the seaman said he had learned, upon entering the harbor, not to proceed until three lights on shore lined up in a straight line before him. He had read the instructions in a forgotten nautical book.

In praying to know God's will in any matter, we will do well to wait until the three "lights" named above line up and agree.

In any decision, small or large, we must ask, "What do I understand the Bible to say about this?" Avoid prooftexts; seek to know what is the "whole counsel of God" on the matter.

Second, what about circumstances. Ask, "Do outward circumstances indicate that this is the will of God?" Circumstances, like feelings, are unreliable when trusted alone. But God sovereignly allows circumstances to "line up" when it is His will to go.

Third, do I have inner peace about this. Paul said, "The peace that Christ gives is to guide you in the decisions you make" (Colossians 3:15 TEV). This is another way of saying, "What is the Spirit telling me, in my inner heart?" Taken alone, this can be very subjective and can be misleading; but taken with the Word of God and the outward circumstances—if these three agree—we can proceed with confidence.

Questions for Discussion
Make use of these questions to involve your students in learning and to test their understanding of the lesson.
1. Who were Paul's traveling companions from Troas into Macedonia?   2. How did the Lord show Paul He wanted him in Macedonia? How does He guide us today?   3. What was so significant about Paul's going to Macedonia?   4. What does the account of Lydia reveal concerning the possibilities that existed for women in those days?   5. Why might Paul have known to seek worshipers at the river side?   6. Did any lasting spiritual fruit result from the mission to Philippi? If so, what was it?   7. How did the slave girl differ from Lydia? In what ways were they similar?

Illustrating the Scripture
Examples and quotations to help the teacher communicate the lesson.
SHE WAS BAPTIZED WITH HER HOUSEHOLD   "When Lydia had the right to baptism, by reason of her faith in Jesus Christ, all her family whom she could undertake to bring up in the knowledge of Christ were admitted to that ordinance also; as all the servants, and such others as were born in his house, or bought with his money, were circumcised with Abraham (Genesis 17:12).

"Now the Gospel does not contract in any way, but enlarges the privileges of believers in all things. And if they might under the Law have their children and servants admitted into a covenant with God (which could not but rejoice religious parents and masters, who value the relation they and theirs have to God, above all earthly things) surely under the Gospel none of our families are excluded, unless they wilfully exclude themselves" (Matthew Poole).

HOSPITALITY   "The primitive Christians made one principal part of their duty to consist in the exercise of hospitality; and they were so exact in the discharge of it that the very heathens admired them for it. They were hospitable to all strangers, but chiefly to those that were of the same faith and communion. Believers scarce ever went without letters of communion, which testified the purity of their faith; this was sufficient to procure them reception in all those places where the name of Jesus Christ was known" (Alexander Cruden).

WHAT IS MISSIONS? "No man anywhere is *getting along* without Jesus Christ. If sophistication has robbed you of concern for the lost, then you need to confess your sins and seek God.

"There is a need for missionaries—for doing the task and to express the international character of the Church. Missions is basically crossing the frontier of faith in Christ and unbelief that exists wherever we find it. The home base is everywhere the Church is. Who is a missionary? Any obedient Christian. David Taylor says that since God has caused you to be born in this country and culture, you are likely to spend the greater part of your life in this country. Divine compulsion to communicate a message ought to typify missionaries.

"The obstacles are psychological. To commit oneself today to be a missionary is to commit oneself to a career of being misunderstood. Today a call to be a missionary may also be a call to danger. 'He who wants to live in peace and quiet, has simply chosen the wrong generation in which to live' said Trotsky" (Warren Webster, Conservative Baptist Missionary).

Topics for Youth

HOW DO YOU DELIGHT YOURSELF IN GOD'S WILL?—"I entered SMU with my personal philosophy, 'Make the best of all situations or they'll get the best of you' (1 June 3:16)," writes June Hunt in her book, *Above All Else.*

"I really majored in extracurricular activities, but they didn't have a tassel that color for graduation, so I walked in line with all the music majors. The experience I gained working in varied organizations with people of different backgrounds laid the foundation for me in my future work. But I didn't know it at the time. God knew what He was doing all along. . . .

"After completing a year of postgraduate courses, the pastor of the First Baptist Church of Dallas, D. W. A. Criswell, called me to his study. He wanted me to join his staff as the junior-high director. Never having *considered* attending seminary or being a youth director, I was astonished! After all, this wasn't like teaching a beginner Sunday School class. He was asking me to head a division of six hundred fifty students in the world's largest Southern Baptist church.

"Immediately I knew God wanted me to accept the position, so I did; however, my heart didn't want it. The peculiar thing is that usually you know God wants you to do a certain thing because you feel joy about it, but to be perfectly honest, when I walked away I was really down.

"I remember being puzzled over this Scripture: 'Delight thyself also in the

Lord; and he shall give thee the desires of thine heart' (Psalms 37:4). I wondered about this statement because I knew that the desires of our hearts aren't always right. After thinking about it awhile it dawned on me that God *changes* those desires of ours which are not good for us—*if* we let Him. As we delight ourselves in Him, He changes our desires to be what they *should* be.

"But how do you delight yourself in the Lord, or for that matter, in any person? You spend time talking with Him, listening to Him, putting His desires ahead of your own, doing things to please Him—even when you'd rather not. *You spend time.* And so I was learning and God was working. He did indeed change the desires of my heart. Ten weeks later I wouldn't have traded jobs with anyone. It was God's timing again."

LESSON 10   MAY 8

Conflict in Corinth

Background Scripture: Acts 18; 1 Corinthians 1
Devotional Reading: 1 John 3:19–24

Acts 18:1, 4–17

1 After these things Paul departed from Athens, and came to Corinth;
4 And he reasoned in the synagogue every sabbath, and persuaded the Jews and the Greeks.
5 And when Silas and Timotheus were come from Macedonia, Paul was pressed in the spirit, and testified to the Jews that Jesus was Christ.
6 And when they opposed themselves, and blasphemed, he shook his raiment, and said unto them, Your blood be upon your own heads; I am clean: from henceforth I will go unto the Gentiles.
7 And he departed thence, and entered into a certain man's house, named Justus, one that worshipped God, whose house joined hard to the synagogue.
8 And Crispus, the chief ruler of the synagogue, believed on the Lord with all his house; and many of the Corinthians hearing believed, and were baptized.
9 Then spake the Lord to Paul in the night by a vision, Be not afraid, but speak, and hold not thy peace:
10 For I am with thee, and no man shall set on thee to hurt thee: for I have much people in this city.
11 And he continued there a year and six months, teaching the word of God among them.
12 And when Gallio was the deputy of Achaia, the Jews made insurrection with one accord against Paul, and brought him to the judgment seat,

13 Saying, This fellow persuadeth men to worship God contrary to the law.
14 And when Paul was now about to open his mouth, Gallio said unto the Jews, If it were a matter of wrong or wicked lewdness, O ye Jews, reason would that I should bear with you:
15 But if it be a question of words and names, and of your law, look ye to it; for I will be no judge of such matters.
16 And he drave them from the judgment seat.
17 Then all the Greeks took Sosthenes, the chief ruler of the synagogue, and beat him before the judgment seat. And Gallio cared for none of those things.

KEY VERSE: "Be not afraid, but speak, and hold not thy peace: for I am with thee, and no man shall set on thee to hurt thee: for I have much people in this city." Acts 18:9, 10.

Home Daily Bible Readings
May 2	M.	How Paul Preached the Gospel at Corinth, 1 Corinthians 2:1-5.
May 3	T.	Paul at Berea, Acts 17:11-15.
May 4	W.	Paul at Athens, Acts 17:16-21.
May 5	T.	Fellow Workers With God, 1 Corinthians 3:1-15.
May 6	F.	When They Heard the Gospel, Acts 17:32-34.
May 7	S.	Paul Works at His Trade, Acts 18:1-4.
May 8	S.	Paul Goes to the Gentiles, Acts 18:5-11.

Lesson Aim: As a result of this lesson adult Christians should deliberately commit a specific fear of theirs to God, trusting in the presence of Christ.

LESSON OUTLINE
Background to the Scripture
Looking at the Scripture Text
  I. Upheaval Among Corinth's Jews (Acts 18:1, 4-6)
 II. Cause of the Upheaval (Acts 18:7, 8)
III. Jesus Encourages Paul (Acts 18:9-11)
IV. The Jews' Last-Ditch Effort Fails (Acts 18:12-17)
Applying the Scripture

Background to the Scripture

In your imagination, what would a typical day be like for Paul in Corinth? Some might imagine him rising at daybreak for morning prayers after which he would enjoy a snack of fruit and cheese with Aquila and Priscilla, his hosts. Then he would retire for the morning to a private room to study the

Scriptures or to write letters to one of the young churches he had planted. The early afternoon might find him in the synagogue or the marketplace, engaging Jew and Gentile in discussion, sometimes preaching, sometimes going with an earnest seeker to his house to lead an entire family to faith in Christ. Toward sundown, he might join one of the Christian families for supper and then, perhaps in that home, an extended session of teaching would follow.

If we think by this that we have pegged a typical day for Paul, we had better think again. What is missing? Work—that is what! Paul did not expect the infant Church to support him. The chapter before us today reveals that Paul had a trade—tentmaking. In Corinth, Aquila and Priscilla invited him to lodge with them because they were of the same trade. Paul's work more than offset the expense of his lodging for he "worked day and night so that we would not be any trouble to you (Thessalonians) . . ." (1 Thessalonians 2:9 TEV). Paul carried on a full-time ministry in addition to toil which more than once he referred to as by night and day (2 Thessalonians 3:8).

Looking at the Scripture Text

Upheaval Among Corinth's Jews (vv. 1, 4-6) A brief summary of what transpired after Paul and his companions left Philippi will help us gain a better feel for what happened at Corinth. After at least three weeks' preaching in Thessalonica, the Lord rewarded Paul's labors with the conversion of a few Jews, some "leading women," and "a great multitude" of Greeks. These Greeks had evidently first become proselytes to the Jewish faith and the Jewish population got so worked up against "the Way" that Paul had to flee for his life under cover of darkness.

He, Silas, and Timothy had similar success in Berea, a smaller city of Macedonia, but a company of angry Thessalonian Jews soon came there, pushing Paul on to Athens. There he evidently remained from two to four weeks before going on to Corinth.

These two cities were most prominent of all in Achaia—Athens, the center of education, and Corinth, the capital of the province and center of commerce. Julius Caesar had refounded Corinth and named it a Roman colony in 46 B.C. There Paul breathed the heady atmosphere of the empire and rubbed shoulders with people from Rome. Situated on the central maritime route between Rome and the East, Corinth would prove to be a strategic spot for a church in the missionary advance into the first-century world.

A teeming, sensuous city, "its name had become a byword for vice." Sailors and soldiers knew the meaning of the slang phrase, "to Corinthianize." One scholar has likened Corinth to London and Paris, all in one.

A very large population of Greeks shared this city with Romans, immigrants from many nations of the Mediterranean region, and a great many Jews. As was his custom, Paul went to the synagogue to tell his fellow Jews of the Savior. From Luke's words, "every Sabbath" it is apparent that Paul had been there some time before Silas and Timothy rejoined him (v. 5).

The phrase "pressed in the spirit" (v. 5) requires special explanation. Moffatt's translation of those words—"was engrossed in this preaching of the word"—fairly represents how some modern versions have tried to handle the phrase. It seems that in Corinth Paul was gripped with "a greater concentration of purpose and simplicity of method" (says the *Expositor's Greek Testament*) than before. Some commentators on the other hand interpret the phrase in another way, suggesting that Silas and Timothy brought with them gifts from the Macedonian churches, allowing Paul to devote all his energies to preaching. This interpretation is reflected in the NIV—"devoted himself exclusively to preaching. . . ."

Addressing himself to a predominantly Jewish audience, Paul made the issue of the Messiah the central thrust of his message. He testified that "Jesus was Christ" or, perhaps more accurately, "that the Messiah is Jesus."

Luke does not describe how soon the tide turned in Corinth, but it definitely turned. We have reason to believe that the Jews burst out in an outrage during one of their Sabbath services while Paul preached Christ and His Resurrection. They "opposed Paul" and "blasphemed." Their great opposition seems to have been equally aimed at Paul and at his Lord. The Living Bible says they began "hurling abuse at Jesus." At that, the apostle who had endured so much already from the Jews, turned and so much as said, "If you are lost, you yourselves must take the blame for it! I am not responsible" (v. 6 TEV).

In a gesture symbolic of his Lord (Matthew 10:14), he "shook out the skirts of his cloak" (NEB) and told them "your blood be on your own heads." This astonishing rebuttal should have rung a responsive chord among his Jewish listeners, reminding them that the watchman of the Lord, once he had warned the people of impending doom, was innocent of their blood if they failed to repent (*see* Ezekiel 33:4–9).

Cause of the Upheaval (vv. 7, 8) In verse 8, we seem to have more than an inkling of why the Jews rose up so sharply against Paul. This doctrine he preached, which sounded incredible to them, was finding converts. None other than Crispus, the man who presided over their substantial synagogue, became a believer, and his family with him. Obviously he had to step down as the chief ruler, probably being replaced by Sosthenes who nine verses later is also called the chief ruler.

As we proceed in our study of Acts, more and more reference points crop up in other New Testament books, shedding direct light on the text at hand. The name Crispus is an example of this. His name appears in 1 Corinthians 1:14 when Paul says that he was one of the few whom Paul baptized.

With characteristic exactness, Luke records also the name of the man to whose house Paul resorted for preaching and teaching when he "left the synagogue." Called Justus in the KJV, he is called Titius Justus or Titus in other translations. One Bible student suggests that he also bore the name Gaius and is the man named in Romans 16:23.

Evidently Paul remained with Aquila and Priscilla in their home but held meetings in the home of Justus. Steadily the church grew as "many Corinthians" (both Greeks and Romans) "hearing believed, and were baptized" (v. 8).

***Jesus Encourages Paul* (vv. 9-11)** At this point Luke interrupts the narrative to tell of a vision Paul received of the risen Lord. Probably this happened soon after Paul's falling out with the Jews, at a time when he very likely feared for his life. We ought to take special note of this loving initiative from heaven to Paul, recognizing that for us, too, as William C. Poole wrote, "Just when I need Him most, Jesus is near to comfort and cheer, just when I need Him most." (© Copyright 1908 by Chas. H. Gabriel. Renewed 1936 The Rodeheaver Co. [A Division of Word, Inc.] All Rights Reserved. Used by permission.)

Luke was not with Paul on this leg of the journey and was dependent on Paul for the record of what happened in Corinth, including the vision. Luke had recorded the words of the angel, "Fear not" (Luke 1:13; 2:10) and of Jesus, "Fear not" (5:10; 8:50; 12:7, 32) in his Gospel story. He again records the words here: "Be not afraid, but speak, and hold not thy peace."

How comforting to Paul. Next, the Lord gives Paul two Gibraltar-like promises to keep him from every fear—"I am with thee" and "no man shall set on thee to hurt thee." And then He assured Paul: "I have much people in this city." The vision shows us a glimpse of the spiritual battle that was raging in Corinth, a battle for the eternal souls of men, women, and children, a battle that continues right now all around us.

By Luke's next stating that Paul continued in Corinth for eighteen months, he implies that the vision had a quieting effect on Paul. From his letters, Paul shows the deep faith the Lord gave to him. Free of all anxiousness, he settled down to teaching the Word. It is believed that he penned both letters to the church at Thessalonica at this time (*see* 1 Thessalonians 1:1; 3:2, 6). The *New Bible Commentary, Revised* estimates the date of this stay in Corinth from autumn A.D. 50 to spring 52.

***The Jews' Last-Ditch Effort Fails* (vv. 12-17)** With one more stroke, Luke completed his portrayal of Paul's conflict at Corinth. Perhaps a year or more had passed. The Jews, still smarting from their conflict with Paul and the Gospel, thought they saw their opportunity with the appointment of Gallio as deputy or proconsul of the province.

Secular history knows Gallio, though it knows his younger brother, Seneca, much better. In one of Seneca's writings, he speaks of Gallio being ill in Achaia, but he does not mention that Gallio had been appointed proconsul, an appointment made by the emperor. His affable, easygoing personality earned this man the nickname, *dulcis Gallio*. Historians set his proconsulate at approximately A.D. 49-65 or 66. "Luke is most accurate," notes the *Pulpit Commentary*, "in calling him proconsul. Achaia recently was made a senatorial province by Claudius."

Perhaps the Jews "made (their) insurrection" against Paul soon after Gallio took office, hoping to spring a punishing judgment on Paul from the new governor. The judgment seat or *bema* to which they brought Paul was a raised seat where the governor held court. It could be moved from place to place. Luke does not say where Gallio's judgment seat was placed, but some public site was obvious from the context.

If we close our eyes and forget we are reading of Paul in Corinth, we might well think we were in Thessalonica where the Jews brought accusation against him, or in Jerusalem as the trial of Jesus proceeded. It is a blessed thing to be accused of the same crime for which our Lord was accused. Paul was like his Lord in so many ways; we do well to follow his example, even in this. The Jews sought to squelch Paul and the young Church by charging the believers with teaching a religion "contrary to the law"—the Mosaic Law, that is.

But they miscalculated *dulcis Gallio*. He was not another Pilate, who would capitulate to their demands. He was no soft touch for their hateful purposes. Before Paul could say anything in his defense, Gallio ridiculed them and ejected them. He saw their dispute for what it was, an argument over religion and not worthy of his time and attention.

Paul may have gained the respect of the authorities and leading persons of Corinth. His use of the home of a Greek (Justus) may have given him access to the more educated people of the city. True, as his first epistle states, "not many wise . . . mighty . . . noble" (1 Corinthians 1:26) were in their number, but there were some. Perhaps the treasurer of the city is the same Erastus named in Romans 16:23. When Gallio dismissed Paul's case, this popularity might explain why the mob did not jump on Paul. Instead, the onlookers and spectators, most of whom were probably Greeks, vented their wrath on the Jews by beating up the current ruler of the synagogue, Sosthenes. Some think that Sosthenes later became a believer and is the one Paul names in his first letter to this church (1 Corinthians 1:1). But no solid evidence exists to prove the theory.

Paul's delivery from this assault of the Jews proved the faithfulness of God's promise to him in the vision. The Gospel had much against it in Corinth. As one writer so well states: "In Corinth the Gospel had been put to a supreme test, and nowhere had it triumphed more gloriously."

Applying the Scripture
Ask: When was the last time you were really afraid?

Invite responses from class members. One may volunteer, "The time when Mom was near death and I had to fly home—my first time ever on an airplane." Or, "Last month when we thought someone was trying to break into our house." Or, "The night a week ago when I had to take a late bus home and had to walk the distance from the bus stop to my house in darkness."

If you have time, try to give each person a chance to name their fear, something for which they have been genuinely frightened—fears for their kids, about their health, about their job which is too demanding, their boss, their need to speak up to someone whom they fear. . . .

People must have a host of fears because the words *fear not* are among the most oft-repeated words in the Old and New Testaments. The dictionary defines fear as "an emotion excited by danger, evil, or pain; apprehension, dread."

Discuss in your class that, in the light of that definition, fear is a "given" in life. Our life demands that we do things that sometime bring us into danger, confront us with evil, or cause pain.

We must learn to live with fear, without being fearful. The Bible says "perfect love casteth out fear, because fear hath torment." Fear must be a result of our fall, and its chief cause is the Evil One. The devil tried to intimidate Paul and he will try to intimidate us.

How do we conquer our fears? Some in your class may make suggestions. The following may be helpful.

1. Share what you fear with someone else. Ask if it has not been of some comfort and encouragement to members of the class for them to learn that their fellow Christians also have fears. But chiefly, *tell the Lord*. Encourage your class members to tell the Lord all about their fears.
2. Remember the "fear nots" in the Bible. If God appeared to Paul in a vision, it was because Paul did not have the entire revelation of God. We have something even Paul did not have! The Scriptures, complete with their full record of how God has delivered all of His people from fear, tells us that we do not need to fear.
3. Remember the other promise: "I am with you." Sure, this was made to Paul in a very personal way. But ask your class if it is any less personal for them to read in the Word such verses as Matthew 28:20—"Lo, I am with you alway"?

Close the class period in solemn prayer, asking each class member to take one specific fear of theirs before God in silent prayer. Ask them to visualize Jesus saying to them, "Do not be afraid." Then ask them to visualize Jesus with them, saying, "I am with you all of the time; fear not."

Questions for Discussion
Make use of these questions to involve your students in learning and to test their understanding of the lesson.
1. What made Corinth such an important place for the church to be planted? 2. What did Paul mean by "Your blood be upon your own heads"? What Old Testament prophet may have inspired such an expression? 3. How long did Paul remain in Corinth teaching and preaching? 4. Which two of his pastoral epistles did the Apostle Paul write from Corinth? 5. What two promises did the Lord make to Paul in the vision? What assurance was given him of the success of his work? 6. How do you explain the apparent contradiction that both Sosthenes and Crispus are named as the chief ruler of the Corinthian synagogue? 7. Who beat up Sosthenes? What do you think was the cause?

Illustrating the Scripture
Examples and quotations to help the teacher communicate the lesson.

CORINTHIAN CONVERTS Paul made it a matter of record that the Corinthian church was comprised, in the main, of people from the lowest social grade. In his first epistle to Corinth he says: "For look at your own calling as Christians, my brothers. You don't see among you many of the wise (according to this world's judgment) nor many of the ruling class, nor many from the noblest families. But God has chosen what the world calls foolish to shame the wise; he has chosen what the world calls weak to shame the strong. He has chosen things of little strength and small repute, yes and even things which have no real existence, to explode the pretensions of the things that are—that no man may boast in the presence of God" (1 Corinthians 1:26–29 PHILLIPS).

John Stirling, in *An Atlas Illustrating The Acts of the Apostles and The Epistles*, lists these Corinthian converts and where they are found in Scripture:

Crispus, Acts 18:8.
Stephanas, 1 Corinthians 16:15.
Fortunatus, 1 Corinthians 16:17.
Achaicus, I Corinthians 16:17.
Erastus, Romans 16:23.
Gaius, 1 Corinthians 1:14.
Tertius, Romans 16:22.
Quartus, Romans 16:23.
Sosthenes, 1 Corinthians 1:1.
Chloe, 1 Corinthians 1:11.
Phoebe of Cenchrea, Romans 16:1.

Quite a list! That Paul acknowledges that there were "not many mighty, not many noble" "indicates that there were some in the higher social ranks and some versed in the learning of the schools who welcomed the Gospel; to a Crispus, a Gaius, a Stephanas, we may add Erastus, the public treasurer of the city, an office which in a place like Corinth carried with it considerable influence and position . . . and the readiness with which the Corinthian Church responded to St. Paul's appeal for the poor saints indicates that many of its members had some means at their disposal" (*Expositor's Greek Testament*).

"WHY SO MANY PUBLIC OFFICIALS GO ASTRAY" *The U.S. News & World Report* (February 18, 1981) devoted two pages to an interview with Dr. Bertram S. Brown, a senior psychiatrist at the RAND Corporation, on the above subject. In light of our study of one public official, Gallio, who did not give in to stress (unlike Pilate), Dr. Brown's comments are to the point. Speaking of members of Congress, he agrees that they are under more strain than they used to be, working "six and seven days a week, with constant visits, constant movement . . . under greater re-election pressure."

"The demands on them are incessant and overwhelming, whether they represent 450,000 people, a state or an entire nation," said Dr. Brown. "In this atmosphere it takes great strength and sense of will to make sure that you tend to personal things. Many officials cannot handle this demand for balance. Their family lives are poor and are carried on in a superficial way rather than in a substantive way. They eventually suffer from this, be it anxiety, depression, alcoholism, or what have you."

Topics for Youth

FEARS, FEARS, FEARS!—All of us have them, but for every young person they are certainly not the same. Some people are like the girl who was frightened of height. When her boyfriend wanted to step to the edge of a wall atop a low hill in the foothills of the Appalachians, she drew back. That is a normal fear; many of us have it.

Remember the times you used to be afraid to go out in the backyard at night, or even to be the only one upstairs at night—especially if you had to go upstairs into the dark and then turn on a light!

A leading national magazine ran a feature on this subject in mid-1980. Their editors had received the findings from a survey of preteens who were asked to rate the things they worried about most. Then the editors asked their readers, "What worries kids most?" and invited the readers to rate the same things that thousands of preteens had rated, to see if the readers (parents in this case) really understood what does upset children and young people.

Below are listed eleven of the most frequently named things that brought fear or anxiety into the lives of kids. Young people who would like to test themselves on these same items should be asked to place these in order, from the first (which would cause the most anxiety) to the last (which they would hardly fear at all).

1. Being made fun of in class
2. Getting lost
3. Having an operation
4. Being sent to the principal's office
5. Receiving a bad report card
6. Being suspected of lying
7. Being caught stealing
8. Hearing parents quarrel
9. Being held back a year in school
10. Going blind
11. Losing a parent

There are many other causes of fear in a young person's life, but these are surely some that could cause a flutter of fear or throw a person into panic—depending upon which one it is. A review of the verses in today's lesson, showing how the Lord encouraged Paul when he was in great danger, should be a helpful way to prepare any young person to cope with his or her fears.

Also, the "Applying the Scripture" section will further assist the individual in facing fear.

Oh yes—you wanted to know how those fears were rated by the preteens who took the test? If you begin the list from No. 11 and go up the list you will have the exact order in which kids ranked the things that worry them most.

LESSON 11   MAY 15

Riot in Ephesus

Background Scripture: Acts 19, 20
Devotional Reading: John 17:20–26

Acts 19:23–29, 35–40

23 And the same time there arose no small stir about that way.

24 For a certain man named Demetrius, a silversmith, which made silver shrines for Diana, brought no small gain unto the craftsmen;

25 Whom he called together with the workmen of like occupation, and said, Sirs, ye know that by this craft we have our wealth.

26 Moreover ye see and hear, that not alone at Ephesus, but almost throughout all Asia, this Paul hath persuaded and turned away much people, saying that they be no gods, which are made with hands:

27 So that not only this our craft is in danger to be set at nought; but also that the temple of the great goddess Diana should be despised, and her magnificence should be destroyed, whom all Asia and the world worshippeth.

28 And when they heard these sayings, they were full of wrath, and cried out, saying, Great is Diana of the Ephesians.

29 And the whole city was filled with confusion: and having caught Gaius and Aristarchus, men of Macedonia, Paul's companions in travel, they rushed with one accord into the theatre.

35 And when the townclerk had appeased the people, he said, Ye men of Ephesus, what man is there that knoweth not how that the city of the Ephesians is a worshipper of the great goddess Diana, and of the image which fell down from Jupiter?

36 Seeing then that these things cannot be spoken against, ye ought to be quiet, and to do nothing rashly.

37 For ye have brought hither these men, which are neither robbers of churches, nor yet blasphemers of your goddess.

38 Wherefore if Demetrius, and the craftsmen which are with him, have a matter against any man, the law is open, and there are deputies: let them implead one another.

39 But if ye inquire any thing concerning other matters, it shall be determined in a lawful assembly.
40 For we are in danger to be called in question for this day's uproar, there being no cause whereby we may give an account of this concourse.

KEY VERSE: "We are troubled on every side, yet not distressed; we are perplexed, but not in despair." 2 Corinthians 4:8.

> **Home Daily Bible Readings**
> May 9 M. John's Disciples at Ephesus, Acts 19:1-7.
> May 10 T. In the School of Tyrannus, Acts 19:8-12.
> May 11 W. The Growth of the Word, Acts 19:13-20.
> May 12 T. The All-Night Service, Acts 20:7-12.
> May 13 F. Paul's Farewell Address, Acts 20:17-27.
> May 14 S. Paul's Message to the Elders, Acts 20:28-35.
> May 15 S. They Kneeled Down and Prayed, Acts 20:36-38.

Lesson Aim: As a result of this lesson, adult Christians will decide to choose Christ and His will rather than lesser standards in questions of morals.

LESSON OUTLINE
Background to the Scripture
Looking at the Scripture Text
 I. Root Cause of the Riot (Acts 19:23-27)
 II. Two Caught in the Riot (Acts 19:28, 29)
 III. Town Clerk Calms the Riot (Acts 19:35-40)
Applying the Scripture

Background to the Scripture

The Apostle Paul has been the main object of our study in Acts since the church at Antioch laid hands on him and Barnabas and sent them on their first journey. Undoubtedly, for most members of your class, this series of lessons has afforded a closer look at Paul's life than ever before. We have perhaps seen qualities that had not impressed us in his life before—such as his personal magnetism, his untiring labors as a tentmaker, his unswerving dedication to preaching Christ.

Today's lesson continues the series, following Paul to the city of Ephesus, but the apostle is not in the foreground. Here we see the effect of his life and ministry from the vantage point of pagan Ephesians whose way of life was threatened by the success of the Gospel.

Paul stayed longer in Ephesus than in any other city on his missionary tours—almost three years. After interrogating some twelve Ephesians who previously had been baptized only with a limited understanding of the Gospel, Paul laid hands on them, imparting to them the Spirit. A church was born in Ephesus! But this city, which Lenski calls "the most important city in all Asia Minor," had other allegiances. The young Church was bound to clash with the devotees of the goddess Artemis, patron saint of this great metropolis. And since roads radiated out from Ephesus to the entire province of Asia, a conflict in Ephesus would be felt by the other churches springing up there (*see* Revelations 1:11).

Looking at the Scripture Text

Root Cause of the Riot (vv. 23–27) To understand what Luke meant by "and the same time," we need to take note of an unusual incident which brought Paul and the Church into direct confrontation with the pagan Ephesians.

Paul did miraculous works by the power of the Spirit in Ephesus, even to the healing of the sick by means of "handkerchiefs and aprons" that had touched him. Evil spirits were cast out in the same way. Seeing this wonderful power in action, seven sons of one Sceva, a Jewish priest, tried in vain to exorcise demons from a man by using the Name Paul invoked. The man turned on them and beat them up so that they "ran out of the house naked and bleeding" (v. 16 NIV).

As word of the incident circulated, a holy fear came on the believers. Many of them had continued to practice occult arts, so common in Ephesus, but now they openly confessed their sin of compromise and those who had scrolls by which they "practiced sorcery" burned them all. This was done in public, so that their testimony spread to the larger population.

Purified of their sin, the Christians of Ephesus grew in power and "the word of the Lord spread widely" (v. 20 NIV). But as so often happens, persecution was soon to follow. Opposition that had been coming from the Jewish quarter in other places now arose out of the Gentile element. J. C. Macaulay says this seems to be the beginning of the persecution of the Church by the pagan world.

As an obvious result of this revival and its spread throughout Ephesus, the demand for idolatrous shrines and trinkets took a sharp downward turn. Chiefly affected was the worship of the highly revered goddess, Artemis, also called Diana. Her temple in Ephesus, constructed of the purest marble with 127 columns 60 feet high, was among the seven wonders of the ancient world.

"Ephesian Artemis bore the same name as the 'queen and huntress, chaste and fair' of Greek mythology, but, far from being a virgin-goddess, she was a local manifestation of the great mother of gods and men who had been worshiped in Asia Minor from time immemorial," says F. F. Bruce. "Her many-breasted image at Ephesus, 'the sacred stone that fell from the sky' (19:35) was housed in a shrine...." Tradition said that the stone had fallen out of the sky. It may have been a meteor, or it may have been an idol from an earlier age, dug up and thought to have fallen.

Man's commercial instincts being what they are, the silversmiths of Ephesus had begun years earlier to sculpt small replicas of the temple of Artemis. These "silver shrines" they sold to the people who placed them in their houses as a talisman of protection bestowed by the goddess. These were sold the year-round, but no time was so advantageous for their sale as at the annual festival honoring Artemis. This was held in May and many scholars believe that the festival was fast approaching just as the demand for shrines had fallen off.

Enter Demetrius. Luke calls him a silversmith although he seems also to have been a proprietor. Moved by genuine material concerns he called a meeting of his fellow silversmiths (Greek—technicians) and also artisans from related trades (Greek—workmen). These latter may have been ones who made the shrines of terra cotta, a reddish clay; many of these have been found in ruins of the ancient world.

In his impassioned speech before this meeting of the artisans' guild, Demetrius paid a backhanded compliment to the Church. Even if his words were exaggerated, the man recognized that Paul "has convinced and led astray large numbers of people here in Ephesus and in practically the whole province of Asia" (v. 26 NIV).

He directly blamed Paul and the success of the Church for the dangers that now ate away the profits from their livelihood. The word *wealth* in verse 25 need not suggest riches; it is not clear how affluent the craftsmen had become. What is clear is that the true motive behind Demetrius's complaint was not to enhance the worship of Diana, but to encourage high sales, greater profits, a secure future—even if it meant deluding people about "man-made gods are no gods at all" (NIV). His talk about the danger that the temple would be "discredited" and the goddess herself "robbed of divine majesty" (NIV) was a thinly-veiled attempt to hide the true concern.

Demetrius claimed that the worship of Artemis was universal—"all of Asia and the world worship" (NASB). History does reveal that this form of worship existed in at least thirty cities throughout the world then. In contrast, he notes that Christianity was spreading "in practically the whole province of Asia." He could not have known that it was also spreading in Galatia, Cilicia, Cyprus, Syria, Judea, Achaia, Macedonia, and elsewhere. Today the Church that once confronted haughty Artemis in first century Ephesus is planted in virtually every nation on earth. And where is Artemis?

Two Caught in the Riot (vv. 28, 29) The other silversmiths could not but agree with the concern voiced by Demetrius. They, too, had begun to suffer in the "pocketbook" and needed to blow off steam. We should probably grant that their spirited chant—"Great is Diana of the Ephesians"—arose partly out of misguided but sincere reverence, partly out of tradition and a sort of patriotism.

With the exception of Christians and Jews, any citizen of Ephesus could enter wholeheartedly into their chant. And they did. The "they" of verse 29 includes a large crowd of Ephesians who now rushed into the amphitheatre. Various estimates say that from 20,000 to 25,000 people could be seated in the amphitheatre at Ephesus. The *Pulpit Commentary* quotes one scholar as saying "The theatre at Ephesus, of which 'ruins of immense grandeur' still remain, is said to be the largest of which we have any account."

The two Christians whom the crowd seized and thrust into the arena—Gaius and Aristarchus—were taken by accident probably. They would have loved to have had Paul, and it is providential that they did not. Luke describes these two as Macedonians. He later identifies Aristarchus as a man from Thessalonica (20:4). The Gaius named there, of Derbe, would be a different man. Gaius was a common name. Very likely, the two believers supplied Luke with the details of this incident.

This indignation meeting, as it has been called, began as a blowing-off-steam session among silversmiths. But it had erupted into an explosive mass public meeting. Confusion reigned. As verse 32 notes, "and the more part knew not wherefore they were come together." Paul tried to go into the arena, but his Christian brethren restrained him. The large colony of Jews in the city put forward one of their men, Alexander, perhaps in an attempt to dissociate the Jewish community from the Christians. But his identification as a Jew only fanned the flames of the people's devotion so that for two hours they did nothing but chant, "Great is Diana of the Ephesians! Great is Diana of the Ephesians!"

Town Clerk Calms the Riot (vv. 35-40) Any incident could have touched off a bloody retaliation against the Christians. But the government, doing what God ordained it to do, stepped in.

A town clerk in such a free city was a person of high office. He was the head of the free municipal administration in Ephesus and the chief liaison officer between it and the Roman provincial government. Luther called the town clerk the chancellor. He evidently had charge of the city funds and was the one who read documents publicly, probably at the lawful assembly.

Apparently this highly respected officer had little difficulty in quieting the throng. His message is tactful and pointed. He began by recognizing what every citizen knew—"the city of Ephesus is the guardian of the temple of the great Artemis and of her image, which fell from heaven" (v. 35 NIV). Ephesus was so wedded to Artemis that she proudly bore the title, "Temple-Warden of Artemis," a title which has been found on coins from the first century.

He reasoned that since "everyone" accepted this as true, they had no reason for carrying on. He counseled calm and quiet. Carefully avoiding the mention of Paul's name, he turned to the two Christians and identified them as men who were neither "robbers of churches" nor persons who had defamed Artemis. What he says of Aristarchus and Gaius ought to be said of every Christian—they have a clean slate, nothing can be found in them as grounds for any accusation.

Next the clerk told the crowd what they most certainly knew. If Demetrius or others had an accusation, "the law is open"—that is, the courts are open, the regular court-days are kept—and "there are deputies" or proconsuls. Roman rule provided a certain framework for handling grievances. All voting citizens were called out to the regular or "lawful assembly" three times a month by the Roman authority. There they could voice their concerns.

The word usually translated *church* is here written "assembly" (*ekklesia*). It is formed from *ek*, "out of" and the verb to call. "It is an excellent illustration of God's true church," writes one commentator. "The assembly is a group of people 'called out' of their various pursuits, to gather together about a common cause . . . we are called out about Christ."

The address of the clerk was as successful as it was pointed. Paul's life and the lives of his companions were spared and the riot averted. In a short while, Paul departed and headed for Macedonia on his third missionary journey. In approximately a year he would arrive in Jerusalem in the year A.D. 57, says John Stirling, there to face continued conflict in behalf of his Lord and ours, Jesus Christ.

Applying the Scripture
Read the following to your class: "The one all-effectual counteractive to social and moral evils is strong, vigorous, noble Christian life; and just this the world so greatly needs today." Ask the members of your class to guess when this was said.

Someone may say, "It could have been written today—or a thousand years ago." How true. In fact, it was written in the late nineteenth century.

In our lesson, Demetrius happened to be an unbeliever. But ask one of your class members to picture what changes the man might make were he to give his allegiance to Christ. To spur discussion, ask the class if they think he might change his profession, or would he change the products he sold?

Now invite the class to consider the question: What should I do if I become a Christian and the Lord convicts me that my work or profession is displeasing to Him? You might talk about what kinds of work a believer could not do. Better yet, ask anyone in the class who had to make such a switch upon becoming a Christian to share what happened with the class. Ask how the difficulty was resolved. Obviously it is easier for us to ask others to give up their jobs or professions or to quit doing certain things, than for us to do the same thing. To have to change work after several years' experience can be very costly and can endanger the standard of living for a family. But is not this the risk we ask people to take when we offer Jesus Christ to them? Of course, we can testify that the Heavenly Father will provide an abundant life and so much more of the things of true value in addition to salvation that to remain a nonbeliever is foolish and shortsighted.

After having discussed the situations that occur at the time of conversion, bring the lesson down to the nitty-gritty of life today with the question: Are there times today when your self-interest wars against the Spirit of Christ in you, in the area of your occupation? Are you tempted to go along with unethical practices at work so that you will not lose your own job, or for fear of being demoted?

Finally, consider what happened in Ephesus. A large number of these pagans had turned to Christ, but they had not surrendered all of their old ways. They still held on to the symbols and idols of their pagan ways. But notice what happened when they turned completely from those things. "The word of the Lord spread widely and grew in power" (v. 20 NIV). Challenge your class with the truth that Christ is either LORD OF ALL or He is not LORD AT ALL. The thing that hampers many a lukewarm church today is the halfhearted obedience and incomplete surrender of we who make up the membership. Close the class with a period of silent prayer and ask each person to search his or her heart to see if God is calling on them to give up anything in order to follow Him completely.

Questions for Discussion
Make use of these questions to involve your students in learning and to test their understanding of the lesson.
1. What made Ephesus an important city for the Church's worldwide mission?   2. Who or what was Artemis (Diana) of the Ephesians? Why was she worshiped?   3. Demetrius, hardly a friend of the Gospel, remarks about the effect of Paul's ministry. How did his description compare with the claims of the worship of Artemis to be a worldwide religion?   4. What caused Demetrius and his fellow craftsmen to stage the indignation meeting?   5. Should we ridicule or belittle the practices of other people's religions? How did Paul and his companions treat false religions, as this passage reveals?   6. What word used in this passage is usually translated *church* in the New Testament? What is its significance?   7. How did God quell the riot and allow Paul's companions to be released unharmed?

Illustrating the Scripture
Examples and quotations to help the teacher communicate the lesson.
    YES, THE MISSION TASK STILL EXISTS FOR THE CHURCH TODAY! In Paul's day, from the provincial viewpoint of a pagan silversmith, the worship of a female idol was practiced all over the world while Christianity was limited to just one province. Not quite true—but today that idolatrous religion is gone (a thousand more are in its place) and the Church of Jesus Christ claims adherents "in virtually every nation and in most of the people groups." So says a 1981 report on "Christianity in the World," published by *World Vision* magazine.

Note the following summary of Christianity's growth in the continents and among "people groups." One-fourth of the world's citizens may be called Christians, though it is impossible to say that all of them are truly believers. *Fully 74 percent of the people on earth* do not claim to be Christians!

"In Latin America, 70–80 percent of the population is considered Christian. Roman Catholicism claims the largest percentage . . . (but) a Catholic writer has estimated that not more than 15 percent of the claimed Catholic church membership is active. Evangelical Protestantism, however, has been growing rapidly in recent years. . . .

"In Africa, the number of Christians of all types is growing rapidly, mainly south of the Sahara. Sub-Saharan Africa will probably be more than 50 percent Christian (at least nominally) by about A.D. 2000. . . .

"In Asia, the largest continental area, Christians have never been a large percentage of the population and do not exceed three or four percent of the total. . . .

"In Europe, the majority of the population is considered Christian, although many people are nominal in their faith and church attendance is generally low. . . .

"Experience has shown that one of the best ways to reach individuals for Christ is through their own culture. Members of every society are organized into 'people groups'—large or small groups made up of persons with the same tribal background, occupation, family relationships, language, religion or other factors.

"A people group may be a remote tribe, a group of drug addicts in a large city, a group of political refugees, or a people who speak a particular dialect of a larger langauge. . . . Thousands of these people groups, scattered throughout the world, have not yet been 'reached.' Estimates are that less than 20 percent of their number have had the Gospel presented to them in an understandable form that they can respond to with a commitment to Jesus Christ." (From *World Vision* magazine, January 1981, pp. 3-5, World Vision International, Monrovia, California. Used with permission.)

WHAT DID DEMETRIUS NEED TO DO? In one word, *surrender!* He was caught in a web of money-making that blinded him from seeing God. The little silver gods were pitiful things to stand between him and Jesus Christ.

Mahalia Jackson is quoted as saying, "God can make you anything you want to be, but you have to put everything in His hands."

Martin Luther said, "I have held many things in my hands, and I have lost them all; but whatever I have placed in God's hands, that I still possess."

Topics for Youth

PEER PRESSURE—Economic pressures were such that Demetrius and his friends felt they had no choice but to unite to eradicate the Christian element. Economic pressures don't affect young people nearly so much as *peer pressure*. Here's what one community is doing to combat the peer pressure among teenagers to drink alcohol.

"In a time when elementary students can buy Snoopy and Mickey Mouse acid stamps and 4 million twelve- to seventeen-year-olds regularly smoke pot, parents, educators and social agencies are banding together to stem the tide of drug and alcohol use.

"One of the most innovative programs is the Peer Group Training Project, the brainchild of Corner House counselor Sharon Powell (in Princeton, New

Jersey). According to Ms. Powell, the project enables high school freshmen to withstand pressure from their peers to drink—pressure that is hard for a teenager who wants to 'belong' to resist.

"This year, about twenty Princeton High juniors and seniors helped sixty incoming ninth graders each semester cope with the confusing issues of the formative years—sex, family relationships, behavior at parties. The 'peer leaders' are usually 'well-rounded and respected' and act as role models for freshmen seeking direction.

"One way the peer leaders convey their message is to stage improvised skits that duplicate that of awkward situations—family arguments, drinking and drug use—that teenagers face in life. These short but realistic 'slice of life' plays have been presented at several other local schools.

" 'I'm concerned when you have kids of fourteen and fifteen say you can't have a party without alcohol or pot present,' said Ms. Powell.

" 'I'm trying to create a situation where you can have a good time without these things. We hope to give the kids the self-confidence to say *no*.'

"The Peer Group Training Project was started in 1980 with a small grant from the state Department of Health. Working with teachers at Princeton High—which awards class credit to peer group participants—Ms. Powell's goal is to 'reach more kids as the years go by.'

"After peer pressure, experts say the second leading cause for teenage drug abuse is family problems. About 28 million children in the U.S. have at least one alcoholic parent." ("Battling Peer Pressure Is Key" by David Salowitz, *The Princeton Packet*, May 20, 1981, p. 1B, Princeton, N.J. Used with permission.)

LESSON 12   MAY 22

On Trial in Jerusalem

Background Scripture: Acts 21:1–26:32
Devotional Reading: Acts 21:7–14

Acts 22:30–23:11
- 30 On the morrow, because he would have known the certainty wherefore he was accused of the Jews, he loosed him from his bands, and commanded the chief priests and all their council to appear, and brought Paul down, and set him before them.
- 23:1 And Paul, earnestly beholding the council, said, Men and brethren, I have lived in all good conscience before God until this day.
- 2 And the high priest Ananias commanded them that stood by him to smite him on the mouth.

3 Then said Paul unto him, God shall smite thee, thou whited wall: for sittest thou to judge me after the law, and commandest me to be smitten contrary to the law?
4 And they that stood by said, Revilest thou God's high priest?
5 Then said Paul, I wist not, brethren, that he was the high priest: for it is written, Thou shalt not speak evil of the ruler of thy people.
6 But when Paul perceived that the one part were Sadducees, and the other Pharisees, he cried out in the council, Men and brethren, I am a Pharisee, the son of a Pharisee: of the hope and resurrection of the dead I am called in question.
7 And when he had so said, there arose a dissension between the Pharisees and the Sadducees: and the multitude was divided.
8 For the Sadducees say that there is no resurrection, neither angel, nor spirit: but the Pharisees confess both.
9 And there arose a great cry: and the scribes that were of the Pharisees' part arose, and strove, saying, We find no evil in this man: but if a spirit or an angel hath spoken to him, let us not fight against God.
10 And when there arose a great dissension, the chief captain, fearing lest Paul should have been pulled in pieces of them, commanded the soliders to go down, and to take him by force from among them, and to bring him into the castle.
11 And the night following the Lord stood by him, and said, Be of good cheer, Paul: for as thou hast testified of me in Jerusalem, so must thou bear witness also at Rome.

KEY VERSE: "I can do all things through Christ which strengtheneth me." Philippians 4:13.

Home Daily Bible Readings
May 16   M.   Paul's Journey to Jerusalem, Acts 21:1-6.
May 17   T.   The Warning of the Holy Spirit, Acts 21:7-15.
May 18   W.   Paul Rescued From the Mob, Acts 21:26-36.
May 19   T.   Paul Before the Sanhedrin, Acts 23:1-8.
May 20   F.   The Promise of the Lord, Acts 23:9-11.
May 21   S.   Paul's Defense Before Felix, Acts 24:10-21.
May 22   S.   Paul Appeals to Caesar, Acts 25:7-12.

Lesson Aim: That adult Christians should take steps to have and to maintain a clear conscience.

LESSON OUTLINE
Background to the Scripture
Looking at the Scripture Text
  I. Before God, a Clear Conscience (Acts 22:30—23:5)

II. Before Sanhedrin, a Wise Witness (Acts 23:6-10)
III. An Encouraging Night Visitor (Acts 23:11)
Applying the Scripture

Background to the Scripture
"If I forget thee, O Jerusalem," wrote the psalmist, "let my right hand forget her cunning. If I do not remember thee, let my tongue cleave to the roof of my mouth; if I prefer not Jerusalem above my chief joy" (Psalms 137:5, 6).

These words, written by a son or daughter of Israel in exile, must have described how Paul felt upon his return to the Holy City from his missionary journeys. There was probably a lump in his throat and perhaps tears were in his eyes as he caught sight of ancient Jerusalem after being away some eight years. Luke says the Christians greeted him gladly (21:17) in Jerusalem. Paul himself must have been overwhelmed with gratitude and joy.

But if his emotions were not pure joy, it was because of the dark cloud that hung over him. The Prophet Agabus had told Paul that if he went to Jerusalem he would be bound and given into the hands of the Gentiles—and so it happened. Jews spotted him in the Temple and dragged him out, thinking to get rid of Paul on the spot. And they would have succeeded, in all probability, were it not for the Roman authorities who once again were used of God to spare Paul's life. Carried from the Outer Court by the soldiers, Paul was allowed to address the crowd. But when he made mention of God's love for the Gentiles, they would listen no longer and so Paul was taken away. To him, "the Tower of Antonia was the one safe place in Jerusalem."

Looking at the Scripture Text
Before God, a Clear Conscience (22:30-23:5) On the day following the riot in Jerusalem, occasioned by Paul's speech, the chief Roman military officer called a meeting of the chief priests and the Jewish Sanhedrin. This tribune, named Claudius Lysias (23:26), surely had better reasons for this meeting than to satisfy his curiosity about Paul. He may have been required to file a report on his use of troops to stop mob action the day before. Or this examination might have been called to determine whether a trial was in order. In Paul's case, if he had violated the Jewish statutes in a matter recognized by Roman law, the Sanhedrin would try the case and issue a decision which, if the sentence were death, would have to be ratified by the Roman governor.

The Sanhedrin or council is named several times in the Gospels. As the chief judicial council of the Jews, it was at first comprised of seventy Levites, priests and chief fathers of Israel (2 Chronicles 19:5-11) under the high priest's executive leadership. As we learn later (v. 6) Pharisees and Sadducees made up the Sanhedrin in New Testament times. The Pharisees were the ultraconservative interpreters of the Law; the Sadducees were wealthy Jews who were in charge of Temple ritual and who "held themselves aloof from the masses and were unpopular with them" (Criswell).

Standing before this august body, Paul "looked intently" at their faces.

While some see in this an indication of Paul's poor eyesight, we have insufficient evidence to suggest such a meaning implied here. Rather, "a fixed steadfast gaze may be fairly called a characteristic of Paul," says one commentator.

Paul opened his defense with a declaration of his innocence. "I have lived in all good conscience before God (or, for the glory of God)," he declared. He knew they would judge otherwise, but this was his sincere position. We agree with Barnhouse that this was "a bold claim which few of us would dare to make."

The Ananias named here as the high priest is not the same one mentioned in the Gospels. This man served an unusually long tenure, from A.D. 47 or 48 to approximately 58, and according to early sources was a "notoriously unscrupulous and avaricious politician." His order that Paul be struck on the mouth is entirely in character with what is known of the man.

Why did he order Paul struck? Ananias considered Paul an apostate, and he could not allow an obviously flawed person to make such a statement of his innocence. Of course, his action shows that he had already judged Paul without hearing his side of things.

Paul's retort reminds us at once of our Lord's condemning words for the hypocritical Pharisees. He called them "whited sepulchres," from the practice of devout Jews. They whitewashed the grave markers so that no one would unexpectedly touch them and defile himself. The stones had a fair appearance, but inside were "dead men's bones" and corruption. This was an apt illustration of hypocrisy. Paul accused the high priest of hypocrisy because he who sat to judge according to the law violated the law by commanding that Paul be struck.

Paul's words, "God shall smite thee" expressed his firm belief that Ananias would not escape punishment for such actions. The manner in which the despised man died seems to bear out Paul's prediction. The *Expositor's Greek Testament* notes that "in A.D. 66, in the days of the last great revolt against the Romans, he (Ananias) was dragged from a sewer in which he had hidden, and was murdered by the weapons of the assassins whom in his own period of power he had not scrupled to employ."

Jesus was struck, as was Paul, when on trial—then before Annas (John 18:22). He did not remain silent, but insisted that He be proven wrong if His words were not true. Paul recovered gracefully from his sharp retort and showed an apologetic tone in his reply once he had learned that it was the high priest against whom he had spoken. The text he quoted is Exodus 22:28. We may see in his soft answer how he could claim to have lived in "all good conscience." The key was instant acknowledging of wrong. In this way, he could seek to fulfill his high goal to "have always a conscience void of offense toward God, and toward man" (24:16).

Before Sanhedrin, a Wise Witness (23:6-10) After Paul's opening statement and the sharp interaction that followed, the noise level in the room probably was elevated several degrees. This may explain why Paul "cried" or shouted in making his second remark.

As he stood before the council, he realized that though they presented a united front, they were not really a homogeneous body. The members of the Sanhedrin of Jesus' day had little in common but their antagonism to Jesus; these shared a common dislike for Paul, but that was about all. Knowing this, Paul next tossed a statement before them that landed like a live grenade in their midst.

"I am a Pharisee, the son of a Pharisee." As we noted in chapter 15, a number of Pharisees had become Christians. For a Pharisee to be born again would be similar to an orthodox Jew today becoming a messianic Jew, a "completed Jew." Paul could still call himself a Pharisee without denying his Lord. It was a wise tactic for the moment.

Also wise was his introduction of the Resurrection into the discussion. The NIV translates this difficult sentence: "I stand on trial because of my hope in the resurrection of the dead." Paul knew the Sadducees did not believe in the resurrection of the dead. The Gospels bear this out also (Matthew 22:23; Mark 12:18) as do the writings of the Jewish historian, Josephus—"the Sadducees reject the permanence or existence of the soul after death, and the rewards and punishments of an invisible world . . . the Sadducees hold that the souls of men perish with their bodies." This idea split the council into the two factions and, forgetting their common foe, they argued with one another.

Luke went on to add that the Sadducees did not believe in angels or "spirit" either—the use of the singular indicating a rejection of the realm of the spirit and thus "spirits." As one Bible student has said, "the faith of the Sadducees is well described by negations."

Paul's shrewd behavior before the council defeated the purpose of these men. How aptly does this illustrate what Jesus foretold when preparing the apostles for the times when they would be brought before "governors and kings as witnesses . . . whenever you are arrested and brought to trial, do not worry beforehand about what to say. Just say whatever is given you at the time, for it is not you speaking, but the Holy Spirit" (Mark 13:9, 11 NIV).

The Pharisees' concession to Paul (v. 9) is surprising. Luke says that over the noise of the debate the biblical scholars within the ranks of the Pharisees acknowledged that they had no objection to what Paul had said, probably an allusion to his public testimony given the day before. "We find no evil in this man," they said. They could not quite go along with Paul's assertion that he had seen Jesus the Messiah on the Damascus Road, but they were willing to allow that a spirit or perhaps an angel had spoken to him.

The words in the KJV "let us not fight against God" (v. 9) do not appear in the older manuscripts. They are almost identical with what Gamaliel said earlier (5:39) and may indeed have been copied into the text here to supply what seemed needed.

Watching the disarray among the Sanhedrin with initial curiosity was Lysias. The in-fighting may have amused him, although we think he had hoped that the issues about which the Jewish authorities differed with Paul would become clear. His concern grew as he observed the mood in the room turning violent. "Fearing lest Paul should have been pulled in pieces" by the council members, he ordered his troops to take Paul to safety. Luke notes that they had to do this "by force." Paul was kept in custody, probably in the Tower of Antonia, and Lysias thought he had his answer—the differences between Paul and the council were religious matters within the Jewish-Christian circle of things. To him, Paul had done no wrong and this he would write to the governor when, in a few days, he had to send Paul away for safety (*see* the letter he wrote to the governor in 23:26–30).

An Encouraging Night Visitor (v. 11)   Twice in two days Paul's life had been in grave danger. Twice he had been spared. As he paced the floor in the cell where he was kept in custody, he may well have wondered if he would ever realize his goal of preaching Christ in Rome. After all, it was *his* dream, *his* ambition—nothing in the scriptural record thus far shows that God had assured him of ever getting there. If he had known what plot some of the radical Jews were cooking up for him even then, he would have perhaps felt his chances were forever gone.

Yet we have no basis for thinking that Paul was discouraged. He had known what lay ahead of him in Jerusalem and so far the Lord had kept him safe. Perhaps he was communing with the Lord in prayer when suddenly the Lord "stood near" and said, "Be of good cheer." This was the second time since his conversion that Paul had received a vision of the Lord Jesus. This text does not say that Jesus appeared to Paul. His presence may have been known chiefly to his spirit and his mind. Once more, on the voyage to Rome, the Lord would again appear to encourage His servant (27:23, 24).

These appearances were timed to encourage Paul at critical times in his service. Here the Lord gave Paul a promise as He had done in the vision at Corinth. "You must also testify in Rome," He promised. Armed with that assurance, he knew he could face the future. With that the apostle fell into a restful sleep.

Applying the Scripture
Ask your class: Who can identify the man who said, "Labor to keep alive in your breast that little spark of celestial fire—conscience"?

Of course, *everybody* remembers that George Washington said that! You may want to turn to the section on "Illustrating the Scripture" for more quotations on this subject. But return to Washington's words. They remind us that in order to have a good conscience, as Paul claimed, effort must be exerted.

First, ask your class if they think it mattered very much for Paul to have a clear conscience. Have them visualize Paul standing before seventy of the most wealthy and influential of his contemporaries and consider whether he could have done what he did without a "good conscience."

The word *conscience* is one of Paul's favorites. Of the thirty times it appears in the New Testament, twenty-two times it is Paul who is using it. He spoke of a "weak conscience" that could be wounded by the uncaring and inconsiderate actions of others (1 Corinthians 8:12). He warned of unbelievers, especially hypocrites, whose conscience was "seared with a hot iron" (1 Timothy 4:2), noting that it is possible to trample conscience underfoot so that it loses its powers of sensibility. The writer to the Hebrews points out that only the blood of Christ can cleanse an "evil conscience" (Hebrews 10:22).

From this overview of what the Scripture says on the subject, we conclude that a conscience is of great importance, it can be harmed or rendered useless and it can be cultivated and nurtured. Ask your class what steps they think a person should take to insure that he has a "good conscience."

Some may suggest:

1. Believe on Christ and accept His forgiveness and cleansing so that our evil conscience—a conscience that keeps reminding us of our guilt and is not a reliable guide—may be washed clean.

2. Avoid questionable practices. Christians in Paul's day received his gentle rebuke for eating meat offered to idols. They knew, and Paul knew, that there was nothing wrong with the meat and that there was no such thing as an idol. But by their liberty, they were wounding the weak conscience of young Christians and weak brethren. If Paul could say that he would not eat meat if it caused a brother to stumble, then we should deny ourselves anything which could harm our fellow Christians.

3. Heed our conscience. The best way to keep the little voice of conscience speaking to us is for us to obey its impulses. In small matters—like giving money back to the cashier when she has made an error and given us more than she should, or putting coins in the parking meter, or exercising self-control when we are alone—we can keep the voice of conscience strong and clear.

4. Realize that conscience is not reliable. It often reflects the standards of society and culture. It needs to be trained by constant correction from God's Word.

Questions for Discussion
Make use of these questions to involve your students in learning and to test their understanding of the lesson.
1. Why was Paul in the custody of the Roman tribune? 2. Why do you think Ananias would order Paul to be slapped on the mouth? 3. Who in the New Testament was also struck on the mouth when on trial before the high priest? 4. How would you define "whited wall" as an expression used in that day? 5. How could Paul say that he was a Pharisee after he had become a Christian? 6. What did Paul do to divide the Sanhedrin so they could not achieve their purpose? 7. Who surprisingly came out on the side of the apostle in this pretrial examination?

Illustrating the Scripture
Examples and quotations to help the teacher communicate the lesson.

SAD—BUT TRUE! "Paul made what seemed to be a casual comment about 'the resurrection.' That did it! A 'dissension arose between the Pharisees and the Sadducees and the assembly was divided.' The next verse explains the theological difference.

"To understand what was happening, perhaps we can imagine a modern-day equivalent. Let's suppose a church meeting of some sort with religious people of various denominational persuasions present—Baptists, Presbyterians, Brethren, Lutherans, Roman Catholics, and so on. In the group is a man who has taken some very unpopular stands. The whole group of church people are challenging him. He realizes that he's outnumbered, so he decides on a clever subterfuge.

"He raises the question of baptism and the Lord's Supper. Immediately, the churchmen start to argue among themselves. The Baptists stand firmly on adult immersion. The covenant groups argue for infant baptism. The Brethren set forth trine-immersion. The Roman Catholics insist that baptism takes away original sin. And on the matter of communion, there is a further division over transubstantiation and consubstantiation, as well as the communion elements being just memorial emblems, etc. In short, there's a free-for-all, and the man upon whom all their wrath had been centered is forgotten in the melee.

"This is precisely what Paul did as he stood before the Sanhedren—drew their attention from himself to an internal battle on doctrine.... I've frequently said that no one can fight like church people. It's a sad testimony, but unfortunately true." (From *Acts, An Expositional Commentary* by Donald Grey Barnhouse with Herbert Henry Ehrenstein. Copyright © 1979 by Zondervan Corporation. Used by permission.)

QUOTES ON CONSCIENCE "Always let your conscience be your guide!"—Jiminy Cricket.

"Look to your health; and if you have it, praise God, and value it next to a good conscience"—Izaak Walton.

"Whose conscience with injustice is corrupted"—Shakespeare.

"O conscience, upright and stainless, how bitter a sting to thee is little fault!"—Dante.

"My conscience is captive to the Word of God"—Luther.

"A good conscience is a soft pillow"—Source unknown.

"A guilty conscience needs no accuser"—English proverb.

"He that loses his conscience has nothing left that is worth keeping"—Nicolas Caussin.

Topics for Youth

THE TRIAL OF JOHN—In 1415, John Hus was placed on trial as was Paul. Here is an account of the outcome:

"On the morning of July 6, Hus was ushered into the cathedral. There sat Prince Sigismund, who had been false to his solemn promises of protection. There were the cardinals and the bishops in their glorious robes. Hus was placed upon a high stool in the middle of the huge building. The Bishop of Lodi preached a funeral sermon saying that the blotting out of heretics was one of the works most pleasing to God. Thirty charges of heresy were read and when Hus attempted to speak he was ordered to remain silent. The vestments of a priest were hung upon his shoulders and a communion cup was placed in his hands. Then the priestly garments were removed one by one and the communion cup was torn from his fingers with the words, 'We take from thee, thou Judas, this cup of salvation!'

"This time the reply of Hus could be distinctly heard: 'But God does not take it from me, and I shall drink of it today in His Kingdom.'

"At length the proceeding came to an end. Attendants placed upon Hus's head a tall fool's cap decorated with a picture of three devils fighting for his soul, and the march to the place of execution began.... Aeneas Sylvius, who later became Pope Pius II, admits that 'not a word escaped him which gave indication of the least weakness.' Over the bridge went the procession to an open field outside the city. Here a post had been firmly driven into the ground. To this stake Hus was bound with wet ropes. Then straw and wood were piled up around him. Once more he was asked if he would recant. 'I shall die with joy,' he replied, 'in the faith of the gospel which I have preached.'

"An officer clapped his hands, and the burning torch was applied to the straw. As the flames flared up around him, Hus began to sing in Latin one of the chants of the church: 'Christ, Thou Son of the Living God, have mercy upon me!'" (From *Through Five Hundred Years* by Allen W. Schattschneider, Comenius Press, Bethlehem, Pennsylvania. Copyright 1956, 1974; used with permission.)

LESSON 13 MAY 29

Paul in Rome

Background Scripture: Acts 27, 28
Devotional Reading: Ephesians 4:1–6

Acts 28:11–23

11 And after three months we departed in a ship of Alexandria, which had wintered in the isle, whose sign was Castor and Pollux.
12 And landing at Syracuse, we tarried there three days.
13 And from thence we fetched a compass, and came to Rhegium: and after one day the south wind blew, and we came the next day to Puteoli:
14 Where we found brethren, and were desired to tarry with them seven days: and so we went toward Rome.
15 And from thence, when the brethren heard of us, they came to meet us as far as Appii forum, and The three taverns: whom when Paul saw, he thanked God, and took courage.

334 THE BOOK OF ACTS

16 And when we came to Rome, the centurion delivered the prisoners to the captain of the guard: but Paul was suffered to dwell by himself with a soldier that kept him.
17 And it came to pass, that after three days Paul called the chief of the Jews together: and when they were come together, he said unto them, Men and brethren, though I have committed nothing against the people, or customs of our fathers, yet was I delivered prisoner from Jerusalem into the hands of the Romans.
18 Who, when they had examined me, would have let me go, because there was no cause of death in me.
19 But when the Jews spake against it, I was constrained to appeal unto Caesar; not that I had ought to accuse my nation of.
20 For this cause therefore have I called for you, to see you, and to speak with you: because that for the hope of Israel I am bound with this chain.
21 And they said unto him, We neither received letters out of Judea concerning thee, neither any of the brethren that came shewed or spake any harm of thee.
22 But we desire to hear of thee what thou thinkest: for as concerning this sect, we know that every where it is spoken against.
23 And when they had appointed him a day, there came many to him into his lodging; to whom he expounded and testified the kingdom of God, persuading them concerning Jesus, both out of the law of Moses, and out of the prophets, from morning till evening.

KEY VERSE: "Be it known therefore unto you, that the salvation of God is sent unto the Gentiles, and that they will hear it." Acts 28:28.

Home Daily Bible Readings
May 23 M. The Dilemma of the Governor, Acts 25:21–27.
May 24 T. Paul's Advice to the Centurion, Acts 27:9–11.
May 25 W. A Word From the Lord, Acts 27:21–26.
May 26 T. Except These Abide in the Ship, Acts 27:27–36.
May 27 F. The Shipwreck, Acts 27:37–44.
May 28 S. On the Isle of Melita, Acts 28:1–7.
May 29 S. Paul's Ministry in Rome, Acts 28:30, 31.

Lesson Aim: That adult Christians will lay plans and execute an evangelistic outreach to some particular ethnic, religious, or age group in their community.

LESSON OUTLINE
Background to the Scripture
Looking at the Scripture Text

I. Excitement With Christian Believers (Acts 28:11-16)
II. Explanation to Jewish Brothers (Acts 28:17-22)
III. Exposition of Messianic Scriptures (Acts 28:23)
Applying the Scripture

Background to the Scripture

"The Rome of the Christian era had extended far beyond its ancient walls," says John Stirling, "and was spread over and beyond the 'seven hills' like an outbreak of unhealthy life. It was a vast dense mass of dwellings thrown together without order or beauty, and scarred by fires, earthquakes, and fevers. Through its narrow dirty streets, moved great crowds of patriots and adventurers, drawn from every nation by the fascination of its imperial position and exciting life. It was the treasure-house and theatre as well as the throne of the world.

"Paul's abode, in which he was allowed to preach to his visitors though a prisoner, was either near to the Praetorian barracks attached to the palace on the Palatine Hill, or to the Praetorian camp in the northeast of the city."

Paul arrived in Rome during the reign of Nero. Goodspeed dated the year A.D. 59. Others say 60, or 61. Though he was not at liberty to attend the Christian services, perhaps still held in house-churches, he was able to do what he most loved—proclaim Christ to all who came to him, including the several Roman guards posted beside him. Here his great pastor's heart poured out some of the Church's most treasured Christian teaching—the so-called prison epistles of Ephesians, Philippians, Colossians, and Philemon.

Looking at the Scripture Text

Excitement With Christian Believers (vv. 11-16)   How appropriately is this book named! Acts is filled with action clear to the end. As we open our Bibles to the final verses of this book, we begin reading a passage that falls hard on the heels of another dramatic action-packed story—that of shipwreck.

The vessel which carried 276 passengers, including Paul, Luke, and Aristarchus (27:2), left Caesarea and providentially came to Malta (Melita) in the middle of the Mediterranean after becoming lost in a terrible storm for fourteen days. Evidently the severe cold rendered sailing too treacherous in winter months, for they waited three months and then boarded an Egyptian ship whose crew had also wintered on the island. It was now, perhaps, late February or early March.

The pagan crewmen, soldiers, and prisoners who, like Paul, transferred to this ship, may have breathed easier when they saw its "sign" was Castor and Pollux. Ships in those days regularly sported a carved or painted figure on the prow and it is possible that the image of these "twin gods" or "Twin Brothers" appeared there. We know this pair today as Gemini. They were thought to "assist sailors in danger of shipwreck." For good reason, they "were the favorite gods of seamen," says one commentator.

These vain gods may have been all these sailors knew to trust. But it is not so today. Though the light of God's revelation has shined through His

Word and through His people in most of the world, even educated people prefer to check their horoscope and look for signs in the stars rather than in that revelation.

Aboard ship with Paul were an unknown number of other prisoners and possibly fare-paying passengers. The Roman centurion Julius, commander of the first ship, exercised control over this mixed group of his passengers by means of a band of soldiers.

From Malta, they traveled north to the island of Sicily, stopping three days at Syracuse (modern Siragossa), probably to await favorable winds. Then they proceeded to Rhegium on the toe of the boot of Italy and next shot a straight, swift course to Puteoli (modern Pozzuoli) on the western coastline, some eight miles from where Naples is today. Puteoli was the principal port south of Rome. From there the party could proceed by land. People in those days thought nothing of walking the 100 or so miles that yet remained to their destination.

"There we found some brothers" (v. 14 NIV), notes Luke. Their discovery of believers at Puteoli would not have been too surprising, given its prominence as a way-station for people traveling to Rome. One of the chief surprises God grants to His people in this life is that of finding "family" in places where they have never been. Some three years earlier, Paul had written his letter to the saints in Rome, more than acknowledging their existence—he was thanking God "because (their) faith is being reported all over the world" (Romans 1:8 NIV).

The believers at Puteoli prevailed upon Paul's group to remain with them a week, no doubt to partake of fellowship and worship together with all the believers there on the Lord's day. That he permitted Paul to interrupt the journey to Rome shows the respect Julius had acquired for the apostle.

Paul must have been anxious once the journey was resumed and especially as they reached the Appian Way which led directly to Rome. At one of the stations, the Appii Forum, approximately forty-three miles south of Rome, the first contingent of Christians from Rome met Paul's party. They would have heard of Paul's arrival while the apostle was enjoying the seven-day visit in Puteoli. Together they proceeded until reaching another station called Three Taverns where more believers were waiting for Paul. Luke notes the effect on Paul of seeing his brethren—Paul "thanked God, and took courage."

Next come those simple words—"we came to Rome." We think that Luke had been in Rome for a year or more when he wrote those words; otherwise it would seem to demand more emotion than he expresses here. "After all the conspiracies of the Jews who sought to take away his life, after the two years' delay at Caesarea, after the perils of that terrible shipwreck, in spite of the counsel of the soldiers to kill the prisoner, and in spite of the 'venomous beast,'—Paul came to Rome. The word of God, 'Thou must bear witness also at Rome' (23:11), had triumphed over all 'the power of the enemy' (Luke 10:19). And doubtless the hearts both of Paul and Luke beat quicker when they first caught sight of the city on the seven hills" (*Pulpit Commentary*).

Explanation to Jewish Brothers (vv. 17-22) We might think it highly unusual that the Roman authorities allowed Paul to live by himself, but this privilege was often granted prisoners who were not suspected of any violent crime. The words, "the centurion delivered the prisoners to the captain of the guard" are not found in most recent translations, indicating insufficient support for them in the best manuscripts. Actually the absence of those words, if correct, serves to show how Luke is solely concerned with tracking Paul's movements. As went Paul, so went the Church!

Evidently Paul's right arm was kept chained to the left arm of the guard who was with him. Being not able to go anywhere, Paul invited the heads of the Jewish community in Rome to come to him. Claudius had expelled all Jews from Rome (*see* 18:2) but his censure is thought to have expired in A.D. 54 when Nero became emperor. It was now approximately five years later and there were large numbers (v. 23) of Jews in the city.

It is remarkable to see Paul, having had nothing but abuse from his countrymen, now even as a prisoner seeking them out. The only explanation that is adequate is the one he gives in his letter to the Romans: "I am speaking the truth . . . I am not lying when I say how great is my sorrow, how endless the pain in my heart for my people, my own flesh and blood! For their sake I could wish that I myself were under God's curse . . ." (Romans 9:1-3 TEV).

"Superficially Paul came to Rome as a prisoner," says Macaulay. "Essentially he came as an *ambassador*." Watch how he goes about presenting the Gospel to his fellow Jews.

1. He took the initiative and called the leaders of the Jews to his apartment.

2. He declared his innocence. "I have done nothing against our people or against the customs of our ancestors" (v. 17 NIV). Also, he testified that they had found "no ground for putting me to death" (NASB).

3. He greatly understated the opposition directed toward him by the Jews—"the Jews objected" or "spake against" his possible acquittal by Festus. He had been at the point of death on numerous occasions because of Jewish opposition, but he would not so much as mention that because he wanted a hearing before the largest representation of Jews in Rome.

4. Paul assured them that if he were placed on trial or permitted to speak to the emperor, he would not use the occasion to bring any charge against "my own people." This was important, for the Jews still had to be very careful lest they bring down accusation on themselves from the Roman authorities. The *Pulpit Commentary* says that Paul "shows himself the constant friend of his own people." He had only appealed to Caesar for his own protection.

5. Finally, he identified his cause and his status as a prisoner with "the hope of Israel." Of course the hope of Israel is its Messiah—he would go into that before the whole assembly.

His Jewish guests were conciliatory. And they were evidently sincere in stating they had received no communication from Judea regarding Paul. The apostle had left Caesarea for Rome shortly after he appealed to Caesar and their party must have been one of the first ships to arrive in Italy after the winter. Little opportunity existed for them to receive a report on Paul.

The apostle's winsome and wise ways won for him the chance he had hoped for. "We want to hear what your views are," they said. He would have his opportunity to explain everything to their people. To these closed-mouth Jews, "the Way" was a "sect," literally a "heresy" which was generally "spoken against." Possibly they were referring only to its treatment by Jews, though it is true that Christians were increasingly being watched because they would not worship the emperor and because they held secret meetings.

Exposition of Messianic Scriptures (v. 23) On a day selected by the Jews' presiding officers, an official hearing took place. Whether this was in Paul's dwelling which he maintained for two years at his own expense (v. 30), or in a temporary lodging, Luke says "even larger numbers" (NIV) came to him. For a whole day and into the evening Paul—the experienced, brilliant, passionate preacher—"expounded and testified." That is, he preached an expository sermon, reasoning from Moses and from the prophets that the Messiah is Jesus; and he testified of the wondrous works He had done through His people.

Sadly, the results were identical to those on his missionary journeys. A few were convinced and believed, but most seemed to disagree. Before they left, Paul had the last word: "the salvation of God is sent unto the Gentiles, and . . . they will hear it" (v. 28).

According to Luke, Paul remained in Rome two years and preached and taught "without hindrance." Did he face a trial on this stay as a prisoner and then meet his death? Or was he released for possibly a further mission to Spain and elsewhere only to return to Rome and his execution? The question is still not settled. F. F. Bruce seems to lean toward the latter. Barnhouse came to the latter position and concludes that "Paul was martyred in the spring of A.D. 67, bringing to a close the career of one of the greatest minds of Christendom."

Applying the Scripture

Reserve at least five minutes at the end of the class period to consider the following questions and a unique but highly important application from today's lesson. Ask the class: How much of the blessing of God is being showered upon our church's evangelistic outreach? Are men and women of the community regularly being confronted with the claims of Jesus Christ?

When was the last time the church made a concerted effort to evangelize the community or a particular segment of it—children, high schoolers, an ethnic group, inmates of a nearby prison, military personnel?

Nothing can be more exciting than having a part in an evangelistic outreach of this kind. While it may be more than your Sunday School class alone can do, it could be that the class can "get the ball rolling."

From our lesson comes the inspiration for a united evangelistic outreach. Since it is always easier to launch a new venture of this kind if we can see how others did it, briefly remind the class of the important elements that led to Paul's "All-Day Exposition and Testimony" meeting.

1. *Find a common ground.* Paul's Jewishness gave him an understanding of

and an entree into the Jewish community. He knew that the Jews had a stake in what he had to say and that it would be possible for them to listen fully to him at least once.

2. *Timing.* Paul's fresh arrival from Judea was very important, probably more so than his identity, for the Jews at Rome did not seem to know much about him. In planning a large or a personal evangelistic appeal, the element of timing can be key. Perhaps if you are trying to reach an ethnic group, meetings could be planned around an important anniversary that is rich with meaning to that people. If you are trying to reach entering freshmen and women at the local college, a fall "Welcome to Our Town" affair may be useful. Strive to find elements that *make sense* to the group of people you are trying to reach, without raising unnecessary fears that they are going to be exploited.

3. *Be tactful.* Review quickly the five points in Paul's approach to the Jews at Rome. It looks easy when we first read it, but remember that Paul was a "pro"—he had learned much in years of experience. For this reason, you will want to depend upon some experienced Christians in the planning and execution of your outreach.

4. *Put the people in your debt.* By this, we mean that if you can put forth the effort to make those whom you are trying to reach feel somehow that they are your "guests," you may find them more receptive. Paul did this by having the whole group of them to come to his lodging. Since they stayed all day, he may have arranged to feed them the evening meal—but perhaps not. A simple comparison is the inviting of international students into one's home. There they share in the warmth of the family, learn about your culture, enjoy food the way you prepare it, and they can hardly refuse your tactful way of telling them the meaning of the Church and of your faith in Christ.

5. *Gear the presentation for the people you are trying to reach.* Paul spoke to them from the familiar Old Testament Scriptures. He had the same message at Athens and elsewhere, but the method was different. Know the group you are seeking to reach well enough (this goes back to No. 1, common ground) so that you can prepare your evangelistic outreach and present it on their "wave length."

In summary, these points are incomplete without prayer and adequate time to develop a strategy. This is more than your class time will provide, but you or someone in your class can be the spark to make this happen. Note: Paul did not win every Jew to Christ that heard him. But he was responsible to deliver the message. So, in your planning you should seek to be faithful to God's Spirit and leave the results to Him. This could become a regular evangelistic outreach and follow-up for your church people—if so, you are in for a rich experience.

Questions for Discussion
Make use of these questions to involve your students in learning and to test their understanding of the lesson.
1. Name two Christians who were traveling with Paul from Malta to Rome. 2. Why would the Christians at Rome be especially eager to see

Paul? 3. To what group of people did Paul want to speak soon after arriving? 4. In addressing the Jewish leaders, Paul took care to disarm any distrust they may have had toward him. Can you identify five precautionary measures he took? 5. From what the Jewish leaders said of the Christian faith, how was it being received or what was its reputation? 6. What did Paul hope to accomplish by addressing the Jewish people at large? 7. What results were achieved from Paul's all-day discourse with the Jews?

Illustrating the Scripture
Examples and quotations to help the teacher communicate the lesson.
"WE DEPARTED IN A SHIP ... WHOSE SIGN WAS CASTOR AND POLLUX" (v. 11).   People then, and people today, are still charting their lives by the stars. No wonder. Look what one "professor" promised to customers in a *National Enquirer* ad recently:

"Thanks to me you can fulfill your hopes. I will reveal to you the strengths in your secret personality and thanks to my help you will be overjoyed to receive at last and immediately all the things you have longed for so long in vain!

"Without asking a dime from you, I will prove this to you, by sending at your request *your free horoscope.* I will teach you how to be victorious in love, how to make money and be lucky. I will tell you the truth about the secret reasons for your problems and will teach you the secrets of instant success.

"I shall transform your life, making it happy and rich in fulfillment. I am not asking you for money. Your free personal horoscope will be mailed to you confidentially in a few days. So that you may live your life to the full and seize all the opportunities within your reach, send me...."

This man made more claims than our Savior Himself made!

Barnhouse wrote in his commentary on Romans:

"I recall one night noticing particularly the stars Castor and Pollux in the evening sky as I came out of my church. Every now and then in the winter season it is possible to see the great star Orion followed by Sirius the great dog star with Procyon heading off—the little dog heading off—toward Castor and Pollux.... The pagan world tried to live by the stars and their superstitions were all gathered about such things. Even in our day there are people who are caught up in this devilish astrology with their attempts to guide their daily lives by the so-called signs of the zodiac. The whole business is satanic and yet great numbers of people cannot take any important action or make any vital decision without consulting their horoscope."

"IT IS EVERYWHERE SPOKEN AGAINST"   The Jewish leaders at Rome told Paul that the way of Christ was a sect which was largely condemned. An English minister, Robert Tuck, catalogued some of the reasons for this in *Biblical Things Not Generally Known:*

"Christianity had enemies on all sides. It offended men by presenting a higher standard of purity than their own. The secrecy attending some portions of the Christian worship aroused suspicions....

"The Agapae (love feast), and the more sacred Supper, furnished material for some of the more horrible charges. It was said that when they met, an infant was brought in covered with flour, and then stabbed to death by a new convert, who was thus initiated in the mysteries. The others then ate the flesh, and licked up the blood. This was the sacrifice by which they were bound together.

"Another charge was that the members of a Christian church met at night, and after a certain time the lights were put out, and dreadful scenes of immorality ensued.

"Their holding aloof from all temples and altars brought on them the charge of Atheism, and it was actually declared that they worshipped their God under the mysterious form of a man with an ass's head."

Topics for Youth

SALVATION: ACCEPT OR REFUSE—"After Paul's day of teaching and persuading concerning Jesus, the Jews prepared to depart. As they were leaving, Paul said, 'Just one more word. Isaiah prophesied well concerning you. The Holy Spirit spoke through Him, saying that your ears and eyes would be closed to the truth, and that you would not be converted and saved, because your hearts were not open to receive God's truth. Now this salvation will be offered to the Gentiles and they will receive it.' These are the last recorded words of Paul. God dealt patiently with the Jews, for hundreds of years. Now He turned from them. The Jew had shut himself out, and the Gospel was passed to the Gentiles. It is seldom now that we see a Jew coming to Christ....

"Several years ago the submarine Squalus dove to the bottom of the Atlantic Ocean in two hundred and forty feet of water. The sailors soon discovered that the submarine was helpless. They could not bring it to the top.

"They sent up a chemical substance which made a red smudge upon the water, and later sent up a buoy. They were hoping that some ship would see their plight and come to their rescue. They realized that their help must come from above.

"Soon the submarine Sculpin set out in search of the Squalus. They found the red smudge and the buoy and knew that the other submarine was on the bottom of the sea at that point. Before they could get their rescue work going, twenty-four hours had passed by. Then they sent down a giant ten-ton diving bell, took out a few men, and brought them safely to the top. They kept this up until all thirty-three of the men on the Squalus were saved. Not one sailor refused to be rescued. All of them gladly accepted the way of salvation.

"How tragic it is when men refuse His way of salvation, when they pass up the only way they have to be saved. The Jews turned away that day when Paul preached, and as they did so they sounded their own death knell for time and for eternity." (From *Simple Sermons from the Book of Acts, Volume II*, by W. Herschel Ford, published by Zondervan Publishing House, copyright 1950; used with permission.)

This book contains lessons through August 1983. The Evangelical Teacher's Guide 1983–84, containing lessons from September 1983 through August 1984, is on sale now at your bookstore.

SUMMER
June, July, August

Old Testament Personalities

UNIT I

Persons Serving in Supportive Roles

LESSON 1 JUNE 5

Aaron: Spokesman and Priest

Background Scripture: Exodus 4:10–17, 27–31; 17:8–13; 28:1–4;
32:1–6; Leviticus 8:6–12; Numbers 20:22–29
Devotional Reading: Exodus 32:30–35

Exodus 4:14–16, 27–30; 17:9–13; 28:1–3

4:14 And the anger of the LORD was kindled against Moses, and he said, Is not Aaron the Levite thy brother? I know that he can speak well. And also, behold, he cometh forth to meet thee: and when he seeth thee, he will be glad in his heart.

15 And thou shalt speak unto him, and put words in his mouth: and I will be with thy mouth, and with his mouth, and will teach you what ye shall do.

16 And he shall be thy spokesman unto the people: and he shall be, even he shall be to thee instead of a mouth, and thou shalt be to him instead of God.

27 And the LORD said to Aaron, Go into the wilderness to meet Moses. And he went, and met him in the mount of God, and kissed him.

28 And Moses told Aaron all the words of the LORD who had sent him, and all the signs which he had commanded him.

29 And Moses and Aaron went and gathered together all the elders of the children of Israel:

30 And Aaron spake all the words which the LORD had spoken unto Moses, and did the signs in the sight of the people.

17:9 And Moses said unto Joshua, Choose us out men, and go out, fight with Amalek: to morrow I will stand on the top of the hill with the rod of God in mine hand.

10 So Joshua did as Moses had said to him, and fought with Amalek: and Moses, Aaron, and Hur went up to the top of the hill.

11 And it came to pass, when Moses held up his hand, that Israel prevailed: and when he let down his hand, Amalek prevailed.

12 But Moses' hands were heavy; and they took a stone, and put it under him, and he sat thereon; and Aaron and Hur stayed up his hands, the one on the one side, and the other on the other side; and his hands were steady until the going down of the sun.

13 And Joshua discomfited Amalek and his people with the edge of the sword.

28:1 And take thou unto thee Aaron thy brother, and his sons with him, from among the children of Israel, that he may minister unto me in the priest's office, even Aaron, Nadab and Abihu, Eleazar and Ithamar, Aaron's sons.

2 And thou shalt make holy garments for Aaron thy brother for glory and for beauty.

3 And thou shalt speak unto all that are wise hearted, whom I have filled with the spirit of wisdom, that they may make Aaron's garments to consecrate him, that he may minister unto me in the priest's office.

KEY VERSE: "And he shall be thy spokesman unto the people: and he shall be, even he shall be to thee instead of a mouth, and thou shalt be to him instead of God." Exodus 4:16.

Home Daily Bible Readings
May 30 M. Speaking for God, Exodus 4:10–12.
May 31 T. Willingness to Be Chosen, Exodus 4:12–17.
June 1 W. God's Credible Witness Through Persons, Exodus 4:27–31.
June 2 T. Obedience Brings Victory, Exodus 17:8–13.
June 3 F. Consecration Involves Community, Exodus 28:1–3.
June 4 S. Worshiping False Gods, Exodus 32:1–6.
June 5 S. Preparing for Ministry, Leviticus 8:6–12.

Lesson Aim: That adult Christians will be willing to take a supportive role with one of God's saints so that God's purposes may be achieved.

LESSON OUTLINE
Background to the Scripture
Looking at the Scripture Text
   I. Special Spokesman for Moses (Exodus 4:14–16)
  II. Committed Co-Worker With Moses (Exodus 4:27–30)
 III. Selfless Supporter of Moses (Exodus 17:9–13)
 IV. Consecrated Clergyman Beside Moses (Exodus 28:1–3)
Applying the Scripture

Background to the Scripture

It was September, the beginning of the school year, and Bill Grant, an entering freshman, was being shown around the campus. He entered one office in the Student Activities Center where there were several girls who knew his older sister, Nancy, a senior.

"Oh, so you're Nancy's kid brother," said one girl. After some small talk, Bill made his way to the door. As he did the girl who had greeted him earlier said, "Nice to meet you, Bill. Who knows, before the year's out you'll probably be so well-known that we'll be introducing Nancy as Bill Grant's sister!"

Well, Bill says it never happened. Some people will always be known in certain circles as "Nancy's brother." Aaron was just such a person. Never anywhere has Moses ever been called, "Aaron's brother"! In our opening text there it is—*"your brother Aaron."*

A lot of people go through life known by their association with someone else. Most especially is this true of women who, until the seventies, were always referred to as "the wife of. . . ." But these people are unique individuals. Getting to know these "lesser lights" is often a discovery of a truly wonderful personality. In this lesson and the following three, we will have opportunity to know this sort of individual.

Looking at the Scripture Text

Special Spokesman for Moses (4:14–16) Moses was on the hot spot. And it was not because the fire burning in the bush was out of control.

Rather, the Lord's anger was about out of control. The Lord had just revealed to Moses that the cry of the Hebrew nation in slavery in Egypt had "come up to" Him and He was acting to deliver His people. *And*, Moses was going to be His chosen instrument to accomplish the deliverance.

To that Moses produced a laundry list of excuses why he was not the one for the task—"Why me?"—"What if they want to know Who You are?"—"What if they won't believe me?"—"I am slow of speech"—*"please send someone else to do it"* (4:13 NIV).

Patiently the Lord dealt with each argument (vv. 3:10–4:12). He knew what He would do about Moses' lack of eloquence. He who "gave man his mouth" would enable Moses to speak such as he never imagined. That is plainly inferred from the context. But since Moses was in no mood to even go back to Egypt, the Lord countered his latest objection by providing another person—Aaron. This was an alternate plan and not the original, but it was to prove a good plan.

The opening reference to Aaron shows us that he was Moses' brother, he could speak well, and he was already on his way to meet Moses. From elsewhere in the Pentateuch, we learn that both he and Moses were sons of Amram and Jochebed, that Miriam was their sister, and that Aaron was eighty-three, three years older than Moses. Aaron had a wife and four sons, one of whom was Eleazar who would become high priest when Aaron died forty years later.

The writer of Exodus was inspired to specially designate Aaron as "the Levite." While some scholars jump on this epithet as a sure sign that Moses could not have written Exodus, and say that it has to date to a period after the priestly tribe was well established, other interpreters do not agree. It is possible that Moses could have so referred to Aaron late in life or that possibly a scribe was authorized later to add the designation, "the Levite."

Taking all of the biblical account into consideration, Aaron is best known as "the Levite," the first head of the Hebrew priesthood. But this and three more "scenes" from his life will reveal other dimensions to his personality as well.

At Horeb, "the mount of God" (3:1) in the Sinai region, the Lord told Moses how the two would work together. "Thou shalt speak unto him, and put words in his mouth . . . and he shall be thy spokesman unto the people. . . ." By declaring that He would teach them what to do, the Lord was saying that He would make His revelations to Moses who would tell everything to Aaron who in turn would speak to the people of Israel or to Pharaoh.

Modern translations help clarify the meaning of verse 16 considerably. The NIV says, for example, "it will be as if he were your mouth and as if you were God to him." Instead of receiving inspiration directly from God, Aaron would receive it through Moses; so, Moses would be like God to him. The *New Bible Commentary, Revised*, notes that this is a clear example of what revelation is, "verbal disclosure both of what God wishes to teach to the unknowing, and also of inspiration and communication . . . sovereignly superintended by God so that what He chooses to reveal may be infallibly communicated."

Committed Co-Worker With Moses (vv. 27–30) In Egypt, the Lord spoke by some means to Aaron, calling him just as certainly as He did Moses. From what we have read already, this "call" occurred before Jehovah appeared to Moses. Aaron perhaps was already planning to go to Midian to see his brother who had been gone forty years. To his credit, he did go immediately when the Lord spoke to him. From the context, it appears that Moses had begun his trek to Egypt but had not gone far because Aaron found him "in the mount of God" (v. 27). Just prior to Aaron's appearance, Moses' wife and sons are mentioned. Moses may have sent his family back to their own people at this time (*see* 18:2–4) for no mention is made of them in Egypt or until the whole nation of Israel reached Sinai.

Aaron "kissed" Moses. The two had not seen each other for so very long. If this expression seems odd to us, we should recall the same show of affection when Jacob and Esau were reunited, and when Joseph revealed himself to his brothers.

From Moses, Aaron learned the true nature of their mission. The journey back to Goshen would allow the two time to talk and think of everything the Lord had revealed to Moses (v. 28). Hard-headed Moses began to believe God as he threw down his rod to show Aaron how it instantly became a serpent, and as he showed him what happened when he put his hand in the folds of his robe (4:6, 7). Gradually God gave to them a strong confidence that He would deliver Israel and just as gradually their two hearts began to beat as one. Aaron immediately executed his office as mouthpiece for Moses when they held their first meeting with the elders of Israel. He spoke and he performed signs. And as they shared their noble vision with the elders, the crowd swelled until a large number of Israelites had assembled. Moses says they "believed." That fact, coupled with his faith and Aaron's obedience marked the turning of the tide in Egypt.

Selfless Supporter of Moses (17:9–13) Months, perhaps a year, had passed since the Lord had formed Aaron and Moses into a team to lead His people. This third "scene" takes place in the desert as they approached Mount Sinai where they would camp. Confronted by the warring desert marauders, the Amalekites, Moses ordered Joshua to choose soldiers and to attack.

Israel was not armed well at all and at this early juncture they knew little about battle tactics. But they did know that Moses' rod held awesome powers. Just days before, Moses had struck the rock on the desert floor and water immediately bubbled forth to slake their thirst. At the Red Sea, the waters had obeyed Moses' outstretched rod as had the elements and creatures when the ten plagues fell upon Egypt. No wonder that it seemed enough to Joshua for Moses to say: "I will stand on the top of the hill with the rod of God in mine hand."

What followed is well-known. Joshua led his men into battle and Moses stood on a hill nearby, perhaps in view, and held high the rod. But anyone who has ever tried such a thing knows that the arms tire quickly. And when Moses dropped his hand, the battle went against Israel. With Moses on that hill were Aaron and Hur, who may have been Miriam's husband. The two of them sat Moses on a stone and then they held up his hands "steady till sunset. So Joshua overcame the Amalekite army with the sword" (v. 13 NIV).

This story is often used to illustrate the power of intercessory prayer. Moses with his hands outstretched toward God typifies the believer whose strong intercession impacts decidedly upon the outcome of the battle somewhere in the world. But it is equally a picture of the validity of "helping hands." Aaron and Hur made the difference, by their actions. They were willing to do something mundane, something "stupid" in order that a wicked enemy would be defeated. For their selfless, thankless task they earned as much of the reward for victory as did Joshua. They remind us to be faithful in "that which is least."

Consecrated Clergyman Beside Moses (28:1-3) One never knows to what an instance of initial obedience to God will lead. David went to play his harp for the king and ended up becoming king; Esther volunteered for the king's beauty contest and lived to save her people. When Aaron went without hesitation to meet Moses in the desert, he learned that he was to serve as Moses' spokesman. But if he thought the duties of his office were all fulfilled in Pharaoh's court, he was to learn that that was but a prelude to his highest calling. The Lord had revealed to Moses the Law and given him the plan for the tabernacle. But priests were required, and here Aaron entered into his true ministry. He became the first high priest of Israel and as such foreshadowed the Messiah, "a great high priest" (Hebrews 4:14), the Lord Jesus Christ.

The chief duty of Aaron was to "minister unto" the Lord (28:1). No service, no calling could be more exalted. Aaron would be the one man in all Israel trusted with the responsibility of the blood atonement, securing Israel's perennial forgiveness and keeping the way open for God's mercy to flow on His people rather than His wrath.

Because of the exalted duties of their office, Aaron and his sons were to wear especially designed clothing—"sacred garments." These were to be created by wise-hearted men particularly gifted by the Lord for their task. Aaron and his sons and the high priest after him would wear the colorful ephod and breastpiece, the robe and turban, so that the people would look on them and their office with greater reverence. They were worn for their "beauty" as well. The multi-colored curtains of the tabernacle and the lovely golden furnishings speak of the love of beauty of our great God and Creator.

Applying the Scripture
Teacher: For this lesson you will need a mouthpiece of some kind to help impress today's truth on the minds of those in your class. See if you can bring to class a mouthpiece—for a horn, or a telephone, even a microphone will do!

As you conclude the Bible lesson and turn to the application, ask your class what office in the spiritual community of Israel did Moses occupy. If your students answer "prophet," they are correct. Moses was the prophet, but he truly needed a mouthpiece, a spokesman, and Aaron was that person.

Next question: Ask your class who in the church (meaning the local church) most often fills the role of prophet today? The pastor or minister or priest, will likely be their answer.

Now, think aloud of the ways your minister may need a spokesman, a mouthpiece. The dictionary definition of a mouthpiece is "someone who speaks for others." At first, it may seem that your minister does not need anyone to serve as his mouthpiece, but encourage discussion of this subject.

Dr. Louis H. Evans, a beloved and longtime Presbyterian pastor, wrote in the preface of his book *Your Marriage—Duel or Duet?* these words: "In appreciation—my sincere appreciation is extended to Mrs. Julia M. C. Drake who during the writing of this book has been a most resourceful and helpful research secretary. Her tireless and efficient search for and arrangement of materials have been of inestimable help to me in the preparing of these messages."

Dr. Evans was such a highly qualified and capable minister that he didn't need someone to do his speaking for him, and most ministers do not. But his acknowledgment shows that Mrs. Drake was like Aaron at his side. Without her aid, he could not have spoken the Word of the Lord, to so many people and for so long a time. (The book was published twenty years ago, yet it still communicates effectively.) Now, this may help us discover areas where our minister may need a spokesman—an Aaron.

Does your pastor have anyone who records his messages so that he could prepare them for publication either in tract form or in a book? If not, he may need an Aaron. Does he have anyone who can devote the hours to transcribing his taped messages so that he can edit them and prepare them for some use in print, to bless not just the congregation, but perhaps thousands of men and women? If not, there's room for another Aaron. Lead a discussion in class of the ways your class members can be *Aarons* and help extend the message of Christ out to the community.

Obviously, there are some people who cannot help in the typing or transcribing of messages. Discuss other ways that an adult can support the minister (or ministers if your church has several ministers serving the congregation) and thus help win the victory. Remember Aaron and Hur, standing there for hours holding up Moses' weary hands. That should help open up the discussion to mundane, ordinary, even "stupid" things that can help the minister, like babysitting his children so that he and his wife can have an evening together—or volunteering to call on all of the first-time visitors to the church and give him a report of those whom he should call on—or putting together that program or ministry for youth or the elderly or for singles which you know is on his heart, but for which he has no time.

Close with a prayer that all in your class may first be willing to say yes to the voice of God now speaking to them, and second, that each will surrender his or her life anew to be a supportive Christian to the prophet in their midst.

Questions for Discussion
Make use of these questions to involve your students in learning and to test their understanding of the lesson.
1. Where was Moses when the Lord revealed to him that Aaron was to go with him? 2. Why did the Lord send Aaron to accompany Moses on his mission to deliver Israel? 3. Did Aaron learn of his role from the Lord, or from Moses? 4. What is the meaning of the words "thou shalt be to him instead of God"? 5. What "signs" would Moses tell and show to Aaron? 6. What is symbolized by the holding up of Moses' hands? 7. Can you name at least two reasons why the priests were to be clothed in beautiful garments?

Illustrating the Scripture
Examples and quotations to help the teacher communicate the lesson.
A SECOND-BEST ARRANGEMENT? "The appointment of Aaron as spokesman to his brother, while in one view of it an act of condescension, and a removal of Moses' difficulty, was in another aspect of it a punishment of his disobedience. It took from Moses the privilege of speaking for God in his own person, and committed the delivery of the message to more eloquent, perhaps, but also to less sanctified lips.

"The arrangement had its advantages. It supplied one's defect by another's gift, it utilized a talent lying unemployed, it gave Aaron a share in the honor of being God's messenger, and it formed a new link of sympathy between the brothers.

"But it was not the best.

"It prevented the development of the gift of speech in Moses himself. Had he relied on God's promise, he would doubtless have acquired a power of speech to which he was at first a stranger.

"The message would lose in force by being delivered through an intermediary. This of necessity. How much of the power of speech lies in its being a direct emanation from the mind and heart of the speaker—something instinct with his own personality! As delivered by Aaron, the messages of God would lose much of their impressiveness. Fluency has its disadvantages. A mind burdened with its message, and struggling with words to give it utterance, conveys a greater impression of force than ready delivery charged with a message that is not its own.

"Moses would be hampered in his work by the constancy of his dependence on Aaron. It limits a man, when he cannot act without continually calling in another to his assistance.

"It divided Moses' authority, and gave Aaron an undue influence with the people (*see* Exodus 32).

"It was a temptation to Aaron himself to assume, or at least aspire to, greater authority than of right belonged to him (*see* Numbers 12).

"We must learn that it is not always good for us to have our wishes granted. God sometimes punishes us by granting us our wishes. His way is ever the best" (*Pulpit Commentary*).

"ALWAYS HOLDING SOMEBODY UP" When Dawson Trotman drowned in Schroon Lake in 1956, the caption under his picture in *Time* magazine read, "Always holding somebody up." This man, who Billy Graham said had influenced his life more than any other man, is best known for his enthusiastic and thorough work in discipling men which led to the formation of the worldwide Navigators organization. He was always in the background in the Billy Graham organization, but his creation and development of follow-up and counseling served as a model that is now used by churches on every continent. Yet he was hardly a household name. At Schroon Lake, when a young person who could not swim was thrown overboard, fifty-year-old Trotman dived in and tried to save her life. The girl's life was spared, but Trotman could no longer stay afloat. He literally died "holding somebody up." He was a follower in the footsteps of Aaron.

Topics for Youth

HOLD HIGH YOUR HANDS—Just for fun, have the young people hold up their hands. See who can hold up his hand for the longest period of time. You might suggest that they start when you reach the point in the lesson dealing with Aaron and Hur holding up the hands of Moses. Tell them that they should surely be able to do as well as Moses, for they are in practice. Don't they raise their hands in class every day, and sometimes have to hold their hands up high for what seems like a long time until they get their teacher's attention?

Of course, they will be doing well if they are able to hold up their hands for more than a few minutes. It's very tiring!

You might conclude this "acting out" of the classroom lesson by having one boy or girl serve as Moses and have two others stand, one on each side, and hold up that person's hands while the class proceeds. Then have someone read Ecclesiastes 4:9, 10, 12—"Two are better off than one, because together they can work more effectively. If one of them falls down, the other can help him up. But if someone is alone and falls, it's just too bad, because there is no one to help him. . . . Two men can resist an attack that would defeat one man alone. A rope made of three cords is hard to break" (TEV).

"I WILL GO DOWN, BUT YOU MUST HOLD THE ROPES!"—William Carey, a shoe cobbler in England, faced insurmountable odds as he made his plans to go to India with the Gospel. The time was near the end of the eighteenth century. He reasoned that if the East India Company could travel as far as India for mercenary reasons, the church could surely go in obedience to Christ's command. But the leaders of the church told him to stay put.

"When God gets ready to convert the heathen He will do it without either your help or mine!" they said.

But Carey would not be denied. He went to India—to learn Bengali and thirty-nine other languages and to leave the Word of God in many tongues in that nation. But his parting words to his faithful church members were, "I will go down, but you must hold the ropes." It was an obvious allusion to Psalm 40 and to the experience of Jeremiah who, when found by a friend in a deep pit, was raised out of the pit by ropes. As the church identified with Carey's achievements by their prayers and sacrificial gifts, so we today can be a part of the missionary task also, by "holding the ropes."

LESSON 2   JUNE 12

Jethro: Wise Adviser

Background Scripture: Exodus 2:15b–3:1; 4:18; 18:1–27
Devotional Reading: John 1:43–51

Exodus 18:13–24

13 And it came to pass on the morrow, that Moses sat to judge the people: and the people stood by Moses from the morning unto the evening.

14 And when Moses' father in law saw all that he did to the people, he said, What is this thing that thou doest to the people? why sittest thou thyself alone, and all the people stand by thee from morning unto even?

15 And Moses said unto his father in law, Because the people come unto me to enquire of God:

16 When they have a matter, they come unto me; and I judge between one and another, and I do make them know the statutes of God, and his laws.

17 And Moses' father in law said unto him, The thing that thou doest is not good.

18 Thou wilt surely wear away, both thou, and this people that is with thee: for this thing is too heavy for thee; thou art not able to perform it thyself alone.

19 Hearken now unto my voice, I will give thee counsel, and God shall be with thee: Be thou for the people to God-ward, that thou mayest bring the causes unto God:

20 And thou shalt teach them ordinances and laws, and shalt shew them the way wherein they must walk, and the work that they must do.

21 Moreover thou shalt provide out of all the people able men, such as fear God, men of truth, hating covetousness; and place such over them, to be rulers of thousands, and rulers of hundreds, rulers of fifties, and rulers of tens:

22 And let them judge the people at all seasons: and it shall be, that every great matter they shall bring unto thee, but every small matter they shall judge: so shall it be easier for thyself, and they shall bear the burden with thee.

23 If thou shalt do this thing, and God command thee so, then thou shalt be able to endure, and all this people shall also go to their place in peace.

24 So Moses hearkened to the voice of his father in law, and did all that he had said.

KEY VERSE: "Thou wilt surely wear away, both thou, and this people that is with thee: for this thing is too heavy for thee; thou art not able to perform it thyself alone." Exodus 18:18.

Home Daily Bible Readings
June 6 M. Caring for Others, Exodus 2:17-21.
June 7 T. Meeting God in Daily Life, Exodus 3:1.
June 8 W. Recognizing the Signs of God, Exodus 4:8.
June 9 T. Rejoicing in Deliverance, Exodus 18:1-12.
June 10 F. The Good Stewardship of Time, Exodus 18:13-27.
June 11 S. Responsible Decision Making, Exodus 18:19-28.
June 12 S. Delegating Authority, Exodus 18:24-27.

Lesson Aim: That adult Christians will be sensitive to situations around them that need to be changed.

LESSON OUTLINE
Background to the Scripture
Looking at the Scripture Text
  I. Moses' Method of Judging (Exodus 18:13-16)
  II. Jethro's Insight and Input (Exodus 18:17-20)
  III. The Heart of Jethro's Plan (Exodus 18:21-23)
  IV. The Happy Outcome (Exodus 18:24)
Applying the Scripture

Background to the Scripture

If you were to suggest to any group—even to a class of Bible students—that they discuss the story of Jethro, you would probably be met with an assortment of wrinkled brows, head-scratching, and squirming in the chairs. Obviously, Jethro is one whose supporting role hardly made his name a household word.

He was a desert-dwelling, idol-worshiping priest of the Midianite people when first we encounter him. Moses had escaped from Egypt and found refuge with Jethro's family in the Sinai. Because he had helped Jethro's seven daughters, Moses was welcomed to stay and was given one of the daughters, Zipporah, to be his wife. Moses herded Jethro's sheep and remained forty years with his father-in-law and when the Lord sent him back to Egypt, he left his wife Zipporah and their two sons with Jethro.

As the early verses of chapter 18 show, Jethro reappeared for a brief visit with Moses shortly after the Lord had delivered Israel at the Red Sea. The occasion seems to be that he was bringing Zipporah and the sons, Gershom and Eliezer, to Moses. Jethro may have anticipated an enjoyable social visit, and he was not disappointed. But he himself was profoundly affected and his sage counsel dramatically altered the way Israel governed its day-to-day affairs from that time on.

Looking at the Scripture Text

Moses' Method of Judging (vv. 13-16) Upon Jethro's arrival in the Israelite camp, Moses took him to his tent where he rehearsed all that Jehovah "had done to Pharaoh and the Egyptians for Israel's sake" (v. 8 NIV). He also shared news of the "hardships" they had encountered, giving glory to the Lord for saving them.

All of the translations say that Jethro "rejoiced" (v. 9) on hearing this. But according to Jewish sources, the meaning is "he circumcised himself" or "he felt stinging in his flesh," meaning that "he was sorry for the loss of the Egyptians, his former coreligionists."

Being in the presence of so great a multitude—an estimated 600,000 people—who were obviously ecstatic about the great wonders the Lord had done among them, overwhelmed poor Jethro. He doubtless felt that his religion of idols and superstition was piddling stuff compared with Jehovah. When Moses witnessed to him all that the Lord had done, Jethro spontaneously burst out with praise to the Lord (vv. 10, 11). His adoration of the Lord above other gods and his subsequent offering of sacrifices may indicate a true change of heart had taken place. At least he had taken a step toward Jehovah.

Moses might well have used the occasion of Jethro's arrival as an excuse for a holiday, at least for himself. But Moses was truly dedicated to the well-being of the people. When the sun rose the next morning, he knew where his duty lay. The King James Version says he "sat to judge the people."

Judges customarily held court at the gates of the city in Old Testament times, but, lacking a settled city, Moses probably sat at the door of his tent. Already, in the brief time since the nation had left Egypt, the people's disputes were so numerous that a great crowd stood all day, waiting to see Moses. There may be something to the suggestion that the division of the spoils of victory after Israel defeated the Amalekites (17:8-13) suddenly led to a large number of disputes among the people. Jethro observed this throughout the day and may have waited until sundown to ask Moses:

"What is this you are doing for the people? Why do you alone sit to judge, while all these people stand around you from morning till evening?" (v. 14 NIV).

An outsider sometimes can see fatal flaws in a situation long before the people who are in the midst of the situation. We can get so close to the trees that we do not see the forest! The brilliant are no less susceptible to this blindness than anyone else as Moses' case proves. Without any apology, he tells Jethro that in this manner the people learned the will of God.

The Law had not yet been given. The people did not have direct access to the Lord. Rather, they sought one whom "they regarded as entitled to speak for God" (*Pulpit Commentary*). As Moses decided each case, he was establishing legal precedent for how such matters were to be handled in the future.

Jethro's Insight and Input (vv. 17-20) Jethro could see that Moses was going about this in the wrong way and he bluntly told him so.

Reason No. 1 Moses himself would "wear away." "The work is too heavy for you" (NIV). He observed that no one could sit all day and listen to case after case without being mentally exhausted and emotionally drained. A steady diet of this would surely have a harmful effect on the health of Moses whose vital leadership had to be preserved for the welfare of the nation. "Earnestness kills itself with excess of work."

Reason No. 2 The people would eventually lose patience at having to wait so long for a decision. Many, seeing that they might have to wait for days, would either take matters into their own hands or try to ignore the problem only to have it become worse.

If we question whether Jethro could come to such insights after observing Moses for only a day, we must remember that Jethro had had forty years to observe Moses. If Moses was highly conscientious, forgetting himself for the good of others, Jethro would know it. A man on fire with the zeal of heaven easily loses perspective on the mundane necessities of life, such as rest, proper nourishment, and change of activity. Jethro was a man Moses needed for his own self-preservation.

The plan Jethro was to suggest is known to have been practiced in Egypt. Moses would have observed the kings there making the laws and leaving the determination of individual cases to the judges. Probably he happened on his own method by accident and with so much occupying his mind, he failed to see that there could be a better way.

A large part of Jethro's wisdom is seen in the approach he made to Moses. He asked him to listen, trying to win a hearing for what he had to say. He even seemed to pray: "may God be with you" (v. 19 NIV). And he began by reenforcing the continued role of Moses as "the people's representative before God" (the NIV's rendition of "be thou for the people to God-ward").

His advice follows in two parts. First, Moses should continue to be their teacher. Jethro probably recognized that God had anointed Moses for the work of prophet and that no one could do what he was doing—showing them "the way to live and the duties they are to perform." Second, he advised a division of labor, a delegation of authority. If Moses had not been commanded by the Lord to use his method—and he was not—and he obviously could not do it by himself for too long, then others should share in the awesome burdens he carried. Jethro's advice harmonizes with the truth which centuries later the Holy Spirit spoke to the church at Antioch: "Separate me Barnabas and Saul. . . ." And it harmonizes with the truth Paul would give to the Church: "Bear ye one another's burdens."

The Heart of Jethro's Plan (vv. 21-23) The specific directions Jethro gave to Moses seem possible only from one who has observed such a plan in operation. Commentators suggest that Arab tribes of the desert must have used such a method of deciding disputes as Jethro was to advise.

"Provide out of all the people able men"—the judges or rulers or magistrates to be appointed were to come from the whole nation Israel. Every tribe would be equally involved. In fact, the "rulers of thousands . . . hundreds . . . fifties . . . tens" would be chosen from within the tribes and would serve their own people.

If we count the first quality—"able men"—then Jethro was saying that four characteristics were necessary in the men chosen to judge Israel. If we consider that as a general description summing up the character of such men, then the three qualities are—"piety, veracity, and strict honesty" (*Pulpit Commentary*). The seventeenth century commentator Matthew Poole pointed out that by "able" Jethro meant "greatness, resolution, courage and constancy of mind."

The first quality named is the fear of God. In giving that priority, Jethro may be showing something of the reverence for the true Lord of the universe which he has so lately gained himself. This is the quality of knowing that one acts in the place of God and that God sees everything that one does. This is the guard against *partiality*.

By "men of truth" is meant "trustworthy men." This is the quality of "diligent labor to find the truth in all cases" and is the guard against *deceit*. The third quality so essential to a judge is "men who cannot be bribed." Note the force of language describing all three radical qualities, particularly this one—"hating covetousness." The men Jethro intended would not be temptable by any offer of dishonest gain. This is the guard against *fraud*.

The Living Bible shows how the hierarchy of Jethro's method would be structured: "One judge for each 1000 people; he in turn will have ten judges under him, each in charge of a hundred; and under each of them will be two judges, each responsible for the affairs of fifty people; and each of them will have five judges beneath him, each counseling ten persons" (v. 21). A threefold appeal system seems built into the plan.

Jethro's final logical advice was that Moses should delegate every dispute possible to these judges. The goals of his advice were two, enabling Moses to endure the strain of leadership and ensuring that the people received a satisfactory judgment and returned "to their place," that is, to home "in peace."

The Happy Outcome (v. 24)   To his credit, Moses did not say to Jethro: "But we've always done it this way," the seven deadliest words any church can utter. Instead, he proved the meekness for which he is known by paying attention ("hearkened") and doing *"all* that he had said."

In later life, Moses described how he went about appointing the rulers Jethro had suggested. In Deuteronomy 1:9–18, we read that he readily admitted "how can I bear your problems and your burdens and your disputes all by myself?" (NIV). Showing that he was not threatened by Jethro's advice, Moses asked the people themselves to choose "wise, understanding and respected men" from their tribes and the people heartily approved. Those whom they nominated Moses appointed and several instances are given of their service (Deuteronomy 16:18, 17:9, 19:17).

Applying the Scripture

Suggest to your class that they may want to take two courses of action in applying today's lesson—in true workaholic fashion! Or they may want to select one and give it their attention in the same manner Moses "hearkened" to what Jethro said and did all that he recommended.

1.   An executive of Life Savers, Inc., the candy company, stood in church to say that 80 percent of all his company's business was done with 20 percent of their customers. "It's about the same way in the church," he continued. "I believe at least 80 percent of all the work in our congregation—teaching, music-making, bookkeeping, prayer-attending, visit-going, nursery-tending, and so on—is done by no more than 20 percent of the congregation."

Does this sound familiar? It probably describes the balance of workers/nonworkers in most churches. If this hits home to your class, then suggest that this lesson can act as a double-edged sword, cutting to the root of a serious problem and having two results. Obviously, there are some who are not bearing their share of the load and others who are trying to do too much.

Begin with the easier corrective. Suggest that each member of the class assume the role of Jethro in the church during the next month. Urge them to be sensitive to situations that are crying for change, people who need some "wise advice" to delegate some of their work so that they do not burn out and become discouraged and drop out of active church life altogether. Remember to stress that if they do the work of Jethro they will succeed with *a tactful, humble approach!*

Suggest to the conscientious ones who are holding down five jobs that they do not have to do it that way. In the congregation, there are able men and women. Many of these would be eager to help if only they were asked. This is a serious problem. Every week in most churches someone is complaining because he or she has too much work thrust upon them; these people need help and the church can prosper if all of the people's talents and energies are harnessed.

2.   A second application is suggested by the scene we glimpse early in this

passage—that of a thronging line of people waiting for their "day in court." If there is something hauntingly familiar about this picture it is because in virtually every one of our municipalities, people are waiting in confinement for their cases to come to trial. And they are not waiting for only a few days as the people of Israel did before seeing Moses. They are waiting months, even years. And our Constitution guarantees the right to a speedy trial!

This should be a concern of God's people because we are called to establish justice and compassion in the land. You may want to open this issue up for discussion or call a meeting of those interested during the week, to explore ways to help speed criminal and civil justice in your town or city or state. This is admittedly a tough problem, but with the aid of God's Spirit, expect a modern-day Jethro to give wise advice!

Questions for Discussion
Make use of these questions to involve your students in learning and to test their understanding of the lesson.
1. Who was Jethro and what was so unusual about his being in the camp of the Israelites?   2. What is the meaning of the words in verse 13, "Moses sat"?   3. How did the people receive answers from God to their questions in those days?   4. Explain the meaning of the words in verse 19, "be thou for the people God-ward"?   5. What does Jethro's advice have to say to the "workaholic syndrome" so many of us are caught up in today?   6. What two results did Jethro think his counsel might achieve?   7. What four qualities did Jethro recommend that Moses should seek in the rulers he appointed among the people? Are these still relevant for the Church and civil government today?

Illustrating the Scripture
Examples and quotations to help the teacher communicate the lesson.

THE EGYPTIAN FIGURE OF JUSTICE   Deuteronomy 1:9–18 is a fine cross reference to be shared with the class in discussing this lesson. Particularly note verse 17 as it details what sort of men Moses chose to be judges in Israel: "Do not show partiality in judging; hear both small and great alike. Do not be afraid of any man, for judgment belongs to God. Bring me any case too hard for you, and I will hear it" (NIV).

From *540 Little Known Facts About the Bible* comes this information about the Egyptian figure of justice, rendering the kind of judgment sought by Moses.

"She was symbolized by a human form, without hands, to indicate that judges should accept no bribes; and not without hands only, but sightless, to indicate that the judge is to know neither father nor mother, nor wife nor child, nor brother nor sister, nor slave nor sovereign, nor friend nor foe, when he occupies the seat of justice. He is not to be the client, but only to hear the cause; and, uninfluenced by fear or favor, to decide the case upon its merits."

THE NEED FOR BALANCE   The advice of Dr. Bertram S. Brown, senior psychiatrist at the RAND Corporation, may be as beneficial to workaholics in the Church as it was to the United States congressmen for whom it was intended.

"The first thing they (congressmen) have to do is recognize the need for balance in their lives in the face of pressures toward imbalance.

"I recommend that no less than one quarter of their time be devoted to personal and family concerns. If they do that, they will be able to utilize the other three quarters of their time twice as effectively. If you have a husband or wife that loves you, a reasonable personal and sexual life and children who give you a sense of satisfaction, you're going to be a better congressman or executive-branch official.

". . . In the executive situation, a very special stress comes from workaholic bosses who are demanding and know no limits. You may have a superior who wants all of your time and 100 percent plus of effort. If there's absolutely no way out of the 100 percent effort, then you have to set a time limit for how long you are going to stay in the job—perhaps two years, and no more than four. If you go beyond four years, you can write off personal and family life." (From an interview with Dr. Bertram S. Brown in "Why So Many Public Officials Go Astray" in *U.S. News & World Report*, February 16, 1981.)

A Baptist church in Somerset County in New Jersey learned how to prevent "lawnmower burnout" while keeping up the four acres of lawn surrounding the church. When the aged riding mower conked out, John, the young layman who was tending to the mowing, suddenly faced the unwelcome task of walking a small push mower across much of the lawn. But he was wise enough to know that he could ruin such a small mower if he operated it constantly for several hours. The solution: two push mowers. While one was cooling in the shade, he could use the other and neither would become overheated.

That may be a good parable for a lot of the Johns and Janes in the churches!

Topics for Youth

YOUTH CAN BE A JETHRO ALSO—Paul had something to say about young people taking part in important matters. He would say that a young person is not too young to serve as a Jethro, to give sound advice. "Don't let anyone think little of you because you are young," wrote Paul to Timothy. "Be their ideal; let them follow the way you teach and live; be a pattern for them in your love, your faith, and your clean thoughts" (1 Timothy 4:12 TLB).

Encourage your young people to speak out and not be silent when they see things being done in the wrong way. Some of the "ways we've always done things" need changing and only a young person or a newcomer to the congregation can see the situation as it really is.

But as each coin has two sides, the coin of wise counsel has another side to it also—those who want to give advice should be willing to receive advice.

Ask your young people to explain their reaction the last time their mother or father gave them some advice. Did they listen attentively and "hearken" to the advice of their elders or were they anxious for it to be over, hardly heeding what the other person had to say? If you encourage the young people to speak up, they should have plenty to say on this subject.

Point out how Moses was the recognized leader of the huge nation of Israel. That Jethro had not even been a worshiper of Jehovah. That Jethro was an outsider and possibly an "old fogey." But Moses listened and carried out what Jethro recommended.

Console your youth by what the Earl of Chesterfield said: "Advice is seldom welcome; and those who want (need) it most always like it least." But liking the advice of others, especially our parents, is worth working at!

LESSON 3   JUNE 19

Caleb: Loyal and Patient

Background Scripture: Numbers 13:1–6, 30–33; 14:24; 32:10–12; Joshua 14:6–15
Devotional Reading: Acts 11:19–26

Numbers 13:30–33; 14:24; 32:10–12; Joshua 14:8, 9.

13:30 And Caleb stilled the people before Moses, and said, Let us go up at once, and possess it; for we are well able to overcome it.

31 But the men that went up with him said, We be not able to go up against the people; for they are stronger than we.

32 And they brought up an evil report of the land which they had searched unto the children of Israel, saying, The land, through which we have gone to search it, is a land that eateth up the inhabitants thereof; and all the people that we saw in it are men of a great stature.

33 And there we saw the giants, the sons of Anak, which come of the giants: and we were in our own sight as grasshoppers, and so we were in their sight.

14:24 But my servant Caleb, because he had another spirit with him, and hath followed me fully, him will I bring into the land whereinto he went; and his seed shall possess it.

32:10 And the LORD's anger was kindled the same time, and he sware, saying,

11 Surely none of the men that came up out of Egypt, from twenty years old and upward, shall see the land which I sware unto Abraham, unto Isaac, and unto Jacob; because they have not wholly followed me:

12 Save Caleb the son of Jephunneh the Kenezite, and Joshua

Joshua 14:8 Nevertheless my brethren that went up with me made the heart of the people melt: but I wholly followed the LORD my God.

9 And Moses sware on that day, saying, Surely the land whereon thy feet have trodden shall be thine inheritance, and thy children's for ever, because thou hast wholly followed the LORD my God.

KEY VERSE: "Surely the land whereon thy feet have trodden shall be thine inheritance, and thy children's for ever, because thou hast wholly followed the LORD my God." Joshua 14:9.

Home Daily Bible Readings
June 13   M.   Spies Sent to Canaan, Numbers 13:1-3, 17-20b.
June 14   T.   An Evil Report of the Land, Numbers 13:20c-33.
June 15   W.   The Challenge of Caleb and Joshua, Numbers 14:1-10a.
June 16   T.   God's Promise Regarding Caleb, Numbers 14:10b-24.
June 17   F.   God Recognizes Caleb's Faith, Numbers 32:10-15.
June 18   S.   Hebron Given to Caleb, Joshua 14:6-14.
June 19   S.   Prayer for Deliverance, Psalm 142.

Lesson Aim: As a result of the class, adults should be able to overcome a particular obstacle which they now face.

LESSON OUTLINE
Background to the Scripture
Looking at the Scripture Text
  I. A Courageous Call (Numbers 13:30-33)
 II. A Different Spirit (Numbers 14:24)
III. A Wholehearted Commitment (Numbers 32:10-12)
IV. A Patient Servant (Joshua 14:8, 9)
Applying the Scripture

Background to the Scripture

In three scenes taken from different points in his life, Caleb emerges as a true patriot, a "faithful follower." He won by his faith the distinction of being one of only two men from all of Israel's adult population to enter the Promised Land. We are more familiar with Joshua, the other man so singly honored by the Lord. But who was Caleb?

The fullest description of Caleb's origin is found in our text—"the son of Jephunneh the Kenezite" (Numbers 32:12). Twice in Genesis the Kenizzites or Kenaz are named. If the Kenizzites of Genesis 15:19 are the same people as mentioned in Numbers, then Caleb's ancestors were already in Palestine in Abraham's day. If they are the offspring of Prince Kenaz (Genesis 36:11, 15), then Caleb would be a descendant of Esau the Edomite. Either way, he was not a Hebrew, of the lineage of Jacob. Apparently Caleb's father or grandfather merged the clan with the Hebrew nation and at some point adopted Israel as their own people.

Caleb was born and grew to maturity in Egypt where he was recognized as an outstanding and promising member of the tribe of Judah. When Israel reached southern Canaan and Moses chose a man from each tribe to explore the land, Caleb was chosen to represent the tribe of Judah. It remained for this adopted son to excel and show himself a "model of unbending integrity."

Looking at the Scripture Text

A Courageous Call (Numbers 13:30-33) We can well imagine the highly charged atmosphere in the camp when the men chosen to explore Canaan returned after forty days. The first spokesman for the spies gave a "yes, but" report. *Yes,* the "land . . . does flow with milk and honey! Here is its fruit!" (v. 27 NIV). With that they held up the largest cluster of grapes any of them had ever seen (v. 23). *But,* they added, the cities of Canaan are strongly fortified and the people are giants.

Although Moses does not say so, there must have been a tremendous uproar at this time. But Caleb could not stand to hear the people complain and grumble. We imagine that God gave Caleb a booming voice and with that voice he calmed the people. "Let us go up *at once,*" he urged. "We are well able to overcome (take possession of) it (the land)."

As we read on, we learn that Caleb was not alone. Joshua also pleaded with the people to enter the land the Lord had promised them. But Joshua did not speak now. As chief minister to Moses, he would be expected to mouth what Moses wanted to hear and so Caleb may have been chosen deliberately to represent what quickly showed itself to be the minority view.

The other members of the exploratory party drowned out Caleb's words and the people were naturally swayed to listen to ten men rather than one. The picture these men portrayed of Canaan was frightening—and false.

"They are stronger than we are." About this statement the *Pulpit Commentary* notes: "In point of numbers the enormous superiority of the Israelites over any combination likely to oppose them must have been evident to the most cowardly. But the existence of numerous walled and fortified towns was (apart from Divine aid) an almost insuperable obstacle to a people wholly ignorant of artillery or of seige operations." Those two factors—that the cities were walled and that "all the people we saw there are of great size" (v. 32 NIV)—are reasonable cause for fear. But not for a people whose God had rescued them from Pharaoh and provided water out of the rocks and manna from heaven. But, of course, they were not now looking to God for help.

A closer look shows that the ten spies exaggerated what they had seen. "The land . . . eateth up the inhabitants thereof" (v. 32), or, as the NEB has it, "the country . . . will swallow up any who go to live in it." This expression sounds incredibly ridiculous to our minds. The TEV seems to attempt to cloak it with serious meaning: "that land doesn't even produce enough to feed the people who live there." But such an interpretation runs against the stated abundance of the land's crops (v. 27).

Several interpreters suggest that what is meant, rather, is the incessant civil strife in Palestine. The population continually changed as marauding tribes swept in from the surrounding desert and displaced other tribes. "The history of Palestine from first to last testifies to the constant presence of this danger. The remarkable variations in the lists of tribes inhabiting Canaan may be thus accounted for," says the *Pulpit Commentary*.

"*All* the people . . . are men of great stature," they said. If their report was true, the ones who recorded Israel's conquest of Canaan forty years later would have said so. But few giants are mentioned. This is another instance of the ten men determining to deceive the people. They "made the heart of the people melt" (Joshua 14:8). They even resorted to scare tactics, linking these imaginary giants to the giants or "Nephilim" (v. 33 NIV) named in Genesis 6:4.

A Different Spirit (14:24) Just how courageous Caleb's call was to Israel can be seen from what followed that night. The people, their hopes dashed to pieces, "wept that night" (14:1). Moses and Aaron prostrated themselves before the gathered assembly while Joshua joined Caleb in trying to convince people that the land was truly good. Far from it eating up the people, "we will swallow them up" they said (v. 9 NIV). "If the Lord is pleased with us, he will lead us into that land . . . and will give it to us" (v. 8 NIV). But the people were in no mood to listen. They were almost ready to stone Joshua and Caleb when suddenly "the glory of the Lord appeared at the Tent of Meeting" (v. 10 NIV).

While the Lord remained in the camp, He said, "But because my servant Caleb has a different spirit and follows me wholeheartedly, I will bring him into the land he went to, and his descendants will inherit it" (v. 24 NIV).

Note the singular way in which the Lord described Caleb. This man might not have been able to trace his family roots very far in Israel's past, but his staunch loyalty to God in the midst of overwhelming opposition won for him the designation, "my servant." The one quality for which Caleb is recognized again and again in Scripture is here given: he "follows me wholeheartedly," said Jehovah. But these words connote an outer, observable way of living. What secret inner quality lay at the heart of this complete devotion? The Scripture says that Caleb "has a different spirit."

This can mean that Caleb was motivated by an entirely different attitude. Or it could mean that the Holy Spirit was active in Caleb's life. The Spirit is "wholly other" or "different" from the spirit of rebellion which worked in the children of Israel. The Living Bible says Caleb was "a different kind of man." He was not worldly, selfish or proud. It would be a wonderful thing to have it said of any of us by the Lord that we are *His servant*, that *we follow Him wholeheartedly*, and that we *have a different spirit*.

A Wholehearted Commitment (32:10–12) Almost forty years later something happened which caused Moses again to recall Caleb's singular devotion to the Lord. The central figure throughout this period of Israel's history was Moses. Sharing the leadership with him were Aaron, now dead and replaced by Eleazar, and Joshua. Nothing is said of Caleb. But he has undoubtedly continued to live up to his reputation. He may well have been one of the judges appointed after Jethro counseled Moses. But that was many years earlier. By this time all of the adults who had rebelled against the Lord had died. Time for possessing the land was near.

While Israel camped near the Jordan River, two of the tribes set their hearts on the region of Gilead to be their land. Reuben and Gad considered that territory choice pastureland for grazing their herds and flocks. The only problem was that the land was on the east bank of the Jordan and Israel had been commanded to possess Canaan west of the Jordan and the Dead Sea.

Moses gave in to their request for the land once he learned that the men of Reuben and Gad would fight with Israel in Canaan until they had broken the back of Canaanite resistance and all the tribes were ready to disperse to their allotted lands. But at first Moses was incensed by the request. Thinking Reuben and Gad were not going to enter Canaan, he was reminded of the time when the spies deterred the whole nation from quickly possessing the land.

At that time, he told the men of Gad and Reuben, "the Lord's anger was kindled." The instances when God revealed His wrath were not many in Moses' lifetime compared with the daily outpourings of His mercy, but Moses never forgot those instances. Perhaps in our time, being constantly reminded of the love of God, we would do well to remember the Lord's hatred of sin and His anger at rebellion. Moses told these men that in His wrath God swore not to allow any Israelite men or women of twenty years of age or older to see Canaan because "they did not remain loyal to me" (TEV). But He made an exception in the case of Caleb and Joshua. The reason—"they wholly followed the Lord." Five times in today's Scripture selections those words appear. What a tribute to Caleb's loyalty! And what a challenge to us to wholly follow Christ today.

A Patient Servant (Joshua 14:8, 9) In this final scene from Caleb's life, the patient loyalty of "my servant" Caleb is rewarded. This ought to encourage us who still walk on through discouraging circumstances, and perhaps amid unbelief, not to lose heart.

The setting of this scene is central Canaan. Israel has scattered her enemies and the time has come to allot the land to the various tribes. Up from the tents of Judah, to see the elder statesman Joshua, walks none other than Caleb to claim what is his. "Here I am today, eighty-five years old! . . . now give me this hill country that the Lord promised me that day" (vv. 10, 12 NIV). Forty-five years earlier he had not been fazed by the giants of Anak who dwelled in Canaan. Now he was given the opportunity of further showing that the God in whom he trusted was able. The fifteenth chapter tells how the city of Hebron, where Abraham first worshiped God in Canaan, was allotted to Caleb. He proceeded to rout three sons of Anak from the hill country and gave his daughter Acsah to the man who captured the city of Kiriath Sepher. He left an indelible impression upon future generations. Harper's Dictionary says, "The Calebites became one of the most important elements in the tribe of Judah." All because one man wholly followed the true and living God.

Applying the Scripture

Teacher: You and your students may remember the lesson from Paul's life in a previous study dealing with the supreme necessity of maintaining a clean conscience. This lesson can be a follow-up on that, as well as serve as a motivator for any in the class who feel the need for more courage.

1. A student of the Bible said of Caleb, "there was a moral unity in Caleb's life. He had obeyed the voice of conscience and discharged manfully the sacred responsibility that was imposed on him forty-five years ago, and now he feels the recollection to be stimulating and strengthening to him. He has been lost to us through all the intermediate time (after the failed exploration by the spies until the conquest of Canaan) but we may be sure that his life in the desert, as a leader of the great tribe of Judah, had sustained the reputation of early days."

Discuss in class the implications for our lives of obeying the voice of conscience through the years when no one apparently notices. Ask if someone will share how the memory of some obedience, either to a parent or to a superior at work, or to the Lord, stimulated them later to live nobly and even gave them more energy to attack a large obstacle in their life.

2. The aim of this lesson is to help each adult overcome a particular obstacle which he or she may be facing.

Ask someone in class to define the obstacle which Caleb faced. Someone might say, "The whole nation Israel was an obstacle for him." Another might say, "He faced the tremendous pressure to conform his report of what he saw in Canaan to that which the other ten said." No matter how we word it, the fact is: Caleb faced a formidable problem and he could have lost his life defending his viewpoint.

Now, ask the class members to think about the one problem or obstacle which each of them faces. You might suggest some:

- A salesman may lack the confidence in himself to succeed at his work.
- A woman or man engaged to be married may fear that their marriage will be an unhappy one.
- Some class members may be out of work and feel discouraged. They do not know why they cannot get a job and they are beginning to feel as if the problem is "them."

If you can, provide a slip of paper and a pen or pencil for each class member. Ask them to write on a piece of paper in one sentence the obstacle which they most fear or which most intimidates them.

Now ask them to write or print below that statement the words of the Key Verse in today's lesson. Have them write it out from the Bible version they prefer, but by all means expect them to write it out while in class.

Finally, challenge each class member to follow the pattern of Caleb and wholly believe God to give them the victory. Urge each one to memorize the Bible verse and claim God's promise daily.

Questions for Discussion
Make use of these questions to involve your students in learning and to test their understanding of the lesson.
1. What had transpired to make it necessary for Caleb to calm the commotion in the camp of Israel? 2. How do you account for two such totally different reports as the two groups of spies gave? 3. The Israelites must have greatly outnumbered the Canaanite tribes. What two factors might have made the spies so afraid of launching a campaign in Canaan? 4. How could Caleb and Joshua be so positive in their report and recommendation? 5. One expression is continually used in speaking of Caleb. What is it and what is meant by it? 6. What great promise did the Lord make to Joshua and Caleb? Why? 7. How long did Caleb have to wait before this promise was fulfilled?

Illustrating the Scripture
Examples and quotations to help the teacher communicate the lesson.
LIFE BEGINS AT EIGHTY—OR IS IT EIGHTY-FIVE? Caleb has a lot of companions today in the group of those whose lives are vibrant in the eighth decade. The Rev. Martin Luther King, Sr., eighty-two, who travels at least twice a month speaking throughout the country, says, "I don't want to stop and just dry up, so I stay active and on the go." Dr. Benjamin E. Mays, eighty-five, became the first elected black president of the Atlanta Board of Education. Vocalist Alberta Hunter, eighty-six, performed two shows a night, five nights a week in 1981 in the Cookery in Greenwich Village, returning to the stage after working as a nurse for twenty years.

A LESSON IN PATIENCE "Years ago I remember seeing a cartoon that showed a farmer with sickle in hand, standing waist-deep in a field of wheat. One hand was over his eyes as he was looking far out on the horizon for signs of the coming of the Lord. Yet all around him stood ripened grain ready for the harvest.

"I'm afraid this tendency is often found among God's people. Too many of us today are standing idly by with eyes gazing heavenward instead of putting in the sickle. Just what should our attitude be in view of the coming of Christ? We believe he is returning to take unto himself his bride, the church, whose membership will be called out of every language group on earth (Revelation 5:9). In light of this, what should our attitude be?

"In James, chapter five, we read, 'Be patient . . . for the coming of the Lord draweth nigh.' One day the Lord indelibly impressed upon me this lesson of patience. It had been my privilege to translate the New Testament into the Cakchiquel language after which God had said to me, 'Move on! Other tribes need the Word.' My first wife was still living and she was in bed with heart trouble. Day after day I was cooking, washing dishes and sweeping floors, all the while longing to go to the uttermost part of the world.

"That day, reading chapter one of Colossians, I came upon this verse, 'Strengthened with all might, according to his glorious power' . . . and I thought, 'This marvelous might and power must be for getting to the tribes that have never been reached—in impossible situations, inaccessible areas. To give them the Word will require his strengthening us "with all might." ' But I read on '. . . unto all patience and long-suffering with joyfulness.' Patience! I wanted to pioneer, but the Lord knew that I needed his strength to get a little joy out of washing dishes." (From "Come, Lord Jesus," by William Cameron Townsend, *Translation*, March–April 1974.)

Like Caleb of old, "Uncle Cam" Townsend at age eighty-four continues to pioneer. In 1980, he and his second wife, Elaine, made their eighth trip to the Soviet Union in the interest of Bible translation for the U.S.S.R.'s minority groups.

Topics for Youth

A FINGER GAME—It was said of Caleb and Joshua, "they wholly followed the Lord." Five times this phrase is used in today's lesson. Have one youth find the five places and read them to the class.

Now note—there are five words in this phrase. To help each one remember the central truth of today's lesson, have each young person draw an outline of his hand and fingers by placing his hand flat on a piece of typewriter paper and tracing an outline. When the tracing is done, have each person write the five words of this phrase over the five fingers on the paper, printing one word across each finger. Now have someone turn to Ecclesiastes 9:10 and read the verse.

A Bible student has said, "Every victory of our better nature over the power of meaner motives lays the foundation for further and completer victories. Even the memory of it becomes an inspiration and a strength to us. The fruit of it is seen after many days. Accustom yourself to do the right and to 'follow wholly' the path the Lord your God marks out, and there shall be stored up within you a fund of strength that will enable you to look calmly in the face of the most formidable difficulties—to storm the strongholds of the Anakims and 'drive them out.' "

The Bible student quotes the following verse: "Our deeds still travel with us from afar, And what we have been makes us what we are" (author unknown).

List the following five characteristics on the chalkboard: independence, truth, courage, unselfishness, wholehearted devotion to God.

Now ask: Which of these characteristics would you like to have in your life? Don't let the youth be satisfied with less than all five! All five of these were present in the life of Caleb, and we can have them in our lives, if we, like Caleb, "wholly follow" the Lord. "Devotion to God makes us independent of men, true in the light of His searching eye, brave with trust in His help and unselfish in obedience to His will. Half-hearted devotion fails of this. We must serve God wholly if we would grow strong and true and brave."

LESSON 4   JUNE 26

Deborah: Supporter and Leader

Background Scripture: Judges 4, 5
Devotional Reading: Acts 16:11–15

Judges 4:4–9, 14–16; 5:1–3

4 And Deborah, a prophetess, the wife of Lapidoth, she judged Israel at that time.

5 And she dwelt under the palm tree of Deborah between Ramah and Bethel in mount Ephraim: and the children of Israel came up to her for judgment.

6 And she sent and called Barak the son of Abinoam out of Kedesh-naphtali, and said unto him, Hath not the Lord God of Israel commanded, saying, Go and draw toward mount Tabor, and take with thee ten thousand men of the children of Naphtali and of the children of Zebulun?

7 And I will draw unto thee to the river Kishon Sisera, the captain of Jabin's army, with his chariots and his multitude; and I will deliver him into thine hand.

8 And Barak said unto her, If thou wilt go with me, then I will go: but if thou wilt not go with me, then I will not go.

9 And she said, I will surely go with thee: notwithstanding the journey that thou takest shall not be for thine honour; for the Lord shall sell Sisera into the hand of a woman. And Deborah arose, and went with Barak to Kedesh.

14 And Deborah said unto Barak, Up; for this is the day in which the Lord hath delivered Sisera into thine hand: is not the Lord gone out before thee? So Barak went down from mount Tabor, and ten thousand men after him.

15 And the Lord discomfited Sisera, and all his chariots, and all his host, with the edge of the sword before Barak; so that Sisera lighted down off his chariot, and fled away on his feet.

16 But Barak pursued after the chariots, and after the host, unto Haro-

sheth of the Gentiles: and all the host of Sisera fell upon the edge of the sword; and there was not a man left.

5:1 Then sang Deborah and Barak the son of Abinoam on that day, saying,

2 Praise ye the LORD for the avenging of Israel, when the people willingly offered themselves.

3 Hear, O ye kings; give ear, O ye princes; I even I, will sing unto the LORD; I will sing praise to the LORD God of Israel.

KEY VERSE: "If thou wilt go with me, then I will go: but if thou wilt not go with me, then I will not go." Judges 4:8.

Home Daily Bible Readings
June 20 M. The Canaanite Oppression, Judges 4:1–3.
June 21 T. Deborah and Barak, Judges 4:4–9.
June 22 W. Defeat of the Canaanites, Judges 4:10–16.
June 23 T. The End of Sisera, Judges 4:17–22.
June 24 F. God Is Our Refuge and Strength, Psalms 46:1–7.
June 25 S. Deborah and Barak Thank the Lord, Joshua 5:1–5.
June 26 S. Bless the Lord for Victory, Judges 5:6–18.

Lesson Aim: As a result of this study, adult Christians ought to be willing to offer their support sacrificially to some other person to help that person achieve a goal for the glory of God.

LESSON OUTLINE
Background to the Scripture
Looking at the Scripture Text
 I. For Deborah, the Battle Plan (Judges 4:4–9)
 II. For Barak, the Battle Victory (Judges 4:14–16)
 III. For Jehovah, the Honor and Glory (Judges 5:1–3)
Applying the Scripture

Background to the Scripture

For the final lesson in this series on persons in supportive roles, it will be helpful to have a map of Palestine handy for classroom use. If your classroom is not blessed with a wall map, have the members of your class turn to the back of their Bibles to the maps there. Have them look for the map of Palestine showing Canaan divided among the twelve tribes.

Last week's lesson climaxed at Hebron in the South. Have your students put their finger on Hebron, just west of the Dead Sea. Now ask them to move their finger up, past Jerusalem, to the town of Bethel. This would be near the tribal name—Ephraim. See how many can also find Ramah, near Bethel. In this region, Deborah lived and judged Israel in the mid-twelfth century B.C.

Having found Deborah's headquarters, again move your finger up to the northern region above the Sea of Galilee (called the Sea of Chinnereth then) until you find the prominent city of Hazor. This was home base for Jabin, the Canaanite king who lorded it over Israel. North of Hazor find Kedesh, the home of Barak who would join Deborah in battle and in judging the nation. Finally, place your finger on Mt. Tabor, just west of the Sea of Galilee's southernmost point, and the River Kishon further west of Tabor. Now we have located the principal sites of action in today's lesson.

Looking at the Scripture Text

For Deborah, the Battle Plan (4:4-9) In the corporate offices of one of America's leading pharmaceutical companies in the East, an executive secretary pasted the following words in plain view on a filing cabinet near her desk: "A woman has to do twice as much as a man to be considered half as good. Fortunately, *it isn't difficult."*

Women have been put down as inferior to men ever since the Fall. It is the most common form of discrimination, to hold certain prejudices against the "weaker sex." Fortunately for woman, she has never had to fear discrimination from the most powerful and important source, the triune God. Our Lord Jesus while on earth demonstrated the high respect God the Father has for woman. And the Holy Spirit still surprises mankind by showing that before God, man and woman are on equal ground with unlimited resources of mind, body, and spirit.

Fortunately for Israel the Holy Spirit, being no respecter of persons, came upon a woman of the tribe of Ephraim for a high responsibility. We know nothing of the childhood and family life of Deborah. The writer of Judges was intent only upon making a record of the major achievements of the various judges and for the sake of recording them all did not concern himself with details of their personal lives. We can be thankful for two golden chapters that tell of Deborah and Barak.

By first describing Deborah as a prophetess, the writer places the emphasis on her relationship with the Lord. Not every one had the Holy Spirit, and very few women in the Old Testament were prophetesses. Besides Deborah, only Miriam and Huldah are named (Exodus 15:20; 2 Kings 22:14). A prophet was one to whom the Lord had given the gift of prophecy, to have special knowledge and to speak for Him.

She was also the "wife of Lappidoth." Some commentators think Lappidoth is the name of a village, but the prevailing view is that this is her husband, indicating her place within the human family. Because of her prophetic gifts, people went to her for aid. After the judge Ehud died, Deborah gradually became recognized as the judge whom God had provided. She lived in the hill country of Ephraim and sat to judge beneath one of the palm trees, an old tree that was well known between the ancient city of Bethel and Ramah. This was almost precisely in the center of Palestine.

As the opening verses of chapter 4 reveal, Israel was in desperate straits once again. King Jabin's power was unequalled in Canaan and his commander, Captain Sisera, making use of the most modern weapons of that Iron Age era, easily kept Israel in submission. He boasted 900 chariots of iron headquartered in the town of Harosheth of the Gentiles (Harosheth Haggoyim) near the Kishon River.

As Jabin lived not far from there in Hazor, we are correct in assuming that the northern tribes—Naphtali, Zebulun, Asher, and Issachar—endured the worst of Jabin's oppression. They perhaps prayed most earnestly for deliverance. Little wonder then that the Word of the Lord came to Deborah directing her to summon Barak of Kedesh in Naphtali to command an army for Israel.

Deborah knew to send for "Barak the son of Abinoam" by name and she knew what message to tell him because the Spirit communicated this to her. We, too, in our churches, could have such prophetic insights for facing our enemy if we were open to the Spirit's ministry. Barak traveled the ninety miles south to receive the command from Deborah: "The Lord, the God of Israel, commands you . . ." (NIV). Barak was to recruit 10,000 fighting men from among his own tribe and from Zebulun and camp on Mt. Tabor awaiting orders. Mt. Tabor, 1,929 feet in elevation, was a prominent landmark at the eastern end of the Plain of Jezreel where the battle was to take place.

"I will draw" or "lure" Sisera and "his chariots and his multitude" to the river the Lord said. "I will deliver him (Sisera) into thine hand." As the Lord had fought for Israel on many occasions before, this again was going to be His battle. He only needed willing human instruments.

Barak's agreeing to go only on condition that Deborah accompanied him betrays a certain weakness in his faith. Later, on the day of battle, he had to be ordered by Deborah to lead his army into the conflict. This "timid, hesitating Naphtalite" needed a companion who would supply what was lacking in his self-confidence. On the other hand, he is to be commended for wanting Deborah to be with him. He recognized that the Lord was with her and he wanted that Presence above all else.

By agreeing to go, Deborah again evidenced her prophetic gifts. She foretold that a woman, not Barak, would receive the honor for defeating Sisera. She probably did not know who the woman was for she might have revealed that also as she did the details of the battle plan.

For Barak, the Battle Victory (vv. 14–16) From the intervening verses, we learn three facts. First, 10,000 men answered Barak's call and moved with Barak and Deborah into position on the slopes of Mt. Tabor. Second, in what appears an unrelated matter, Heber the Kenite and his wife Jael "parted company" with his clan and relocated near Barak's hometown. Third, Sisera played into the Lord's hands by arraying his 900 chariots along the Kishon River.

Seeing the army spread out in the valley below, Deborah shouted, "Up! This day the Lord gives Sisera into your hands. Already the Lord has gone out to battle before you" (v. 14 NEB). There may have been a clap of thunder at the same instant Deborah gave the battle shout for what followed was not the ordinary kind of battle. Barak's men were not mounted on horses and they had but swords in their hands. Evidently not a shield or a spear was among them (*see* 5:8). Like a swarm of bees (Deborah's name means *bee*), they charged down the hill.

The next verse says the Lord "discomfited" the enemy; some translations say, "threw them into confusion" or "panic." From the Song of Deborah which follows (*see* 5:19-22), scholars have concluded that rain fell in torrents on the armies as they engaged. In no time Sisera's vaunted chariot force was mired in mud, an easy prey for the bold Israelites. Barak and his men chased the army of Sisera all the way to Harosheth, killing every soldier except for the captain. Meanwhile, he had slipped unnoticed from his chariot and escaped on foot, running a great distance until he fell exhausted at the entrance of the tent of Jael whom he recognized as a Kenite. The Kenites had a peace treaty with Jabin, so he must have thought he was safe in accepting her hospitality. True to the word of Deborah, he died at the hands of this courageous woman. When Barak came to ask if Sisera had come that way, Jael showed him the proud captain, his head pinned to the earth by a tent peg!

For Jehovah, the Honor and Glory (*5:1-3*) Israel did the only appropriate thing they could do when once the news was given of Sisera's death and of his army's total annihilation. They celebrated. The Song of Deborah which comprises the fifth chapter was sung by Barak and Deborah (v. 1), but is generally thought to be of her composition. It bears the marks of her prophetic gifts.

One scholar calls this "the choicest masterpiece of Hebrew poetry." The *New Bible Commentary, Revised*, notes that this "is the longest and most important" of the early poetical records of "episodes in the conquest of Canaan" and is the "oldest element in Judges."

The song may be divided in this way: "vv. 2, 3—exordium of praise; 4, 5—invocation of Yahweh; 6-8—the desolation under the oppressors; 9-18—the mustering of the tribes; 19-23—the battle of Kishon; 24-27—the death of Sisera; 28-30—the mother of Sisera awaits his coming; and 31a—epilogue."

In her exordium of praise, Deborah spoke of the voluntary self-sacrifice of the men of several tribes who responded to Barak's call. "When the people willingly offer themselves" (NIV). The Song reveals that more than just the men of Naphtali and Zebulun formed the army; others joined from Ephraim, Manasseh, Benjamin, and Issachar. To their shame, however, men of Reuben, Asher, and Dan did not volunteer to help their fellow Israelites.

This battle of Kishon vividly shows how God's people triumph against any odds when they allow the Lord to go ahead of them (as Jesus promised He would for us in John 10:4). They had but to follow and He gave them victory and rest in their land for a period twice the length of Jabin's twenty-year oppression (5:31). But it would not have been possible had not a woman sacrificed herself to lend support to a hesitant leader who needed her. Deborah, the supporting catalyst in this crucial time, evidently continued a low key role as judge and spiritual leader in Israel. When it came time for the writer of the Epistle of Hebrews to draw up his list of "heroes of faith" he passed over this self-sacrificing "mother in Israel" and named Barak instead. "What more shall I say? I do not have time to tell about Gideon, Barak, Samson, Jephthah, David, Samuel, and the prophets.... These were all commended for their faith, yet none of them received what had been promised" (Hebrews 11:32, 39 NIV).

Applying the Scripture
Take a moment toward the end of the class period to ask: What to you is the point of today's lesson? Instruct the class to remain silent for at least thirty seconds before anyone expresses an opinion. Once the class members begin to answer the question, be prepared to write their answers on the chalkboard.

Someone might say that, among other things, this lesson teaches us the value of self-sacrifice in helping others achieve their goals. Deborah certainly exemplified this, in encouraging and going with Barak. Read what one Bible commentator says about this.

"In the battle of life, a great variety of service is requisite for final success. Deborah cannot lead the army, but she can inspire it. Barak cannot prophesy, but he can fight. Thus Deborah cannot secure victory without Barak, nor Barak without Deborah. We are members one of another, and all the members have not the same office. There is work for the seer and work for the warrior. The world always needs its prophets and its heroes. The worker without the thinker will blunder into confusion; the thinker without the worker will fail for want of power to execute his designs. Brain work is at least as important as mechanical work. It is therefore foolish for practical men and women to despise the men and women of thought as mere theorists, and foolish for the thinkers to treat the active men and women of business with philosophical contempt."

Now ask the class members if they see themselves in a helping role to anyone in particular. Do the fathers and mothers think of themselves as supporters of a son or daughter? Invite a parent to tell briefly about a specific goal he or she is helping a child to achieve.

Now invite someone else to tell of someone who is not related to them, but for whom they feel responsible as a "Deborah." A teacher may name one of his or her students. A coach may name a team player. A secretary may name her boss, or an employer may name a younger or weaker employee.

Have someone read Judges 5:2 and point out that if we really want God's redemptive work in our midst as a church or a family or in any context, we ought to be "willingly offering" ourselves. Challenge each class member to be willing to do this and to share with the class on a future Sunday what the Lord is leading them to do.

(Note to teacher: *Be flexible.* Someone may suggest an application for this lesson that is entirely different from what is suggested above. Go ahead and let that application develop and "sacrifice" your own plan, if the application flows from the lesson text.)

Questions for Discussion
Make use of these questions to involve your students in learning and to test their understanding of the lesson.
1. What marks of a prophetess are seen in Deborah in the text? 3. Where in Israel did Deborah reside? Where was she in relation to the Canaanite king Jabin who was oppressing the nation? 3. In agreeing to go to battle only if Deborah accompanied him, what weakness did Barak show? What good quality did his request reveal? 4. Who was the other woman in this story and what did she do to Sisera? 5. How does Deborah's command (v. 14) reveal her utmost trust in the Lord? 6. What natural means do the interpreters believe God used to "discomfort" or throw into a panic the enemy army? 7. What is the grand theme of Deborah's song?

Illustrating the Scripture
Examples and quotations to help the teacher communicate the lesson.

THE BATTLE OF KISHON AND *ARMAGEDDON* The battle which Barak fought against Sisera was not the first nor will it be the last on the famed Plain of Esdraelon. "In this valley Saul was slain by the Philistines (1 Samuel 31:1-3). It has provided the stage for countless pivotal battles, long before Israel faced the plain-dwelling Canaanite chariot kings (Joshua 17:16), and continuing into modern times. Esdraelon has been coveted by every strategist from the generals of Egyptian Thutmose III and Ben-hadad of Syria to Saladin the Moslem (1186), Napoleon (1799), and the British liberator of Palestine from the Turks, Allenby, Viscount of Megiddo (1917). Today it is intensively cultivated" (*Harper's Bible Dictionary*).

The "vast, fertile Plain of Esdraelon or Valley of Jezreel, stretching NE-SW from Mt. Carmel, south of Mt. Gilboa and north of the highlands of Samaria" is the "most conspicuous transverse plain of Palestine" adds Harper's. "In the Plain of Esdraelon ... were such cities as Megiddo and Taanach in the west and the powerful fortress Beth-shan in the east commanding the Jordan Valley. For thousands of years farmers and armies have contended for possession of this plain of Armageddon."

The evangelist, Dr. Anis Shorrosh, an Arab who grew up not far from Megiddo before he found Christ, writes: "The plain of Megiddo or Jezreel, as the region also is known, has been the breadbasket of Palestine along with the Jordan Valley.... The ominous word *Armageddon* is associated geographically with this very area. It is here that the final great battle of history, the war to end all wars, is to be fought. Actually this significance is contained in the very name *Armageddon*, which means literally 'hill of slaughter' or 'hill of the cut off.'

"... According to Hal Lindsey, the emperor Napoleon is said to have stood 'upon the hill of Megiddo and recalled prophecy as he looked over the valley and said, "all the armies of the world could maneuver for battle here."' From its northernmost point not far from modern Haifa, the plain measures some twenty miles long and fourteen miles across" (*Jesus, Prophecy, and the Middle East* by Anis A. Shorrosh).

SELF-SACRIFICE FOR THE GOOD OF OTHERS "Deborah's burst of generous admiration toward those who offered themselves willingly in her time is a stirring call to us to imitate their example. But let us not imagine that such self-sacrifice is confined to extraordinary occasions, or can be executed only on the platform of great emergencies. Unselfish efforts for the good of others find room for their exercise in the common round of everyday life. He who works when he is weary, who overcomes his natural shyness or timidity, who lays aside his own schemes or tastes and takes up work which is distasteful to him, who risks losses in money, in consideration, in convenience, in comfort, in ease, in leisure, that he may do something which he believes will be useful to others, is treading in the steps of these 'willing governors' (5:9) and deserves like them the warm approval of all generous hearts" (*Pulpit Commentary*).

Topics for Youth

EMULATING DEBORAH, BY PRAISING THE LORD!—Deborah's song should encourage us to praise Him also. A writer, upon completing a very long project, wants to open the windows of his study and tell the world, "Hallelujah! It's finished!" A student wants to shout on the housetops when he gets top grades. A musician wants to tell the world when she receives an invitation to perform on the stage of Carnegie Hall.

But how about "Praising God in Everyday Life"? A writer, Derek Prime, gives us these thoughts from an article by that title in *His* magazine (April 1981). "When we rightly affirm that we are *created to praise* God we are implying that praise, happily, does not have to be limited to expressions of praise in song or speech, but that the life we live can be praise. The writer to the Hebrews links the two together when he urges, 'Through Jesus, therefore, let us continually offer to God a sacrifice of praise—the fruit of lips that confess his name. And do not forget to do good and to share with others, for with such sacrifices God is pleased' (13:15, 16)....

"To praise God when we are in difficulties—and not least when some of those difficulties arise from our faithfulness to him (*see* Acts 5:41; 16:25)—may cost us something, but that only enhances our '*sacrifice* of praise.' We have joy in identifying with David who declared, 'I will not *sacrifice* to the Lord my God burnt offerings that cost me nothing' (2 Samuel 24:24)....

"It is worth noting too that the offering of praise when hardship, illness or other trials come is often the first stage in discovering God's deliverance or healing. All the time we are lacking in praise, we fail to exercise faith. But as we exercise faith in God by praising him, we may find him doing the most surprising things for us (*see* Acts 16:25, 26; Psalms 50:23). The path we deliberately tread as we praise God in difficulty so often becomes the path God uses along which to send his blessings."

UNIT II

Persons Choosing Priorities

LESSON 5   JULY 3

Jephthah: Zeal Without Wisdom

Background Scripture: Judges 11:1–12:7
Devotional Reading: Matthew 26:30–35

Judges 11:7-10, 29-35

7 And Jephthah said unto the elders of Gilead, Did not ye hate me, and expel me out of my father's house? and why are ye come unto me now when ye are in distress?

8 And the elders of Gilead said unto Jephthah, Therefore we turn again to thee now, that thou mayest go with us, and fight against the children of Ammon, and be our head over all the inhabitants of Gilead.

9 And Jephthah said unto the elders of Gilead, If ye bring me home again to fight against the children of Ammon, and the LORD deliver them before me, shall I be your head?

10 And the elders of Gilead said unto Jephthah, The LORD be witness between us, if we do not so according to thy words.
29 Then the Spirit of the LORD came upon Jephthah, and he passed over Gilead, and Manasseh, and passed over Mizpeh of Gilead, and from Mizpeh of Gilead he passed over unto the children of Ammon.
30 And Jephthah vowed a vow unto the LORD, and said, If thou shalt without fail deliver the children of Ammon into mine hands.
31 Then it shall be, that whatsoever cometh forth of the doors of my house to meet me, when I return in peace from the children of Ammon, shall surely be the LORD's, and I will offer it up for a burnt offering.
32 So Jephthah passed over unto the children of Ammon to fight against them; and the LORD delivered them into his hands.
33 And he smote them from Aroer, even till thou come to Minnith, even twenty cities, and unto the plain of the vineyards, with a very great slaughter. Thus the children of Ammon were subdued before the children of Israel.
34 And Jephthah came to Mizpeh unto his house, and, behold, his daughter came out to meet him with timbrels and with dances: and she was his only child; beside her he had neither son nor daughter.
35 And it came to pass, when he saw her, that he rent his clothes, and said, Alas, my daughter! thou hast brought me very low, and thou art one of them that trouble me: for I have opened my mouth unto the LORD, and I cannot go back.

KEY VERSE: "There is a way which seemeth right unto a man, but the end thereof are the ways of death." Proverbs 14:12.

Home Daily Bible Readings
June 27 M. Choosing a Leader, Judges 11:1–11.
June 28 T. Message to a King, Judges 11:12–28.
June 29 W. A Tragic Vow, Judges 11:29–40.
June 30 T. The Way of Wisdom, Proverbs 14:8–18.
July 1 F. The Value of Wisdom, Proverbs 3:13–24.
July 2 S. Unwise Promises, Matthew 26:30–35.
July 3 S. God's Wisdom, 1 Corinthians 1:18–31.

Lesson Aim: That adult Christians may manifest the virtue of fidelity in every commitment they make to man and to the Lord.

LESSON OUTLINE
Background to the Scripture
Looking at the Scripture Text
I. Sought by His Countrymen (Judges 11:7–10)

II. Caught by His Vow (Judges 11:29-35)
Applying the Scripture

Background to the Scripture

It could have been said of the period of the Judges: "It was the best of times, it was the worst of times, it was the age of wisdom, it was the age of foolishness, it was the epoch of belief, it was the epoch of incredulity, it was the season of Light, it was the season of Darkness, it was the spring of hope, it was the winter of despair."

Fortune changed for the people of Israel overnight. The Lord told them that because they had not obeyed Him completely He would leave the ungodly Canaanites all about them to test and prove of what Israel was made. In such an environment, Israel more often proved putty than granite.

The people were granted the privilege of blazing the way as a new nation in their own land, but too often they cut a path to luxury and idolatry. The words that best describe Israel's way of life during the period are: "In those days there was no king in Israel; every man did that which was right in his own eyes."

As Criswell points out, "Their terrible state of affairs does not take centuries to evolve; it comes about in the very generation that succeeds Joshua and the elders who survive him (2:11-15). In His mercy, God does not destroy His people for their sin; instead, He raises up deliverers when they turn to Him in repentance...." Jephthah is one of those deliverers, a paradoxical figure in puzzling times.

Looking at the Scripture Text

Sought by His Countrymen (vv. 7-10) The setting for the heroic story of Jephthah is that region of Palestine called Gilead, a high and scenic land east of the Jordan River. In ancient times and throughout the Old Testament period, Gilead was known for its "balm," an aromatic resin with healing properties, extracted from bushes which grew in abundance there. On seeing this well-watered hill country, the tribe of Gad selected it as its tribal inheritance in Israel as did half of the tribe of Manasseh.

Some years after the death of Deborah, in another dark hour of Israel's history (10:6-14), the people of God begged the Lord to send a deliverer. Two old foes—the Philistines and the Ammonites—had Israel tightly under pressure. While the Philistines did their worst on Israel's southern and western flanks, giving rise to the judgeship of Samson, the Ammonites controlled Gilead in the east.

Long before the Israelites in Gilead, whom we will call Gileadites, were in a penitent mood for their sins, the future deliverer was born in a Gileadite household. His name was Jephthah, meaning "He opens" (the womb), which indicates that he was his mother's firstborn. However, his mother was a prostitute. When Jephthah grew to young manhood, the two legitimate sons of his father "drove Jephthah away," telling him he was not about to receive any of the family inheritance. Verses 7 and 8 imply that it was not the brothers alone who expelled Jephthah; evidently it was done with the authority of the Gileadite elders.

The ostracized Jephthah must have felt keenly the rejection of his half-brothers for he traveled to far-away Tob on the edge of the Arabian desert before settling down. This obscure place was home for Aramean people (*see* 2 Samuel 10:6ff) giving rise to the notion that Jephthah's mother was Aramean. This is important for understanding Jephthah's later actions. His was a mixed spiritual heritage, partly based on the monotheistic teachings of the Mosaic Law, partly based upon the superstitions of a heathen people. In Tob, Jephthah became a sort of freedom fighter, the leader of "a group of adventurers" (v. 3 NIV).

As our text implies, Jephthah must have made a name for himself because in time the Gileadites sought him out and implored him to return. They wanted to get the Ammonites off their backs and Jephthah seemed just the man to help them do that.

But Jephthah was skeptical. "Didn't you hate me . . . ? Why do you come to me now, when you're in trouble?" The Living Bible captures his sarcasm exquisitely: " 'Sure!' Jephthah exclaimed. 'Do you expect me to believe that?' "

In telling him you will "be our head over all the inhabitants of Gilead," the Gileadites were offering to Jephthah their highest office—he would be their judge. Jephthah responded warily, like a big-league ballplayer being offered a terrific contract by his one-time owners. "Suppose you take me back to fight the Ammonites and the Lord gives them to me—will I really be your head?" (v. 9 NIV). The committee of Gileadites swore by an oath that he would.

Soldiers of fortune are not always known for their finer personal qualities. But Jephthah's answer seems to betray a sense of gratitude. He was flattered to be asked to come to their rescue. But more than that, he exhibited humility. He knew that his countrymen had their backs to the wall and that only Jehovah could deliver them from their distress. His answer gives us reason to believe he had retained a basic trust in the Lord even though he had been separated from His people and the services of sacrificial worship. But he may not have conceived of Jehovah as being the Lord of the whole earth. In his negotiations with the enemy, he describes the Lord as "our God" (v. 24) as opposed to "Chemosh thy god."

Satisfied that their offer was sincere, Jephthah returned with the Gileadites to Mizpah in Gilead where the people designated him "head" or judge and "commander." His daughter returned with him, and perhaps his wife, though no mention is made of her. As the elders had promised, he was accepted and occupied a house in Mizpah.

Caught by His Vow (vv. 29-35) Jephthah's next action justified even further the astute judgment of Gilead in making him judge, but it hardly prepares us for the irrational act soon to follow. Jephthah did not rush impulsively into battle. First he sent messengers to the Ammonites, asking what reason they had to attack Israel. When they replied that Israel had taken away their land and demanded that it be given back peaceably, Jephthah gave them a short history lesson. This is a remarkable summary of the disposition of the land east of the Jordan (vv. 14–16). Jephthah taunted Ammon: "Will you not take what your god Chemosh gives you? Likewise, whatever the Lord our God has given us, we will possess" (v. 24 NIV). His final words show Jephthah's confidence that "the Lord, the Judge" would show Israel's cause to be just.

Ammon's flat refusal to cease warring against Israel lit the fuse under Jephthah. The words, "The Spirit of the Lord came upon" him are typical of the writer of Judges. They indicate that the Spirit had empowered Jephthah for the great task before him. At crucial points, this same expression is used of other judges—Othniel (3:10), Gideon (6:34), and Samson (13:25, 15:14).

Verse 29 traces Jephthah's course as he raised an army, evidently calling soldiers to him from the tribes of Gad and Manasseh and perhaps Reuben. From Mizpah, he launched his attack. But first, he made a vow. We do not know where he was when he vowed his vow, but it seems likely he did so upon leaving his property. Perhaps as he looked toward the door of his house, he pledged that if the Lord would allow him to defeat the Ammonites he would give to the Lord as a burnt offering "whatever comes out of the door of my house to meet me when I return in triumph . . ." (v. 31 NIV).

His vow was to offer human sacrifice; that is clear. All commentators agree that the word *whatsoever* can only mean "who" as opposed to some animal.

Jephthah and his army went on to devastate the opposing Ammonites who were no match for the Lord and His people. Jephthah liberated twenty cities of Gilead and ended the threat from wicked Ammon—at least for the time being.

What happened on Jephthah's return home is well known. His daughter, on hearing the splendid news that the army of her father was returning in triumph, took her tambourine and spontaneously danced around the room and out the door to meet her father. At that awful moment, Jephthah's ecstatic joy of victory vanished as he remembered his "rash and unhappy" vow. The writer shows the utter tragedy of the scene by stating that this daughter was Jephthah's only child.

Jephthah's reaction bears all the marks of genuine anguish. He had won the greatest victory of his life only to lose the dearest person of all to him. He tore his clothes, the common sign of grief, and exclaimed, "thou hast brought me very low" (literally—"thou hast thoroughly bowed me down"). He had been "troubled" by his Gileadite half-brothers, and lately by the Ammonites, but now sorely troubled by her, he said. A more accurate translation of his meaning may be "you have made me miserable and wretched" (NIV). Of course, the poor man had brought it all upon himself.

Why would Jephthah make such a vow? Psychologists might suggest that, still pained by the rejection of his half-brothers, he so desperately wanted to be accepted in the Mizpah community that he overcompensated to the point of inviting dreadful pain to himself. One commentator explains, "Jephthah may have reasoned that the more precious the gift offered the more likely would Jehovah be to grant what was required. This was the conception of the age."

Though not included in our text, the thirty-sixth verse reveals a noble submission on the part of Jephthah's daughter. "While it reveals a most lovable character," says the *Pulpit Commentary*, "it seems also to show that the idea of a human sacrifice was not so strange to her mind as it is to ours. The sacrifice of his eldest son as a burnt offering by the king of Moab, some 300 years later, as related in 2 Kings 3:27 . . . the sacrifices of children to Moloch, so often spoken of in Scripture; the question in Micah 6:7, 'Shall I give my firstborn for my transgression, the fruit of my body for the sin of my soul?' . . . and many other examples prove the prevalence of human sacrifices in early times, and in heathen lands. This must be borne in mind in reading the history of Jephthah."

Some commentators attempt to soften the outcome of this vow and explain away the natural meaning of "he did to her as he had vowed" (v. 39) by suggesting that she lived on under a perpetual vow of virginity. But we do not doubt that after her two-month period of mourning, Jephthah offered her up. Luther said: "Some affirm that he did not sacrifice her, but the text is clear enough." The Law specifically forbade human sacrifice (Leviticus 18:21; 20:1–5); but that he did this without either his own conscience stopping him or the high priest's intervention shows the decadence of that day when "every man did that which was right in his own eyes."

Applying the Scripture
In applying the truth from today's text, ask God to show you and your class a weakness to avoid and a strength to add to your life.

It is easy to see Jephthah's weakness and condemn it. A vow entered into rashly, impulsively, without due consideration of the consequences is shown in his case to be utterly tragic and totally lacking in wisdom. But we can see why the Holy Spirit included it in Scripture. Remember the words of Paul: "For all those words which were written long ago are meant to teach us today; so that we may be encouraged to endure and to go on hoping in our own time" (Romans 15:4 PHILLIPS). And in 1 Corinthians 10:11—"Now these things that happened to our ancestors are illustrations of the way in which God works, and they were written down to be a warning to us who stand today so near to the end of the world."

Learning from the weakness of this judge, we call to mind what Solomon said: "Do not let your mouth lead you into sin" (Ecclesiastes 5:6 NIV). And the words of Jesus: "Suppose one of you wants to build a tower. Will he not first sit down and estimate the cost to see if he has enough money to complete it?" (Luke 14:28 NIV).

1. We should take very seriously the lesson of a wrongful vow. One Christian said it correctly when he observed that the Church has failed today in teaching the seriousness of the vow, especially the marriage vows. From

Jephthah's weakness, we may learn to weigh thoroughly the consequences of any agreement we enter into before we agree to it.

But, we can also learn from Jephthah's strength. Once he vowed a vow, he would not turn back. This sort of resolution is praised in the Psalms—"who keeps his oath even when it hurts . . ." (Psalms 15:4 NIV). This is fidelity to its utmost. Scripture warns us not to make a vow if we do not intend to keep it (Ecclesiastes 5:4, 5).

2. Think of the positive good we can gain from this story of Jephthah. Ask yourself and your students: am I a person of His word? Do I make a pledge and keep it; do I vow a vow and fulfill it? Examine those relationships and covenants you have made, and are going to make, to see if your fidelity measures up to that of Jephthah. And make it a rule in all future commitments to be fully faithful to keep what you have promised before God and with others.

Questions for Discussion
Make use of these questions to involve your students in learning and to test their understanding of the lesson.
1. For what reason was Jephthah ostracized from his family home? 2. Why did the elders of Gilead now seek Jephthah to be their leader against the Ammonites? What perhaps did they see in Jephthah? 3. By saying, "if the Lord deliver them before me" what good character trait does Jephthah show? 4. How did Jephthah first try to gain peace with the Ammonites? 5. What was his vow? 6. What reasons, both within himself and from the times in which he lived, might be given for his making such a tragic vow? 7. Did he actually sacrifice his daughter?

Illustrating the Scripture
Examples and quotations to help the teacher communicate the lesson.
"I WILL PAY MY VOWS. . . ." The author of the 116th Psalm asks: "What shall I render unto the Lord for all his benefits toward me?" (v. 12). The question is most appropriate. And as we ponder how to answer it ourselves, we see that the psalmist fully gives to us a pattern for our own response. He goes on to declare: "I will take the cup of salvation . . . I will pay my vows unto the Lord . . . I will offer to thee the sacrifice of thanksgiving, and will call upon the name of the Lord" (vv. 13, 14, 17).

A note from John Foxe's *Acts and Monuments* shows us that Christians during the Reformation were not infrequently called upon to "pay their vows" as a servant and disciple of the Lord by enduring martyrdom. "John Philpot went with the sheriffs to the place of execution; and when he was entering into Smithfield the way was foul, and two officers took him up to bear him to the stake. Then he said merrily, What, will ye make me a pope? I am content to go to my journey's end on foot. But first coming into Smithfield, he kneeled down there, saying these words, I will pay my vows in thee, O Smithfield."

"AS LONG AS *LOVE* SHALL LAST"   Maybe it was the imprint of realism. It was certainly no slip of the tongue. On an episode of the TV show "Love Boat" in 1980–81, when it came time for the captain of the ship to preside over the wedding of three couples aboard ship, he said, "I pronounce you man and wife, for as long as love shall last."

With one out of two marriages now ending in divorce, no wonder the scriptwriters poke fun at the notion of "one man and one woman for life." That so many Christians decide to end their marriage is a sure sign of the erosion of the meaning of the vows we make.

The vows a man and woman make in a marriage ceremony are the most sacred of all covenants a person enters into with another person. Though the form of the vow used in Jewish and Christian weddings is not found in Scripture, the vows do find their root in God's revelation of marriage as declared in the Old and New Testaments. Perhaps the expression of vows as found in the *Book of Common Prayer* (1928) is the most commonly used model for wedding vows in the Christian church. In those vows, the minister asks:

"*Name*, wilt thou have this Woman to thy wedded wife, to live together after God's ordinance in the holy state of Matrimony? Wilt thou love her, comfort her, honour, and keep her in sickness and in health; and, forsaking all others, keep thee only unto her, so long as ye both shall live?"

After asking the same of the bride, he leads the couple in vows which are almost exactly identical:

"I, *Name*, take thee Name to my wedded wife, to have and to hold from this day forward, for better for worse, for richer for poorer, in sickness and in health, to love and to cherish, till death us do part, according to God's holy ordinance; and thereto I plight thee my troth."

Topics for Youth

CONSIDER THE CONSEQUENCES—The great thing about reading the Bible and books of biography is that we can see the mistakes other people have made, and we can learn a lesson for ourselves without going through it. We all can see the folly of heroic Jephthah's vow. That was a failure to consider the consequences *in the extreme!*

Young people are typically vulnerable to such extremes, as evidenced by one young person who wrote to his counselor: "There is no communication between my parents and me, and I can't figure out why. I've tried very hard to talk to my parents about so many different things, but they will not listen to me. . . . My problems are not little. They have gotten so big that I've tried to kill myself four times in the past six months, and my parents still won't listen to me. Please tell me what to do."

The counselor responded: "The first thing you should do is stop trying to commit suicide. I don't know how serious your attempts were, but I can assure you that there is a terrific risk of tragedy in doing bizarre things to get attention. You may, through trying a little too hard, end up dead. Or you may end up in an institution.

"In trying to get attention, you focus attention on the wrong things. All the attention is on your bizarre behavior, and not on the poor communication. I've seen kids who had normal problems but did bizarre things wind up in psycho wards. Believe me, the institutional file can follow you all your life. You may have cleared up your problems, but those who hear you were committed to a mental hospital won't know that.

"I think there are better ways to grab your parents' attention. One very powerful way is simply to say, 'I am really feeling some problems, and I'm having a hard time getting you to listen. Can we make an appointment to sit down and have a long talk sometime when you're not busy?' That ought to get their attention, and it should also make sure that you're not getting to them just at the moment when they have a million things on their mind." (*Campus Life*, Oct. 1978, p. 15. "I Never Promised You a Disneyland" by Jay Kesler.)

LESSON 6   JULY 10

Samson: Unfulfilled Destiny

Background Scripture: Judges 13–16
Devotional Reading: Acts 15:6–11

Judges 13:2–5, 24, 25; 16:15–17, 28–30
13:2 And there was a certain man of Zorah, of the family of the Danites, whose name was Manoah; and his wife was barren, and bare not.
 3 And the angel of the LORD appeared unto the woman, and said unto her, Behold now, thou art barren, and bearest not: but thou shalt conceive, and bear a son.
 4 Now therefore beware, I pray thee, and drink not wine nor strong drink, and eat not any unclean thing:
 5 For, lo, thou shalt conceive, and bear a son; and no razor shall come on his head: for the child shall be a Nazarite unto God from the womb: and he shall begin to deliver Israel out of the hand of the Philistines.
 24 And the woman bare a son, and called his name Samson: and the child grew, and the LORD blessed him.
 25 And the Spirit of the LORD began to move him at times in the camp of Dan between Zorah and Eshtaol.
16:15 And she said unto him, How canst thou say, I love thee, when thine heart is not with me? thou hast mocked me these three times, and hast not told me wherein thy great strength lieth.

16 And it came to pass, when she pressed him daily with her words, and urged him, so that his soul was vexed unto death;

17 That he told her all his heart, and said unto her, There hath not come a razor upon mine head; for I have been a Nazarite unto God from my mother's womb: if I be shaven, then my strength will go from me, and I shall become weak, and be like any other man.

28 And Samson called unto the Lord, and said, O Lord God, remember me, I pray thee, and strengthen me, I pray thee, only this once, O God, that I may be at once avenged of the Philistines for my two eyes.

29 And Samson took hold of the two middle pillars upon which the house stood, and on which it was borne up, of the one with his right hand, and of the other with his left.

30 And Samson said, Let me die with the Philistines. And he bowed himself with all his might; and the house fell upon the lords, and upon all the people that were therein. So the dead which he slew at his death were more than they which he slew in his life.

KEY VERSE: "He that hath no rule over his own spirit is like a city that is broken down, and without walls." Proverbs 25:28.

Home Daily Bible Readings
July 4 M. A Promised Birth, Judges 13:1-14.
July 5 T. A Good Beginning, Judges 13:15-25.
July 6 W. An Unwise Marriage, Judges 14:5-20.
July 7 T. Treachery Produces Treachery, Judges 15:1-15.
July 8 F. Secret Strength, Judges 16:1-14.
July 9 S. A Tragic Ending, Judges 16:15-30.
July 10 S. Walk by the Spirit, Galatians 5:13-24.

Lesson Aim: Adult Christians should decide to look to God for the strength to recover from any failure.

LESSON OUTLINE
Background to the Scripture
Looking at the Scripture Text
  I. Announcement and Precautions (Judges 13:2-5)
  II. Birth and Promise (Judges 13:24, 25)
  III. Compromise and Powerlessness (Judges 16:15-17)
  IV. Death and Prayer (Judges 16:28-30)
Applying the Scripture

Background to the Scripture

Palestine is such a common word in the news today and frequently encountered in the study of the Old Testament that most of us have never stopped to find out its origin. The land called Palestine actually received its name indirectly from one of Israel's most bitter enemies, the Philistines.

So far as is known, the historian Herodotus was the first to use the word *Palestine* in referring to that "part of Syria which is called 'Palaistine,'" or "Philistine Syria." "From the Greeks," says *Harper's Bible Dictionary*, "the Romans derived their Latin name, *Palestina*." Palestine is the English derivative.

We are interested in this because of the people whose name, *Philistines*, formed the basis for the name of this whole region south of the Lebanon mountains, west of the Arabian desert, northeast of Egypt and east of the Mediterranean. The Philistines, "those that dwell in villages," lived in the land as early as Abraham's time (*see* Genesis 21:34; 26:14) and even then were not too friendly. They settled all along the coast and during the period of the judges and the first king of Israel, Saul, they offered the stiffest resistance to Israel's efforts at expansion. King David subdued the Philistines ultimately, but the judge whom we study today was the first Israelite to give them serious trouble.

Looking at the Scripture Text

Announcement and Precautions (13:2-5) When we were children, Samson was a hero larger than life to us. We never tired of hearing stories of his exploits—tearing a wild lion to pieces, slaughtering a thousand Philistines with a jawbone of an ass, waltzing off from Gaza under the full moon, the huge city gates atop his broad shoulders. But, as we matured, we saw Samson in an entirely different light. And just maybe we quietly put aside any intention of naming our son after this musclebound "hero."

Yet Samson did begin well. He had excellent parentage. His mother and father were God-fearing and hard working and the account of their behavior in chapter 13 shows that they confided fully in one another and walked together in one mind. While the attention of Israel was fixed upon the heavy-handed Philistines, this devout couple one day received a heavenly guest and heard surprising news. The angel appeared to the wife of Manoah, a woman so humble she is not even named.

Probably she had been praying for a child because to be childless in Israel was a terrible reproach. "You will soon be pregnant and have a son" (TEV) the angel announced. And before she could call her husband, the angel gave her special precautions. Hers was to be no ordinary child. The patriarch Jacob had prophesied that the tribe of Dan "shall judge his people Israel" (Genesis 49:16). This child of Dan's clan would do just that!

The child to be born was to be a Nazirite (preferred spelling), meaning that he was to be "consecrated" or "separated" to God. Of course, every firstborn was separated unto the Lord, but this baby was to be a Nazirite for life. That is, he was to abide by the strict code of those taking the Nazirite vow: (1) he would not drink wine or even eat grapes or raisins; (2) his hair would never be shorn, and (3) he was never to touch a dead carcass of man or beast (Numbers 6:1-21). Only Samuel and John the Baptist, with Samson, among all the men named in the Bible, were called to live as Nazirites perpetually.

Because her son was to follow such a holy calling, the mother was to abide by certain rules once she conceived and while she carried this son. "Drink not wine nor strong drink, and eat not any unclean thing" the angel warned. Of course, whatever entered her blood stream would affect this son; since he was to be pure, she was also to be pure. No Israelite was to eat "unclean" animals—such as pigs or camels or rabbits, certain kinds of fowl and sea creatures (see Leviticus 11)—but Israelites were undoubtedly "fudging" on these commandments. Thus the angel warned her.

Birth and Promise (vv. 24, 25) Following an unforgettable second encounter with the angel, her husband Manoah being present (vv. 9–23), this woman conceived and gave birth to Samson. The writer of Judges does not explain why the name Samson was chosen. Possibly it derives its significance from the Chaldee word *shemash*, to minister, especially in sacred things. The *Pulpit Commentary* says that "if this were the derivation, it would be a reference to his dedication to God as a Nazirite from his mother's womb, the only thing his mother knew about him when she gave him the name." Some suggest that his name meant "the sun"; however, the Hebrew word for sun, *shemesh*, is not quite the same as his name. Josephus held that the name meant "he is strong," but failed to say in what language this meaning was conveyed.

The name's significance is not so important as the facts next stated: "the child grew," the Lord "blessed him" and God's Spirit "began to move" or "strengthen him." These words sound hauntingly familiar, calling to mind what Luke said:

"Jesus increased in wisdom and stature, and in favour with God and man" (Luke 2:52). This is but one instance of the subtle similarities between this man, born to deliver Israel, and the Redeemer. Like Jesus, Samson's birth was announced by an angel and he was the firstborn. And both would voluntarily die at the hands of their enemies.

Verse 25 is the first of four references to the Spirit of the Lord in Samson's life. "The Spirit of the Lord began to move him at times...." In Old Testament times, God sent the Holy Spirit upon certain individuals for special tasks. But not until after the Resurrection of Christ would the Spirit inhabit man as His temple (John 14:17; 1 Corinthians 6:19). This is why David would pray "take not thy holy Spirit from me" (Psalms 51:11).

Samson received a special anointing of power when he encountered a lion in the field (14:6) and when battling the Philistines (14:19; 16:14). Chapters 14 and 15 describe the exploits of this man of great strength. At this early stage, Samson's life was brimming with promise. The Spirit was his secret of strength. But, of course, there is a vital link between purity and power and Samson's carelessness would eventually catch up with him.

Compromise and Powerlessness (16:15–17) Samson judged Israel (the NIV says "led") twenty years so at this point he may have been forty-five years of age. What is this man, called to "begin to deliver Israel" from the Philistines, doing in the lap of Delilah, an ally of the Philistines? Is this the Nazirite consecrated to Jehovah? Apparently not. Early in his adventuresome life he showed a disregard for his vows by taking honey from a lion's carcass (14:8,

9). Nowhere does the record say that he drank wine, but if he would sleep with a prostitute (16:1) it seems highly unlikely that he would strictly abide by the prohibition against the fruit of the vine.

Only in the matter of his hair could it be said of him that he was still a Nazirite. But Satan knew how to take that from him, too—through his weakness for seductive women. Delilah may have been a Philistine herself. His ability to spend time with her while the enemy sought to kill him shows how highly they regarded him. But it also shows his stupidity. He walked into a trap, for the Philistine lords had baited Delilah, offering her 1,100 shekels of silver (or 28 pounds) apiece if she would deliver Samson into their hands. There were evidently five lords (Joshua 13:3).

Three times Samson resisted Delilah's attempts to learn the secret of his strength (vv. 6–14). But when she began insinuating that he did not love her, he weakened. True, he had not shown her real love, else he would have taken her to his own home as his wife and shared all of himself with her. And she was clearly playing him along as well, no doubt enjoying his attention but motivated by her greed to know more about him. The name of their game was lust, not love, although Samson would have contended that he loved her.

Finally Samson wearied of her nagging and "told her everything." " 'No razor has ever been used on my head,' he said, 'because I have been a Nazirite set apart to God since birth. If my head were shaved, my strength would leave me, and I would become as weak as any other man' " (v. 17 NIV).

Delilah knew that finally he had told her the truth. Probably she gave him a potion which helped put him to sleep on her lap, and then she called a "man to shave off the seven braids of his hair ... and his strength left him" (v. 19). When she awakened him and he went out to fight the Philistines as he had done before, he was weak. Saddest of all, "the Lord was departed from him" and he hadn't known it.

Death and Prayer (vv. 28–30) A Methodist evangelist of the previous generation preached a stirring sermon from a simple outline on Samson's life— "Sin blinds, sin binds, sin grinds." Once captured, that is exactly what happened to this promising deliverer. The Philistines held a celebration and paraded Samson before the jeering crowd. The worst part of the humiliation for Samson must have been the constant gnawing of his anguished conscience. What might have been! But the final act of his life shows that in prison he evidently found repentance and though he could not see with his physical eyes, he saw the Lord's purpose for him once more.

In bringing him to the temple, probably in Gaza, the enemy overleaped their advantage. Samson must have known the building well. Other much smaller buildings of a similar plan to this one have been reconstructed from ruins of the period and they show that the roof was supported "by two wooden pillars which had been set on round, well-made stone bases. There were traces of timber still adhering to these bases, and on analysis it was proved that the pillars that had held up the roof were made of cedar of Lebanon" writes Magnus Magnusson in *Archaeology of the Bible*. The only problem is that the writer of Judges says that 3,000 people were on the roof and no ruins have been found suggesting that the Philistines ever built a temple that large. But a lack of evidence cannot disprove what the biblical writer records. Matthew Poole noted that the Philistines were "either a part of, or very near neighbors to, the Phoenicians from whom it is confessed the arts came to the Grecians," so they evidently had the skill to erect such a building.

Samson's intense prayer, only the second recorded prayer in his life story (*see* 14:18), was followed by his self-sacrificing act in pulling the house down on top of himself and all the assembled multitude. The value of his life is not just that of a bad example to shun. As the story of Samson unfolded, he gave the nation Israel several occasions of genuine rejoicing. Further, his dying act proves again the longsuffering, patient, forgiving nature of God. And, he did what the Lord said he would: "he began to deliver Israel out of the hands of the Philistines."

Applying the Scripture
Teacher: Two ways are suggested for drawing an application from this lesson. However, you may choose an altogether different truth to emphasize. Be sure it flows from the Scriptures for this particular lesson.
1.   Self-control—The obvious lesson from Samson's life is his failure to exercise self-control. Our Key Verse for this lesson speaks of this as "ruling one's spirit." Have one member of the class read the Key Verse and paraphrase its meaning for the class.

Invite the members of the class to name the areas of life that come to their mind when they think of self-control. Probably the first one will have to do with food. Someone else may name sex or passions. Or TV viewing? List on the chalkboard the areas of life in which a Christian needs to exercise self-control.

Now ask someone to read the passage about the fruit of the Spirit, in Galatians 5:22, 23. Notice that the fruit of temperance or "self-control" is named among them. But obviously we do not all appear to enjoy the benefits of self-control in our lives. Suggest to the class that a lack of self-control in one area of our life could be a measure of just how far short we fall in allowing the Spirit to control our lives, to "fill" us. Urge class members to allow the Spirit to search their hearts for evidence of lack of self-control, and then to pray for the grace to allow the Spirit to take over those areas. Urge them to make this an on-going prayer, remembering the sad example of Samson's life.

2.   Failure isn't final—A lesson we may miss from Samson's life is that even when he was at his lowest point he could reach out to God. Note the quotations in the section of this lesson under "Illustrating the Scripture" which show how his strength returned.

If you know of someone in class who has suffered a setback, a failure—and you know they would be willing to talk about it—invite that person to share particularly the steps the Lord led them through toward recovery.

There may be persons in your class whose marriage has failed, or who have gone bankrupt, or whose son or daughter faces failure. Suggest to them that the slogans we hear about making lemonade out of the lemon life has handed us, or learning more from our failures than our successes, are not just empty words. Above all, urge them to know that God is with them even in the pit of despair—as Samson's story proves.

Questions for Discussion
Make use of these questions to involve your students in learning and to test their understanding of the lesson.
1. What two restrictions did the angel place upon the wife of Manoah when he announced the birth of Samson? 2. What is the meaning of Nazirite? 3. What three requirements did the Law make of a Nazirite? Was Samson careful to fulfill these throughout his lifetime? 4. The Spirit of the Lord is spoken of as coming on or stirring Samson four times at least. In what basic way is the Spirit's work in the lives of Christians different from Old Testament times? 5. What was the secret of Samson's strength? 6. In what respects are the details of Samson's life similar to that of the Lord Jesus? In what important respects are the two very different?

Illustrating the Scripture
Examples and quotations to help the teacher communicate the lesson.
WE MAY LEARN LESSONS FROM OUR FAILURES "The death of Samson was more honorable to the man and more useful to his nation than any event in his previous career. The heroism of his death followed the return of God's strength.

"1. *It followed a great fall.* We may learn lessons from our failures. Through our very weakness we may discern the secret of strength. The humility which should accompany failure is one of the first steps toward wiser conduct.

"2. *It came in a season of distress.* Samson was a prisoner, defeated, insulted, mutilated. Sorrow is one road to God's grace, (a) as it teaches us the folly of the evil conduct that produced it, (b) as it leads us into a mood of serious and heart-searching reflection in which true wisdom is found, and (c) as it teaches us our helplessness, and compels us to turn to God for deliverance.

"3. *The return of strength followed a return to obedience.* This was suggested by the growing of Samson's hair and the return to fidelity to his vow. It was gradual. We are received into God's favor immediately we return in penitent faith; but we only conquer evil consequences of sin and regain lost powers and position by degrees.

"4. *The return of strength was realized through prayer.* Samson now knows his weakness. In his own soul he is weak. Strength must come from above. There is no prayer which God will more certainly hear than that which invokes his aid in our performance of some great self-sacrificing duty" (*Pulpit Commentary*).

Topics for Youth

FAILURE TO REMEMBER AND RECOVERY—*"I was sitting at my amateur radio in my home in the Eastern Highlands Province of Papua New Guinea on Friday night (April 7, 1972) at 6:30 p.m. talking to someone in the United States when I received a telephone call from the hangar at which I worked. The person on the other end of the line said, 'The Aztec just crashed at Nadzab.' Nadzab was about sixty miles east of where I lived. I couldn't believe what was told to me. It couldn't be! Not our plane."*

Craig Nimmo, an American aviation mechanic, learned that night the meaning of failure. It was to plunge him to the depth of despair. He was in Papua New Guinea with the Jungle Aviation and Radio Service, assisting Wycliffe Bible Translators in taking the Bible to Bibleless tribes. On that particular day, Craig was doing a routine 100-hour inspection on the right engine of the twin-engine Piper Aztec. Just when he was replacing the fuel unit filter screen, another mechanic signalled that he needed Craig's help. Craig replaced the vital fuel line *finger tight*, intending to return with his wrench and complete the job. But when he returned to the Aztec, the fuel line slipped his mind. Hours later the plane crashed, killing the pilot and six passengers.

"What was wrong? As a teenager I felt God's call in my life," Craig wrote, "to serve in missionary aviation. I had gone to Bible college and graduated, learned to fly, attended seminary in Portland, Oregon, gone to aircraft maintenance school, got a job with a Cessna dealer, applied to Wycliffe and was accepted. I went through all this preparation and was very much aware of God's leading and providing all for the specific purpose of serving my Lord where I knew He wanted me. Now, there it was, seven people thrust into eternity, one totally destroyed airplane and me. How could I face it?"

Craig immediately told his supervisor of his error, in tears and anguish. The next few days were a blur, but somehow he got through the funeral. The next most difficult thing was returning to work in the hangar. He recalls that this would have been impossible if he were left alone, but two other pilot/mechanics worked with him.

"I got through that week with their help and love—or should I say with Christ's help and love demonstrated through two of the members of the body of Christ."

The most difficult task of all was facing the wife and family of the pilot who lost his life in the accident. But Craig met them as they waited to board a flight back to their native New Zealand. He broke down, but they comforted him.

"Glennis (the pilot's widow) sat by me and held the hand that took her husband's life. Ken (the Wycliffe director) sat on my other side with a demonstration of love, comfort and forgiveness. That was the most significant first step in the healing process that was to be my experience over the next few years."

After a furlough in the States, Craig returned to his post in Papua New Guinea "to do the job that God had placed on my wife's and my heart."

LESSON 7   JULY 17

Hannah: A Promise Kept

Background Scripture: 1 Samuel 1:1–2:10
Devotional Reading: Luke 1:8–20

1 Samuel 1:9-11, 19, 20, 24-28

9 So Hannah rose up after they had eaten in Shiloh, and after they had drunk. Now Eli the priest sat upon a seat by a post of the temple of the LORD.

10 And she was in bitterness of soul, and prayed unto the LORD, and wept sore.

11 And she vowed a vow, and said, O LORD of hosts, if thou wilt indeed look on the affliction of thine handmaid, and remember me, and not forget thine handmaid, but wilt give unto thine handmaid a man child, then I will give him unto the LORD all the days of his life, and there shall no razor come upon his head.

19 And they rose up in the morning early, and worshipped before the LORD, and returned, and came to their house to Ramah: and Elkanah knew Hannah his wife; and the LORD remembered her.

20 Wherefore it came to pass, when the time was come about after Hannah had conceived, that she bare a son, and called his name Samuel, saying, Because I have asked him of the LORD.

24 And when she had weaned him, she took him up with her, with three bullocks, and one ephah of flour, and a bottle of wine, and brought him unto the house of the LORD in Shiloh: and the child was young.

25 And they slew a bullock, and brought the child to Eli.

26 And she said, Oh my Lord, as thy soul liveth, my lord, I am the woman that stood by thee here, praying unto the LORD.

27 For this child I prayed; and the LORD hath given me my petition which I asked of him:

28 Therefore also I have lent him to the LORD; as long as he liveth he shall be lent to the LORD. And he worshipped the LORD there.

KEY VERSE: "For this child I prayed; and the LORD hath given me my petition which I asked of him: therefore also I have lent him to the LORD; as long as he liveth he shall be lent to the LORD." 1 Samuel 1:27, 28.

Home Daily Bible Readings
July 11 M. Hannah Weeps, 1 Samuel 1:1-8.
July 12 T. Hannah Makes a Promise, 1 Samuel 1:9-18.
July 13 W. Hannah Has a Son, 1 Samuel 1:19-23.
July 14 T. Hannah Keeps Her Promise, 1 Samuel 1:24-28.
July 15 F. Hannah Praises God, 1 Samuel 2:1-11.
July 16 S. God Seeks a Faithful Priest, 1 Samuel 2:26-36.
July 17 S. Samuel Answers God's Call, 1 Samuel 3:1-10.

Lesson Aim: That adult Christians may so strongly desire the Lord's way in a particular need of theirs that they will make a sacrifice in order to receive God's answer.

LESSON OUTLINE
Background to the Scripture
Looking at the Scripture Text
  I. Where to Go With Bitter Disappointment (1 Samuel 1:9-11)
  II. Who Remembers Our Prayers (1 Samuel 1:19, 20)
  III. How to Show Gratitude (1 Samuel 1:24-28)
Applying the Scripture

Background to the Scripture

To author Edith Deen, Hannah personifies "the ideal in motherhood in the Old Testament."

In her book *All of the Women of the Bible*, Mrs. Deen refers to Hannah as "the prayerful mother." Hannah, she says, was "the fourth great woman in sacred history who grieved because she had not conceived, and among the four she was the most prayerful. Sarah had laughed when she learned a child would be born to her in old age. Rebekah bore her trial with listlessness and indifference. Rachel, irritated at her long wait for a child, exclaimed, 'Give me children, or else I die.' Hannah sought her call as a mother in the power of God, for she desired a son as a poet desires a song."

Her times followed hard on the heels of the period of Samson's judgeship. Mrs. Deen calls this environment "not conducive to prayer" because it was marked by a sharp decline in Israel's "standards of morality and spirituality." Hannah may have considered her day in just the opposite light—a season so dark that it demanded earnest, fervent prayer. True, Hannah was praying a prayer of personal anguish, seeking a son who would take away her reproach for being barren. But in her prayer she made a promise that moved the Lord of the universe not only to give her a son—but to give her a Samuel!

Looking at the Scripture Text

***Where to Go With Bitter Disappointment* (vv. 9-11)** Our text opens, "So Hannah rose up after they had eaten in Shiloh." Notice that it does not say "*she* had eaten," but *they*. Who were *they*? And what were *they* doing in Shiloh?

For a number of years Hannah and her husband Elkanah had gone to Shiloh from their home in Ramah (v. 19) to offer sacrifices to Jehovah. Since Joshua had allotted to the various tribes the land for their inheritance, at least 200 years earlier, Shiloh in the middle of Palestine had been Israel's center of worship. There the tabernacle stood and the high priest ministered.

But Hannah could not look forward to these annual spiritual pilgrimages because Elkanah's other wife, Peninnah, also accompanied them, and the children she had given Elkanah. Scripture is not explicit, but probably Hannah was Elkanah's first wife. She is named first (v. 2). But because she was infertile after several years, Elkanah also took Peninnah as a wife. By her he had sons and daughters, assuring him of children to take care of him in his old age and of heirs to his name.

It would have been difficult for Hannah to enjoy these rare occasions when she was thrown together with "her rival" (v. 6) as Peninnah is called. But Peninnah used such occasions to heap abuse on her because she could not become pregnant.

A clue which may show why Peninnah "provoked" Hannah is given in verse 5. At the feast, probably the Passover, Elkanah presented a peace offering to Jehovah and on that particular evening the family would banquet on the portion of meat which the priests gave to them. Elkanah dealt portions of the savory meat to Peninnah and the children, but he gave a "double portion" (v. 5 NIV) to Hannah "because he loved her."

We don't know how many years this went on. But there came a time when Hannah was so upset that she could not eat. Peninnah's lively children around the table, thoroughly relishing the feast, were a harsh reminder to her that "the Lord had closed her womb." Elkanah's assurances (v. 8) were no comfort to her. Hannah, feeling as if her heart would burst, stood when the meal was finished and walked from their tent the short distance to where the tabernacle stood.

There Eli the priest—in reality, the high priest—sat at the entryway. As the Living Bible says, this was his "customary place." His seat was more a throne than a chair, for at this time he was as much judge in Israel as he was the high priest.

Hannah "wept much and prayed unto the Lord" evidently standing in the outer room of the tabernacle. So overcome with "bitterness of soul," she did not pray aloud (v. 13). It is clear that what she did there was no spur-of-the-moment act; from deep within her she offered a singular petition and a vow.

"O Lord of hosts,"— she addressed Jehovah with simple faith in His supreme and exalted position as the Lord over all the heavenly hosts, which may be taken either as meaning angels or the myriads of stars. This is the second time this popular title of Jehovah (the first appearance in Scripture is in verse 3), used 260 times, appears.

"Thine handmaid"—three times she refers to herself as the maidservant of the Lord, a sincere indication of her deep humility. Three times she also reaches out to the Lord: "look on . . . remember me . . . forget not"—revealing the earnestness of her petition.

In her vow, she asked not merely for a child, but especially for a *male child*, pledging that he would be consecrated to the Lord all of his life. The rule for all sons of the tribe of Levi was that they were to devote their lives totally to Jehovah's service once they reached age twenty-five and until they were fifty (*see* Numbers 8:24). Samuel was of the tribe of Levi, as the genealogical list in 1 Chronicles 6:22–25, 33, 34 shows (rather than of the tribe of Ephraim as we might conclude from verse 1; that is a geograhical designation). If the Lord honored her request, Hannah was pledging to make her son a Nazirite unto God for his entire life (review previous lesson for a discussion of the Nazirite vow).

Who Remembers Our Prayers (vv. 19, 20) As verse 18 indicates, Hannah returned to the banquet table, composed and no longer downcast, and "ate something." In the tabernacle, Eli had taken notice of her and joined in her petition that "the God of Israel" would grant her request. By eating now she was expressing the assurance that comes to those whose heartfelt prayer is seconded by another human being (Matthew 18:19).

In verse 19, the writer speaks in the same breath of the family's religious devotion and of Elkanah's and Hannah's sexual intimacy, as if to say that sex is as much a part of the normal husband-wife relationship as is spirituality, and vice versa. Again and again, the Hebrew writers use explicit language in speaking of the most private and sacred of human relationships. We should learn from this that married couples neglect either of these two at their peril. Hannah can be sure to have worshiped with renewed faith after the crisis experience the evening before. And with the same eagerness she received Elkanah's intimate attentions after the family had returned to Ramah. In due time, Hannah's heart was overjoyed as she learned that the Lord had remembered her; He who had closed her womb now opened it.

At some point before Samuel's birth, Hannah no doubt told her husband of the vow she had made. It would be highly irregular for a Hebrew wife to make a vow without her husband's approval. But in this case Hannah knew best and the absence of any discussion of her telling Elkanah shows that he, too, covenanted with her to keep the promise she had made.

Barren for probably a dozen years or more, Hannah had no difficulty in naming Samuel. Our Bibles say that his name means "asked of God." But Hebrew scholars agree that that is the meaning of "Saul" not "Samuel." The *New Bible Commentary, Revised* says that "Samuel means something like 'his name is God' or 'a godly name.'" One commentator suggests that Hannah "may have uttered some sentence like 'I asked for him a godly name.'"

How to Show Gratitude (vv. 24–28) Precious beyond all else to a young mother are the early months when she is nursing her firstborn. Nothing her baby does escapes her loving attention. She remembers Baby's first smile, the first look of recognition in his eyes, the first time he reaches to grasp her finger. All the more because she had waited so long, and because she would only have Samuel a short while, Hannah treasured Samuel's early days. But when she had weaned him, she knew it was time to follow through on her promise.

In those days in the East, a child was not weaned as early as even the first year. One apocryphal book mentions that a child was three years old when weaned (2 Maccabees 7:28). Samuel was probably that age when Hannah took him to Shiloh to Eli. Since no mention is made of her husband, we might assume that she went alone. But that seems unlikely because she took not only Samuel but things for a sacrifice, including a live ox.

The preference in modern translations for one three-year-old bull rather than three, as the King James says in verse 24, serves to illustrate the value of an earlier manuscript of the Book of Samuel that has come to light with the discovery of the Dead Sea Scrolls in 1947. Until this manuscript began to be studied in the early 1950s, many uncertainties surrounded a good many verses in the books of 1 and 2 Samuel. (Actually, the two books are on one continuous scroll in the Hebrew language.) But the manuscript discovered at the Dead Sea is a full thousand years older than any previously known manuscript. According to it, Hannah took with her one bull to offer as a sacrifice.

The children of Israel were "not to appear before (the Lord) empty-handed" (Exodus 23:15). Hannah's offering seems to be a peace or fellowship offering which was given when fulfilling a vow (Leviticus 7:16). In offering these sacrifices, the Hebrews were reminded that only by the offering of blood could they remain within the favor of the Lord. It was a costly sacrifice, but she offered it with a glad heart.

In approaching aged Eli, she reminded him of her vow and testified how "the Lord has granted me what I asked of him" (v. 27 NIV). Then she did not shrink from the more costly sacrifice to which she had pledged herself. "So now I give him to the Lord. For his whole life he will be given over to the Lord" (v. 28 NIV).

Our text closes with "he worshipped the Lord there," only we cannot be sure who is intended—Samuel? Eli? Or perhaps Elkanah? Some versions say *"they* worshiped there."

As chapter 2 indicates, Hannah's devotion to her child continued, though she saw him only on the occasions when the family went to Shiloh to worship. Once as she brought little Samuel a handsewn robe to wear, Eli pronounced an added blessing upon her and Elkanah; the Lord gave her in the ensuing years three sons and two daughters as compensation for the great sacrifice she made in giving the godly Samuel to Him.

Applying the Scripture

Teacher: The personal application of today's lesson, as suggested below, should find a responsive chord in the life of every member of your class. Approach this part of the study in two steps.

First, from our vantage point, we can see these events and know something of what the Lord was about to do in Israel, and actually, in world history.

After all, His purpose is what really matters. He was setting the stage for a significant development in the near future. He foresaw Israel's need of a king; He saw David and Solomon, and the establishment of a "house of David" from which would issue the Messiah to Israel and to all the world.

But Israel was in no condition to do honor to a king. After all of the ups and downs of the period of the judges, she was in national disarray, intimidated by her enemies, shot through with idolatry, and disunited. Someone was needed to prepare the way for the monarchy, to rally Israel around one central focus and to teach her the ways of the Law.

But where was such a leader to be found? Israel's high priests were nondescript figureheads. (Eli's sons, for example, led wicked lives.) Samson, the latest judge, had utterly failed to raise the spiritual and moral standards of Israel.

Enter Hannah—the *second* step in our application. Hannah was "all bent out of shape," as we would say, because of a particularly painful reproach. She must have thought many times that God did not even know about her. Or if He did, He certainly didn't care. But from our vantage point, we can see that He never stopped caring. Finally His high purpose meshed exactly with Hannah's great longing. He had waited until someone was willing to make a special sacrifice so that He could do a very special thing.

According to Isaiah 30:18, this is ever God's way. That verse says, "therefore will the Lord wait, that he may be gracious unto you, and therefore will he be exalted, that he may have mercy upon you . . . blessed are all they that wait for him."

Each of us may identify with Hannah in her need. We may have a painful longing for some answer from God. We may feel our hearts will break if a certain prayer is not answered. From this lesson, we should seek to look at our need from the Lord's viewpoint. He waits to be gracious to us. His answer is probably delayed because we are not yet ready, or the conditions are not right. While we want an answer now, He sees the good that will come by waiting.

It may help us to remember the familiar axiom that "it takes only sixty days to make a squash, but sixty years to grow an oak." We should be encouraged to be patient. *But*, we should each go before God alone as Hannah did. If He is asking us to sacrifice something—and we are unwilling—that may be the hindrance. In such cases, urge your students—and yourself—to offer the sacrifice that God demands, knowing that "underneath are the everlasting arms."

Questions for Discussion
Make use of these questions to involve your students in learning and to test their understanding of the lesson.
1. What were Hannah and her family doing in Shiloh? 2. What was her "affliction" from which she sought relief? 3. How could she make a binding vow without her husband? 4. What marks this as a religious family?

What distinguishes Hannah as being more than merely religious? 5. About what age was Samuel when Hannah took him to the temple? 6. What was Hannah's sacrifice? What does her deed say to us who want spiritual blessing and answers to prayer today? 7. How did the Lord compensate Hannah for giving up her son?

Illustrating the Scripture
Examples and quotations to help the teacher communicate the lesson.

A nineteenth-century poet, known only as Mrs. Homans, captured something of the joy and sacrifice which Hannah knew on that day when she fulfilled her vow and kept her promise:

> The boy was vowed
> Unto the temple service. By the hand
> She led him, and her silent soul, the while,
> Oft as the dewy laughter of his eye
> Met her sweet serious glance, rejoiced to think
> That aught so pure, so beautiful, was hers,
> To bring before her God.
>
> I give thee to thy God—the God that gave thee
> A well-spring of deep gladness to my heart!
>   And precious as thou art,
> And pure as dew of Hermon, he shall have thee,
> My own, my beautiful, my undefiled!
>   And thou shalt be his child.
>
> Therefore, farewell!—I go, my soul may fail me,
> As the stag panteth for the water brooks,
>   Yearning for thy sweet looks.
> But thou, my first-born, droop not, nor bewail me!
> Thou in the Shadow of the Rock shalt dwell,
>   The Rock of Strength.—Farewell!

THE DISCIPLINE OF WAITING "In God's laboratory of building men and women, strengthening character, healing the spirits and restoring confidence, He has a very important area called: The Waiting Room! . . .

"Impetuous youth says: 'Go man, go!' Maturity and wisdom say: 'Wait . . . take time . . . hold tight!' I am prone to say: 'Up and at 'em.' God usually says: 'Blessed are all they that wait. . . .'

"It's tough enough to wait for that plane or letter, but how we 'chomp at the bit' *waiting for God to make His next move.*

"Can you imagine Abraham waiting till he was over 100 years old for the birth of his first boy? Moses waiting forty years in the desert? The children of Israel 'standing still' on the shores of the Red Sea with the Egyptians moving in on their rear-guard?

" 'Rest in the Lord, and wait patiently for him: fret not thyself . . .' (Psalms 37:7).

"The discipline of waiting does much for God's child. It teaches us patience and faith (Psalms 27:4); it enables us to watch God at work (Psalms 26:5); it matures us through struggle and stress as the butterfly coming from the cocoon (Isaiah 64:4); and best of all, the person who waits has the touch of God upon his life (Lamentations 3:22–27).

"Think on this—God waits so He may be gracious to you. Happy, satisfied, and completely honored in this confidence is the man who will wait for Him. He waits for you . . . will you wait for Him?" (From *The Challenge*, a monthly letter written by Robert D. Foster.)

Topics for Youth

DOES GOD ANSWER YOUR PRAYERS?—What if Hannah had given up praying for a son? What if she took all of the long years of silence from heaven as evidence that God was either unconcerned or didn't know about the way she felt? There would never have been a Samuel, and Israel would have very likely disappeared as a nation of any real consequence.

"It is easy to become a fatalist in reference to prayer," says J. Oswald Sanders. "It is easier to regard unanswered prayer as the will of God than to deliberately reason out the causes of defeat. But should we be less honest in our approach to this perplexing problem than a merchant to his adverse balance sheet? Perhaps our reluctance to analyze our failures in prayer is rooted in a mistaken solicitude for God's honor. God is more honored when we ruthlessly face our failure and diligently search for its cause than when we piously ignore it.

"The underlying reason for *every* unanswered prayer is that in some way we have asked amiss (James 4:3). Could it be that we have substituted faith in *prayer* for faith in *God*? We are nowhere exhorted to have faith in prayer, but we are counseled: 'Have faith in God' (Mark 11:22). Faced with this problem the disciples asked: 'Why could not we . . . ?' 'Because of your unbelief,' replied the Master. An analysis of our prayers might afford the disconcerting discovery that many of them are not the *prayer of faith* at all, only the *prayer of hope*, or even of despair. We earnestly hope they will be answered, but have no unshakable assurance to that effect. God has, however, undertaken to answer only the prayer of faith. 'Whatever you pray for and ask, believe that you have got it, and you shall have it' (Mark 11:24 MOFFATT). Don't think the translator has his tenses wrong! It is we who have our attitude wrong!

"Another prolific cause of defeat in the prayer life is a secret sympathy with sin. 'If I regard (cling to) iniquity in my heart, the Lord will not hear me.' Then let us search out and rectify the causes of our unanswered petitions." (From the booklet, *Effective Prayer*, by J. Oswald Sanders.)

LESSON 8

JULY 24

Naaman: Reluctant Follower

Background Scripture: 2 Kings 5
Devotional Reading John 3:1–12

2 Kings 5:1–5, 9–14

1 Now Naaman, captain of the host of the king of Syria, was a great man with his master, and honourable, because by him the LORD had given deliverance unto Syria: he was also a mighty man in valour, but he was a leper.

2 And the Syrians had gone out by companies, and had brought away captive out of the land of Israel a little maid; and she waited on Naaman's wife.

3 And she said unto her mistress, Would God my lord were with the prophet that is in Samaria! for he would recover him of his leprosy.

4 And one went in, and told his lord, saying, Thus and thus said the maid that is of the land of Israel.

5 And the king of Syria said, Go to, go, and I will send a letter unto the king of Israel. And he departed, and took with him ten talents of silver, and six thousand pieces of gold, and ten changes of raiment.

9 So Naaman came with his horses and with his chariot, and stood at the door of the house of Elisha.

10 And Elisha sent a messenger unto him, saying, Go and wash in Jordan seven times, and thy flesh shall come again to thee, and thou shalt be clean.

11 But Naaman was wroth, and went away, and said, Behold, I thought, He will surely come out to me, and stand, and call on the name of the LORD his God, and strike his hand over the place, and recover the leper.

12 Are not Abana and Pharpar, rivers of Damascus, better than all the waters of Israel? may I not wash in them, and be clean? So he turned and went away in a rage.

13 And his servants came near, and spake unto him, and said, My father, if the prophet had bid thee do some great thing, wouldest thou not have done it? how much rather then, when he saith to thee, Wash, and be clean?

14 Then went he down, and dipped himself seven times in Jordan, according to the saying of the man of God: and his flesh came again like unto the flesh of a little child, and he was clean.

402 OLD TESTAMENT PERSONALITIES

KEY VERSE: "Then went he down, and dipped himself seven times in Jordan, according to the saying of the man of God: and his flesh came again like unto the flesh of a little child, and he was clean." 2 Kings 5:14.

Home Daily Bible Readings
July 18   M.   The Priest Tests for Leprosy, Leviticus 13:9-17.
July 19   T.   A Syrian Maiden Suggests a Cure, 2 Kings 5:1-7.
July 20   W.   Naaman Is Cured of Leprosy, 2 Kings 5:8-14.
July 21   T.   Elisha Refuses a Present, 2 Kings 5:15-19.
July 22   F.   A Deceitful Servant Becomes a Leper, 2 Kings 5:19-27.
July 23   S.   Jesus Recalls Naaman, Luke 4:16-28.
July 24   S.   Jesus Sends Ten Lepers to the Priest, Luke 17:11-19.

Lesson Aim: That adults will not be offended by the simplicity of the Gospel.

LESSON OUTLINE
Background to the Scripture
Looking at the Scripture Text
  I. Hindered by a Disease (2 Kings 5:1)
 II. Helped by a Maiden (2 Kings 5:2-5)
III. Humbled by the Jordan (2 Kings 5:9-13)
IV. Healed by His Obedience (2 Kings 5:14)
Applying the Scripture

Background to the Scripture

Today we leap forward in Israel's history, from the period of the judges to the time of the prophets, when Israel was divided into the northern (Israel) and southern (Judah) kingdoms. We shall be studying a small section of what is called "the Elisha cycle" of the Book of Kings—those several events in the northern kingdom's history which revolved around the Prophet Elisha.

The date is approximately 850 B.C. As a number of scholars suppose, the kings of Israel and of Syria, respectively, are Joram and Benhadad II. But they go unnamed for they are really backstage in the scenes of this account. Front and center are Elisha, a little Israelite girl, and Naaman. Often the courage and loyalty of the maiden has been praised in Bible classes. And Elisha's exploits have made his name almost a household word, even if we do confuse him with his predecessor Elijah. But Naaman, the forgotten Syrian, has not often been the subject of Bible lesson. In what promises to be a richly rewarding study, we turn our attention to him today.

Looking at the Scripture Text

Hindered by a Disease (v. 1)   To the Syrians, the civilized world is indebted for the introduction of the alphabet into public and private use. But the Syrians of the ninth century (more properly called Arameans; Syria is their Greek name) were indebted to the strong and wise rule of their kings, Benhadad and his son. Benhadad habitually led his troops into battle, as instances in 1 and 2 Kings show, but in Benhadad II's later years the honor of commanding the troops passed to Naaman.

This man had made a name for himself in many spheres of human endeavor. He was *high in rank*, "commander of the army"—*great in honor*, "a great man in the sight of his master"—*successful in war*, "through him the Lord had given victory to Aram" (NIV)—and *distinguished for personal bravery*, "a valiant soldier."

But one thing spoiled Naaman's life so that the lowest slave in Syria would not have exchanged skins with him. "He was a leper." As the footnotes to the New International Version point out, the word *leper* was used for "various diseases affecting the skin—not necessarily leprosy." The *New Bible Commentary, Revised* says the word as used in the Bible "rarely if ever refers to Hansen's disease, commonly called 'leprosy' today."

What Naaman's affliction was we cannot be sure. Today's English Version translates it "he suffered from a dreaded skin disease." But it seems fair to conclude that his "leprosy" or skin disease was painful, loathsome, and fatal. Perhaps Naaman suffered increasingly and could only ignore the pain by immersing himself in a flurry of activity. Yet the repulsive appearance of his diseased body could have driven him more and more into isolation. His life became filled with fear and angry frustration. Though the text does not say so, the disease was probably considered incurable and fatal.

King Benhadad II would have empathized with the suffering of his great captain for to Naaman's wise generalship the Syrian people were consciously indebted for the peace they enjoyed. But as our text shows, the king was most indebted to Jehovah, though not conscious of Him. He it was who gave the Syrians "victory." This is one of the earliest instances where, during Israel's existence, the Lord's care for Gentiles is clearly spoken of. As we will see, His love extended not just to the great masses of non-Jewish people; He reached in grace to particular Gentiles who would acknowledge Him (vv. 15-18).

Helped by a Maiden (vv. 2-5) Without question, the capture of a Hebrew girl by Israel's archenemy Syria would be considered most unfortunate. It is like the sad and tragic events of which we learn daily through the news media. But the writer of 2 Kings shows how God turned this evil circumstance to the benefit of Naaman and his unbelieving household. The incident should encourage the children of God to know that, with Him there are no "accidents"; He is ever bringing good out of evil.

The little girl may only have observed Naaman once, and knew immediately that dreaded disease. Or she may have been exposed to his pain and discomfort for a longer period of time. At home, the great captain would give way to affliction and her heart would go out to him in sympathy until one day she would exclaim: "If only my master would see the prophet who is in

Samaria! He would cure him of (literally, take away) his leprosy" (v. 6 NIV).

Her singular witness set in motion a turn of events that might well have amazed the girl. Perhaps Naaman's wife, whom the girl served, told Naaman what she said. He would probably have the girl repeat it and explain in detail who this prophet was and what she had meant. Then he went straight to "his master," Benhadad, who acted with characteristic swiftness. "By all means, go" the NIV translates his remarks (v. 5).

Ten talents of silver would be 12,000 ounces, or 340 kilograms. The gold, 6,000 pieces (coins were not in use as yet) weighed 150 pounds (a whopping $1.5 million in today's inflated currency). This rich bounty Naaman took with him in his search for a cure reminds us that this was before the days of Blue Cross and Blue Shield. The riches he carried ought to pay for an extended stay in any Mayo Clinic of his day. On a more serious note, the silver and gold and "ten changes of clothes" denote at once the wealth of Syria's king and Naaman's worth to his king. It also shows that, in some sense, Naaman intended to buy his health. He would learn that such is not God's way.

Humbled by the Jordan (vv. 9–13) Israel was hardly on equal terms with Syria at this time. She was more a "vassal state" of her northern neighbor. For that reason, King Joram feared any provocation from Benhadad and he interpreted Benhadad's command to cure Naaman's leprosy as a ruse to start a quarrel. The king's lack of spiritual insight is revealed in his failure to send Naaman to Elisha who lived in the same city, Samaria; the prophet himself had to send for Naaman.

From the splendor of the king's palace, Naaman and his party proceeded to Elisha's dwelling, which may have been quite humble. While the proud Syrian horses snorted and stomped, Naaman, thinking that the moment of his cure was come, waited impatiently in his beautifully crafted chariot for "the man of God" to appear. But instead, a house servant emerged at the door and made his way to Naaman's chariot.

This "messenger" announced a simple directive to Naaman in the hearing of all his retinue of attendants—"Go, wash yourself seven times in the Jordan, and your flesh will be restored and you will be cleansed" (v. 10 NIV).

Verse 11 shows that Naaman was instantly insulted and outraged. As a great man, one on whom the king leaned (v. 18), he was "accustomed to extreme deference, and all the outward tokens of respect and reverence." He had imagined "a striking scene, whereof he was to be the central figure," says the *Pulpit Commentary*, "the prophet descending, with perhaps a wand of office, the attendants drawn up on either side, the passers-by standing to gaze—a solemn invocation of the Deity, a waving to and fro of the wand in the prophet's hand, and a sudden manifest cure, wrought in the open street of the city before the eyes of men, and at once noised abroad through the capital...."

But God's ways are not our ways, and Naaman's were surely not Elisha's. He was offended at being directed by a servant and at the thought of dipping in the Jordan. "Are not Abana and Pharpar . . . better than any of the waters of Israel?" Those who have visited Syria testify to the purity and vitality of those rivers of Damascus identified today as the Barada and the Awaj. But of course Naaman was yet going on the strength of his physical senses alone. His spiritual blindness, like his leprosy, could be "cleansed" by obeying Elisha's simple command which he would have to take by faith.

The proud Syrian most surely would have failed to be healed were it not for his own servants who persuaded him. Their part in the story underlines the crucial role more than a half dozen persons played in Naaman's healing—the wife of Naaman, the Hebrew girl, King Benhadad, Elisha's servant, Elisha, and these servants. God continues to work in this manner through His people today.

Because leprosy was one of those conditions that prevented an Israelite from approaching the tabernacle to worship or even to live in his own tent or house, a leper was called unclean. To be healed was to be cleansed, and an elaborate ritual of cleansing accompanied the declaration by the priest that a leper was "clean." When the disease was active, he was cut off from fellowship with God and man and was required to call to any whom he met, "Unclean! Unclean" (Leviticus 13:45, 46). It was a pathetic, humiliating ailment, in many ways typical of sin.

Healed by His Obedience (v. 14) Naaman's better judgment told him to accept Elisha's advice and yield to his servants' persuasions. The account of his going down to the Jordan has been retold thousands of times, in story and sermon. Yet it is not diminished in impact to read once more that "he . . . dipped himself seven times in Jordan, according to the saying of the man of God. . . ."

His skin restored "fresh and pure" like that of a young man, Naaman could have proceeded on to Damascus; at the Jordan he was only three or four days' journey from home. But instead, he retraced his steps and stood once more at Elisha's house, a changed, grateful, humble man. This time he spoke with Elisha and testified, "Now I know that there is no god but the God of Israel . . . from now on I will not offer sacrifices or burnt offerings to any god except the Lord" (vv. 15, 17 TEV).

Elisha staunchly refused any reward, showing Naaman something of God's free gift. Gehazi, Elisha's servant, did later seek a portion of the bounty on false pretences and subsequently contracted leprosy (vv. 19-27). But Naaman, like the Ethiopian eunuch, "went on his way rejoicing." The two mule loads of dirt he took with him (vv. 17, 18) merely reflect the state of his understanding at that time. He thought the Lord could only be worshiped on His soil, for that was what the heathen peoples believed. Who can doubt that upon his return to Damascus, Naaman led his whole household to worship the true and living God—the God who had cleansed him.

Applying the Scripture

This lesson leads naturally to the grand theme: salvation. Although you may feel that everyone in class has already embraced the Gospel and is trusting Jesus Christ for salvation, you should use the occasion to drive home the truth of salvation. Someone may need to hear the simple Gospel message and everyone who knows Christ will be happy once more to think on "the old, old story."

The story of Naaman is a graphic illustration of these points of the Gospel:

1. *Sin*—leprosy is a biblical representation of sin, because it was hereditary, painful, contagious, loathsome, and fatal.

2. *Man's efforts to buy his salvation*—It is almost universally accepted that man must somehow merit heaven. Naaman's rich rewards were typical of how man in his pride and independence attempts to obtain healing for his soul but finds that God refuses all such attempts.

3. *Cleansing*—The healing of an illness portrays the cleansing of the soul, our inner man, which we know to be filled with pride, greed, selfishness, lying, lust, gluttony, and a hundred other vices.

4. *Dipping in the Jordan*—The order to "dip in the Jordan" was a humbling directive. So it is to accept the death of Christ by faith for salvation. What could be more simple than to dip oneself in the Jordan? Anyone could do that, and so *anyone* can put his trust in Jesus. Note that the figures of speech Jesus used in John are all simple acts—eat the bread of life (6:35), drink of the water of life (7:37), walk through the door (10:9). All of these are simple acts within the reach of everyone. So, salvation is free to all who will simply call on the Name of the Lord (Romans 10:13).

5. *"According to the saying of the man of God"*—The only way to salvation is to follow what God has said in His Word.

Close the class period with a minute of silent prayer. Invite anyone in class who is not certain that their sins are forgiven "to dip in the Jordan"—to pray and receive Christ. You may want to lead the class in an audible prayer of concession, asking God to forgive their sins for Christ's sake and to come into their hearts. Ask that anyone who has asked Christ to come into his heart to tell you after class.

Questions for Discussion
Make use of these questions to involve your students in learning and to test their understanding of the lesson.
1. From the text, name two factors which would show that a Gentile person and/or nation could also be "chosen" of Jehovah. 2. Why was Naaman's disease so particularly dreadful? 3. When He referred to Naaman (Luke 4:27), what point did the Lord Jesus seek to make? 4. What in this passage shows the pride of this commander-in-chief? What reveals the humility Elisha's advice required? 5. Why was Naaman's comment about the Abana and Pharpar rivers beside the point? 6. Why is a person healed of leprosy spoken of as clean, or cleansed (vv. 10, 13)? 7. Of what great biblical truth is Naaman's healing symbolic? How is it symbolic?

Illustrating the Scripture
Examples and quotations to help the teacher communicate the lesson.
"ACCORDING TO THE SAYING OF THE MAN OF GOD" Naaman obeyed the instruction of Elisha; as the text says, he went to the Jordan and

dipped "according to the saying of the man of God." In this case, the "man of God" represented the Word of God. We can have as absolute confidence in the Word as Naaman did in Elisha's word.

Writing on the authority of the Bible, Donald E. DeGraaf said in *His* magazine (March 1981): "Scientists are puzzled by the problem of accounting for the data from quasars in terms of the law of conservation of energy. Yet, even this major unsolved problem does not really shake our belief in the universal validity of conservation of energy. Scientists continue to use and depend on the law—because it works, even though our understanding of it may not yet be complete.

"It seems we can use and depend on Scripture in the same way: we can accept and rely on the Bible in spite of unresolved difficulties in the text. In deciding whether the Bible is trustworthy and authoritative, the place to begin is not with the problems, but with the Bible as a whole.

"Martyn Lloyd-Jones said in *Authority*, 'We are . . . to start with the whole Bible first, and to consider the details in the light of the whole and not in the reverse order.' When we do this, the overall thrust of the evidence strongly supports the general conclusion that our Bible is indeed a trustworthy document. Followers of Christ can accept the Bible's own affirmation that it carries the authority of God himself. They are then free to view the difficulties in a proper perspective and proceed to deal with them.

"What should we do, though, about the problems?

"For one thing, we should not concede that an alleged 'error' is really an error, when it is only a *difficulty*. Some writers seem to take a delight in collecting as many difficulties as they can find. Thus, a casual reader can get the impression that the whole Bible is a mass of contradictions and problems. Thoughtful study, however, has shown that the great majority of these difficulties can be resolved.

"In dealing with internal discrepancies the first step is to thoughtfully compare Scripture with Scripture. By using several translations and reading the text with care, the Bible student can often find a satisfactory reconciliation between passages which initially seemed to conflict. . . .

"When faced with difficulty that persists even after diligent study, it is often helpful to consult the works of scholars who accept the authority of Scripture. Some writers have addressed themselves to these difficulties with care and thoroughness. Here are three books by Christian scholars which can be strongly recommended: *The New Testament Documents: Are They Reliable?* by F. F. Bruce (InterVarsity Press); *Introduction to the Old Testament* by Roland K. Harrison (Eerdmans); *Ancient Orient and Old Testament* by Kenneth A. Kitchen (InterVarsity Press)."

Topics for Youth

DON'T ALLOW THE GOSPEL'S SIMPLICITY TO OFFEND YOU—"Oh, that's too easy. That can't be true—it's too simple!"

Ever hear that said about being born again, about becoming a Christian? So, what's so wrong about a thing being simple? Is there virtue in complexity? Here's what several people from different eras have said about the notion of simplicity.

Winston Churchill said, "All great things are simple, and many can be expressed in a single word: freedom, justice, honor, duty, mercy, hope."

"The greatest truths are the simplest, and so are the greatest men," said August W. Hare. Henry Wadsworth Longfellow said: "In character, in manners, in style, in all things, the supreme excellence is simplicity."

Think of Naaman. What offended him about going to the Jordan River? He saw no sense in it. It was intellectual suicide. It hurt his pride. Funny how he was prepared to pay big money to get healed, but he scoffed at the rude suggestion of going to the Jordan. He thought the prophet would come out of his house, call a crowd about him, say the magic words, wave his hand over the leprosy and *zingo!* he would be well!

But to go to the Jordan, the muddy Jordan, where no one but his servants would see him. *Yuk!* The simplicity of it offended him. But we know that when he did swallow his pride and go down into the Jordan, the simple orders of the prophet were enough. He came out well!

How simple is the approach to Christ. The statements of Scripture make that plain: "Everyone who calls on the name of the Lord will be saved" (Romans 10:13 NIV). "For God so loved the world that he gave his one and only Son, that whoever believes in him shall not perish but have eternal life" (John 3:16 NIV). "They replied, 'Believe in the Lord Jesus, and you will be saved—you and your household" (Acts 16:31 NIV).

The Gospel is simple so that a young child can understand it. And it is simple so that we will not have anything of ourselves of which to boast. Jesus Christ saves us by grace. We come to Him in humility. "Nothing in my hand I bring, simply to Thy cross I cling."

LESSON 9   JULY 31

Joash: A King Led Astray

Background Scripture: 2 Chronicles 24
Devotional Reading: Matthew 27:3–10

2 Chronicles 24:1–7, 17–20
1 Joash was seven years old when he began to reign, and he reigned forty years in Jerusalem. His mother's name also was Zibiah of Beersheba.
2 And Joash did that which was right in the sight of the LORD all the days of Jehoiada the priest.

3 And Jehoiada took for him two wives; and he begat sons and daughters.
4 And it came to pass after this, that Joash was minded to repair the house of the LORD.
5 And he gathered together the priests and the Levites, and said to them, Go out unto the cities of Judah, and gather of all Israel money to repair the house of your God from year to year, and see that ye hasten the matter. Howbeit the Levites hastened it not.
6 And the king called for Jehoiada the chief, and said unto him, Why hast thou not required of the Levites to bring in out of Judah and out of Jerusalem the collection, according to the commandment of Moses the servant of the LORD, and of the congregation of Israel, for the tabernacle of witness?
7 For the sons of Athaliah, that wicked woman, had broken up the house of God; and also all the dedicated things of the house of the LORD did they bestow upon Baalim.
17 Now after the death of Jehoiada came the princes of Judah, and made obeisance to the king. Then the king hearkened unto them.
18 And they left the house of the LORD God of their fathers, and served groves and idols: and wrath came upon Judah and Jerusalem for this their trespass.
19 Yet he sent prophets to them, to bring them again unto the LORD; and they testified against them: but they would not give ear.
20 And the Spirit of God came upon Zechariah the son of Jehoiada the priest, which stood above the people, and said unto them, Thus saith God, Why transgress ye the commandments of the LORD, that ye cannot prosper? because ye have forsaken the LORD, he hath also forsaken you.

KEY VERSE: "Thus saith God, Why transgress ye the commandments of the LORD, that ye cannot prosper? because ye have forsaken the LORD, he hath also forsaken you." 2 Chronicles 24:20.

Home Daily Bible Readings		
July 25	M.	The Way of the Wicked, Psalm 1.
July 26	T.	Trust in the Lord, Psalm 4.
July 27	W.	The Shield of Favor, Psalm 5.
July 28	T.	Walking Blamelessly, Psalm 15.
July 29	F.	Forgiven Transgressions, Psalm 32.
July 30	S.	Walking in Integrity, Psalm 26.
July 31	S.	Trust Not in Princes, Psalm 146.

Lesson Aim: That your class members will want to make Christ-honoring choices independent of others' influence.

410 OLD TESTAMENT PERSONALITIES

LESSON OUTLINE
Background to the Scripture
Looking at the Scripture Text
I. Good Beginning Under Godly Influence (2 Chronicles 24:1-7)
II. Evil Ending Under Idolatrous Influence (2 Chronicles 24:17-20)
Applying the Scripture

Background to the Scripture

"Certainly Judah never fully recovered from Joash's apostasy," says one Old Testament scholar in commenting on the subject of this final lesson in the series on "Persons Choosing Priorities."

Joash lived right in the middle of the period of Israel's monarchy. Some 200 years preceded his reign, from the anointing of Saul to approximately 837 B.C., and another 200 years of slow, gradual decline followed his death in approximately 796 B.C. until the fall of Jerusalem in 586.

Why did this man go astray and end up so devoid of honor that the people would not even accord him a burial among the kings of Judah? What bearing does the moral and spiritual decline of Judah have upon our own nation's future? And what can we personally learn from this man's life that will protect us from doing the same thing? Our study today should help us discover some answers to these very important questions. For a fuller understanding of Joash and his times, consult 2 Kings 12 which treats this same time period.

Looking at the Scripture Text

Good Beginning Under Godly Influence (vv. 1-7) A cartoon in the *New Yorker* showed a king sitting in his private study, penning an entry in his journal. He wrote, "Reigned all day." King Joash could have written that 14,600 times! His forty years as the king over Judah was one of the longest reigns in Israelite history.

But more important than the quantity of days on the throne is the quality of that reign. Before this study is finished, we will see that not all of his forty years were a sign of the blessing of God.

Yet Joash (he is sometimes called Jehoash) surely had an auspicious start. He was a child king, crowned and anointed in the regal palace of Solomon when he was but seven years old. He was there because of the high priest, Jehoiada, and Jehoiada's wife, Jehosheba. When Joash was still an infant his father, King Ahaziah, was murdered and Queen Mother Athaliah strongarmed her way to the throne. In doing so she had all of Ahaziah's sons killed—except Joash. This little one-year-old was taken by Jehosheba into Solomon's temple and hid there for six years.

When Jehoiada sensed that the time was right, he called for Levites and "leaders of hundreds" to come to Jerusalem. They heartily consented to installing the "king's son" on the throne of David. Athaliah was executed and so began Joash's rule. "The extremely interesting circumstances under which Joash came to the throne make us wish that there was something satisfactory to record of him when he sat upon it," notes the *Pulpit Commentary*. Perhaps that is a little too harsh a judgment to make, as we will see; but after such a beginning, marked by the providence of God in sparing his life, Joash is a sharp disappointment.

The chronicler states that "he reigned ... in Jerusalem" to indicate that these events are taking place in the southern kingdom of Judah of which Jerusalem was the capital. Last week's lesson on Naaman centered in the northern kingdom of Israel whose capital was Samaria.

The chronicler, generally assumed to be the priest Ezra, described the nature of Joash's reign in the customary way, but with a slightly different twist: "he did that which was right in the sight of the Lord *all the days of Jehoiada the priest*" (italics ours). We know something is amiss by the words—"all the days of Jehoiada." It seems that when one first reads this he is prepared for Ezra to say "all the days of his life." Thankfully, Jehoiada lived to be 130 years old. He would have been about 100 years old when little Joash became king.

There is nothing strange about his choosing a wife for Joash. One commentator suggests that he may have selected two wives in order to prevent Joash from taking numerous wives as did Solomon. We cannot know the reason, but the priest's action in Joash's behalf in such an important matter implies an overbearing, smothering quality in Jehoiada. And that may be the prime clue to Joash's weakness of character which later revealed itself. He grew up in the shadow of a man all Judah respected and perhaps never developed strength independent of him.

However, the decision to renovate the temple was King Joash's. A hundred years had passed since the beautiful temple of Solomon had been dedicated. During that time the people were to contribute a half-shekel per adult annually for the temple upkeep as Moses had commanded (*see* v. 6; Exodus 30:11-16). From our text, it is clear that this collection was not currently in effect. Without it the temple would have been neglected. Additionally, the sons of the "corrupt" Queen Athaliah had "broken into" the temple (v. 7) and looted its treasury of the "dedicated (sacred) things"—holy vessels and furniture were put to use in the worship of Baal. Perhaps with failing eyesight and wearied of the heavy responsibilities which were his for so long, Jehoiada grew accustomed to the rundown condition of the temple. It took a new set of eyes to see what had to be done.

That the "Levites did not act at once" in obeying Joash's command to collect the half-shekel reflects both the priest's waning powers of leadership and, as well, the indifference of the people. According to the parallel account in 2 Kings 12:6, by the king's twenty-third year on the throne "the priests still had not repaired the temple" (NIV).

As verses 8-16 indicate, Joash initiated a new plan which proved effective. To this day, it is called in some quarters "Joash's Box." Monies were given freely by the people so that the chronicler could write: "The men in charge of the work were diligent and the repairs progressed under them. They rebuilt the temple of God according to its original design and reinforced it" (v. 13 NIV).

Evil Ending Under Idolatrous Influence (vv. 17–20) To this point we have had nothing but good news about Joash. But with the death of Jehoiada, a new page is turned in the life of Joash and unfortunately it is bad news from here on.

In one of Joseph's dreams, the sheaves of his brothers' wheat bowed down to Joseph's sheaf. It is this verb, *to bow down*, that the writer uses to describe the action of the princes or nobles of Judah. They "made obeisance" or "paid homage" to the king. Calculating that by flattering the king with feigned worship, they could gain his approval for their evil purpose, they approached him with outward humility. Their calculations were correct; he "listened to them," which means he gave in to them.

From the next verse, it is clear that they had wanted to ease out from under the yoke of obedience to the Law. Perhaps they approached Joash from the standpoint of how inconvenient it was always to be coming to the temple to make sacrifices and to worship Jehovah. They would have rationalized to him that they could worship God as well in their own towns. Satan still uses this same tactic today! What was left unsaid, of course, was that the holiness of Jehovah-worship crimped their life-style. But that was not necessary to state. Joash could well have been chafing under the strict moral code of the Law. So, although he himself had launched the work of temple repairs, he OK'd a decided return to heathen worship. "They"—the leaders, and also the masses—"abandoned" the house of the Lord.

Joash's decision cut across the covenant he and some of these same leaders had entered into at the start of his reign (23:16). Sometimes when man does such a thing, he gives little thought to how the Lord, the silent third party to such a covenant, will look upon his actions. The holy God could only view this action in one way, with angry disapproval; and being a God who acts, He could not remain silent.

The chronicler records three steps Jehovah took to recover His people from idol worship.

First, "wrath came upon Judah and Jerusalem. . . ." Exactly how God showed His wrath is not said. But 2 Kings 12:17, 18 may give a clue. The king of Syria, Hazael, who caused Elisha to weep because Elisha could foresee the cruel punishment the king would inflict upon Israel, cut across Judah with apparent ease, conquered the town of Gath southwest of Jerusalem and turned toward Jerusalem. A desperate Joash bought him off by emptying the temple treasury and giving riches to Hazael.

Next, Jehovah sent prophets to the people and to the king, "to bring them again unto the Lord." In the books of Chronicles at least ten prophets are named—Nathan, Ahijah, Azariah, Hanani, Micaiah, Jehu, Jahaziel, Elijah, Elisha, and Zechariah—and there were evidently others. Nothing could show more clearly the Lord's mercy and longsuffering toward His people. But, tragically, "they would not give ear" (v. 19).

Finally, the last prophet appeared, not to offer a call to repentance but to pronounce judgment. It was none other than Zechariah, a son of Jehoiada. From a platform, he spoke to the people as the Holy Spirit "took control of" or "clothed" him. "Ye have forsaken the Lord," he declared, "he hath also forsaken you." Joash and his ruling princes could not stand to hear such things. There in the outer court of the temple, they stoned Zechariah to death, the man who owed his very life to Jehoiada giving the order to kill Jehoiada's son. Zechariah's death startled even the princes who had used Joash for their own purposes. The "weakling king" proved himself erratic and brutal when acting on his own. In time, these same princes put Joash to death for slaying Zechariah (v. 25).

Centuries later, a Prophet greater than Zechariah stood in the same city, Jerusalem, and denounced the hypocrisy of those religionists who stoned the prophets and all whom Jehovah sent. In the only biblical reference to the lifetime of Joash, the Lord Jesus named Zechariah as the last of the great prophets whom Israel put to death (*see* Matthew 23:35; Luke 11:51).

Applying the Scripture
Teacher, consider for a moment the lesson aim—that your class members will want to make Christ-honoring choices independent of others' influence.

This does not mean that we should seek to be completely independent of others. We do need the advice and counsel of friends, family, associates, and other people with expertise. But we must learn to make independent choices, to stand alone, and stand up for something because we believe in it. Joash's life sadly shows the results when we fail to do this.

Joash, as we have seen, was too much of a "wishy-washy Charlie Brown." He lacked backbone. So long as godly Jehoiada was at his side, he could sail a steady course toward good. But once he was alone, and others began to pressure him, he went along and was led astray.

Ask: From what little we know of Joash, what do you think caused him to be led astray? Let your class discuss this to see if the suggested reasons given in the lesson are adequate; put forth your own reasons or solicit reasons from the students.

Now ask: What do you recommend as a corrective for a person, who, like Joash, is susceptible to the wrong influences of powerful pressure groups? As a starter, have someone read Ephesians 4:14: "As a result, we are no longer to be children, tossed here and there by waves, and carried about by every wind of doctrine, by the trickery of men, by craftiness in deceitful scheming" (NASB).

This passage is speaking of the very subject of today's lesson and ought to contain a clue to our questions. "As a result" points to something that comes before. Paul is saying that our goal is to be mature, as Jesus Christ was mature. And this maturity is attained as we exercise and receive the gifts He has given His Church. By these we are built up and equipped, giving us inner strength and understanding of what we believe (v. 13)—sure protection from the influences that would lead us astray.

But this is only a part of the answer. Invite others to express any idea that would contribute toward one's independence and strong maturity in Christ. Then close in prayer: *Heavenly Father, we praise You for the truth that we see in this portion of Your Word. We confess too often that we do not want to choose the course that pleases You. Grant us grace to always follow Jesus Christ and not be led astray. Change our wants until they become Your wants. In the Name of Jesus Christ our Lord, Amen.*

Questions for Discussion
Make use of these questions to involve your students in learning and to test their understanding of the lesson.
1. Becoming king at age seven is quite unusual. What were the special circumstances leading to Joash's being crowned at such an early age? 2. Why would the chronicler specify that Joash reigned "in Jerusalem"? 3. Who was Athaliah, who is mentioned in verse 7? 4. After the apostasy of the people, what does our text say the Lord did to try to call the people back to Himself? 5. What was so wicked and ironic about Joash having Zechariah the prophet killed? 6. How did Joash's life end? 7. Can you name in a word or one sentence the chief character flaw in Joash?

Illustrating the Scripture
Examples and quotations to help the teacher communicate the lesson.

"The Set of the Sail"

> One ship sails east
> and another sails west
> by the very same wind that blows.
> It's the set of the sail,
> and not the gale,
> that determines the way that it goes.
>
> Like the winds of the sea
> are the ways of God
> as we sail along through life.
> It's the set of the soul
> that determines the goal,
> and not the stress or the strife.
> —Ella Wilcox

Paul Tournier, the Swiss physician who is known for his many fine books (*A Place to Stand, The Strong and The Weak, The Healing of Persons*) and is so often mistaken for a psychiatrist, had this to say about *advice* in *Escape from Loneliness:*

"Advice is the only form of social activity of which many are capable of conceiving. Those whom life has wounded have met givers of advice on every hand. Often advice is good, but if they follow it, they remain children. If they do not follow the advice given, they are isolated. Often they are surprised that I do not give them any advice. They would prefer at times to be led rather than to assume personal responsibility for themselves. Thus I patiently apply myself to giving back self-confidence to the client who has completely lost it. It is very important that he dare to affirm his own personal conviction."

LIKE JOASH, OR LIKE PETER? Simon Peter was in some ways like King Joash. He was easily influenced by those around him. The Lord Jesus saw that tendency in him and said, "Cephas is your name, but you shall be called Peter—a rock." Later He told the boastful Peter, "When you have turned back (converted), strengthen your brothers" (Luke 22:32 NIV). That must have been hard to take, only hours before Jesus was crucified. Of course, during the dark hours of Jesus' trial, Peter faced his "Waterloo" and failed. But he was fully repentant and came back to God with humility. But even then, many years after Pentecost and after becoming a prominent preacher, he weakened in Antioch to the pressure of the Jewish brethren around him (Galatians 2:11-14). Yet that seems to have been his last time to fall into such temptation. More and more his life took on the rock-like independence in Christ that is a sign of spiritual maturity.

Topics for Youth

FEW CHRISTIANS END WELL!—Does that startle you? It probably does. Does it worry you? It should. Is it true? Well, as the youth say: "Check it out."

Thousands respond to evangelistic crusades, church invitations, Christian camp altar calls, all year long. But where are all of them today? The Sunday School rolls of all churches in America add up to several million, but most of them are children and teenagers. Where are all of the "Christians" from last generation's Sunday School rolls?

Sadly, many drop by the wayside. Do you want some examples from the Bible? Think of the approximately 600,000 Hebrew children who crossed the Red Sea with Moses. And how many of those adults walked over the Jordan River bed into the Promised Land? *Two*—Caleb and Joshua. Or, read 2 Timothy and see how many times Paul mentions so-called Christians who were no longer following the Lord. "Everyone in the province in Asia, including Phygelus and Hermogenes, has deserted me . . . Hymeneus and Philetus . . . have left the way of truth . . . Demas fell in love with this present world and has deserted me" (1:15; 2:17, 18; 4:10 TEV).

How can it *not* happen to you? How can you be sure you are not a Joash? First, determine and commit yourself to follow Jesus Christ no matter what. Write down this commitment in your Bible or somewhere so that you can frequently look on it and renew your covenant with the Lord.

Second, be sure you are in the family of God. A good beginning, in which you attach yourself to Christ firmly and fully, will be as important as perseverance.

When Arthur Reed was asked how he had lived to be the person who supposedly is the oldest in the world, he answered: "They made me out of good dirt. They took the time and made me good!" He was 121 on June 28, 1981. Be sure you were "made good" as God's child through Christ and that is half of the problem solved already.

UNIT III

Persons with Family and Friendship Ties

LESSON 10 **AUGUST 7**

Naomi and Ruth: Shared Loyalty

Background Scripture: Ruth
Devotional Reading: Luke 10:38–42

Ruth 1:16–20; 3:1–5; 4:13–17

16 And Ruth said, Intreat me not to leave thee, or to return from following after thee: for whither thou goest, I will go; and where thou lodgest, I will lodge: thy people shall be my people, and thy God my God:

17 Where thou diest, will I die, and there will I be buried: the LORD do so to me, and more also, if ought but death part thee and me.

18 When she saw that she was stedfastly minded to go with her, then she left speaking unto her.

19 So they two went until they came to Bethlehem. And it came to pass, when they were come to Bethlehem, that all the city was moved about them, and they said, Is this Naomi?

417

20 And she said unto them, Call me not Naomi, call me Mara: for the Almighty hath dealt very bitterly with me.

3:1 Then Naomi her mother in law said unto her, My daughter, shall I not seek rest for thee, that it may be well with thee?

2 And now is not Boaz of our kindred, with whose maidens thou wast? Behold, he winnoweth barley to night in the threshing-floor.

3 Wash thyself therefore, and anoint thee, and put thy raiment upon thee, and get thee down to the floor: but make not thyself known unto the man, until he shall have done eating and drinking.

4 And it shall be, when he lieth down, that thou shalt mark the place where he shall lie, and thou shalt go in, and uncover his feet, and lay thee down; and he will tell thee what thou shalt do.

5 And she said unto her, All that thou sayest unto me I will do.

4:13 So Boaz took Ruth, and she was his wife: and when he went in unto her, the LORD gave her conception, and she bare a son.

14 And the women said unto Naomi, Blessed be the LORD, which hath not left thee this day without a kinsman, that his name may be famous in Israel.

15 And he shall be unto thee a restorer of thy life, and a nourisher of thine old age: for thy daughter in law, which loveth thee, which is better to thee than seven sons, hath born him.

16 And Naomi took the child, and laid it in her bosom, and became nurse unto it.

17 And the women her neighbours gave it a name, saying, There is a son born to Naomi; and they called his name Obed: he is the father of Jesse, the father of David.

KEY VERSE: "Intreat me not to leave thee, or to return from following after thee: for whither thou goest, I will go; and where thou lodgest, I will lodge: thy people shall be my people, and thy God my God." Ruth 1:16.

Home Daily Bible Readings		
Aug. 1	M.	Three Widows, Ruth 1:6–14.
Aug. 2	T.	A Kind Kinsman, Ruth 2:1–13.
Aug. 3	W.	A Happy Mother-In-Law, Ruth 2:14–23.
Aug. 4	T.	An Act of Love, Ruth 3:1–13.
Aug. 5	F.	A Grateful Man, Ruth 3:14–4:6.
Aug. 6	S.	Witnesses of Mercy, Ruth 4:7–12.
Aug. 7	S.	Blessings of the Lord, Ruth 4:13–17.

Lesson Aim: That adult Christians can be confident of rebuilding after any loss if they can develop loyalties to humans and faith in the Lord.

LESSON OUTLINE
Background to the Scripture
Looking at the Scripture Text
  I. "Intreat Me Not to Leave Thee" (Ruth 1:16-20)
 II. "Shall I Not Seek Rest for Thee?" (Ruth 3:1-5)
III. "There Is a Son Born to Naomi" (Ruth 4:13-17)
Applying the Scripture

Background to the Scripture
Is the Book of Ruth a piece of real history?

To the person who has the faith to accept the Bible as the inspired and inerrant Word of God, such a question has probably never crossed his mind. But circumstances today require that we face this question and its implications. One can hardly read widely in commentaries about Ruth without encountering the notion that the unknown author of this universally acclaimed literary masterpiece was writing "historical fiction" to impart a moral.

To deny that Ruth is actual history is to fly in the face of some fairly obvious features about the book's contents. For instance, the author's first words, "it came to pass" (KJV) are identical to those used to introduce such books as Joshua and Judges, obviously historical books.

More important, it cannot be contended that two of the book's main characters, Ruth and Boaz, are "nowhere else known." Luke the historian listed Boaz in his genealogy of the Messiah (Luke 3:32). And Matthew's genealogy goes even further: "Boaz begat Obed of Ruth; and Obed begat Jesse: and Jesse begat David the king . . ." (1:5, 6).

More could be said in defense of the historicity of Ruth, but does anything further need to be said? Let us feed our minds and hearts and souls on this true story within God's sacred Scriptures.

Looking at the Scripture Text
"Intreat Me Not to Leave Thee" (1:16-20) "It is not difficult to account for the wide appeal of this little book," says the *New Bible Commentary, Revised*. "From a literary standpoint alone it has outstanding merit: symmetry of form, convincing characterization, restraint, dignity, and a gently repetitive style which accords well with the speech of peasant people."

In the opening verses which precede this portion of the lesson text, Elimelech of the tribe of Judah, a dweller of Bethlehem, thought it well to leave home temporarily when a drought struck the region. Taking with him his wife Naomi and their two sons, he migrated to the land of Moab, east of the Dead Sea, and settled in its well-watered plains. But then Naomi suffered her first setback; Elimelech died. Her heart would have been cheered when her sons married Moabite girls, but then both sons died, all in the course of "about ten years" (v. 4).

Bereft of her husband and sons, and hearing that the drought had ended in her homeland, she made plans to return to Judah. Orpah and Ruth, her daughters-in-law, had been living with her and had evidently grown dear to her. Leaving them meant driving one more wedge of pain into her sad heart. But she could not expect them to go with her. Came the moment of her departure, and Orpah, weeping, said an affectionate good-by. But Ruth clung to her (v. 14).

"Look, your sister-in-law is going back to her people and her gods. Go back with her" (NIV), Naomi pleaded. To which Ruth made her poignant reply (vv. 16, 17).

"Nothing could be said more fine, more brave," commented Matthew Henry on Ruth's immortal words. Another commentator, after stating that "her vow has stamped itself on the very heart of the world . . . because it expresses in a worthy form, and once for all, the utter devotion of a genuine and self-conquering love" adds that the spirit that "breathes through these melodious words makes them so precious and also renders it impossible to utter any fitting comment on them." Yet who cannot but comment! J. G. Baldwin says her words are "the epitome of utter loyalty and selfless devotion."

Naomi had set Ruth free of all obligation, but Ruth had a loyalty to all that Naomi represented and feared lest her mother-in-law would dash all hope by not permitting her to go with her. Her words reveal a thoroughgoing commitment to whatever fortunes lay ahead with Naomi. She would be content—no, more than that—she desired to "lodge" where Naomi lodged. This implies both on the difficult journey and in Judah.

The people of Israel would be "my people," not a small thing for anyone to say. The proud Moabites traced their ancestry back to Lot, Abraham's nephew (Genesis 19:30–38) and were at times hated enemies of Israel.

Naomi's faith in Jehovah (or Yahweh) might well have been the pivotal factor feeding Ruth's desire to cling to Naomi. Moabites worshiped gods represented by idols, Melchom and Chemosh. No splendor, nothing of moral uplift, and very little joy attended such Moabite worship, which in actuality was bondage. Naomi may have felt that her lamp of faith burned very low, if at all, in her misfortune. But to Ruth, as is often the case with onlookers, Naomi's trust in the Lord was tenderly appealing. So attractive was "the Lord" to her that she sealed her pledge of loyalty to the Lord ("your God, my God") with an oath typical of the Hebrew people (v. 17). She invoked "Yahweh's severest penal displeasure if she should suffer anything less uncontrollable than death to part her from her mother-in-law," says the *Pulpit Commentary*.

Some interpreters overdo the element of Naomi's age upon her return to her native Bethlehem, calling her "aged." From the evidence in the text, it seems fair to assume that she may have been in her early fifties. But she evidently looked much older. When suddenly she appeared in Bethlehem, the women who knew her gawked and said, "Can this be Naomi?" (v. 19 NIV). "The whole town was stirred" or was "in commotion" because of her arrival accompanied by a lone Moabitess, without the husband and sons they had known.

"How serious the eye, how sober the mien, of this woman as she came into the city," says one Bible student in speaking of Naomi. Yes, and how bitter the heart. All of the resentment toward the Lord which Naomi had been carefully nurturing came tumbling out as she soberly corrected the women who stood about her.

"Call me not Naomi . . . call me Mara," she said. Naomi—*pleasant, delightful.* Mara—*bitter* (*see* Exodus 15:23). "The Almighty," she continued, "has made my life very bitter. I went away full, but the Lord has brought me back empty" (vv. 20, 21 NIV). Her use of the title, *El Shaddai*, "the Omnipotent," signified the estrangement she felt toward Jehovah.

"Shall I Not Seek Rest for Thee?" **(3:1-5)** Ruth is more than a beautiful love story, more than an account of the life of one of David's ancestors. Since all Scripture ultimately finds its true meaning in relation to Christ, this book also finds its unique significance from the truth it teaches about Him. In this section is introduced the biblical concept of redemption. Ruth sheds light on the place of the kinsman-redeemer in Israel's life, giving rich texture to the revelation that awaited fulfillment in the Redeemer, Jesus Christ. (*See* "Illustrating the Scripture" for this lesson.)

Naomi and Ruth had arrived in Bethlehem at a fortuitous season—the beginning of barley harvest, probably in the month of April. Chapter 2 shows how "the Almighty" had not forsaken Naomi, directing Ruth to glean in the fields of Boaz whose warm approval she immediately won. Naomi was cheered by this happy turn of events (2:20).

After perhaps two months, Naomi felt ready to fulfill her obligation to Ruth. According to what was termed the levirate law (*see* Deuteronomy 25:5-10), she should take the initiative to see that her husband's name was perpetuated. Through her daughter-in-law, a grandson could inherit the family estate and carry on the name.

For one to qualify as a *go'el* or kinsman-redeemer, he must be related to the family. And Naomi, noting the obvious attention Boaz gave Ruth, intuitively decided on a course of action to provide "rest," literally a home, for Ruth. We do not know why she did not speak to Boaz directly. The course she chose certainly could not have been more interesting, but it subjected Ruth to serious risks. What if Boaz were tempted by Ruth's presence at his feet all night and took advantage of her? That that possibility existed proves the trust which Naomi had in both Ruth and Boaz.

To the slumbering Boaz Ruth went, uncovered his feet, and lay down. One can hardly imagine that she slept! In the night, when he awakened, because of the large outer garment which she wore for warmth and because of the dark, he could not identify her. But she made herself known and whispered, "Spread the corner of your garment over me, since you are a kinsman-redeemer." His response shows his personal interest in—if not love for—her, and his pure ideals. Yes, he said, he was a kinsman-redeemer, but another man was of closer kin and must be asked first. He would look into the matter "first thing tomorrow." Obviously he was busy in the harvest, but love takes precedence over all.

"There Is a Son Born to Naomi" (4:13-17) Before this final section of our text, Boaz is the principal character, going to the gate of the city and there declaring his intentions (vv. 9, 10). But in these closing verses, Naomi again becomes the central figure.

The women in Bethlehem declare God's gift of a son to Naomi (v. 17) rather than Ruth. This is understood because of their sympathy for Naomi whose despair had caused them grief. The real reason for their rejoicing lies in the fact that the name of Elimelech will now not be obliterated, for a son meant that the family name would be carried on. Boaz had performed the duty of a kinsman-redeemer; it is he who is meant in verse 14, rather than the infant, although the son, Obed, would in time be the one to "redeem" or keep alive the family name.

How much is communicated by those three words regarding Ruth—"which loveth thee" (v. 15)! Ruth's unselfish loyalty to Naomi, through the depressing months of her seeming failure, proved her love. By saying that she was "better to thee than seven sons" they were crowning their tribute with utmost praise.

Subtly the Holy Spirit allows the attention to turn at the close to David. Obed would be David's grandfather, making Naomi the great-grandmother of the king. And David would be the "founder of the united kingdom of Israel," yes; but even more important, a forerunner of the Redeemer of Israel, our kinsman-redeemer, Christ.

Applying the Scripture

Look again at the lesson aim: That adult Christians can be confident of rebuilding after any loss if they can develop loyalties to humans and faith in the Lord.

Ruth abounds in lessons for our daily living. But today's lesson aim has been chosen with the title of this four-lesson section in mind: "Persons with Family and Friendship Ties." Try to guide the discussion of today's application toward a goal that will encourage especially the cooperation of people with common loyalties and common faith in Christ.

Ask your class what were the problems which surfaced early in the Book of Ruth. Someone may say: a broken home. Another might reply, poverty. An obvious problem is the economic one—the drought forced the family out of their home and then the deaths of the "breadwinners" forced Naomi to return home emptyhanded. Others may name loneliness, failure, depression.

Now ask the class to name the "plusses" in today's lesson. They might say: Ruth's devotion, Naomi's loyalty to her roots, Boaz's near kinship and sound economic status. And, most important, the Lord whose people they were and who sovereignly took care of them all.

With these minuses and plusses in mind (you may want to write them on a chalkboard), invite discussion of the question: "Do any of you expect ever to be brought low as Naomi was? Do you think bankruptcy or the loss of most of your family could happen to you?" Most in the class will be willing to admit that it could happen. If someone wants to explain how this has already happened to him, seek to determine if you should allow him to use valuable class time for this. It may be just what is needed, but your knowledge of the individual will guide you as to whether you relinquish class time for him to tell his story.

Strive to show the class that Naomi was steering a course dangerously close to disaster by harboring bitterness toward God *and* by almost forcing the one human being who clung to her to stay away. With Ruth, the pathway of life opened up with promise as together they faced each obstacle. The obvious lesson from their experience is:

- Develop strong loyalties to one or a few individuals. With such friends (or husband, or wife, or Christian brother or sister), the rebuilding process can begin.
- But second, and equally as important, is a steadfast faith in the Lord. Though Naomi doubted His goodness and His grace, He proved faithful.

Close the class period in prayer that each of us may store away these lessons and live by them.

Questions for Discussion
Make use of these questions to involve your students in learning and to test their understanding of the lesson.
1. What relation was Ruth to Naomi? What had happened to the husbands of these two women? **2.** Who were Ruth's "people" before she left them to go with Naomi? Who were her adopted "people"? Who was to be her "God"? **3.** Why did they choose Bethlehem for a home? **4.** What was the meaning of the names, Naomi and Mara? **5.** In searching for the right husband for Ruth, why would Naomi point out that "Boaz is . . . a kinsman of ours"? **6.** What praiseworthy qualities of Ruth's character are revealed in vv. 1:16, 17 and 3:5? **7.** What is perhaps a better translation of the word *kinsman* (v. 14)? How did Boaz serve as a redeemer?

Illustrating the Scripture
Examples and quotations to help the teacher communicate the lesson.
THE REDEEMER "The twenty occurrences of the verb *to redeem* (Hebrew *ga'al*) in so short a book are a reminder that the word was in common use in Israel. It belonged to the realm of family law: each member of the family had obligations to protect the other, and none should be lonely or destitute. The near relative who bought back family property (Leviticus 25:25), or secured the freedom of an enslaved brother (Leviticus 25:47–55), or avenged a murder (Numbers 35; Deuteronomy 19:6), was known as the *go'el*.

"The book of Ruth extends his duties to providing an heir for a relative who has died childless. The law of levirate marriage, outlined in Deuteronomy 25:5-10, envisaged several brothers and their families sharing one home. If one brother died without having a son, the next brother was to take the widow and provide an heir for his dead brother. In the case of Ruth, who had no brothers-in-law, a more distant relative was expected to marry her. When the Old Testament asserted that Yahweh was Israel's *Go'el*, it underlined His covenant promise, by which Israel became His own possession (Exodus 19:5). He dwelt among His people (Exodus 25:8) and was their divine Kinsman, ready to deliver and protect them.

"The special contribution of this book to the subject is to make clear that the *go'el* alone possessed the right to redeem, and yet was under no obligation to do so. The willing, generous response of Boaz was, in a very small way, a foreshadowing of the great *Go'el*, who was to descend from him." (From the "Introduction to the Book of Ruth," by J. G. Baldwin, in the *New Bible Commentary, Revised*.)

DID YOU CATCH THE JOY? No wonder the Book of Ruth is a favorite. It is seasoned throughout with little oases of joy. You were probably not conscious of the "joy-notes" that brightened up the hard times and cheered despairing hearts—but look at them now.

After Ruth had begun to glean in the harvest field of Boaz, she told Naomi whose heart forgot about her despair for the moment and exclaimed: "Praise the Lord for a man like that! God has continued his kindness to us as well as to your dead husband!" (2:20 TLB.)

Then when Ruth approached Boaz and asked him to consider performing the duties of a kinsman-redeemer, he burst out: "Thank God for a girl like you!" (3:10.)

And finally, when Ruth's baby was born the women of the city said to Naomi: "Bless the Lord who has given you this little grandson; may he be famous in Israel . . ." (4:14 TLB.)

No wonder one interpreter wrote—"This book, like the Psalms, shows us how joyous and satisfying Israel's religion was and how attractive it became to others when God's people reflected His faithful love to them in their dealings with one another."

Topics for Youth

FAITH COMES FIRST—When Ruth left her native Moab and her family and her friends and committed her total devotion to Naomi, it was a little like her singing, "I Have Decided to Follow Jesus. . . . No Turning Back, No Turning Back."

Cliff Richard, the British pop singer and actor, told in a recent interview what happened when he became a Christian while at the same time being one of Britain's most popular rock and roll entertainers.

"A lot of people said to me, 'You know you could lose a lot of fans when it becomes public knowledge that you are a Christian.'

"I had to make a decision at that time whether or not my career was more important than my faith. My faith was far more important. I didn't have any fans, actually. I know my position with God and I'm open to him. If he wants me to leave show business, he'll obviously find me something else to do."

The writer in the *Christian Herald* interview said that Evangelist Billy Graham taught him to be authoritative. "There's only one way to do that and that's to know from the Bible what you are going to say. The things I say I can base on biblical truth. Opinions are nice but if you want to speak to people authoritatively, then there's one way to do it—that's to quote Scripture."

Richard was named an officer in the Order of the British Empire by the Queen in 1980. He believes it is important to be a "relevant Christian."

"A few years after he had become a Christian," notes the interviewer, "Cliff was doing his first TV series. 'I went through the script and crossed out in red everything I didn't like—dubious jokes. The next time I did a series with the same producer, before he gave me the script, he had red lines through sections he knew I wouldn't say. It's fantastic when you make your stand as a Christian. People may think you're a bit crazy at first, but suddenly they see what you are doing is valid.'" (From "Cliff Richard," in *Christian Herald,* May 1981, pp. 46, 47, by Twila Knaack; used with permission.)

LESSON 11   AUGUST 14

Hophni and Phinehas: Corrupt Priests

Background Scripture: 1 Samuel 1:3; 2:12–17, 22–25; 4
Devotional Reading: Acts 5:1–12

1 Samuel 1:3; 2:12-17, 22-25; 4:11

1:3   And this man went up out of his city yearly to worship and to sacrifice unto the LORD of hosts in Shiloh. And the two sons of Eli, Hophni and Phinehas, the priests of the LORD, were there.

2:12   Now the sons of Eli were sons of Belial; they knew not the LORD.

13   And the priest's custom with the people was, that, when any man offered sacrifice, the priest's servant came, while the flesh was in seething, with a fleshhook of three teeth in his hand;

14   And he struck it into the pan, or kettle, or caldron, or pot; all that the fleshhook brought up the priest took for himself. So they did in Shiloh unto all the Israelites that came thither.

15   Also before they burnt the fat, the priest's servant came, and said to

the man that sacrificed, Give flesh to roast for the priest; for he will not have sodden flesh of thee, but raw.

16 And if any man said unto him, Let them not fail to burn the fat presently, and then take as much as thy soul desireth; then he would answer him, Nay; but thou shalt give it me now: and if not, I will take it by force.

17 Wherefore the sin of the young men was very great before the LORD: for men abhorred the offering of the LORD.

22 Now Eli was very old, and heard all that his sons did unto all Israel; and how they lay with the women that assembled at the door of the tabernacle of the congregation.

23 And he said unto them, Why do ye such things? for I hear of your evil dealings by all this people.

24 Nay, my sons; for it is no good report that I hear: ye make the LORD's people to transgress.

25 If one man sin against another, the judge shall judge him: but if a man sin against the LORD, who shall intreat for him? Notwithstanding they hearkened not unto the voice of their father, because the LORD would slay them.

4:11 And the ark of God was taken; and the two sons of Eli, Hophni and Phinehas, were slain.

KEY VERSE: "For the LORD knoweth the way of the righteous: but the way of the ungodly shall perish." Psalms 1:6.

Home Daily Bible Readings		
Aug. 8	M.	The Wicked Sons of Eli, 1 Samuel 1:1–3.
Aug. 9	T.	The Sins of Hophni and Phinehas, 1 Samuel 2:12–17, 22–25.
Aug. 10	W.	The Capture of the Ark, 1 Samuel 4:1–10.
Aug. 11	T.	The Doom of Eli's House, 1 Samuel 2:27–36.
Aug. 12	F.	Philistines Return the Ark, 1 Samuel 6:1–15.
Aug. 13	S.	Good and Evil Ways, Psalm 1.
Aug. 14	S.	Men Good and Evil, Jeremiah 17:5–10.

Lesson Aim: That adult Christians will administer correction when and how it is needed.

LESSON OUTLINE
Background to the Scripture
Looking at the Scripture Text
 I. Abusing the People and Their Sacrifice (1 Samuel 1:3; 2:12–17)
 II. Seducing the Women at the Sanctuary (1 Samuel 2:22)

III. Ignoring the Rebuke of Their Father (1 Samuel 2:23-25)
IV. Dying in Battle as Was Prophesied (1 Samuel 4:11)
Applying the Scripture

Background to the Scripture

During the summer months when it is difficult to make yourself sit down and prepare for yet another Sunday School class session, it's nice to happen onto a lesson from a text you've previously studied. Especially is this true for studies in the Old Testament! And that is exactly our experience this week as we return to the familiar scene of Israel during the period of the judges, at the time when Hannah sought a son from the Lord and subsequently dedicated this son, Samuel, to a lifetime of service (*see* Lesson 7).

But though we will be ploughing in already-broken ground, we will have to force ourselves to realize that this is the same cheerful, hope-filled time of Samuel's birth and early introduction to tabernacle services in Shiloh. For this lesson takes us to the ugly "other side" of professional religion. It is as if we are forced to play the same song, but in a minor key. Or, having spent the day in Walt Disney World, where dreams seem to come true, we return the following day to visit an insane asylum and view the ravages of unbridled human greed and passion.

Be prepared to allow the Lord to stir your soul with this lesson and to use you to teach a valuable truth to your class.

Looking at the Scripture Text

Abusing the People and Their Sacrifice (1:3; 2:12-17) Abraham Lincoln is quoted as saying, "The Lord must love the common people. He made so many of them." In the common people, the common virtues of honesty, decency, hard work, patriotism, and piety thrive. It was this sort of people who flocked to Shiloh year by year during the mid-eleventh century B.C. in Israel to offer their sacrifices to Jehovah. Elkanah and his wives, Hannah and Peninnah, were among them.

In the lesson on Hannah, we saw why this annual trip became very unpleasant for Hannah. It was becoming distasteful for a majority of devout Israelites also, but not for the same reason. At Shiloh, the people came to the altar to present their sacrifices, following the strict ritual established by Moses and Aaron. But they were thwarted in their worship by the very men who ought to have brought them blessing—the priests, Hophni and Phinehas.

The writer of 1 Samuel describes these two sons of Eli as "sons of Belial." Modern translations substitute "scoundrels" or "wicked men" for "Belial," because it is not the name of any person. To be a son of Belial was to be vile, wretched, and lawless, with reverence for neither man nor God. This is admittedly a harsh judgment to make of anyone, but Hophni and Phinehas deserved it fully.

Eli, Israel's spiritual leader at the time, was both judge and high priest. The last reference to him in 1 Samuel indicates that he judged or "led" Israel forty years (4:18). Due to his advanced age (2:22) and his position as judge, he had evidently turned over the day-to-day responsibilities of priestly service to his two sons even though "they had no regard for the Lord" (v. 12 NIV). Our text shows two ways in which they displayed their total disregard for the Lord—in their treatment of the ones who offered sacrifices and in their relations to the young women who served at the tabernacle.

Israel's national life was so constituted that the Levites were dependent upon the members of the other eleven tribes; priests could not own land. They would receive their portion of food and goods through the various required sacrifices and the tithes of the people. As their "due and legal portion" of the peace (or fellowship) offering, for instance, a shoulder and the breast of an animal brought as a sacrifice were given to the priests (see Leviticus 7:31-34).

But the sons of Eli were not content with these. While a man would be stewing his family portion in "a pan, or kettle, or caldron, or pot" (v. 14), a servant of Hophni and Phinehas would dip his three-pronged brass fork into the man's pot and "whatever the fork brought up" he would take for the priest. "This is how they treated all the Israelites who came to Shiloh" (NIV).

But that was not all. After the offerer killed the animal he had brought for a sacrifice, and the priest had sprinkled its blood against the sides of the altar, the priest was to burn the fat of the meat. This was "an offering made by fire, an aroma pleasing to the Lord" (Leviticus 3:5 NIV). Moses had declared "all the fat is the Lord's." Criswell explains that the fat belonged to the Lord "because it was looked upon as being the choicest part."

Hophni and Phinehas did not care that the fatty meat belonged to Jehovah. Over the objections of the people, they demanded raw meat. Boiled meat day after day did not suit their taste; they would rather have a roast now and then. So calloused were they, according to verse 16, that if the worshiper was slow to give the servant the raw meat they would threaten him: "No, hand it over now; if you don't, I'll take it by force."

"This sin of the young men was very great in the Lord's sight, for they were treating the Lord's offering with contempt" notes the writer. Often the writers of Scripture use the words "in the Lord's sight." All of our actions are committed in plain view to Him, but it was a more serious thing to defile the Lord in His holy place. The sons of Eli had no regard for the Lord's tabernacle. Many of the people perhaps chose not to go to Shiloh during the years when Hophni and Phinehas were officiating. They were damned if they did go, and damned if they didn't. It was a very sad time to be a worshiper of Jehovah.

Seducing the Women at the Sanctuary (v. 22) And yet the priests sank even deeper in their sin. Like their heathen counterparts in Canaan's idolatrous "high places," they had sexual intercourse with "the women who served at the entrance to the Tent of Meeting" (NIV). It evidently became a practice with them, finally gaining the attention of old Eli.

Who the women were it is not clear. The verb *assembled*, sometimes translated "served," is used of an army and suggests large numbers. Matthew Poole thought that these would be female worshipers who went to the tabernacle in large numbers. But as the *Pulpit Commentary* points out it probably has reference to the women who had regular duties at the tabernacle. "The frequent sacrifices, with the feasts which followed, must have provided occupation for a large number of hands in the cleaning of the utensils and the cooking of the food." How wretched these so-called priests were, then, to corrupt the morals of girls who had devoted themselves to the Lord's service. Phinehas at least, was married (4:19); Hophni probably was also, which shows how they both ran roughshod over every ordinance of God and man.

Ignoring the Rebuke of Their Father (vv. 23-25) After this had continued for some time, Eli tried at least once to talk sense into the heads of his sons. But he had waited too long. And his rebuke was too mild. Nothing in our text suggests that he was greatly moved or that he exerted much effort beyond saying, "Stop it, my sons."

In verse 25, "God shall judge him" or "God can defend him" (TEV) are preferred over "the judge shall judge." The second part of this verse should read "who shall act as judge for him?" or "who shall interpose as arbitrator between him and Jehovah to settle the question?" Eli's counsel is—if one man sins against another, God will judge between the two of them. But if a man sins against God, who is a third party that can help such a man?

Of all people, Eli should have known that man can "stand in the gap" and divert a course Jehovah has chosen to take. Had not the Lord provided the sacrifices as means by which a penitent man could regain peace with God? But of course the one thing Jehovah does not provide is a penitent heart. Hophni and Phinehas would have been capable of repentance at an earlier point, but by now they had transgressed against God's patience. The writer says they did not listen to Eli "for the Lord had decided to kill them" (TEV). As one interpreter has said, "the punishment of sin may consist in the sinner's loss of free will." Pharaoh reached that point. The willfully sinful, of whom Paul wrote, rebelled and "God gave them up . . ." (Romans 1:24, 26, 28).

In the brief interchange with his sons, Eli is much too gentle. "In the case where the rebuke should have descended like a bolt from heaven we hear nothing but low and feeble murmurings, coming, as it were, out of the dust," says the *Pulpit Commentary*. Eli merely slapped their wrists. They deserved capital punishment after being banished from the priesthood (Leviticus 18:20, 29). By neglecting his duty, Eli was sealing both their doom and his own.

Dying in Battle as Was Prophesied (4:11) Shortly after Eli confronted his sons, an unnamed prophet appeared and rebuked Eli (2:27-36), telling him that because of his failure and that of his sons (v. 29), God would put both Hophni and Phinehas to death on the same day (v. 34).

Then, in Samuel's oft-told vision, the subject matter again was the same:

God had warned Eli but he had "failed to restrain" his sons; "the guilt of Eli's house will never be atoned for by sacrifice or offering" (3:11–14 NIV). In the morning after the Lord had spoken to Samuel, Eli demanded to know what the Lord had said. But he only shrugged it off: "He is the Lord; let him do what is good in his eyes" (v. 18 NIV).

Shortly Israel suffered defeat by the Philistines. In an attempt to gain victory, the elders of Israel decided in a desperate act of superstition that Israel's ark of the covenant, which resided in the holiest place in the tabernacle, should go out to battle with Israel's armies. Hophni and Phinehas were commandeered to accompany the ark and in the battle which ensued, 30,000 Israelite warriors were killed and the ark was captured. Hophni and Phinehas were both killed. Old Eli was more concerned about the ark than his sons. He waited beside the road for a report of the battle. When a Benjamite brought news of the death of Hophni and Phinehas and the ark's capture, Eli fell backward and broke his neck. He and his sons all died on the same day. Nearby, Phinehas's pregnant wife heard of the capture of the ark. She was so shocked that she went into labor and died as the baby was born. With her dying breath she called him, "Ichabod"—"the glory has departed from Israel" (v. 21). Such was the sad end of Hophni and Phinehas, corrupt priests.

Applying the Scripture

In keeping with the theme for this month, "Persons With Family and Friendship Ties," we have again chosen an objective that can be realized between or among a few people: That adult Christians will administer correction when and how it is needed.

The aim is deliberately worded in a broad, general way so that every member of the class will be challenged to make an application. Most of your class members may be parents and they will see this lesson in the light of their responsibilities as parents. But your class members may be older and have no children yet living with them or of minor age—or there may be a number of singles. You will want an aim that each of them can "bite into."

Rephrasing the Lesson Aim in your own words, ask your class in what areas of life they can see themselves applying the truth of this lesson. Encourage them to think of the areas of their life in which they find themselves involved with at least one person, but probably more, on a constant basis. Obviously the home and work situations will be named; some will name the church, clubs, or neighborhood. Now add the word *responsibility*. Obviously we are associated with people for whom we have *some* responsibility. Eli was triply responsible for his sons—as their father, as the high priest (their supervisor), and as the judge (the governor). We can see that he failed to correct his sons *when* he should have and *how* he should have. And his failure seems to indicate that he did not care really all that much for them.

Suggest that the first prerequisite for the right kind of discipline in any situation is love, a sincere caring attitude. (Note the book quoted in "Illustrating the Scripture"—*Parenting With Love and Limits*.) Whether we seek to discipline a daughter or an employee who is careless or a fellow Christian whose life is a stumbling block, we will be driven to discipline by our care for that person's well being. And love will help guide us to the *how* also.

If time permits, allow an adult to tell how he or she is thankful for the correction a fellow church member gave when they needed it. In our day, the practice of church discipline has harsh overtones and is rarely exercised on a one-to-one basis among the fellowship. Thus, an example of this kind may help others to see the value of giving and receiving Christian correction. If no one can give such an example from church life, furnish one from your own experience.

Close by recommending that persons who want to go more in depth into this subject should make a study of Proverbs and the Epistles of Paul as a starter. Suggest that they may also want to pick a good book to read, such as Bruce Narramore's *Parenting With Love and Limits*.

Questions for Discussion
Make use of these questions to involve your students in learning and to test their understanding of the lesson.
1. Why were Hophni and Phinehas fulfilling the service of priests rather than Eli?   2. What was wrong with the way Hophni and Phinehas treated the people who offered sacrifices (v. 14)?   3. Why was their selfish grasping for the fatty meat such a contemptible practice?   4. What would the people probably choose to do rather than submit to the shameful abuses when they offered sacrifices at Shiloh?   5. Was Eli's discipline harsh enough for his sons? What should he have done to punish them for their sacrilege and fornication?   6. According to verse 25, the two priests could not change their ways because the Lord had already purposed their destruction. What does this teach us about man's free will?

Illustrating the Scripture
Examples and quotations to help the teacher communicate the lesson.
ACCOUNTABILITY—PARENT AND CHILD   "We cannot justifiably expect obedience and maturity from our children unless we first fulfill their needs.... Let's suppose the father of a teen-age girl is rarely home. When he is, he is too busy to be lovingly involved in his daughter's life. He may also be critical and judgmental and not supportive of her friends. Her mother is also extremely busy, or perhaps she is prone toward depression. She isn't really happy in her role of wife and mother and finds it difficult to participate in her daughter's world. On top of this the parents are quite restrictive, and there is a great deal of tension and hostility in the home.

"After years in this environment, the girl reaches adolescence with major unmet needs. She does not feel loved and accepted by her father. She lacks a sense of pride in her femininity. She has a serious lack of self-confidence and worth. She also harbors a great deal of anger and resentment toward her parents.

"When this girl begins to date, she will bring all of this background of resentment and unfulfilled needs to her new relationships. She may withdraw for fear of further rejection. Or she may get deeply involved with the first boy she begins to date. When sexual temptations come, she will probably be more susceptible than if she had a more positive family life. In her search to fill previously unmet needs she is more likely to become sexually promiscuous. Since she doesn't feel loved by the most important man in her life she will do rash things to gain a temporary sense of love or satisfaction.

"Obviously this girl bears a responsibility for her actions. She could have responded to her parents' rejection of her differently.... One reason so many people are deeply troubled by the issue of responsibility is their unresolved sense of guilt. Guilt always seeks a scapegoat. Grace, however, desires to pull together for the future. Once a parent or a child has come to grips with his own sinfulness and God's forgiveness, the strained issue of responsibility begins to fade into the background. We no longer need to blame our children because we can freely acknowledge our responsibility and accept divine forgiveness.

"Until both parents and children perceive and appropriate God's grace and His forgiveness, they will smolder or argue endlessly about who is to blame—and the failures will proliferate. Accepting responsibility allows everyone concerned to stop blaming others and begin taking steps toward improvement." (From *Parenting With Love and Limits* by Bruce Narramore, published by Zondervan, Grand Rapids, Michigan; Copyright 1979. Used with permission.)

Topics for Youth

GETTING ENOUGH DISCIPLINE LATELY!—If Hophni and Phinehas lived today, they would have had most everything that doting parents could provide. Their "needs" would have included a late model, souped-up hot rod, each, the best and loudest stereo tape equipment, money for skiing at the winter lodge and surfing in the Mediterranean. But they still would have been without a very important ingredient of life. Their life reveals a woeful lack of *discipline*.

You might ask your young people: "Getting enough discipline lately?"

If they are honest they will probably say, "No."

In February 1980, four sisters and two brothers sat around the breakfast table one morning and talked. The death of their father had brought them to Dallas, Texas. The funeral was over and now they were engrossed in remembrances of "Daddy." He had been widowed five years after the birth of the youngest child, had remarried a couple of years later and many years had passed since that last one had left home, married and entered a career. By all outward signs, "Daddy"—despite obvious flaws and failings—had succeeded in raising his "kids."

One of the sisters, now in her late fifties, recalled how the quality of discipline, which she learned at home, served to keep her on a steady course when tragedy struck her life. She was very happily married to a petroleum engineer and they were raising their three children when Marsh became ill with what was diagnosed as a tumor of the brain. He became very ill, was in and out of hospitals and sometimes it appeared as though he would recover—but eighteen months later he died.

"The discipline instilled in me by Mother and Daddy saw me through those very difficult months and years," this sister confessed.

And actually, if one were to have to say which quality in "Daddy" stood out to all the brothers and sisters, one would have to say discipline—the thing most of us do not want until it is too late. So, young people, if you are not getting enough discipline from your parents, ask them for it. Later in life you'll be glad you did!

LESSON 12   AUGUST 21

Jonathan and David: Loyal Friends

Background Scripture: 1 Samuel 18:1–9; 19:1–7; 20:1–42; 23:15–18; 2 Samuel 1
Devotional Reading: 1 Thessalonians 3

1 Samuel 18:1–4; 19:4–6; 23:15–18; 2 Samuel 1:26

18:1 And it came to pass, when he had made an end of speaking unto Saul, that the soul of Jonathan was knit with the soul of David, and Jonathan loved him as his own soul.

2 And Saul took him that day, and would let him go no more home to his father's house.

3 Then Jonathan and David made a covenant, because he loved him as his own soul.

4 And Jonathan stripped himself of the robe that was upon him, and gave it to David, and his garments, even to his sword, and to his bow, and to his girdle.

19:4 And Jonathan spake good of David unto Saul his father, and said unto him, Let not the king sin against his servant, against David; because he hath not sinned against thee, and because his works have been to thee-ward very good:

5 For he did put his life in his hand, and slew the Philistine, and the LORD wrought a great salvation for all Israel: thou sawest it, and didst rejoice: wherefore then wilt thou sin against innocent blood, to slay David without a cause?

6 And Saul hearkened unto the voice of Jonathan: and Saul sware, As the LORD liveth, he shall not be slain.

23:15 And David saw that Saul was come out to seek his life: and David was in the wilderness of Ziph in a wood.
16 And Jonathan Saul's son arose, and went to David into the wood, and strengthened his hand in God.
17 And he said unto him, Fear not: for the hand of Saul my father shall not find thee; and thou shalt be king over Israel, and I shall be next unto thee; and that also Saul my father knoweth.
18 And they two made a covenant before the Lord: and David abode in the wood, and Jonathan went to his house.

2 Samuel 1:26
I am distressed for thee, my brother Jonathan: very pleasant hast thou been unto me: thy love to me was wonderful, passing the love of women.

KEY VERSE: "Then Jonathan and David made a covenant, because he loved him as his own soul." 1 Samuel 18:3.

Home Daily Bible Readings
Aug. 15 M. David's Abilities Recognized by Saul, 1 Samuel 17:50-58.
Aug. 16 T. Jonathan's Covenant With David, 1 Samuel 18:1-5.
Aug. 17 W. Cause of Saul's Jealousy, 1 Samuel 18:6-10.
Aug. 18 T. Jonathan Reconciles Saul to David, 1 Samuel 19:1-7.
Aug. 19 F. Jonathan's Plan to Protect David, 1 Samuel 20:12-17.
Aug. 20 S. Jonathan Accepts David as His King, 1 Samuel 23:13-18.
Aug. 21 S. David's Lament on Jonathan's Death, 2 Samuel 1:23-27.

Lesson Aim: That adult Christians as a result of this lesson will celebrate God's gift of friendship by renewing one friendship by some specific action this week.

LESSON OUTLINE
Background to the Scripture
Looking at the Scripture Text
 I. A Great Friendship Born (1 Samuel 18:1-4)
 II. Friendship Tested (1 Samuel 19:4-6)
 III. Friendship Renewed (1 Samuel 23:15-18)
 IV. Friendship Praised (2 Samuel 1:26)
Applying the Scripture

Background to the Scripture
Out of the ashes of her humiliation at losing the Ark of the Covenant to the Philistines who also killed 30,000 of her soldiers, Israel arose and gradually began to gather strength. Young Samuel led the way in this ascent out of the abyss by teaching the people the laws of Jehovah. In time, Samuel the

Prophet anointed Saul as Israel's first king (1 Samuel 9:15, 16; 10:1) only to see the promising Benjamite fail to obey the Lord at critical junctures.

So, once again with the anointing oil in his bag, Samuel sought a king for Israel. This time the Lord directed him to the family of Jesse where he poured oil on the head of the young shepherd, David, and signified that he would be king after Saul (16:13).

Subsequently David was sent to take rations to his three older brothers in Saul's army and, while he was in camp, the Philistine, Goliath, made one of his periodic taunts at Israel. The rest of the story is well known. Fearless in his faith in Jehovah, David approached the giant with his slingshot, toppled him with one smooth stone, and cut off his head with the giant's own weapon. Israel routed the Philistines and King Saul ordered the brave warrior brought to his tent. Still with Goliath's head in his hand, David stood before Saul and answered his questions. It is this conversation that is in progress as our Lesson Text begins.

Looking at the Scripture Text

A Great Friendship Born (1 Samuel 18:1-4) The Today's English Version says, "Jonathan was deeply attracted to David." The New International Version has it: "Jonathan became one in spirit with David." But in this case nothing equals the imagery of the Authorized Version (King James): "the soul of Jonathan was knit with the soul of David." Jonathan evidently shared in the conversation David had with the king and in those moments the friendship was born. No freak this relationship; it developed gradually even as a garment that is woven takes shape, thread by thread. The verb *knit* suggests that.

Jonathan took the initiative in this, "One of the great friendships of history"; yet both were mutually attracted to one another. In David, Jonathan saw the ideal of his own life and David saw in Jonathan a man more experienced and untainted by the artificial airs that always attend any royal court.

Jonathan "deserved to be known in his own right," notes Andrew Blackwood. His reputation as a warrior was known already. He had led a garrison against the Philistines, and once when he inadvertently broke a rule his father had made, he was saved from execution by the immense popularity he had among the people for his exploits (14:45). He had several strong points—bravery, success in battle, courage, fidelity, and selfless devotion. He is one of the rare persons in Scripture about which not one evil blemish is recorded concerning his character.

"And Saul took him that day"—this marks a new chapter in David's life. No more would he make frequent trips home. He remained in Saul's citadel in Gibeah, a fortress whose ruins have been unearthed and identified as the oldest datable fortifications in Israel (*Harper's Bible Dictionary*). Gibeah was located three miles north of Jerusalem which then was ruled by the Jebusites (2 Samuel 5:6).

As one of Saul's bodyguards at Gibeah, David would have ample time to be with Prince Jonathan. Their friendship flourished from the start. The covenant which they entered into (v. 3) was not an immediate thing, but neither would they have required a lengthy time to learn how perfectly matched were their ideals and spirits. We are commanded to love our neighbor as we love ourselves. Jonathan and David had that kind of love for each other almost from the start. How rare! As someone has said, much that is called friendship is not worthy of the name. Blackwood notes that "as friendship is here employed (concerning David and Jonathan), it refers to the sort of intimate relationship that comes to a strong man only once or twice in his earthly career."

We may interpret Jonathan's next actions in one of two ways. David certainly would need apparel appropriate to his new station in life. Unselfishly and as a mark of the covenant between them, Jonathan gave him his own—his tunic and outer robe, his sword and bow, and his belt. Criswell offers the opinion that in doing this Jonathan was indicating that he, as prince, was changing positions with David. He would normally be in line as the next king, but he may have sensed very early that David was God's man for the throne (especially if David had told of Samuel's anointing David). We know that Jonathan later was fully confident that David would be king (23:17).

Friendship Tested (19:4–6) Those early days in Saul's citadel were filled with tranquil pleasure, but they were not to last long. The people had made Saul king to set them free from the hated Philistines and Saul pursued that mandate vigorously. He went out to battle with David and Jonathan at his side. They were invincible. However, Saul was too insecure to take pleasure in David's successes. When the people chanted on their return from battle, "Saul hath slain his thousands, and David his ten thousands . . ." Saul became jealous. From then on he "eyed David" (v. 9). Samuel had told Saul that the Lord would take the kingdom away from him and instead of humbly seeking the Lord, he withdrew from godly counsel and became more and more influenced by the evil spirit which the Lord sent to trouble him (16:14; 19:9).

Impelled by this spirit, his jealousy boiled to the point of insanity. Twice he tried to kill David with his own spear. Failing that, he gradually became obsessed with plans for murdering David until, in the verses prior to this section, he confided in his officers "that they should kill David."

The only member of that coterie of officers to oppose Saul's mad plan was his son. He faced Saul with the truth, presenting facts to his conscience. David "has benefited you greatly" (NIV) he said. "Everything he has done has been a great help to you" (TEV). He reminded Saul how David had risked his life in killing the Philistine, Goliath. And he brought to mind the "great salvation" or "victory" that this gave to Israel and how the king himself had rejoiced in it.

Jonathan put his argument on behalf of David in calm terms to his father. Had he been angry, his father would probably have only hardened his heart. But he is sure to have prayed also as he commended David to the king. And his defense succeeded in "buying time" for David. Saul, an erratic man given to extremes, made a solemn oath. "As the Lord liveth, he shall not be slain" (v. 6). In a hard test, the bond of friendship between Jonathan and David had remained strong. But still severer tests were to come.

Friendship Renewed (23:15-18) These verses of our text afford us a final observation of these two "kindred spirits," Jonathan and David. In the interim, Jonathan has remained loyal to his father and faithful to David. In one touching incident not included in our text, Jonathan again withstood Saul and was himself cursed and almost speared by his father (chapter 20). Jonathan went out in a rage, arranged a clandestine meeting with David, and bid him good-by since it was no longer safe for David to be near Saul. Tearfully they recommitted themselves to the love they had for one another. From then on, David was a fugitive.

An army of the three D's—"everyone in distress . . . in debt . . . discontented" (22:2)—rallied to David's side in the wilderness of Judah. But what were 400 men against Saul's army? Slowly it appeared that Saul would close the noose around David's neck.

David would easily be subject to confusing thoughts at this time, causing him to doubt whether God was with him. A report of the slaughter of eighty priests at Nob saddened him, for he thought himself somehow responsible (22:18-22). Next, he and his men went to the aid of fellow Israelites in the wilderness town of Keilah and fought off the Philistines successfully, only to see the villagers turn traitor to David. Word reached Saul that David and his men were in Keilah which evidently was a walled city (23:7).

The one advantage David had over Saul was that the Lord gave him sure guidance. Being warned by the Lord that the Keilites would turn him over to Saul, he and his men went into the wilderness (v. 15). Yet it would be hard for David to remain optimistic about his chances of evading Saul. The Psalms show how desperate he became. The 57th Psalm may have been penned at this time; in that song he cries, "Be merciful unto me, O God . . . they have prepared a net for my steps: my soul is bowed down" (vv. 1, 6).

Just as David was feeling low, God "was mercifully operating in the heart of the noblest man at the court of Saul to bring him sweetest consolation" (*Pulpit Commentary*). Saul did pursue David, but with Saul came Jonathan. Somehow Saul never did find David, but Jonathan did and the writer says he "strengthened his hand in God" (a lovely phrase).

Jonathan encouraged David most of all with his presence. But he also buoyed his courage by his words. He recited what God had done already—He had taken care of David, had sent Samuel to anoint him. He charged David not to fear, giving David's faith a boost by the exercise of his own. Looking into the future he said, "You will be king over Israel, and I will be second to you. Even my father Saul knows this" (v. 17 NIV). They climaxed this brief meeting together with a renewal of their covenant "before the Lord." Earlier Jonathan had secured a pledge from David to protect his family in case anything happened to him, and David had heartily agreed

(20:13-15). But no mention is made of that now. Jonathan evidently had no premonition that he would never see David, that he would die in battle with his father Saul, that this sweet reunion was their last on earth.

Friendship Praised (2 Samuel 1:26) In this song of David, we find one of the most moving passages of all Old Testament Scripture. David's soul ascended to the heights when he rejoiced; and he felt the deepest losses with the same intensity. His lament for Absalom and his sorrow for his own sin are on a par with this emotional outburst for the man whom he "loved as his own soul." Blackwood perceptively attributes "much of the goodness in David" to Jonathan for "as long as Jonathan lived to befriend him, David went on in the path of honor."

Often in this life, it seems the most virtuous suffer most keenly. It was so with David. He had lost his dearest friend whose love surpassed the love of any woman to him. One interpreter describes the friendship between the two in six qualities. It (1) exists only in noble souls; (2) is founded on mutual esteem; (3) consists of disinterested affection; (4) unites in a steadfast bond; (5) is confirmed by a solemn compact; and (6) is manifested in generous gifts.

Applying the Scripture
Teacher, several possibilities exist for application of this lesson text. Choose the one suited best for your class.
1. Try this approach. Tell the class that they must go out and make a friend this week. Watch their reactions. Some of them might even say, "No way."

As someone said, friendships are born, not made. They are a gift from God. We can be thankful that friendships are possible. Still, we do have to put forth some effort if we are going to have friends. David and Jonathan would never have been such strong friends had they not spent time with each other and shared on an increasingly deeper level and ultimately committed their all to each other.

Tell your class that there ought to be a familiar ring to the words that described this friendship: "he loved him as he loved his own soul." Isn't this the type of love the Lord has charged us to have for our fellow Christian? If it is then we should be careful not to shy away from it and say it is so rare that we could never attain it.

Encourage your class members to think of those whom they might especially regard as friends. Suggest that in the coming week they do something—spend time with, write a letter, call on the telephone, buy a gift—for that friend and renew the friendship.
2. You may want to toss out the statement: "Friendship in some degree is a necessity of life." Some diehards will argue that this is not so, but it does appear to be true. Having one to share our joys and our trials with is the essence of friendship. Who can do without a friend? Perhaps the point of the quotation is found in the words, "in some degree." Probably no one in class has experienced a friendship to the depth of Jonathan's and David's. Invite a discussion of how a friendship can be made stronger.

3. Or, you may invite discussion of the statement: "few things are more sad to think on than a broken friendship."

Immediately you will need to acknowledge that some friendships, if not most, are for a season. Especially is this true today when friends move away, come and go. But this is not what is meant by the quotation. Ask your class if they agree with the statement. Perhaps you or a class member can offer an example. Conclude the discussion by returning to Jonathan and David, noting how tragic it would have been for them to allow anything to come between them. If any class member feels that he has reason to break a friendship sincerely entered into, suggest that he review the Scriptures in this lesson that show what storms David's and Jonathan's friendship had to weather.

Questions for Discussion
Make use of these questions to involve your students in learning and to test their understanding of the lesson.
1. What well-known feat of heroism had young David performed prior to his being brought to King Saul? 2. Was David older than Jonathan? Which one reached out first to befriend the other? 3. How was Jonathan's generous, unselfish nature manifested? 4. According to 19:4, 5, what did Jonathan do that showed his loyalty to his friend David? 5. Why was David particularly needing encouragement when Jonathan went to him in the wilderness of Ziph? What means did Jonathan employ to encourage David? 6. Why do we need occasionally to renew the agreements we have with another person?

Illustrating the Scripture
Examples and quotations to help the teacher communicate the lesson.
WHAT THE SCRIPTURES SAY ABOUT "FRIENDS" Alexander Cruden in his Concordance says, "friend is taken for one whom we love and esteem above others, to whom we impart our minds more familiarly than to others, and that from a confidence of his integrity and good will toward us. Thus Jonathan and David were mutually friends.

"Solomon in his book of Proverbs gives the qualities of a true friend. Proverbs 17:17—*'A friend loveth at all times.'* Not only in prosperity, but also in adversity. Chapter 18:24—*'There is a friend that sticketh closer than a brother.'* He is more hearty in the performance of all friendly offices. He reproves and rebukes when he sees any thing amiss. Proverbs 27:6—*'Faithful are the wounds of a friend.'* His sharpest reproofs proceed from an upright and truly loving and faithful soul. He is known by his good and faithful counsel as well as by his seasonable rebukes. Proverbs 27:9—*'Ointment and perfume rejoice the heart: so doth the sweetness of a man's friend by hearty counsel.'* By such counsel as comes from his very heart and soul, and is the language of his most inward and serious thoughts. The company and conversation of a friend is refreshing and reviving to a person, who when alone is sad and dull and inactive. Proverbs 27:17—*'Iron sharpeneth iron, so a man sharpeneth the countenance of his friend.'*"

WHAT OTHERS HAVE SAID ABOUT FRIENDS Robert Louis Stevenson said, "So long as we love we serve; so long as we are loved by others, I would almost say that we are indispensable; and no man is useless while he has a friend."

> Every one that flatters thee
> is no friend in misery.
> Words are easy, like the wind;
> faithful friends are hard to find.
> Every man will be thy friend
> whilst thou hast wherewith to spend:
> But, if store of crowns be scant,
> No man will supply thy want. . . .
> He that is thy friend indeed,
> he will help thee in thy need.
> —from *Address to the Nightingale*
> by Richard Barnfield, 1598.

Willa S. Cather said, "Only solitary men know the full joys of friendship. Others have their family; but to a solitary and an exile his friends are everything."

Topics for Youth

"JESUS IS A NEVER-FAILING FRIEND"—As the story of David and Jonathan illustrates, human friendships of the kind they knew are rare indeed. And human friendships end. Too soon, a friend moves away and we gradually lose all contact. One of the difficult things for young people is seeing their friends move away—or having to move away from a bosom companion.

Still, we should not hesitate to make new friends and to seek to cultivate friendships even when distance separates us. Yet to the Christian, the truest friend is He who is always with us, who is utterly faithful, loving, and gentle. It is He of whom Joseph Scriven wrote when he composed, "What A Friend We Have in Jesus."

Robert Harvey, in *Best-Loved Hymn Stories*, tells how Scriven came to write the hymn. Ira Sankey was the gospel singer who accompanied D. L. Moody in evangelistic services in England and there the hymn "was much used during the revival services." Sankey "told how it came to be discovered.

"A neighbor was once sitting up with Scriven when the latter was ill and happened upon the piece of paper containing the hymn. He read it with delight and asked Mr. Scriven about it. Scriven replied that he had composed it for his mother to comfort her when she was passing through a time of special sorrow and had not intended that anyone else should see it. Once found, such a hymn could not be kept hidden and so it was given to the world. All his other hymns are unknown today. . . .

"In the hymn he emphasizes that while Jesus is a Savior from sin, He is especially a Savior from sorrow. In all our lost peace, our sorrows, our burdens, or being forsaken by those we love, we may find comfort and healing in the touch of Jesus Christ. Friends once learned from Scriven that he had paid a visit back home, but had received anything but a hearty welcome. This experience may find an echo in the line, 'do thy friends despise, forsake thee? Take it to the Lord in prayer.' "

LESSON 13   AUGUST 28

Mordecai and Esther: Challenge and Commitment

Background Scripture: Esther
Devotional Reading: Psalms 31:19–24

Esther 2:7; 4:13-16; 8:3-8

2:7 And he brought up Hadassah, that is, Esther, his uncle's daughter: for she had neither father nor mother, and the maid was fair and beautiful; whom Mordecai, when her father and mother were dead, took for his own daughter.

4:13 Then Mordecai commanded to answer Esther, Think not with thyself that thou shalt escape in the king's house, more than all the Jews.

14 For if thou altogether holdest thy peace at this time, then shall there enlargement and deliverance arise to the Jews from another place; but thou and thy father's house shall be destroyed: and who knoweth whether thou art come to the kingdom for such a time as this?

15 Then Esther bade them return Mordecai this answer,

16 Go, gather together all the Jews that are present in Shushan, and fast ye for me, and neither eat nor drink three days, night or day: I also and my maidens will fast likewise; and so will I go in unto the king, which is not according to the law: and if I perish, I perish.

8:3 And Esther spake yet again before the king, and fell down at his feet, and besought him with tears to put away the mischief of Haman the Agagite, and his device that he had devised against the Jews.

4 Then the king held out the golden sceptre toward Esther. So Esther arose, and stood before the king,

5 And said, If it please the king, and if I have found favour in his sight, and the thing seem right before the king, and I be pleasing in

442 OLD TESTAMENT PERSONALITIES

his eyes, let it be written to reverse the letters devised by Haman the son of Hammedatha the Agagite, which he wrote to destroy the Jews which are in all the king's provinces:

6 For how can I endure to see the evil that shall come unto my people? or how can I endure to see the destruction of my kindred?

7 Then the king Ahasuerus said unto Esther the queen and to Mordecai the Jew, Behold, I have given Esther the house of Haman, and him they have hanged upon the gallows, because he laid his hand upon the Jews.

8 Write ye also for the Jews, as it liketh you, in the king's name, and seal it with the king's ring: for the writing which is written in the king's name, and sealed with the king's ring, may no man reverse.

KEY VERSE: "And who knoweth whether thou art come to the kingdom for such a time as this?" Esther 4:14.

Home Daily Bible Readings
Aug. 22   M.   The Luxury Living King of Persia, Esther 1:1–12.
Aug. 23   T.   Mordecai Prepares Esther for Presentation, Esther 2:2–11.
Aug. 24   W.   Esther Shown Grace and Favor, Esther 2:15–20.
Aug. 25   T.   A Jewish Pogrom Planned, Esther 3:8–15.
Aug. 26   F.   Esther Plans to Defy Persian Law, Esther 4:5–16.
Aug. 27   S.   Esther and Haman's Opposing Plans, Esther 5:6–14.
Aug. 28   S.   Esther Saves Jewish Lives, Esther 8:5–16.

Lesson Aim: That adult believers will be willing to join with others at times in a just cause which could cost them dearly.

LESSON OUTLINE
Background to the Scripture
Looking at the Scripture Text
  I. Esther, the Beautiful Foster-Daughter (Esther 2:7)
 II. Challenging the Queen to Duty (Esther 4:13, 14)
III. The Queen's Daring Commitment (Esther 4:15, 16)
IV. A Jewish Duo in Xerxes' Court (Esther 8:3–8)
Applying the Scripture

Background to the Scripture

"The story of Esther is set, not in Palestine, nor even in Babylon," says the *New Bible Commentary, Revised,* "but farther east still in a capital of the Persian Empire, throughout which Jews of the post-exilic period were scattered. Cyrus the empire-builder, well known for his liberal attitude to conquered peoples, allowed Jews to return to Jerusalem after he had conquered Babylon in 539 B.C. Darius, the Persian king mentioned in Haggai and Zechariah, organized the administration of his huge empire during his reign (522–486). Ahasuerus, the Persian monarch of Esther, was his successor."

Ahasuerus, or Xerxes I as he is better known, ruled from 486–464 B.C. over the vast Persian Empire which stretched from Egypt to India and encompassed a hundred million subjects. Scholars date the Book of Esther at approximately 400 B.C. The author is unknown, but it is generally agreed that he was a Jew living in Persia.

A large number of interpreters consider Esther as legendary, without basis in history. Yet an equally large number accept its historicity without question. They have their reasons for repudiating the skeptics' claims, one of which is that the Jewish Feast of Purim which celebrates God's deliverance through the instrumentality of Esther, could hardly have been based on myth.

Looking at the Scripture Text

Esther, the Beautiful Foster-Daughter (2:7)   Mordecai and Esther are not introduced into the narrative until this point. Prior to this, the author is concerned to describe the events that led to Esther's surprising leap from ignominy as a young exiled Jewess to honor as queen of the Persian Empire.

Xerxes I, who had deposed Queen Vashti, ordered a search to be made through all 127 of Persia's provinces for a new queen. It was a beauty search, more than a talent search, and among the women selected in Susa, the empire's winter capital, was young Hadassah. The girl made an immediate impression upon Hegai, the eunuch in charge of the young women, but right away he insisted that she adopt a Persian name. The name *Esther* was decided upon, possibly inspired by *Ishtar*, the Babylonian goddess of love, or by the Persian word *stara*, star.

As any historian would do, the writer informs us of Esther's background: she was a cousin of Mordecai who raised her after the death of her parents. He is identified as a Jew of Benjamin's tribe who was taken captive by King Nebuchadnezzar. Since that took place in 586 B.C. and we are now talking of events nearer 478, a literal interpretation would make Mordecai over 100 years old and Esther almost as old. What is probably intended is that Mordecai's immediate forefathers were carried into exile. He and Esther were probably born in Persia. For some time, she had looked to him as her father, and he to her as his daughter.

Challenging the Queen to Duty (4:13, 14)   The scene in the fourth chapter is this: Esther has enjoyed the honor and privilege of being queen for five years. But she has just learned of a grave threat to all Jews in the empire. (The commentators Keil and Delitzsch estimated there were two to three million Jews in the empire.) Haman, the king's prime minister, had been granted unlimited power to wipe out the Jews—all because Mordecai, whom he learned was a Jew, would not bow to him when he came and went at the palace.

Mordecai, who was among the royal officials charged with duties at the entrance of the palace, learned of the decree and reacted by tearing his clothes and putting on the sackcloth and ashes typical of mourners. When Esther heard of this she could not understand her cousin's actions for the Persian court insulated her from news of the empire. But Mordecai not only told her the news but challenged her to go into the king's presence to beg for mercy (*see* 4:8).

He may not have understood the risks such a venture involved. No one, not even the queen, saw the king unless permitted to do so. But though he loved Esther dearly, Mordecai insisted that she intervene on behalf of the Jews, making a statement which has become a classic expression of the high purpose attached to a responsible position: "who knoweth whether thou art come to the kingdom for such a time as this?" (4:14).

This communication from Mordecai touches on the central theme of the book and on one of its chief problems. He was confident that the Jews would be spared. If not by Esther's intervention, "relief and deliverance" would arise from some other quarter. He warned her though that she should not consider herself immune from harm just because she was "in the king's house." A king who would remove a lovely Vashti would just as quickly depose an Esther.

Devout Jews and Christians have usually read into Mordecai's statement the thought of the sovereign Lord. Because the whole book is testimony to the Lord's sovereignty in the affairs of people, we think that Mordecai must certainly have intended that Jehovah would come to the rescue of His people. But that introduces the *problem*. Not once is God mentioned in Esther. She herself has not yet told the king that she is Jewish; Mordecai had instructed her to hide this fact (2:10, 20). And Mordecai's unwillingness to bow to Haman is not explained on any religious basis. He said that he would not do it because he was a Jew.

John Whitcomb thinks that the only satisfactory explanation for the absence of God's name in Esther is that "the Jews of Susa not only were outside of the promised land but, moreover, were not even concerned about God's theocratic program centered in that land" (*Esther: The Triumph of God's Sovereignty*, Moody Press). He suggests that Esther and her older cousin, like the majority of Jews in exile, were unregenerate. Quoting an earlier scholar he says, " 'the history of God's work in the earth can never be associated' with the unbelieving Jews who deliberately detach themselves from God's revealed program." While thousands of Jews remained in Susa, a remnant of the faithful were rebuilding Jerusalem and resettling in the Promised Land. Perhaps the absence of any reference to God or to Jerusalem or the temple in this book reveals that the Jews were bitter toward the Lord for the humiliation of their exile and they were trying to live as though He did not exist. If true, the sovereign, watchful care of Jehovah is all the more astounding.

The Queen's Daring Commitment (vv. 15, 16)   Esther possessed uncommonly good sense and her willingness to listen to her "father" shows that her being queen had not gone to her head. She replied to Mordecai that she was willing to risk the king's wrath if he would gather all of the Jews in the capital city and fast for her sake for three days. Her request for complete abstinence from either food or drink for three days (and nights) shows her determination to meet the challenge facing her.

Her maids were to fast with her, giving rise to our wondering if they also were Jews, or whether her influence was such that they would join her in anything she asked of them. No mention is made of prayer, but it almost certainly is implied. "Here again the thought of God underlies the narrative," says the *Pulpit Commentary*.

"Which is not according to law" (v. 16) is better rendered "even though it is against the law" (NIV). She had not been summoned to the king in thirty days (4:11) and she did not know if he would grant her favor. The three days of fasting—and prayer—would allow her to prepare her approach, and then she would ask for an audience with Xerxes.

A Jewish Duo in Xerxes' Court (8:3-8) Commenting on the teamwork of Mordecai and Esther, the *New Bible Commentary* says, "Mordecai made prudent use of his privileged position 'in the gate,' while Esther for her part had to resolve to do what was right and carry her resolve into action." Her resolve carried her to the king's court where she shrewdly invited the king and Haman to banquet with her the following day. Then, at the banquet, she extended a second invitation for the next day when she would make a request of the king. But before that second dinner, one of those coincidences occurred which so illustrates to the believer the hand of a sovereign God helping His covenant people.

Unable to sleep, Xerxes ordered the record books brought to him and there he learned how Mordecai had prevented an assassination attempt on the king's life. The next morning he ordered Haman to honor Mordecai immediately and publicly. The angry Haman had no sooner completed this distasteful task than he was summoned to the banquet where Esther revealed to the king his plan to annihilate "my" people. The king ordered Haman hanged on the gallows he had hoped to use on Mordecai, and then he promoted "Mordecai the Jew" as his prime minister.

Although Haman was dead, the threat against the Jews still existed and it appears that Esther had to make another appeal to the king for an audience to complete her mission. Her tears (v. 3) and her obvious sincerity (v. 6) moved the king. The repetitiveness of verse 5 shows something of the pressure she still felt, not knowing how Xerxes would react to her request to revoke Haman's orders (she tactfully avoided calling it the king's decree). Xerxes could not go back on his decree; for the Medes and Persians, to change one's word was a sign of weakness. But he trusted Esther and Mordecai so implicitly that he allowed them to draft a letter "as it seems best to you" and seal it with his ring which Mordecai then wore.

They decided to grant the Jews the power to defend themselves and sped the new decree to every province by means of the same postal system that had carried the earlier document. This was months before the day of disaster chosen by Haman. The book concludes with the report of how the Jews were spared and how Mordecai ordered that the feast of Purim ("lots") be observed on the fourteenth and fifteenth day of Adar every year after that. To this day the scroll of Esther is read at this feast and the names of Mordecai and Esther are remembered as Jews who responded with commitment to an extraordinary challenge.

Applying the Scripture
This final of four lessons on "Persons With Family and Friendship Ties" could be an effective follow-up to last week's study on friends.

Look once again at that quotation a few paragraphs above: "Mordecai made prudent use of his privileged position 'in the gate' while Esther for her part had to resolve to do what was right and carry her resolve into action." It is obvious that *both* Mordecai and Esther were needed to block Haman's plan. Had Mordecai not informed Esther, she may not have heard of the scheme until it was too late. And it was not enough for Mordecai to know for he did not have access to the king.

Not many wrongful schemes are on so grand a scale as was Haman's, but evil forces are nonetheless at work to oppress people and rob them of their rights—and this happens right before our eyes. Sometimes the wrong that needs correcting is not a deliberate evil aimed at any person, but is the result of human failing.

Three years ago, a bicyclist was killed instantly in a Bay Area city of California when he fell from his bike and was thrown beneath the wheels of a bus. The uncle of this young man, from Colorado, traveled to the Bay Area to gather the deceased's personal effects. The man's girl friend met the uncle and they went together to the scene of the accident. Immediately they noticed a broken rain "catch basin" at the curb, exactly where the bicyclist had fallen. Upon reading the police report of the accident, they noticed that no mention was made of the broken catch basin.

Further investigation revealed a large number of these deep catch basins were in similarly unsafe condition—accidents just waiting to happen. The two, a man from Colorado and the girl friend, began to call on City Hall, the city council, attorneys, and the police in order to correct the situation. They feared that the police might be covering up negligent maintenance by the city transit company in order to protect the city from lawsuits. These two who were not even acquainted before they started their study were able to get the city to change its police reporting procedures. And though they failed to secure special bicycle routes in the city, they did get the city council to approve funds for repair of the catch basins. Only, at last report the funds had been siphoned off for another emergency need.

This is but one example of the kind of evil that can be corrected if two people join forces to do something. The Lord has not called us to sit idly by when evil of any form is present. Like Esther and Mordecai, we will be called upon to do something about an injustice, an unsafe condition, a morally threatening situation. Will we be as willing to sacrifice what is dear to us and do something about it?

Questions for Discussion
Make use of these questions to involve your students in learning and to test their understanding of the lesson.
1. What feast which the Jews keep to this day derives its origin from events recorded in Esther? 2. Why did Esther have two names? Can you name another prominent Jew who was in exile and who also was given a new name? 3. Why was Esther so reluctant to ask for an appointment with the king? 4. In being asked to join her and her maids in a three-day fast, in what spiritual exercise would Mordecai be expected to take part? 5. After Haman's death, why is Esther still so burdened? What request did she make of Xerxes? 6. What explanation would you offer for the complete absence of the name of God in this book? 7. What truth does the Book of Esther teach us about God's dealing with His people?

Illustrating the Scripture
Examples and quotations to help the teacher communicate the lesson.
A REASON FOR FASTING "Some of my friends have been fasting through the years; I really had never done it. But four years ago I became interested in it, so I went back to the Bible. I believe the Bible, and I believe in prayer. What interests me is that prayer in Scripture is frequently connected with fasting, so I asked myself, 'What is the purpose of fasting?'

"Some people fast in order to give the money to people who are hungry, and some people fast for a variety of other reasons. But when I read the Scripture, I realized that fasting is to create within my heart a sense of humiliation as I stand before God—as if I take my shoes off my feet because the ground on which I stand is holy ground. Not only is fasting connected to humiliation, but to a recognition of my utter, complete and absolute dependence upon God. . . .

"As I studied the Scriptures, I discovered that there are three different relationships in which fasting was used in the Bible. The first had to do with the individual as a person, with his problems. The second had to do with the people of God in what I think of as a church relationship. The third had to do with people together in a national or political situation. . . .

"(This) third kind of fasting is by people in a national situation, as seen in 2 Chronicles 20. This is the tremendous national crisis where the Moabites, the Ammonites, and the Meunites came against Jehoshaphat in battle. Some people told Jehoshaphat, 'A great multitude is coming against you . . . from beyond the sea.' Then Jehoshaphat feared and set himself to seek the Lord and proclaim a fast throughout all Judah. Judah assembled to seek help from the Lord; and when they had fasted, Jehoshaphat offered a prayer. Jehoshaphat declared a time of fasting and prayer, and when he prayed he exhibited in that prayer what I think should always be our attitude. He claimed every promise of God that was written in the Book, and then he said, '(Lord) we do not know what to do, but our eyes are upon thee.' And there was a great deliverance." (Taken from "Are You Fasting?" by Harold Lindsell, *Decision* magazine, July 1980. Used with permission.)

Topics for Youth

THOUGHTS ON "PURPOSE"—The crucial question Mordecai raised to the queen concerned *purpose:* "Who knows but that you have come to royal position for such a time as this?"

Jay Kesler, writing in *Campus Life* (October 1978) tried to answer a high-school student who worried about his purpose in studying for school. "Whatever I do I can't get my mind off school," the junior said. "When I go out to a church social or a football game I feel guilty for not staying home to study."

This is a part of what Kesler said: "It might help to think through school a little. You've taken studying too far, but recognize that what you're doing is basically good. It's much better than not studying at all, which is a more common problem.

"People who have an overactive conscience, who are perfectionists, who are overly pious, have the same problem—taking a good thing too far.

"Too much of a good thing is poison. It's like over-fertilizing your lawn: it does the opposite of what you intend it to do. What is the purpose of school? Most definitions I've heard stress that school is meant to equip people to live in the world. Your preoccupation with grades is actually doing just the opposite of what school is supposed to accomplish.

"But I don't think it does much good to tell someone, 'Stop worrying,' You're probably too intense to just relax. You ought to channel your energy into other interests. You can find hobbies where your intensity will be a good thing, where it will help you excel, rather than destroy the very purpose of the activity."

MORE THOUGHTS ON "PURPOSE"—Francis A. Schaeffer once said, "Man, made in the image of God, has a purpose—to be in relationship to God, who is there. Man forgets his purpose and thus he forgets who he is and what life means."

"More men fail through lack of purpose than through lack of talent," said Billy Sunday.

Charles R. Hembree said, "Our lives will be complete only when we express the full intent of the Master."

This book contains lessons through August 1983. The Evangelical Teacher's Guide 1983-84, containing lessons from September 1983 through August 1984, is on sale now at your bookstore.